Fodor's 95
Spain

D1298569

PRAISE FOR FODOR'S GUIDES

"Fodor's guides . . . are an admirable blend of the cultural and the practical."
—The Washington Post

"Researched by people chosen because they lived or have lived in the country, well-written, and with good historical sections . . . Obligatory reading for millions of tourists."
—The Independent, *London*

"Usable, sophisticated restaurant coverage, with an emphasis on good value."
—Andy Birsh, Gourmet restaurant columnist, quoted by Gannett News Service

"Packed with dependable information."
—Atlanta Journal Constitution

"Fodor's always delivers high quality . . . thoughtfully presented . . . thorough."
—Houston Post

"Valuable because of their comprehensiveness."
—Minneapolis Star-Tribune

Fodor's Travel Publications, Inc.
New York • Toronto • London • Sydney • Auckland

**Copyright © 1994
by Fodor's Travel Publications, Inc.**

Fodor's is a registered trademark of Fodor's Travel Publications, Inc.

All rights reserved under International and Pan-American Copyright Conventions. Published in the United States by Fodor's Travel Publications, Inc., a subsidiary of Random House, Inc., New York, and simultaneously in Canada by Random House of Canada Limited, Toronto. Distributed by Random House, Inc., New York.

No maps, illustrations, or other portions of this book may be reproduced in any form without written permission from the publisher.

ISBN 0–679–02763–7

Fodor's Spain

Editor: Christopher Billy
Contributors: Steven Amsterdam, Hilary Bunce, Philip Eade, Echo Garrett, Anita Guerrini, Sean Hignett, Michael Jacobs, Dawn Lawson, Deborah Luhrman, Bevin McLaughlin, Mark Potok, Mary Ellen Schultz, George Semler, Nancy van Itallie
Creative Director: Fabrizio La Rocca
Cartographer: David Lindroth
Illustrator: Karl Tanner
Cover Photograph: Joe Viesti/Viesti Associates

Design: Vignelli Associates

Special Sales

Fodor's Travel Publications are available at special discounts for bulk purchases for sales promotions or premiums. Special editions, including personalized covers, excerpts of existing guides, and corporate imprints, can be created in large quantities for special needs. For more information, contact your local bookseller or write to Special Markets, Fodor's Travel Publications, 201 East 50th Street, New York, NY 10022. Inquiries from Canada should be directed to your local Canadian bookseller or sent to Random House of Canada, Ltd., Marketing Department, 1265 Aerowood Drive, Mississauga, Ontario L4W 1B9. Inquiries from the United Kingdom should be sent to Fodor's Travel Publications, 20 Vauxhall Bridge Road, London, England SW1V 2SA.

MANUFACTURED IN THE UNITED STATES OF AMERICA
10 9 8 7 6 5 4 3 2 1

Contents

Glossary *541*

Index *543*

Maps

Foreword

We would like to express our gratitude to Pilar Vico, Director of Public Relations, and Roberta Cores of the Spanish National Tourist Office in New York City for their valuable assistance during the preparation of this edition of *Fodor's Spain.*

While every care has been taken to ensure the accuracy of the information in this guide, the passage of time will always bring change, and consequently, the publisher cannot accept responsibility for errors that may occur.

All prices and opening times quoted here are based on information supplied to us at press time. Hours and admission fees may change, however, and the prudent traveler will avoid inconvenience by calling ahead.

Fodor's wants to hear about your travel experiences, both pleasant and unpleasant. When a hotel or restaurant fails to live up to its billing, let us know and we will investigate the complaint and revise our entries where the facts warrant it.

Send your letters to the editors of Fodor's Travel Publications, 201 E. 50th Street, New York, NY 10022.

Highlights '95 and Fodor's Choice

Highlights '95

In 1995 the citizens of **Granada** will grab the spotlight in Spain, first by hosting the **World Ski Championships** in February and then continuing throughout the year with celebrations promoting the Moorish heritage of Andalucía. The Spanish National Tourist Office has launched a program called **"The Andalus Legacy,"** which includes the creation of 10 different tourism routes through the region's most picturesque and historic pueblos. All itineraries terminate in Granada, home of the magical Alhambra palace and the last capital of the Moors in Spain.

In addition, organizers are mounting 10 exhibitions showcasing aspects of Spanish life that derive from the country's 800-year legacy of Moorish rule. One of these shows will focus on the ingenious irrigation methods employed by the Moors to provide relief from the scorching Andalusian sun. Others will focus on the architectural, agricultural, and scientific contributions made by the Moors, as well as the influence of Arabic on the Spanish language. These expositions will be held April–August in all the provincial capitals of Andalucía and in Ronda, Almuñécar, and Algeciras. Further information and brochures describing the tourism routes are available from the Oficina de Comunicacíon, El Legado Andalusi, Callejon Atarazana Vieja 1, 18010 Granada, tel. 958/20–64–62, fax 958/20–63–58.

Also new to Spain in 1995 is the **Port Aventura theme park** in Salou on the Costa Dorada, which is scheduled to open in April. Owned in part by the U.S. brewery Anheuser Busch, the park will have five main theme areas: Polynesia, China, Mexico, the Wild West, and Catalonia.

Visitors to Spain in 1995 will likely face **climbing hotel and restaurant** prices brought on by the tourism boom of last summer. The biggest price hikes, however, will be at coastal resorts and in the Balearic and Canary islands. Prices in Madrid and Barcelona should remain relatively stable, with especially good deals for tourists who schedule their city visits on weekends.

Securing accommodations in rural areas is an increasingly popular budget option for travelers in Spain. Catering to a trend toward rural tourism, numerous small privately owned inns have opened, many in historic buildings, and these make a charming alternative to the civil service attitudes of the paradors and the impersonality of the high-rise chains. Farmhouses are also being converted into charming bed-and-breakfast inns throughout the country. Besides providing a low-cost way to travel, these lodgings usually also make it easier for visitors to mix with the locals. Ask in small-town tourism offices for accommodations in *turismo rural* or *agroturismo*. Majorca has an especially well developed system of rural inns in comfortable farmhouses, where you are treated like one of the family and have a unique opportunity to learn about traditional ways of life on the island.

Fodor's Choice

No two people will agree on what makes a perfect vacation, but it can be fun and helpful to know what others think. We hope you'll have a chance to experience some of Fodor's Choices yourself while visiting Spain. For detailed information on individual entries, see the relevant sections of this guidebook.

Castles and Palaces

Alhambra, Granada
Castle, Coca
Castle, Sigüenza
Palace of Archbishop Gelmírez, Santiago de Compostela
Palacio Real, Aranjuez
Palacio Real, La Granja
Palacio Real, Madrid
Palau Güell, Barcelona

Towns and Villages

Arcos de la Frontera
Ares del Maestre
Ciudad Rodrigo
Elanchove
Grazalema
Luarca
Peñíscola
Taüll
Trujillo
Valldemossa

Churches and Monasteries

Basilica of San Isidoro, León
Capilla Real, Granada
Cathedral, Burgos
Cathedral, León
Cathedral, Santiago de Compostela
Cathedral, Seville
Convent of Las Dueñas, Salamanca
Convent of the Descalzas Reales, Madrid
El Escorial, Madrid
El Salvador Cathedral, Orihuela
Mezquita, Córdoba
Monastery of Guadalupe
Monastery of Lluc, Mallorca
La Moreneta shrine, Montserrat
New Cathedral, Salamanca
Santa Maria Cathedral, Seu d'Urgell
Santa Maria del Mar, Barcelona

Sant Climent, Taüll
Temple Expiatori de la Sagrada Família, Barcelona

Museums

Archbishop's Palace (Museo del Camino), Astorga
Centro de Arte Reina Sofía, Madrid
Fundació Miró, Barcelona
Museo Taurino, Ronda
Museu Picasso, Barcelona
Museum of Roman Art, Mérida
National Museum of Religious Sculpture, Valladolid
Prado, Madrid
Thyssen-Bornemísza, Madrid

Squares and Parks

Aigües Tortes National Park, Espot
Cazorla Nature Park, Cazorla
Doñana National Park, Huelva province
Huerto del Cura, Elche
Parc Güell, Barcelona
Parque del Retiro, Madrid
Plaza de España, Madrid
Plaza Mayor, Madrid
Plaza Mayor, Salamanca
Plaza Mayor, Trujillo

Hotels

Formentor, Port de Pollença, Mallorca, *$$$$*

Hostal de los Reyes Católicos, Santiago de Compostela, *$$$$*

Palace, Madrid, *$$$$*

Ritz, Barcelona, *$$$$*

Colón, Barcelona, *$$$*

Parador Nacional Castillo de Sigüenza, Sigüenza, *$$$*

Parador Nacional Zurbarán, Guadalupe, *$$$*

Reina Victoria, Madrid, *$$$*

Restaurants

Eldorado Petit, Barcelona, *$$$$*
Zalacaín, Madrid, *$$$$*
Arzak, San Sebastián, *$$$*
El Molino, Durcal, *$$$*
Rincón de Pepe, Murcia, *$$$*
Ariatza, Bilbao, *$$*
El Asador de Aranda, Barcelona, *$$*
Ca'n Olga, Mercadal, Menorca, *$$*

Hostal Pizarro, Trujillo, *$$*
La Pampa, Madrid, *$$*

Other Sights

Cape Formentor, Mallorca
Palau de la Música, Barcelona
Roman ruins, Mérida
Roman ruins, Tarragona
University, Salamanca

Spain

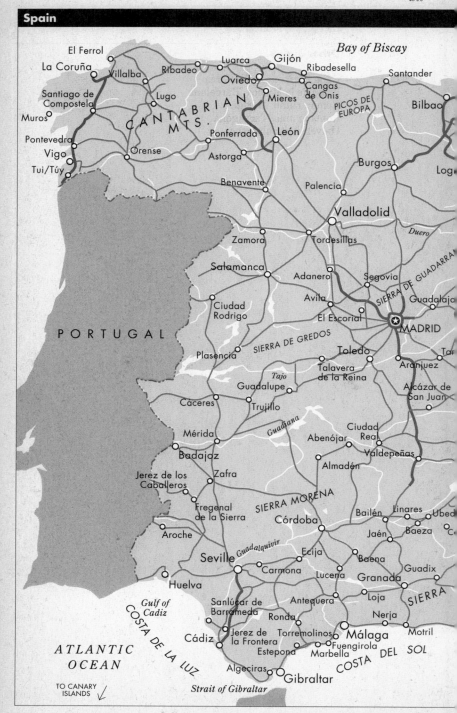

Bay of Biscay

El Ferrol
La Coruña
Villalba
Ribadeo
Luarca
Gijón
Ribadesella
Santander
Santiago de Compostela
Lugo
Oviedo
Cangas de Onis
Mieres
PICOS DE EUROPA
Bilbao
Muros
CANTABRIAN MTS.
Pontevedra
Orense
Ponferrada
León
Vigo
Astorga
Burgos
Tui/Túy
Benavente
Palencia
Log
Zamora
Tordesillas
Valladolid
Duero
Salamanca
Adanero
Segovia
SIERRA DE GUADARRA
Ciudad Rodrigo
Avila
Guadalajo
El Escorial
MADRID
PORTUGAL
SIERRA DE GREDOS
Toledo
Tar
Plasencia
Talavera de la Reina
Aranjuez
Tajo
Guadalupe
Alcázar de San Juan
Cáceres
Trujillo
Mérida
Guadiana
Abenójar
Ciudad Real
Badajoz
Valdepeñas
Almadén
Jerez de los Caballeros
Zafra
Fregenal de la Sierra
SIERRA MORENA
Córdoba
Bailén
Linares
Ubed
Aroche
Jaén
Baeza
C
Seville
Guadalquivir
Ecija
Baena
Guadix
Huelva
Carmona
Lucena
Granada
SIERRA
Gulf of Cadiz
Sanlúcar de Barrameda
Antequera
Loja
COSTA DE LA LUZ
Ronda
Nerja
ATLANTIC OCEAN
Cádiz
Jerez de la Frontera
Torremolinos
Málaga
Motril
Fuengirola
Estepona
Marbella
COSTA DEL SOL
Algeciras
Gibraltar
Strait of Gibraltar
TO CANARY ISLANDS

Autonomous Regions and Provinces

PAIS VASCO
(EUSKADI)
San
Sebastián
GUIPUZCOA
Victoria ÁLAVA   Pamplona
TREVIÑO
   Logroño   NAVARRA
A RIOJA
Soria
SORIA
ZARAGOZA
GUADALAJARA
Tajo
Cuenca
CUENCA
NCHA
Júcar
Albacete
ALBACETE
Segura
MURCIA
Murcia
Lorca
ALMERIA
Almería
COSTA DE
ALMERIA

FRANCE

ANDORRA

HUESCA
Huesca
LERIDA
GERONA
Ebro
Zaragoza   Lérida   CATALUNYA
(CATALONIA)
ARAGON   BARCELONA   Gerona
   Barcelona   COSTA
TARRAGONA   BRAVA
   Tarragona
TERUEL   Tortosa   COSTA
   DORADA   Balearic
Teruel   Sea
CASTELLON   Menorca →
   Castellón
   de la Plana   Palma
Valencia   Mallorca
Requena   Ibiza
VALENCIA   BALEARIC
   ISLANDS
Játiva   Eivissa
ALICANTE   Formentera
Alicante
   COSTA   Menorca
   BLANCA   Ciudadela
   Mahón
   Cartagena
COSTA   Mediterranean
CALIDA   Sea

COSTA DEL AZAHAR

N

ALGERIA

KEY
—·—· Regions
— — — Provinces
◉ Provincial
capitals

0   50 miles
0   75 km

Europe

NORWAY
Bergen○

○ Reykjavík
ICELAND

NORTHERN
IRELAND

SCOTLAND
Edinburgh✪

*North
Sea*

Skagerrack

Belfast✪

IRELAND

*Irish
Sea*

UNITED

DENMARK

Dublin✪

KINGDOM

WALES

ENGLAND

NETHERLANDS

Hamburg○

Cardiff✪

London✪

The Hague✪

Amsterdam✪

English Channel

Brussels✪

Rotterdam○

G E R M

Bonn○

**ATLANTIC
OCEAN**

BELGIUM

Paris✪

LUXEMBOURG

Frankfurt○

F R A N C E

Zürich○

Munich○

Bern✪

SWITZERLAND

LIECHTENSTEIN

Lyon○

Milan○

L

Venice○

**Monte
Carlo**

Nice✪

Marseille○

MONACO

ANDORRA

Florence○

PORTUGAL

✪**Madrid**

Corsica

✪**Lisbon**

S P A I N

Barcelona○

Seville○

○**Granada**

*Balearic
Islands*

Sardinia

Tyrrhenian

○**Gibraltar**

Mediterranean Sea

MOROCCO

ALGERIA

0 ──────── 400 miles

0 ──────── 600 km

TUNISIA

World Time Zones

Numbers below vertical bands relate each zone to Greenwich Mean Time (0 hrs.).
Local times frequently differ from these general indications,
as indicated by light-face numbers on map.

Algiers, **29**	Berlin, **34**	Delhi, **48**	Istanbul, **40**
Anchorage, **3**	Bogotá, **19**	Denver, **8**	Jerusalem, **42**
Athens, **41**	Budapest, **37**	Djakarta, **53**	Johannesburg, **44**
Auckland, **1**	Buenos Aires, **24**	Dublin, **26**	Lima, **20**
Baghdad, **46**	Caracas, **22**	Edmonton, **7**	Lisbon, **28**
Bangkok, **50**	Chicago, **9**	Hong Kong, **56**	London (Greenwich), **27**
Beijing, **54**	Copenhagen, **33**	Honolulu, **2**	Los Angeles, **6**
	Dallas, **10**		Madrid, **38**
			Manila, **57**

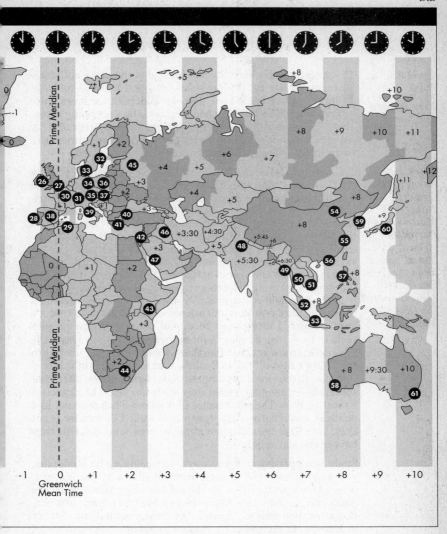

Introduction

By Mark Potok

French-born and American-raised journalist Mark Potok has lived in Greece, Italy, and Madrid. He currently lives in Texas, where he is the Southwest correspondent for USA Today.

In a place where heretics once burned at the stake with fearsome regularity, topless—and even bottomless—sunbathing is now rife. Where poverty and backwardness were legend, a hustling, bustling middle class is on a shopping spree. The hidebound morality of the past has faded—replaced by ubiquitous public romance, young men and women embracing in every street, plaza, park, and bar.

The sense of excitement in Spain today is contagious. Probably the first thing that will strike the visitor to this long-isolated land is this palpable exhilaration, a feeling that seems to electrify Spain from remote mountain villages to the ritzy avenues in Madrid and Barcelona. Naturally, there are many dark spots in the picture—beggars in the streets, continuing Basque terrorism, huge economic adjustments required by the country's 1986 entry into the European Community—and yet it's difficult not to be infected by the overall optimism. You can see its results, in the general sprucing up of recent years. You can feel it, especially in the bars and restaurants—even if you don't understand a word, Spaniards speak with such wonderful expression that it's hard to miss. Life is loved here, and celebrated; few peoples seem to have such a capacity for enjoyment. In many ways, the Spanish have always been like this—Richard Wright, visiting in the 1950s, called it "pagan Spain"—but for 36 years of this century, its citizens lived and labored under a repressive, ultra-conservative regime that ended only with the death of Francisco Franco in 1975. The renaissance that followed has been not just political, but creative and economic as well. The wonder is not that there have been disappointments since then, but that they have been relatively few.

Spain is surprising in many ways. In imagining its landscape, you may picture the orange-scorched plains of La Mancha, where Don Quixote tilted, or the softly rolling hills of southern Andalucía, or even the overdeveloped Mediterranean beaches. But after Switzerland, Spain is the most mountainous country in Europe, crisscrossed by rugged mountain ranges, some of them completely Alpine in appearance (skiing is a popular sport). It is also one of the most geographically diverse: from the soggy northwest (wetter than Ireland) to the airless plains of the central Meseta, from the cascading trout streams of the Pyrenees to the marshes and dunes of the Coto Doñana National Park on its southwest Atlantic coast. There are deep caves, lonely coves, rock canyons. There are also mountain meadows, coastal rice paddies, volcanic island peaks. That the great, snowy wall of the Pyrenees has always isolated Spain, making her people "different," is well known (Europe, historians have scoffed, ends at the Pyrenees). But Spain's peculiar climate and geography have had another effect on inhabitants of the peninsula: they keep the people apart from one another.

At a time when regionalism is sweeping Europe, Spain is an old hand. More than almost any country its size—the second largest in Europe after France—Spain is characterized by the distinct nature of its many regions and peoples. The Galicians, who live in the northwest, are descended from the same Celtic tribes that colonized the British isles. Bagpipes are a local instrument there, and kilts not unheard of; the local language, Gallego, is a mix of Spanish and Portuguese spoken by more and more Galicians. The Basque Country, east of Galicia and abutting the northern border with France, also has its own language: Euskera, a tongue so strange that linguists are baffled as to where it began. They also have a tough work ethic, derived from thousands of years of grueling farm labor in their long-isolated region, that is not shared by all of their Spanish neighbors. Some paleontologists believe the Basques, with their barrel chests and jutting brows, are directly descended from Neanderthals who inhabited the caves of the Pyrenees. Be that as it may, local pride is fiercest of all here, where independence movements have been strong for centuries. The most famous expression of this separatist yen, of course, is the terrorist group ETA (Euskadi Ta Askatasuna), which has killed more than 700 Spaniards over the course of 25 years (the violence is extremely unlikely to affect visitors). The Catalans, who populate northeastern Spain around Barcelona, are hard-working and industrious. They also speak the country's third regional language, Catalan, which is related to old Provençal; inhabitants of the Balearic islands and Valencia province boast their own local variants. All of these areas, and several others that are less obviously distinct, suffered terribly under Franco's virulent centralism (regional languages were actually banned). Today, these regions are enjoying a renaissance with their local language, traditions, and arts.

Most first-time visitors expect to find the swarthy features of most southern European countries, or the dark hair and eyes traditionally associated with Spain. But Spaniards resemble no one so much as Americans—they are an utterly mixed bag of people. There are blondes, brunettes, and even redheads. Most people used to be short—a byproduct of poor nutrition—but today they come in all sizes (as a rule, better-fed young people are much taller than their parents). These differences came about through an almost unequaled history of racial mingling. The peninsula's early peoples included Basques, Celts, Iberians, Greeks, Romans, and Visigoths. But more importantly, Christians in the centuries after Christ widely intermarried with Jewish and Arabic minorities. Today, most Spaniards see themselves as purely Catholic, but in fact, almost all have ancestors who were Jewish and Muslim.

Spain changed from a peasant economy to a modern, capitalist one in remarkably little time—so little, in fact, that it's been called the "Spanish miracle." In the last 40 years, huge numbers of Spaniards left the poorer regions of Spain and flooded the cities looking for jobs. When they reached the cities, many moved into the shantytowns of *chabolas* (shacks) that sprang up around every major city. But all that has changed. The shantytowns are almost gone, and a lively economy reaches even small provincial towns. Roads, trains, and telephones—once legendary for their poor quality—are being modernized. Even a recession in the 1980s didn't seem to slow Spain's generally brisk pace.

Modernity has come at a price. For generations, Spain was the destination of choice for the penniless artist, the adventurer willing to forego comfort for rugged romance. That is now decidedly not true. After years of inflation, and a value-added tax imposed as a condition of entry into the European Community, Spain's cost of living compares to that of partners like France. The festivities of 1992—the Olympic Games in Barcelona and the International Exposition in Seville—further inflated hotel and restaurant prices in those cities. And for Americans, sticker shock is compounded by the chronically weak dollar. Still, there are bargains to be had; it's just that you'll have to shop harder to find them. The government-run chain of *paradores*—luxurious but moderately priced hotels ensconced in renovated castles, monasteries, and other historic buildings—is certainly one of them. One salutary effect of the changed economy has been new tourist interest in the relatively cheap interior and northern regions, where Spain is often at her most beautiful.

Surprisingly, perhaps, this is a nation that retains much of what's always attracted the foreigner: an extraordinary heritage of history, art, and architecture. It begins with the caves at Altamira, where men wearing skins for warmth painted delicate animals on the contours of a rock ceiling. From hardscrabble Extremadura, Spain's poorest province, robust adventurers—many of them illiterate—left to explore the New World. Some never returned, but many did return rich and built great stone palaces in the stark, scrubby landscape. Stretched across northern Spain are the Romanesque churches of the Camino de Santiago (Way of St. James), which in the Middle Ages became the most famous religious pilgrimage in Europe; the journey culminated at the soaring Cathedral of Santiago de Compostela. Cave churches of the early Christians, scattered across the north, are a graphic counterpoint. Seville, the pastel-colored city of Don Juan, still clusters elegantly along the banks of the Guadalquivir; the undulating fantasy of Catalan architect Antoni Gaudí, the Sagrada Familia (Holy Family) Cathedral, towers over Barcelona. Contrary to popular belief, today's bullfights and at least some flamenco are very much a product of Spanish history; they were not concocted as mere tourist attractions. More than ten thousand castles dot the peninsula, many of them merely ruins, but many also in extraordinarily good shape, living testaments to the harsh and brutish life of another era. Villages of whitewashed buildings, harbors crowded with brightly painted fishing boats, and majestic towns welded to craggy mountaintops all are commonplace. Perhaps above all, the Spanish countryside remains unchanged, still washed by that beautiful, subtle light that inspired Velázquez and other Spanish painters, past and present.

The story of this land, a romance-tinged tale of counts and caliphs, crusaders and kings, begins long before men began to formally record history. The Basques were among the first here, huddling in the cold mountain valleys of the north. The Iberians came next, apparently crossing the Mediterranean from North Africa around 3,000 BC. The Celts arrived from the north about a thousand years later. The seafaring Phoenicians founded Gadir (now Cádiz) and several southern coastal cities. The parade continued with the Greeks, who settled parts of the east coast, and then the Carthaginians, who founded Cartagena around 225 BC—and who dubbed the country they found Spania. It was a wild, forested place these peoples came to, quite unlike present-day Spain; it was said a monkey could make its way from the Strait of Gibraltar to the Bay of Biscay without touching the ground once. Spain's trees had yet to be felled.

Modern civilization really began with the Romans, who expelled the Carthaginians and turned the peninsula into three important imperial provinces; the two making up today's Spain produced four Roman emperors. The Romans didn't manage to subdue the fiercely resisting natives for the two centuries ending shortly before the birth of Christ, but their influence was lasting. Evidence of the Roman epoch is found today in the great ruins in Mérida, Segovia, Tarragona, and other cities, in the peninsula's legal system, and in the Latin base for its three Romance languages, Spanish, Catalan, and Gallego. In the early fifth century invading barbarians crossed the Pyrenees to attack the weakening Roman empire. The Visigoths, who later adopted Christianity, became the dominant force in northern Spain by 419, establishing their kingdom at Toledo.

But they, too, were to fall before the might of invaders, this time a Berber-led Arab force, commanded by one Tariq ibn Ziyad, which crossed the Strait of Gibraltar from North Africa. (Gibraltar's name is a corruption of Gebel-Tariq, or "Tariq's Rock.") The Moors swept through the country in an astonishingly short time, meeting only token resistance and beginning almost eight centuries of Muslim rule—a period that in many respects was the pinnacle of Spanish civilization. Unlike the semibarbaric Visigoths, they were extremely cultured and promoted public works, education, and religious tolerance. During their reign, Jews, Arabs, and Christians lived together in peace, although many Christians did convert to Islam. The Moors also brought with them many of the features of Spain today: the complex irrigation system still used around Valencia, citrus fruits, rice, cotton, sugar, palm trees, glassmaking, and numerous other crafts, to name but a few. Their influence is evident in modern Spanish, where most words beginning with "al" are Arabic in origin (for instance, *albondiga*, or meatball; *alcalde*, or mayor; *almohada*, pillow; and *alcazar*, fortress). To the visitor, the most spectacular evidence of Moorish culture will be found in modern-day Andalucía, the region the Moors called al-Andalus. The fairy-tale Alhambra, an ochre-colored palace made of stucco and mud that crowns the southern city of Granada, is testimony to the delicacy of the Moorish aesthetic. In the Mezquita (Mosque) of Córdoba, 800 candy-striped marble columns support an amazing series of symmetrical arches—and surround the Christian cathedral that Charles V later ordered built smack in the middle of this beautiful space.

Although the Moors had driven all the way across the Pyrenees during their initial invasion, they were stopped in France in 732. More important to Spain, they never managed to subdue northwestern Galicia and Asturias, and it was in the latter that a minor Christian king, Pelayo, began the long crusade that came to be known as the *Reconquista* (Reconquest). By 1085, Alfonso VI of Castile had captured Toledo, giving the Christians a firm grip on the north. During the 13th century, Valencia, Seville, and finally Córdoba—the former capital of the Muslim caliphate in Spain—fell to Christian forces, leaving only Granada in Moorish hands. For a time, that beautiful city continued to flourish. It would be some two centuries yet before two Catholic monarchs, Ferdinand of Aragón and Isabella of Castile, were joined in a marriage that would change the world.

The year 1492 is a watershed in Spanish history, the beginning of the nation's political golden age and also the moment of some of its worst excesses of intolerance. That year, the twenty-third of Ferdinand and Isabella's marriage, Christian forces conquered Granada to unify Spain as a single kingdom at last, though at the expense of Jews and Muslims who didn't embrace Christianity and were expelled from the country *en masse*. Christopher Columbus, under the sponsorship of Isabella, landed in the Americas that same year, initiating the age of discoveries. But the seeds of future disaster were sown simultaneously. The departure of educated Muslims and Jews was a blow to the nation's economy from which it would never recover; the Inquisition, established in 1478, further hurt those who chose to stay. The lands of the New World would greatly enrich Spain at first, but massive shipments of Peruvian and Mexican gold later produced terrible inflation. The so-called Catholic Monarchs and their centralizing successors maintained the unity of Spain, but they sacrificed the spirit of free trade among nations that was beginning to bring capitalist prosperity to other European countries.

Ferdinand and Isabella were succeeded by their grandson, Carlos, who became the first Spanish Habsburg and one of the most powerful rulers known to history. Under him, Córtes reached Mexico and Pizzaro conquered Peru; tales of these New World adventurers were frequently heard at court. He also inherited Austria and the Netherlands, and in 1519, three years into his reign, was elected Holy Roman Emperor (as Charles V), and he wasted little time in annexing Naples and Milan. He championed the Counter-Reformation, and the Jesuit order was created to help defend Catholicism against European Protestantism. But Charles cost the nation by his penchant for waging war, particularly against the Ottomans and German Lutherans. His son,

Philip II, followed in the same, expensive path. Philip also established the capital at Madrid, defeated the Turks at the Battle of Lepanto, and ordered the building of the Escorial, a somber monastery outside Madrid. It was there he died, in a small chamber adjoining the chapel, 10 years after losing his Armada in an attack on Protestant England.

S pain's greatest contribution to world culture is its painting, and great painters flourished throughout this period and to the end of the 17th century, thanks largely to royal patronage paid for by American booty. The best known included the Greek immigrant El Greco (1541–1614), famed for his curiously elongated figures; Francisco de Zurbarán (1598–1664); Bartolome Esteban Murillo (1617–82); and most important of all, Diego Rodríguez de Silva Velázquez (1599–1660), whose *Las Meninas*, an unflattering portrayal of Philip IV's family, is considered by many to be Spain's finest single painting. Drama and poetry flourished as well, although it was a novelist—Miguel de Cervantes (1547–1616), author of *Don Quixote*—who would become universally famous.

The War of the Spanish Succession was ignited by the death, without issue, in 1700 of Charles II, the last Habsburg. In the end, Philip of Anjou was crowned Philip V, and he inaugurated the Bourbon line of Spain (a representative of whom sits on the throne today). The Bourbons of that era, a Frenchified lot, copied many of the attitudes and fashions of their northern neighbors. But the infatuation ended with the 1808 installation by Napoleon of his brother, Jose Bonaparte. Mocked bitterly as "Pepe Botella" for his fondness for drink (*botella* means bottle), Bonaparte was widely despised, and an 1808 uprising in Madrid—chronicled harrowingly by the great painter, Francisco de Goya y Lucientes (1746–1828)—began the War of Independence, known to foreigners as the Peninsular War. Britain, siding with Spain, sent the Duke of Wellington to the rescue. With the aid of Spanish guerillas, the French were finally expelled, but not before they had looted Spain's major churches and cathedrals. It didn't help that most of Spain's American colonies took advantage of the war to claim their independence.

The rest of the century was not a happy one for Spain, as conservative regimes grappled with civil wars and revolts inspired by the currents of European republicanism. The final blow came with the loss of Cuba, Puerto Rico, and the Philippines in 1898, in a military disaster that ironically sparked a remarkable literary renaissance. The so-called Generation of '98, whose members included writers Miguel de Unamuno and Pío Baroja and poet Antonio Machado, agonized over the reasons for the nation's decline. In 1902, Alfonso XIII came to the throne, but rising civil strife got the better of him and ended in his self-imposed exile in 1931. A fledgling republic followed, to the delight of most Spaniards, but the 1936 election of a left-wing Popular Front government ignited bitter opposition from the right. In the end, a young general named Francisco Franco used the assassination of a monarchist leader as an excuse for a military revolt.

The Spanish Civil War (1936–39) was one of the most costly, and tragic, episodes in Spanish history. More than half a million people died in the conflict, which was marked by appalling atrocities, deadly reprisals, and ferocious fighting. For a sense of how the war shattered Spain, visit the ruins of Belchite—this once-proud Zaragozan town changed hands several times in bitter, house-to-house fighting, and its clean-swept streets and the rubble of its destroyed houses have been left as a horrifying national reminder. Intellectuals and leftists the world over sympathized with the elected government, and the Soviet Union sent some aid. The International Brigades, which included many American, British, and Canadian volunteers, took part in some of the worst fighting, including the storied defense of Madrid. But Franco, backed by the Catholic Church, got far more help from Nazi Germany, whose Condor legions destroyed the Basque town of Guernica in a horror made infamous by Picasso's monumental painting, and from Fascist Italy. For three years, European governments stood quietly by as Franco's armies vanquished Barcelona, Madrid, and finally, the last capital of the Republic, Valencia.

What followed were 36 years of bleak, moralistic dictatorship. The first years were the worst, as surviving opponents were severely repressed. Republican prisoners of war were set to work hollowing the inside of a granite hill for Franco's giant monument to the civil war dead, the Valle de los Caídos (Valley of the Fallen) outside Madrid. Spain, officially neutral during World War II but sympathetic to the Axis powers, was largely shunned by the world until the United States finally recognized her, and provided aid in a 1953 agreement, in exchange for the building of NATO bases in Spain. Gradually, the shattered economy began to pick up, especially with the boom in tourism that gathered steam in the late 1960s. But when Franco announced in 1969 that his successor would be Juan Carlos, the grandson of Alfonso XIII whose militaristic education had been strictly overseen by the aging general, the hopes of a nation longing for freedom sagged. Imagine Spaniards' surprise when, six years later, Franco died and the young monarch revealed himself to be a closet democrat—indeed, it seemed that Juan Carlos had carefully planned for this moment throughout the last years of the general's life, and had even met secretly with the dictator's political opponents. Under his nurturing, a new constitution restoring civil liberties and freedom of expression was adopted in 1978. On February 23, 1981, the king proved his mettle again, when a disgruntled Guardia Civil colonel named Antonio Tejero burst into the nation's parliament, the Córtes, and held its members at gunpoint for some 24 hours. The coup attempt, aimed at bringing back a right-wing government, was by all accounts only routed through the heroism of the king, who personally called military commanders across the country to ensure their loyalty to the elected government. A massive, emotional demonstration in favor of democracy followed the arrest of the plotters.

Since 1982, the Socialists have ruled Spain, and there appear to be no other strong contenders for power on the horizon. The artistic flowering of the first third of the 20th century—which produced poet Federico García Lorca, filmmaker Luis Buñuel, and painters Pablo Picasso, Joan Miró, and Salvador Dalí—ended in their exile and the cultural wasteland of the Franco years. But today, the arts are blossoming everywhere; look, for instance, at the gorgeous posters being created in even small provincial towns. The world has come to know Spanish artists such as filmmaker Pedro Almodóvar, who directed the madcap but ingenious *Women on the Verge of a Nervous Breakdown*. In 1989, Camilo José Cela, whose first novel, *The Family of Pascual Duarte*, subtly described life in the Franco years, won the Nobel Prize.

Spain is an experience that is addictive for many. Take it a little at a time, as the Spaniards do, and you'll better enjoy the delights of this complicated country. That familiar hum of excitement is everywhere, and before you know it, you'll be joining Spaniards at what they do best: living life to the hilt.

1 Essential Information

Before You Go

Government Information Offices

Contact the Spanish government tourist offices for information on all aspects of travel to and in Spain.

In the U.S. 665 5th Ave., New York, NY 10022, tel. 212/759–8822, fax 212/980–1053; Water Tower Pl., Suite 915, 845 N. Michigan Ave., Chicago, IL 60611, tel. 312/642–1992, fax 312/642–9817; 1221 Brickell Ave., Miami, FL 33131, tel. 305/358–1992, fax 305/358–8223; 8383 Wilshire Blvd., Suite 960, Beverly Hills, CA 90211, tel. 213/658–7188, fax 213/658–1061.

U.S. Government Travel Briefings The Department of State's **Overseas Citizens Emergency Center** (Room 4811, Washington, DC 20520; enclose S.A.S.E.) issues Consular Information Sheets, which cover crime, security, political climate, and health risks as well as embassy locations, entry requirements, currency regulations, and other routine matters. For the latest information, stop in at any passport office, consulate, or embassy; call the interactive hotline (tel. 202/647–5225, fax 202/647–3000); or, with your PC's modem, tap into the Bureau of Consular Affairs' computer bulletin board (tel. 202/647–9225).

In Canada 102 Bloor St. W, Suite 1450, Toronto, Ontario M5S 1M8, tel. 416/961–3131, fax 416/961–1992.

In the U.K. 57–58 St. James's St., London SW1A 1LD, tel. 71/499–0901, fax 71/629–4257.

Tours and Packages

Should you buy your travel arrangements to Spain packaged or do it yourself? There are advantages either way. Buying packaged arrangements saves you money, particularly if you can find a program that includes exactly the features you want. You also get a pretty good idea of what your trip will cost from the outset. You have two options: fully escorted tours and independent packages. Escorted tours mean having limited free time and traveling with strangers. Escorted tours are most often via motorcoach, with a tour director in charge. Your baggage is handled, your time rigorously scheduled, and most meals planned. Escorted tours are therefore the most hassle-free way to see Spain, as well as generally the least expensive. Independent packages allow plenty of flexibility. They generally include airline travel and hotels, with certain options available, such as sightseeing, car rental, and excursions. Independent packages are usually more expensive than escorted tours, but your time is your own.

While you can book directly through tour operators, you will pay no more to go through a travel agent, who will be able to tell you about tours and packages from a number of operators. Whatever program you ultimately choose, be sure to find out exactly what is included: taxes, tips, transfers, meals, baggage handling, ground transportation, entertainment, excursions, sports or recreation (and rental equipment if necessary). Ask about the level of hotel used, its location, the size of its rooms, the kind of beds, and its facilities and amenities, such as pool, room service, or programs for children, if they're important to you. Find out the operator's cancellation penalties. Nearly everyone charges them, and the only way to avoid them is to buy trip-cancellation insurance (*see* Insurance, *below*). Also ask about the single supplement, a surcharge assessed to solo travelers. Some operators do not make you pay it if you agree to be matched up with a roommate of the same sex, even if one is not found by departure time. Remember that a program that has features you won't use may not be the most cost-wise choice.

Fully Escorted Tours Escorted tours are usually sold in three categories: deluxe, first-class, and tourist or budget class. The most important differences are the price and the level of accommodations. Some operators specialize in one category, while others offer a range. In the deluxe category, try **Maupintour** (Box 807, Lawrence, KS 66044, tel. 913/843–1211 or 800/255–4266) or the "Club Petrabax" tours sponsored by **Petrabax** (97-45 Queens Blvd., Rego Park, NY 11374, tel. 718/897–7272 or 800/367–6611). First-class programs are offered by **Abreu Tours** (317 E. 34th St., New York, NY 10016, tel. 212/532–6550 or 800/223–1580), **Caravan** (401 N. Michigan Ave., Chicago, IL 60611, tel. 800/227–2862), **Certified Vacations** (Box 1525, Fort Lauderdale, FL 33302, tel. 305/522–1414 or 800/233–7260), **Collette Tours** (162 Middle St., Pawtucket, RI 02680, tel. 401/725–3805 or 800/832–4658), **El Corte Inglés** (500 5th Ave., Suite 1044, New York, NY 10110, tel. 212/944–9400 or 800/333–2469), **Gadabout Tours** (700 E. Tahquitz Way, Palm Springs, CA 92262, tel. 619/325–5556 or 800/952–5068), **Globus** (5301 S. Federal Circle, Littleton, CO 80123, tel. 303/797–2800 or 800/221–0090), **Petrabax, Perillo Tours** (Perillo Plaza, 577 Chestnut Ridge, Woodcliff Lake, NJ 07675, tel. 201/307–1234 or 800/431–1515), **Tauck Tours** (11 Wilton Rd., Box 5027, Wilton, CT 06881, tel. 800/468–2825, fax 203/454–3081), and **Trafalgar Tours** (21 E. 26th St., New York, NY 10010, tel. 212/689–8977 or 800/854–0103). In the budget category, look into **Cosmos Tourama,** a sister company of Globus (*see above*), and the "Cost Saver" programs offered by **Trafalgar Tours.**

Also look into programs from **Abreu Tours** (*see above*), **Bravo Tours** (182 Main St., Ridgefield, NJ 07660, tel. 201/641–0655 or 800/272–2674), **Hispanidad Holidays** (99 Tulip Ave., Floral Park, NY 11001, tel. 516/488–4700 or 800/274–4400), **Spanish Heritage Tours** (116–47 Queens Blvd., Forest Hills, NY 11375, tel. 718/544–2752 or 800/221–2580), and **V E Tours** (1150 N.W. 72nd Ave., Suite 450, Miami, FL 33126, tel. 800/222–8383).

Most itineraries are jam-packed with sightseeing, so you see a lot in a short amount of time (usually one place per day). To judge just how fast-paced the tour is, review the itinerary carefully. If you are in a different hotel each night, you will be getting up early each day to head out, travel to your next destination, do some sightseeing, have dinner, and go to bed; then you'll start all over again. If you want some free time, make sure it's mentioned in the tour brochure; if you want to be escorted to every meal, confirm that any tour you consider does that. Also, when comparing programs, be sure to find out if the motorcoach is air-conditioned and has a restroom on board. Make your selection based on price and stops on the itinerary.

Independent Packages Independent packages, which travel agents call FITs (for foreign independent travel), are offered by airlines, tour operators who may also do escorted programs (such as American Express Vacations, Gadabout, Petrabax, and most of the others), and any number of other companies from large, established firms to small, new entrepreneurs.

U.S. **American Airlines Fly AAway Vacations** (tel. 800/321–2121), **Continental Airlines' Grand Destinations** (tel. 800/634–5555), and **Delta Dream Vacations** (tel. 800/872–7786) have Barcelona and Madrid city packages; airline operators also include **TWA Getaway Vacations** (tel. 800/438–2929) and **United Airlines' Vacation Planning Center** (tel. 800/678–0949). Other programs are available from **El Corte Inglés** (*see above*), **Spain Tours and Beyond** (261 W. 70th St., New York, NY 10023, tel. 212/595–2400), **Travel Bound** (599 Broadway, New York, NY 10012, tel. 212/334–1350 or 800/456–8656), **V E Tours** (*see above*), **Wright Travel** (57 E. 77th St., New York, NY 10021, tel. 212/570–0969 or 800/877–3240) for Marbella, and **Odysseys Adventures** (537 Chestnut St., Cedarhurst, NY 11516, tel. 516/569–2812 or 800/344–0013).

U.K. **Mundi Color** (276 Vauxhall Bridge Rd., London SW1V 1BE, tel. 071/828–6021) is an established, Spanish-owned specialist in Spanish holidays. **Page & Moy Ltd.** (136–140 London Rd., Leicester LE2 1EN, tel. 0533/552521) has a 10-day tour to Andalucia, as well as escorted tours to Spain's historic cities.

Programs come in a wide range of prices based on levels of luxury and options—in addition to hotel and airfare, sightseeing, transfers, admission to local attractions, and (except on American Express programs), car rentals. Note that when pricing different packages, it sometimes pays to purchase the same arrangements separately, as when a rock-bottom promotional airfare is being offered, for example. Again, base your choice on what's available at your budget for the destinations you want to visit.

Special-Interest Tours Special-interest programs may be fully escorted or independent. Some require a certain amount of expertise, but most are for the average traveler with an interest and are usually hosted by experts in the subject matter. When the program is escorted, it enjoys the advantages and disadvantages of all escorted programs; because your fellow travelers are apt to be passionate or knowledgeable about the subject, they can prove as enjoyable a part of your travel experience as the destination itself. The price range is wide, but the cost is usually higher—sometimes a lot higher—than for ordinary escorted tours and packages, because of the expert guiding and special activities.

Adventure **Mountain Travel Sobek** (6420 Fairmount Ave., El Cerrito, CA 94530, tel. 510/527–8100 or 800/227–2384, fax 510/525–7710) and **Wilderness Travel** (801 Allston Way, Berkeley, CA 94710, tel. 510/548–0420 or 800/368–2794, fax 510/548–0347) have treks in the mountains of Spain.

Art and Architecture **Prospect Art Tours** (454–458 Chiswick High Rd., London W4 5TT, tel. 081/995–2163), and **Swan Hellenic** (77 New Oxford St., London WC1A 1PP, tel. 71/831–1616). **Archeological Tours** (271 Madison Ave., New York, NY 10016, tel. 212/986–3054, fax 212/370–1561) visits monuments, ancient cities, and great museums of Madrid and Barcelona. **The Smithsonian Institution's** Study Tours and Seminars (1100 Jefferson Dr. SW, Room 3045, Washington, DC 20560, tel. 202/357–4700) explores the Roman, Moorish, and explorers' legacies on one tour and museums of Madrid, Toledo, and Cuenca on another. **Swan Hellenic/Esplanade Tours** (581 Boylston St., Boston, MA 02116, tel. 617/266–7465 or 800/426–5492) offers several art and archaeology tours. **Welcome Tours/Hispanidad Holidays** (99 Tulip Ave., Suite 208, Floral Park, NY 11001, tel. 516/488–4700 or 800/274–4400) visits sites and museums throughout the country.

Bicycling **Backroads** (1516 5th St., Suite L101, Berkeley, CA 94710, tel. 510/527–1555 or 800/462–2848) tours the northwestern region of the Iberian peninsula. **Butterfield & Robinson** (70 Bond St., Toronto,

Ontario, Canada M5B 1X3, tel. 416/864–1354 or 800/387–1147) has two tours that meander through the wine province of Rioja.

Food and Wine **Odysseys Adventures** (*see above*) does wine-tasting tours coupled with meals in fine restaurants around the country. **Altamira Tours** (Box 20163, Denver, CO 80220, tel. 800/474–2869) serves up two wine-and-cuisine tours, one focusing on Catalunya and the other taking in all of northern Spain from Barcelona to Santiago de Compostela. Wine tours starting out from the United Kingdom are arranged by **Arbaster & Clarke** (104 Church Rd., Steep, Petersfield, Hants GU32 2DD, tel. 0730/266883, fax 0730/268620) and **Blackheath Wine Trails** (13 Blackheath Village, London, SE3 9LA, tel. 081/463–0012).

Gardens **Coopersmith's England** (6441 Valley View Rd., Oakland, CA 94611, tel. 510/339–2499) explores the gardens, art, and architecture of Madrid and Andalucía.

Jewish **Abreu Tours** (*see above*), **Kesher Tours** (370 Lexington Ave., New
Heritage York, NY 10017, tel. 212/949–9580 or 800/582–8330), **Odysseys Adventures** (*see above*), and **Wright Travel** (*see above*) have programs that visit synagogues in Cordoba and Toledo and other remnants of Jewish culture.

Golf **Petrabax** and **Odysseys** (*see above*) have programs to the famous courses of the Costa del Sol. **ITC Golf Tours** (4134 Atlantic Ave., Suite 205, Long Beach, CA 90807, tel. 310/595–6905 or 800/257–4981) and **Golf International** (275 Madison Ave., New York, NY 10016, tel. 212/986–9176 or 800/833–1389) have similar programs with optional Mallorca and Madrid extensions.

History **Holt's Battlefield Tours** (Golden Key Bldg., 15 Market St., Sandwich, Kent CT13 9DA, tel. 0304/612248, fax 0304/614930) offers visits to historic sites related to the 19th-century War of Independence.

Horseback **FITS Equestrian** (685 Lateen Rd., Solvang, CA 93463, tel. 805/688–
Riding 9494 or 800/666–3487) has rides through Andalucía, the Costa de la Luz, and Extremadura.

Nature Spanish wildlife and natural wonders are the focus of tours by **Cox and Kings Travel Ltd.** (St. James Court, Buckingham Gate, London, SW1E 6AF, tel. 071/873–5002, fax 071/873–5008).

Pilgrimages **Pilgrimage Tours and Travel** (39 Beechwood Ave., Manhasset, NY 11030, tel. 516/627–2636 or 800/669–0757), **V E Tours** (*see above*), and **Wright Travel** (*see above*) arrange pilgrimages to Santiago de Compostela and other religious sites in Spain.

Vintage Train **Marketing Ahead** (433 5th Ave., New York, NY 10016, tel. 212/686–
Travel 9213, fax 212/686–0271) sells packages to Andalucía and other regions aboard the restored Andalusian Express, whose carriages date from the 1920s and '30s; accommodations and meals are aboard the train. The more economical, somewhat less luxurious **Transcantabrico Express** makes weeklong trips from San Sebastián to Santiago de Compostela with frequent stops for sightseeing; you can book this train through **EC Tours** (10153 Riverside Dr., Toluca Lake, CA 91602, tel. 800/388–0877, fax 213/851–3405).

When to Go

May and October, when the weather is generally warm and dry, are considered the best months for touring Spain. May gives you more hours of daylight for sightseeing, while October offers a chance to enjoy the harvest season, especially colorful in Spain's many wine regions.

April is good for catching a glimpse of some of Spain's most spectacular Semana Santa (Holy Week) fiestas. Weather in the southern part of the country warms up enough by April to make sightseeing comfortable.

Because Spain is the number-one destination for European tourists, the months of June, July, August, and September tend to be crowded and more expensive, especially along the coasts. Most people find the waters of the Mediterranean too cold for swimming the rest of the year. Beach season on the Atlantic coast is slightly shorter. August is the month when Spaniards take vacations; the annual migration to the beach causes huge traffic jams on August 1 and 31. During August big cities are delightfully relaxed and empty. Small shops and some restaurants shut down for the entire month, but museums remain open.

Summers in Spain are hot; temperatures frequently hit 100°F (38°C), and air-conditioning is not widely used. Try to limit your touring to the morning hours and take a siesta in the afternoon. Warm summer nights are one of the most enjoyable things about Spain.

Winters in Spain are mild and rainy along the coasts, especially in Galicia. Elsewhere winter blows bitterly cold. Snow is infrequent except in the mountains, where skiing is possible from December to March in the Pyrenees and other resorts near Granada, Madrid, and Burgos.

Climate The following are average daily maximum and minimum temperatures for major cities in Spain.

Madrid	**Jan.**	48F	9C	**May**	70F	21C	**Sept.**	77F	25C
		36	2		50	10		57	14
	Feb.	52F	11C	**June**	81F	27C	**Oct.**	66F	19C
		36	2		59	15		50	10
	Mar.	59F	15C	**July**	88F	31C	**Nov.**	55F	13C
		41	5		63	17		41	5
	Apr.	64F	18C	**Aug.**	86F	30C	**Dec.**	48F	9C
		45	7		63	17		36	2

Barcelona	**Jan.**	55F	13C	**May**	70F	21C	**Sept.**	77F	25C
		43	6		57	14		66	19
	Feb.	57F	14C	**June**	77F	25C	**Oct.**	70F	21C
		45	7		64	18		59	15
	Mar.	61F	16C	**July**	82F	28C	**Nov.**	61F	16C
		48	9		70	21		52	11
	Apr.	64F	18C	**Aug.**	82F	28C	**Dec.**	55F	13C
		52	11		70	21		46	8

Seville	**Jan.**	59F	15C	**May**	81F	27C	**Sept.**	90F	32C
		43	6		55	13		64	18
	Feb.	63F	17C	**June**	90F	32C	**Oct.**	79F	26C
		45	7		63	17		57	14
	Mar.	68F	20C	**July**	97F	36C	**Nov.**	68F	20C
		48	9		68	20		50	10
	Apr.	75F	24C	**Aug.**	97F	36C	**Dec.**	61F	16C
		52	11		68	20		45	7

Córdoba	Jan.	55F	13C	May	79F	26C	Sept.	88F	31C
		41	5		55	13		63	17
	Feb.	61F	16C	June	90F	32C	Oct.	77F	25C
		43	6		63	17		55	13
	Mar.	66F	19C	July	99F	37C	Nov.	66F	19C
		46	8		68	20		48	9
	Apr.	73F	23C	Aug.	97F	36C	Dec.	57F	14C
		50	10		68	20		41	5

Granada	Jan.	54F	12C	May	73F	23C	Sept.	84F	29C
		36	2		50	10		59	15
	Feb.	57F	14C	June	86F	30C	Oct.	73F	23C
		37	3		59	15		50	10
	Mar.	63F	17C	July	93F	34C	Nov.	63F	17C
		41	5		63	17		43	6
	Apr.	68F	20C	Aug.	91F	33C	Dec.	54F	12C
		45	7		63	17		37	3

Information Sources For current weather conditions and forecasts for cities in the United States and abroad, plus the local time and helpful travel tips, call the **Weather Channel Connection** (tel. 900/932–8437; 95¢ per minute) from a touch-tone phone.

Festivals and Seasonal Events

From solemn pre-Easter processions to hilarious wine and tomato battles, Spain has a fiesta for every occasion. The best known is probably the Running of the Bulls in Pamplona, immortalized by Ernest Hemingway in *Fiesta*, or *The Sun Also Rises*. The Fallas (end-of-winter celebrations) in Valencia and Seville's Semana Santa (Holy Week) and April Fair also top the list. All require hotel reservations far in advance.

January: Epiphany, on the 6th, is a Spanish child's Christmas. Youngsters leave their shoes on the doorstep to be filled with gifts by the three wise men, or Three Kings. In towns throughout Spain the Kings arrive by camel or car in a parade the night of January 5.

February: Carnival dances through Spain as a final fiesta before Lent. The most flamboyant parades take place in Santa Cruz de Tenerife, Cadiz, and Sitges (Barcelona).

March: Papier-mâché figures up to 30 feet tall are torched for the **Fallas,** lighting up the sky of Valencia.

April: The **April Fair** of Seville brings out the best of Andalucían hospitality. Horse parades and flouncy-skirted women make this one of Spain's most picturesque fiestas. April 9 to 15 is **Semana Santa,** Spain's most spectacular fiesta. The most famous Semana Santa processions take place in Seville, Valladolid, Toledo, Murcia, Lorca, and Cuenca. This year, during the last week of April, the **Battle of the Moors and Christians** brings history alive as townspeople in Alcoy (Alicante) reenact the battle of 1275 in which the Catholic knights, aided by St. George, ousted the infidel invaders. Similar festivals take place throughout southeastern Spain: in Altea (3rd Sunday in May), Villajoyosa (July 24–31), and Murcia (Sept. 1–15).

May: The **Jerez Horse Fair** (2nd week of May) prances out a pageant of equestrian events, bullfighting, flamenco music, and dance. **San Isidro** (May 15) begins two weeks of the best bullfighting in Spain in honor of the patron saint of Madrid. **Romería del Rocío** (May 18–20) rolls across the dusty fields of Almonte (Huelva) and across a hip-deep river, as religious statues are carried on backs and in covered wagons.

June: Beginning in mid-month, the **International Festival of Music and Dance** in Granada brings symphony orchestras, opera companies, and ballet corps from around the world to perform on the grounds of the Alhambra through mid-July. The **Classical Theater Festival** uses the beautifully preserved 1st-century BC Roman Theater in Mérida (Badajoz) to present Greek and Roman dramas in Spanish from mid-June through mid-August.

Corpus Christi (June 25) is celebrated with processions throughout Spain, but the most magnificent are in Toledo and Sitges (Barcelona). The **Wine War** in Haro (La Rioja, on June 29) wastes thousands of gallons of delicious Rioja wine and proves that a bota bag makes a better squirt gun than a canteen.

July and August: Veranos de la Villa cools off Madrid's summer nights with a series of outdoor films, and concerts of everything from flamenco to rock and roll all summer long. The **Running of the Bulls** (July 6–13) through the streets of Pamplona (Navarra) unleashes wine-drinking, merrymaking, and macho bravado. For four weeks in August, the **International Music and Ballet Festival** brings world-class performances to the popular beach resort of Santander. **El Místeri** of Elche (Alicante, August 11–15) is Europe's oldest Christian mystery play. Also in mid-month, the upper-crust resort of San Sebastián lets down its hair for **Big Week,** with parades, fireworks, sporting events, and cardboard-bull running. **Tomato Battle** (August 28) turns the entire town of Buñol (Valencia) red.

September: In late August or early September, the **International Folkloric Gala** kicks off five days of folk dance and song from around the world at the elegant bullring in Ronda (Málaga). **La Merced** is celebrated in Barcelona on September 24 with concerts, fireworks, and parades featuring people wearing giant papier-mâché heads.

October: On the 12th, **El Pilar** gives the children of Zaragoza a chance to dress up in regional costumes for parades and *jota* dance contests.

December: New Year's Eve ticks away at Madrid's Puerta del Sol, where crowds gather to eat 12 grapes, one on each stroke of midnight.

What to Pack

Pack light. Although baggage carts are free and plentiful in most Spanish airports, they are rare in train and bus stations.

Clothing On the whole, Spaniards dress up more than Americans or the British. What you bring will depend a great deal on what time of year you visit. Summer will be hot nearly everywhere, but don't forget a raincoat or an umbrella. Visits in winter, fall, and spring call for warm clothing and boots.

It is sensible to wear casual, comfortable clothing and shoes when sightseeing, but dressier outfits are required for the cities, especially at fine restaurants and nightclubs. American tourists can be spotted easily in Spain because they are the ones wearing sneakers. If you want to blend in, wear leather shoes.

On the beach, anything goes; it is common to see females of all ages wearing only bikini bottoms, and many of the more remote beaches allow nude bathing. Bring a cover-up to wear over your bathing suit when you leave the beach.

Electricity The electrical current in Spain is 220 volts, 50 cycles alternating current (AC); the United States runs on 110-volt, 60-cycle AC current.

Unlike wall outlets in the United States, which accept plugs with two flat prongs, outlets in Spain take continental-type plugs, with two round prongs.

Adapters, To use U.S.-made electric appliances abroad, you'll need an adapter
Converters, plug. Unless the appliance is dual voltage and made for travel, you'll
Transformers also need a converter. Hotels sometimes have 110-volt outlets for low-wattage appliances marked "For Shavers Only" near the sink; don't use them for a high-wattage appliance like a blow-dryer. If you're traveling with an older laptop computer, carry a transformer. Newer laptop computers are auto-sensing, operating equally well on 110 and 220 volts (so you need only the appropriate adapter plug). When in doubt, consult your appliance's owner's manual or the manufacturer. Or get a copy of the free brochure "Foreign Electricity is No Deep Dark Secret," published by adapter-converter manufacturer Franzus Company (Customer Service, Dept. B50, Murtha Industrial Park, Box 142, Beacon Falls, CT 06403, tel. 203/723–6664; send a stamped, self-addressed envelope when ordering).

Miscellaneous Bring an extra pair of eyeglasses or contact lenses in your carry-on luggage. If you have a health problem that requires a prescription drug, pack enough to last the duration of the trip or have your doctor write a prescription using the drug's generic name, because brand names vary from country to country. Always carry prescription drugs in their original packaging to avoid problems with customs officials. Don't pack them in luggage that you plan to check in case your bags go astray. Pack a list of the offices that supply refunds for lost or stolen traveler's checks.

Luggage Free airline baggage allowances depend on the airline, the route,
Regulations and the class of your ticket; ask in advance. In general, on domestic flights and on international flights between the United States and foreign destinations, you are entitled to check two bags—neither exceeding 62 inches, or 158 centimeters (length + width + height), or weighing more than 70 pounds (32 kilograms). A third piece may be brought aboard; its total dimensions are generally limited to less than 45 inches (114 centimeters), so it will fit easily under the seat in front of you or in the overhead compartment. In the United States, the Federal Aviation Administration gives airlines broad latitude to limit carry-on allowances and tailor them to different aircraft and operational conditions. Charges for excess, oversize, or overweight pieces vary.

If you are flying between two foreign destinations, note that baggage allowances may be determined not by the piece method but by the weight method, which generally allows 88 pounds (40 kilograms) of luggage in first class, 66 pounds (30 kilograms) in business class, and 44 pounds (20 kilograms) in economy. If your flight between two cities abroad *connects* with your transatlantic or transpacific flight, the piece method still applies.

Safeguarding Before leaving home, itemize your bags' contents and their worth in
Your Luggage case they go astray. To minimize that risk, tag them inside and out with your name, address, and phone number. (If you use your home address, cover it so that potential thieves can't see it.) Put a copy of your itinerary inside each bag, so that you can easily be tracked. At check-in, make sure that the tag attached by baggage handlers bears the correct three-letter code for your destination. If your bags do not arrive with you, or if you detect damage, immediately file a written report with the airline before you leave the airport.

Taking Money Abroad

Traveler's Checks Traveler's checks are preferable in metropolitan centers, although you'll need cash in rural areas and small towns. The most widely recognized are **American Express, Citicorp, Diners Club, Thomas Cook,** and **Visa,** which are sold by major commercial banks. Both American Express and Thomas Cook issue checks that can be countersigned and used by you or your traveling companion. Typically the issuing company or the bank at which you make your purchase charges 1% to 3% of the checks' face value as a fee. Some foreign banks charge as much as 20% of the face value as the fee for cashing traveler's checks in a foreign currency. Buy a few checks in small denominations to cash toward the end of your trip, so you won't be left with excess foreign currency. Record the numbers of checks as you spend them, and keep this list separate from the checks.

Currency Exchange Banks offer the most favorable exchange rates. If you use currency exchange booths at airports, rail and bus stations, hotels, stores, and privately run exchange firms, you'll typically get less favorable rates, but you may find the hours more convenient.

You can get good rates and avoid long lines at airport currency-exchange booths by getting a small amount of currency at **Thomas Cook Currency Services** (630 5th Ave., New York, NY 10111, tel. 212/757–6915 or 800/223–7373 for locations in major metropolitan areas throughout the United States) or **Ruesch International** (tel. 800/424–2923 for locations) before you depart.

Getting Money from Home

Cash Machines Many automated-teller machines (ATMs) are tied to international networks such as **Cirrus** and **Plus.** You can use your bank card at ATMs to withdraw money from an account and get cash advances on a credit-card account if your card has been programmed with a personal identification number, or PIN. Check in advance on limits on withdrawals and cash advances within specified periods. Ask whether your bank card or credit-card PIN will need to be reprogrammed for use in the area you'll be visiting. Four digits are commonly used overseas. Note that Discover is accepted only in the United States. On cash advances you are charged interest from the day you receive the money from ATMs as well as from tellers. Although transaction fees for ATM withdrawals abroad may be higher than fees for withdrawals at home, Cirrus and Plus exchange rates are excellent because they are based on wholesale rates offered only by major banks. They also may be referred to abroad as "a withdrawal from a credit account."

Plan ahead: Obtain ATM locations and the names of affiliated cash-machine networks before departure. For specific foreign Cirrus locations, call 800/424–7787; for foreign Plus locations, consult the Plus directory at your local bank.

Wiring Money You don't have to be a cardholder to send or receive a **MoneyGram from American Express** for up to $10,000. Go to a MoneyGram agent in retail and convenience stores and American Express travel offices, pay up to $1,000 with a credit card and anything over that in cash. You are allowed a free long-distance call to give the transaction code to your intended recipient, who needs only present identification and the reference number to the nearest MoneyGram agent to pick up the cash. MoneyGram agents are in more than 70 countries (call 800/926–9400 for locations). Fees range from 3% to 10%, depending on the amount and how you pay.

You can also use **Western Union.** To wire money, take either cash or a cashier's check to the nearest agent or call and use MasterCard or Visa. Money sent from the United States or Canada will be available for pickup at agent locations in 100 countries within minutes. Once the money is in the system, it can be picked up at *any* one of 25,000 locations (call 800/325–6000 for the one nearest you; 800/321–2923 in Canada). Fees range from 4% to 10%, depending on the amount you send.

Spanish Currency

The peseta is Spain's currency unit. Bills are 10,000, 5,000, 2,000, and 1,000. Coins are 500, 200, 100, 50, 25, 10, 5, and 1 peseta. Be careful not to mix up the 100- and 500-peseta coins—they are the same color and almost the same size. There are two types of 25 peseta coins, large silver ones and small bronze ones with a hole in the center. Five-peseta coins are always called *duros*, but watch out for the new microsized 1- and 5-peseta coins. At press time (spring 1994) the currency markets of Europe were highly unstable, with exchange rates of 142 pesetas to the U.S. dollar, 108 pesetas per Canadian dollar, and 213 pesetas to the pound sterling.

What It Will Cost

Spain's rush to catch up with the rest of Europe has kept prices climbing; annual inflation runs about 5%. But devaluations of the peseta have brought prices down substantially for foreigners, while hotels and restaurants have moderated their tariffs in order to attract more visitors. Still, Madrid and Barcelona are nearly as expensive as any international capital and harder on the pocketbook than many big cities in the United States and Great Britain. The popular Costa del Sol, Costa Blanca, and Costa Brava can also be expensive, but lower-priced hotels and restaurants catering mainly to the package-tour trade do exist. Substantially less expensive lodging and food awaits the traveler who heads inland and off the beaten path.

Restaurants and clothing are among the most expensive items in Spain. World-famous Spanish leather jackets and shoes may be beautiful, but they are no bargain. Hotels are generally reasonably priced, and the government-run parador hotel chain is a good value.

Transportation is economical in Spain, and new competition with Iberia on domestic routes has brought airfares down. Train and bus travel are inexpensive. The price of gas throughout the country is also low; however, highway tolls along the Mediterranean coast are high.

Taxes Value-added tax (or sales tax) is called IVA in Spain. It is charged on services, such as hotels and restaurants, and many categories of consumer products. Restaurant menus will generally say at the bottom whether tax is included *(IVA incluido)* or not *(más 6% IVA)*. The highest category restaurants are required to charge 15% IVA. Five–star hotels also charge 15% tax, but all other hotels charge only 6% IVA. A special tax law for the Canary Islands allows all hotels and restaurants there to charge 4% IVA. When in doubt as to whether tax is included in a price, ask, *Está incluido el IVA* (ee-vah)*?*

Sample Prices Coffee in a bar: 125 pesetas (standing), 150 pesetas (seated). Beer in a bar: 125 pesetas (standing), 150 pesetas (seated). Small glass of wine in a bar: 100 pesetas. Soft drink: 150–200 pesetas a bottle. Ham and cheese sandwich: 300–450 pesetas. One-mile taxi ride: 400 pesetas, but the meter keeps ticking in traffic jams. Local bus or subway ride: 150 pesetas. Movie-theater seat: 600 pesetas. Foreign newspaper: 225 pesetas.

Long Distance Calling

AT&T, MCI, and Sprint have several services that make calling home or the office more affordable and convenient when you're on the road. Use one of them to avoid pricey hotel surcharges. **AT&T** Calling Card (tel. 800/225–5288) and the AT&T Universal Card (tel. 800/662–7759) give you access to the service. With AT&T's USA Direct (tel. 800/874–4000 for codes in the countries you'll be visiting) you can reach an AT&T operator with a local or toll-free call. **MCI's** Call USA (MCI Customer Service, tel. 800/444–4444) allows that service from 85 countries or from country to country via MCI WorldReach. From MCI ExpressInfo in the United States you can get 24-hour weather, news, and stock quotes. MCI PhoneCash (tel. 800/925–0029) is available through American Express and through several convenience stores and retailers nationwide. **Sprint** Express (tel. 800/793–1153) has a toll-free number travelers abroad can dial using the WorldTraveler Foncard to reach a Sprint operator in the United States. The Sprint operator can offer international directory assistance to 224 countries in the world. All three companies offer message delivery services to international travelers and have added debit cards so that you don't have to fiddle with change.

Passports and Visas

All visitors are required by law to carry their passports at all times. Visitors who are stopped by police and found not to be carrying their passports are sometimes jailed. If you are worried about losing your passport by chance or to pickpockets, make a photocopy to carry with you during your visit and leave the passport in the hotel safe.

If your passport is lost or stolen, report the loss immediately to the nearest embassy or consulate and to the local police. If you can provide the consular officer with the information contained in the passport, he or she will usually be able to issue you a new passport promptly. For this reason, keep a photocopy of the data page of your passport separate from your money and traveler's checks. Also leave a photocopy with a relative or friend at home.

U.S. Citizens   All U.S. citizens, even infants, need a valid passport to enter Spain for stays of up to 90 days. You can pick up new and renewal application forms at any of the 13 U.S. Passport Agency offices and at some post offices and courthouses. Although passports are usually mailed within four weeks of your application's receipt, allow five weeks or more from April through summer. Call the Department of State Office of Passport Services' information line (tel. 202/647–0518) for details.

Canadian Citizens   Canadian citizens need a valid passport to enter Spain for stays of up to 90 days. Application forms are available at 23 regional passport offices as well as post offices and travel agencies. Whether for a first or subsequent passport, you must apply in person. Children under 16 may be included on a parent's passport but must have their own to travel alone. Passports are valid for five years and are usually mailed within two weeks of an application's receipt. For more information in English or French, call the passport office (tel. 514/283–2152 or 800/567–6868).

U.K. Citizens Citizens of the United Kingdom need a valid passport to enter Spain for stays of up to 90 days. Applications for new and renewal passports are available from main post offices as well as at the six passport offices, located in Belfast, Glasgow, Liverpool, London, Newport, and Peterborough. You may apply in person at all passport offices, or by mail to all except the London office. Children under 16 may travel on an accompanying parent's passport. All passports are valid for 10 years. Allow a month for processing.

A British Visitor's Passport is valid for holidays and some business trips of up to three months to Spain and other countries. It can include both partners of a married couple. A British visitor's passport is valid for one year and will be issued on the same day that you apply. You must apply in person at a main post office.

Customs and Duties

On Arrival Limits on transportation of goods from one EC country to another have been eliminated. From other countries, visitors age 15 and over are permitted to bring into Spain up to 200 cigarettes or 50 cigars, up to one liter of alcohol over 22 proof, and up to two liters of wine. Dogs and cats are admitted, providing they have up-to-date vaccination records from the home country.

Returning Home
U.S. Customs If you've been out of the country for at least 48 hours and haven't already used the exemption, or any part of it, in the past 30 days, you may bring home $400 worth of foreign goods duty-free. So can each member of your family, regardless of age; and your exemptions may be pooled, so one of you can bring in more if another brings in less. A flat 10% duty applies to the next $1,000 of goods; above $1,400, the rate varies with the merchandise. (If the 48-hour or 30-day limits apply, your duty-free allowance drops to $25, which may not be pooled.) Please note that these are the *general* rules, applicable to most countries, including Spain.

Travelers 21 or older may bring back 1 liter of alcohol duty-free, provided the beverage laws of the state through which they reenter the United States allow it. In addition, 100 non-Cuban cigars and 200 cigarettes are allowed, regardless of your age. Antiques and works of art more than 100 years old are duty-free.

Gifts valued at less than $50 may be mailed to the United States duty-free, with a limit of one package per day per addressee, and do not count as part of your exemption (do not send alcohol or tobacco products or perfume valued at more than $5); mark the package "Unsolicited Gift" and write the nature of the gift and its retail value on the outside. Most reputable stores will handle the mailing for you.

For a copy of "Know Before You Go," a free brochure detailing what you may and may not bring back to the United States, rates of duty, and other pointers, contact the **U.S. Customs Service** (Box 7407, Washington, DC 20044, tel. 202/927–6724).

Canadian Customs Once per calendar year, when you've been out of Canada for at least seven days, you may bring in C$300 worth of goods duty-free. If you've been away less than seven days but more than 48 hours, the duty-free exemption drops to C$100 but can be claimed any number of times (as can a C$20 duty-free exemption for absences of 24 hours or more). You cannot combine the yearly and 48-hour exemptions, use the C$300 exemption only partially (to save the balance for a later trip), or pool exemptions with family members. Goods claimed under the C$300 exemption may follow you by mail; those claimed under the lesser exemptions must accompany you on your return.

Alcohol and tobacco products may be included in the yearly and 48-hour exemptions but not in the 24-hour exemption. If you meet the age requirements of the province through which you reenter Canada, you may bring in, duty-free, 1.14 liters (40 imperial ounces) of wine or liquor *or* two dozen 12-ounce cans or bottles of beer or ale. If you are 16 or older, you may bring in, duty-free, 200 cigarettes, 50 cigars or cigarillos, and 400 tobacco sticks or 400 grams of manufactured tobacco.

An unlimited number of gifts valued up to C$60 each may be mailed to Canada duty-free. These do not count as part of your exemption. Label the package "Unsolicited Gift—Value under $60." Alcohol and tobacco are excluded.

For more information, including details of duties on items that exceed your duty-free limit, ask the Revenue Canada Customs and Excise and Taxation Department (2265 St. Laurent Blvd. S, Ottawa, Ontario, K1G 4K3, tel. 613/957–0275) for a copy of the free brochure "I Declare/Je Déclare."

U.K. Customs If your journey was wholly within EC countries, you no longer need to pass through customs when you return to the United Kingdom. According to EC guidelines, you may bring in 800 cigarettes, 400 cigarillos, 200 cigars, and 1 kilogram of smoking tobacco, plus 10 liters of spirits, 20 liters of fortified wine, 90 liters of wine, and 110 liters of beer. If you exceed these limits, you may be required to prove that the goods are for your personal use or are gifts.

For further information or a copy of "A Guide for Travellers," which details standard customs procedures as well as what you may bring into the United Kingdom from abroad, contact HM Customs and Excise (Dorset House, Stamford St., London SE1 9PY, tel. 071/928–3344).

Traveling with Cameras, Camcorders, and Laptops

Film and Cameras If your camera is new or if you haven't used it for a while, shoot and develop a few test rolls before you leave. Store film in a cool, dry place—never in the car's glove compartment or on the shelf under the rear window.

Airport security X-rays generally aren't harmful to film with ISO below 400. To protect your film, carry it with you in a clear plastic bag and ask for a hand inspection. Such requests are honored at U.S. airports but are up to the inspector abroad. Don't depend on a lead-lined bag to protect film in checked luggage—the airline may increase the radiation to see what's inside. Call the Kodak Information Center (tel. 800/242–2424) for details.

Camcorders Before your trip, put camcorders through their paces, invest in a skylight filter to protect the lens, and check all the batteries. Most newer camcorders are equipped with batteries that can be recharged with a universal or worldwide AC adapter charger (or multivoltage converter), usable whether the voltage is 110 or 220. All that's needed is the appropriate plug.

Videotape Videotape is not damaged by X-rays, but it may be harmed by the magnetic field of a walk-through metal detector, so ask for a hand-check. Airport security personnel may ask you to turn on the camcorder to prove that it's what it appears to be, so make sure the battery is charged. Note that rather than the National Television

System Committee video standard (NTSC) used in the United States and Canada, Spain uses PAL/SECAM technology. You will not be able to view your tapes through the local TV set or view movies bought there in your home VCR. Blank tapes bought in Eastern Europe can be used for NTSC camcorder taping, but they are pricey.

Laptops Security X-rays do not harm hard-disk or floppy-disk storage, but you may request a hand-check, at which point you may be asked to turn on the computer to prove that it is what it appears to be. (Check your battery before departure.) Most airlines allow you to use your laptop aloft except during takeoff and landing (so as not to interfere with navigation equipment). For international travel, register your foreign-made laptop with U.S. Customs as you leave the country. If your laptop is U.S.-made, call the consulate of the country you'll be visiting to find out whether it should be registered with customs upon arrival. Before departure, find out about repair facilities at your destination, and don't forget any transformer or adapter plug you may need (*see* Electricity, *above*).

Language

Although Spaniards exported their language to all Central and South America, you may be surprised to find that Spanish is not the principal language of many regions of Spain. The Basques speak Euskera; in Catalunya (Catalonia), you'll hear Catalan; in Galicia, Gallego; and in Valencia, Valenciana. While almost everyone in these regions also speaks and understands Spanish, local radio and television stations broadcast in these languages and road signs are either printed or spray-painted over with the preferred regional language. Spanish is referred to as Castellano, or Castilian.

Roughly half the people you come in contact with will speak some English. But they speak the British variety, so don't be surprised if you are told to queue (line up) or take the lift (elevator) to the loo (toilet). All your attempts at Spanish are genuinely appreciated, and Spaniards will not make fun of your mistakes. Try to use at least the following basic phrases: *por favor* (please), *gracias* (thank you), *buenos días* (hello—until 2 PM), *buenas tardes* (good afternoon—until 8 PM), *buenas noches* (hello—after dark), *adiós* (good-bye), *encantado* (pleased to meet you), *sí* (yes), *no* (same as English), *los servicios* (the toilets), *la cuenta* (bill/check), *habla inglés?* (do you speak English?), *no comprendo* (I don't understand). Many guided tours offered at museums and historic sites are in Spanish; ask about the language that will be spoken before signing up.

Staying Healthy

Two problems frequently encountered during Spanish summers are sunburn and sunstroke. On hot, sunny days, even people who are not normally bothered by strong sun should cover themselves with a long-sleeve shirt, a hat, and long pants or a beach wrap. These are essential for a day at the beach but are also advisable for a long day of touring. Carry some sun-block lotion for nose, ears, and other sensitive areas, such as eyelids or ankles. Be sure to drink enough liquids. Above all, limit your sun time for the first few days until you become accustomed to the heat.

No special shots are required before visiting Spain.

Finding a The **International Association for Medical Assistance to Travellers**
Doctor (IAMAT, 417 Center St., Lewiston, NY 14092, tel. 716/754–4883; 40

Regal Rd., Guelph, Ontario N1K 1B5; 57 Voirets, 1212 Grand-Lancy, Geneva, Switzerland) publishes a worldwide directory of English-speaking physicians whose qualifications meet IAMAT standards and who have agreed to treat members for a set fee. Membership is free.

Assistance Companies Pretrip medical referrals, emergency evacuation or repatriation, 24-hour telephone hot lines for medical consultation, dispatch of medical personnel, relay of medical records, cash for emergencies, and other personal and legal assistance are among the services provided by several membership organizations specializing in medical assistance to travelers. Among them are **International SOS Assistance** (Box 11568, Philadelphia, PA 19116, tel. 215/244–1500 or 800/523–8930; Box 466, Pl. Bonaventure, Montréal, Québec H5A 1C1, tel. 514/874–7674 or 800/363–0263), **Medex Assistance Corporation** (Box 10623, Baltimore, MD 21285, tel. 410/296–2530 or 800/874–9125), **Near Services** (450 Prairie Ave., Suite 101, Calumet City, IL 60409, tel. 708/868–6700 or 800/654–6700), and **Travel Assistance International** (1133 15th St. NW, Suite 400, Washington, DC 20005, tel. 202/331–1609 or 800/821–2828). Because these companies will also sell you death-and-dismemberment, trip-cancellation, and other insurance coverage, there is some overlap with the travel-insurance policies discussed under Insurance, *below*.

Publications *The Safe Travel Book* by Peter Savage ($12.95; Lexington Books, 866 3rd Ave., New York, NY 10022, tel. 212/702–4771 or 800/257–5755, fax 800/562–1272) is packed with handy lists and phone numbers to make your trip smooth. *Traveler's Medical Resource* by William W. Forgey ($19.95; ICS Books, Inc., 1 Tower Plaza, 107 E. 89th Ave., Merrillville, IN 45410, tel. 800/541–7323) is also a good, authoritative guide to care overseas.

Insurance

For U.S. Residents Most tour operators, travel agents, and insurance agents sell specialized health-and-accident, flight, trip-cancellation, and luggage insurance as well as comprehensive policies with some or all of these features. Before you make any purchase, review your existing health and homeowner policies to find out whether they cover expenses incurred while travelling.

Health-and-Accident Insurance Specific policy provisions of supplemental health-and-accident insurance for travelers include reimbursement for from $1,000 to $150,000 worth of medical and/or dental expenses caused by an accident or illness during a trip. The personal-accident, or death-and-dismemberment, provision pays a lump sum to your beneficiaries if you die or to you if you lose a limb or your eyesight; the lump sum awarded can range from $15,000 to $500,000. The medical-assistance provision may reimburse you for the cost of referrals, evacuation, or repatriation and other services, or it may automatically enroll you as a member of a particular medical-assistance company (*see* Assistance Companies, *above*).

Flight Insurance Often bought on a last-minute impulse at the airport, flight insurance pays a lump sum when a plane crashes, either to a beneficiary if the insured dies or sometimes to a surviving passenger who loses eyesight or a limb. Like most impulse buys, flight insurance is expensive and basically unnecessary. It supplements the airlines' coverage described in the limits-of-liability paragraphs on your ticket. Charging an airline ticket to a major credit card often automatically entitles you to coverage and may also embrace travel by bus, train, and ship.

Baggage Insurance In the event of loss, damage, or theft on international flights, airlines' liability is $20 per kilogram for checked baggage (roughly about $640 per 70-pound bag) and $400 per passenger for unchecked baggage. On domestic flights, the ceiling is $1,250 per passenger. Excess-valuation insurance can be bought directly from the airline at check-in for about $10 per $1,000 worth of coverage. However, you cannot buy it at any price for the rather extensive list of excluded items shown on your airline ticket.

Trip Insurance **Trip-cancellation-and-interruption insurance** protects you in the event you are unable to undertake or finish your trip, especially if your airline ticket, cruise, or package tour does not allow changes or cancellations. The amount of coverage you purchase should equal the cost of your trip should you, a traveling companion, or a family member fall ill, forcing you to stay home, plus the nondiscounted one-way airline ticket you would need to buy if you had to return home early. Read the fine print carefully, especially sections defining "family member" and "preexisting medical conditions." **Default** or **bankruptcy insurance** protects you against a supplier's failure to deliver. Such policies often do not cover default by a travel agency, tour operator, airline, or cruise line if you bought your tour and the coverage directly from the firm in question. Tours packaged by one of the 33 members of the United States Tour Operators Association (USTOA, 211 E. 51 St., Suite 12B, New York, NY 10022, tel. 212/750–7371), which requires members to maintain $1 million each in an account to reimburse clients in case of default, are likely to present the fewest difficulties.

Comprehensive Policies Companies supplying comprehensive policies with some or all of the above features include **Access America, Inc.** (Box 90315, Richmond, VA 23230, tel. 800/284–8300); **Carefree Travel Insurance** (Box 310, 120 Mineola Blvd., Mineola, NY 11501, tel. 516/294–0220 or 800/323–3149); **Tele-Trip** (Mutual of Omaha Plaza, Box 31762, Omaha, NE 68131, tel. 800/228–9792); **The Travelers Companies** (1 Tower Sq., Hartford, CT 06183, tel. 203/277–0111 or 800/243–3174); **Travel Guard International** (1145 Clark St., Stevens Point, WI 54481, tel. 715/345–0505 or 800/826–1300); and **Wallach and Company, Inc.** (107 W. Federal St., Box 480, Middleburg, VA 22117, tel. 703/687–3166 or 800/237–6615).

U.K. Residents Most tour operators, travel agents, and insurance agents sell specialized policies covering accident, medical expenses, personal liability, trip cancellation, and loss or theft of personal property. You can also buy an annual travel-insurance policy valid for every trip (usually of less than 90 days) you make during the year in which it's purchased. Make sure you will be covered if you have a preexisting medical condition or are pregnant.

For advice by phone or a free booklet, "Holiday Insurance," that sets out what to expect from a holiday-insurance policy and gives price guidelines, contact the Association of British Insurers (51 Gresham St., London EC2V 7HQ, tel. 071/600–3333; 30 Gordon St., Glasgow G1 3PU, tel. 041/226–3905; Scottish Providence Bldg., Donegall Sq. W, Belfast BT1 6JE, tel. 0232/249176; call for other locations).

Car Rentals

Spain's leading car-rental firm is **ATESA** (Orense 83, Madrid, tel. 91/571–2145; Plaza Carmen Benitez 7, Seville, tel. 95/441–9712). In addition, most major car-rental companies are represented in Spain, including **Avis** (tel. 800/331–1084, 800/879–2847 in Canada); **Budget** (tel. 800/527–0700); **Hertz** (tel. 800/654–3001, 800/263–0600 in Canada); and **National** (tel. 800/227–3876), the latter two known internationally as InterRent and Europcar, respectively.

In cities, unlimited-mileage rates range from $46 per day for an economy car to $125 for a large car; weekly unlimited-mileage rates range from $180 to $450. This does not include IVA tax, which in Spain is 15% on car rentals.

Requirements Your own driver's license is not acceptable. An International Driver's Permit, available from the American or Canadian Automobile Association, is necessary.

Extra Charges Picking up the car in one city and leaving it in another may entail substantial drop-off charges or one-way service fees. The cost of a collision or loss-damage waiver (*see below*) can be high, also. Some rental agencies will charge you extra if you return the car *before* the time specified on your contract. Ask before making unscheduled drop-offs. Be sure the rental agent agrees *in writing* to any changes in drop-off location or other items of your rental contract. Fill the tank when you turn in the vehicle to avoid being charged for refueling at what you'll swear is the most expensive pump in town. In Europe, manual transmissions are standard and air-conditioning is a rarity and often unnecessary. Asking for an automatic transmission or air-conditioning can significantly increase the cost of your rental.

Cutting Costs If you are planning to begin your visit with a city stay, don't pick up your car until the day you want to start traveling. If you are already in Spain and decide to rent a car, it can pay to have a friend at home book your car. Or ask a travel agent about fly-drive and train-drive packages and special weekend deals.

Major international companies have programs that discount their standard rates by 15%–30% if you make the reservation before departure (anywhere from 24 hours to 14 days), rent for a minimum number of days (typically three or four), and prepay the rental. More economical rentals may come as part of fly/drive or other packages, even bare-bones deals that only combine the rental and an airline ticket (*see* Tours and Packages, *above*).

Several companies operate as wholesalers. They do not own their own fleets but rent in bulk from those that do and offer advantageous rates to their customers. Rentals through such companies must be arranged and paid for before you leave the United States. Among them are **Europe by Car** (mailing address, 1 Rockefeller Plaza, New York, NY 10020; walk-in address, 14 W. 49th St., New York, NY 10020, tel. 212/581–3040, 212/245–1713, or 800/223–1516; 9000 Sunset Blvd., Los Angeles, CA 90069, tel. 213/252–9401 or 800/223–1516); **Foremost Euro-Car** (5658 Sepulvada Blvd., Suite 201, Van Nuys, CA 91411, tel. 818/786–1960 or 800/272–3299); and **The Kemwel Group** (106 Calvert St., Harrison, NY 10528, tel. 914/835–5555 or 800/678–0678). You won't see these wholesalers' deals advertised; they're even better in summer, when business travel is down. Always ask whether the prices are guaranteed in U.S. dollars or foreign currency and if unlimited mileage is available. Find out about any required deposits, cancellation penalties, and drop-off charges, and confirm the cost of any required insurance coverage.

Insurance and Collision-Damage Waiver Until recently, standard rental contracts included liability coverage (for damage to public property, injury to pedestrians, and so on) and coverage for the car against fire, theft, and collision damage with a deductible. Due to law changes in some states and rising liability costs, several car rental agencies have reduced the type of coverage they offer. Before you rent a car, find out exactly what coverage, if any, is provided by your personal auto insurer. Don't assume that you are covered. If you do want insurance from the rental company, secondary coverage may be the only type offered. You may already have secondary coverage if you charge the rental to a credit card. Only Diners Club (tel. 800/234–6377) provides primary coverage in the United States and worldwide.

In general if you have an accident, you are responsible for the automobile. Car rental companies may offer a collision damage waiver (CDW), which ranges in cost from $4 to $14 a day. You should decline the CDW only if you are certain you are covered through your personal insurer or credit card company.

Leasing For trips of 21 days or longer, you may save money by leasing a car. With the leasing arrangement, you are technically buying a car and then selling it back to the manufacturer after you've used it. Although leasing is not common in Spain, companies that offer some leasing arrangements include **Europe by Car** and **Kemwel**—both listed above.

Rail Passes

Spain Flexipasses give you three, five, or 10 days of travel during any one-month period; cost is $185, $265, and $470 for first class, $145, $225, and $345 for second class. Various rail/drive packages are also available. The **Spain Rail 'N Drive Pass** gives you three days of rail travel in Spain and three days' use of an Avis car with unlimited mileage in both Spain and Portugal; cost ranges from $325 for an economy car to $475 for a small automatic if you opt for first-class train travel, $279–$435 if you go second class ($265–$339 in first-class, $219–$295 in second, per person, for two adults traveling together). Prices include local tax and free drop-off. (None of the above rail passes are valid for the Andalusia Express nor the Pablo Casals, and you must pay extra, in local currency, to ride the AVE, Talgo, and some other trains.)

Spain is also one of 17 countries in which you can use **EurailPasses,** which provide unlimited first-class rail travel during their period of validity. If you plan to rack up the miles, they can be an excellent value. Standard passes are available for 15 days ($498), 21 days ($648), one month ($728), two months ($1,098), and three months ($1,398). **Eurail Saverpasses,** valid for 15 days, cost $430 per person, 21 days for $550, one month for $678 per person; you must do all your traveling with at least one companion (two companions from April through September). **Eurail Youthpasses,** which cover second-class travel, cost $578 for one month, $768 for two; you must be under 26 on the first day you travel. **Eurail Flexipasses** allow you to travel first class for five ($348), 10 ($560), or 15 ($740) days within any two-month period. **Eurail Youth Flexipasses,** available to those under 26 on their first travel day, allow you to travel second class for five ($255), 10 ($398), or 15 ($540) days within any two-month period. Another option is the **Europass,** featuring a minimum of five and a maximum of 15 days (within a two-month period) of unlimited rail travel in your choice of three to all five of the participating countries (France, Germany, Italy, Spain, and Switzerland); cost for five days is $280 first class, $198 second class (three countries); for eight days, $394 first class, $284 second class (four countries), and for 11 days, $508 first class, $366 second class (all five countries). Each extra day costs $38 for first class and $28 for second class. Apply through your travel agent or Rail Europe (226–230 Westchester Ave., White

Plains, NY 10604, tel. 914/682–5172 or 800/848–7245; or 2087 Dundas E, Suite 105, Mississauga, Ontario L4X 1M2, tel. 416/602–4195), **DER Tours** (Box 1606, Des Plaines, IL 60017, tel. 800/782–2424, fax 800/282–7474), or **CIT Tours Corp.** (342 Madison Ave., Suite 207, New York, NY 10173, tel. 212/697–2100 or 800/248–8687; 310/670–4269 or 800/248–7245 in western U.S.).

All of these passes must be purchased before you reach Spain. Apply through your travel agent, or **Rail Europe** (226–230 Westchester Ave., White Plains, NY 10604, tel. 914/682–5172 or 800/848–7245 from the East and 800/848-7245 from the West).

Seat Reservations Don't make the mistake of assuming that your rail pass guarantees you seats on the trains you want to ride. Seat reservations are required on some trains, particularly high-speed trains, and are a good idea on trains that may be crowded. You will also need reservations for overnight sleeping accommodations. Rail Europe can help you determine if you need reservations and can make them for you (about $10 each, less if you purchase them in Europe at the time of travel).

Student and Youth Travel

Travel Agencies **Council Travel Services (CTS)**, a subsidiary of the nonprofit Council on International Educational Exchange (CIEE), specializes in low-cost travel arrangements abroad for students and is the exclusive U.S. agent for several discount cards. Newly available from CTS are domestic air passes for bargain travel within the United States. CIEE's twice-yearly *Student Travels* magazine is available at the CTS office at CIEE headquarters (205 E. 42nd St., 16th Floor, New York, NY 10017, tel. 212/661–1450) and in Boston (tel. 617/266–1926), Miami (tel. 305/670–9261), Los Angeles (tel. 310/208–3551) and at 43 branches in college towns nationwide (free in person, $1 by mail). **Campus Connections** (1100 E. Marlton Pike, Cherry Hill, NJ 08034, tel. 800/428–3235) specializes in discounted accommodations and airline fares for students. The **Educational Travel Centre** (438 N. Frances St., Madison, WI 53703, tel. 608/256–5551) offers low-cost domestic and international airline tickets, mostly for flights departing from Chicago, and rail passes. Other travel agencies catering to students include **TMI Student Travel** (1146 Pleasant St., Watertown, MA 02172, tel. 617/661–8187 or 800/245–3672), and **Travel Cuts** (187 College St., Toronto, Ontario M5T 1P7, tel. 416/979–2406).

Discount Cards For discounts on transportation and on museum and attractions admissions, buy the **International Student Identity Card** (ISIC) if you're a bona fide student or the **International Youth Card** (IYC) if you're under 26. In the United States the ISIC and IYC cards cost $16 each and include basic travel accident and illness coverage and a toll-free travel assistance hotline. Apply to **CIEE** (*see* address *above*, tel. 212/661–1414; the application is in *Student Travels*). In Canada the cards are available for $15 each from **Travel Cuts** (*see above*). In the United Kingdom they cost £5 and £4 respectively at student unions and student travel companies, including Council Travel's London office (28A Poland St., London W1V 3DB, tel. 071/437–7767).

Hostelling There are some 55 youth hostels (*albergues juveniles*) throughout Spain, and more open during the summer months. But because of the abundance of unsupervised cheap lodging at pensions, hostels are not as popular in Spain as in other European countries. A youth hostel card is needed. Spanish hostels are listed in the international

YHA directory, or you can contact the **Red Nacional de Albergues Juveniles** (Ortega y Gasset 71–3A, 28006 Madrid, tel. 91/347–7700).

A **Hostelling International** (HI) membership card is the key to more than 5,000 hostels in 70 countries; the sex-segregated, dormitory-style sleeping quarters, including some for families, go for $7 to $20 a night per person. Membership is available in the United States through **Hostelling International-American Youth Hostels** (HI-AYH, 733 15th St. NW, Suite 840, Washington, DC 20005, tel. 202/783–6161), the U.S. link in the worldwide chain, and costs $25 for adults 18 to 54, $10 for those under 18, $15 for those 55 and over, and $35 for families. Volume 1 of the *AYH Guide to Budget Accommodation* lists hostels in Europe and the Mediterranean ($13.95, including postage). HI membership is available in Canada through **Hostelling International-Canada** (205 Catherine St., Suite 400, Ottawa, Ontario K2P 1C3, tel. 613/748–5638) for $26.75, and in the United Kingdom through the **Youth Hostel Association of England and Wales** (Trevelyan House, 8 St. Stephen's Hill, St. Albans, Hertfordshire AL1 2DY, tel. 0727/855215) for £9.

Tour Operators Contiki (300 Plaza Alicante #900, Garden Grove, CA 92640, tel. 714/740–0808 or 800/266–8454) specializes in package tours for travelers from 18 to 35.

Traveling with Children

Spaniards love children, and bringing them along on your trip should not be a problem. You will see children accompanying their parents everywhere, including bars and restaurants. Shopkeepers will shower your child with *caramelos* (sweets), and even the coldest waiters tend to be friendlier when you have a youngster with you. But although you will not be shunted into a remote corner when you bring children into a Spanish restaurant, you won't find high chairs or special kids' menus. Children are expected to eat what their parents do, and it is perfectly acceptable to ask for an extra plate and share your food. Museum admissions and bus and metro rides are generally free for children up to age five. Be prepared for late bedtimes. Especially in summer, it is surprisingly common to see under-fives playing cheerfully outdoors until midnight. Disposable diapers (*pañales*), formula (*papillas*), and bottled baby foods are readily available at supermarkets and pharmacies.

Publications *Family Travel Times,* published 10 times a year by Travel With Your
Newsletter Children (TWYCH, 45 W. 18th St., New York, NY 10011, tel. 212/206–0688; annual subscription $55), covers destinations, types of vacations, and modes of travel. TWYCH also publishes *Cruising with Children* ($22) and *Skiing with Children* ($29).

Books *Traveling with Children—And Enjoying It,* by Arlene K. Butler ($11.95 plus $3 shipping per book; Globe Pequot Press, Box 833, 6 Business Park Rd., Old Saybrook, CT 06475, tel. 800/243–0495, or 800/962–0973 in CT) helps you plan your trip with children, from toddlers to teens. *Innocents Abroad: Traveling with Kids in Europe,* by Valerie Wolf Deutsch and Laura Sutherland ($15.95 or $4.95 paperback; Penguin USA, 120 Woodbine St., Bergenfield, NJ 07621, tel. 800/253–6476), covers child- and teen-friendly activities, food, and transportation.

Getting There On international flights, the fare for infants under age 2 not occupy-
Air Fares ing a seat is generally either free or 10% of the accompanying adult's fare; children ages 2 through 11 usually pay from half to two-thirds of the adult fare. On domestic flights, children under 2 not occupying

a seat travel free, and older children currently travel on the "lowest applicable" adult fare.

Baggage In general, infants paying 10% of the adult fare are allowed one carry-on bag, not to exceed 70 pounds or 45 inches (length + width + height), and a collapsible stroller; check with the airline before departure, because you may be allowed less if the flight is full. The adult baggage allowance applies for children paying half or more of the adult fare.

Safety Seats The FAA recommends the use of safety seats aloft and details approved models in the free leaflet "**Child/Infant Safety Seats Recommended for Use in Aircraft**" (available from the Federal Aviation Administration, APA–200, 800 Independence Ave. SW, Washington, DC 20591, tel. 202/267–3479); information hotline, tel. 800/322–7873). Airline policy varies. U.S. carriers allow FAA-approved models bearing a sticker declaring their FAA approval. Because these seats are strapped into regular passenger seats, airlines may require that a ticket be bought for an infant who would otherwise ride free.

Facilities Aloft Some airlines provide other services for children, such as children's meals and freestanding bassinets (only to those with seats at the bulkhead, where there's enough legroom). Make your request when reserving. Biennially the February issue of *Family Travel Times* details children's services on three dozen airlines ($12; *see above*). "Kids and Teens in Flight" (free from the U.S. Department of Transportation's Office of Consumer Affairs (R-25, Washington, DC 20590, tel. 202/366–2220) offers tips for children flying alone.

Lodging Spanish hotels have no trouble providing a crib or cot for children who share a room with their parents, but there is almost always a small extra charge. The **Novotel** hotel chain (tel. 800/221–4542) allows up to two children to stay free in their parents' room. Many of the hotels include playgrounds. In addition, many Spanish ski resorts, including Baqueira Beret, have child-care facilities.

Baby-Sitting Services While there is no such thing as a babysitting agency in Spain, reliable child minders can be located through your hotel. With a few hours' notice, the concierge or reception desk can find a babysitter, usually a moonlighting maid who will charge about 800 pesetas an hour.

Hints for Travelers with Disabilities

Unfortunately, Spain has done little to make traveling easy for visitors with disabilities. Only the newest museums, such as the Reina Sofia and the Thyssen-Bornemisza museum in Madrid, have wheelchair entrances or elevators. Most of the churches, castles, and monasteries on a tourist's itinerary involve quite a bit of walking and climbing uneven terrain.

Organizations Several organizations provide travel information for people with disabilities, usually for a membership fee, and some publish newsletters and bulletins. Among them are the **Information Center for Individuals with Disabilities** (Fort Point Pl., 27–43 Wormwood St., Boston, MA 02210, tel. 617/727–5540 or 800/462–5015 in MA between 11 AM and 4 PM, or leave message; TTY 617/345–9743); **Mobility International USA** (Box 10767, Eugene, OR 97440, tel. and TTY 503/343–1284, fax 503/343–6812), the U.S. branch of an international organization based in Britain (*see below*) that has affiliates in 30 countries; **MossRehab Hospital Travel Information Service** (tel. 215/456–9603, TTY 215/456–9602); the **Travel Industry and Disabled Exchange** (TIDE, 5435 Donna Ave., Tarzana, CA 91356, tel. 818/344–3640, fax 818/344–0078); and **Travelin' Talk** (Box 3534, Clarksville, TN 37043, tel. 615/552–6670, fax 615/552–1182).

In the United Kingdom Important information sources include the **Royal Association for Disability and Rehabilitation** (RADAR, 12 City Forum, 250 City Rd., London EC1V 8AF, tel. 071/250–3222), which publishes travel information for people with disabilities in Britain, and **Mobility International** (228 Borough High St., London SE1 1JX, tel. 071/403–5688), an international clearinghouse of travel information for people with disabilities.

Travel Agency **Flying Wheels Travel** (143 W. Bridge St., Box 382, Owatonna, MN 55060, tel. 507/451–5005 or 800/535–6790) is a travel agency specializing in domestic and worldwide cruises, tours, and independent travel itineraries for people with mobility problems.

Publications Two free publications are available from the U.S. Consumer Information Center (Pueblo, CO 81009): "New Horizons for the Air Traveler with a Disability" (include Dept. 608Y in the address), a U.S. Department of Transportation booklet describing changes resulting from the 1986 Air Carrier Access Act and from the 1990 Americans with Disabilities Act, and the Airport Operators Council's *Access Travel: Airports* (Dept. 5804), which describes facilities and services for people with disabilities at more than 500 airports worldwide.

Travelin' Talk Directory (*see* Organizations, *above*) was published in 1993. This 500-page resource book ($35 check or money order with a money-back guarantee) is packed with information for travelers with disabilities. Twin Peaks Press (Box 129, Vancouver, WA 98666, tel. 206/694–2462 or 800/637–2256) publishes the *Directory of Travel Agencies for the Disabled* ($19.95), listing more than 370 agencies worldwide. Add $2 for shipping.

Hints for Older Travelers

In Spain seniors are called *Tercer Edad* (literally "third age"). Older travelers should have no problems visiting Spain provided they do not try to cram too much sightseeing into one day, especially in the scorching months of July and August. Discounts on admissions and transportation for seniors are not common, but Spanish travel agencies offer retired folks lots of special deals on beach holidays to the Balearic and Canary islands during the off season. The RENFE Gold Card for half-price train tickets is available only to Spanish citizens and legal foreign residents over 60.

Organizations The **American Association of Retired Persons** (AARP, 601 E St. NW, Washington, DC 20049, tel. 202/434–2277) provides independent travelers who are members of the AARP (open to those age 50 or older; $8 per person or couple annually) with the Purchase Privilege Program, which offers discounts on lodging, car rentals, and sightseeing. AARP also arranges group tours, cruises, and apartment living through AARP Travel Experience from American Express (400 Pinnacle Way, Suite 450, Norcross, GA 30071, tel. 800/927–0111 or 800/745–4567).

Two other organizations offer discounts on lodgings, car rentals, and other travel products, along with such nontravel perks as magazines and newsletters: the **National Council of Senior Citizens** (1331 F St. NW, Washington, DC 20004, tel. 202/347–8800 (membership $12 annually) and **Mature Outlook** (6001 N. Clark St., Chicago, IL 60660, tel. 800/336–6330; $9.95 annually).

Note: Mention your senior-citizen identification card when booking hotel reservations for reduced rates, not when checking out. At restaurants, show your card before you're seated; discounts may be limited to certain menus, days, or hours. If you are renting a car, ask about promotional rates that might improve on your senior-citizen discount.

Educational Travel The nonprofit **Elderhostel** (75 Federal St., 3rd Floor, Boston, MA 02110, tel. 617/426–7788) has offered inexpensive study programs for people 60 and older since 1975. Held at more than 1,800 educational and cultural institutions, courses cover everything from marine science to Greek myths and cowboy poetry. Participants generally attend lectures in the morning and spend the afternoon sightseeing or on field trips; they live in dormitory-type lodgings. Unique home-stay programs are offered in a few countries. Fees for the two- to three-week international trips—including room, board, tuition, and transportation from the United States—range from $1,800 to $4,500.

Interhostel (University of New Hampshire, 6 Garrison Ave., Durham, NH 03824, tel. 603/862–1147 or 800/733–9753) caters to a slightly younger clientele—50 and over—and runs programs in some 25 countries. The idea is similar: Lectures and field trips mix with sightseeing, and participants stay in dormitories at cooperating educational institutions or in modest hotels. Programs usually last two weeks and cost $1,500–$2,100, excluding airfare.

Publications *The 50 + Traveler's Guidebook: Where to Go, Where to Stay, What to Do* by Anita Williams and Merrimac Dillon ($12.95; St. Martin's Press, 175 5th Ave., New York, NY 10010) is available in bookstores and offers many useful tips. "The Mature Traveler" (Box 50820, Reno, NV 89513, tel. 702/786–7419; $29.95), a monthly newsletter, contains many travel deals.

Hints for Gay and Lesbian Travelers

Organizations The **International Gay Travel Association** (Box 4974, Key West, FL 33041, tel. 800/448–8550), which has 700 members, will provide you with names of travel agents and tour operators who specialize in gay travel. The **Gay & Lesbian Visitors Center of New York Inc.** (135 W. 20th St., 3rd Floor, New York, NY 10011, tel. 212/463–9030 or 800/395–2315; $100 annually) mails a monthly newsletter to its members with information about domestic and international destinations.

Travel Agencies and Tour Operators The dominant travel agency in the market is **Above and Beyond** (3568 Sacramento St., San Francisco, CA 94118, tel. 415/922–2683 or 800/397–2681). Tour operator **Olympus Vacations** (8424 Santa Monica Blvd., #721, West Hollywood, CA 90069, tel. 310/657–2220) offers all-gay-and-lesbian resort holidays. **Skylink Women's Travel** (746 Ashland Ave., Santa Monica, CA 90405, tel. 310/452–0506 or 800/225–5759) handles individual travel for lesbians all over the world and conducts two international and five domestic group trips annually.

Publications The premier international travel magazine for gays and lesbians is **Our World** (1104 N. Nova Rd., Suite 251, Daytona Beach, FL 32117, tel. 904/441–5367; $35 for 10 issues). **Out & About** (tel. 203/789–8518 or 800/929–2268; $49 for 10 issues, full refund if you aren't satisfied) is a 16-page monthly newsletter with extensive information on resorts, hotels, and airlines that are gay-friendly.

Further Reading

Spain's people and history are explained through the metaphors of their monuments and landscapes in Jan Morris's brilliant series of essays entitled *Spain;* James A. Michener fills us in on all the anecdotes that make sightseeing worthwhile in *Iberia: Spanish Travels and Reflections;* and Ted Walker has more of a vagabond approach to travel in his book *In Spain.* Madrid-based journalist John Hooper examines the post-Franco era in *The Spaniards.*

Ernest Hemingway is the writer most responsible for embellishing the image of Spain. Read *The Sun Also Rises*, also known as *Fiesta,* for a vicarious visit to the Running of the Bulls in Pamplona. *For Whom the Bell Tolls* depicts the physical and psychological horrors of the Spanish civil war, and *Death in the Afternoon* contains a convincing argument on bullfighting.

H. V. Morton *(A Stranger in Spain)*, George Orwell *(Homage to Catalonia)*, V. S. Pritchett *(The Spanish Temper)*, and Washington Irving (the romantic and mystical *Tales of the Alhambra*) have all paid their respects to Spain.

Among Spanish writers, the story of the errant knight *Don Quixote,* by Miguel de Cervantes, will always be Spain's towering classic. The disturbing drama of Spain's repressed women is told in Federico García Lorca's play *Blood Wedding.*

For more modern fare try translations of the realism-drenched novels of Galician Camilo José Cela, the 1989 recipient of the Nobel Prize for literature. *The Beehive* and *The Family of Pascual Duarte* are his best-known works. *The Story of Spain*, by Mark Williams, is a fascinating account of the role Spain has played in world events throughout the centuries.

Gourmet Janet Mendel Searl's *Cooking in Spain* goes beyond the recipes to offer mouth-watering explanations of the country's regional specialties; Penelope Casas's *The Food and Wine of Spain* and *Tapas* both capture the flavor of Spanish life in essays and recipes; *404 Spanish Wines*, by Frank Snell, includes information on wine-growing regions; Author Colman Andrews's contagious enthusiasm for that region's foods is revealed in *Catalan Cuisine: Europe's Last Great Culinary Secret.*

Arriving and Departing

All transatlantic flights arriving in Spain from the United States and Canada pass through Madrid. Some stop briefly to let off passengers, while others require you to change planes to get to a farther destination in Spain.

From North America by Plane

Flights are either nonstop, direct, or connecting. A **nonstop** flight requires no change of plane and makes no stops. A **direct** flight stops at least once and can involve a change of plane, although the flight number remains the same; if the first leg is late, the second waits. This is not the case with a **connecting** flight, which involves a different plane and a different flight number.

Airports and Airlines Madrid's airport is called **Barajas** (tel. 91/305–8343), Barcelona's is **El Prat de Llobregat** (tel. 93/478–5000).

The seven airlines that fly nonstop from North America are **Iberia** (tel. 800/772–4642), from New York, Montreal, Miami; **TWA** (tel. 800/892–4141), from New York; **Continental** (tel. 800/231–0856), from Newark, New Jersey; **American Airlines** (tel. 800/433–7300), from Dallas/Ft. Worth and Miami; **United Airlines** (tel. 800/241–6522), from Washington, D.C.; **Delta** (800/221–1212), from Atlanta; and **AeroMexico** (tel. 800/237–6639), from Miami. For flights from New York to the Canary Islands, *see* Chapter 16. Two of the best-known charters for flights to Spain are **Air Europa** (tel. 718/244–6016) and **Spanair** (tel. 212/695–8660).

If you are arriving early in the morning on an overnight flight, be sure to let your hotel know in advance so it can have a room ready and you can get a nap.

Flying Time to Madrid From New York: 7 hours. From Dallas/Ft. Worth: 10½ hours. From Los Angeles (including one stop): 14½ hours.

Cutting Costs The Sunday travel section of most newspapers is a good source of deals. When booking, particularly through an unfamiliar company, call the Better Business Bureau and your local or state Consumer Protection Bureau to find out whether any complaints have been registered against the company, pay with a credit card if you can, and consider trip-cancellation and default insurance (*see* Insurance, *above*). A helpful resource is *Airfare Secrets Exposed*, by Sharon Tyler and Matthew Wonder ($16.95; Universal Information Publishing), available in bookstores.

Promotional Airfares Less expensive fares, called promotional or discount fares, are round-trip and involve restrictions, which vary according to the route and season. You must usually buy the ticket—commonly called an APEX (advance purchase excursion) when it's for international travel—in advance (seven, 14, or 21 days are usual), although some of the major airlines have added no-frills, cheap flights to compete with new bargain airlines on certain routes.

With the major airlines, the cheaper fares generally require minimum and maximum stays (for instance, over a Saturday night or at least seven and no more than 30 days). Airlines generally allow some return date changes for a $25 to $50 fee, but most low-fare tickets are nonrefundable. Only a death in the family would prompt the airline to return any of your money if you cancel a nonrefundable ticket. However, you can apply an unused nonrefundable ticket toward a new ticket, again with a small fee. The lowest fare is subject to availability, and only a small percentage of the plane's total seats will be sold at that price. Contact the U.S. Department of Transportation's Office of Consumer Affairs (I–25, Washington, DC 20590, tel. 202/366–2220) for a copy of "Fly-Rights: A Guide to Air Travel in the U.S." *The Official Frequent Flyer Guidebook*, by Randy Petersen ($14.99, plus $3 shipping and handling; 4715-C Town Center Dr., Colorado Springs, CO 80916, tel. 719/597–8899 or 800/487–8893), yields valuable hints on getting the most for your air travel dollars. Also new and helpful is *202 Tips Even the Best Business Travelers May Not Know*, by Christopher McGinnis, president of the Travel Skills Group ($10 in bookstores; Box 52927, Atlanta, GA 30355, tel. 404/659–2855).

Consolidators Consolidators or bulk-fare operators—"bucket shops"—buy blocks of seats on scheduled flights that airlines anticipate they won't be able to sell. They pay wholesale prices, add a markup, and resell the seats to travel agents or directly to the public at prices that still undercut the airline's promotional or discount fares (higher than a charter ticket but lower than an APEX ticket, and usually without the advance-purchase restriction). Moreover, some consolidators sometimes give you your money back. Carefully read the fine print detailing penalties for changes and cancellations. If you doubt the reliability of a company, call the airline once you've made your booking and confirm that you do, indeed, have a reservation on the flight.

The biggest U.S. consolidator, C.L. Thomson Express, sells only to travel agents. Well-established consolidators selling to the public include **UniTravel** (Box 12485, St. Louis, MO 63132, tel. 314/569–0900 or 800/325–2222); **Council Charter** (205 E. 42nd St., New York, NY 10017, tel. 212/661–0311 or 800/800–8222); and **Travac** (989 6th Ave., New York, NY 10018, tel. 212/563–3303 or 800/872–8800).

Discount Travel Clubs Travel clubs offer members unsold space on airplanes, cruise ships, and package tours at as much as 50% below regular prices. Membership may include a regular bulletin or access to a toll-free hotline giving details of available trips departing from three or four days to several months in the future. Most also offer 50% discounts off hotel rack rates, but double-check with the hotel to make sure it isn't offering a better promotional rate independent of the club. Clubs include **Discount Travel International** (114 Forrest Ave., Suite 203, Narberth, PA 19072, tel. 215/668–7184; $45 annually, single or family), **Entertainment Travel Editions** (Box 1014, Trumbull, CT 06611, tel. 800/445–4137; $28–$48 annually), **Great American Traveler** (Box 27965, Salt Lake City, UT 84127, tel. 800/548–2812; $29.95 annually), **Moment's Notice Discount Travel Club** (425 Madison Ave., New York, NY 10017, tel. 212/486–0503; $45 annually, single or family), **Privilege Card** (3391 Peachtree Rd. NE, Suite 110, Atlanta, GA 30326, tel. 404/262–0222 or 800/236–9732; domestic annual membership $49.95, international, $74.95), **Travelers Advantage** (CUC Travel Service, 49 Music Sq. W, Nashville, TN 37203, tel. 800/548–1116; $49 annually, single or family), and **Worldwide Discount Travel Club** (1674 Meridian Ave., Miami Beach, FL 33139, tel. 305/534–2082; $50 annually for family, $40 single).

Publications The newsletter "Travel Smart" (40 Beechdale Rd., Dobbs Ferry, NY 10522, tel. 800/327–3633; $44 a year) has a wealth of travel deals in each monthly issue. The monthly "Consumer Reports Travel Letter" (Consumers Union, 101 Truman Ave., Yonkers, NY 10703, tel. 800/234–1970) is filled with information on travel savings and indispensable consumer tips.

Enjoying the Flight Fly at night if you're able to sleep on a plane. Because the air aloft is dry, drink plenty of fluids while on board. Drinking alcohol contributes to jet lag, as do heavy meals. Bulkhead seats, in the front row of each cabin—usually reserved for people who have disabilities, are elderly, or are traveling with babies—offer more legroom, but trays attach awkwardly to seat armrests, and all possessions must be stowed overhead.

Smoking Since February 1990, smoking has been banned on all domestic flights of less than six hours' duration; the ban also applies to domestic segments of international flights aboard U.S. and foreign carriers. On U.S. carriers flying to Spain and other destinations abroad, a seat in a no-smoking section must be provided for every passenger who requests one, and the section must be enlarged to accommodate such passengers if necessary, as long as they have complied with the airline's deadline for check-in and seat assignment. If smoking bothers you, request a seat far from the smoking section.

Foreign airlines are exempt from these rules but do provide no-smoking sections, and some nations, including Canada as of July 1, 1993, have gone as far as to ban smoking on all domestic flights; other countries may ban smoking on flights of less than a specified duration.

Smoking has been banned on all flights within the Iberian Peninsula and to the Balaeric Islands. Flights to the Canary Islands, however, still allow smoking on board.

The International Civil Aviation Organization has set July 1, 1996, as the date to ban smoking aboard airlines worldwide, but the body has no power to enforce its decisions.

From the U.S. by Ship

There are no regular transatlantic crossings from the United States to Spain, but **Cunard Line** (555 5th Ave., New York, NY 10017, tel. 212/880–7545 or 800/221–4770) usually includes a stop in the Canary Islands on its repositioning crossings between Fort Lauderdale, Florida, and either Malaga or Barcelona (the schedule varies each year). **Royal Viking** (95 Merrick Way, Coral Gables, FL 33134, tel. 800/422–8000) includes a stop in Barcelona on some of its cruises.

From the U.K. by Plane, Train, Car, and Bus

By Plane It's important to distinguish between scheduled services to Spain, operated chiefly by **Iberia** and **British Airways,** and inexpensive charter flights, operated by a whole range of companies, that serve the holiday airports in the summer. If you're looking for bargains, don't mind traveling at inconvenient times, and are prepared for delays—up to 48 hours at peak periods—then consider a charter flight. But if you value reliability—and don't mind paying for it— you're better off with a scheduled flight.

Between them, Iberia and British Airways serve 15 Spanish airports from Heathrow, Gatwick, Birmingham, and Manchester. There are up to seven flights a day to Madrid from London, and up to six to Barcelona. Flying time is between 2 and 2½ hours. At both Madrid and Barcelona you can plug into Iberia's internal air network. The lowest fares require a Saturday night stayover.

Charter flights offer substantial savings, though booking conditions can be strict. You'll need to buy your ticket some time in advance (between two and four weeks), and most charter flights allow stays of no more than four weeks. On the other hand, there are charter flights to practically every Spanish airport from practically every British regional airport. Most flights, naturally, are in summer. Prices vary so much, however, that it's hard to give guidelines, though you can generally expect to pay between 10% and 15% less than on the cheapest scheduled flight. Check what's available with a good travel agent, take your time, and shop around.

Further bargains are available if you buy at the last minute off-season or want only a one-way ticket. Check the advertisements in *Time Out* and the Sunday papers.

For reservations and information: **British Airways** (tel. 71/897–4000), **Iberia** (tel. 71/437–5622).

By Train Train services to Spain are not as frequent, fast, or inexpensive as airplane travel.

To reach Spain from Britain, you have to change trains (and rail stations) in Paris. It's worth paying extra for a "TALGO" express or for the "Puerta del Sol" express to avoid having to change trains again at the Spanish border. Journey time to Paris is around six hours; to Madrid from Paris, an additional 13 hours. Allow at least two hours in Paris for changing trains.

International overnight trains run from Madrid to Lisbon (11½ hours) and Barcelona to Paris (11½ hours). A daytime trip is offered from Barcelona to Grenoble and Geneva (10 hours).

Eurotrain (52 Grosvenor Gardens, London SW1W OAG, tel. 071/730–3402) and **Transalpino** (71–75 Buckingham Palace Rd., London SW1W ORE, tel. 071/834–9656) both offer excellent deals for those under 26. Otherwise, book through **British Rail Travel Centers** (tel. 071/834–2345).

By Car Potentially the cheapest route to Spain by car, though not the fastest, is by cross-Channel ferry to France and then overland to Spain. The drawbacks are that the shortest, and thus the cheapest, ferry crossings (Dover–Calais or Folkestone–Boulogne) leave you with the greatest amount of driving, which can be not only tiring but also expensive, depending on whether you take toll autoroutes through France and how many nights you spend en route. Even the longer ferry crossings leave you with a significant amount of driving. Cherbourg, for example, with ferries from Portsmouth, is 980 km (610 mi) from the Spanish border.

An alternative is to put your car on the train in France, at either Calais or Boulogne, and travel overnight to Narbonne, 80 km (50 mi) from Spain's northeast border, or Biarritz, right on Spain's northwest border. Though fast and restful, this option is significantly more expensive. Similarly, direct ferry links between Britain and Spain are also expensive, but they get you there in 24 hours with no strain, weather permitting. Brittany Ferries runs between Plymouth and Santander, while P&O European Ferries operates from Plymouth to Bilbao.

For reservations and information: **Brittany Ferries** (tel. 0752/221–321), **Hover-Speed** (tel. 071/554–7061), **P&O European Ferries** (tel. 081/575–8555), **Sealink** (tel. 0223/47047), **SNCF** (for Motorail, tel. 071/409–3518).

By Bus The **Eurolines/National Express** consortium runs regular bus services to more than 45 destinations in Spain. Journey times are around 32 hours to Madrid from London and around 26 hours to Barcelona. There's a daily bus to Barcelona at peak periods and never fewer than two a week the rest of the year. There are two buses a week to Madrid year-round. Other destinations, especially the major summer resorts on Spain's east and south coasts, are also well served. Fares are reasonable.

For reservations and information: **Eurolines/National Express** (tel. 071/730–0202).

Staying in Spain

Getting Around

By Plane **Iberia** (tel. 901/333–111) and its sister carrier, **Aviaco,** are the main airlines offering domestic service, with flights from Madrid to all major cities and many interregional flights. Travel in Spain can be time-consuming, hot, and dusty. Trains are slow, and roads are sometimes bad, so flying is often the best option. Be sure to ask for your boarding time as you may be denied a seat on your flight even if you check in before the scheduled departure time.

Between Madrid and Barcelona, Iberia operates the *Puente Aereo* (Air Bridge) commuter service. Flights leave every half-hour or hour, depending on the time of day, and no advance booking is needed; just show up at the airport, buy a ticket, and take the next flight out.

If you buy a round-trip transatlantic ticket on Iberia, you might want to purchase a *Visit Spain* pass, good for four domestic flights during your trip. It must be purchased before you arrive in Spain, all flights must be booked in advance, and the cost is $300, or $350 if you want to include flights to the Canary Islands.

On certain days of the week, Iberia also offers *minifares*, which can save you 40% on domestic flights. Tickets must be purchased in advance, and you must stay over Saturday night.

Two independent airlines, **Air Europa** (tel. 91/305–5130) and **Spanair** (tel. 902/131–415), began operations in 1994; both offer a number of domestic routes, including Madrid–Barcelona, at prices about one-third less than Iberia.

By Train In 1992 Spain launched its first high-speed train, the AVE, which travels between Madrid and Seville in less than three hours. However, the rest of the government-run railroad, RENFE, remains below par by European standards. Train travel can be tediously slow, and most long-distance runs are made at night. While overnight trains have comfortable sleeper cars, first-class fares that include a sleeping compartment are about the same as those for air travel.

For most journeys, however, trains are the most economical way to go. First- and second-class seats are reasonably priced, and you can get a bunk in a compartment with five other people for a supplement of about $25. The most comfortable train is called a TALGO, and has a special inverted suspension system designed to give a faster and smoother ride on winding rails. Food in the dining cars and bars is overpriced and uninspired.

Most Spaniards buy train tickets in advance by standing in long lines at the station. But the overworked clerks rarely speak English, so you are better off going to a travel agency that displays the blue and yellow RENFE sign; the price is the same.

RENFE also operates the luxurious turn-of-the-century *Al Andalus Express,* which makes three- and five-day trips in Andalucía for sightseeing in Córdoba, Granada, and Seville, and runs from Barcelona to Santiago de Compostela along the Way of St. James in summer.

This is how kings and queens used to travel through Europe. The train has been splendidly restored down to the smallest etched-glass and wood-inlay details in the lounge, dining cars, and 19th-century sleeping compartments. The only new parts of the passenger train now are the two spacious shower cars. Cost for a three-day journey is approximately $1,700 per person. Reservations and information can be obtained from **Marketing Ahead** (433 5th Ave., New York, NY 10016, tel. 212/686–9213).

Fares Those planning extensive train travel during their stay should weigh the benefits of buying a *tarjeta tourista*, which allows unlimited travel during a 15-day or 30-day period. Large families are also eligible for substantial discounts, but there are no special fares for foreign senior citizens. Another option is to consider traveling on *valles* (literally, "valleys"), a special category of cheaper trains that leave at unpopular times, usually early in the morning.

If you are under 26 and have not invested in a Eurail Youthpass or any of the other rail passes, inquire about discount travel fares under a *Billet International Jeune* (BIJ) scheme. The special one-trip tariff is offered by **EuroTrain International,** with offices in London, Dublin, Paris, Madrid, Lisbon, Rome, Zurich, Athens, Brussels, Budapest, Hannover, Leiden, Vienna, and Tangier. You can purchase a EuroTrain ticket at one of these offices, or through travel agent networks, mainline rail stations, and specialist youth travel operators.

Smoking RENFE provides nonsmoking cars on many short runs and all long-distance service; ask for a seat or bunk in these areas when you reserve. But be prepared for second-hand smoke: Many Spaniards happily ignore all posted signs.

By Bus An array of private companies operate Spain's buses, providing service that ranges from knee-crunching basic to luxurious. Some buses have television and free drinks. Fares are lower than for rail travel. If you want to reach a town not served by train, you can be sure a bus will go there. Spanish towns don't usually have a central bus depot, so ask at the tourist office where to pick up a bus to your destination.

Bus tours are a popular way to see large cities and the surrounding sights. Among the largest operators, most with tours in English, are **Julia Tours** (Gran Vía 68, Madrid, tel. 91/571–5300); **Pullmantur** (Plaza de Oriente 8, Madrid, tel. 91/541–1805); **Marsans** (Gran Vía 59, Madrid, tel. 91/547–7300). In most cases you can book bus tours through your hotel.

By Car Driving is the best way to see rural areas and get off the beaten track. Roads are classified as follows: A for *autopista* (tollroad or *peaje*); N for *nacional* (main roads that are either divided highways or two lanes); and C for *comarcal* (local roads that crisscross the countryside).

Road Spain's highway system was overhauled for 1992 and the improve-
Conditions ment is startling. It now includes some 6,000 km (3,600 mi) of superhighways. Still, however, you find some stretches of major national highways that are two lanes wide, where traffic often backs up behind heavy trucks. Autopista tolls are steep.

Most Spanish cities have notoriously long morning and evening rush hours, which can try any driver's patience. Traffic jams *(atascos)* are especially bad in and surrounding Barcelona and Madrid, where the morning rush hour can last until noon! Evening rush hour runs from 7 PM to 9 PM.

Rules of the Residents of EC countries can use their national driver's license in
Road Spain; others should have an International Driving Permit (*see* Car

Rentals in Before You Go, *above*), although this rule is rarely enforced. Driving is on the right, and horns are banned in cities, but that doesn't keep Spaniards from blasting away. Children under 10 may not ride in the front seats, and seat belts are compulsory everywhere. Speed limits are 60 km per hour (37 mph) in cities, 100 km per hour (62 mph) on N roads, 120 km per hour (74 mph) on the autopista, and 90 km per hour (56 mph) unless otherwise signposted on other roads.

Gas Gas stations are plentiful. Prices, decontrolled in 1993, were 101 pesetas a liter for *normal* (regular; 92 octane) and 106 pesetas a liter for *super* (97 octane) at press time. Many small town service stations do not sell unleaded gas. Credit cards are frequently accepted, especially along main routes.

Breakdowns The large car-rental companies, Hertz and Avis, have 24-hour breakdown service. If you are a member of an automobile club (AAA, CAA, or AA), you can get help from the Spanish auto club RACE (Jose Abascal 10, Madrid, tel. 91/447–3200; emergency assistance, 91/593–3333).

By Boat Spain's Mediterranean islands of Mallorca, Menorca, and Ibiza can be reached by ferryboats operated by the **Trasmediterranea** company from Barcelona, Valencia, and Denia. The trip takes seven to nine hours, and tickets can be purchased through travel agents.

By Bicycle Spain is Europe's second most mountainous country, after Switzerland, and even country roads are often crowded with speeding trucks. For these reasons, a bicycle trip requires careful preparation. A detailed 20-day cycling tour called *The Route of El Cid*, mapped out by the tourist office, crosses Spain from Burgos to Valencia; a booklet describing it is available from the Consejo Superior de Deportes (Martín Fiero s/n, 28040 Madrid, tel. 91/589–6600). Guided cycling tours are offered by **Bicibus** (Puerta del Sol 14, 2nd Floor, Madrid, tel. 91/522–4501).

Telephones

Pay Phones There are three types of pay phones in Spain, all of them bright green. The most common kind has a digital readout, so you can see your money ticking away. You need at least 15 pesetas for a local call, 50 pesetas to call another province. Simply insert coins and wait for a dial tone. (At older models, you must line coins up in a groove on top of the dial and they drop down as needed.) Neither model accepts the new micro-size 5 and 10 peseta coins, nor the small 25 peseta coins.

Newer pay phones work on special telephone credit cards, which can be purchased at any tobacco shop for 1,000 or 2,000 pesetas.

Long-Distance Calls To call other provinces from within Spain, both from pay and private phones, dial the area code first. Large cities such as Madrid (91), Barcelona (93), Bilbao (94), Sevilla (95), and Valencia (96), have a two-digit area code followed by a seven-digit local number. A massive overhaul of the telephone system aims to install this pattern throughout Spain, but less-populated regions still have a three-digit area code followed by a six-digit local number. All provincial codes begin with a 9, but you don't need to use the 9 when dialing from outside Spain.

International Calls International calls are awkward from public pay phones and can be expensive from hotels, which often add a surcharge. The best way to make them is to go to the local telephone office. Every town has one, and big cities have several. When the call is connected, you will be sent to a quiet cubicle, and you will be charged according to the meter. If the price is 500 pesetas or more, you can pay with Visa or MasterCard.

In Madrid the main telephone office is on Gran Vía 28. There is another at the main post office and a third on Paseo Recoletos 43, just off Plaza Colón. In Barcelona calls can be placed from the office on Carrer de Fontanella 4, off Plaça de Catalunya.

To make an international call yourself, dial 07 and wait for a loud tone. Then dial the country code (1 for the United States and Canada, 44 for the United Kingdom), followed by the area code and number.

It is worthwhile to sign up for a U.S. long-distance service before you travel. For example, you can save about half the cost of phone calls from Spain to the states by using **AT&T USA Direct** (access tel. 900–99–0011), **Sprint** (access tel. 900–99–0013), or **MCI** (access tel. 900–99–0014). Simply dial the number from any phone in Spain and you will be connected to an English-speaking operator who will place the call. Collect calls are also cheaper and more convenient this way. **British Telecom** (access tel. 900–99–0044) has a similar service for its customers to ring the U.K.

Operators and Information For general information in Spain, dial 003; the international information and assistance operator is at 025. Information on hotels, transportation, museum hours, and the like is dispensed by friendly multi-lingual operators on the **Tourist Information Line** (tel. 901–300–600) daily 10–2.

Mail

Postal Rates Airmail letters to the United States and Canada cost 90 pesetas up to 15 grams. Letters to the United Kingdom and other countries in the European Community cost 45 pesetas up to 20 grams. Letters within Spain are 27 pesetas. Postcards are charged the same rate as letters. Stamps can be bought at post offices and government-run tobacco shops.

Receiving Mail Because mail delivery in Spain can often be slow and unreliable, it is best to have your mail sent to **American Express** or **Thomas Cook** (call 800/528–4800 for a list of foreign American Express offices). Mail-holding service is free if you are a card member. An alternative is to have mail held at a Spanish post office; have it addressed to **Lista de Correos** (general delivery) in a town you will be visiting. Postal addresses should include the name of the province in parentheses, e.g., Marbella (Málaga).

Tipping

Pride keeps Spaniards from acknowledging tips, but waiters and other service people are poorly paid, and you can be sure your contribution will be appreciated. On the other hand, if you run into some bad or surly service, don't feel obligated to leave a tip.

Restaurant checks may or may not include service, but no more than 10% of the bill is necessary for a tip, and if you eat *tapas* or sandwiches at a bar, leave less, enough to round out the bill to the nearest 100. Cocktail waiters get 25–50 pesetas a drink, depending on the bar.

Taxi drivers get about 25 pesetas, but more for long rides or extra help with luggage, although there is an official surcharge for airport runs and baggage.

Hotel porters are tipped 50 pesetas a bag; 50 pesetas also goes to someone who brings you room service. A doorman who calls you a taxi gets 25 pesetas. If you stay in a hotel for more than two nights, tip the maid about 100 pesetas per night. A concierge should be tipped for any additional help he or she gives you.

Tour guides should be tipped about 200 pesetas, ushers in theaters or bullfights 25–50 pesetas, barbers 100 pesetas, and ladies' hairdressers at least 200 for a wash and set. Washroom attendants are tipped 5–10 pesetas.

Opening and Closing Times

Public Holidays January 1 (New Year's Day), January 6 (Epiphany), March 19 (St. Joseph), April 14 (Good Friday), April 17 (Easter Monday—Barcelona and Palma de Mallorca), May 1 (Labor Day), August 15 (Assumption), October 12 (International Hispanic Day–Columbus Day), November 1 (All Saints Day), December 6 (Constitution), December 8 (Immaculate Conception—except Barcelona), December 25 (Christmas), and December 26 (Boxing Day—Barcelona and Palma de Mallorca).

In addition, each city and town has its own holidays honoring political events and patron saints. Madrid is closed May 2 (Madrid Day), May 15 (San Isídro), and November 9 (Almudena). Barcelona celebrates April 23 (St. George), September 11 (Catalunya Day), and September 24 (Merced). Valencia's community day is October 9.

If a public holiday falls on a Tuesday or Thursday, many businesses also close on the Monday or Friday in between for a long weekend called a *puente* (bridge).

Banks Banks are generally open weekdays 8:30 to 2, Saturdays 8:30 to 1, but in the summer most banks close at 1 PM weekdays and do not open on Saturday. Money exchanges at airports and train stations stay open later. Traveler's checks can also be cashed at the Corte Inglés department stores until 9 PM.

Museums Most museums are open from 9:30 to 2 and from 4 to 7, and are closed one day a week, usually Mondays, but opening hours vary widely, so check before you set off. A few big museums, such as the Prado, the Reina Sofía Museum in Madrid, and the Picasso Museum in Barcelona, do not close at midday.

Shops One of the most inconvenient things about Spain is that almost all shops close at midday for at least three hours, except for the two big department store chains (Corte Inglés and Gallerías Preciados). Generally store hours are from 10 to 1:30 and 5 to 8. Shops are closed all day Sunday, and in Madrid and several other places they are also closed Saturday afternoons.

Shopping

Ceramics and leather goods are what most tourists shop for in Spain. Distinctive country-style ceramics can be purchased throughout the country; most are made in Talavera, Puente del Arzobispo (Toledo), and Seville. Leather clothing, purses, and shoes can also be found across Spain, with the best selection in Madrid, although shoes are generally made in Alicante and the Balearic Islands.

Madrid has begun to earn an international reputation for high fashion. Clothes are pricey. Search out Calle Almirante off Paseo Recoletos, if only for window shopping.

If you're buying a gift for a child, duck into any stationery shop and you will find a wide selection of unusual pen and pencil boxes, the likes of which can't be bought in the States.

Other shopping in Spain will probably have something to do with alcohol. Each region produces its own wine, with the sherries of Jerez, the riojas of the north, and the sparkling wines of Catalunya famous around the world.

Tax Refunds A number of shops, particularly large stores and boutiques in holiday resorts, offer a refund of the 15% IVA sales tax on large purchases. The purchase must be a single item worth more than $500. You show your passport, fill out a form, and the store then mails you the refund at your home.

Galerías Preciados department stores issue foreign shoppers a card good for a 10% discount on all nonsale merchandise.

Sports and the Outdoors

Spaniards still seem more at home watching a soccer match on TV in a bar than swinging a racket on a tennis court, but the fitness revolution is beginning to make some inroads, and sports facilities are widely available, especially in the coastal resorts.

Thousands of pedal pushers turn out each year when the roads are closed off for Madrid's annual bicycle day. While **bicycling** is impossible in crowded cities, many coastal resorts offer bike rentals.

Sailing, boating, and **water sports** are popular all along the Mediterranean coast and in the Balearic Islands. Spain's best-known sailing enthusiast is King Juan Carlos, who keeps his fleet in Mallorca. The tourism office publishes a map listing the facilities available at hundreds of marinas, and for further information you can contact the **Federación Española de Vela** (Spanish Sailing Federation, Juan Vigon 23, 28003 Madrid, tel. 91/519–5008).

The mountain streams of the Pyrenees and other ranges offer excellent **fishing;** for permits and information, contact **ICONA** (Instituto Nacional para la Conservación de la Naturaleza, Madrid, tel. 91/347–6000) and the **Federación Española de Pesca** (Navas de Tolosa 3, 28013 Madrid, tel. 91/532–8353).

Another sports map is available with information about Spain's 84 golf courses. **Golf** is one of the country's main attractions. The course at El Saler, south of Valencia, is considered the best in continental Europe. Marbella, on the Costa del Sol, has 14 excellent courses; there are two on the Costa Brava and several on the Costa Blanca, including the two championship 18-hole courses at the superb La Manga complex near Cartagena. The **Real Federación Española de Golf** (Capitán Haya 9, 28020 Madrid, tel. 91/555–2757) can answer all your questions.

Hiking is possible in the interior of Spain. The numerous national parks range from the marshy Doñana, Prime Minister Felipe Gonzalez's favorite place for walking, to the mountainous Picos de Europa. The Pyrenees and the Sierra de Gredos are also popular with hikers. Tourist offices can provide details, or contact the

Federación Española de Montañismo (Alberto Aguilera 3, 28015 Madrid, tel. 91/445–1382).

Hunting is possible on private game preserves. Contact **ICONA** (*see above*) or **Federación Española de Caza** (Av. Reina Victoria 72, 28003 Madrid, tel. 91/553–9017) for permits and information.

Spain has excellent **skiing and winter sports** facilities. The major resorts include Baqueira-Beret, Port del Compte, Llessui, and Formigal in the Pyrenees. Skiing is also excellent at Sierra Nevada, near Granada, and close to Madrid at Navacerrada, Valcoto, and Valdesqui. A ski map is provided by the tourist office, or you can contact the **Federación Española de Deportes de Invierno** (Infanta Maria Terésa 14, 28016 Madrid, tel. 91/344–0944).

Beaches

With more than 2,000 miles of coastline, Spain has been promoting and developing her beaches since the tourist boom started some 20 years ago. Unfortunately, little thought has been given to protecting this precious natural resource. As a result, it's hard to find an unspoiled Spanish beach.

Sewage and industrial wastes have made swimming dangerous on beaches surrounding Barcelona, Tarragona, Valencia, Cadiz, Bilbao, Aviles, and La Coruña. High-rise development casts an unpleasant shadow over popular resorts on the Costa del Sol and Costa Blanca.

Try beaches in the provinces of Almería, Murcia, Huelva, and the Rías Bajas of Galicia for cleaner water and smaller crowds, but you may still have to fish plastic bottles and bags out of the sea before taking a dip.

Dining

Cuisine Seafood and roast meats are the national specialties; foods are lightly seasoned. Salads are delicious and are usually served topped with canned tuna and olives. If you get tired of adventurous dining, order an *ensalada mixta* (mixed salad) and a *solomillo* (filet mignon).

Spaniards eat paella, the delicious seafood and rice dish, exclusively at midday and preferably at a beachside restaurant, but it is served to tourists at dinnertime as well.

Lunch usually consists of the first plate, which is a salad, soup, vegetable, or smoked fish or cured meat; the second plate, almost always meat or fish; and dessert, which can be ice cream, yogurt, or flan, but is more typically a piece of fresh fruit. All this is accompanied by bread (no butter) and washed down with a bottle of wine. In big cities some businessmen now grab a quick sandwich instead of stopping for the traditional three-course lunch, but not many.

Restaurants are required by law to offer a *menú del día* at lunch that includes all the above at a price that is 80% of what each course would cost separately. Restaurants that specialize in a menú del día will post it at the door; in other establishments you have to ask to see the menú del día, and then it is often a couple of unappetizing choices designed to get you to order from the regular menu.

Supper is another three courses, sometimes with lighter fare replacing the meat course. Some restaurants may offer a menú del día, but it is usually leftover lunch.

Breakfast in Spain is usually coffee and a roll; in Madrid, it's *choco-late* and *churros* (strips of fried dough dipped in a cup of thick hot cocoa). Spanish coffee is strong espresso taken straight *(café solo)* or with hot milk *(café con leche);* if you prefer weaker coffee, ask for *café américano.*

Mealtimes The hardest thing to get used to about Spanish meals is not the food but the hours. Mealtimes are late. Lunch, considered the main meal of the day, is eaten between 2 and 4 PM. Supper is served anytime between 9 and midnight.

Restaurants that cater to tourists in coastal resorts may serve meals earlier, but Spanish restaurants generally open for lunch at 1:30 and dinner at 9. Foreigners are usually the first to arrive, so at least there's never a wait for a table.

You will enjoy your trip more if you can adapt to Spanish mealtimes. But there are tricks you can use to get around eating two big meals a day. Eat a big lunch, then just a snack for supper at a tapas bar. Eat a sandwich at a bar or fast-food restaurant for lunch and then a full dinner. Order just a salad course at lunch; restaurants have no trouble accepting this, but if you're dining with others who are eating more, be sure to tell the waiter when you want your salad served.

Precautions Tap water is perfectly safe throughout Spain, but mineral water is routinely ordered with meals. If you want a pitcher of tap water, ask for *una jarra de agua.*

Ratings The government rates restaurants from five forks (deluxe) down to one fork (basic). We use four categories ($$$$, $$$, $$, $) to indicate average prices in pesetas (ptas) for a three-course meal excluding wine.

Lodging

The government has spent decades buying up old castles and historic buildings and converting them into outstanding lodging for its parador hotel chain. The rest of Spain's hotels tend to be newish high rises, although there is a growing trend toward the restoration of historic buildings. By law, prices must be posted at the reception desk and should indicate whether tax is included (IVA is 6%, 15% for 5-star hotels). Breakfast is not included in the price of a room in Spain.

Hotels Hotels are rated by the government with one to five stars. While quality is a factor, the ratings also indicate how many extra facilities the hotel offers. You may find a three-star hotel just as good as a four-star hotel, but without a swimming pool, for example.

The major private hotel groups in Spain include the upscale **Melia** chain and the moderately priced **Tryp** and **Sol** chains. Dozens of reasonably priced beachside high rises along the coast cater to package tours. The new **Estancias de España** (Velázquez 111, 4–D, 28006 Madrid, tel. 91/561–0170, fax 91/561–0172) is an association of 20 independently owned hotels located in restored palaces, monasteries, mills and post houses, generally in rural Spain; a free directory is available.

High season rates prevail not only in summer, but also during Easter week and local fiesta periods.

Paradors There are about 100 of these. Some are in castles on a hill with sweeping views. Others are in historic monasteries or convents filled with art treasures. Still others are in modern buildings on

Spain's choicest beachfront property. Prices are reasonable, considering that most paradors are four- and five-star hotels. Paradors are immaculate and tastefully furnished, often with antiques or reproductions. All have restaurants that serve some regional specialties. You can stop for a meal or a drink at a parador and look around without spending the night. Breakfast, however, is an expensive buffet, and you'll do better to go down the street for a cup of coffee and a roll.

Because paradors are extremely popular with foreigners and Spaniards alike, make reservations well in advance. You can contact the central reservations office (**Paradores de España,** Central de Reservas, Requena 3, Madrid 28013, tel. 91/559–0069, fax 91/559–3233); in the United States, **Marketing Ahead** (433 5th Ave., New York, NY 10016, tel. 212/686–9213); in the United Kingdom, **Keytel International** (402 Edgeware Rd., London W2 1ED, tel. 71/402–8182).

Home Exchange You can find a house, apartment, or other vacation property to exchange for your own by becoming a member of a home-exchange organization, which then sends you its annual directories listing available exchanges and includes your own listing in at least one of them. Arrangements for the actual exchange are made by the two parties to it, not by the organization. For more information, contact the **International Home Exchange Association** (IHEA, 41 Sutter St. Suite 1090, San Francisco, CA 94104, tel. 415/673–0347 or 800/788–2489). Principal clearinghouses: **Homelink International** (Box 650, Key West, FL 33041, tel. 800/638–3841), with thousands of foreign and domestic listings, publishes four annual directories plus updates; the $50 membership includes your listing in one book. **Intervac International** (Box 590504, San Francisco, CA 94159, tel. 415/435–3497) has three annual directories; membership is $62, or $72 if you want to receive the directories but remain unlisted. **Loan-a-Home** (2 Park La., Apt. 6E, Mount Vernon, NY 10552, tel. 914/664–7640) specializes in long-term exchanges; there is no charge to list your home, but the directories cost $35 or $45 depending on the number you receive. **Villa Leisure** (Box 30188, Palm Beach, FL 33420, tel. 407/624–9000 or 800/526–4244) facilitates swaps.

Apartment and Villa Rentals If you want a home base that's roomy enough for a family and comes with cooking facilities, a furnished rental may be the solution. It's generally cost-wise, too, although not always—some rentals are luxury properties (economical only when your party is large). Home-exchange directories do list rentals—often second homes owned by prospective house swappers—and some services search for a house or apartment for you (even a castle if that's your fancy) and handle the paperwork. Some send an illustrated catalogue and others send photographs of specific properties, sometimes at a charge; up-front registration fees may apply.

Among the companies are **At Home Abroad** (405 E. 56th St., Suite 6H, New York, NY 10022, tel. 212/421–9165), **Europa-Let** (92 North Main St., Ashland, OR 97520, tel. 503/482–5806 or 800/462–4486), **Interhome Inc.** (124 Little Falls Rd., Fairfield, NJ 07004, tel. 201/882–6864), **Overseas Connection** (31 North Harbor Dr., Sag Harbor, NY 11963, tel. 516/725–9308 or 800/542–4007), **Property Rentals International** (1 Park West Circle, Suite 108, Midlothian, VA 23113, tel. 804/378–6054 or 800/220–3332), and **The Invented City** (*see* IHEA, *above*); **Hideaways International** (767 Islington St., Box 4433, Portsmouth, NH 03802, tel. 603/430–4433 or 800/843–4433) functions as a travel club. Membership ($99 yearly per person or family at the same address) includes two annual guides plus quarterly newsletters; rentals are arranged directly between members, not by the club staff.

In Britain, try **Jean Harper Holidays** (20 Walton Rd., Stockton Heath, Warrington WA4 6NL, tel. 925/64234) or **Bartle Holidays** (Wingfield, High Drive Woldingham, Caterham, Surrey CR3 7ED, tel. 883/652257).

Camping Camping in Spain is not a wilderness experience. There are more than 500 campgrounds, and many of them have excellent facilities, including hot showers, restaurants, swimming pools, tennis courts, and even discothèques! But during the summer months, especially August, the best campgrounds are filled with Spanish families who move in with their entire household: pets, grandparents, even the kitchen sink and stove! A government guide listing all Spanish campgrounds can be obtained from the tourist office or purchased at the main post office in Madrid.

Credit Cards

The following credit card abbreviations have been used: AE, American Express; DC, Diners Club; MC, MasterCard; V, Visa. It's a good idea to call ahead to check current credit card policies.

Great Itineraries

Essential Spain for First-time Visitors

The best of historic and modern Spain awaits the visitor who follows this basic itinerary: Take in the sophistication of Madrid and Barcelona, the medieval luster of Toledo and Segovia, the Moorish splendor of Granada and Cordoba, and end up in romantic Seville.

Duration 14 days

Getting Around This tour can easily be followed by auto on divided highways, train, bus, or plane. A one-hour plane trip will save a day's travel time between Barcelona and Madrid. A rented car between Granada, Cordoba, and Seville will allow you to see more of the famous Andalucian countryside and will be faster than the train, which tends to stop in every village. For the trip home, the high speed train (AVE) can return you from Seville to Madrid in less than three hours.

The Main Route **Day 1: Barcelona.** Try to stay near the center of the city. Visit the cathedral and stroll through the Gothic Quarter. Promenade along the Ramblas and duck into the Boquería market. Sample *paella* or seafood at one of the outdoor restaurants on the Barceloneta peninsula by the port.
Day 2: Barcelona. Visit the fantasylike Sagrada Familia cathedral, which was designed by Gaudí and is still under construction. Walk by one of Gaudí's other eye-opening buildings, the Casa Milà, and visit the Renaissance palace that houses the Picasso museum.
Day 3: Barcelona–Madrid. If you go by car, stop outside Barcelona at the mountaintop monastery of Montserrat.
Day 4: Madrid. Visit the Royal Palace, then stroll through old Madrid. Stop and people-gaze from one of the bars of the Plaza Mayor.
Day 5: Segovia. Using Madrid as your base, make a day trip to Segovia to see the Roman aqueduct, cathedral, and turreted castle. Have a big Segovian lunch of roast suckling pig or push on to see the huge gray palace of Felipe II at El Escorial.

Day 6: Madrid. Stroll the leafy Paseo del Prado, visit the Prado museum, and then recuperate with a stop at Retiro Park.

Day 7: Toledo. Less than an hour from Madrid, Toledo is the spiritual center of Spain. It can be a seen as a day trip from Madrid or for those traveling by car, as the first stop on the way to Granada. Soak up history from its cobbled alleyways, explore the cathedral, visit the synagogue, and get a glimpse of daily life in medieval Spain at El Greco's house.

Day 8: Madrid–Granada. En route, detour to the sleepy town of Consuegra in La Mancha to see the windmills of Don Quixote.

Day 9: Granada. Explore the lush Moorish palace and gardens of the Alhambra. Visit the Royal Chapel adjoining the cathedral, where Ferdinand and Isabella are buried, and dine in the hillside Arab quarter, the Albaicín.

Day 10: Granada–Cordoba. In Cordoba, at one time headquarters of all the Moorish kingdoms in Spain, see the red- and white-striped mosque with its jewel-encrusted altar.

Day 11: Cordoba–Seville. Make a stop in Carmona, one of the oldest villages in Spain. Then in Seville, stroll the walkways alongside the Guadalquivir river and loose yourself amid the winding streets and patios of the romantic barrio Santa Cruz.

Day 12: Seville. Visit the splendid Moorish palaces of the Alcazar, climb the Giralda, stick your nose in the sweet-smelling orange blossom patio by the cathedral, and hire a horse-drawn carriage to take you to the tile-encrusted Plaza de España.

Day 13: Jerez de la Frontera and Arcos de la Frontera. Visit a sherry winery in Jerez and then make your way to the white hilltop town of Arcos in time for the sunset.

Day 14: Seville–Madrid. Return by highway, plane, or the ultra-modern AVE high-speed train.

Architectural Treasures

From north to south, this unique tour avoids the big cities, while concentrating on Spain's rich architectural treasures. Enjoy a dose of Spanish history through its art and architecture—this route offers superb examples of every major building style since the Romans.

Duration 12 days

Getting Around A car is essential for following this route, which sometimes winds over steep back roads and through narrow gates into walled cities.

The Main Route **Day 1: Oviedo.** The capital of the province of Asturias, Oviedo is home to Europe's best examples of pre-Romanesque art. Visit the primitive yet graceful 9th-century chapels of Santa Maria del Naranco and San Miguel de Lillo on a hill overlooking the city. Don't miss the treasures of Oviedo's Gothic cathedral, which include Visigoth-style jeweled crosses that commemorate the first Christian victory over the Moors in 718.

Day 2: Oviedo–León. Cross the Pajares pass and descend to the high plains of Castile. In León, stay at the Parador San Marcos, a sumptuous Renaissance monastery that was once the headquarters for the Knights of St. James. Visit the basilica of San Isidoro, with its primitive medieval frescoes, spend time in the 13th century Gothic cathedral that glitters with stained glass, and visit the arcaded Plaza Mayor with its half-timber houses.

Day 3: León–Segovia. Follow the back roads and stop at the imposing castles of Peñafiel and Coca, two of Spain's best.

Day 4: Segovia. Visit the Roman aqueduct and the turreted castle filled with furnishings from the period of Spain's Catholic Kings. From here it is possible to take excursions to the French-inspired palace of La Granja or the medieval stone village of La Pedraza.

Day 5: Segovia–Avila–Salamanca. In Avila, walk the ramparts of the city walls, the best preserved in Spain. A detour through Puerto del Pico pass in the Gredos Mountains allows you to walk over a still-intact Roman road, the likes of which once crisscrossed this countryside.

Day 6: Salamanca. The arched Plaza Mayor and the Plateresque buildings of the University make the entire city of Salamanca an architectural monument.

Day 7: Salamanca–La Alberca–Caceres. Nestled in one of the poorest and most primitive corners of Spain, La Alberca has changed little since medieval times. Its winding streets are full of rustic half-timber houses and squares. In Caceres, stay in the unspoiled old town; its stone palaces and plazas served as backdrops for Ridley Scott's film on the life of Columbus.

Day 8: Caceres–Merida. Explore the Roman theater (24 BC), the amphitheater, and the archaeology museum.

Day 9: Merida–Seville. Travel day.

Day 10: Seville. Visit the splendid Moorish palaces of the Alcazar, climb the Giralda, a 12th-century minaret, and tour the immense cathedral—the largest in Spain. Stroll under flowered Andalucian balconies in the barrio Santa Cruz and hire a horse-drawn carriage to take you to the tile-encrusted Plaza de España. Some of Spain's most modern architecture, including two soaring suspension bridges, can be found on the island of La Cartuja, site of the 1992 Expo.

Day 11: Seville–Cordoba. In Cordoba, stroll the narrow streets and poke your head into the flowering patios typical of Andalucia. Visit the red- and white-striped mosque with its jewel-encrusted altar, once the spiritual center of Spain's Moorish kingdoms.

Day 12: Cordoba–Granada. End your trip with a stop at the lush palaces and gardens of the Alhambra, the last Moorish outpost in Europe. Explore the old Arab quarter with its unforgettable views of the Alhambra.

Castles in Spain

The Spanish countryside is packed with castles—this one-week tour takes you to some of the best and allows you to spend the night in medieval splendor. The route fans out from Madrid and zigzags through Spain's midsection, where the castles of Castile and La Mancha once served as the front line of defense between Christian and Moslem Spain. Children will especially enjoy this tour and any of the days described could also stand on its own as a briefer excursion from the capital.

Duration 5 days

Getting Around A car is essential for following this tour, which goes through some fairly hilly, rugged territory. Rent in Madrid.

The Main Route **Day 1: Madrid–Belmonte–Alarcón.** On the way to Belmonte stop by the Royal Palace of Aranjuez, the inspiration of Spain's romantic composers and poets. The 15th-century Belmonte castle is a powerful fortress overlooking the La Mancha plains. Crossing the narrow bridge into the walled city and castle of Alarcón will take you back to medieval times. The castle is a national parador; try to book a room in the tower.

Day 2: Alarcón–Siguenza. The ruined castle of Jadraque is worth a stop en route to Siguenza, where a crenelated 14th-century castle lords over the village. The castle is one of the most popular national paradors. Be sure to ask to see the chapel.

Day 3: Siguenza–Manzanares El Real–Segovia. Crossing back through Madrid, head for the charming foothill village of Manzanares El Real, whose square castle is storybook perfect and one of Spain's best examples of double-walled fortification.

Day 4: Segovia. The turreted castle of Segovia, although scorned by purists because of its massive reconstruction, is one of Spain's most famous landmarks. Unlike most Spanish castles, which are empty inside, this one houses a fine collection of armor and furnishings from the period of the Catholic Kings.

Day 5: Turégano–Coca–Peñafiel. Using Segovia as a base, make an excursion through the castle-rich countryside of Castile. The 12th-century castle of Turégano contains a beautiful church, while the brick fortress of Coca shows unmistakable Moorish influence in its design. The shiplike 14th-century castle of Peñafiel sits on a plateau with commanding views of three valleys.

Day 6: Segovia–Avila. While Avila does not have a castle as such, the thick city walls turn the entire city into a fortress. Walk the ramparts and be sure to see the walls lit up at night (the best viewpoint is at Cuatro Postes below the city). You can stay in a national parador built into the walls.

Day 7: Avila–Madrid. Make your way back to Madrid through the Gredos mountains and over the Puerto del Pico with its Roman road. Just below the pass visit the romantic castle of Mombeltran built in the 14th century by the Duke of Albuquerque.

The Way of St. James

Pilgrims making the lengthy and dangerous journey to the shrine of St. James (Santiago) in Santiago de Compostela have used this route to cross Spain over the past thousand years. They left in their wake a wealth of Romanesque buildings and art treasures. A number of books and tourist-office brochures describe the route and the attractions along the way. It is also possible to pick up the road in León and still see a good representation of its offerings.

Duration 6 days

Getting Around The whole trail is signposted, and it is possible to walk the entire distance, but the less energetic can make their pilgrimage by car.

The Main Route
Day 1: Roncesvalles–Estella. This pass in the Pyrenees was the traditional entry point for pilgrims arriving from France. Visit the Chapel. In Estella, see the 12th-century Dukes of Granada Palace and the early churches.

Day 2: Estella–Burgos. Visit the church of Santiago in Logroño, the Cathedral in Santo Domingo de la Calzada, the many monasteries along the way, and the arcaded square of Belorado. In Burgos, see the massive cathedral.

Day 3: Burgos–León. Explore the half-timbered medieval section of León; see the cathedral, decorated with 125 stained-glass windows.

Day 4: León–Villafranca del Bierzo. Stop at the pilgrims' museum in Astorga, housed in a palace designed by Gaudí. Explore the Knights Templar Castle in Ponferrada. In Villafranca, see the Church of Santiago.

Day 5: Villafranca–Santiago de Compostela. Examine the primitive, round Celtic houses in O Cebreiro. In Santiago, the cathedral and the Hotel of the Catholic Monarchs are masterpieces of stone carving.

Day 6: Santiago. Explore the city and the nearby town of Padrón.

For more information, refer to Chapters 5, León, Galicia, and Asturias, and 6, Burgos, Santander, and the Basque Country.

2 Portraits of Spain

Spain at a Glance:
A Chronology

c. 12,000 BC	Paleolithic (Old Stone Age) settlement; caves of Altamira painted.
c. 2000	Copper Age culture; stone megaliths built.
c. 1100	Earliest Phoenician colonies, including Cadiz, Villaricos, Almuñecar, and Málaga. Native peoples include Iberians in south, Basques in Pyrenees, and Celts in northwest.
c. 650	Greeks begin to colonize east coast.
237	Carthaginians land in Spain; found Cartagena c. 225 BC.
206	Romans expel Carthaginians from Spain, gradually conquer peninsula over next two centuries. Spain becomes one of Rome's most important colonies.
AD 67	St. Paul is said to have visited Spain.
74	Roman citizenship extended to all Spaniards.
380	Christianity declared sole religion of Rome and her empire.
409	First Barbarian invasions.
419	Visigothic kingdom established in northern Spain, with capital at Toledo.

Moorish Spain

711–712	Christian Visigothic kingdom destroyed by invading Muslims (Moors) from northern Africa, who create emirate, with capital at Córdoba, of Ummayyad Caliphate at Damascus.
756	Independent dynasty established in Spain under Abd al-Rahman I.
778	Charlemagne establishes rule north of Ebro.
899	Miraculous discovery of remains of St. James the Greater; church of Santiago de Compostela, a major pilgrimage site, is built.
912–961	Reign of Abd al-Rahman III: height of Moorish culture, although it flourishes throughout Reconquest.

The Reconquest

1085	Alfonso VI of Castile captures Toledo.
1099	Death of Rodrigo Diaz de Bivar, known as El Cid, who served both Christian and Muslim kings; buried at Burgos Cathedral (completed 1126), first Gothic cathedral.
1137	Aragón unites with Catalunya.
1209	First Spanish university founded at Valencia by Moors.
1212	Victory at Las Navas de Tolosa by united Christian armies: Moorish power crippled.
1236–48	Valencia, Córdoba, and Seville fall to Christians.

1270 End of main period of Reconquest: Portugal, Aragón, and Castile emerge as major powers.

1347 Black Death reaches Europe.

1435 Alfonso V of Aragón and Sicily conquers Naples and southern Italy.

1469 Isabella, princess of Castile, marries Ferdinand, heir to the throne of Aragón.

1474 Printing press arrives in Spain.

1478 The Spanish Inquisition is established.

1479–1504 Isabella and Ferdinand jointly rule.

1492 Granada, last Moorish outpost, falls. Christopher Columbus, under the sponsorship of Isabella, discovers America, setting off a wave of Spanish exploration.

1494 Treaty of Tordesillas: Portugal and Spain divide the known world between them.

1499 *La Celestina*, by Fernando de Rojas, considered the first novel, is published.

1516 Death of Ferdinand. His grandson and heir, Charles I, inaugurates the Habsburg dynasty and Spain's Golden Age.

The Habsburg Dynasty

1519 Charles I is elected Holy Roman Emperor as Charles V. From his father, Philip of Habsburg, he inherits Austria, the Spanish Netherlands, Burgundy, and nearly continuous war with France. Hernán Cortés conquers the Aztec Empire in Mexico.

1519–22 First circumnavigation of the world by Magellan's ships.

c.1520–c.1700 Golden Age. Funded by its empire, Spain's culture flourishes. Artists include El Greco (1541–1614), Velázquez (1599–1660), and Murillo (1617–82). In literature, the poet Quevedo (1580–1645), dramatists Lope de Vega (1562–1635) and Calderón (1600–1681), and novelist Miguel de Cervantes (1547–1616) were known throughout Europe. Counter-Reformation Catholicism took its lead from St. Ignatius of Loyola (1491–1556), founder of the Jesuit order (1540), and the mystic St. Teresa of Ávila (1515–82).

1531 Pizarro conquers the Inca empire in Peru.

1554 Charles's heir, Philip, marries Queen Mary of England ("Bloody Mary," c. 1558).

1556 Charles abdicates in favor of his son Philip II, who inherits Spain, Sicily, and the Netherlands; the Holy Roman Empire goes to Charles's brother Ferdinand. Philip II leads cause of Counter-Reformation against Protestant states in Europe.

1561 Capital established at Madrid; construction of El Escorial begins in 1563.

1567–1648 Dutch Revolt.

1588 Philip attacks Protestant England with the Spanish Armada, but is defeated.

1598 Death of Philip II.

1609 *Moriscos* (converted Muslims) expelled and independence of the Netherlands recognized during reign of Philip III.

1618 Beginning of Thirty Years' War; originally a religious dispute, it became a dynastic struggle between Habsburgs and Bourbons.

1621–65 Reign of Philip IV; his minister, Count-Duke Olivares, reforms regime on absolutist model of France.

1640–59 Revolt in Catalunya; republic declared for a time.

1648 Peace of Westphalia ends Thirty Years' War; Spanish Netherlands declared independent.

1659 Treaty of the Pyrenees ends war with France and Spanish ascendancy in Europe.

1665–1700 Reign of Charles II, last of the Spanish Habsburgs.

The Bourbon Dynasty

1701–14 War of the Spanish Succession: Three claimants to the throne are Louis XIV of France, Leopold I of Bavaria, and Philip of Anjou. Philip is recognized as Philip V, first Bourbon king, by the Treaty of Utrecht, 1713. By the Treaty of Rastatt, 1714, Spain loses Flanders, Luxembourg, and Italy to Austrian Habsburgs; it spends much of its energy in the 18th century trying to regain these.

1756–63 Seven Years' War: Spain and France versus Great Britain. 1756: Spain regains Menorca, lost to Great Britain in 1709. 1762: Treaty of Paris: Spain cedes Menorca and Florida to Great Britain and receives Louisiana from France in return.

1779 Spain supports rebels in American War of Independence, regains Florida and Menorca.

1793 Revolutionary France declares war.

1795 By Treaty of Basel, Spain allies with France against Great Britain.

Napoleonic Rule

1808 King Charles IV abdicates in favor of Joseph Bonaparte, Napoleon's brother. Napoleon takes Madrid in December. Artist Francisco Goya (1746–1828) chronicles a dying culture.

The Peninsular War

1809–14 Reconquest of Spain by British under Wellington.

Restoration of the Bourbons

1814 Bourbons restored under Ferdinand VII, son of Charles IV. Like other restored monarchs of the era, he was a reactionary and crushed liberal movements.

1833 Ferdinand deprives brother Don Carlos of succession in favor of his infant daughter, Isabella; her mother, María Cristina, becomes regent.

1834–39 First Carlist War: Don Carlos (an extreme conservative in a land of conservatives) contests the crown and begins an era of upheaval.

1835 Suppression of monasteries (disentailment).

1836 Revolt of progressives in Andalucía, Aragón, Catalunya, and Madrid.

1840 Coup d'état: General Baldomero Espartero becomes dictator, exiles María Cristina, ushers in a series of weak and unpopular regimes.

1843 Espartero ousted; Isabella II restored to throne. Guardia Civil created.

Period of Troubles

1868 Revolution, supported by liberals, topples Isabella II but ushers in the Period of Troubles: Attempts to establish a republic and then to find an alternate monarch fail.

1873 First Spanish Republic declared; Second Carlist War (to 1876). With their vineyards decimated by phylloxera, the French begin to import Spanish wine.

Restoration of the Bourbons

1874 Alfonso XII, son of Isabella, brought to the throne.

1890 Universal manhood suffrage declared.

1892 Peasant revolt, inspired by anarchist doctrine; revolt again in 1903.

1895 Revolution in Cuba, one of the few remaining Spanish colonies. Spain moves to suppress it.

1898 Spanish-American War: United States annexes Spanish colonies of Puerto Rico and the Philippines; Cuba is declared independent.

1902–31 Reign of Alfonso XIII: increasing instability and unrest. Artists, including Pablo Picasso (1881–1973) and Juan Gris (1887–1927), leave for France.

1914 Spain declares neutrality in World War I.

1923 Coup d'état of General Manuel Primo de Rivera, who models his government on Italian Fascism.

1928 Luis Buñuel (1900–1983) and Salvador Dalí (1904–88) collaborate on the Surrealist film *Un Chien Andalou (An Andalusian Dog)*.

Republic, Civil War, and Fascism

1930–31 Primo de Rivera is ousted; a republic is declared, and Alfonso XIII is deposed. Liberals attempt to redistribute land and diminish the power of the Church.

1936–39 Spanish Civil War: Electoral victory of Popular Front (a coalition of the left) precipitates rightist military insurrection against the Republic, led by General Francisco Franco. Europe declares neutrality, but Germany and Italy aid Franco, and the USSR and volunteer brigades aid (to a lesser extent) the Republic. More than 600,000 die, including the poet Federico García Lorca. Franco is victorious and rules Spain for the next 35 years.

1939 Fascist Spain declares neutrality in World War II.

1945 Spain is denied membership in the United Nations, but is admitted in 1950.

1953 NATO bases are established in Spain in return for economic and military aid.

1969 Franco names Prince Juan Carlos de Borbón, heir to the vacant throne, his successor.

1970 Basque uprising.

1973 Franco's prime minister, Carrero Blanco, is assassinated by Basque separatists.

Restoration of the Bourbons

1975 Franco dies and is succeeded by Juan Carlos, grandson of Alfonso XIII.

1977 The first democratic elections in 40 years are won by the Center Democratic Union.

1978 A new constitution restores civil liberties and freedom of the press.

1981 An attempted coup by Colonel Antonio Tejero fails.

1982 Spain becomes a full member of NATO. Socialists win a landslide victory in the general election.

1985 The frontier with Gibraltar, closed since 1968, is reopened.

1986 Spain enters European Community (Common Market); in a national referendum, Spain votes to stay in NATO. The Socialists win for a second time.

1988 Pedro Almodóvar's award-winning film *Women on the Verge of a Nervous Breakdown* becomes a hit in the United States and Europe, symbolic of Spain's post-Franco cultural ferment.

1989 Camilo José Cela is awarded the Nobel Prize for Literature; Socialists lose majority, but continue in office.

1992 The Olympic Games are held in Barcelona. The 1992 Universal Exposition (Expo) is held in Seville.

Flamenco

By Michael
Jacobs

Born in
Italy,
Michael
Jacobs
received his
Ph.D. in Art
History
from the
Courtauld
Institute
at the
University of
London. He
has visited
and lived in
Spain and is
the author of
a number of
books on art
and on travel
in Spain.

The poet Federico García Lorca described the dance and musical form known as flamenco as "the most gigantic creation of the Spanish people." Flamenco, as it is generally performed today, is also one of the greatest travesties of Spanish culture. Spanish tourist industry promotion has so shamelessly exploited flamenco that the guitars, polka-dotted dresses, and anguished wails characteristic of this music are for many people essential components of their image of Spain. As with the region of Andalucía, where flamenco was born, the music expresses much that is genuinely mysterious about Spain, but also much that is bogus.

The numerous myths about flamenco are propagated as much by the serious lover of the music (the so-called aficionado) as by the writer of tourist brochures. Probably the greatest of these myths is that the flamenco artist is respecting traditions that go back to ancient times. Some even believe that the predecessors of flamenco dancers were the dancing girls of Roman Cádiz, who were celebrated for their sensuality and much in demand all over the Roman Empire. As for flamenco singing, many see its roots both in the Byzantine chants introduced into Spain by the Visigoths and in the music of the Spanish Muslims. Another school of thought, particularly popular today, emphasizes the similarities between flamenco and Jewish Festival songs, and even claims that the term used to describe the purest form of flamenco, *Cante Jondo*, is derived from the Hebrew *jon tob*, meaning "good day" or "good festival." Frequently, the discussion of flamenco's origins evaporates completely into hot air, as it did with García Lorca, who described flamenco as a blend of many influences in which "the emotion of history, its lasting lights, without dates or facts, takes refuge."

Everyone is at least agreed that flamenco is essentially the creation of Andalusian Gypsies, who are often referred to as *flamencos*. Why they are called flamencos—a word that means either "Flemish" or "flamingos"—is, unfortunately, another thorny and endlessly debated issue. Some suggest that the Gypsies acquired the name because they wore colorful costumes similar to those brought back by Spanish soldiers from Flanders. Others believe that the name alluded to the flamingolike appearance of Gypsy men, with their brightly colored trousers clinging to spindly legs. There is also the possibility that the word derives from the Arabic *felagmengu* (fugitive peasant), or even from the 18th-century Spanish slang for "boaster." In any case, the first known use of the word is as late as 1835, a good 400 years after the Gypsies had come to Spain.

Much of the aura that surrounds flamenco music can undoubtedly be attributed to romantic attitudes toward Gypsies, a people whose origins are suitably mysterious. They probably came from India originally—the physical similarities between the Indian and Spanish Gypsies are very striking; inevitably certain writers on flamenco have found parallels between flamenco and Hindu dancing. The Gypsies in Spain seem to have arrived by way of Egypt—the most common Spanish word for them is *gitanos*, which originally meant "Egyptians."

Although they are thought to have forged the projectiles that the Catholic Monarchs, Ferdinand and Isabella, used in the Siege of Granada in 1492, they did not manage to endear themselves to the royal pair, who in 1499 issued a decree ordering Gypsies to stop their wanderings and find stable employment or else leave the country. At least 12 other laws were to be passed limiting their activities and lifestyle, laws that the Gypsies did their best to ignore. Finally, in 1783, Charles III made a serious attempt to integrate the Gypsies into Spanish society and to inspire greater tolerance toward them. Though he, too, forbade them their wanderings, he made it an offense for Spaniards to refuse them employment or prohibit them access to a public place. Thereafter, Spanish Gypsies adopted Spanish, rather than Romany, as their first language, and settled permanently in places like the Seville suburb of Triana and the Granada cave district of Sacromonte. Prejudices against the Gypsies continued, but were matched by a growing romantic fascination. Furthermore, in Andalucía—the Gypsy capital of Spain—Gypsies and non-Gypsies *(payos)* have a remarkable amount in common. They share the same superstitious fears, machismo, love of spectacle, and refusal to be tied down by practical considerations.

Flamenco appears to have been born in the wake of Charles III's edict, and certainly its lyrics and forms are difficult to date earlier than the late 18th century. There is evidence also to suggest that its exact place of origin is the triangle of land formed by Seville, Jerez, and Cádiz, the three Atlantic-facing towns that are often regarded as the "Holy Trinity" of flamenco. Flamenco evolved in Gypsy homes and was performed at weddings, baptisms, funerals, and *juergas* (spontaneous gatherings of musicians and aficionados). At first, the Gypsies kept their music very much to themselves, especially because it reflected, in its sad tone and tragic lyrics, the suffering of their people. One of the first payos to attend a Gypsy festival was a journalist named Estébanez Calderón, who, in 1847, published an account of dancing and singing in the Gypsy suburb of Triana. Much of what he wrote about flamenco was ridiculous, and the Gypsies to whom he spoke about their music were clearly having a joke at his expense. To this day, Gypsies love to exploit the gullibility of payos, who have often been made to believe that they are witnessing the "real flamenco," rather than something put on for the benefit of tourists. It was, at any rate, only shortly after Estébanez Calderón's article appeared that Gypsies became aware of the potential financial rewards of flamenco and made it public.

Flamenco, with its complex, ever-changing rhythms, is not an easy music, and those who are able to perform it well have generally been exposed to it from an early age: Many of the greatest Gypsy artists of today belong to musical dynasties that stretch back for generations. Like jazz, flamenco depends heavily on improvisation, while obeying strict rules. To the uninitiated, flamenco singing has a monotonous, unvarying quality. The singer is usually seated and performs with hands outstretched and shaking, the face becoming ever redder and the veins on the forehead more and more prominent: The very act of singing appears to be painful. There are numerous types of song, though sometimes not even the greatest aficionados can distinguish among them. The two main groups are the *cante chico* (small song) and the *cante grande* or *jondo* ("big" or "deep" song). The former, confusingly known also as *cante flamenco*, comprise the more lightweight, lyrical, and cheerful songs of the flamenco canon, such as *fandangos, bulerías, alegrías,* and *malagueñas.* Far more primitive and unmelodic are the sounds of the cante jondo, which all aficionados consider to be the more important of the two groups. Among its songs are the *martinetes* and *deblas,* which today are unaccompanied but might once have been sung to the hammering of metal in the Gypsy forges. The most famous of the cante jondo songs are the *siguirillas* and *soleas,* which are unrelievedly austere and sad, the word *solea* being, in fact, derived from the Spanish for "solitude." To this same group also belong the *saetas,* which you will hear during Andalucía's celebrated Holy Week processions. Someone standing in the crowd or on a nearby balcony will suddenly burst into song when the statue of Christ or the Virgin passes by.

Song is the main element in a flamenco performance, though today it is generally the dancer who receives most of the attention, especially from the foreigners in the audience. The flamenco dancer moves the hands and torso, rather than the feet, intermittently bursting into frenetic, hysterical passion. Castanets, which have come to be thought of as one of the symbols of Spain, are not traditional to flamenco and are rarely used by the best dancers. The only accompaniments to flamenco singing and dancing are the guitar and what is known as the *jaleo,* a word used to describe stamping of feet, clapping of hands, and the shouting of encouragements such as *"olé!"* Tourists frequently join in the clapping without realizing that it is quite an art in itself.

Vital to any performance of flamenco is the elusive quality of *duende.* A singer or dancer might have exceptional skills but leave the audience unmoved. Lorca related how one singer with a beautiful voice began to engage the audience only after downing half a bottle of *aguardiente,* whereupon she sang "with scorched throat, without voice, without breath or color, but with duende." A considerable mystique is attached to duende, but Lorca's anecdote unwittingly shows how this quality can be induced by something as straightforward as drink and drugs. The great Gypsy singers have tended to die young, and of heart attacks, and writers on flamenco love to stress how these were brought on by the emotional intensity required of their performances. Yet the excessiveness of their lifestyle seems a more likely reason. Gypsy juergas are notorious for the amount of drink and drugs consumed and last for hours on end, stamina usually being maintained with cocaine. Sadly, the most outstanding flamenco singer of today, El Camarón de la Isla, is able to sing less and less, owing to his heroin addiction.

It goes without saying that most public performances of flamenco generally lack the spontaneity and high spirits that are so necessary to this music. Flamenco might perhaps never have survived at all had it not been commercialized after 1850. Yet as soon as flamenco gained international recognition, it suffered in quality. By the 1920s Gypsy singers had become more self-conscious in their looks and performances, castanets and other accessories had been introduced, and the more accessible cante chico had come to be preferred to the difficult cante jondo. Flamenco in its public form had once flourished mainly in the sympathetic and informal environment of bars known as *cafés cantantes*, but after 1900 the fashion for these places was gradually replaced by one for the *tablao*, or flamenco floor show. Most tourists to Spain today experience flamenco only in the context of these tablaos, the best known of which are those put on in the caves of Granada's Sacromonte. These caves have not been lived in by Gypsies since the early 1960s, but long before then, many of the caves had been transformed into tackily decorated nightclubs specializing solely in flamenco shows. A typical show begins with an offer of a weak glass of wine punch known as sangría; this is then followed by an appalling display of singing and dancing, after which members of the audience may be encouraged to join in themselves. The main excitement comes from the possibility of being pickpocketed or of being charged more than you had originally bargained for.

Other than genuinely befriending a group of Gypsies, your best chance of seeing and hearing good flamenco is to go to one of the numerous flamenco festivals that are held throughout Andalucía during the summer months. These festivals were started in the late 1950s, at a time when intellectuals calling themselves "flamencologists" were eager to revive the dying art of cante jondo. The festivals attract the finest performers, are attended by relatively few tourists, and retain something of the character of the juergas, in that they always start several hours late, never really get going until the early hours of the morning, and last until dawn. Much of their success is also dependent on the proximity of the stage to the bar.

To be subjected to many hours of serious flamenco, however good, can seem as exhausting as having to perform it. Not surprisingly, attendance at the festivals is beginning to decline seriously, and many good flamenco artists have had to adapt their music to modern tastes in order to survive: Among the liveliest flamenco performers of today are Pata Negra, a Gypsy group that combines flamenco with rock. Other flamenco artists have had to search for employment abroad—above all, in Japan, where there appear to be far more flamenco clubs than there are in Spain. The future of flamenco as other than an exotic entertainment expressive of "Spanish color" is in jeopardy.

The same could not be said of *sevillanas*, a type of music and dancing that stems from the cante chico and is commonly confused with flamenco by foreigners. The fashion for sevillanas is greater now than ever before and has spread well beyond the confines of its native Seville. This music has nothing specifically Gypsy about it; neither is it at its best in its commercial form, which is a mixture of folk and pop music. Sevillanas are the songs and dances that everyone in Andalucía knows and will spontaneously perform at bars, in the streets, at parties. Unlike most flamenco today, sevillanas are among the strongest and most genuine of European folkloric traditions. The three traditional occasions for the performing of sevillanas are the *ferias* (the town festivals), the spring parties known as *Cruces de Mayo,* and the annual pilgrimage to the Virgin of the Rocío. These are also the times of the year when the women of Andalucía, to be able to enjoy themselves without the slightest inhibitions, dress up in polka-dotted flamenco or Gypsy costumes. On these occasions of endless singing, dancing, and drinking, the similarities between Gypsies and Andalusian payos become particularly apparent. The pursuit of pleasure is carried by both peoples to a degree rarely reached elsewhere in Western society.

Spain's Food and Wine

By Michael
Jacobs

The cuisine of Spain is among the most varied and sophisticated in Europe. Favored by a wealth of natural produce almost unrivaled, Spain has traditionally been an agricultural country, famous since ancient times for its extensive wheat fields, vineyards, and olive groves and for pig and cattle raising. A recent medical report has even concluded that the Spaniards eat more healthily than any other Western nation, largely because they insist on fresh produce and avoid canned and convenience foods.

The geographic variety of the peninsula accounts, of course, for the extremely varied nature of Spain's produce: For instance, the snowcapped mountains of the Sierra Nevada have Nordic cultures on their upper slopes, while those lower down yield tropical fruits unique to Europe, such as custard apples. Furthermore, with both an Atlantic and a Mediterranean coastline, Spain boasts an exceptional range of fish and seafood.

Another major influence on Spanish cuisine has been the 7½ centuries of Moorish presence in the peninsula. The Moors gave the local cooking an exotic quality by using new ingredients, such as saffron, almonds, and peppers; they introduced the art of making sweets and pastries and created refreshing dishes such as *ajo blanco* that still remain popular. The Moors produced one of the world's pioneering gastronomes, Ziryab, an Arab who worked in 10th-century Córdoba and brought over to Europe the new Arab fashion for eating a regular sequence of dishes, beginning with soup and ending with dessert.

Whether inherited from the Moors or not, the Spanish love of food stretches back at least several centuries. A famous poem by the 16th-century Seville writer Baltasar del Alcázar expresses this feeling:

> There are three things
> That hold my heart Love's captive
> My fair Inés, cured ham,
> And aubergines and cheese

Spaniards, when traveling around their country, often seem to prefer hunting down local gastronomic specialties to visiting museums and monuments. They tend to assume that foreigners do not have the same interest in food as they do, largely because so many of these foreigners are not adventurous in their tastes and refuse to adapt to Spain's idiosyncratic eating times and traditions. You are more likely to find outstanding food in some remote and dirty village bar where olive stones and shrimp heads are spat out onto the floor than in many of the luxury restaurants: The Spaniards aren't as snobbish about eating as, say, the French are. But if you decide to have lunch before 2 PM or to dine before 10, the only restaurants that you will probably find open are those that cater to bland international tastes.

The most Spanish of culinary traditions is undoubtedly that of the *tapa* (bar snack). Many people who dismiss Spanish food as un-imaginative will make an exception of the tapa, without realiz-ing that these snacks are miniature versions of dishes that you can find in restaurants or in Spanish homes. The tradition origi-nated in Andalucía, where a combination of heat and poverty made it impractical to sit down to a heavy meal in a restaurant. Today tapas are generally taken as appetizers before lunch or supper, but in the south they are still often regarded as a meal in themselves. The eating of tapas makes you aware of the variety of Spanish food and also prevents you from getting too drunk, especially if you decide to go on the Spanish equivalent of a bar crawl, a *tapeo*. In some of the more old-fashioned bars, a tapa of the barman's choice is automatically presented to you when you order a drink. Having to choose a tapa yourself is not always easy, for the barman often recites at great speed a seemingly interminable list. The timid, baffled tourist usually ends up pointing to some familiar tapa that is standing on the counter.

The Spaniards' love of tasting small quantities of many dishes is evident also in their habits in restaurants, where they normally share food and order dishes *para picar* (to nibble at). If you go to a restaurant in a group, a selection of *raciones* (larger versions of tapas) makes a popular starter.

Soups in Spain tend not to be smooth and creamy, as they are in France, but watery, highly spiced, and very gar-licky. One of the most common hot soups is a *sopa de ajo* (garlic soup), which consists of water, oil, garlic, paprika, stale bread, and cured ham. This is far more appetizing than it sounds, as is the famous gazpacho, a cold blend of water, bread, garlic, tomatoes, and peppers. Most people today make gazpacho in a blender, but it is at its best when prepared by hand in a terra-cotta mortar, the ingredients slowly pounded with a pestle. There are several variations on gazpacho, including *salmorejo*, which comes from Córdoba and has a denser texture. Particularly good is the *ajo blanco*, the basis of which is almonds rather than tomatoes: Served always with peeled muscatel grapes or slices of honeydew melon, this dish encapsulates the Moorish love of combining sweet and savory flavors.

The Spanish egg dish best known abroad is the *tortilla* (not the same as the Mexican tortilla—instead it's an omelet of onions and potatoes), which is generally eaten cold. *Huevos flamencos* ("Gypsy eggs") is a traditional Seville dish now found in all parts of Spain, consisting of eggs fried in a terra-cotta dish with cured ham, tomatoes, and a selection of green vegetables. The exact ingredients vary as much as does Gypsy cooking itself, which tends cleverly to incorporate whatever is at hand.

The Spaniards—and the Andalusians and Galicians, in particu-lar—are known for the vast quantities of fish and seafood they consume. Some of the finest seafood can be found in western Andalucía and in Galicia, the former being renowned for shrimp, prawns, and crayfish, the latter for its oysters, lobsters, and crabs, and the much sought after if also revolting-looking *percebes* (goose barnacles). Another specialty of the Galician coast is scallops chopped up with breadcrumbs, onions, parsley, and peppers and served in their shells (the same shells that are worn by pilgrims on their way to Santiago de Compostela). *Changurro*, a stuffed king crab, is a specialty of the Basque country, where you will also find one of Spain's most interesting fish dishes, *bacalao al pil-pil* (cod fried in garlic and covered in a green sauce made from the gelatin of the fish). A fish dish now common all over Spain is *trucha a la Navarra* (trout wrapped in pieces of bacon). In Andalucía most fish is deep-fried in batter—which is why the place is sometimes disparagingly referred to by outsiders as the land of the fried fish, an unattractive image. You, in fact, need considerable art, as well as spanking-fresh fish, to be able to fry the fish as well as they do here and achieve the requisite texture of crispness on the outside and succulence inside. The *chancetes* (whitebait) and *sardinas* (sardines) are especially good in Málaga, while along the Cádiz coast, you should try the *salmonetes* (red mullet) and *acedías* (miniature soles). *Adobo*, also delicious, is fried fish marinated in wine.

The cold meats and sausage products of Spain are renowned—in particular, the cured hams of Trevélez and Jabugo, the *chorizo* (spicy paprika sausage), and the *morcilla* (blood sausages) of Granada and Burgos, the latter sometimes incorporating nuts. Meat, when served hot, is usually unaccompanied by a sauce or vegetables and presented rare. The great meat-eating center of Spain is Castile, which is famous for its *cochinillo* (suckling pig), a specialty of Segovia, and *cordero* (lamb), both of which are roasted in wood or clay ovens. The most sophisticated and elaborate poultry dishes in Spain are prepared in the Catalan district of Gerona and include chicken with lobster and turkey stuffed with raisins, pine nuts, and *butifarras* (spicy Catalan sausages).

Fish, meat, and seafood come together in *paella*, a saffron-flavored rice dish that many consider to be the most typical of Spanish dishes. Originating in Valencia, paella, in fact, dates no earlier than the late 19th century. The one Spanish dish that can truly claim to be the most national and traditional is the meat stew referred to by the people of Madrid as *cocido*, by the Andalusians as *potaje*, and by the Catalans as *escudella*. Despite the slight regional variations, the three basic ingredients remain the same—meats, legumes, and vegetables. The dish is usually served in three courses, beginning with the broth in which everything is cooked and finishing with the meats, which Spaniards sometimes shred and mix together on their plates to form what they call *pringa*.

The range and quality of Spanish cheeses is impressive, but most of them are little known and can be bought only in the area where they are made. The hard cheeses of La Mancha are best well matured: A good *Manchego viejo* is almost the equal of an Italian Parmesan. If you find it, you should try *Cabrales*, an exquisite sheep's cheese that is rather like a melting Roquefort.

Spaniards do not usually finish a meal with a dessert. They tend to bake the many almond- and honey-based sweets and pastries of Moorish derivation, such as *polvorones*, around Christmas or Easter time. Ever since St. Teresa devised *yemas* (egg-yolk sweets), Spanish convents have specialized in all kinds of sweet products. The yemas were once distributed free to the poor, but their production has now become a profitable industry for the nuns. The correct procedure for buying anything from a convent is to ring the bell and then address the nun (who is usually hidden behind a rotating drum) with the words *Ave María Purísima*. This religious formality over with, you can then proceed to order your yemas, *bizcochos* (sponge biscuits), *tocinos de cielo* (an excellent variant of crème caramel), or whatever else appears on the list pinned up in the convent's entrance hall.

Spain claims to be more extensively covered with vineyards than is any other country in the world. Until recently, the quality of Spanish wines was considered by foreigners to be barely equal to the quantity, and Spanish "plonk" was thought suitable only for parties where people would be too drunk to notice. The Spaniards themselves, as unpretentious in their drinking as in their eating habits, did not help matters with their love of wine washed down with *gaseosa* (carbonated lemonade) and their tendency to buy wine from great barrels simply marked *tinto* (red) or *blanco* (white), along with a figure indicating the alcohol content. Recently, increased tourism has led to the enormous promotion of Spanish wines, which are now very much in fashion. Villages with excellent wine that has yet to be commercialized still do exist.

The cheap variety of Spanish wines comes mainly from Valdepeñas, in the middle of the dreary plains of La Mancha, Spain's largest wine-growing area. On the other end of the scale are the celebrated red wines of Rioja, which have a full-bodied woody flavor resulting from their having matured for up to eight years in casks made of American oak (the oldest and best of these wines are labeled *Reserva*). The technique of aging the wine in this way was introduced by French vintners from Bordeaux and Burgundy, who moved to the Rioja area in the last century, hoping to escape the phylloxera epidemic that was destroying the vines in their own country; curiously, however, there are few places today in France where the aging process is as long as it is here. Among the better Riojas are those of Imperial, Marqués de Murrieta, and Marqués de Riscal. Marqués de Riscal, in fact, has recently moved into the nearby Rueda district, where it has marketed one of Spain's most distinguished white wines. Sparkling white wines are the specialty of Catalunya (the most renowned being Codorniu and Freixenet), which is also the Spanish area with the greatest variety of wine production.

The one Spanish wine that has always been popular with foreigners is sherry. The English have dominated the sherry trade in Jerez de la Frontera since the 16th century, and most of the famous labels are foreign (for instance, Domecq, Harvey, Sandeman). The classic dry sherry is the *fino;* amontillado is deeper in color and taste, and *oloroso* is really a sweet dessert wine. Another fortified wine from the area is Manzanilla, which is made in the delightful coastal town of Sanlúcar de Barrameda and is dependent for its production on the cool sea breezes there; this wine, with a faint tang of the sea, does not travel well, and there are even those who believe that it tastes better in the lower part of Sanlúcar than in the upper town. Sherry and Manzanilla tend to be thought of as aperitif wines, and indeed they are the ideal accompaniment to tapas; to eat a Sanlúcar prawn with a glass of Manzanilla is many Spaniards' idea of paradise. Spaniards tend also to drink sherry and Manzanilla when sitting down to a meal, a custom that has yet to catch on outside the country. In England, sherry still has the genteel associations of an Oxford college, but the Spaniards have a more robust attitude toward it. You will probably never think of sherry in the same way again if you attend the Seville *Feria*, where reputedly more sherry and Manzanilla are drunk in a week than in the whole of Spain in a year. Manzanilla, incidentally, has a reputation for not giving a hangover, and some make the dubious claim that it is an excellent cure for gout.

Some of Spain's finest brandies, such as Osborne, Terry, Duque de Alba, and Carlos III, also come from Jerez. Málaga has a sweet dessert wine that enjoyed a vogue with the English in the last century (look for the label Scholtz). *Aguardientes* (aquavits) are manufactured throughout Spain, famous brands being from Chinchón, near Madrid. A sweet and popular liquor called *Ponche Caballero* comes in a silver-coated bottle that looks like an amateur explosive. Sangría, which is usually drunk by tourists, should consist of fruits, wine, brandy, and Cointreau, but usually served as a watered-down combination of wine and lemonade with the odd piece of orange thrown in. If you truly wish to appear a tourist, you should try drinking wine from a *porrón*, a glass vessel from which you pour the wine into your mouth from a distance of at least one foot: A raincoat is recommended.

You are truly initiated into Spanish ways after your first night spent drinking until dawn. Ideally, this experience is followed by a snack of *churros* (doughnut fritters) dipped into hot chocolate; the more hardened souls will be ordering the morning's glass of aguardiente. After a few hours' sleep, you will have a proper breakfast (around 11 o'clock), consisting, if you are brave, of toast rubbed in garlic or covered in *manteca colorada* (spicy pig's fat). Soon it will be time for the midday tapas. And so a typical Spanish day continues.

3 Madrid

*By Mark
Potok and
Deborah
Luhrman*

At the heart of Spain, Madrid's pulsing energy and openness make it Europe's most lively capital. Its people—called Madrileños—are a joyful lot, famous for their seeming ability to defy the need for sleep. Life here is lived in the crowded streets and in the noisy cafés, where endless rounds of socializing last long into the night. The publicness of Madrid's lifestyle makes it especially easy for visitors to get involved, and its allure is hard to resist.

Madrid's other chief attraction is its unsurpassed collection of paintings by some of the world's great artists, among them: Goya, El Greco, Velázquez, Picasso, and Dalí. Nowhere else will you find such a concentration of masterpieces as in the three museums—the Prado, the Reina Sofia, and the Thyssen-Bornemisza—that make up Madrid's so-called golden triangle of art.

The bright blue sky, as immortalized in Velázquez' paintings, is probably the first thing you'll notice about Madrid. Despite 20th-century pollution, that same color sky is still much in evidence thanks to breezes that sweep down from the Guadarrama mountains, blowing away the urban smog.

The city's skyline has its share of soaring modern skyscrapers but the more typical Madrid towers of red brick crowned by gray slate roofs and spires far outnumber them. This Habsburg-era architecture, built in the 1500s and 1600s by Spain's Austrian kings who made Madrid capital of the realm, gives parts of town a timeless, Old World feel.

Monumental neoclassical structures like the Prado Museum, the Royal Palace, and the Puerta de Alcalá arch make up Madrid's other historic face. These are the sights most visited by tourists and most were built in the 1700s during the reign of Bourbon monarch Charles III, who, inspired by the enlightened ideas of the age, also created Retiro Park, and the broad, leafy boulevard called Paseo del Prado.

Modern-day Madrid sprawls northward in block after block of dreary high-rise brick apartment buildings and office towers. A swelling population of 3.2 million is also moving into surrounding villages and new suburbs, creating tremendous traffic problems in and around the capital.

While these new quarters and many of Madrid's crumbling old residential neighborhoods may seem unappealing to the visitor, don't be put off by first impressions. The city's attractiveness has mostly to do with its people and the electricity they generate—whether at play in the bars and discotheques or at work in the advertising, television, and film industries headquartered here.

Situated on a plateau 646 meters (2,120 feet) above sea level, Madrid is the highest capital in Europe. It can also be one of the world's hottest cities in summer, and freezing cold in winter. Spring and summer are the most delightful times to visit when a balmy evening has virtually everyone in town lingering at an outdoor café, but each season has its own charms; in winter steamy café windows beckon and the famous blue skies are especially crisp and bright. That's when Madrid, as the local bumper stickers will tell you, is the next best place to heaven.

The sophistication of Madrid stands in vivid contrast to the ancient ways of the historic villages close to the capital. Less than an hour away from the downtown skyscrapers you can find villages where farm fields are still plowed by mule. Like city dwellers the world over, Madrileños like to visit the countryside, and getaways to the dozens of Castilian hamlets nearby, and excursions to Toledo, El

Escorial, and Segovia are a favorite pastime of locals, as well as being regular stops on the tourist trail.

Essential Information

Arriving and Departing by Plane

Airports and Airlines Madrid is served by **Barajas Airport,** 12 km (7 mi) east of the city; it's a rather grim-looking facility, although the national terminal was recently renovated. Major carriers, including American, Delta, TWA, and United, provide regular service to the United States. Most connections are through Miami, Washington, or New York, but American offers daily direct flights to and from Dallas–Fort Worth International Airport (reserve well in advance because they're very popular). Many carriers serve London and other European capitals daily, but if you shop around at Madrid travel agencies, you'll generally find better deals than those available abroad (especially to and from Great Britain). For more information on getting to Madrid by air, *see* Arriving and Departing in Chapter 1. For general information and information on flight delays, call the airport (tel. 91/305–8343/44/45).

Between the Airport and Downtown For a mere 300 pesetas, there's a convenient **bus** to the central Plaza Colón, where taxis wait to take you to your hotel. The buses run between 5:40 AM and 2 AM, leaving every 15 minutes—slightly less often very early or late in the day. Be sure to watch your belongings, as the underground Plaza Colón bus station is one of the favorite haunts of purse snatchers and con artists. **Taxis** are usually waiting outside the airport terminal near the clearly marked bus stop. Expect to pay up to 2,000 pesetas, or even more in heavy traffic, plus small holiday, late-night, and luggage surcharges. Make sure the driver works on the meter—off-the-meter "deals" almost always cost more.

Arriving and Departing by Car, Train, and Bus

By Car Felipe II made Madrid the capital of Spain because it was at the geographic center of his peninsular domains, and today many of the nation's highways radiate out from it like the spokes of a wheel. Originating at Kilometer Zero, marked by a brass plaque on the sidewalk of the central Puerta del Sol, these highways include A6 (Segovia, Salamanca, Galicia); A1 (Burgos and the Basque Country); the N II (Guadalajara, Barcelona, France); the N III (Cuenca, Valencia, the Mediterranean Coast); the A4 (Aranjuez, La Mancha, Granada, Seville); N401 (Toledo); and the N V (Talavera de la Reina, Portugal). The city is surrounded by M30, the inner ring road, and M40, the outer ring road, from which most of these highways are easily picked up.

By Train Madrid has three train stations: Chamartín, Atocha, and Norte. **Chamartín** Station, near the northern tip of the Paseo Castellana, serves trains heading for points north, including Barcelona, France, San Sebastián, Burgos, León, Oviedo, La Coruña, Segovia, Salamanca, and Portugal. The **Atocha** Station, at the southern end of the Paseo del Prado, was renovated in honor of the inauguration of high-speed AVE train service in 1992, and serves points south and east, including Seville, Malaga, Córdoba, Valencia, Castellon, and Toledo. The **Norte** Station is used primarily as a terminal for local trains serving Madrid's western suburbs, including El Escorial. For schedules and reservations call RENFE (tel. 91/563–0202, in Spanish only) or go to the information counter in any of the train stations.

Reservations can be made by phone, and tickets can be charged on a credit card and delivered to your hotel. Most major travel agencies can also provide information and tickets.

By Bus   Madrid has no central bus station, and, in general, buses are less popular than trains (though they can be faster). Most of southern Spain is served by the **Estación del Sur** (Canarias 17, tel. 91/468–4200), while buses for much of the rest of the peninsula, including Cuenca, Extremadura, Salamanca, and Valencia, depart from the **Auto-Rés Station** (Plaza Conde de Casal 6, tel. 91/551–7200). There are several other smaller stations, however, so inquire at travel agencies for the one for your destination.

Other bus companies of interest include **La Sepulvedana** (Paseo de la Florida 11, near the Norte Station, tel. 91/527–9537), serving Segovia, Ávila, and La Granja; **Herranz** (departures from Fernandez de los Ríos s/n, metro: Moncloa, tel. 91/543–3645 or 91/543–8167), for the Escorial and Valle de los Caidos; **Continental Auto** (Alenza 20, metro: Ríos Rosas, tel. 91/533–0400), serving Cantabria and the Basque region; and **La Veloz** (Mediterraneo 49, metro: Conde de Casal, tel. 91/409–7602), with service to Chinchón.

Getting Around

Madrid has a distinctly different feel depending on the neighborhood—from winding medieval streets to superchic shopping boulevards, regal formal parks to seedy red-light districts. While you will probably want to start out in the old city, where the majority of attractions are clustered, further adventures are likely to call you to other parts of town.

By Metro   The metro is quick, frequent, and, at 125 pesetas no matter how far you travel, cheap. Vastly cheaper is the 10-ride *billete de diez*, which costs 600 pesetas and has the added merit of being accepted by automatic turnstiles (lines at ticket booths can be long). The system is open from 6 AM to 1:30 AM, although a few entrances close earlier. Ten metro lines crisscross the city, and there are system maps in every station. Note the end station of the line you need, and just follow the signs to the correct corridor. Exits are marked *salida*. Crime is still rare on the system.

By Bus   Red city buses run between 6 AM and midnight and cost 125 pesetas per ride. Signs listing stops by street name are located at every stop but are hard to comprehend if you don't know the city well. Pick up a free route map from EMT kiosks on the Plaza de Cibeles or the Puerta del Sol, where you can also buy a 10-ride ticket (*bonobus*, 600 pesetas). If you speak Spanish, you can call for information (tel. 91/401–9900).

Drivers will make change for you, generally up to a 1,000-peseta note. If you've bought a 10-ride ticket, step up just behind the driver and insert it in the ticket-punching machine you see there until you hear the mechanism make a ding.

By Taxi   Taxis are one of the few truly good deals in Madrid. Meters start at 150 pesetas and add 70 pesetas a kilometer thereafter; numerous supplemental charges, however, mean your total cost often bears little resemblance to what you see on the meter. There's a 150-peseta supplement on Sundays and holidays, and between 11 PM and 6 AM; 125 pesetas to sports stadiums and the bullring; and 300 pesetas to or from the airport, plus 50 pesetas per suitcase.

Taxi stands are numerous, and taxis are easily hailed in the street—except when it rains, when they're exceedingly hard to come by. Free

Madrid Metro

KEY
1 Metro Terminals
○ Metro Stations
▭ Transfer Stations
— Railway Lines
• Train Stations

cabs will display a *libre* sign during the day, a green light at night. Generally, a tip of about 25 pesetas is right for shorter in-city rides, while you may want to go as high as 10% for a trip to the airport. Radio-dispatched taxis can be ordered from **Tele-Taxi** (tel. 91/445–9008), **Radioteléfono Taxi** (tel. 91/547–8200), or **Radio Taxi Independiente** (tel. 91/447–5180).

By Motorbike Motorbikes, scooters, and motorcycles can be rented by the day or week at **Moto Alquiler** (Conde Duque 13, tel. 91/542–0657). If driving in a strange city doesn't bother you, this is a fast and pleasant way to see the city. You'll need your passport, your driver's license, and either a cash deposit or a credit card.

By Car Driving automobiles in Madrid is best avoided by all but the most adventurous. Parking is nightmarish, traffic extremely heavy almost all the time, and the city's drivers can be frightening. An exception may be August, when the streets are largely emptied by the mass exodus of Madrileños on vacation.

Important Addresses and Numbers

Tourist Information There are four provincial tourist offices in Madrid, but the best is on the ground floor of the Torre Madrid building, on the **Plaza España** (Princesa 1, tel. 91/541–2325; open weekdays 9 AM–7 PM, Sat. 9:30–1:30, closed Sun. and holidays). Others are at **Barajas Airport** (tel. 91/305–8656; open weekdays 8 AM–8 PM, Sat. 9–2); the **Chamartín railroad station** (tel. 91/315–9976; open weekdays 8–8, Sat. 9–2); and **Duque de Medinaceli 2** (tel. 91/429–4951; open weekdays 9–6, Sat. 9–1). The city tourism office on the Plaza Mayor (tel. 91/366–5477; open weekdays 10–8) is good for little save a few pamphlets.

Embassies **United States** (Serrano 75, tel. 91/577–4000), **Canada** (Nuñez de Balboa 35, tel. 91/431–4300), and **United Kingdom** (Fernando el Santo 16, tel. 91/319–0200).

Emergencies **Police** (tel. 091), **ambulance** (tel. 91/522–2222 or 91/588–4400), and English-speaking **doctors** (Conde de Aranda 7, tel. 91/435–1823). Major **hospitals** include La Paz (tel. 91/358–2600) and 12 de Octubre (tel. 91/390–8000).

English-Language Bookstores **Turner's English Bookshop** (Génova 3, tel. 91/319–0926) has a very large collection of English-language books. It also offers a useful bulletin board exchange. **Booksellers** (José Abascal 48, tel. 91/442–8104) also has a large English-language selection.

Late-Night Pharmacies Forty percent of all pharmacies are required by law to be open 24 hours a day, on a rotating basis. Listings of those pharmacies are found in all major daily newspapers.

Travel Agencies Travel agencies, found almost everywhere in Madrid, are generally the best bet for obtaining deals, tickets, and information without hassles. Some major agencies: **American Express,** located next door to the Cortés, the parliament building on Génova (Plaza de las Cortés 2, tel. 91/322–5500); **Wagons-Lits** (Paseo de la Castellana, tel. 91/563–1202); and **Pullmantur,** across the street from the Royal Palace (Plaza de Oriente 8, tel. 91/541–1807).

Guided Tours

Orientation Standard city tours, in English or Spanish, can be arranged by your hotel; most include **Madrid Artístico** (Royal Palace and Prado Museum included), **Madrid Panorámico** (half-day tour for first-time visitors), **Madrid de Noche** (combinations include a flamenco or a nightclub show), and **Panorámico y Toros** (on Sundays, a brief city overview followed by a bullfight). **Trapsatur** (Saw Bernardo 23, tel. 91/542–6666) runs the *Madridvision* tourist bus, which makes a one-hour sightseeing circuit of the city with recorded commentary in English. No advance reservation is needed. Buses leave from the front of the Prado Museum every 1½ hours, beginning at 10:45 Monday–Saturday, 10:30 on Sunday. A round-trip ticket costs 500 pesetas, while a day pass, which allows you to get on and off at various attractions, is 1,000 pesetas.

Personal Guides Contact the **Asociación Profesional de Informadores** (Ferraz 82, tel. 91/542–1214 or 91/541–1221) if you wish to hire a personal guide to take you around the city.

Exploring Madrid

Madrid is a compact city, and most of the things visitors want to see are concentrated in a downtown area barely a mile across, stretching between the Royal Palace and Retiro Park. Broad avenidas, twisting medieval alleys, grand museums, stately gardens, and tiny tiled taverns are all jumbled together in an area easily explored on foot.

In fact, the texture of Madrid is so rich that walking is the only way to experience those special moments—peeking in on a guitar maker at work or watching a child dip churros into a steamy cup of chocolate—whose images linger long after the holiday photos have faded.

This Exploring section is divided into five tours: the first is the longest (covering about 2 miles) and is designed to help you get your bearings on a leisurely walk across town, stopping at the Plaza Mayor and strolling up the leafy Paseo del Prado; the second tour takes in Madrid's famous museum mile, said to have more masterpieces per meter than anywhere else in the world; the third tour focuses on regal Madrid, with stops at the royal convent, the sumptuous royal palace, the Almudena cathedral, and the king's gardens; the fourth tour winds through the narrow streets of medieval Madrid, tracing the city's history from its beginnings as an Arab fortress; and our fifth tour explores the humble but vibrant neighborhoods known as *castizo* or "authentic" Madrid, where Miguel de Cervantes once lived and where today poets, musicians, and average people still do.

Highlights for First-time Visitors

Centro de Arte Reina Sofía (*see* Tour 2)
Paseo del Prado (*see* Tour 1)
Plaza de Paja (*see* Tour 4)
Plaza Mayor (*see* Tour 1)
Prado Museum (*see* Tour 2)
Retiro Park (*see* Tour 1)
Royal Palace (*see* Tour 3)
Tapas bars (*see* Tour 4)

Tour 1: Introduction to the City

Numbers in the margin correspond to points of interest on the Madrid map.

❶ Begin at the stately **Plaza de Oriente** in front of the Royal Palace, where you'll find yourself surrounded by stone statues of all the Spanish kings from Ataulfo to Fernando VI. These massive sculptures were meant to be mounted on the railing atop the palace,

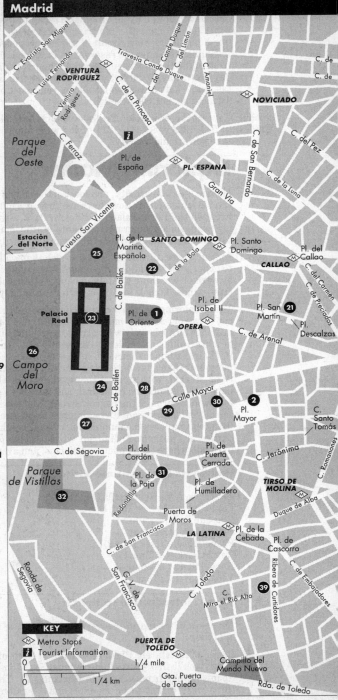

Madrid

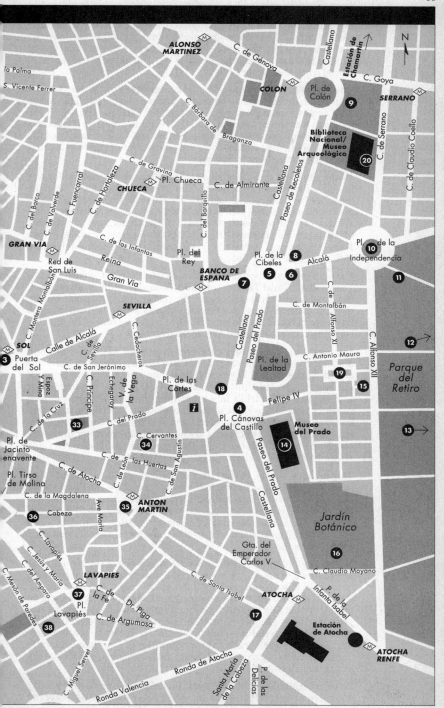

where there are now stone urns. But Queen Isabel de Farnesio, one of the first royals to inhabit the palace, had them taken off because she was afraid their enormous weight would bring the roof down. At least that's what she *said*. Palace insiders reported the Queen wanted the statues removed because her own likeness had not been placed front and center.

The statue of King Felipe IV in the center of the plaza was the first equestrian bronze ever to be cast of a horse rearing up. This action pose comes from a painting of the king by Velázquez by which the monarch was so smitten that in 1641 he commissioned an Italian artist, Pietro de Tacca, to turn it into a sculpture. De Tacca enlisted the help of the scientist Galileo to figure out the feat of engineering that keeps the statue from falling over.

In the minds of most Madrileños, the Plaza de Oriente is forever linked with Francisco Franco. The *generalissimo* liked to make speeches from the roof of the Royal Palace to his thousands of followers crammed into the plaza below. Even now, on the November anniversary of Franco's death, the plaza fills with his supporters, most of whom are old-timers, although lately the occasion has also drawn Nazi flag-waving skinheads from other European countries in a chilling pro-fascist tribute.

Turn away from the palace and walk to the right (south) of the **Teatro Real** (Royal Theater) on calle Carlos III. Built in about 1850, the neoclassical theater was once the center of Madrid's cultural society. It has been closed for renovations and was set to reopen as the city's opera house by the end of 1995. From the front of the theater continue straight up Calle Arenal for four blocks.

Just past the 14th-century church of San Ginés, one of the oldest in Madrid, turn right onto the narrow **San Ginés passageway** that runs alongside the church. Wooden stalls selling used books and prints of old Madrid are built into the church wall. Across the way is Joy Eslava, one of Madrid's late-night discotheques. Where the passageway jogs to the right is the **Chocolatería San Ginés,** a Madrid institution known for its chocolate and churros, and the final stop on many a night owl's bar crawl. Continue along the passageway past a couple more old-fashioned cafés, then cross the traffic-clogged Calle

② Mayor and climb the short hill into the **Plaza Mayor.**

This arcaded square is the heart of Madrid. Austere, grand—and surprisingly quiet compared to the rest of the city—the Plaza Mayor has seen it all: *autos da fe* (public burnings of heretics); the canonization of saints; criminal executions; royal marriages, such as that of Princess Maria and the King of Hungary in 1629; bullfights (until 1847); masked balls; fireworks displays; and all manner of events and celebrations.

Measuring 110 by 90 m (360 by 300 ft), this is one of the largest public squares in Europe, and considered by many to be one of the most beautiful. It was designed by Juan de Herrera, the architect to Felipe II and the same man who designed the forbidding El Escorial monastery outside Madrid. Construction of the plaza lasted just two years and was completed in 1620 during the reign of Felipe III, whose **equestrian statue** stands in the center. The inauguration ceremonies included celebrating the canonization of four Spanish saints: Teresa of Ávila, Ignatius of Loyola, Isidro (Madrid's male patron saint), and Francis Xavier.

Prior to becoming the Plaza Mayor, this space was occupied by a city market, and many of the surrounding streets retain the names of the trades and foodstuffs once ensconsed there. Nearby is *Calle de Cuchilleros* (Knife Makers' Street), *Calle de Lechuga* (Lettuce Street), *Calle de Fresa* (Strawberry Street), and *Calle de Botoneros* (Button Makers' Street). The oldest building on the plaza is the one with the brightly painted murals and the gray spires, *Casa de la Panadería* (the bakery) in honor of the bread shop it was built on top of. Opposite it is the *Casa de la Carniceria* (the butcher shop) which now houses a police station.

The plaza is closed to motorized traffic, making this a pleasant place to sit in the sun or while away a warm summer evening at one of the sidewalk cafés, watching alfresco portrait artists, street musicians, and Madrileños from all walks of life. At Christmas the plaza fills with stalls selling trees, ornaments, and nativity scenes, as well as all types of practical jokes and tricks to be used on December 28, the *Dia de los Inocentes*, a Spanish version of April Fool's Day.

Leave the Plaza Mayor through the arch in the northeast corner to the right of the *Casa de la Panadería* onto *Calle de la Sal* (Salt Street) and follow this pedestrian walkway back down to Calle Mayor. A right turn will bring you to the **Puerta del Sol**.

Always crowded with people and exhaust fumes, this busy square is Madrid's traffic nerve center. The city's main subway interchange is located below, and buses fan out through the city from here. A brass plaque in the sidewalk on the south side of the plaza marks **Kilometer 0**, the spot from which all distances in Spain are measured. The restored 1756 French neoclassic building by the marker now houses government offices, but during the Franco period it was used as a political prison and is still known as the "house of screams." Across the square is a bronze statue of Madrid's official symbol, a bear and a *madroño* (strawberry) tree.

Head east on Carrera San Jeronimo, past the jumble of shops and cafés. At number 8 peek into the ground-floor delicatessen of **Lhardy,** one of Madrid's oldest and most traditional restaurants. Shoppers stop in here on cold winter mornings for steamy cups of *caldo* (chicken broth). As you continue down Carrera San Jeronimo, be sure to have a look at the beautifully tiled and decorated tops of buildings, especially at the corner of Calle Sevilla. The big white granite building on the left with the lions out in front is the **Congress,** the lower house of Spain's parliament.

Past the Palace Hotel and the boutique-filled Galeria del Prado shopping center is the Plaza Canovas del Castillo with its **Fuente de Neptuno** (Neptune's fountain). This plaza is the hub of Madrid's so-called "golden triangle of art," made up of the red brick Prado Museum spreading out along the east side of the boulevard, the Thyssen-Bornemisza Museum across the plaza, and five blocks to the south, the Reina Sofia Museum.

Leaving the museums until later (*see* Tour 2, *below*), continue north along the wide, landscaped walkway that runs down the center of the Paseo del Prado to the Plaza de la Cibeles, which is home to the **Fuente de la Cibeles.** Sybil, the wife of Saturn, is depicted atop this fountain driving a chariot drawn by lions. Even more than the officially designated bear and the strawberry tree, this monument, beautifully lit at night, has come to symbolize Madrid—so much so that during the civil war, patriotic citizens risked life and limb sandbagging it as Nationalist aircraft bombed the city.

On the southeast side of the plaza is the ornate **Palacio de Comunicaciónes,** otherwise known as the main post office, and the place to go for all your postal and telecommunications needs. *Open for stamps weekdays 9 AM–10 PM, Sat. 9–8, Sun. 10–1; open for telephone, telex, telegrams, and fax weekdays 8 AM–midnight, weekends 8 AM–10 PM.*

7 Across the Paseo del Prado from the post office is the massive 1884 **Banco de España** (Spain's equivalent of the U.S. Federal Reserve) that takes up the entire city block, and where it's said the nation's gold reserves are held in great vaults that stretch under the traffic circle all the way to the fountain. If you want to risk dodging traffic to reach the median strip in front of the bank, you can get a fine photo of the fountain and the palaces with the monumental Puerta de Alcalá arch in the background.

8 Continuing north up the boulevard, the first building on the right is the **Casa de las Americas,** a cultural center and art gallery focusing on Latin America. It opened in 1992 in the allegedly haunted Palacio de Linares, which was built by a man who made his fortune in the New World and returned to a life of incestuous love and strange deaths. *Paseo Recoletos 2, tel. 91/576–3590. Admission: Palace tour 300 ptas.; art gallery, free. Palace tours Mon.–Sat. 9–11:30; art gallery open daily 11–8.*

To the left behind the trees is the red brick neoclassical **Palacio de Buenavista,** which now serves as a headquarters for the army, but was built in 1747 by the duchess of Alba, whose clothed and unclothed portraits by Goya hang in the Prado Museum (*see* Tour 2, *below*).

The grand mansions that once lined the paseo have been replaced with modern high-rise buildings or converted to other purposes, such as the elegant yellow **Banco Argentaria** (formerly Banco Hipotecario), on the right. This was the home of the Marquis of Salamanca who, at the turn of the 20th century, built the exclusive shopping and residential neighborhood that bears his name.

Time Out To rest your feet and sip a cup of coffee or a beer, pull up a chair on the shady terrace or inside the air-conditioned, stained-glass bar of **El Espejo** (Paseo Recoletos 31, tel. 91/308–2347. Open daily 10 AM–2 AM), located right in the center of the paseo, and decorated in the style of Belle-Epoque Paris.

9 Two more blocks north is the modern **Plaza Colón.** Named for Christopher Columbus, a statue of the explorer (identical to one in the port of Barcelona), looks west from atop a high tower in the middle of the square. Behind Plaza Colón is **Calle Serrano,** the city's number-one shopping street. Turn right onto Serrano for some window shopping. The big gray building on the right side of the street is Spain's **archaeology museum** (*see* Tour 2, *below*). Four blocks south **10** along Serrano brings you to the **Puerta de Alcalá,** a triumphal arch built by Carlos III in 1778 to mark the spot of the former city gates. Bomb damage inflicted on the arch during the civil war is still visible.

11 This plaza is also the main entrance to **Parque del Retiro** (Retiro Park). Once royalty's private playground, Retiro is a vast expanse of green that includes formal gardens, fountains, lakes (complete with rentable rowboats), exhibition halls, children's play areas, and a puppet theater. It is especially lively here on weekends, when it fills with street musicians, jugglers, clowns, gypsy fortune tellers, and sidewalk painters, along with hundreds of Spanish families out for a walk. During May the park hosts a month-long book fair, and in summer flamenco concerts often take place here.

If you head straight towards the center of the park, you'll find the
⑫ **Estanque** (lake), presided over by a grandiose equestrian statue of King Alfonso XII, erected by his mother. One of the best of the many cafés within the park is behind the lake, just north of the statue. Or if you're feeling more energetic, you can rent a boat and work up an appetite rowing around the lake.

⑬ The 19th-century **Palacio de Cristal** (Crystal Palace), southeast of the lake, was built to house a collection of exotic plants from the Philippines, a Spanish possession at the time. This airy marvel of steel and glass sits on a base of decorative tile, and now occasionally hosts exhibitions of sculpture. A small lake with ducks and swans is next door. A 10-minute walk south brings you to the **Rosaleda** (rose garden), an English garden design bursting with color and heavy with the scent of flowers for most of the summer. Nearby look for a statue called the **Ángel Caído** (fallen angel), which Madrileños claim is the only one in the world depicting the prince of darkness before—during, actually—his fall from grace.

Tour 2: Museum Mile

⑭ This tour starts at the **Museo del Prado** (Prado Museum), which for many visitors is Madrid's chief attraction. It was commissioned in 1785 by King Carlos III, and was originally meant to be a natural science museum. The king, popularly remembered as "Madrid's best mayor," intended the museum, the adjoining botanical gardens, and the elegant Paseo del Prado to serve as a center of scientific enlightenment for his subjects. By the time the building was completed in 1819, its purpose had been changed to exhibiting the vast collection of art gathered by Spanish royalty since the time of Ferdinand and Isabella.

Painting represents one of Spain's greatest contributions to world culture, and the jewels of the Prado are the works of the nation's three great masters: Francisco Goya, Diego Velázquez, and El Greco. The museum also contains masterpieces of Flemish and Italian artists, collected when those lands were part of the Spanish Empire. The museum benefitted greatly from anticlerical laws in 1836, which forced monasteries, convents, and churches to turn over many of their art treasures so that they could be enjoyed by the general public.

The visit begins on the **upper floor** (primera planta) of the museum, where you enter through a series of halls dedicated to **Renaissance painters.** While many visitors hurry through these rooms to get to the Spanish canvases, don't miss the *Portrait of Emperor Charles V* by Titian, and Raphael's exquisite *Portrait of a Cardinal*.

Next comes a hall filled with the passionately spiritual works of **El Greco** (Doménikos Theotokópoulos, 1541–1614). This Greek-born artist, who lived and worked in Toledo, is known for his mystical, elongated faces. His style was quite shocking to a public accustomed to strict, representational realism; and as he intended his art to provoke emotion, El Greco is sometimes called the world's first "modern" painter. *The Resurrection* and the *Adoration of the Shepherds*, considered two of his greatest paintings, are on view here.

Straight ahead and to the left are the rooms dedicated to **Velázquez** (1599–1660). The artist's meticulous brushwork is visible in numerous portraits of kings and queens. Be sure to look for the magnificent painting *Las Hilanderas* (The Spinners)—evidence of the artist's talent for painting light. One hall is reserved exclusively for the Prado's most famous canvas, Velázquez's *Las Meninas* (the Maids of Honor). It combines a self portrait of the artist at work with a mirror reflection of the king and queen in an astounding interplay of space and perspectives. Picasso was obsessed with this work and painted numerous copies of it in his own abstract style, which can be seen in the Picasso Museum in Barcelona.

The south end of this floor is reserved for **Goya** (1746–1828), whose works span a staggering range of tone, from bucolic to horrific. Among his early masterpieces are numerous portraits of the family of King Carlos IV, to whom he was court painter. A glance at their unflattering and imbecilic expressions, especially in the painting *The Family of Carlos IV*, reveals the loathing Goya developed for these self-indulgent and reactionary rulers. His famous side-by-side canvases, *The Clothed Maja* and *The Nude Maja*, represent the young duchess of Alba, whom Goya adored and frequently painted. It is not known whether she ever returned his affection. Adjacent rooms house a series of bucolic scenes of Spaniards at play, painted by Goya as designs for tapestries.

His paintings take on political purpose starting in 1808, when the population of Madrid rose up against occupying French troops. The *2nd of May* portrays the insurrection at the Puerta del Sol, and the even more terrifying companion piece *3rd of May*, depicts the nighttime executions of patriots who had rebelled the day before. The garish lighting effects of this work typifies the romantic style, which favors drama over detail, and makes it one of the most powerful indictments of violence ever committed to canvas.

Downstairs you'll find the extreme of Goya's range in a hall that features his "black paintings," dark, disturbing works completed late in his life that reflect the inner turmoil he suffered after losing his hearing and his deep embitterment over the bloody War of Independence. The rest of the ground floor is taken up with Flemish paintings including the bizarre masterpiece *Garden of Earthly Delights* by Hieronymous Bosch. *Paseo del Prado s/n, tel. 91/420–2836. Admission: 400 pesetas. Open Tues.–Sat. 9–7, Sun. 9–2; closed Mon.*

⑮ The **Casón del Buen Retiro** (Calle Alfonso XII, s/n) is a museum annex five-minutes' walk from the Prado that can be entered on the same ticket. This building, once a ballroom, and the formal gardens in nearby Retiro Park are all that remains of Madrid's second royal palace complex, which until the early 19th century occupied the entire neighborhood. On exhibit here are 19th-century Spanish painting and sculpture, including works by Sorolla and Rusiñol.

⑯ Just south of the Prado is the entrance to the **Jardín Botánico** (Botanical Gardens), a pleasant place to stroll or sit under the trees. True to the wishes of King Carlos III, the garden holds an array of plants, flowers, and cacti from around the world. *Plaza de Murillo 2, tel. 91/585–4700. Admission: 100 pesetas, children under 10 free. Open daily, summer 10–8, winter 10–6.*

Time Out   Instead of eating in the Prado's so-so basement cafeteria, head across the paseo and up one block on Calle Lope de Vega to the tiny Plaza de Jesus, where you'll find **La Dolores** (Pl. de Jesus 4), one of Madrid's most atmospheric old tiled bars, and the perfect place for a beer or glass of wine and a plate of olives.

At the south end of the Paseo del Prad
Glorieta del Emperador Carlos V, you'll
ing of painted tiles and winged statue
Ministerio de Agricultura (Agriculture
ing to acquire this building in order to dis
remains in storage for lack of space. Across the
train station, thoroughly restored in 1992. The high-
Seville leaves from here, as do local trains to Toledo and
tance trains to points south.

On the far side of the traffic circle you'll see Madrid's modern art museum, the **Centro de Arte Reina Sofía.** Often called "the Sofidu," after Paris's Pompidou modern art center, the museum is housed in a
converted hospital, whose classic granite austerity is somewhat relieved (or ruined, depending upon who you ask) by the two transpar-
ent glass elevator shafts that have been added to the facade.

Like the Prado, the collection focuses on three great Spanish artists, this time modern masters: Pablo Picasso, Salvador Dalí, and
Joan Miró. Take the elevator to the second floor to see the permanent collections; the other floors house visiting exhibits.

The first rooms are dedicated to the beginnings of Spain's modern
art movement and contain paintings completed around the turn of
the century. The focal point is Picasso's 1901 *Woman in Blue*—hardly beautiful, but surprisingly representational compared to his later
works.

Moving on to the **Cubist collection,** which includes nine works by
Juan Gris, be sure to see the splintered, blue-gray *Self-Portrait* by
Dalí, in which he painted his favorite things, a morning newspaper
and a pack of cigarettes. The other highlight here is Picasso's *Musical Instruments on a Table*, one of many variations on this theme
created by the Spanish-born artist.

The museum's showpiece is Picasso's famous *Guernica,* which occupies the center hall and is surrounded by dozens of studies for individual figures within it. It depicts the horror of the Nazi Condor
Legion's bombing of the ancient Basque town of Guernica in 1937,
which helped bring Spanish dictator Francisco Franco to power.
The work, in many ways a 20th-century version of Goya's *3rd of
May*, is something of a national shrine, as evidenced by the solemni-
ty of Spaniards viewing it. The painting was not brought into Spain
until 1981. Picasso, an ardent anti-fascist, refused to allow it to enter the country while Franco was alive.

The room in front of *Guernica* contains a collection of **surrealist**
works, including six canvases by Miró, known for his childlike
graphicism. On the opposite side of *Guernica* is a hall dedicated to
the surrealist **Salvador Dalí,** and hung with paintings bequeathed to
the government in the artist's will. Although Dalí is perhaps best
known for works of a somewhat whimsical tone, many of these canvases are dark and haunting, and bursting with symbolism. Among
the best known are *The Great Masturbator* (1929) and *The Enigma
of Hitler* (1939), with its broken, dripping telephone.

The rest of the museum is devoted to more recent art, including the
massive, gravity-defying sculpture *Toki Egin* by Eduardo Chillida,
considered Spain's greatest living sculptor, and five textural paintings by Barcelona artist Antoní Tàpies, who incorporates materials
such as wrinkled sheets or straw into his works. *Santa Isabel 52, tel.
91/467–5062. Admission: 400 pesetas. Open Mon. and Wed.–Sat.
10–9, Sun. 10–2:30; closed Tues.*

To complete the triangle, head back north on the Paseo del Prado to
(18) the third and newest art center, the **Museo Thyssen-Bornemísza**,
which opened in 1992 in the Villahermosa Palace—elegantly renovated to include lots of airy space and natural light. This ambitious
collection of 800 paintings attempts to trace the history of Western
art with examples from all the important movements beginning
with 13th-century Italy.

The artworks were gathered over the past 70 years by industrialist
Baron Hans Heinrich Thyssen-Bornemisza and his father. At the
urging of his Spanish wife, a former Miss Spain, the baron agreed to
donate the collection to Spain. While the museum itself is beautiful
and its Impressionist paintings are the only ones on exhibit in the
country, critics have characterized the collection as the minor works
of major artists and the major works of minor artists.

Among the museum's gems are the *Portrait of Henry VIII* by Hans
Holbein (purchased from Princess Diana's grandfather, who used
the money to buy a new Bugatti sports car). American artists are
also well represented. Look for the Gilbert Stuart portrait of
George Washington's black cook, and note how much the composi-
tion and rendering resembles the artist's famous painting of the
founding father himself. Two halls are devoted to the Impressionists
and Postimpressionists, including many works by Pissarro, and a
few each by Renoir, Monet, Degas, Van Gogh, and Cézanne.

Of 20th-century art, the baron shows a weakness for terror-filled
(albeit dynamic and colorful) German Expressionism, but there are
also soothing paintings by Georgia O'Keefe and Andrew Wyeth.
*Paseo del Prado 8, tel. 91/420-3944. Admission: 600 pesetas, chil-
dren under 12 free. Open Tues.–Sun. 10–7; closed Mon.*

(19) Also along the "museum mile" is the **Museo del Ejército** (Army Museum), located in the pink palace just behind the Ritz Hotel, and displaying arms and armor. Among the 27,000 items on view are a
sword allegedly belonging to Spanish hero El Cid, suits of armor,
bizarre-looking pistols with barrels capable of holding scores of bul-
lets, Moorish tents, and a cross carried by Christopher Columbus.
This is an unusually entertaining museum of its genre. *Mendez
Nuñez 1, tel. 91/522-8977. Admission: 50 pesetas. Open Tues.–Sun.
10–2.*

The nearby **Museo Naval** (Navy Museum) has on display the first
map of the New World, drawn by cartographer Juan de la Cosa in
1500. Scale models of ships through the ages and lush reproductions
of two ships' cabins are also on exhibit. *Calle de Montalbán 2, tel.
91/521-0419. Admission: 50 pesetas. Open Tues.–Sun. 10:30–1:30.*

About six blocks north on the paseo you'll come to the **Biblioteca
Nacional** (National Library). The back side of this neoclassical
(20) building is the **Museo Arqueológico** (Archeology Museum). The biggest attraction here is a replica of the prehistoric Altamira cave
paintings, located underground in the garden. Inside the museum,
look for the *Dama de Elche*, a bust of a wealthy woman of the 4th-
century Iberian culture. Notice how her headgear is a rough precur-
sor to the mantillas and hair combs still associated with traditional
Spanish costumes. Be sure to see the ancient Visigothic votive
crowns discovered in 1859 near Toledo and believed to date back to
the 8th century. *Calle Serrano 13, tel. 91/577-7912. Admission: 200
pesetas. Open Tues.–Sat. 9:30–8:30, Sun. 9:30–2:30; closed Mon.*

Tour 3: Regal Madrid

㉑ Our tour of royal Madrid begins at the Co... ales (Convent of the Royal Barefoot Nuns), j... west of the Puerta del Sol. The 16th-century conve... for 200 years to women of royal blood, and its plain bri... facade hides a treasure trove of riches. Inside there are pan... Zurbarán, Titian, and Breughel the Elder, as well as a hall of su... tuous tapestries crafted from drawings by Rubens. The convent was founded in 1559 by Juana of Austria, whose daughter shut herself up here rather than endure marriage to Felipe II. A handful of nuns (not necessarily royal) still live here, cultivating their own vegetables in the convent's garden. Unfortunately you must visit as part of a tour, which is conducted only in Spanish. *Plaza de las Descalzas Reales 3, tel. 91/559–7404. Admission: 350 pesetas. Open Tues.–Thurs. and Sat. 10:30–12:30 and 4–5:30; Fri. 10:30–12:30; Sun. 11–1:30; closed Mon.*

㉒ From here, walk two blocks down to Calle Arenal. Turn right and follow the street around the right side of the royal theater, heading up Calle Arrieta to the **Convento de la Encarnación** (Convent of the Incarnation), which can be entered on the same ticket as the Convent of Descalzas Reales. Once connected to the Royal Palace by an underground passageway, this Augustinian convent was founded in 1611 by the wife of Felipe III. It houses many artistic treasures, but the convent's biggest attraction is the reliquary chamber where among the sacred bones is a vial containing the dried blood of St. Pantaleón, which is said to liquify every year on July 27th. *Plaza de la Encarnación 1, tel. 91/547–0510. Admission: 350 pesetas. Open Wed. and Sat. 10:30–1 and 4–5:30, Sun. 4–5:30.*

Behind the convent is the restored **Palacio del Senado,** yellow, neoclassical headquarters for Spain's upper house of parliament. Just north of here you'll find the unappealing *Plaza de España*, which has been taken over by trinket vendors and homeless immigrants.

Time Out Stop for a drink or a snack in the Royal Palace neighborhood at the **Taberna del Alabardero** (Felipe V 6). Named for a regiment of the king's guards, this cozy bar stocks a dozen types of tapas. Try the garlicky *patatas à la pobre* (poor man's potatoes).

㉓ Now head across the Plaza del Oriente to the entrance of the **Palacio Real** (Royal Palace). Standing on the same strategic spot where Madrid's first Alcazar or Arab fortress was built in the 9th century, the Royal Palace was commissioned in the early 1700s by the first of Spain's Bourbon rulers, Felipe V. But before building began, the old fortress-palace burned to the ground in a terrible fire on Christmas Eve 1734, and the king decided to use its site instead.

Before entering, take time to walk around the graceful **Patio de Armas** and admire the classical French architecture. It's clear that King Felipe was inspired by his childhood days spent with his grandfather, Louis XIV, at Versailles. Look for the stone statues of Inca Prince Atahualpa and Aztec King Montezuma, perhaps the only tributes in Spain to these pre-Columbian American rulers. Notice how the steep bluff drops down to the Manzanares River to the west. On a clear day this vantage point also commands a good view of the mountain passes leading into Madrid from Old Castile and it becomes obvious as to why the Moors picked this particular spot for a fortress.

compete with each other for over-
nour guided tour in English winds a
...lace. Highlights include: the **Salón de**
... private apartments, a riot of Rococo
...nlaid floors, curlicued ceramic wall and
...ening in the light of a two-ton crystal chan-
...ono, an exceedingly grand throne room that
...ts of King Juan Carlos and Queen Sofia; and
...ich is the palace's largest room and seats up to
... dinners. No monarch has lived here since 1931,
...I was hounded out of the country by a populace fed
...es of royal oppression. The current king and queen
...simpler Zarzuela Palace on the outskirts of Madrid,
...oyal Palace only for state functions and official occa-
s... ...as the first Middle East peace talks in 1991.

Within the palace you can also visit the **Biblioteca Real** (Royal Library), which has a first edition of Cervantes' *Don Quixote;* the **Museo de Música** (Music Museum), where the five stringed instruments by Stradivarius make up the world's largest collection; the **Armería Real** (Royal Armory), with its vast array of historic suits of armor and some frightening medieval torture implements; and the **Real Oficina de Farmacía** (Royal Pharmacy), boasting an assortment of vials and flasks used for concocting the king's medicines. *Calle Bailén s/n, tel. 91/559-7404. Admission: 500 pesetas for entire complex, 350 pesetas for palace alone. Open Mon.–Sat. 9:30–5, Sun. 9–2; closed during official receptions.*

24 Adjoining the palace to the south is the **Catedral de la Almudena,** which, after 110 years of construction, was consecrated by Pope John Paul II in 1993. The first stone was laid in 1883 by King Alfonso XII, and at the time it was planned as a Gothic-style structure of needles and spires, but as time ran long and money ran short the design was simplified by Fernando Chueca Goltia to become the more austere classical building you see today. The cathedral houses the remains of Madrid's male patron saint, St. Isidro, and a wooden statue of Madrid's female patron saint, the Virgin of Almudena, which was said to have been discovered following the Christian reconquest of Madrid in 1085. Legend has it that a divinely inspired woman named Maria led authorities to a secret spot in the old wall of the Alcazar (which in arabic can also be called *almudeyna*), where the statue was found framed by two lit candles inside a grain storage vault. That wall is part of the cathedral's foundation. *Calle de Bailén s/n, tel. 91/548-3514. Admission free. Open daily 10–1:30 and 6–8.*

25 Walking north past the palace, explore the formal **Jardínes Sabatini** (Sabatini Gardens). Crawling with stray cats, the gardens are a pleasant place for a rest and a good spot from which to watch the sunset. Below the gardens, but accessible only by walking around to **26** an entrance on the far side, is the **Campo del Moro.** This park's clusters of shady trees, winding paths, and long lawn that leads up to the palace offer a prime spot for photographing the building. Even without considering the riches inside, the palace's immense size (twice as large as Buckingham Palace) is awe-inspiring.

Tour 4: Medieval Madrid

Madrid's historic quarters are not so readily apparent as the ancient neighborhoods that characterize Toledo, Segovia, and Ávila. Nor are they so grand. But the visitor who takes time to explore the quiet, winding streets of medieval Madrid will be rewarded with an impression of the city that is light-years away from today's traffic-clogged avenues.

Our tour starts where the city began, on Calle Cuesta de la Vega at the ruins of the **Arab Wall,** which protected a fortress built on this site in the 8th century by Emir Mohammed I. In addition to being an excellent defensive position, the site had plentiful water and was called *Mayrit,* which is Arabic for "water source" and the likely origin of the city's name. All that remains of the Arab *medina* or early city that formed within the walls of the fortress is this neighborhood's crazy-quilt of streets and plazas, which likely follow the same layout as they did more than 1,100 years ago. The park Emir Mohammed I, alongside the wall, is a venue for summertime concerts and plays.

Walking uphill across Calle Bailén, head up Calle Mayor for three short blocks and turn left onto the tiny Calle San Nicolás, where you'll see the red-brick *mudéjar* tower of the **Iglesia de San Nicolás de las Servitas** (Church of St. Nicholas). The tower is one of the oldest buildings in Madrid and there's some debate over whether it once formed part of an Arab mosque. More likely it was built after the Christian reconquest of Madrid in 1085, but the brickwork and horseshoe arches are clear evidence that it was crafted by either Moorish workers or Spaniards well versed in the style. Inside the church are exhibits detailing the Islamic history of early Madrid. *Pl. de San Nicolás, tel. 91/559–4064. Admission: free. Open daily 5:30–6:30 or by appointment.*

Back on Calle Mayor continue two blocks uphill to the **Plaza de la Villa,** a medieval-looking complex of buildings that is now Madrid's city hall. Once called the Plaza de San Salvador for a church that used to stand here, this site has been the meeting place for the town council since the Middle Ages. The oldest building is the one with the *mudéjar* tower on the east side of the plaza, known as the **Casa de los Lujanes.** Built as a family home in the late 15th century, the Lujanes' crest can be seen over the main doorway. Directly across the plaza is the **Casa de la Villa,** built in 1629. This brick-and-stone building is a classic example of Madrid design with its clean lines and spire-topped corner towers. It is joined by an overhead walkway to the **Casa de Cisneros,** commissioned in 1537 by the nephew of Cardinal Cisneros, and one of Madrid's rare examples of the flamboyant Plateresque style, which has been likened to splashing water—liquid exuberance wrought in stone. *Buildings are open to the public for guided tours in Spanish Mon. 5 PM.*

The narrow picturesque streets behind the Plaza de la Villa are also worth exploring. Head three more blocks up Calle Mayor and turn right onto **Cava de San Miguel.** With the Plaza Mayor on your left and the iron-and-glass San Miguel market on your right, walk downhill past the row of ancient tapas bars built right into the retaining wall of the plaza above. Each one specializes in something different: Mesón de Champiñones has mushrooms, Mesón de Boquerones serves anchovies, Mesón de Tortilla cooks up excellent Spanish omelettes, and so on. Madrileños and tourists flock here each evening to sample the food and sing along with raucous musicians, who delight in playing foreign tunes for tourists.

About halfway down the street is the oldest of the taverns, the **Cuevas de Luis Candelas,** named for a 19th-century Madrid version of Robin Hood who was famous for his ingenious ways of tricking the rich out of their money and jewels. Farther down on the left is Casa

Botín (*see* Dining, *below*), Madrid's oldest restaurant and a favorite haunt of Ernest Hemingway. This curving street was once a moat just outside the walls of old Madrid. The plaza with the bright murals at the intersection of Calle Segovia is called the **Puerta Cerrada** (Closed Gate) for the entrance to the city that once stood here.

Turn right onto Calle Segovia, one of the main streets of Madrid during the Middle Ages. The first street on the left, Costanilla del Nuncio, is a ramp with steps that lead up to the **Palacio de la Nunciatura** (Palace of the Nunciat). Although it's not open to the public, you can peek inside the Renaissance garden of this mansion that once housed the Pope's ambassadors to Spain, and is now the official residence of the Archbishop of Madrid.

Time Out The **Café del Nuncio** (Costanilla del Nuncio s/n) on the corner of Calle Segovia is a relaxing Old World–style spot for coffee or a beer where classical music plays in the background.

Continue down Calle Segovia another block to the Plaza Cruz Verde and turn left up another ramp street, Costanilla de San Andrés, which leads to the heart of the old city. Halfway up the hill, look left down the narrow Calle Príncipe Anglona for a good view of the *mudéjar* tower of the **church of San Pedro el Viejo,** which, after San Nicolás, is one of the city's oldest. The brick tower is believed to have been built in 1354 following the Christian reconquest of Algeciras, in southern Spain. Be sure to notice the tiny defensive slits designed to accommodate crossbows.

31 At the top of the hill is the **Plaza de Paja,** the most important square of medieval Madrid. Although a few upscale restaurants have moved in, the quiet plaza remains unpaved and atmospheric. The jewel of this square is the **Capilla del Obispo** (Bishop's Chapel) built between 1520 and 1530. This was where peasants deposited their tithes called *diezmas*, literally one-tenth of their crop. Reference to this is made by the stacks of wheat shown on the ceramic tiles on the chapel. Architecturally, the chapel marks a transition from the blockish Gothic period—the basic shape of this structure—to the Renaissance, as evidenced by its decorations. Try to get inside to see the intricately carved polychrome altarpiece by Francisco Giralta, featuring scenes from the life of Christ. Opening hours of the chapel are erratic; the best time to visit is during Mass or on feast days.

The chapel forms part of the complex of the **church of San Andres,** whose dome was raised to house the remains of Madrid's male patron saint San Isidro Labrador. Isidro was a peasant who worked fields belonging to the Vargas family. The 16th-century **Vargas** palace forms the eastern side of the Plaza de Paja. According to legend, Isidro actually worked little, but thanks to many hours spent in prayer had the best-tended fields. When Señor Vargas came out to investigate the phenomenon, Isidro made a spring of sweet water spurt from the ground to quench his master's thirst. Because Saint Isidro's power had to do with water, in times of drought his remains were paraded through the city to bring rain (even as recently as the turn of the century). His bones now reside in another church.

Walk west from the Plaza de Paja on Calle de la Redondilla for one block to the **Plaza Moreria,** which is really no more than a wide spot in the street. This neighborhood was once the home of Moors who had chosen to stay in Madrid after the Christian reconquest. Although most of the buildings date from the 18th and 19th centuries, the steep, narrow streets and twisting alleyways are reminiscent of the much older *medina*.

Climb the stairway and cross Calle Bailén near the **viaduct,** a metal bridge that spans a ravine 31 meters (100 ft) above Calle Segovia. The viaduct has won grisly fame as the preferred spot in Madrid for suicides.

❸❷ On the opposite side of the street is the neighborhood of **Las Vistillas,** named for the pleasant park on the bluffs that overlooks Madrid's western edge. A great place to watch the sun go down or catch a cool breeze on a sweltering summer's night, the best thing to do here is find an empty outdoor table and order a drink and some tapas.

Tour 5: Castizo Madrid

Castizo is a Spanish word that means "authentic," and while there are few "sights" in the usual sense on this tour, our walk wanders through some of the most traditional and lively neighborhoods of Madrid.

❸❸ Begin at the **Plaza Santa Ana,** the heart of the theater district in the 17th century—the Golden Age of Spanish Literature—and today the center of Madrid's thriving nightlife. In the plaza is a statue of playwright Pedro Calderón de la Barca on a base depicting scenes from his works. His likeness faces the **Teatro Español,** which is adorned with the names of Spain's greatest playwrights. The theater, rebuilt in 1980 following a fire, stands in the same spot in which plays were performed as early as the 16th century, at that time in a rowdy outdoor setting called a *corral.* These makeshift theaters were usually installed in a vacant lot between two apartment buildings and families with balconies overlooking the action rented out seats to wealthy patrons of the arts. On the opposite side of the plaza is the ceramic tile facade of the **Casa de Guadalajara,** one of the most beautiful buildings in Madrid and currently a popular nightspot. On the same side of the plaza stands the recently refurbished **Hotel Victoria,** now an upscale establishment but once a rundown residence frequented by famous and not-so-famous bullfighters, including Manolete.

To the side of the hotel is the diminutive **Plaza del Angel,** home of one of the city's best jazz clubs, the Café Central. Back on Plaza Santa Ana is one of Madrid's most famous cafés, the **Cervecería Alemana.** Another Hemingway haunt, the café's marble-topped tables still attract struggling writers, poets, and beer-lovers.

Walk east on the street where the Alemana sits, Calle del Prado, for two blocks and turn right onto Calle León, named for a lion kept here **❸❹** long ago by a resident Moor. At the corner of **Calle Cervantes** you'll see a plaque marking the house where the author of *Don Quixote* lived and died. Miguel de Cervantes's 1605 epic story of the man with the impossible dream is said to be the world's second most-widely translated and read book, after the Bible.

The **home of Lope de Vega,** a contemporary of Cervantes, is at number 11 Calle Cervantes, and has been turned into a museum that shows how a typical home of the period was furnished. Considered the Shakespeare of Spanish literature, Lope de Vega (1562–1635) wrote some 1,800 plays and enjoyed huge success during his lifetime. *Tel. 91/429–9216. Admission: 200 pesetas. Open Mon.–Fri. 9:30–2:30, Sat. 10–1:30; closed Sun.*

Continuing down Calle León one block, turn left onto Calle Huertas, the premier street of bars in bar-besotted Madrid. One block down Huertas turn right onto **Calle Amor de Dios,** the center of the city's flamenco community. Look for the music shops and guitar makers. At number 4 Calle Amor de Dios is a flamenco dancing school that attracts students from around the world. If you stop and listen, you may hear the staccato sound of stamping heels.

Amor de Dios ends at busy Calle Atocha. The ugly modern church you see across the street is **San Nicolás.** The burning of this church in 1936 is vividly described by writer Arturo Barea in his autobiographical *The Forge.* Like many other churches during that turbulent period, the original building here fell victim to the wrath of working-class crowds who felt themselves to be the victims of centuries of clerical oppression. Next door is the **Pasaje Doré,** home to a colorful assortment of market stalls typical of most Madrid neighborhoods. At the end of the market turn left for a look at the **Cine Doré,** a rare example of Art Nouveau architecture in Madrid. The theater shows movies from the Spanish National Film Archives.

Cross the street and walk down Calle de la Rosa, which turns into Calle de la Cabeza. This is the beginning of the **Barrio Lavapiés**—the old *judería* (Jewish Quarter). Today it remains one of the most typical or *castizo* of all working-class Madrid neighborhoods, although there are some recent signs of creeping gentrification. Don't be surprised to see graffiti reading "Yuppies No!"

Jews as well as Moors were forced to live outside the city walls in old Madrid, and this was one of the suburbs they founded. For a chilling reminder of the depth of Catholic Spain's intolerance, stop at the southeast corner of Calle Cabeza and Calle Lavapiés. Here, unmarked by any historical plaque, is the former **Cárcel de la Inquisición** (Inquisition Jail). Today a lumber warehouse, in this little building, Jews, Moors, and others designated as unrepentant heathens and sinners suffered the many tortures devised by the merciless inquisitors.

Walk down the long hill traced by Calle Lavapiés until you reach the **Plaza Lavapiés,** the heart of this historic neighborhood. To the left is the *Calle de la Fe* (Street of Faith), which was called Calle Synagogue up until the expulsion of the Jews in 1492. At the top of this narrow way is the **Church of San Pedro el Real,** built on the site of the razed synagogue. Legend has it that Jews and Moors who accepted baptism over exile were forced to walk up this street barefoot to be baptized in the church, as a demonstration of the sincerity of their newfound faith.

Leave the plaza heading southwest on Calle Sombrerete two blocks until you reach the intersection of Calle Mesón de Paredes. On the corner you'll see a lovingly preserved example of popular Madrid architecture called the **Corrala.** Life in this type of balconied apartment building is lived very publicly, with laundry flapping in the breeze, babies crying, and old ladies dressed in black gossiping over the railings. In the past, common kitchen and bathroom facilities in the patio were shared among neighbors. This building is not unlike the *corrales* that were used as the city's early theater venues and there is a plaque to remind us that the setting for the famous 19th-century *zarzuela* or light opera called *La Revoltosa* was a *corrala* like this one. In summer, city-sponsored musical theater events are occasionally held here. The ruins across the street were once the Escalopios de San Fernando—another church and parochial school that fell victim to anti-Catholic sentiments in this neighborhood during the civil war.

Time Out   Drop in at Madrid's oldest bar, the **Taberna de Antonio Sanchez** (Me-són de Paredes 13), for a glass of wine and some tapas or just a peek inside. The dark walls lined with bullfighting paintings, zinc bar, and pulley system used to lift casks of wine from the cellar look much the same as they did when the place was first opened in 1830. Meals are also served in a dining room in back. Specialties include *rabo de buey* (bull's tail stew) and *morcillo al horno* (a beef stew).

39   Continue west on Calle de los Abades, crossing Calle de Embaja-dores into the neighborhood known as **"El Rastro."** Filled with tiny shops selling antiques and all types of used stuff (some of it junk), the rastro becomes an overcrowded flea market on Sunday mornings from 10 to 2. The best time for exploring is any other morning, when a little browsing and bargaining are likely to turn up such treasures as old iron grillwork, marble tabletops, or gilt picture frames. The main street of the rastro is Ribera de Curtidores and the best streets for shopping are the ones to the west.

Excursion: El Escorial and the Valley of the Fallen

Numbers in the margin correspond to points of interest on the Madrid Excursions map.

Felipe II was certainly one of history's most deeply religious and forbidding monarchs—not to mention one of its most powerful—and the great granite monastery he had constructed in a remarkable 21 years (1563–84) offers enduring testimony to that austere charac-
1   ter. Severe, rectilinear, and unforgiving, the **Real Monasterio de San Lorenzo de El Escorial** (El Escorial Monastery) stands 50 km (31 mi) from Madrid on the slopes of the Guadarrama Mountains, one of the most massive yet simple examples of architecture on the Iberian Peninsula.

Felipe built the monastery in the village of San Lorenzo de El Escorial to commemorate Spain's crushing victory over the French at Saint-Quentin on August 10, 1557, and as a final resting place for his all-powerful father, the emperor Carlos V. The vast rectangle it traces, along with 16 courts, is modeled on the red-hot grille upon which San Lorenzo was martyred—appropriate, given that August 10 was the saint's day (it's also said that Felipe's troops accidentally destroyed a church dedicated to the saint during the battle, and he sought to make amends). A Spanish psychohistorian recently theorized that it is actually shaped like a prone woman, an unintended emblem of Felipe's sexual repression. Perhaps most surprising is not the fact that this thesis was put forward by a serious academic, but that it provoked several heady newspaper articles and other commentary.

El Escorial can be easily reached by car, train, bus, or organized tour; simply inquire at a travel agency or the appropriate station. While the building and its adjuncts—a palace, museum, church, and more—can take hours or even days to tour, you should be able to include a visit to the Valley of the Fallen, where General Franco is buried, in a day trip. At the monastery, be prepared for the mobs of tourists who visit daily, especially during the summer.

The Escorial was begun by Juan Bautista de Toledo but finished in 1584 by Juan de Herrera, who was to give his name to a major Spanish architectural school. It was completed just in time for Felipe to die here, gangrenous and in great pain from the gout that had plagued him for years, in the tiny, sparsely furnished bedroom that resembled a monk's cell more than the resting place of a great mon-

Madrid Excursions

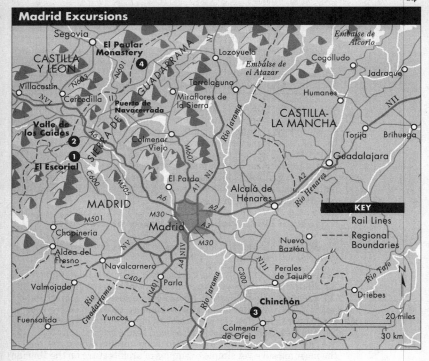

arch. It is in this bedroom—which looks out, through a private entrance, into the royal chapel—that one most appreciates the Spartan nature of this man. Later, Bourbon kings, such as Carlos III and Carlos IV, had clearly different tastes, and their apartments, connected to Felipe's by the Hall of Battles, are far more luxurious.

Perhaps the most interesting spot in the entire Escorial is the **Royal Pantheon,** which contains the body of every king since Carlos I save three—Felipe V (buried at La Granja palace), Ferdinand VI (in Madrid), and Amadeus of Savoy (in Italy). The body of Alfonso XIII, who died in Rome in 1941, was brought to the Escorial only in January 1980. The bodies of the rulers lie in 26 sumptuous marble and bronze sarcophagi that line the walls (three of which are empty, awaiting future rulers). Only those queens who bore sons later crowned lie in the same crypt; the others, along with royal sons and daughters who never ruled, lie nearby in the **Pantheon of the Infantes.** Many of the child infantes are in a single, circular tomb made of Carrara marble.

Another highlight is the uncharacteristically lavish and beautiful **Library,** with 40,000 rare manuscripts, codices, and ancient books including St. Teresa of Ávila's diary and the gold-lettered, illuminated *Codex Aureus.* **Tapestries** woven from cartoons by Goya, Rubens, and El Greco cover almost every inch of wall space in huge sections of the building, and extraordinary canvases by Velázquez, El Greco, David, Ribera, Tintoretto, Rubens, and other masters have been collected from around the monastery and are now displayed in the New Museums. In the **Basilica,** don't miss the fresco over the choir depicting heaven or Titian's fresco of *The Martyrdom*

Apartamentos de Felipe II, **14**

Biblioteca (Library), **9**

Colegio, **11**

Convento (Convent), **10**

Coro (Choir), **3**

Main Entrance, **1**

Museos, **13**

Palacio Real, **12**

Patio de los Evangelistas (Court of the Evangelists), **7**

Patio de los Reyes (Court of the Kings), **2**

Sacristía (Sacristy), **6**

Salas Capitulares (Chapter Houses), **8**

Stairway to the Panteon de los Reyes (Royal Pantheon), **5**

Templo, **4**

Tour Entrance, **15**

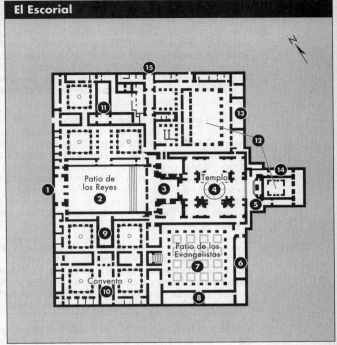

El Escorial

of St. Lawrence, showing the saint being roasted alive. *San Lorenzo de El Escorial, tel. 91/890–5905. Admission: 800 pesetas. Open Apr.–Sept., Tues.–Sun. 10–6; Oct.–Mar., Tues.–Sun. 10–5; closed Mon.*

Time Out Many Madrileños consider El Escorial the perfect place for a huge weekend lunch. Topping the list of favorite eating spots is the outdoor terrace of **Charoles** (Floridablanca 24, tel. 91/890–5975, reservations advised), where imaginative seasonal specialties round out a menu of Spanish favorites like *bacalao al pil-pil* (spicy cod) and grilled *chultetón* (steak).

Just a few miles north of El Escorial on C600 is the **Valle de los Caídos** (Valley of the Fallen). You'll drive through a pine-studded state park to this massive basilica, which is carved out inside a hill of solid granite and commands magnificent views to the east. Topped with a cross nearly 150 m (500 ft) high, this is the tomb of both Franco and José Antonio Primo de Rivera, founder of the Spanish Falange. It was built with the forced labor of Republican prisoners after the civil war and dedicated rather disingenuously to *all* those who died in the three-year conflict. The inside of this gigantic hall is more reminiscent of the palace of the Wizard of Oz than of anything else, with every footstep resounding loudly off its stone walls. Tapestries of the Apocalypse add to the generally terrifying flavor of the place. *Tel. 91/890–5611. Admission: 600 pesetas, 300 pesetas for funicular to top of the hill. Open Apr.–Sept., daily 10–7; Oct.–Mar., daily 10–6.*

Excursion: Chinchón

③ The picturesque village of **Chinchón** lies only 54 km (28 mi) southeast of Madrid, off the N III highway to Valencia on the C300 local road; yet it seems a good four centuries away in time, a true Castilian town. It's an ideal place for a day trip and lunch at one of its many rustic restaurants—the only down side being that swarms of Madrileños have the very same idea, so it's often difficult to find a table for lunch on weekends.

The high point of Chinchón is its charming Plaza Mayor, an uneven circle of ancient three- and four-story houses embellished with wooden balconies resting on granite columns. It's reminiscent of an open-air Elizabethan theater, but with a Spanish flavor. In fact, the entire plaza is converted to a bull ring from time to time, with temporary bleachers erected in the center and seats on the privately owned balconies being rented out for a splendid view of the festivities. (It should be noted that these fights are rare, and tickets hard to come by, as they are snatched up by Spanish tourists as soon as they go on sale.)

Time Out Two of the best and most popular restaurants on Chinchon's arcaded plaza are **Mesón de la Virreina** (Plaza Mayor 21, tel. 91/894–0015) and **Café de la Iberia** (Plaza Mayor 17, tel. 91/894–0998). Both have balconies for dining outside and it's a good idea to call and reserve an outdoor table ahead of time. The food in each is hearty Castilian fare such as roast lamb and suckling pig or thick steaks.

On the way back to Madrid, you'll pass through the valley of Jarama, just at the point where C300 joins the main highway. This is the scene of one of the bloodiest battles in which the Abraham Lincoln Brigade, American volunteers fighting with the Republicans against Franco in the Spanish Civil War, played a major role (immortalized by folksinger Pete Seeger, who sang, "There's a valley in Spain called Jarama . . ."). Until just a few years ago, you could find bones and rusty military hardware in the fields here; today, there are still a number of clearly discernible trenches.

Excursion: The Valley of Lozoya and the El Paular Monastery

Behind the great meseta where Madrid sits, the Guadarrama Mountains rise like a dark, jagged shield that separates New and Old Castile. The mountains, snowcapped for much of the year, are indeed rough-hewn in many spots, particularly so on their northern face, but there is a dramatic exception—the **Valley of Lozoya.**

About 100 km (62 mi) north of the capital, this valley of pine, poplar, and babbling brooks is a cool and green retreat from the often searing heat of the plain. In it, Madrileños often take a day for a picnic or a simple driving tour, rarely joined by foreign tourists, to whom the area is virtually unknown.

A car is required for visiting this place, but the drive will be a pleasant one. Take the A6 motorway northwest from the city, exiting at signs for the Navacerrada Pass on the N601 highway. As you climb toward the 6,100-ft mountain pass, you'll come to a road bearing off to the left toward Cercedilla. This little village, also reachable by train from Madrid, is a favorite spot for mountain hikers. Just above the town an old Roman road leads up to the ridge of the Guadarrama, where an ancient fountain, known as Fuenfría, long provided the spring water that fed the Roman aqueduct of Segovia (*see* Chapter 4, Around Madrid). The path traced by this cobble road is very close to the route Hemingway had his hero Robert Jordan take in his novel of the civil war, *For Whom the Bell Tolls;* eventually it will take you near the bridge that Jordan blew up in the novel.

If you continue past the Cercedilla road, you'll come to a ski resort at the highest point of the Navacerrada Pass. Take a right here on the C604 and you'll follow the ridge of the mountains for a few miles before descending into the Lozoya Valley.

❹ The **El Paular Monastery** will loom up on your left as you approach the valley floor. This was the first Carthusian monastery in Castile, built by King Juan I in 1390, but it has been badly neglected since the Disentailment of 1836. Fewer than a dozen Benedictine monks still live here, eating and praying exactly as their predecessors did centuries ago. One of them gives tours—as well as abundant advice on the state of your soul—at noon, 1, and 5.

The monastery is physically connected to the Santa María del Paular hotel (reserve in advance: tel. 91/869–1011, fax 91/869–1006). This hotel is tastefully furnished and charming, but very expensive and not as grand as similarly priced paradors.

The valley is filled with spots to picnic along the Lozoya River, including several campgrounds. Afterward, take the C604 north a few kilometers to Rascafría, where you turn right on a smaller road marked for Miraflores de la Sierra. In that town you'll turn right again, following signs for Colmenar Viejo, where you pick up a short expressway back to Madrid.

What to See and Do with Children

Spaniards love children. Take a baby into a restaurant, and chances are he or she will be whisked away by a waiter wanting to show the little darling off to the kitchen staff (don't worry; the child is in good hands). Walk into almost any park, and a swing set and other child-oriented amenities will be waiting. There's hardly a bar or restaurant that would look askance at you for bringing a child of any age with you, whatever the time of day or night.

Park Attractions That said, there are a few attractions of special interest for those of lesser years. A leading candidate is the **Parque de Atracciones,** a large amusement park in the Casa de Campo, a sprawling park northwest of the city. *Metro: Batán; bus No. 33 from Plaza de Isabel II. Admission and 2 rides: 600 pesetas. All-ride ticket: 1,375 pesetas, 800 pesetas children 7 and under. Open weekends noon–10.*

The Casa de Campo also has a large, well-laid-out **zoo,** with most of the animals allowed to roam free behind deep trenches. Most popular are the pandas donated by the People's Republic of China, but there are many other animals, too. There's also a dolphinarium with regular performances. *Metro: Lago; bus No. 33. Admission: 730 pesetas adults, 490 pesetas children under 8; admission with dolphin show: 940 pesetas adult, 695 pesetas children. Open Mon.–Fri. 10–7:30.*

Children love the **cable car** (*see* Off the Beaten Track, *below*) that takes you from just above the Rosaleda gardens in the Parque del Oeste to the center of Casa de Campo. Be warned, however, that it's at least a mile from where the cable car drops you off to both the zoo and the amusement park, and you'll have to ask directions.

Museums Another favorite with children—this one located downtown—is the **Wax Museum.** Along with such world figures as Mikhail Gorbachev and President Kennedy, there are grisly reconstructions of famous Spanish crimes. The complete line of Spanish royalty is intriguing for adults, too; if you read Spanish the plaques that accompany them provide a marvelous history lesson. *Paseo de Recoletos 41. Admission: 750 pesetas adults, 500 pesetas children. Open daily 10:30–2 and 4–9.*

While not properly a museum, the **planetarium** is a perennial children's favorite. *Parque de Tierno Galván, tel. 91/467–3898. Metro: Méndez Alvaro. Admission: 275 pesetas. Shows Tues.–Fri. 5:30 and 6:45; weekends 11:30, 12:45, 5:30, 6:45, and 8.*

Boating Rowboats can be rented at **El Estanque,** the lake in the center of Retiro Park, where you'll paddle around with scores of other parents and children. Or you can rent similar watercraft in the larger lake in Casa de Campo, near the Lago metro stop.

Puppet Shows Retiro Park is also the location of an outdoor puppet theater for children, featuring slapstick routines that even non-Spanish speakers will enjoy. Shows take place on Saturday at 1 PM and on Sunday at 1, 6, and 7. Free admission. The theater is located near the Puerta de Alcalá gate.

Off the Beaten Track

For a visit to the parks of northwest Madrid and the university, follow Calle Ferraz (the extension of Bailén) north from the Plaza de España. Atop a hill in the first park area to your left, you'll see the **Templo de Debod** (Debod Temple), an authentic 4th-century BC Egyptian temple donated to the Spanish in recognition of their engineering help during the construction of the Aswan Dam. It sits near the site of the former Montaña barracks, where Madrileños bloodily crushed the beginnings of a Francoist uprising in 1936.

If you continue down Pintor Rosales, the street that follows the upper edge of the park, you'll come to the **teleférico** (cable car; in the Rosaleda Gardens, tel. 91/541–7440; 445 pesetas; open Apr.–Sept., daily noon–sundown; Oct.–Mar., weekends noon–sundown) that will carry you high over the Manzanares River and out into **Casa de Campo** (*see* What to See and Do with Children, *above*), which contains a zoo, an amusement park, a convention center, major outdoor concerts, and a half-dozen cafés. Pintor Rosales ends at Paseo de Moret, where you'll turn right to climb up the hill that follows the hilly **Parque del Oeste** (West Park), a perfect place for a picnic. At the top of the hill you'll come into the Moncloa traffic circle.

For a panoramic view of Madrid from 92 meters (304 ft) up, ride the elevator to the top of the modernistic **Faro de Moncloa** (Moncloa Lighthouse). From this landmark's vantage point, the city's gray slate roofs and Habsburg spires look like pictures from a storybook. *Intersection of Avenida Reyes Católicos and Arco de la Victoria. Admission: 200 pesetas. Open Tues.–Sun. 10:30–1:45 and 2:30–7:15.*

The **Royal Tapestry Factory** has been in operation continuously since 1721, laboriously crafting rugs and tapestries for Spain's royal family. Here you can see the artisans working with modern methods and demonstrating traditional tapestry-making techniques. While most of the output of this workshop is on display in palaces throughout the country, there is also a exhibition of tapestries and the drawings on which they were based. *Fuenterrabia 2, tel. 91/551–3400. Admission: 50 pesetas. Open Mon.–Fri. 9–12:30, closed Aug.*

If you're in the mood for museums, head up Alcalá from the Puerta del Sol to the **Academia de Bellas Artes de San Fernando.** Designed by Churriguera in the early 18th century, the waning years of the Baroque period, this little visited museum is Madrid's second great showcase of painting and the other plastic arts. The same building houses the **Instituto de Calcografía,** where limited-edition prints from original plates engraved by Spanish artists—including Goya—are sold. *Alcalá 13, tel. 91/532–1249. Admission: 200 pesetas. Open Tues.–Fri. 9–7, Sat.–Mon. 9–2:30.*

Behind an elaborately sculpted stone portal, the **Museo Municipal** (Municipal Museum) offers a carefully selected collection of historical artifacts, including a huge, remarkably detailed wooden model of the city exactly as it was in 1830. Take a look at the riotous Carnaval posters of the creative 1930s; then compare them to those that came later, the bland and soulless official "art" of the Franco era. *Fuencarral 78, tel. 91/522–5732. Open Tues.–Sat. 10–2 and 5–9; Sun. 10–2.*

The Municipal Museum stands at the entrance to the area known as **Malasaña** (named after a heroine executed by the French). This neighborhood, in the narrow streets directly across from the museum, is filled with music clubs and is where much of the city's famed cultural reawakening was centered in the years following Franco's death. Today, the clubs and bars are still fascinating, often offering such intriguing fare as a kind of flamenco-jazz fusion, but drug use is rampant.

Around the corner from the Municipal Museum lies another museum that's not often visited by foreigners but makes for an offbeat adventure: the **Museo Romántico** (Romantic Museum). The Marquís of Vega Inclán established this museum in 1920 as a tribute to the movement that swept Europe in the 19th century, a literary current that brought scores of writers and artists to Spain to chronicle the "rustic" life that had already disappeared in neighboring lands. Note the *Satire of Romantic Suicide*, a painting by Leonardo Alenea, for an amusingly sarcastic view of these ideas. *San Mateo 13, tel. 91/448–1071. Admission: 200 pesetas. Open Tues.–Sat. 9–2:45, Sun. 9–1:45.*

Shopping

Beyond the popular Lladro porcelains, castanets, and bullfight posters, Madrid offers a great selection of gift items and unique souvenirs. In recent years Spain has achieved recognition as one of the world's top design centers. You'll have no trouble finding traditional crafts such as ceramics, guitars, and leather goods, but don't stop there. Madrid is famous for contemporary furniture and decorator items, as well as chic clothing, shoes, and jewelry. Most major credit cards are accepted at all shops.

Shopping Districts

Madrid has two main centers of shopping. The first is around the **Puerta del Sol** (*see* Tour 1, *above*) in the center of town and includes the two major department stores and a large number of midline shops in the streets nearby. The second area, far more elegant and expensive, is in the northwest Salamanca district, bounded, roughly, by Serrano, Goya, and Conde de Peñalver. In 1989, the Mercado Puerta de Toledo (Ronda de Toledo 1) opened south of the city center and has since become another major shopping area. It is a government-subsidized, ultraslick mall of dozens of shops that market only the most upscale goods, at prices to match. Another new, attractive mall also opened in 1989 underneath the Palace Hotel on the Paseo del Prado. Stores in this elegant, two-story complex include fine shops for books, gourmet foods, clothing, leather goods, art, and more.

Flea Market

On Sundays, Calle de Ribera de Curtidores, the main thoroughfare of **El Rastro** (*see* Tour 5, *above*), is closed to traffic and absolutely jammed with outdoor booths selling all manner of objects. The crowds grow so thick that day that it takes a while to advance just a few feet amid the hawkers and the gawkers. A word of warning: Hang on to your purse and wallet, and be especially careful if you choose to bring a camera—pickpockets abound. The flea market sprawls into most of the surrounding streets, with certain areas specializing in one product or another. Many of the goods sold here are wildly overpriced.

But what goods! You'll find everything from antique furniture to exotic parrots and cuddly puppies; from pirated cassette tapes of flamenco music to keychains emblazoned with symbols of the old anarchist trade union, the CNT; there are paintings, colorful Gypsy oxen yokes, heraldic iron gates, new and used clothes, and even hashish for sale.

Off the Ribera are two *galerías*, courtyards where small shops offer higher-quality, higher-priced antiques and other goods. The whole spectacle shuts down around 2 PM.

Department Stores

Non-Spanish-speaking visitors will find the department stores surprisingly good, and an easy way to shop. **Corte Inglés** is the better of the two chains, with a wider range of higher quality goods. There are four stores: on Calle de Preciados, just off the Puerta del Sol; at the corner of Goya and Alcalá; on Raimundo Fernández Villaverde, just west of the Castellana; and at the corner of Princesa and Alberto Aguilera. **Galerías Preciados** is this chain's main competitor. Its main store is on Plaza del Callao, just off Gran Vía and a few steps from the Puerta del Sol Corte Inglés. Another branch is at Calle Arapiles near the Glorieta de Quevedo, and a third is on Goya, corner of Peñalver, and a fourth is on Calle Serrano. Both chains offer interpreters and shipping services.

Specialty Stores

Ceramics The best of these is probably **Antigua Casa Talavera** (Isabel la Católica 2). Despite its name, the finest ware sold here is from Manises, near Valencia, although the blue-and-white Talavera is first-rate as well. Another good bet is **Cerámica El Alfar** (Claudio Coello 112). Distinctive, modern Spanish ceramics are made in Galicia, and an excellent selection of breakfast sets, coffee pots, and *objets d'art* can be found at **Sargadelos** (Zurbano 46).

Costume Chunky necklaces and dangling earrings can be found in abundance
Jewelry at **Del Pino** (Serrano 48) and **Musgo** (Hermosilla 36). Original crea-

tions with African and Indian motifs are crafted in silver and bronze by one of Spain's hottest designers, **Joaquín Berao,** at his own shop/ studio (Conde de Xiquena 13). The gift shop of the **Prado Museum** is the source of classically styled jewelry, many of the pieces copied from the museum's paintings.

Crafts Contemporary handicrafts from all over Spain are sold at **El Arco** (Plaza Mayor 9), which has a good selection of modern ceramics, hand-blown glassware, jewelry, and leather items, as well as a whimsical collection of pendulum clocks. The best decorator furniture, lamps, and rugs are displayed stylishly at **Artespaña** (Hermosilla 14), a store run by the government to encourage Spanish craftsmanship.

Fans These quintessentially Spanish objects can be found in all variations at the **Casa de Diego** (Puerta del Sol 12).

Guitars Some of Spain's best guitar makers are in Madrid. Founded in 1882, the firm **José Ramirez** (Concepción Jerónimo 2) exports guitars around the world (prices start at 15,000 pesetas). The shop includes a museum of antique instruments. Another good place to look is the workshop of **Conde Hermanos** (Felipe II 2), where three generations of the same family have been building and selling guitars since 1917.

Hats There are two first-rate hat shops on the Plaza Mayor, offering everything from the Guardia Civil tricornered patent leather hat to the berets worn by the guardia's oft-time enemy, the Basques. These berets are much wider than those worn by the French Basques and make excellent gifts.

Leather Goods Leather goods are another fine Spanish tradition, but you'll find that, for the most part, deals are few and far between. You'll still pay in the neighborhood of $400 and up for a first-class man's leather jacket, for instance, but it will probably outrank anything you would find back home in quality. **Loewe** (Gran Vía 8 and Serrano 26 and 34) is the best-known leather shop for men and women, but it's outrageously expensive. You can find top leather goods and clothes at the more reasonable **Duna** (Lagasca 7). Designer leather purses and accessories at reasonable prices can also be found at **Piamonte** (Piamonte 16). Bargain hunters should check out the *muestrarios* or shoe showrooms just west of the market on Calle Augusto Figueroa, where you can find samples and one-of-a-kind pairs for half price or less. **Caligae** (Augusto Figueroa 27) shods Madrid's dress-for-less crowd with the avant-garde designs of Parisian Stephane Kélian.

Men's and Women's Clothing Many of the leading fashion designers' outlets are concentrated in the Salamanca district, particularly along Calle Serrano. Take a stroll along that street between Diego de León and Jorge Juan for a gander at a wide array of these shops, or head straight to some of the leading design shops: **Adolfo Domínguez** (Serrano 96), the best-known contemporary Spanish designer for men and women; **Ascot** (Serrano 88), featuring Maria Teresa de Vega's garments for women; **Irene Prada** (Columela 3), clothes by a woman who has dressed some members of the British royal family; or **Sybilla** (Jorge Juan 8), a women's shop.

Miscellaneous Excellent **cutlery** is sold at **Simon** (Espoz y Mina 12). For **kitchenware** try a shop that also offers world-renowned cooking classes, **Alambique** (Encarnación 2). **Books on Madrid,** all of them in Spanish, are the specialty at **La Librería** (Señores de Luzón 8). **Musical instruments** are sold at **Garrido-Bailén** (Bailén 19). A marvelous array of adult and children's **games** can be found at **Naipe** (Meléndez Valdes

55). The shop at the **Municipal Museum** (Fuencarral 78) sells gifts for children, such as wooden toys and puzzles.

Sports

Spectator Sports

Bullfighting For better or for worse, bullfighting is a spectacle, not a sport. Nevertheless, for those not turned off by the death of six bulls each Sunday afternoon from April to early November, it has all the elements of any major stadium event. Nowhere in the world is bullfighting better than at Madrid's **Las Ventas** (formally called the Plaza de Toros Monumental, Calle Alcalá 231; metro: Las Ventas). The city's *afición*, the sophisticated audience that follows the bulls intensely, is more critical in Madrid than anywhere, and you'll be amazed at how confusing their reactions to the fights are; cheers and hoots are difficult at first to distinguish, and it takes years to understand what has prompted the wrath of this most difficult-to-please audience. Tickets may be purchased at the ring or, for a 20% surcharge, at the agencies on Calle Victoria, just off the Puerta del Sol. Most fights start in the late afternoon, and the best of all—the world's top venue of bullfighting—come during the three weeks of consecutive daily fights in May marking the festival of San Isídro. Tickets can be tough to get through normal channels, but they'll always be available from scalpers in the Calle Victoria and at the stadium. You can bargain, but even Spaniards pay prices of perhaps 10 times the face value, up to 10,000 pesetas or even more.

Soccer Spain's number-one sport is soccer, or *fútbol*, as it's known locally. Madrid has two teams, both of them among Europe's best, and two stadia to match. The 130,000-spectator **Santiago Bernabeu Stadium** (Paseo de la Castellana 140) is home to the more popular Real Madrid, while the **Vicente Calderón Stadium** (Paseo de Melancólicos s/n), located on the outskirts of town, is where Atlético Madrid defends. Generally you'll have to stand in line at the stadia to get tickets, but for many major games tickets are available at agencies inside the Galerías Preciados and Corte Inglés department stores (*see* Shopping, *above*).

Participant Sports

Horseback Riding On the other side of Casa de Campo, **Club El Trebol** (tel. 91/711–8512) rents both animals and equipment to the public at reasonable prices.

Jogging The best bet is **Retiro Park,** where one path makes the circumference of the entire park, and numerous others weave their way under trees and through formal gardens. **Casa de Campo** is crisscrossed by numerous less shady trails.

Swimming Madrid has devised a perfect antidote to the sometimes intense dry heat of the summer months—a superb system of clean, popular, and well-run municipal swimming pools (about 350 pesetas for adults; there are several reduced-price multiple-ticket options). There are pools in most neighborhoods, but the biggest and best is in the **Casa de Campo** (take the metro to the Lago stop and walk up the hill a few yards to the entrance). **La Elipa** (Av. de la Paz s/n) has a nude sunbathing area. More expensive, and fitted with a comfortable, tree-shaded restaurant by the pool, is the private **Piscina El Lago** (Av. de Valladolid 37), a trendy young people's hangout.

Tennis **Club de Tenis Chamartín** (Federico Salmon 2, tel. 91/345–2500), with 28 courts, is open to the public. There are also public courts in the **Casa de Campo** and on the Avenida de Vírgen del Puerto, behind the Palacio Real (ask for details at the tourist office).

Dining

Unlike most regions of Spain, Madrid does not really have a native cuisine. But, as capital of the realm and home of the king, Madrid has attracted generations of courtiers, foreign diplomats, politicians, and tradesmen, all of whom brought their own styles of and tastes in cooking, whether from another region of Spain, or from abroad.

The roast meats of Castile and the seafood dishes of the Cantabrian coast are just as at home in Madrid as they are in their native lands. Basque cooking, Spain's haute cuisine, is the specialty of Madrid's best restaurants, and seafood houses take advantage of the capital's abundant supply fish and shellfish, trucked in nightly from the coast. Spaniards joke that Madrid is Spain's biggest seaport.

The only truly local dishes are *cocido a la Madrileño* (garbanzo bean stew) and *callos a la Madrileño* (stewed tripe). Given half a chance, Madrileños will spend hours waxing lyrically over the mouth-watering merits of both. *Cocido* is a delicious and hearty winter meal consisting of garbanzo beans, vegetables, potatoes, sausages, and pork. The best *cocidos* are slowly simmered in earthenware crocks over open fires, and served as a complete meal in several courses, first the broth which comes with angel hair pasta, then the beans and vegetables, and finally the meat. *Cocido* can be found in the most elegant restaurants, such as Lhardy and at the Ritz hotel, as well as the most humble eateries, and is usually offered as a midday selection on Monday or Wednesday. *Callos*, on the other hand, is a much simpler concoction of veal tripe stewed with tomatoes, onions, and garlic, and is served in *tascas* or taverns.

Although the countryside near the capital produces some wines, they are not very good. The house wine in nearly all Madrid restaurants is a sturdy, uncomplicated *Valdepeñas* from La Mancha. A traditional anise-flavored liqueur called *Anís* is manufactured just outside the village of Chinchón.

Madrileños tend to eat their meals even later than other Spaniards. Restaurants generally open for lunch at 1:30 and fill up by 3. Dinnertime begins at 9, but reservations for 11 are common. A meal in Madrid is usually a lengthy (up to three hours) and rather formal affair, even at inexpensive places. Restaurants are at their best at midday, when most places offer a *menu del día* (daily special) consisting of two courses, dessert, wine, and coffee.

Dinner, on the other hand, can present something of a problem if you don't want to eat such a big meal so late. One solution is to take your evening meal at one of Madrid's many foreign restaurants. Good-quality Italian, Mexican, Russian, Argentine, and American places abound, and on the whole tend to be less formal, more lively, and open earlier.

The other alternative is to make a dinner of *tapas* and Madrid offers some of the best *tapa* bars in Spain. A *tapa* is a bit of food that usually comes free with a drink; it might be a few olives, a mussel in vinaigrette, a sardine, or spicy potatoes. A larger plate of the same sort food called a *ración* can also be ordered, and is meant to be eaten with toothpicks and shared among friends. While a *tapa* bar crawl is fun and filling, it isn't necessarily a way to save money and usually ends up costing the same, if not more, than a sit-down, three-course meal. Dress in most Madrid restaurants and *tapa* bars is stylish, but casual. The more expensive places tend to be a bit more formal, and men generally wear jackets and ties, and women wear skirts.

Highly recommended restaurants are indicated by a star ★.

Category	Cost*
$$$$	over 6,000 ptas
$$$	4,000–6,000 ptas
$$	1,800–4,000 ptas
$	under 1,800 ptas

per person, excluding drinks, service, tip, and tax

$$$$ ★ **Horcher.** Housed in a luxurious mansion at the edge of Retiro Park, this classic restaurant is renowned for its hearty but elegant fare served with impeccable style. Specialties include the types of game dishes favored by Spanish aristocracy. Try the wild boar, venison, or roast wild duck with almond croquettes. The star appetizer is lobster salad with truffles. Offerings like Stroganoff with mustard, pork chops with sauerkraut, and *baumkuchen*, a chocolate-covered fruit and cake dessert, reflect the restaurant's Germanic roots (the Horcher family operated a restaurant in Berlin at the turn of the century). The intimate dining room is decorated with antique Austrian porcelains and rust brocade fabric on the walls. A wide selection of French and German wines rounds out the menu. *Alfonso XII 6, tel. 91/532–3596. Reservations required. Jacket and tie advised. AE, DC, MC, V. Closed Sun.*

Lhardy. Serving Madrid specialties from the same central city locale for more than 150 years, Lhardy's dark wood paneling, brass chandeliers, and red velvet chairs look pretty much the same as they have since day one. The menu features international fare, but most diners come for the traditional *cocido madrileño* (garbanzo beans with sausage, pork, and vegetables) and *callos madrileño* (stewed tripe). Sea bass in champagne sauce, game, and dessert soufflés are also very well prepared. The dining rooms are upstairs, and the ground-floor entryway doubles as a delicatessen and stand-up coffee bar that, on chilly winter mornings, is filled with shivering souls sipping *caldo* (chicken broth) ladled steaming hot from silver urns. *Carrera de San Jerónimo 8, tel. 91/521–3385. Reservations advised. Jacket and tie recommended. AE, DC, MC, V. Closed Sun. evening and holidays.*

Viridiana. The trendiest of Madrid's gourmet restaurants, Viridiana has the relaxed atmosphere of a bistro and black-and-white decor punctuated by prints from the classic Luis Buñuel anticlerical film after which this establishment is named. Iconoclast chef Abraham Garcia says "market-based" is too narrow a description for his creative menu, though the list does change every two weeks depending on what's locally available. Offerings include such varied fare as red onions stuffed with *morcilla* (black pudding); soft flour tortillas wrapped around marinated fresh tuna; and filet mignon in white truffle sauce. If it's available, be sure to try the superb duck pâté drizzled with sherry and served with Tokay wine. The tangy grapefruit sherbet is a marvel. *Juan de Mena 14, tel. 91/531–5222.*

Reservations required. Dress: stylish but casual. No credit cards. Closed. Sun., Easter week, and Aug.

★ **Zalacaín.** The deep apricot color scheme, set off by dark wood and gleaming silver, suggests the atmosphere of an exclusive villa. One of only two Spanish restaurants to be awarded three Michelin stars, Zalacaín introduced *nouvelle cuisine* to Spain and continues to set the pace after twenty years at the top. Splurge on prawn salad in avocado vinaigrette, scallops and leeks in Albariño wine, and roast pheasant with truffles. Service is correct but somewhat stuffy. A fixed-price tasting menu allows you to sample the best of Zalacaín for about 6,500 pesetas. *Alvarez de Baena 4, tel. 91/561–5935. Reservations required. Jacket and tie recommended. AE, DC, V. Closed Sat. lunch, Easter week, and Aug.*

$$$ **El Cenador del Prado.** A mecca for those with gourmet palates, Cenador features an innovative menu with French and Asian touches and some exotic Spanish dishes not often found in restaurants. Dine in the baroque salmon-and-gold salon or the less formal plant-filled conservatory. The house specialty is *patatas à la importancia*—sliced potatoes fried in a sauce of garlic, parsley, and clams. Equally rewarding are the shellfish consommé with ginger raviolis, veal and eggplant in béchamel, or wild boar with prunes. For dessert try *cañas fritas*, a cream-filled pastry treat once served only at Spanish weddings. *Calle del Prado 4, tel. 91/429–1561. Reservations advised. Jacket and tie recommended. AE, DC, MC, V. Closed Sat. lunch, Sun., Easter week, and 1st half of Aug.*

★ **Gure-Etxea.** Located in the heart of medieval Madrid on the trendy Plaza de Paja, this is the capital's most authentic Basque restaurant. The ground-floor dining room is airy, high-ceilinged, and elegant, while brick walls lining the downstairs eating area give it a rustic, farmhouse feel. As in the Basque country (but uncommon elsewhere in Europe), you are waited on by women. Classic dishes here include *bacalao pil-pil* (spicy cod fried in garlic and oil, making the "pil-pil" sound), *rape en salsa verde* (monkfish in green parsley sauce), and for dessert *leche frita* (fried custard). On weekdays a hearty and inexpensive plate of the day is added to the lunchtime menu. *Plaza de Paja 12, tel. 91/365–6149. Reservations advised. AE, DC, V. Closed Sun., Aug., and Easter week.*

Mentidero de la Villa. The decor of this intimate eatery is a bewitching blend of pastel colors, pale wood, and candlelight, with fanciful, rough-hewn rocking-horse sculptures. The menu is adventuresome—the chef's salad mixes fresh kelp and lettuce. Specialties include breast of squab in cherry vinegar, pheasant and chestnuts in wine, and halibut with a black-olive sauce. Apropos of the restaurant's moniker (the name means "gossip shop"), service is informal and chatty. *Santo Tomé 6, tel. 91/308–1285. Reservations advised. AE, MC, V. Closed Sat. lunch, Sun., and Aug.*

★ **El Pescador.** Spaniards swear that the seafood in Madrid is fresher than in the coastal towns where it was caught. That's probably an exaggeration, but it *seems* plausible, at least judging from El Pescador, one of Madrid's best-loved seafood restaurants. Stop for a drink at the bar before sitting down to dinner, and take in the delicious aromas wafting from the kitchen, where skilled chefs dressed in fishermen's smocks prepare shellfish just behind the counter. As tapas at the bar or as a first course of your meal, definitely try the incredible *salpicón de mariscos* (mussels, lobster, shrimp, and onions in vinaigrette). Named for the restaurant's owner, the *lenguado Evaristo* (grilled sole) is the best dish on the menu. The place is cheerful and noisy, and the decor is "dockside rustic," with lobster-pot lamps, red-and-white checked tablecloths, and rough-

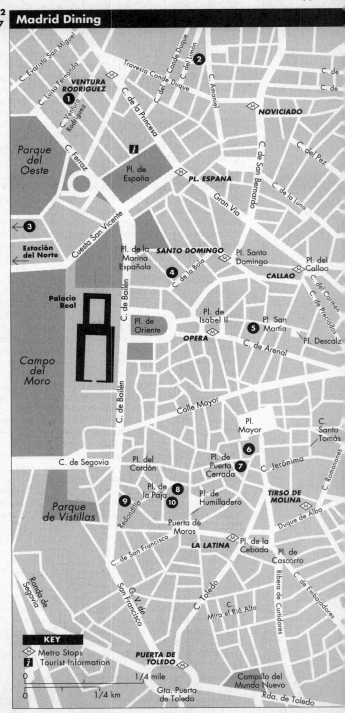

Madrid Dining

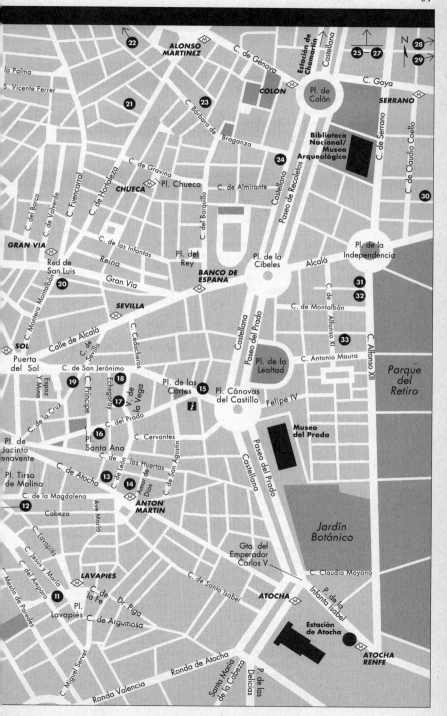

hewn posts and beams. *José Ortega y Gasset 75, tel. 91/402–1290. Reservations advised. MC, V. Closed Sun. and Aug.*

La Trainera. Fresh seafood—the best quality money can buy—is what La Trainera is all about. For decades this informal restaurant, with its nautical decor and maze of little dining rooms, has reigned as the queen of Madrid's seafood houses. Crab, lobster, shrimp, mussels, and a dozen other types of shellfish are served by weight in *raciones.* While most Spanish diners share several plates of these delicacies as their entire meal, the grilled hake, sole, or turbot make an unbeatable second course. Skip the listless house wine and go for a bottle from the cellar. *Lagasca 60, tel. 91/576–8035. Reservations advised. MC, V. Closed Sun. and Aug.*

$$ ★ **La Bola.** First opened as a *botelleria* or wine shop in 1802, La Bola developed slowly into a tapas bar and eventually a full-fledged restaurant. Tradition is what La Bola offers, from the blood-red paneling outside to the original bar and cozy dining nooks decorated with polished wood, Spanish tile, and lace curtains inside. It still belongs to the founding family, with the seventh generation currently in training to take over. Although it's open for dinner, La Bola's specialty is that quintessential Madrid meal, *cocido madrileño,* which is served only at lunch, and accompanied by crusty bread and a hearty red wine. *Bola 5, tel. 91/547–6930. Reservations advised for lunch. No credit cards. Closed Sun.*

Brasserie de Lista. For a gourmet meal in a comfortable, informal setting this bistro-style spot in a neighborhood of designer boutiques can't be beat. A long marble bar, lots of brass, and frosted glass create a turn-of-the-century ambience. Waiters in long white aprons serve Spanish specialties with nouvelle touches, grilled monkfish with toasted garlic or steak with *cabrales* blue cheese sauce, for example. The varied menu also includes international fare such as chicken and avocado salad with chutney and beef carpaccio. The weekday lunchtime special is a good value. *Ortega y Gasset 6, tel. 91/435–2818. Reservations advised for lunch and on weekends. AE, MC, V.*

La Cacharrería. The name of this restaurant in medieval Madrid means junkyard and it's reflected in the funky decor, a mix of dusty calico, old lace, and gilt mirrors. The cooking, however, is decidedly upscale, with a market-based menu that changes daily, and an excellent selection of wines. Venison stew and fresh tuna steaks with cava and leeks were among the specialties on a recent visit. Whatever else you order, save room for the homemade lemon tart. *Moreiria 9, tel. 91/365–3930. AE, DC, MC, V. Closed Sun.*

Café Balear. A sophisticated yet informal eatery that attracts a crowd of creative types from the fashion and advertising world, the Café Balear serves some of the best *paella* (rice dishes) in Madrid. Art prints and potted palms are the only nods to decoration in the stark white dining room. Specialties include *paella centolla* (rice with crab) and *arroz negro* (rice with squid in its ink). The perfectly prepared *paella mixta* combines seafood, pork, and vegetables. Also worth trying is the excellent and very affordable house cava. *Sagunto 18, tel. 91/447–9115. Reservations advised. AE, V. Closed Sun. and Mon. evenings.*

Cañas y Barro. Hidden away on an unspoiled plaza that was the 19th-century center of Madrid's university, this Valencian restaurant specializes in rice dishes with flair. The most popular is *arroz à la banda* (rice with peeled shrimp cooked in seafood broth). Another good choice is the *paella* Valenciana, made with chicken, rabbit, and vegetables. The service is friendly and unpretentious, and white plaster friezes lend the pink dining room a touch of elegance.

Amaniel 23, tel. 91/542–4793. Reservations advised on weekends. AE, DC, MC, V. Closed Sun. evening, Mon., and Aug.

★ **Casa Botín.** The *Guinness Book of World Records* calls this the world's oldest restaurant (1725) and Hemingway called it the best. The latter claim may contain a bit of hyperbole, but the restaurant *is* excellent and extremely charming, despite the hordes of tourists. There are four floors of tiled and wood-beamed dining rooms, and ovens dating back several centuries—which you'll pass if you're seated upstairs. There are also visits from traditionally garbed musical groups called *tunas*. Must-try specialties are *cochinillo asado* (roast suckling pig) and *cordero asado* (roast lamb). It is said Francesco Goya was a dishwasher here before he became successful as a painter. *Cuchilleros 17 (just off Plaza Mayor), tel. 91/366–4217. Reservations strongly advised (or you're in for a wait). AE, DC, MC, V.*

★ **Casa Paco.** This is a popular Castilian tavern that wouldn't have looked out of place two or three centuries ago. Squeeze your way past the old zinc-topped bar, always crowded with Madrileños downing shots of red wine, and into the tiled dining rooms. People come here to feast on thick slabs of red meat, served sizzling on plates so hot that it continues to cook at your table. The beef is superb and the Spanish consider overcooking a sin, so if you ask for your meat well done be prepared for nasty glares. You order the meat by weight, so remember that a *medio kilo* is more than a pound. For starters try the *pisto manchego* (the La Mancha version of ratatouille). *Puerta Cerrada 11, tel. 91/366–3166. Reservations advised. DC, V. Closed Sun. and Aug.*

Casa Vallejo. With its homey dining room, friendly staff, creative menu, and reasonable prices, this restaurant is the well-kept secret of Madrid's budget gourmets. Try the tomato, zucchini, and cheese tart or artichokes and clams for starters, then follow up with duck breast in prune sauce or meatballs made with lamb, almonds, and pine nuts. The fudge and raspberry pie alone makes it worth the trip. *San Lorenzo 9, tel. 91/308–6158. Reservations required. AE, MC, V. Closed Sat. lunch and Sun.*

Ciao Madrid. Always noisy and packed with happy diners, Ciao Madrid is the city's best Italian restaurant. Homemade pastas like tagliatelle with wild mushrooms or panzerotti stuffed with spinach and ricotta are popular as inexpensive main courses, but the kitchen also turns out credible versions of osso buco and veal scaloppine, accompanied by a good selection of Italian wines. The decor—mirrored walls and sleek black furniture—convincingly evokes fashionable Milan. A second location (Apodaca 20, tel. 91/447–0036), run by the owner's sons and daughter, also serves pizza. *Argensola 7, tel. 91/308–2519. Reservations essential. AE, MC, V. Closed Sat. lunch and Sun.*

Cornucopia en Descalzas. Run by former Boston caterer Deborah Hansen and her Madrid-born husband Julio de Haro, this young and friendly restaurant on the first floor of an old mansion just off the historic Plaza de las Descalzas Reales features a creative blend of nouvelle Spanish and American dishes. The menu changes with the seasons: In winter expect dishes like duck soup with duck meatballs, roast pork loin stuffed with apricots, or scallops in wine and cream; the lighter summer menu includes cold almond and garlic soup and grilled calamares with garlic mayonnaise. The mustard-and-burgundy-colored dining room is a tad ornate. *Flora 1, tel. 91/547–6465. Reservations advised for dinner. AE, MC, V. Closed Sat. and Sun. lunch, Mon., and Aug. 15–Sept. 15.*

★ **El Cosaco.** This romantic, candlelit Russian restaurant, tucked away on the ancient Plaza de Paja, is a favorite of young couples in love. While they may only have eyes for each other, the food here is definitely worth a look—savory blini stuffed with caviar, smoked trout, or salmon, and hearty beef dishes like woronof and stroganoff. The dining rooms are decorated with paisley wallpaper and dark red linens, and if the crackling fireplace's cheery glow in winter isn't enough to warm you there are eight types of vodka that ought to do the trick. *Plaza de Paja 2, tel. 91/365–3548. Reŝervations advised. AE, DC. Open for dinner only; lunch served on Sun.*

La Galette. Located just one block from Madrid's main shopping street, Calle Serrano, this is an intimate restaurant for a romantic lunch or supper by candlelight. The menu is primarily vegetarian, but includes some inventive meat dishes. Avoid the tasteless onion soup and go straight for the *Pimiento Persa* (green pepper stuffed with vegetables, rice, and cheese) or the *Cocotte Rusia* (beef stewed with laurel and plums, served over basmati rice). Luscious fruit tarts and brownies de Boston are irresistible dessert choices. *Conde de Aranda 11, tel. 91/576–0641. Reservations recommended. AE, V. Closed Sun.*

★ **La Gamella.** American-born chef Dick Stephens has created a new, reasonably priced menu at this hugely popular dining spot. The sophisticated rust-red dining room, batik tablecloths, oversize plates, and attentive service remain the same, but much of the nouvelle cuisine has been replaced by more traditional fare such as chicken in garlic, boeuf Bourguignon, or steak tartar à la Jack Daniels. A few of the old-favorite signature dishes like sausage and red pepper quiche and bittersweet chocolate pâté remain. The lunchtime *menú del día* is a great value at 1,700 pesetas. *Alfonso XII 4, tel. 91/532–4509. Reservations advised. AE, DC, MC, V. Closed Sun., Mon., and Aug. 15–Sept. 15.*

★ **La Pampa.** This excellent Argentine restaurant is secluded on a side street in the Lavapíes neighborhood. As you enter there's a small eating area to the left, but most patrons prefer to sit in the rustic dining room to the right. The massive and delicious *bife* La Pampa is the specialty of the house (enough steak, fried eggs, peas, and tomatoes for two light eaters), and contains sufficient protein for a week. Pasta dishes, such as cannelloni Rossini, are also good. The appearance of a second, more centrally located La Pampa (Bola 18, tel. 91/542–4412), testifies to its popular success. *Amparo 61, tel. 91/528–0449. AE, DC, MC, V. Closed Mon.*

Si Señor. One of Madrid's new crop of entertaining restaurants, Si Señor specializes in Mexican food and tequila slammers. There's a big bar in the entryway, which serves Mexican-style tapas (quesadillas or chips with guacamole). The huge, noisy dining hall is lined with oversized paintings, artfully executed in a unique Mexican pop-art style. While the drinks here are far better than the food, do try the beef enchiladas or *pollo pibil*, a spicy Yucatan-style chicken dish. *Paseo de la Castellana 128, tel. 91/564–0604. Reservations recommended. AE, DC, MC, V.*

$ ★ **Bodegon Logroñes.** This is a hidden treasure, a quiet, inexpensive restaurant masquerading as a gaudy cafeteria-style bar. At the back of the bar, walk downstairs and you'll emerge in the dining room in an old brick wine cellar with vaulted ceilings, decorated with hunting prints and lots of wrought iron. The sole waiter is friendly, even with those who speak no Spanish, and he'll help you pick a wine from the surprisingly fine list. The *pisto manchego* (vegetable stew) and the *paella* are good for starters. The *pimientos rellenos* (green peppers stuffed with meat) are excellent. *Plaza Tirso de Molina 5, tel. 91/369–1137. Reservations advised for Sun. lunch. No credit cards. Closed Mon.*

La Bodeguita del Caco. Salsa music and pink linoleum-topped tables give this place a tumble-down tropical feel that's just right for the Caribbean and Canary Island dishes served here. You won't go wrong ordering the avocado stuffed with shrimp or the *ropa vieja al estilo Canario,* which, although it literally means "old Canarian clothes," is in fact a tender brisket of beef stewed with potatoes, raisins, and olives. Be sure to ask for a plate of the *papas arrugadas* (wrinkled potatoes) that come with a garlicky sauce for dipping. *Echegaray 27, tel. 91/429–4023. No reservations. V. Closed Mon. and Aug.*

Cactus Charlie's. Homesick Americans aren't the only ones drawn to this spot just uphill from the Puerta del Sol. Young Spaniards are also attracted by the boisterous combination of rock and roll, hamburgers, and happy hour. The Mexican food is not as good as you can get back home, but the ribs are passable, and the cheeseburgers are terrific. Genuine Baskin Robbins 31 flavors of ice cream are available for dessert. *Caballero de Gracia 10, tel. 91/532–1976. Reservations advised on weekends. DC, MC, V.*

Café La Plaza. Strategically positioned between the Prado and Thyssen-Bornemisza art museums and open 10 AM to midnight, the Café La Plaza is an indispensable rest stop for tourists exploring Madrid. This is an upscale, self-service restaurant with a green-and-white, garden-party decor, situated among the exclusive boutiques of the Galería del Prado shopping center. Food is arranged on several circular tables. There's a do-it-yourself salad bar, a pasta bar, and an economical *menú del día,* which, depending on the day, might be Spanish-style chicken, breaded fish, or beef stew served with vegetables, bread, and wine. Breakfast, including bacon and eggs, is available until 12:30 PM, and the café is also a good place to remember for afternoon coffee and pastries. *Plaza de las Cortes 7, tel. 91/429–6537. AE, V.*

★ **Casa Mingo.** Resembling an Asturian cider tavern, Casa Mingo is built into a stone wall beneath the Estación del Norte train station, across the street from the hermitage of San Antonio de la Florida. It's a bustling place where you'll share long plank tables with other diners, and the only dishes offered are succulent roast chicken, salad, and sausages, all to be washed down with numerous bottles of *sidra* (hard cider). In summer small tables are set up on the sidewalk. *Paseo de la Florida 2, tel. 91/547–7918. No reservations. No credit cards.*

Inti de Oro. This Peruvian restaurant, located on one of Madrid's premier restaurant streets, is a big hit, thanks largely to the care the owners put into such traditional specialties of their native Peru as *cebiche de camarones* (shrimp in lime juice), *conejo con maní* (rabbit in peanut sauce), and *seco de cabrito* (goat meat stew). The dining room is light and the walls are adorned with handicrafts. *Ventura de la Vega 12, tel. 91/429–6703. No credit cards. Closed Sun. evening and Mon.*

El Molino de Siguero. One of the best bets for an inexpensive and tasty lunchtime *menú del día* in the Plaza España area, El Molino offers home-style Castilian food, such as lentil stew, roast meats, breaded fish, and excellent house wine. The busy dining room has dark wood wainscoting and is decorated with strings of sausages, hams, and antique farm implements. If you come here at night or order à la carte, prices rise from inexpensive to the moderate category. *Ventura Rodriguez 8, tel. 91/542–3524. AE, MC, V. Closed Sun.*

Puebla. Although the dining room decor lacks charm (the fake wood beams fool no one), you'd be hard pressed to find better-prepared food at such affordable prices anywhere in Madrid. Puebla opened in 1992 and is always crowded with bankers and congressmen from the nearby Cortes. There are two prices ranges for the *menú del día*, with more than a dozen choices in each. The selection changes frequently, but be sure to try the *berenjenas a la romana* (batter fried eggplant) if it's offered. The soups are always great, and other dishes include roast lamb, trout, calamari, and chicken. *Ventura de la Vega 12, tel. 91/429–6713. No credit cards. Closed Sun.*

Sanabresa. You can tell by the clientele what a find this place is. Working men and women who demand quality but don't want to spend much money come here daily, as does an international assortment of starving students from the nearby flamenco school. The menu is classic Spanish fare—hearty, wholesome meals like *pechuga villaroy* (chicken breast in béchamel, breaded and fried) and *paella* (Thursday and Sunday lunch only). The functional, green-tiled dining room is always crowded, so be sure to arrive by 1:30. *Amor de Dios 12, no phone. No reservations. No credit cards. Closed Sun. evening and Aug.*

Lodging

Hotel prices in Madrid have come down significantly since the glory days of the early '90s, especially in the upper price brackets. The Ritz and the Villamagna both once charged upward of $600 a night, but they each now offer a room rate comparable to that found in other world capitals—$250 to $300 a night. If that's still too steep, try bargaining. Surveys show that only 15% of hotel guests pay the posted room rate in Madrid. More savvy customers take advantage of a dizzying array of special offers. Be sure to ask for a business or professional discount, which can amount to up to 40% off. Since most hotels cater to business travelers, special weekend rates are widely available. You can generally save 50% on a Friday, Saturday, or Sunday night, and many hotels throw in extras, like meals or museum admissions.

There are booking services at the airport and the Chamartin and Atocha train stations. You can also contact the La Brujula agency (6th Floor, Torre de Madrid, Plaza de España, tel. 91/559–9705); the fee's a modest 150 pesetas. The staff speaks English and can book rooms and tours all over Spain.

If you're willing to embark on a serious hunt, you can also find *hostals* for 2,500 pesetas or even less. Most of these very cheap rooms are found in tiny hostals on the upper floors of apartment buildings. They are frequently full, however, and don't take reservations, so there is little use in listing them here; you simply have to go door to door and trust your luck. Many such places are concentrated in the old city between the Prado Museum and the Puerta del Sol. Start by looking around the Plaza Santa Ana.

All the rooms listed below come with complete baths. Highly recommended hotels are indicated by a star ★.

Category	Cost*
$$$$	over 20,000 ptas
$$$	12,000–20,000 ptas
$$	7,000–12,000 ptas
$	under 7,000 ptas

*All prices are for a standard double room, excluding tax.

$$$$ **Fenix.** A magnificent marble lobby greets guests at this Madrid institution, overlooking Plaza de Colón on the Castellana, where a giant monument to the discoverers of the New World rises. The hotel is also just a few steps from the posh shopping street of Serrano. Its spacious rooms, decorated in beiges and golds, are carpeted and amply furnished. Flowers abound. *Hermosilla 2, 28001, tel. 91/431–6700, fax 91/576–0661. 204 rooms, 12 suites. Facilities: café, bar, catering, hairdressers, boutiques. AE, DC, MC, V.*

★ **Palace.** Built in 1912, this enormous Belle Epoque grand hotel is a creation of Alfonso XIII. At less than two thirds the price of the nearby Ritz, the Palace is a pleasure, though its attractions are concentrated in the opulent public areas, including a large cupola with a stained-glass ceiling. The rooms aren't impressive for a hotel of this caliber—they're plain and often small, with a pronounced 1960s American flavor. Bathrooms are spacious, however, with double sinks, tubs and separate shower stalls, and other welcome touches such as bathrobes and magnifying mirrors. The Palace looks and feels like a great aristocratic institution, and it is: President John F. Kennedy, the Aga Khan, and Mata Hari (just before she was captured and executed) stayed here. Long a symbol of bourgeois decadence, it was transformed during the civil war into a war orphanage. On the night of February 23, 1981, when a mad Civil Guard colonel held the nearby parliament at gunpoint in an attempt to return Spain to a Francoist dictatorship, the Palace became the de facto seat of Spanish government. *Plaza de las Cortes 7, 28014, tel. 91/429–7551, fax 91/429–8266. 480 rooms, 20 suites. Facilities: restaurant, bar, garage, shops, beauty salon. AE, DC, MC, V.*

★ **Ritz.** When Alfonso XIII was preparing for his marriage to the granddaughter of Queen Victoria of England, he realized, to his dismay, that Madrid had not a single hotel that could meet the exacting standards of his royal guests. Thus, the Ritz was born. Opened in 1910 by the king, who had personally overseen its construction, the Ritz is a monument to the Belle Epoque, furnished with rare antiques in every public room, hand embroidered linens from Robinson & Cleaver of London, and all manner of other luxurious details. The rooms are carpeted, hung with chandeliers, and decorated in pastel colors; many have good views of the Prado or the Castellana. A major renovation has made it, once again, Madrid's most exclusive hotel, just across the street from the Prado Museum. Visit the garden terrace even if you're not staying here. *Plaza de Lealtad 5, 28014, tel. 91/521–2857, fax 91/532–8776. 158 rooms. Facilities: restaurant, bar, beauty salon, garage. AE, DC, MC, V.*

Santo Mauro. A turn-of-the-century mansion that once housed the Canadian embassy was opened in 1992 as an intimate luxury hotel. The neoclassical architecture is complemented by contemporary furnishings such as suede armchairs, and sofas in such colors as mustard, teal, and eggplant. Twelve of the rooms are in the main building, which also houses a popular gourmet restaurant. Other rooms are in a new annex, are all split-level, and have stereo systems and VCRs. *Zurbano 36, 28010, tel. 91/319–6900, fax 91/308–5477. 37 rooms. Facilities: restaurant, bar, garden, garage, satellite TV. AE, DC, MC, V.*

Villamagna. Favored by visiting financiers and reclusive rock stars, the modern Villamagna ranks among Madrid's most exclusive hotels and boasts a staff dedicated to personal attention. Its green-and-white lobby exudes elegance, and a pianist provides soothing music in the lounge at lunchtime and during the cocktail hour. Rooms all have desks and working space, as well as luxury details such as hidden TVs, VCRs, and green plants in the bathrooms. The restaurant, Berceo, has cozy walnut paneling and the feel of an English library;

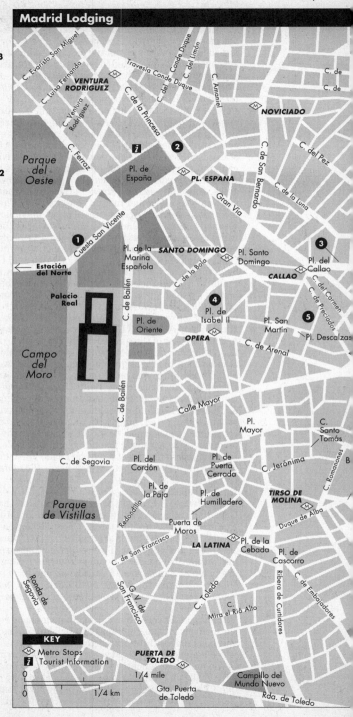

Madrid Lodging

C. Evaristo San Miguel
Travesía Conde Duque
C. del Limón
C. Conde Duque
C. de
C. de
C. Luisa Fernanda
VENTURA RODRIGUEZ
C. del
C. Amaniel
NOVICIADO
C. del Pez
C. de Ventura Rodríguez
C. de la Princesa
C. de San Bernardo
C. de la Luna

Parque del Oeste
C. Ferraz
Pl. de España
PL. ESPANA
Gran Via

Cuesta San Vicente
Pl. de la Marina Española
SANTO DOMINGO
Pl. Santo Domingo
Pl. del Callao
CALLAO
C. del Carmen
C. de Preciados

Estación del Norte
C. de la Bola
C. de Bailén

Palacio Real
Pl. de Oriente
Pl. de Isabel II
Pl. San Martín
Pl. Descalzas
OPERA
C. de Arenal

Campo del Moro
C. de Bailén

Calle Mayor
Pl. Mayor
C. Santo Tomás
C. de Segovia
Pl. del Cordón
Pl. de Puerta Cerrada
C. Jerónima
C. Romanones
B

Parque de Vistillas
Pl. de la Paja
Pl. de Humilladero
TIRSO DE MOLINA
Redondilla
Puerta de Moros
Duque de Alba
LA LATINA
Pl. de la Cebada
Pl. de Cascorro
C. de San Francisco
C. de Embajadores
Ronda de Segovia
G. V. de San Francisco
C. Toledo
C. Mira el Rió Alto
Ribera de Curtidores
Ronda de Curtidores

KEY
Metro Stops
Tourist Information

0 ———————— 1/4 mile
0 ———————— 1/4 km

PUERTA DE TOLEDO
Gta. Puerta de Toledo
Campillo del Mundo Nuevo
Rda. de Toledo

its garden terrace is open for dinner in warm weather. *Paseo de la Castellana 22, 28046, tel. 91/576–7500, fax 91/575–9504. 164 rooms, 18 suites. Facilities: restaurant, bar, sauna, beauty salon, garage, shops. AE, DC, MC, V.*

Villa Real. If you're looking for a luxury hotel that combines elegance, modern amenities, and great location, this may be the ticket. Opened in 1989, its simulated 19th-century facade gives way to large lobbies dotted with potted palms and a tiny bar that seats about half a dozen people. Each room has a character of its own, albeit with an overall French feel. The hotel faces the Cortes and is convenient to almost everything. *Plaza de las Cortes 10, 28014, tel. 91/420–3767, fax 91/420–2547. 94 rooms, 20 suites. Facilities: bar, garage, boutiques. AE, DC, MC, V.*

$$$ **Gran Hotel Colón.** You'll have some traveling to do to get to the old city from this sprawling hotel on the far side of Retiro Park, but the prices are somewhat less than they'd be elsewhere, given the many amenities it offers. It's a massive, functional structure that went up in the 1960s, and its lobbies have the airport-lounge look typical of that era. The rooms, which are sizable and well lit, are brightly furnished with kelly-green bedspreads, aqua curtains, and brown carpeting. *Calle Dr. Esguerdo 117–119, 28007, tel. 91/573–5900, fax 91/573–0809. 390 rooms. Facilities: 3 restaurants, 2 cafeterias, outdoor pool, sauna, 3 bars, shops, beauty salon. AE, DC, MC, V.*

Lagasca. Opened in 1993 in the heart of the elegant Salamanca neighborhood, this hotel combines large brightly decorated rooms with an unbeatable location two blocks from Madrid's main shopping street, Calle Serrano. The marble lobbies border on the coldly functional, but are fine to use as a meeting place. *Lagasca 64, 28001, tel. 91/575–4606, fax 91/575–1694. 100 rooms. Facilities: restaurant, bar, garage, satellite TV. AE, DC, MC, V.*

Plaza. This aging hotel, overlooking the Plaza de España, is a bit dreary, with leatherette overstuffed furniture setting the tone in its lobby. The rooms are a step up, fairly bright and comfortable enough. A major attraction is the rooftop swimming pool and bar—a marvelous spot to look out over one of Madrid's major squares at night. *Gran Vía 84, 28013, tel. 91/547–1200, fax 91/548–2389. 306 rooms. Facilities: cafeteria, restaurant, bar, child care, hairdresser, barbershop. AE, DC, MC, V.*

El Prado. Wedged in between the classic buildings of Old Madrid, this skinny new hotel is within stumbling distance of the city's best bars and nightclubs. Rooms are surprisingly spacious, and are virtually soundproofed from street noise by double-paned windows. Decorative touches include pastel floral prints and gleaming marble baths. *Calle Prado 11, 28014, tel. 91/369–0234, fax 91/429–2829. 50 rooms. Facilities: cafeteria, garage, satellite TV. AE, DC, MC, V.*

★ **Reina Victoria.** The Tryp chain recently bought and extensively renovated what is one of Madrid's most historic and loved hotels. Now, besides the remarkable glass and steel exterior that faces two of Madrid's most charming squares, the Victoria boasts a ritzy lobby and far more upscale clientele than in the era when it served down-at-the-heels bullfighters and American writers like Ernest Hemingway. The rooms are huge and bright, with new furnishings, and the best have views of the Plaza Santa Ana. Reservations usually are needed because it's becoming very popular. *Plaza del Angel 7, 28014, tel. 91/531–4500, fax 91/522–0307. 110 rooms. Facilities: bar. AE, DC, MC, V.*

Suecia. The chief attraction of the Suecia is its location right next to the superchic Círculo de Bellas Artes (arts society/café/movie/theater complex). It's on a very quiet street, a definite advantage in Madrid. Though recently remodeled, its lobby is still somewhat soulless. The rooms are trendy, with modern art on the walls and futuristic light fixtures. *Marqués de Riera 4, 28014, tel. 91/531–6900, fax 91/521–7141. 119 rooms, 9 suites. Facilities: 2 restaurants and bar. AE, DC, MC, V.*

★ **Tryp Ambassador.** Ideally located on an old street between Gran Vía and the Royal Palace, this hotel opened in 1991 in the renovated 19th-century palace of the Dukes of Granada. A magnificent front door and a graceful three-story staircase are reminders of the building's aristocratic past; the rest has been transformed into an elegant hotel favored by business executives. The lobby, in the palace's former patio, is decorated in French Provincial style, with a glass roof that gives the space a bright and airy feel. Bedrooms are large, with separate sitting areas, and have mahogany furnishings and floral drapes and bedspreads. A greenhouse bar filled with plants and songbirds is especially pleasant on cold days. *Cuesta Santo Domingo 5 and 7, 28013, tel. 91/541–6700, fax 91/559–1040. 182 rooms. Facilities: restaurant, bar, garage. AE, DC, MC, V.*

Zurbano. Just a few steps from the Castellana, in the northern part of the city, the Zurbano is a hotel of gleaming modern lobbies and equally gleaming rooms. The decor, in a word, is minimalist; the rooms, like the lobby, have tile floors, and the linens, walls, and rugs are generally monochromatic—muted blues, greens, or other colors. *Zurbano 79–81, 28003, tel. 91/441–4500, fax 91/441–3224. 269 rooms. Facilities: restaurant, cafeteria, bar. AE, DC, MC, V.*

\$\$ Atlántico. Don't be put off by the location on a noisy stretch of Gran Vía, or by the rather shabby third-floor lobby. Bright, clean accommodations at good prices is what the Atlántico is all about. Rooms are small but comfortable, with fabric wall-coverings and new furniture. All have tile baths. A member of the Best Western chain, this hotel is a favorite with British travelers and is almost always full, so it's a good idea to book well in advance. *Gran Vía 38, 28013, tel. 91/522–6480, fax 91/531–0210. 60 rooms. Facilities: snack bar. AE, MC, V.*

Carlos V. For those who like to be right in the center of things, this classic hotel in a quiet pedestrian zone may be one of the best options for value and convenience. It's just a few steps away from the Puerta del Sol and Plaza Mayor. A suit of armor decorates the tiny lobby, while crystal chandeliers add elegance to a second-floor guest lounge. All rooms are bright and carpeted. *Maestro Victoria 5, 28013, tel. 91/531–4100, fax 91/531–3761. 67 rooms. AE, MC, V.*

★ **Inglés.** This little gem is smack in the center of the old city's bar and restaurant district. Virginia Woolf was one of its first discoverers, but since then it's attracted more than its share of less famous artists and writers. The interior is a bit faded, but its offbeat rooms and lobby—which has a glass-cased model ship—are still appealing. Many of the rooms are gigantic—suites for the price of normal doubles. The balconies overlooking Calle Echegaray give you an unusual view of the medieval look of the old city from the air, all red Mediterranean tiles and ramshackle gables. *Echegaray 8, 28014, tel. 91/429–6551, fax 91/420–2423. 58 rooms. Facilities: cafeteria, bar, parking lot (essential in this neighborhood), gym. AE, DC, MC, V.*

★ **Paris.** For a remarkably fair price, the Paris offers delightful Old-World charm, right at the corner of the busy Puerta del Sol and Calle de Alcalá; you can't get more central than this. The odd-shaped rooms are clean, spacious, and decorated with orange bedspreads and curtains. The lobby is dark, woody, and somehow redolent of times long past. There's no bar, but three meals are served in a bright second-floor restaurant. All in all, the Paris is an unusual deal. *Alcalá 2, 28014, tel. 91/521–6496. 114 rooms. Facilities: restaurant. MC, V.*

Príncipe Pío. This hotel appears to have seen better days, but despite the fading velveteen and linoleum look of the lobby, it's convenient to much of Madrid's west side: the Royal Palace and its gardens, Plaza de España, and the Norte railway station. The rooms are surprisingly pleasant once you're past the lobby; they're bright, with fine views of the Royal Palace, and furnished with white bedside tables and orange carpeting. Also offered are "apartosuites," complete with kitchen and up to two bedrooms. *Cuesta de San Vicente 14–16, 28008, tel. 91/547–0800, fax 91/541–1117; for apartosuites, tel. 91/542–5900. Facilities: restaurant, bar, garage. AE, DC, MC, V.*

$ **Lisboa.** Clean, small, and central, the Lisboa has for years been a well-kept secret just off the Plaza Santa Ana. It offers no frills, but is in a marvelous location on a busy bar and restaurant street and is easy on most budgets. Past a tiny lobby, the rooms tend to vary greatly in size and quality. Most of them are sparsely furnished, with tile floors and papered walls, and the linen doesn't always match; but they are clean and functional. *Ventura de la Vega 17, 28014, tel. 91/429–9894. 22 rooms. AE, DC, MC, V.*

Monaco. Just a few steps from the tiny Plaza de Chueca, the Monaco is an eccentrically opulent delight. The lobby's resplendent with red carpeted stairs, potted plants, brass rails, and mirrors—and the rooms are similar, with Louis XIV–style furniture and mirrored walls. The owner is Portuguese and very gracious. *Barbieri 5, 28004, tel. 91/522–4630, fax 91/521–1601. 33 rooms. Facilities: cafeteria, bar. AE, MC, V.*

★ **Mora.** Directly across the Paseo del Prado from the Botanical Gardens, the Mora underwent a complete renovation in 1994 and now offers a sparkling faux-marble lobby and bright, carpeted hallways. The guest rooms are modestly decorated but large and comfortable; those on the street side have great views of the gardens and Prado Museum (they're also fairly quiet, thanks to double-paned windows). *Paseo del Prado 32, 28014, tel. 91/420–1569, fax 91/420–0564. 61 rooms. AE, DC, MC, V.*

Ramón de la Cruz. If you don't mind a longish metro ride from the center, this medium-size hotel is a find. The rooms are large, with modern bathrooms, and the lobby's spacious and stone-floored. Given Madrid prices, it's a bargain. *Don Ramón de la Cruz 94, 28006, tel. 91/401–7200, fax 91/402–2126. 103 rooms. Facilities: cafeteria. MC, V.*

The Arts and Nightlife

The Arts

Madrid's cultural scene is so lively that it's hard to keep pace with the constantly changing offerings and venues. As its reputation has skyrocketed in recent years, artists and performers of all kinds are coming here. The best way to stay abreast of events is through the weekly *Guía de Ocio* (published Mondays) or daily listings in the leading newspaper, *El País*. Both sources are relatively easy to figure out, even if you don't read Spanish. Tickets to performances usually are best purchased at the venues themselves; in the case of major popular concerts, the larger Corte Inglés and Galerías Preciados department stores have **Discoplay** outlets that sell advance tickets.

The city puts on major arts festivals in each of the four seasons. While you'll have to look up ever-changing details, events include world-class jazz, salsa, African music, and rock; arts exhibitions of all kinds; movie festivals; and more—all at more than reasonable prices. The venues are more often than not outdoors in city parks and amphitheaters.

Theater English-speaking performances are a rarity, and when they do come to town, they may play on any of a dozen Madrid stages; you'll have to check local newspapers. One you won't need the language for is the **Teatro de la Zarzuela** (Jovellanos 4, tel. 91/429–8225), which puts on the traditional Spanish operettas known as *zarzuela*, a kind of bawdy comedy. The **Teatro Español** (Príncipe 25, tel. 91/429–6297) specializes in Spanish Golden Age classics.

Concerts Opened in 1988, the **Auditorio Nacional de Música** (Príncipe de Vergara 136, tel. 91/337–0100) is Madrid's principal concert hall for classical music, and regularly hosts major orchestras from around the world.

Movies Almost a dozen theaters regularly show undubbed foreign films, the majority of them English-language. These are listed in newspapers and in the *Guía de Ocio* under "V.O."—meaning original version. Leading V.O. theaters include the **Alphaville** and **Renoir**, both on Martín de los Heros, just off Plaza de España, and each with four theaters. The city offers excellent classic V.O. films that change daily at the **Filmoteca Cine Dore** (Santa Isabel 3).

Nightlife

It's a commonplace in Spain that Madrileños hardly sleep, and that's largely because of the amount of time they spend in bars—not drunk, but socializing in the easy, sophisticated way that is unique to the capital. This is true of old as well as young, though the streets that are famous for their bars tend to be patronized by a younger clientele (these include Huertas, Moratín, Segovia, Victoria, and the areas around Plaza Santa Ana, Plaza de Anton Martin). Adventuresome travelers may want to explore the scruffier bar scene around the Plaza Dos de Mayo in the Malasaña neighborhood, where trendy, smoke-filled places line both sides of Calle San Vicente Ferrer.

Tapas Bars Spending the early evening hours going from bar to bar and eating tapas is so popular that the Spanish have a verb to describe it: *tapear*. The selection is endless and the best-known tapas bars are the *cuevas* that cluster around Cava de San Miguel (*see* Tour 4, *above*). Here are a few more suggestions:

Aloque (Torrecilla del Leal 20) is one of Madrid's few wine bars, with more than 200 offerings by the bottle and half a dozen Spanish varieties sold by the glass. Plates of hearty stews and tapas are also served as classical music plays in the background.

Bocaíto (Libertad 6) is said by some to serve the best tapas in all Madrid—a heady claim. In any case, you can have a full meal here or just partake of a few tapas before heading on to the many other fine places in the immediate vicinity.

Las Bravas (Alvarez Gato 3), hidden away in an alley off the Plaza Santa Ana, isn't much to look at, but it's here that *patatas bravas* (potatoes in a spicy tomato sauce) were invented. They're now a classic Spanish tapa.

Casa Alberto (Huertas 18) is an atmospheric place with a pewter and marble bar, beautifully carved wooden ceilings, and some great tapas. Like many Madrid bars, there's no seating—you're meant to stand while you imbibe.

La Chuleta (Echegaray 20) is a cheery corner bar hung with bullfight memorabilia and offering a colorful selection of tapas on the bar. You *can* sit down here.

La Dolores (Plaza de Jesús 4) is a crowded, noisy, and wonderful place that's rightly reputed to serve the best draft beer in Madrid. Located just behind the Palace Hotel, it offers a very few tables in the back.

Mesón Gallego (León 4) is a hole in the wall that serves a wonderfully hearty Galician potato soup (a famous cure for those who've drunk too much) called *caldo gallego*. Not for everyone is the *ribeira* (the somewhat acidic white wine made with grapes from Galician riverbanks).

The Reporter (Fúcar 6), true to its English name, is hung with great Spanish and world news photos. Its other great attraction is a garden terrace shaded by a grapevine trellis. The raciones are very good, and the pâté plate is terrific.

El Rey de Pimiento (Plaza Puerta Cerrada) serves some 40 different kinds of tapas including *pimientos* (peppers)—the roasted red variety, as well as the intermittently hot *pimientos de padrón*.

Taverna del Alabardero (Felipe V 6) is an upscale and cheerful bar with a twin in Washington, DC. Their specialty is garlicky *patatas a la pobre*.

La Trucha (Manuel Fernández y Gonzalez 3) is hung with hams and garlic and has the feel of an inn of the Middle Ages. It's also a restaurant, but the wonderful tapas that line its aging bar are a far better bet.

El Ventorrillo (Bailén 14) is a place to go between May and October, when tables are set up in the shady park of Las Vistillas overlooking the city's western edge. Specialties include croquettes and mushrooms. This is Madrid's premier spot from which to watch the sun go down.

Other Bars There are countless bars in Madrid, and while almost all offer something to eat, some are known more for their atmosphere than their food. Some recommendations:

Cafe Gijon (Paseo de Recoletos 24) may be Madrid's most famous café-bar. For more than a century, it's been the venue of the city's most highfalutin *tertulias* (discussion groups that meet regularly to muse on all manner of topics).

Casa Pueblo (corner of calles del Prado and León) stays open later than most (4 AM on weekends) and has a wonderful Jazz Age feel to it.

Cervantes (León 8) is a bright, tiled bar where you can also get a pizza or pasta in a small dining room at the back. It caters to a young neighborhood crowd.

La Champañeria Gala (Moratín 24) is one of the city's better-known champagne bars, offering especially good Catalan *cavas* (as Spanish champagnes are known).

Chicote (Gran Vía 12) was immortalized in several Hemingway short stories of the Spanish civil war and still makes an interesting stop.

Los Gabrieles (Echegaray 17) is featured in most of the tourist literature on Madrid for its remarkable tile walls, but the place's clientele is mostly hip Spaniards, not foreigners.

Hermanos Muñiz (Huertas 29) is the quintessential Spanish neighborhood bar, neither trendy nor touristy. The tapas here are uniformly excellent, and the men who serve them both friendly and superbly professional.

Palacio de Gaviria (Arenal 9) is an impeccably restored 19th-century baroque palace hidden away on the upper floors of a tawdry commercial street between Puerta del Sol and the Royal Palace. Allegedly built to house one of the queen's lovers, the palace now serves drinks in an elegant setting with live jazz late at night.

Taberna de Antonio Sanchez (Meson de Paredes 13) is reputedly the oldest bar in Madrid (the proprietors claim it's been in business since 1830). Order wine and tapas at the old zinc bar in front; head to the back to order a full meal.

La Venecia (Echegaray 7) is a trendy but engaging sherry bar in a rustic 19th-century setting. Examples of the best sherries, both sweet and dry, are available.

Viva Madrid (Manuel Fernández y Gonzalez 7) is an extremely popular and atmospheric bar with a Brassai motif. Packed with Spaniards and foreigners, it has become something of a hip singles scene recently. There are tables—and food served—in the rear.

Nightclubs   Jazz, rock, flamenco, and classical music are all popular in the many small clubs that dot the city. Here are a few of the more interesting:

Café Central (Plaza de Ángel 10), the city's best-known jazz venue, is chic and well run. The musicians are often very good, with performances generally beginning at 10 PM.

Cafe del Foro (San Andrés 38) is a funky, friendly club on the edge of the Malasaña neighborhood with live music every night starting at 11:30.

Café Jazz Populart (Huertas 22) is a club featuring jazz, Brazilian music, reggae, and salsa.

Café Maravilla (San Vicente Ferrer 33) is physically reminiscent of the futuristic milk bar in Stanley Kubrick's film *A Clockwork Orange*, but the music—often a kind of flamenco-jazz fusion—is more trendsetting still. Prices can be outrageous.

Clamores (Albuquerque 14), another famous jazz club, offers a wide selection of French and Spanish champagnes.

La Fídula (Huertas 57) features nightly chamber music (starting around 11:30 PM) in a subdued and pleasant setting.

Teatriz (Hermosilla 15) is a restaurant that converts to a sophisticated nightspot after hours. Its theatrical decor is entertaining in and of itself, plus the place includes a tiny discotheque.

Torero (Cruz 26), a thoroughly modern club despite the name, is one of Madrid's chicest spots. You'll have to come looking good, though—a doorman ensures that only those judged *gente guapa* (beautiful people) may enter.

Flamenco   Madrid is not a great city for flamenco, but for those who aren't traveling south, here are a few possibilities:

Café de Chinitas (Torija 7, tel. 91/547–1502) is the city's best-known show, and the tourists it draws have included such diplomatic guests as former Nicaraguan president Daniel Ortega. It's expensive, but the food and dancing are good. Plan to reserve in advance; it often sells out.

Corral de la Moreria (Moreria 17, tel. 91/365–8446) serves dinners à la carte, and features well-known flamenco stars who perform along with the resident group.

Corral de la Pacheca (Juan Ramon Jiménez 26, tel. 91/359–2660) offers good performances, if a little touristy, and the prices are more reasonable than those of Chinitas.

Cabaret   If you're looking for Las Vegas–style topless revues, head for **La Scala Melía**, a cabaret in the gigantic Melía Castilla Hotel (Rosario Pino 7, tel. 91/571–4411).

Casino   **Casino Gran Madrid,** 29 km (18 mi) northwest of the capital on N VI, is said to handle more money per year than any of its counterparts at

Monte Carlo, Deauville, and Baden Baden. The casino, with a night-club, three restaurants, and four bars, is open daily from 5 PM to 4 AM. Men are required to wear jackets and ties, October to April. Free buses to the casino depart from in front of Plaza de España 6 at 5, 7, and 9 every evening, with return trips at 7, 8, and 10. Bring your passport. (Admission: 500 pesetas. Tel. 91/856–1100.)

 Madrid's hottest new discotheque is in a converted public bathhouse predictably called **Baños** (Escalinata 10). Owned by the same people behind Viva Madrid and Archy's, the locale doubles as a café during the day, but a pounding disco beat takes over from midnight to 4. **Joy Eslava** (Arenal 11), a downtown disco in a converted theater, remains popular, as does **Pacha** (Barceló 11), while the well-heeled crowd likes to be seen at **Archy's** (Marqués de Riscal 11). Salsa music has become a permanent fixture of the Spanish capital and the best place to dance to these Latin-American rhythms is the **Café del Mercado** (Ronda de Toledo 1).

4 Around Madrid

By Michael Jacobs

Updated by Deborah Luhrman

Traveling around Madrid will take you to an enormous variety of landscapes and places. The impressive Sierras of Guadarrama and Gredos to the north and west of Madrid attract skiers. Farther north runs the fertile valley of the Duero, with extensive vineyards producing excellent wines. Bare hills alternating with densely wooded valleys make up much of the landscape northeast of Madrid, while south of here, the river courses turn into harsh and dramatic gorges. South of Cuenca and Toledo begin the vast, featureless plains of La Mancha. In the course of your travels, you will find, furthermore, that each of the main towns that you visit has a very distinctive character in terms of architecture, gastronomy, popular traditions, and the inhabitants themselves.

Yet for all the many facets that make up the surroundings of Madrid, there is an underlying unity. The region covered in this section is Castile—more accurately Old and New Castile, the former north of Madrid, the latter south (and known as "New" because it was captured from the Moors at a slightly later date). Castile is essentially a vast, windswept plateau, famed for its clear skies and endless vistas. Over the centuries poets and others have characterized it as an austere and melancholy region, most notably Antonio Machado, whose experiences early this century at Soria inspired his memorable and haunting *Campos de Castilla (Fields of Castile)*.

Stone is one of the dominant elements of the Castilian countryside and it has, to a large extent, molded the character of the region. Gaunt mountain ranges frame the horizons, gorges and rocky outcrops break up many a flat expanse, and the fields around Ávila and Segovia are littered with giant boulders. The villages are predominantly of granite, and their solid, formidable look contrasts markedly with the whitewashed walls of most of southern Spain. The presence of so much stone perhaps helps to explain the rich sculptural tradition of this region—few parts of Europe have such a wealth of outstanding sculptural treasures as does Castile, a wealth testified to by the unrivaled National Museum of Sculpture at Valladolid.

Whereas southern Spaniards are traditionally passive and peace loving, Castilians have been a race of soldiers. The very name of the region refers to the great line of castles and fortified towns built in the 12th century between Salamanca in the west and Soria in the east. The Alcázar at Segovia, the intact surrounding walls of Ávila, and countless other military monuments are among the greatest tourist attractions of Castile, and some of them—for instance, the castles at Sigüenza and Ciudad Rodrigo—are also splendid hotels.

Faced with the austerity of the Castilian environment, many here have taken refuge in the worlds of the spirit and the imagination. Ávila is closely associated with two of the most renowned of Europe's mystics, St. Teresa and her disciple St. John of the Cross; Toledo, meanwhile, was the main home of one of the most spiritual of all western painters, El Greco. As for the escape into fantasy, this is famously illustrated by Cervantes's hero Don Quixote, in whose formidable imagination even the dreary expanse of La Mancha—one of the bleakest parts of Spain—could be transformed into something magical. A similarly fanciful mind has characterized many of the region's architects. Castile in the 15th and 16th centuries was the main center of the Plateresque, a style of ornamentation of extraordinary intricacy and boundless fantasy, suggestive of silverwork. Developed in Toledo and Valladolid, it reached its exuberant clímax in the university town of Salamanca.

Essential Information

Arriving and Departing by Plane

The only international airport in both Old and New Castile is Madrid Barajas. Valladolid Airport has flights to Barcelona.

Getting Around

By Train   All the main towns covered in this section are accessible by train from Madrid, and it is quite possible to visit each in separate day trips. There are commuter trains from Madrid to Segovia (3 hours), Alcalá de Henares (30 minutes), Guadalajara (50 minutes), and Toledo (1½ hours). Train travel, however, is generally slow, and it is always quicker, if not as interesting, to get to your destination by bus. The one important town that can be reached only by train is Sigüenza, which, like most places surrounding Madrid (including Segovia, Ávila, and Salamanca), is served by Madrid's Chamartín Station. Atocha is the station for trains to Toledo, Cuenca, and other destinations south of Madrid.

By Bus   The bus connections between Madrid and the two Castiles are excellent. Two of the most popular services with tourists and day-trippers are to Toledo (1 hour) and Segovia (1½ hours); buses to the former leave every half hour from the Estación del Sur (Canaria s/n, tel. 91/468–4200) and to the latter every hour from La Sepulvedana (Paseo de la Florida 11, tel. 91/527–9537). Buses to Soria (3 hours) and Burgo de Osma (2½ hours) leave from Continental Auto (Calle Alenza 20, tel. 91/533–0400), while Auto Res (Plaza Conde de Casal 6, tel. 91/551–7200) runs services to Ávila (2 hours), Cuenca (2 hours, 50 minutes), Valladolid (2½ hours), and Salamanca (3 hours). Services between the provincial towns are not as good as those to and from Madrid: If you are traveling between, say, Cuenca and Toledo, you will find it quicker to return to Madrid and make your way from there. Reservations are rarely necessary; in cases of extra demand, additional buses are usually put into service.

By Car   A series of major roads with extensive stretches of divided highway—the N I, II, III, IV, and V—radiate from Madrid in every direction and make communications with the outlying towns only too easy; if possible, however, you should avoid returning to Madrid on these roads at the end of a weekend or public holiday. The side roads are variable in quality and rarely of the high standard that you find, say, in provincial France. Nonetheless, these roads constitute one of the great pleasures of traveling around the Castilian countryside by car—you are constantly coming across unexpected architectural delights and wild and spectacular vistas; above all, you can enjoy the feeling that you have all these beautiful places to yourself because you will rarely come across other tourists.

Important Addresses and Numbers

Tourist Offices   The main provincial tourist office in Madrid is on the Plaza de España (Princesa 1, tel. 91/541–2325). Useful information and excellent town plans can be obtained from the following local offices:

Alcalá de Henares (Callejón de Santa María, tel. 91/889–2694), **Aranjuez** (Plaza Santiago Rusiñol, tel. 91/889–2694), **Ávila** (Plaza de la Catedral 4, tel. 918/21–13–87), **Ciudad Real** (Av. Alarcos 21, tel. 926/21–29–25), **Ciudad Rodrigo** (Puerta de Amayuelas 5, tel. 923/

46–05–61), **Cuenca** (Calle Dalmacio García Izcara 8, tel. 966/22–22–31), **Guadalajara** (Plaza Mayor 6, tel. 911/22–06–98), **Salamanca** (Gran Vía 41, tel. 923/26–85–71), **Segovia** (Plaza Mayor 10, tel. 911/43–03–28), **Soria** (Plaza Ramón y Cajal s/n, tel. 975/21–20–52), **Toledo** (Puerta de Bisagra s/n, tel. 925/22–08–43), **Valladolid** (Plaza de Zorrilla 3, tel. 983/35–18–01), and **Zamora** (Calle Santa Clara 20, tel. 988/53–18–45).

Car Rental It is often cheaper to rent cars in advance, while still in the United States, through international firms such as Hertz and Avis (*see* Before You Go in Chapter 1). Spain's leading car rental agency is **Atesa** (Infanta Mercedes 90, Madrid, tel. 91/571–2145).

Guided Tours

City Tours Current information on city tours can be obtained from the local tourist offices, where you can also find out about hiring guides. You should be especially wary of the local guides at Ávila and Toledo; they can be quite ruthless in trying to impose their services on you. Do not buy goods in the shops that they take you to because you will probably end up paying more than the normal prices.

Special-Interest Tours For a special art tour of Castile, including Salamanca, contact **Prospect Music & Art Tours Ltd.**, a London-based company (10 Barley Mow Passage, Chiswick, London W4 4PH, tel. 081/995–2163). At the same address is by far the best of Great Britain's cultural tour specialists, **Martin Randall Travel** (tel. 081/994–6477), which offers an excellent five-day trip that includes Madrid and Toledo.

Exploring Around Madrid

Orientation

Aranjuez, Ávila, Segovia, and Toledo tend to be visited by tourists on day trips from Madrid. Salamanca and all the other major places discussed in this section can also be seen on a day's outing from the capital, but in these cases you will find yourself spending more time traveling than actually being there. Ideally, especially if you have a car, you should undertake at least a four-day trip around the area, staying at Toledo, Segovia, and Salamanca and passing through Ávila. Both Toledo and Segovia have an extra charm at night, not only because their monuments are so beautifully illuminated, but also because they are free of the great crowds of tourists that congest them by day. To visit all the main sights around Madrid would require at least another three to six days and feature overnight stays as well in Zamora, Soria, Sigüenza, and Cuenca.

Highlights for First-time Visitors

The walls of Ávila (*see* Tour 2)
The Casas Colgadas, Cuenca (*see* Tour 7)
The fountains of La Granja (*see* Tour 1)
The National Museum of Religious Sculpture, Valladolid (*see* Tour 5)
Salamanca (*see* Tour 3)
Segovia (*see* Tour 1)
Toledo (*see* Tour 8)

Tour 1: Segovia and Its Province

Numbers in the margin correspond to points of interest on the Around Madrid and Segovia maps.

Outstanding Roman and medieval monuments, embroideries and textiles, and excellent cuisine make beautifully situated **Segovia** one of the most popular destinations for excursions from Madrid. An important military town in Roman times, Segovia was later established by the Arabs as a major textile center. Captured by the Christians in 1085, the town was enriched by a royal residence, and indeed, in 1474 the half-sister of Henry IV, Isabella the Catholic (Isabel la Católica, of Castile, wife of Ferdinand of Aragón), was proclaimed queen of Castile here. By that time Segovia was a bustling city of about 60,000 inhabitants (there are 54,000 today), but its importance was soon to diminish as a result of its taking the side of the Comuneros in the popular revolt against the Emperor Charles V. Though the construction in the 18th century of a royal palace at nearby La Granja helped somewhat to revive its fortunes, it was never to recover its former vitality. At the turn of the century, its sleepy charm came to be appreciated by numerous artists and writers—for instance, the painter Ignacio Zuloaga and the poet Antonio Machado. Today, it swarms with tourists and day-trippers from Madrid and you may want to avoid it in the summer months, especially on weekends or public holidays. On weekdays in the winter you can appreciate fully the haunting peace of the town.

When you approach Segovia driving west from Madrid along N603, the first building that you see is the cathedral, which seems from here to rise directly above the fields. Between you and Segovia lies, in fact, a steep and narrow valley, which shields the old town from view. Only when you descend into this valley does the spectacular position of the old town begin to become apparent, rising as it does on top of a narrow rock ledge shaped like a ship. As soon as you reach the modern outskirts of Segovia, turn left onto the Paseo E. Gonzalez and follow the road marked **"Ruta Panorámica."** Soon you will find yourself descending on the narrow and winding Cuesta de los Hoyos, a road that takes you to the bottom of the wooded valley that dips to the south of the old town. Above, in the old town, you can see the Romanesque church of San Martín to the right; the cathedral in the middle; and on the far left, at the point where the rock ledge tapers out, the turrets, spires, and battlements of the castle, known as the Alcázar.

The Cuesta de los Hoyos comes to an end at a bridge crossing the River Eresma, which runs below the northern side of the town; turn right on the other side of the bridge and then, after 100 m (328 ft), make a short detour to the left, up several hundred yards to the church of **Vera Cruz.** This isolated Romanesque structure, in the warm orange stone of the area, was built in 1208 for the Knights Templar; like other buildings associated with this order, it is round, inspired by the Holy Sepulcher in Jerusalem. A visit here is rewarded by the climb up the bell tower for a view of the whole town profiled against the Sierra de Guadarrama, which in the winter is capped with snow. *Admission: 150 pesetas. Open May–Sept., Tues.–Sun. 10:30–1:30 and 3:30–7; Oct.–Apr., Tues.–Sun. 10:30–1:30 and 3–6.*

Return to the road, turn left (east), and you will soon cross the river again. Continue to drive below the walls, and you will pass on your left a 15th-century building that functioned from 1455 until 1730 as the **mint** where all Spanish coinage was struck. Farther on is the

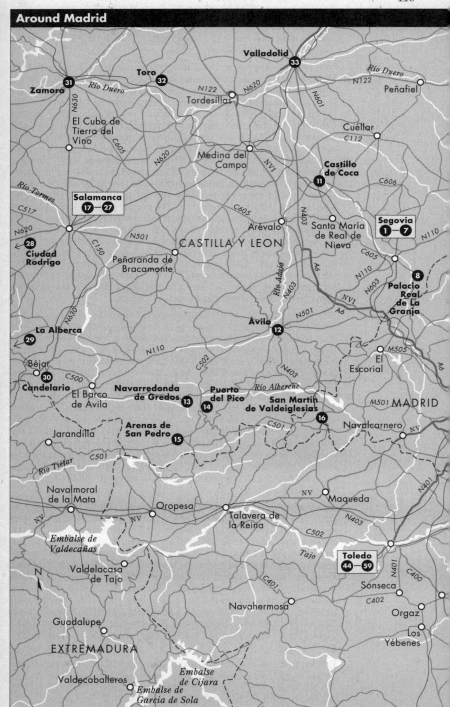

Around Madrid

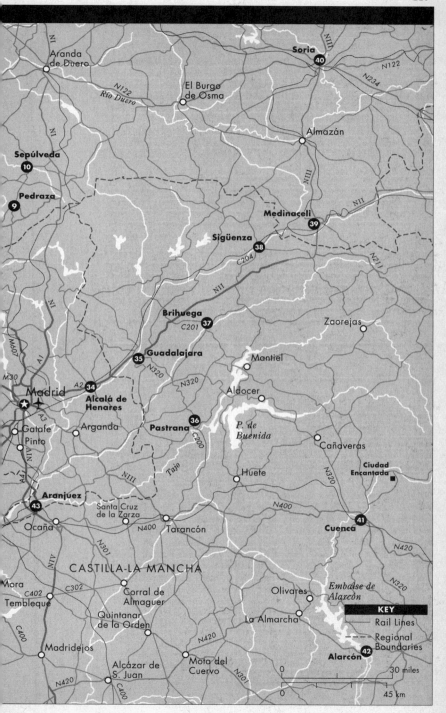

N1 Aranda de Duero

N122 Río Duero

El Burgo de Osma

Almazán

N122 N234

NIII

N1

Sepúlveda 10

Pedraza 9

Medinaceli 39

Sigüenza 38

NII NII

C204

N211

NII

Brihuega 37
C201

Zaorejas

M607

A1

35 **Guadalajara**
N320

Mantiel

M30

A2 34
NI

Alcalá de Henares

N320

Aldocer

Madrid

A3

Gatafe
Pinto

Arganda

Pastrana
C200

36

P. de Buenida

Cañaveras

NIII

Tajo

Húete

Ciudad Encantada ■

N320

Aranjúez
43

Santa Cruz de la Zarza

N400

N400

Tarancón

41 **Cuenca**

Ocaña

N301

Embalse de Alarcón

N420

Mora

C402
Tembleque

C302

Corral de Almaguer

Olivares

N320

CASTILLA-LA MANCHA

Quintanar de la Orden

La Almarcha

C400

Madridejos

N420

Alcázar de S. Juan

Mota del Cuervo

N301

42 **Alarcón**

N420

C400

KEY

—— Rail Lines

--- Regional Boundaries

0   30 miles

0   45 km

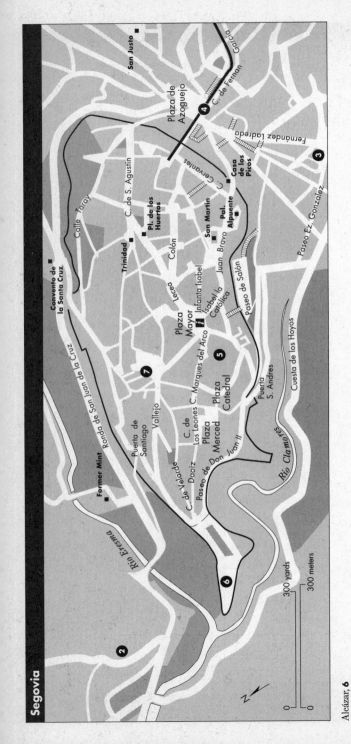

Segovia

San Justo

Plaza de Azoguejo

C. de Fernan Garcia

Fernández Ladreda

Casa de los Picos

Paseo Ez. Gonzalez

C. Cervantes

C. de S. Agustín

San Martín

Pal. Alpuente

Juan Bravo

Paseo de Salón

Calle Taray

Pl. de los Huertos

Colón

Trinidad

Convento de la Santa Cruz

Lecea

Plaza Mayor

Infanta Isabel

Isabel la Católica

Ronda de San Juan de la Cruz

Former Mint

Río Eresma

Puerta de Santiago

C. de Velade

Daoiz

C. de Vallejo

C. de Los Leones

C. Marqués del Arco

Plaza Merced

Plaza Catedral

Paseo de Don Juan II

Puerta S. Andres

Cuesta de los Hoyos

Río Clamores

0   300 yards

0   300 meters

N

Alcázar, **6**
Catedral, **5**
Roman aqueduct, **4**
San Esteban, **7**
San Millán, **3**
Vera Cruz, **2**

Convento de la Santa Cruz, founded in the 13th century near a cave inhabited by Santo Domingo de Guzmán, founder of the Dominican order; the church was rebuilt in the 15th century by Ferdinand and Isabella. At the church the road forks; a left turn takes you up to the modern parador, from which there is another extensive panorama of Segovia and the Guadarrama. If you take the right-hand turn, you will come to Segovia's Roman aqueduct, on the other side of which is the Avenida Fernández Ladreda, the main street through the lower, modern half of town. Near its end is the Paseo E. Gonzalez. Continue your visit on foot.

❸ The 12th-century church of **San Millán,** nearby on Fernández Ladreda, is a perfect example of the Segovian Romanesque and perhaps the finest church in town, apart from the cathedral. The exterior is notable for its arcaded porch, where church meetings were once held. The virtually untouched Romanesque interior is dominated by massive columns supporting capitals beautifully carved with such scenes as the Flight into Egypt and the Adoration of the Magi; the vaulting of the crossing shows the Moorish influence on Spanish medieval architecture. *Admission free. Open for mass only, daily 10:30 AM and 7 PM.*

From San Millán, walk down the Avenida Fernández Ladreda until
❹ you come to the **Roman aqueduct,** which ranks with the Pont du Gard in France as one of the greatest surviving examples of Roman engineering. Spanning the dip that stretches from the walls of the old town to the lower slopes of the Sierra de Guadarrama, it is about 900 m (2,952 ft) long, and—above the square to which Avenida Fernández Ladreda leads—rises in two tiers to a height of 35 m (115 ft). The raised section of stonework in the center originally carried an inscription, of which only the holes for the bronze letters remain. The massive granite blocks that make up the vast structure are held up by neither mortar nor clamps. Nonetheless, the aqueduct has managed to remain standing from the time of the emperor Augustus (3rd century BC), and the only damage it has suffered is the demolition of 35 of its arches by the Moors (these were later replaced on the orders of Ferdinand and Isabella).

Steps at the side of the aqueduct lead up to the walls of the old town, offering at the top a breathtaking side view of the structure. Turn left along a narrow alley that follows the walls, and you will eventually emerge beside the late-15th-century **Casa de los Picos,** so called because its walls are studded with diamond shapes. The Calle de Juan Bravo, a pedestrian shopping street, leads from here toward the center of the old town. Just off to the left, a few meters from the Casa de los Picos, is the Late Gothic **Palacio de los Condes de Alpuente** (Palace of the Counts of Alpuente), covered with plasterwork incised with regular patterns; this type of plasterwork, known as *esgrafiado*, is characteristic of the buildings of Segovia and was probably introduced by the Moors. Head once more toward the center and you will soon cross the small, delightful Plaza Martín, on which rises another porticoed Romanesque church, San Martín.

A turning from the south side of the square will lead you down to the Paseo de Salón, a small promenade at the foot of the town's southern walls that was very popular with Spain's 19th-century queen, Isabel II; it offers good views over the wooded valley to the south and toward the Guadarrama range. Back on the Calle de Juan Bravo, turn right at the Calle Isabel la Católica and into the arcaded main square, on which stand the 17th-century **Ayuntamiento** (Town Hall), the tourist office, and the cathedral.

Time Out The Plaza Mayor, lined with bars and terraces, makes an ideal place for a lunch break or early evening drink. The most elegant of the bars, and the one with the most renowned *tapas* (savory tidbits), is **La Concepción** (Plaza Mayor 15), adjacent to the cathedral; excellent homemade pâtés are served here.

⑤ The **catedral** (cathedral) was begun in 1525 to replace an earlier one near the Alcázar that was destroyed during the revolt of the Comuneros. Completed only 65 years later, it is one of the most harmonious in Spain, and one of the last great examples of the Gothic style in the country. The designs were drawn up by the leading Late Gothicist Juan Gil de Hontañon, but executed by his son Rodrigo, in whose work can be seen a transition between the Gothic and Renaissance styles. The tall proportions and buttressing are pure Gothic, but much of the detailing—for instance, on the crossing tower—is classical. The golden interior, illuminated by 16th-century Flemish windows, is remarkably light and uncluttered, the one major distracting detail being the wooden neoclassical choir. You enter the building through the north transept, and the first chapel you come to on the right has a lamentation group in polychromed wood by the Baroque sculptor Gregorio Fernández.

On the southern transept is a door opening into the Late Gothic cloister; this and the delightfully elaborate door leading into it were transported from the old cathedral and are the work of Juan Guas, the architect of the church of San Juan de Los Reyes, in Toledo. Under the pavement immediately inside the cloisters are the tombs of Juan and Rodrigo Gil de Hontañon: That these two men should lie in a space designed by Guas is appropriate, for these three men together dominated the last phase of the Gothic style in Spain. Off the cloister a small museum of religious art, installed partly in the first-floor chapter house, is worth a visit for the white-and-gold paneled ceiling of the 17th century, a late and splendid example of Mudéjar *artesonado* work. *Admission to museum: 200 pesetas. Open June–Sept., daily 10–7; Oct.–May, 10–1 and 3–6, Sun. and holidays 9:30–6.*

The Calle de Los Leones, lined with tourist shops, slopes gently down from the cathedral toward the western extremity of the old town's ridge. Finally, you'll come to the partially shaded Plaza del Alcázar, where there are excellent views to the north and south. At **⑥** the western end of the square is the famous **Alcázar,** which dates possibly to Roman times, but was considerably expanded in the 14th century, remodeled in the 15th, altered again toward the end of the following century, and completely redone after being gutted by a fire in 1862, when the building was used as an artillery school. The exterior, especially when seen from the Ruta Panorámica, is certainly imposing, but it is little more than a medieval sham, with the exception of the keep through which you enter, the last remnant of the original structure. Crowned by crenellated towers that seem to have been carved out of icing sugar, the keep can be climbed and offers superb views. The rest of the garishly colored interior of the Alcázar is disappointing. *Tel. 911/43–01–76. Admission: 350 pesetas. Open May–Sept., daily 10–7; Oct.–Apr., daily 10–6.*

You can return to the Roman aqueduct through the northern half of town, leaving the Plaza del Alcázar on the Calle de Velarde, and **⑦** passing shortly afterward the porticoed church of **San Esteban,** the third of the town's major Romanesque monuments. Though the interior has a Baroque facing, the exterior has kept some splendid capitals, as well as an exceptionally tall and elegant tower. Due east of the attractive square on which the church stands is the Capilla de San Juan de Dios, next to which is the former pension where the poet Antonio Machado spent his last years in Spain. The family who looked after him still own the building and will show you on request the poet's room, with its paraffin stove, iron bed, and round table.

Numbers in the margin correspond to points of interest on the Around Madrid map.

The major attraction within the immediate vicinity of Segovia is ❽ without question the **Palacio Real** (Royal Palace) **de La Granja,** which is built in the town of La Granja de San Ildefonso on the northern slopes of the Guadarrama range, 11 km (7 mi) southeast of Segovia on the N601 (the route is well-marked with road signs). It stands on a site previously occupied by a hunting lodge and a shrine to San Ildefonso administered by Hieronymite monks from the Segovian monastery of El Parral. Commissioned by the Bourbon king Philip V in 1719, the palace has sometimes been described as the first great building of the Spanish Bourbon dynasty; the English 19th-century writer Richard Ford likened it to "a theatrical French chateau, the antithesis of the proud, gloomy Escorial, on which it turns its back." The architects who brought the building to completion in 1739 and gave it its distinction were, in fact, not French but Italian—Juvarra and Sachetti. They were responsible for the imposing garden facade, a Late Baroque masterpiece articulated throughout its whole length by a giant order of columns. The interior has been badly gutted by fire, and the few rooms that were undamaged are heavy and monotonous; the main interest is the collection of 15th- to 18th-century tapestries, which have been gathered together in a special museum. It is the gardens of La Granja that you should come to see. Terraces, ornamental ponds, lakes, classical statuary, woods, and elaborate Late Baroque fountains dot the slopes of the Guadarrama, permitting hours of wandering. On Wednesday, Saturday, and Sunday evenings in the summer (from 6 to 7, May 1–Sept. 30), the fountains are turned on, one by one, creating one of the most exciting spectacles to be seen in Europe (*see* What to See and Do with Children, *below*). *Tel. 911/47–00–20. Admission: 500 pesetas. Open Oct.–May, Tues.–Sat. 10–1:30 and 3–5, Sun. 10–2; June–Sept., Tues.–Sun. 10–6. Admission to gardens: free. Open daily 10–sunset.*

Another delightful excursion from Segovia is to the villages of Pedraza and Sepúlveda. Head northeast from Segovia on N110, following the northern slopes of the Guadarrama range; after 24 km (15 mi), turn left (north) onto the road marked "Pedraza" and continue for another 10.5 km (6½ mi). Though it has been commercialized and ❾ overprettified in recent years, **Pedraza** is still a striking 16th-century village. Crowning a rocky outcrop and completely encircled by its walls, it is perfectly preserved, with wonderful views of the Guadarrama Mountains. Farther up, at the very top of the tiny village, is a Renaissance castle, which was bought in this century as a private residence by the painter Ignacio Zuloaga. Two sons of the French king Francis I were kept hostage here after the Battle of Pavia, together with their majordomo, the father of the Renaissance poet Pierre de Ronsard. In the center of the village is the attractive main square, irregularly shaped, lined with rustic wooden porticoes, and dominated by a Romanesque bell tower.

❿ **Sepúlveda,** another walled village with a commanding position, lies 24 km (15 mi) to the north of Pedraza. It, too, has a charming main square, but its principal attraction is the 11th-century Church of El Salvador, the highest monument within the walled perimeter. Older than any of Segovia's Romanesque churches, it has a crude but amusing example of the porches that are to be found in later Segovia buildings: The carvings of its oversize capitals, probably the work of a Moorish convert, are purely fantastical and have little to do with Christianity.

① Perhaps the most famous medieval sight in the Segovia area is the **Castillo de Coca** (Castle of Coca), situated near recently planted forests, 52 km (32 mi) northwest of Segovia; it merits a detour between Segovia or Ávila and Valladolid. The shortest approach from Segovia is to take C605 northwest to Santa María la Real de Nieva and then, just beyond the town, turn right and head north for 20½ km (13 mi) on the tiny and poorly surfaced SG341. Built in the 15th century for Archbishop Alonso de Fonseca I, the castle is a turreted structure in plaster and red brick, surrounded by a deep moat. It looks like a stage set for a fairy tale and, indeed, was intended not for any defensive function, but as a place for the notoriously pleasure-loving Archbishop Fonseca to hold riotous parties. The interior, now taken over by a forestry school, can be visited only with special permission (tel. 911/58–60–62). The once-lavish rooms have been modernized, with only fragments of the original decoration preserved.

Tour 2: Ávila and the Sierra de Gredos

② **Ávila** looks wild and slightly sinister in the middle of a windswept plateau littered with giant primeval-looking boulders. Ugly modern development on the outskirts of the town only partially obscures Ávila's intact surrounding **walls.** Though restored in parts, these walls look exactly as they would have in the Middle Ages. Begun in 1090, shortly after the town had been reclaimed from the Moors, they were completed in only nine years—a feat accomplished by the daily employment of an estimated 1,900 men. Featuring nine gates and 88 cylindrical towers bunched closely together, these walls are unique to Spain in form and very unlike the Moorish defense system that the Christians adapted elsewhere. For the most extensive view, cross the Adaja River and walk to a large cross off the Salamanca road.

The walls of Ávila are a telling reflection of the town's importance in the Middle Ages. Populated by Alfonso VI mainly with Christians from Asturias, the town soon came to be known as "Ávila of the Knights," on account of the high proportion of nobles among the inhabitants. Decline set in at the beginning of the 15th century, with the gradual departure of the nobility to the court of Charles V at Toledo. Ávila's fame in later years was due largely to St. Teresa, patroness of Spain (St. James, the apostle, is Spain's male patron saint). Born here in 1515, she spent much of her life in Ávila, leaving a legacy of various convents and the ubiquitous *yemas* (egg-yolk sweets), originally distributed free to the poor, but now sold for high prices to tourists. Ávila today is well preserved, but with a sad, austere, and slightly desolate atmosphere.

Any tour of the town should begin with the **catedral** (cathedral), whose battlemented apse forms the most impressive part of the town's walls. The apse was built mainly in the late 12th century, but the construction of the rest of the cathedral continued until the 18th century. Entering the town gate to the right of the apse, you'll reach the sculpted north portal (originally the west portal until it was moved in 1455 by the architect Juan Guas) by turning left and walking a few steps. The present west portal, flanked by 18th-century towers, is notable for the crude carvings of hairy male figures on each side. These figures, known as "wild men," are often found in Castilian palaces of this period, but are of disputed significance.

The Transitional Gothic interior, with its granite nave, is heavy and austere. The Lisbon earthquake of 1755 deprived the building of its Flemish stained glass, so the main note of color appears in the curious mottled stone in the apse, tinted yellow and red. Exceptionally elaborate Plateresque choir stalls built in 1547 complement the powerful high altar of c. 1504 by the painters Juan de Borgoña and Pedro Berruguete. On the wall of the ambulatory, look for the extraordinary early 16th-century marble sepulcher of Bishop Alonso de Madrigal, a remarkably lifelike representation of the bishop seated at his writing table. Known as "El Tostado" for his swarthy complexion, the bishop was a tiny man of enormous intellect, the author of 54 books. When on one occasion Pope Eugenius IV ordered him to stand—mistakenly thinking him to be still on his knees—the bishop indicated the space between his eyebrows and hairline, retorting, "A man's stature is to be measured from here to here!" *Tel. 918/21– 16–41. Admission: 200 pesetas. Open May–Sept., daily 10–1 and 3:30–7; Oct.–Apr., daily 10–2.*

Outside the walls, a few minutes' walk to the east of the cathedral apse, is the 15th-century **Casa de Deanes** (Dean's House), now a cheerful provincial museum of local archaeology and folklore. *Tel. 918/21–10–03. Admission: 200 pesetas. Open Tues.–Fri. 10–2 and 4:30–7:30.*

Just north of the museum is the Romanesque **Basilica de San Vicente** (Basilica of St. Vincent), a much-venerated church founded on the supposed site where St. Vincent was martyred in 303, together with his sisters Saints Sabina and Cristeta. The west front, shielded by a narthex, has damaged but expressive Romanesque carvings featuring the death of Lazarus and the parable of the rich man's table. The sarcophagus of St. Vincent, surrounded with delicate carvings of this period, forms the centerpiece of the basilica's Romanesque interior; the extraordinary, Oriental-looking canopy that rises over the sarcophagus is a 15th-century addition, paid for by the Knights of Ávila. *Admission: 50 pesetas. Open May–Sept., Tues.–Sun. 10–2 and 4–7; Oct.–Apr., Tues.–Sun. 10–2 and 4–6.*

Reenter the walled town through the splendid gate directly in front of San Vicente and follow the quiet Calle de Lopez Nuñez until you reach the **Capilla de Mosen Rubi.** Try to persuade the nuns in the adjoining convent to let you inside this particularly elegant chapel (c. 1516), illuminated by Renaissance stained glass by Nicolás de Holanda.

Continue parallel to the town's north walls and you will soon come to the parador, housed in one of the austere granite palaces characteristic of old Ávila. One of the ancient stone bulls that the Iberians mysteriously deposited on the Castile landscape occupies the middle of its courtyard. From the gardens of the parador, you can climb up to the town's battlements and walk for 100 m (328 ft) or so along them.

At the bottom of the walls, just above the river, is the small but memorable **Ermita de San Secundo** (Hermitage of St. Secundus). This Romanesque structure, partly hidden by poplars in an enchanting farmyard setting, was founded on the site where the remains of St. Secundus, a follower of St. Peter, were reputedly found. Inside is a realistic and expressive marble monument to the saint, carved by Juan de Juni. *Admission: tip to caretaker in adjoining house. Open any reasonable hour if caretaker is in.*

Return to the old town through **La Puerta del Puente** (the bridge gate) and walk uphill to the Palace of the Counts of Polentinos (now a police station), one of the grandest palaces of 15th-century Ávila. Turn right here and you will come to the **Convento de Santa Teresa,** which was founded in the 17th century on the site of the saint's birthplace. Her famous written account of an ecstatic vision she had, involving an angel piercing her heart, was to influence many Baroque artists, including the Italian Bernini. There are three small museums dedicated to the saint in Ávila alone, one of which is in this convent; you can also see the small and rather gloomy garden where Teresa —the daughter of a noble family of Jewish origin—played as a child. *Admission free. Open daily 9:30–1 and 3:30–7.*

The other two museums are on the outskirts of the city, in the Convento de La Encarnación (due north of the parador) and the Convento de San José, or de Las Madres (due east of the cathedral). The **Convento de la Encarnación** is where the saint first took orders, and where she was to remain based for more than 30 years; its museum has an interesting drawing of the crucifixion by her disciple, St. John of the Cross, and a reconstruction of the cell used by the saint when she was a prioress here. *Admission: 50 pesetas. Open May–Sept., daily 9:30–1 and 4–7; Oct.–Apr., daily 9:30–1:30 and 3:30–6.*

The museum in the **Convento de San José** displays the musical instruments used by the saint and her nuns at Christmas; she herself specialized in percussion. *Admission: 50 pesetas. Open May–Sept., daily 10–1:30 and 4–7; Oct.–Apr., daily 10–1:30 and 4–6.*

On the town's outskirts the chief monument of architectural interest is the **Monasterio de Santo Tomás.** Leave the old town through the Puerta de Santa Teresa (next to the convent of that name), walk east along the walls to the neighboring Puerta de Rastro, and then take the street that descends from here in a southeasterly direction. The monastery's location, a good 10-minute walk from the walls among blackened housing projects, is certainly not where you would expect to find one of the most important religious institutions in Castile. The founders were Ferdinand and Isabella, assisted financially by the notorious Inquisitor-General Tomás de Torquemada, who is buried in the sacristy here; further funds were provided by the confiscated property of converted Jews who fell foul of the Inquisition. Three extensively decorated cloisters, each progressively larger, lead you to the church. Inside, a masterly high altar (c. 1506) by Pedro Berruguete overlooks a delicate and serene marble tomb by the Italian artist Domenico Fancelli. This influential work was one of the earliest examples of the Italian Renaissance style in Spain; it was made for Prince Juan, the only son of Ferdinand and Isabella, who died when only 19 while at Salamanca University. After his burial here, his heartbroken parents found themselves unable to return to the institution that they had founded. In happier times, they had frequently attended Mass in the church, seated in the upper choir behind a balustrade exquisitely carved with their coats of arms; the choir can be reached from the upper part of the Kings' Cloister. *Admission to cloister: 50 pesetas. Admission to Museum of Eastern Art, containing works collected in Dominican missions in Vietnam: 50 pesetas. Open daily 10–1 and 4–7.*

Return to the Puerta de Rastro and walk due north (past the imposing Palacio de Abrantes) to end your tour in the pleasant but distinctly unlively main square (the Plaza de la Victoria). Due east from here is the cathedral, in front of which is the grand 15th-century palace housing the Palacio de Valderrábanos hotel (*see* Dining and Lodging, *below*).

The gaunt Sierra de Gredos, the most dramatic mountain range in Castile, lies just to the south of Ávila and provides in the winter months a majestic snowy backdrop to the town. To approach it, take N110 southwest toward Piedrahita, then turn left at the fork about 5 km (3 mi) onto the small C502. Head south and about 26 km (16 mi), past the village of Mengamuñoz, the road begins to ascend steeply, and its surface rapidly degenerates. You enter a rocky, treeless landscape. After another 15 km (9 mi), there is a turning to the right (west on the C500, which will be marked "Parador"), which will take

⑬ you 12½ km (7¾ mi) to the modern parador at **Navarredonda de Gredos** (*see* Dining and Lodging, *below*), an excellent base for skiing in the winter and hiking excursions in the summer. Back on C502,

⑭ you continue to ascend in a southerly direction to the **Puerto del Pico** (1,352 m/4,435 ft), from which there are extensive views. The route you have taken from Ávila has followed a road dating to Roman times, when it was used for the transport of oil and flour from Ávila in exchange for potatoes and wood. Soon after you descend from the Puerto del Pico, you will see below you a perfectly preserved stretch of the Roman road, zigzagging its way down into the valley and crossing the modern road every now and then. Today it is used by hikers, as well as by shepherds transporting their flocks to lower pastures in early December.

⑮ The medieval town of **Arenas de San Pedro,** farther down the mountain (turn right, or west, of the C501 when you cross it), is surrounded by pretty villages, such as Mombeltrán, Guisando, and Candeleda, with wooden balconies decorated with flowers. A common and colorful sight in Candeleda is wicker baskets with pimiento for sale. Guisando, incidentally, has nothing to do with the famous stone bulls of that name, which are situated 60 km (37 mi) to the east.

If you decide to see the bulls, head back east from Arenas on the

⑯ C501 to **San Martín de Valdeiglesias.** This is a pleasant drive through green and fertile countryside bordered to the north by the southern side of the Gredos range. Just 6 km (3¾ mi) before San Martín, on the right-hand side of the road, is a stone inscription placed in front of a hedge; this records the site where in 1468 Isabella the Catholic was acknowledged as rightful successor to Henry IV by the assembled Castilian nobility. On the other side of the hedge stand the forlorn stone bulls of Guisando, now a symbol of the Spanish Tourist Board. These are just three of many such bulls that once were scattered around the Castilian countryside; probably they marked the frontier of a Celto-Iberian tribe. The three here, in their evocative rustic setting, have an undoubted pathos and power. Return to Ávila by turning left and heading north on N403 from San Martín de Valdeiglesias, a 58-km (36-mi) drive along a winding but well-surfaced road, past a beautifully situated reservoir.

Tour 3: Salamanca and Its Province

Numbers in the margin correspond to points of interest on the Around Madrid and Salamanca maps.

⑰ Approached from Ávila and Madrid, **Salamanca** is first seen rising up on the northern banks of the wide and murky River Tormes. In the foreground is its sturdy 15-arch Roman bridge, while, above this, dominating the view, soars the bulk of the old and new cathedrals. Piercing the skyline to the right is the Renaissance monastery and church of San Esteban, the second most prominent ecclesiastical structure in Salamanca. Behind both San Esteban and the cathedrals, and largely out of sight from the river, extends a stunning

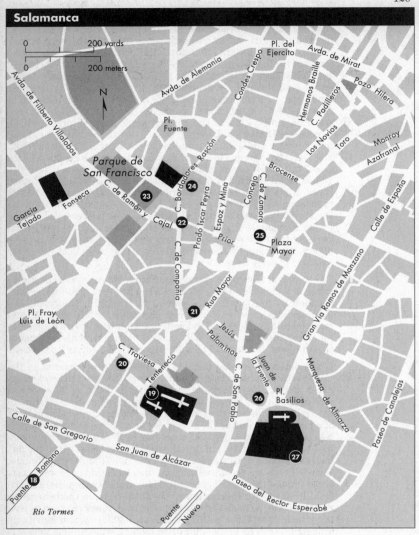

Salamanca

0 — 200 yards
0 — 200 meters

N

Parque de San Francisco

Pl. del Ejercito
Avda. de Mirat
Avda. de Alemania
Condes Crespo
Hermanos Braille
C. Padilleros
Pozo Hilera
Los Novios
Toro
Monroy
Azafranal
Pl. Fuente
C. Bordadores Rascón
Brocense
Avda. de Filiberto Villalobos
Fonseca
C. de Ramón y Cajal
García Tejado
Prado Iscar Peyra
Espoz y Mina
Concejo
C. de Zamora
Calle de España
Prior
Plaza Mayor
C. de Compañia
Rua Mayor
Pl. Fray Luis de León
Jesús
Palominos
Gran Via Ramos de Manzano
C. Traviesa
Tentenecio
C. de San Pablo
Juan de la Fuente
Pl. Basilios
Marquesa de Almarza
Paseo de Canalejas
Calle de San Gregorio
San Juan de Alcázar
Puente Romano
Puente Nuevo
Paseo del Rector Esperabé
Río Tormes

18 19 20 21 22 23 24 25 26 27

Casa de Las Conchas, **21**
Casa de Las Muertes, **24**
Catedral, **19**
Convento de las Dueñas, **26**
Convento de Las Ursulas, **23**
Palacio de Monterrey, **22**
Plaza Mayor, **25**
Puente Romano, **18**
San Esteban, **27**
Universidad, **20**

series of palaces, convents, and university buildings, culminating in the Plaza Mayor, one of the most elegant squares in Spain. Despite considerable damage over the centuries, Salamanca remains one of Spain's greatest cities architecturally and certainly one of the show-pieces of the Spanish Renaissance. The beauty of its buildings is enhanced by the color of the local stone, a soft sandstone that has worn over the centuries to a golden reddish brown.

Already an important settlement in Iberian times, Salamanca was captured by Hannibal in 217 BC and later flourished as a major Roman station on the road between Mérida and Astorga. Converted to Christianity by at least the end of the 6th century, it later passed back and forth between Christians and Moors and began to experience a long period of stability only after the Reconquest of Toledo in 1085. The later importance of the town was due largely to its university, which grew out of a college founded around 1220 by Alfonso IV of León.

Salamanca thrived in the 15th and early 16th centuries, and the number of students in attendance at its university rose to almost 10,000. Its greatest royal benefactor was Isabella the Catholic, who generously financed both the magnificent New Cathedral and the rebuilding of the university. A dual portrait of her and her husband, incorporated into the facade of the main university building, commemorates her patronage.

The other outstanding buildings of Renaissance Salamanca nearly all bear the five-star crest of the all-powerful and everostentatious Fonseca family. Alonso de Fonseca I, the most famous of the Fonsecas, was archbishop first of Santiago and then of Seville; Alonso was also a notorious womanizer and one of the major patrons of the Spanish Renaissance.

Salamanca and its university began to decline in the early 17th century, corrupted by ultraclericalism and devastated by a flood in 1626. Something of the town's former glory was recovered in the 18th century with the construction of the Plaza Mayor by the Churrigueras; natives of Salamanca, they were among the most influential architects of the Spanish Baroque. The town suffered in the Peninsular War of the early 19th century and was damaged by ugly modern development initiated by Franco after the civil war. In compensation, the university has revived in recent years and is again one of the most prestigious in Europe.

18 Both chronologically and in terms of available parking space, the well-preserved **Puente Romano** (Roman Bridge) makes a good starting point for a tour of Salamanca. This is a quiet and evocatively decayed part of town, with a strong rural character. Next to the bridge is an Iberian stone bull, and, opposite the bull, a recent statue commemorating Lazarillo de Tormes, the eponymous young hero of an anonymous 16th-century work that is one of the masterpieces of Spanish literature.

19 In front of the bridge the narrow Tentenecio climbs up steeply toward the **catedral** (cathedral) complex. For a complete tour of the buildings' exterior (an arduous 10-minute walk), take the first street to the right and circle the complex in a counterclockwise direction. Nearest the river stands the **Catedral Vieja** (Old Cathedral), which was built in the late 12th century. It is one of the most interesting examples of the Spanish Romanesque. Because the dome of the crossing tower features strange plumelike ribbing, it is known as the Torre del Gallo (the rooster's tower). The much larger **Catedral Nueva** (New Cathedral) dates mainly from the 16th century, though some parts, including the dome over the crossing and the bell tower attached to the west facade, had to be rebuilt after the Lisbon earthquake of 1755. Work was begun in 1513 under the direction of the distinguished Late Gothic architect Juan Gil de Hontañon. As at Segovia cathedral, Juan's son Rodrigo took over the work after his father's death in 1526. Of the many outstanding architects active in 16th-century Salamanca, Rodrigo Gil de Hontañon left the greatest mark, becoming one of the leading exponents of the Classical Plateresque. The New Cathedral's north facade (where the main entrance is situated) is ornamental enough, but the west facade is dazzling in its sculptural complexity. Try to come here in the late afternoon, when the sun shines directly on it.

The interior of the New Cathedral is as light and harmonious as that of Segovia cathedral, but larger. Furthermore, you are treated to a triumphant Baroque conception designed by the Churrigueras. From a door in the south aisle, steps descend into the Old Cathedral, where boldly carved capitals supporting the vaulting feature a delightful range of foliage, strange animals, and touches of pure fantasy. Then comes the extraordinary crossing of the dome, which seems to owe much to Byzantine architecture: It is a remarkably light structure raised on two tiers of arcaded openings. Not the least of the Old Cathedral's attractions are its furnishings, including many sepulchers of the 12th and 13th centuries and a curved high altar, comprising 53 colorful and delicate scenes by the mid-15th-century artist Nicolás Florentino. In the apse above, Florentino painted an astonishingly fresh Last Judgment fresco.

From the south transept of the Old Cathedral, a door leads into the cloister, which was begun in 1177. From about 1230 until the construction of the main university building in the early 15th century, the chapels around the cloister served as classrooms for the university students. In the chapel of St. Barbara, on the eastern side, theology students answered the grueling questions put to them by their doctoral examiners. The chair in which they sat is still there, directly in front of a recumbent effigy of Bishop Juan Lucero, on whose head the students would place their feet for inspiration. Also attached to the cloister is a small cathedral museum that contains a 15th-century triptych of St. Catherine by Salamanca's greatest native artist, Fernando Gallego. *Admission to New Cathedral free. Admission to Old Cathedral: 200 pesetas. Open daily 10–2 and 4–7.*

20 After seeing the two cathedrals, your next stop should be the main building of the **universidad** (university), the plain back of which faces the New Cathedral's west facade. Its walls, like those of the cathedral and of numerous other structures in Salamanca, are covered with large ocher lettering recording the names of famous university graduates—it is this golden coloring, which seems to glow throughout the city, that you will remember above all things after leaving Salamanca. The earliest names are said to have been written in the blood of the bulls killed celebrating the successful completion of a doctorate. To reach the main facade, walk along the Calle Calderón and then turn right into the enchanting quadrangle known as the **Patio de Las Escuelas** (Schools' Square). The main university building (Escuelas Mayores) is to your right, while adjacent to it, on the southern side of the square, is the Escuelas Menores, which was built in the early 16th century as a secondary school preparing candidates for the university proper. In the middle of the square is a modern statue of the 16th-century poet and philosopher Fray Luis de León, one of the greatest teachers in the history of the university.

The **Escuelas Mayores** dates to 1415, but it was not until more than 100 years later that an unknown architect provided the building with its gloriously elaborate frontispiece, generally acknowledged as one of the finest works of the Classical Plateresque. Immediately above the main door is the famous double portrait of Isabella and Ferdinand, surrounded by ornamentation that makes much play on the yoke-and-arrow heraldic motifs of the two monarchs. The double-eagle crest of Charles V flanked by portraits of the emperor and empress in classical guise dominates the middle layer of the frontispiece. On the highest layer is a panel recently identified as representing Pope Martin V (one of the greatest benefactors of Salamanca University), accompanied by cardinals and university rectors. The whole is crowned by a characteristically elaborate Plateresque balustrade.

The interior of the Escuelas Mayores, which has been drastically restored in parts, comes as a slight disappointment after the splendor of the facade. The fancifully shaped arches of the courtyard (a form peculiar to Salamanca, known as Salamantine) lost some of their charm in a recent glazing. The large classrooms that lie off the courtyard, though medieval in date, have a similarly modern, institutional character. The *aula* (lecture hall) of Fray Luis de León, the place where Cervantes, Calderón de la Barca, and numerous other luminaries of Spain's Golden Age sat, is of particular interest. Here Fray Luis, returning after five years' imprisonment for having translated the Song of Solomon into Spanish, began his lecture, "As I was saying yesterday. . . ."

Your ticket to visit the Escuelas Mayores also permits entrance to the Escuelas Menores nearby. Passing through a gate crowned with the double-eagle crest of Charles V, you'll come to a large green, on the other side of which is a modern building housing a strange and fascinating ceiling fresco of the zodiac, originally in the library of the main university building. This painting, a fragment of a much larger whole, is generally attributed to Fernando Gallego. *Tel. 923/29–44–00, ext. 1150. Admission: 200 pesetas. Open Mon.–Sat. 10–2 and 4–8; Sun. 10–1.*

You might like to pay a quick visit to the **Museo de Salamanca,** on the west side of the Patio de Las Escuelas. Consisting mainly of minor 17th- and 18th-century paintings, it is interesting largely for the 15th-century building, which belonged to the physician to Isabella the Catholic, Alvárez Abarca. *Tel. 923/21–22–35. Admission: 200 pesetas. Open Tues.–Sat. 10–2 and 4–8; Sun. 10–2.*

As you head now toward the Plaza Mayor, numerous distractions **㉑** may slow your progress, beginning with the **Casa de Las Conchas** (House of Shells), which looms in front of you as you walk north from the Patio de Las Escuelas on the Calles Libreros and San Isidro. It was built around 1500 for Dr. Rodrigo Maldonado de Talavera, professor of medicine at the university and a doctor at the court of Isabella. The scallop shell motif was a reference to his recently having been made chancellor of the Order of Santiago, whose symbol is the shell. Among the playful Plateresque details, note the two lions over the main entrance in a fearful tug-of-war with the Talavera crest. The interior has been converted into a public library. You can also visit the elaborate courtyard, which has an upper balustrade carved with virtuoso intricacy in imitation of basketwork. *Tel. 923/26–93–17. Admission free. Open Mon.–Fri. 9–9, Sat. 9–2.*

Turn left at the Casa de Las Conchas and head north along the Calle de Compañía. The next palace that draws attention is at the inter-

22 section of Calle Agustinas. This building, the **Palacio de Monterrey** (Palace of Monterrey), was built after 1538 by Rodrigo Gil de Hontañón for an illegitimate son of Alonso de Fonseca I. Only one of its four wings was completed, but this alone makes the palace one of the most imposing in Salamanca. As in Rodrigo's other palaces in this town, the building is flanked on each side by towers and has an open arcaded gallery running the whole length of the upper level. Such galleries—which, in Italy, you would expect to see on the ground floor of a building—are common features in Spanish Renaissance palaces and were intended as areas where the women of the house could exercise unseen and undisturbed; they also had the advantage of cooling the floor below during the summer months.

You can make an interesting detour from here to the **Colegio de Los Irlandeses** by turning left up the Calle de Ramón y Cajal and then left again past the Monastery of San Francisco (which faces the park of that name). This university college was founded in 1521 by Alonso de Fonseca II and is referred to as the Irish College because it served at one time as an institution for the training of young Irish priests. Today, it is a residence hall for guest lecturers at the university. The surroundings are not attractive; this part of town was the most severely damaged during the Peninsular War and still has a slightly derelict character. The interior of the building, however, is a treat. Immediately inside to the right is an elegant and spacious Late Gothic chapel, while beyond is one of the most classical and genuinely Italianate of Salamanca's many beautiful courtyards; the architect was possibly Diego de Siloe, Spain's answer to Michelangelo. *Tel. 923/21–45–02. Admission: 100 pesetas. Open Tues.–Sun. 10–2 and 4–6.*

Return to the Calle de Compañía along the northern side of the Parque de San Francisco, passing the **Convento de Las Ursulas** (Con- **23** vent of the Ursulines). Archbishop Alonso de Fonseca I lies buried here, in a splendid marble tomb by Diego de Siloe. *Tel. 923/21–98–77. Admission: 100 pesetas. Open daily 10–1 and 4:30–7.*

Facing the apse of the convent church, on the other side of a small square, is the bizarre **Casa de Las Muertes** (House of the Dead). **24** Built in about 1513 for the majordomo of Alonso de Fonseca II, it received its sinister name on account of four small skulls that decorate the facade. Alonso de Fonseca II had them put there to commemorate his recently deceased uncle, the licentious archbishop who lies in the church opposite. For this reason, too, the facade bears a portrait of the archbishop.

The square on which the House of the Dead stands was a favorite haunt of the poet, philosopher, and university rector Miguel de Unamuno, whose statue stands here. At the outbreak of the civil war of 1936–39, Unamuno supported the Nationalists under Franco, but then turned decisively against them. Placed under virtual house arrest, he died in the house adjacent to the House of the Dead in 1938 (plaque). During the Franco period, his statue was frequently daubed red by students, as a symbol that his heart still bled for Spain.

Head down the Calle de Compañía, and you come back to the Monterrey. From here, it is a five-minute walk along Calle Prior to the **25** **Plaza Mayor.** One of the largest squares in Spain, the Plaza Mayor was built in the 1730s by Alberto and Nicolás Churriguera; it is dominated on its northern side by the grandly elegant, pinkish **Ayuntamiento** (Town Hall). Along the square's arcades and in its traffic-free center gather most of Salamantine society.

Time Out The Plaza Mayor and its surroundings offer innumerable possibilities for a leisurely drink, a snack, or a full meal. One of the most popular cafés is on the north side, the **Cafetería Las Torres** (at No. 26), a very large establishment with an enormous array of snacks and pastries.

Leave the Plaza Mayor and walk down the Calle de San Pablo. Halfway down, on your left, you will pass a verdant square, bordered on the northern side by a late-15th-century tower topped by fantastic battlements (the **Torre del Clavero,** built for the *clavero,* or key warden, of the order of Alcántara). To your right is the **Palacio de La Salina,** another Fonseca palace designed by Rodrigo Gil de Hontañón. Try to pop inside to have a glimpse of the courtyard, where you will find a projecting gallery supported by wooden consoles carved with expressive nudes and other dynamic forms.

26 Toward the end of the street, on the left-hand side, is the Dominican **Convento de las Dueñas** (Convent of Las Dueñas). Founded in 1419, it has a 16th-century cloister that is the most fantastically decorated in Salamanca, if not in the whole of Spain. The capitals of its two superimposed Salamantine arcades are crowded with a baffling profusion of grotesques that could absorb you for hours. There is another good reason for visiting this convent: The nuns here make excellent sweets and pastries. *Tel. 923/21–54–42. Admission: 100 pesetas. Open daily 10:30–1 and 4:15–5:30 (until 7 in summer).*

27 Facing Las Dueñas, atop a monumental flight of steps, is the church and monastery of **San Esteban.** The vast size of this building is a measure of its importance in the history of the town: Its monks were among the most enlightened teachers at the university, among the first to take Columbus's ideas seriously (hence his statue in the square below), and helpful in gaining his introduction to Isabella the Catholic. The architecture of San Esteban was the work of one of its monks, Juan de Alava. The door to the right of the west facade leads you into a gloomy cloister with Gothic arcading, interrupted by tall, spindly columns adorned with classical motifs. From the cloister, you enter the church at its eastern end. The interior is unified and uncluttered, but also dark and severe. The one note of color is provided by the sumptuously ornate and gilded high altar of 1692, a Baroque masterpiece by José Churriguera. The most exciting feature of San Esteban, though, is the massive west facade, a thrilling Plateresque work in which sculpted figures and ornamentation are piled up to a height of over 30 m (98 ft). *Tel. 923/21–50–00. Admission: 150 pesetas. Open May–Sept., daily 9–1 and 5–8; Oct.–Apr., daily 9–1 and 4–7.*

From San Esteban, it is a short walk to the river and back to the Roman bridge.

Numbers in the margin correspond to points of interest on the Around Madrid map.

28 The most interesting town in Salamanca province outside the capital is **Ciudad Rodrigo,** which lies 88 km (54 mi) to the west, along N620. Surveying the fertile valley of the River Agueda, Ciudad Rodrigo is entirely surrounded by its medieval walls, within which little has changed over the centuries. This small and surprisingly little-visited town (which makes an excellent overnight stop on the way between Spain and Portugal) has numerous well-preserved palaces and churches.

The **cathedral** is a combination of Romanesque and Transitional Gothic styles, with much fine sculpture. Among its furnishings, the early 16th-century choir stalls by Rodrigo Alemán, elaborately carved with entertaining grotesques, deserve attention. The cloister has carved capitals, and the four cypresses in its center contribute to its tranquillity. Note that the cathedral's outer walls are still scarred by cannonballs fired during the Peninsular War. *Admission: 50 pesetas. Open daily 8–1 and 4–8.*

The town's other chief monument is its sturdy medieval **castillo** (fortress), part of which has been turned into a parador. From here, you can climb the town's battlements.

A half-hour's drive due east of Ciudad Rodrigo on the C515 will take you into wild, mountainous scenery bordering on the once-savage and notoriously poor Extremaduran region of Las Hurdes. Follow C515 for 49 km (30 mi) until you reach the village of El Cabaco, and then head south into the wooded range known as the Sierra de La Peña de Francia (there's only one right turn possible in the village). After 10 km (6 mi), you will come to **La Alberca,** a pretty village full of narrow alleys overhung with wooden balconies supporting a riot of flowers. The place has been overexploited in recent years, and its balcony-lined main square is now almost cloyingly quaint. At La Alberca head east, following signs for **Miranda del Castañar,** a hilltop village of equally excessive prettiness. Farther east still, you hit the C512; turn left, and after a short drive you rejoin C515. Once across the River Alagón, this road climbs in an easterly direction into the wilder Sierra de Béjar, a continuation of the Gredos range. The small medieval town of **Béjar,** 30 km (18 mi) from Miranda del Castañar, makes a good base for skiing and hiking. Southward 4 km (2½ mi) is the village of **Candelario,** singularly attractive if also slightly spoiled, with balconied houses overlooking steep alleys and rushing streams. It is known for its folklore, and some of the older women still wear their hair in a style that could only be described as baroque. The local sausages are excellent; one of the more famous 18th-century tapestries at El Escorial is even entitled *The Sausage-Seller from Candelario.* From Béjar, Salamanca is 70 km (43 mi) north along N630.

Tour 4: Zamora and Toro

The province of Zamora is densely fertile country, divided by the River Duero into two distinct zones, the "land of bread," to the north, and the "land of wine," to the south. The province is of interest, above all, for its Romanesque churches, the finest of which are concentrated in the towns of Zamora and Toro.

Zamora, rising on a bluff above the Duero, is not a conventionally beautiful place, as its many interesting monuments are isolated from one another by ramshackle 19th- and 20th-century development. It does have a lively, old-fashioned character, making it a pleasant stop for a night or two. Calle Santa Clara leads from Avenida Alfonso IX, near the old bus station, to the medieval center of town. On the south side of the Plaza Mayor is the Romanesque **Church of San Juan,** remarkable for its elaborate rose window. *Admission free. Open for Mass only.*

The rest of the square seems to have changed little since the 19th century. North of the Plaza Mayor, at the end of Calle Reina, is one of the surviving medieval gates of the town, and if you turn left here along the Avenida Santa María, you will reach the Romanesque church of that name.

Zamora is famous for its Holy Week celebrations, and next to the Church of Santa María is a hideous modern building housing the **Museo de Pasos,** a museum of the processional sculptures that are paraded around the streets during that week. These works, of relatively recent date, have an appealing provincial quality. You will find, for instance, a Crucifixion group filled with apparently all the real contents of a hardware shop, including bales of rope, a saw, a spade, and numerous nails. *Admission: 300 pesetas adults, 150 pesetas children. Open Mon.–Sat. 11–2 and 4–6 (until 8 in summer).*

From the Church of Santa María, the Calle Carniceros leads west to a large square. Continue west along the Calle Ramos Carrión to the hauntingly attractive cathedral square, situated at the highest and westernmost point of old Zamora. The bulk of the **cathedral** is Romanesque, and the most remarkable feature of the exterior is its dome, which is flanked by turrets, articulated by spiny ribs, and covered in overlapping stones like scales. The dark interior is notable for its early 16th-century choir stalls. The austere late-16th-century cloister has a small museum upstairs, with an intricate *custodia* (monstrance, or receptacle for the Host) by Juan de Arce and some badly displayed but intriguing Flemish tapestries of the 15th and 16th centuries. *Admission: 200 pesetas adults, 100 pesetas children. Open daily 11–2 and 4–6 (until 8 in summer).*

Surrounding the cathedral to the north is an attractive park incorporating the town's much-restored **castle.** The Calle Trascastillo, which descends south from the cathedral to the river, affords views of the fertile countryside to the south and of the town's old Roman bridge. Follow the river east until you reach the bridge and then turn onto Calle del Puente. Shortly, on your left, you will see an amusing 15th-century house with a sculpted rope decorating its facade. Turning north from here, you now climb up to the **parador,** which is located in a Renaissance palace, with excellent views and a patio adorned with classical medallions of mythological and historical personages (*see* Dining and Lodging, *below*). The main entrance to this building overlooks the principal street through old Zamora. Turn east and you will pass to your right the Calle Herreros, a small street lined with 14 bars, most serving good tapas. One street farther on and you will be back at the Plaza Mayor.

㉜ **Toro,** 33 km (20 mi) east of Zamora along N122, stands above a loop of the River Duero and commands particularly extensive views over the vast plain to the south. It, too, was a provincial capital, but was absorbed into Zamora province in 1833, a loss of status that, in some ways, was to its advantage. Zamora developed into a thriving modern town, but Toro slumbered and thus was able to preserve its old appearance. The latter is crowded with Romanesque churches, of which the most important is the **Colegiata,** begun in 1160. The protected west portal (the Portico de La Gloria) has colorfully painted early 13th-century statuary that is perfectly preserved. Famous, too, is its Serbian-Byzantine dome. In the sacristy is an anonymous 15th-century painting of the Virgin: This touching work, in a so-called Hispano-Flemish style, is called *The Virgin of the Fly* because of the fly painted on the Virgin's robe, a most unusual detail. *Admission free, but you'll have to arrange a visit by asking at the tourist office or calling a local association of English-speaking personal guides (tel. 988/52–69–53).*

Tour 5: Valladolid

③ **Valladolid** is a large, dirty, and singularly ugly modern-looking town
in the middle of one of the flattest and dreariest parts of the Castilian countryside. It has one outstanding attraction, however—the
Museo Nacional de Escultura Religiosa (National Museum of Religious Sculpture)—as well as many other interesting sights. It is also
historically one of the most important Spanish towns. Ferdinand
and Isabella were married here, Philip II was born and baptized
here, and Philip III turned the town, for six years, into the capital of
Spain.

To cope with this chaotic city, take a taxi—from the bus station, the
railway station, or wherever you have parked your car—and head
for the National Museum of Religious Sculpture, in the northernmost part of the old town. The late-15th-century Colegio de San
Gregorio in which this museum is housed would alone make a trip to
Valladolid worthwhile. It's a masterpiece of the so-called Isabelline
or Gothic Plateresque, an ornamental style of exceptional intricacy
featuring a plethora of playful, naturalistic detail. The retable facade is especially fantastic, with ribs in the form of pollarded trees,
branches sprouting everywhere, and—to accentuate this forest im-
agery—a row of wild men bearing mighty clubs.

The museum is beautifully arranged in rooms off an elaborate
arcaded courtyard. Its collections do for Spanish sculpture what
those in the Prado do for Spanish painting. The only difference between the museums is that while most people have heard of Velázquez, El Greco, Goya, and Murillo, few know anything about Alonso
de Berruguete, Juan de Juni, and Gregorio Fernández, the three
great names represented here.

Arrows and attendants encourage you to tour the museum in a chro-
nological order, beginning on the ground floor with Alonso de
Berruguete's remarkable sculptures from the dismantled high altar
in the Valladolid church of San Benito (1532). Berruguete, who
trained in Italy under Michelangelo, is the most widely appreciated
of Spain's postmedieval sculptors. He strove for pathos rather than
realism, and his works have an extraordinarily expressive quality.
The San Benito altar was the most important commission of his life,
and fragments in this museum at least allow one to study, at close
hand, his powerful and emotional art. In the museum's elegant chapel (which you normally see at the end of the tour) is a retable by him,
dated 1526, his first known work. On either side of Berruguete's retable kneel gilt bronze figures by the Italian-born Pompeo Leoni,
whose polished and very decorative art is diametrically opposed to
that of Berruguete.

To many critics of Spanish sculpture, decline set in with the late-
16th-century artist Juan de Juni, who used glass for eyes, and pearls
for tears. But to his many admirers, the sculptor's works are intensely exciting; they comprise the highlights of the museum's upper floor. Many of the 16th-, 17th-, and 18th-century sculptures on
this floor were originally paraded around the streets during
Valladolid's celebrated Easter processions; should you ever attend
one of these thrilling pageants, the power of Spanish Baroque sculpture will become evident to you.

Dominating Castilian sculpture of the 17th century was the Gali-
cian-born Gregorio Fernández, in whose works the dividing line between sculpture and theater becomes a tenuous one. Respect for
Fernández has been diminished by the large number of vulgar

imitators that his work has spawned, right up to the present day. At Valladolid you see his art at its very best, and the enormous, dramatic, and very moving sculptural groups that have been assembled in the museum's last series of rooms (on the ground floor near the entrance) form a suitably spectacular climax to this impressive collection. *Calle Cadenas San Gregorio 1, tel. 983/25–03–75. Admission: 200 pesetas. Open Tues.–Sat. 10–2 and 4–6; Sun. 10–2.*

Turn right from the museum and walk toward the Plaza de San Pablo. **Felipe II's birthplace** is the brick mansion on the Plaza at the corner of Calle Angustias. The late-15th-century **Church of San Pablo** has another overwhelmingly elaborate retable facade. The city's **cathedral,** which can be reached by walking the length of the Calle Angustias, is disappointing. Though its foundations were laid in Late Gothic times, the building owes much of its appearance to designs executed in the late 16th century by Juan de Herrera, the architect of the Escorial; further work was carried out by Alberto de Churriguera in the early 18th century, but even so, the building remains only a fraction of its intended size. The altarpiece by Juni is the one bit of color and life in an otherwise cold and intimidatingly severe place. *Tel. 983/30–43–62. Admission: 200 pesetas. Open Tues.–Fri. 10–1:30 and 4:30–7; weekends 10–2.*

Far more appealing is the main **university** building, which stands on the southern side of the verdant space south of the cathedral. The exuberant and dynamic Late Baroque frontispiece is by Narciso Tomé, the creator of the remarkable *Transparente* in the Toledo cathedral (*see* Tour 8, *below*). The Calle Librería will lead you south from this building to the magnificent **Colegio de Santa Cruz,** a large university college begun in 1487 in the Gothic style and completed in 1491 by Lorenzo Vázquez in a tentative and pioneering Renaissance mode; inside is a harmonious courtyard.

Turning west onto Calle del Cardenal Mendoza, you will come to Calle Colón, where you can see the extensively rebuilt house where Columbus died in 1506; within is the excellent **Museo de Colón,** featuring a well-arranged collection of objects, models, and information panels relating to the life and times of the explorer. *Tel. 983/29–13–53. Admission free. Open Tues.–Sat. 10–2 and 4–6; Sun. 10–2.*

A more interesting survival from Spain's Golden Age is the tiny house where the writer Miguel de Cervantes lived from 1603 to 1606, **Casa de Cervantes.** A haven of peace set back from a noisy commercial thoroughfare, this house is far from the other main monuments in town and is best reached by taxi. Furnished in the early 20th century in a pseudo-Renaissance style by the Marquis of Valle-Inclan—the creator of the El Greco Museum in Toledo—it has a cozy, appealing atmosphere. *Calle Rastro s/n, tel. 983/30–88–10. Admission: 200 pesetas. Open Tues.–Sat. 10–3:30, Sun. 10–3.*

Tour 6: East of Madrid: Alcalá de Henares, Guadalajara, Sigüenza, Medinaceli, and Soria

Though off the main tourist routes, the provinces of Guadalajara and Soria have much to offer and, what is more, are—for a change—easily accessible by train. The line from Madrid to Zaragoza passes through all the towns mentioned above, making possible a manageable and interesting excursion of about two to three days. If you travel by car, you can extend this trip by detouring into beautiful, unspoiled countryside.

③④ **Alcalá de Henares** is on the eastern edge of Madrid province, 30 minutes from the capital off the A2/N II (entrances to the town are well-marked on both roads). Its fame in the past was due largely to its university, founded in 1498 by Cardinal Cisneros. In 1836 the university was moved to Madrid, and Alcalá's decline was hastened. The civil war destroyed much of the town's artistic and architectural heritage, and in recent years Alcalá has emerged as a dormitory town of Madrid, with extensive high-rise development. Nevertheless, enough survives of old Alcalá to give a good impression of what it must have been like during its Golden Age heyday.

The town's main monument of interest is its enormous **Universidad Complutense** (university) building, constructed between 1537 and 1553 by the great Rodrigo Gil de Hontañón. Though it is one of the earliest and most important examples in Spain of a building in an Italian Renaissance style, most Italian architects of the time would probably have had a fit had they seen its principal facade. The use of the classical order is all wrong, the main block is out of line with the two that flank it, and the whole is crowned by a heavy and elaborate gallery. All this is typically Spanish, as is the prominence given to the massive crest of Cardinal Cisneros and to the ironwork, both of which form an integral part of the powerful overall design. Inside are three patios, of which the most impressive is the first, comprising three superimposed arcades. A guided tour of the interior will take you to a delightfully decorated room where exams were once held and to the chapel of San Ildefonso, with its richly sculpted Renaissance mausoleum of Cardinal Cisneros. *Plaza San Diego s/n. Admission: 150 pesetas (free to citizens of EC countries). Open May–Sept., Tues.–Sun. 11–2 and 5–8; Oct.–Apr., Tues.–Sun. 11–2 and 4–7.*

On one side of the university square is the **Convento de San Diego,** where Clarissan nuns make and sell the *almendras garrapiñadas* (caramelized almonds) that are a specialty of the town. The other side adjoins the large and arcaded **Plaza de Cervantes,** the animated center of Alcalá. Off this runs the arcaded Calle Mayor, which still has much of the appearance that it had in the 16th and 17th centuries.

Miguel de Cervantes y Saavedra was born in a house on this street in 1547; a charming replica, **Casa de Cervantes,** built in 1955, contains a small Cervantes museum. *Mayor 48. Admission free. Open Tues.–Fri. 10–2 and 4–7; weekends 10–2.*

③⑤ **Guadalajara,** 17 km (10 mi) east of Alcalá on N II, is a provincial capital that was severely damaged in the civil war of 1936–39. The **Palacio del Infantado,** built between 1461 and 1492 by Juan Guas, is one of the most important palaces of its period in Spain, a bizarre and potent mix of Gothic, classical, and Mudéjar influences. The main facade is rich, the lower floors studded throughout with diamond shapes, and the whole crowned by a complex Gothic gallery supported on a frieze pitted with intricate Moorish cellular work (honeycomb motif). Inside is a fanciful and exciting courtyard, though little else, the magnificent Renaissance frescoes that once covered all the palace's rooms having largely been obliterated in the civil war. On the ground floor is a modest provincial art gallery. *Admission: 100 pesetas. Open Tues.–Sat. 10–2 and 4–7; Sun. 10–2.*

East of Guadalajara extends the Alcarria, an area of high plateau intercut with rivers forming verdant valleys. It was made famous in the 1950s by one of the great classics of Spanish travel literature, Camilo José Cela's *Journey to the Alcarria.* Cela evoked the backwardness and remoteness of an area barely an hour away from Madrid. Even today, despite growing numbers of day-trippers, you can feel far removed from the modern world here. **Pastrana,** 42 km (26 mi) southeast of Guadalajara on C200 (south from N320), is high on a hill, its narrow, secretive lanes merging into the landscape. It is a pretty village of Roman origin, once the capital of a small duchy. The tiny museum (admission: 125 pesetas; open weekends only 1–3 and 4–6) attached to its Collegiate Church displays a glorious series of Gothic tapestries. The village of **Brihuega** has kept its medieval fortifications and a castle dating to Moorish times. From Guadalajara, continue northeast on N II and turn right at Torija (22 km/13 mi); Brihuega lies 15 km (9 mi) to the east.

The next major stop on the journey east from Madrid is **Sigüenza,** one of the most beautiful of all the Castilian towns. From the Brihuega turning, continue east along N II for another 30 km (18 mi), and then head due north along C204 for 26 km (16 mi). The journey by train between Guadalajara and Sigüenza is beautiful, following as it does the narrow, poplarlined valley of the River Henares. An attractive shaded promenade leads from the station up the hill on which this small town lies. Halfway up the hill, turn left onto the Calle del Cardenal Mendoza, and you will come soon to Sigüenza's remarkable **cathedral.** Begun around 1150 and not completed until the early 16th century, the building presents an anthology of Spanish architecture from the Romanesque period to the Renaissance. The sturdy west front has a forbidding, fortresslike appearance, and your first impression of the interior might well be one of austere Romanesque gloom. It contains, however, a wealth of ornamental and artistic masterpieces. Go directly to the sacristan (the Sacristy is at the north end of the ambulatory) for an informative guided tour of the building; he will turn on lights and unlock doors for you. The Sacristy is an outstanding Renaissance structure, covered in a barrel vault designed by the great Alonso de Covarrubias; its coffering is studded with hundreds of portrait heads, which stare at you disarmingly. The tour will take you, among other places, into the Late Gothic cloister, off which is situated a room lined with Flemish 17th-century tapestries. You will also have illuminated for you the ornate late-15th-century sepulcher of Dom Fadrique of Portugal (in the north transept), an early example of the Classical Plateresque. The cathedral's high point is the Chapel of the Doncel (to the right of the sanctuary), in which is to be found the most celebrated of Spain's funerary monuments, the tomb of Don Martín Vázquez de Arca. It was commissioned by Isabella the Catholic, to whom Don Martín served as *doncel* (page) before dying young at the gates of Granada in 1486. The reclining Don Martín is portrayed in a most lifelike way, an open book in his hands and a wistful melancholy in his eyes. More than a memorial to an individual, this tomb, with its surrounding Late Gothic foliage and tiny mourners, is like an epitaph of the Age of Chivalry, a final flowering of the Gothic spirit. *Admission: 150 pesetas. Open daily 11:30–2:30 and 4–6.*

Adjacent to the cathedral's west facade, in a refurbished early 19th-century house, is the **Museo Diocesano de Arte Sacro** (Diocesan Art Museum), with a prehistoric section and much religious art from the 12th to the 18th century, including an outstanding painting by Zurbarán. *Admission: 50 pesetas. Open Tues.–Sun. 11:30–2 and 3–7:30 (4–8:30 in summer).*

The south side of the cathedral overlooks the arcaded Plaza Mayor, a harmonious Renaissance square commissioned by Cardinal Mendoza. By now you will have entered a virtually intact Old Quarter, full of small palaces and cobbled alleys. Walk the length of the square and continue uphill along the Calle Mayor, past the palace that belonged to the doncel's family. At the top is the **castle,** founded by the Romans but rebuilt at various later periods; most of the present structure was put up in the 14th century, when it was transformed into a residence for the queen of Castile, Doña Blanca de Borbón, who was banished here by her husband, Peter the Cruel. This enchanting castle, above Sigüenza and overlooking wild, hilly countryside, is now a parador (*see* Dining and Lodging, *below*).

Continuing toward Soria, take C114 east to Alcolea del Pinar (20 km/ 12 mi), where you will rejoin N II. Your first stop within Soria province should be **Medinaceli,** 19 km (12 mi) farther on. The original village of Medinaceli commands an exhilarating position on top of a long, steep ridge and can be reached from the train station by a sharply winding 2-km (1-mi) side road or by a more direct but arduous footpath (an exhausting 20minute walk). Dominating the skyline is a Roman triumphal arch of the 2nd or 3rd century AD, the only triple archway of this period to survive in Spain. (The arch's silhouette is now featured in signposts to national monuments throughout the country.) The surrounding village, once the seat of one of Spain's most powerful dukes, had virtually been abandoned by its inhabitants by the end of the 19th century, and if you come here during the week, you will find yourself in almost a ghost town. Numerous Madrileños have weekend houses here, and there are also various Americans in part-time residence. It is undeniably beautiful, with extensive views, picturesquely overgrown houses, and unpaved lanes leading directly into wild countryside. The former palace of the dukes of Medinaceli is currently undergoing restoration, and Roman excavations are also being carried out in one of the squares.

The town of **Soria** lies 74 km (46 mi) north of Medinaceli on N III. This provincial capital, which has prospered for centuries as a center of sheep farming, has been spoiled by modern development and is frequently beset by biting cold winds. Yet its situation in the wooded valley of the Duero is splendid, and it has a number of fascinating Romanesque buildings. The main roads to Soria converge onto the wide modern promenade called El Espolón, where you will find the **Museo Numantino,** a collection of local archaeological finds that was founded in 1919. A large postmodern structure has recently been built for it, which opened in September 1989. Few other museums in Spain are laid out quite as well or as spaciously as this; the collections are rich in prehistoric and Iberian finds, and there is one section—on the top floor—dedicated to the important Iberian/Roman settlement at nearby Numantia (*see below*). Tel. 975/22–13–97. *Admission: 200 pesetas. Open May–Sept., Tues.–Sat. 10–2 and 5–9, Sun. 10–2; Oct.–Apr., Tues.–Sat. 9:30–6:30, Sun. 10–2.*

Soria has strong connections with Antonio Machado, Spain's most popular 20th-century poet after García Lorca. From the eastern end of the Espolón, follow the pedestrian Calle Marqués de Vadillo to the Plaza San Esteban; to the right is the fine Romanesque church of **San Juan de Ribanera,** but turn left instead, to reach (at the junction of Calles La Aduana Vieja and Instituto) the **school** where Machado taught from 1909 to 1911. A large bronze head of the poet is set outside the building, and, in the room where he taught (now called the Aula Machado), there's a tiny collection of memorabilia relating to him. The Seville-born poet lived a bohemian life in Paris for many years, but returned to Spain and became a French teacher at Soria. Here he fell in love with and married the 16-year-old daughter of his landlady. When she died only two years later, the heartbroken poet felt he could no longer stay in this town so full of her memories. He moved on to Baeza in his native Andalucía, and then went to Segovia, where he spent his last years in Spain (he died early in the civil war, shortly after escaping to France). His most successful work, the *Campos de Castilla*, was greatly inspired by Soria and by his dead wife, Leonor; the town and this woman both haunted him until his death.

At the top of the Calle Aduana Vieja is the late-12th-century church of **San Domingo**, with its richly carved Romanesque west facade. Turn right down the Calle Estudios, on the left of which is the imposing 16th-century palace of the counts of Gomara (now a law court). Calle Estudios will take you to Calle Collado, which ends in the uninspiring Plaza Mayor. Walking down the ugly Calle Real toward the River Duero, you pass between two hills, the one to the south dominated by the parador Antonio Machado (*see* Dining and Lodging, *below*), which stands in a park that also contains the ruins of the town's castle. Machado loved the views of the town and valley from this hill. Calle de Santiago, which leads to the parador, passes on its way the church and cemetery of El Espino, where Leonor is buried. Just before the river stands the **catedral** (cathedral)—a Late Gothic hall church attached to a large Romanesque cloister.

On the other side of the river, you are virtually in open countryside. To the left of the bridge, in a wooded setting overlooking the river, is the deconsecrated church of **San Juan de Duero**, once the property of the Knights Hospitalers. Outside the church are the curious ruins of a Romanesque cloister, featuring a rare Spanish example of interlaced arching; the church itself, now looked after by the Museo Numantino, is a small, didactic museum of Romanesque art and architecture. *Admission: 200 pesetas. Open Apr.–Oct., Tues.–Sat. 10–2 and 4–6, Sun. 10–2; Nov.–Mar., Tues.–Sat. 10:30–2 and 3:30–6, Sun. 10:30–2.*

It is an evocative half-hour walk along the Duero to the **Ermita de San Saturio.** Return to the bridge and follow the Zaragoza road until it turns away from the river. From here, a riverside path (accessible by car) lined by poplars leads to the hermitage, which was built above a cave where the Anchorite San Saturius fasted and prayed. Entering the cave, you can climb up to the 18th-century hermitage. *Admission free. Open daily 10–2 and 4–sundown.*

Seven km (4 mi) north of Soria, off the Logroño road and accessible only by car, are the bleak hilltop ruins of **Numantia,** an important Iberian settlement, which was viciously besieged by the Romans in 135–134 BC; the inhabitants chose death rather than surrender. Most of the foundations that have been unearthed are from the time of the Roman occupation. *Admission: 200 pesetas. Open Apr.–Oct., Tues.–Sat. 10–2 and 4–7, Sun. 10–2; Nov.–Mar., Tues.–Sat. 10:30–1:30 and 3:30–6, Sun. 10:30–2.*

The N122 back to Madrid passes through **El Burgo de Osma,** 56 km (35 mi) west of Soria. This village is a virtually intact medieval and Renaissance town, dominated by a Gothic cathedral and a Baroque bell tower. Thirteen km (8 mi) farther west, turn south onto N110, and join N I after 71 km (44 mi); from this point, it is 98 km (61 mi) to Madrid.

Tour 7: Cuenca

Situated in wild and rocky countryside intercut with dramatic gorges, **Cuenca** offers a haunting atmosphere and outstanding cuisine. Arriving either by bus or by train, you reach the old town by heading due north along the Calle Ramón y Cajal until you come to a small bridge crossing the narrow River Huécar. On the other side of the river, the old town rises steeply, hugging a spine of rock thrust up between the gorges of the Huécar and the Júcar and bordered on two sides by sheer precipices, over which plunges the odd hawk or eagle. The lower half of the old town is a maze of tiny streets, any of which will take you up to the Plaza del Carmen. From here the town narrows, and just a single street, the Calle Alfonso VIII, continues the ascent up to the Plaza Mayor, which you reach after passing under the arch of the Town Hall.

You have still some way to climb before reaching the very top of the town, but from this point onward, all is sheer enchantment. Walk up the central Calle San Pedro and take the first alley to your left, which will lead you to the tiny **Plaza San Nicolás,** a picturesquely dilapidated square clinging to the western edge of the town. Continue from here along the unpaved Ronda del Júcar, which hovers over the Júcar gorge and commands remarkable views over the mountainous landscape. The best views of all are from the square in front of the **castle,** at the very top of Cuenca, where the town tapers out to the narrowest of ledges. Gorges are on each side of you, while directly in front, old houses sweep down toward a distant plateau. The castle itself, which for many years served as the town prison, is expected to open as a parador by 1994. Inquire at the tourist office for more information.

Return to the Plaza Mayor by following the Calle de Julian Romero, a street hung over the town's eastern precipice. Back at the Plaza Mayor, take the Calle Obispo Valero, which skirts the southern side of the undistinguished cathedral, and follow signs pointing toward the Casas Colgadas. Halfway down on the left, in what were formerly the cellars of the Bishop's Palace, a **Museo Diocesano de Arte Sacro** (Diocesan Museum of Sacred Art) has recently been installed; in its beautifully clear display you will find a jewel-encrusted Byzantine diptych of the 13th century, a Crucifixion by the 15th-century Flemish artist Gerard David, and two small El Grecos. *Tel. 966/21–20–11. Admission: 150 pesetas. Open Tues.–Sat. 11–2 and 4–6, Sun. 11–2.*

At the bottom of the street is one of the finest and most curious of Spain's museums, housed in the most famous of Cuenca's buildings, the **Casas Colgadas** (Hanging Houses). This group of joined houses, literally projecting over the town's eastern precipice, originally formed a 15th-century palace; later they served as a town hall, before falling into disuse and decay in the 19th century. During the restoration campaign of 1927, the cantilevered balconies that had once hung over the gorge were rebuilt. Finally, in 1966, the painter Fernando Zóbel decided to create inside them the first museum in the world devoted exclusively to abstract art. The works he gathered are almost all by the remarkable generation of Spanish abstract artists who grew up in the 1950s and were forced to live abroad. The major names include Carlos Saura, Eduardo Chillida, Muñoz, Millares, Antoni Tàpies, and Zóbel. Even if you have had no previous interest in abstract art, this museum is likely to win you over, with its honeycomb of dazzlingly white rooms and vistas of sky and gorge.

Admission: 200 pesetas. Open Tues.–Fri. 11–2 and 4–6, Sat. 11–2 and 4–8, Sun. 11–2:30.

From the museum, you can walk down to the Puente de San Pablo, an iron footbridge built over the Huécar gorge in 1903 for the convenience of the Dominican monks of San Pablo, who live on the other side. If you have a head for heights, cross the narrow bridge, with its vertiginous view down to the river below and equally thrilling panorama of the Casas Colgadas. A path from the bridge descends to the bottom of the gorge, landing you by the bridge that you crossed to enter the old town.

The most popular car excursion from Cuenca is to the **Ciudad Encantada** (Enchanted City). (Drive north for 30 km/18 mi along CU991, then turn right, following signs, and continue 5 km/3 mi.) The so-called city comprises a series of large and fantastic rock formations erupting in a landscape of pines.

42 South of Cuenca (69 km on N320, then right onto N111) is the village of **Alarcón,** also situated on the River Júcar. This fortified village on the edge of the great plains of La Mancha stands impressively on a high spur of land encircled almost entirely by a bend of the river. The principal monument is its **castle,** which dates to Visigothic times; in the 14th century it came into the hands of the infante Don Juan Manuel, who wrote a collection of moral tales that rank among the great treasures of Spanish medieval literature. The castle is today one of the finest of Spain's paradors (*see* Dining and Lodging, below).

Tour 8: South of Madrid: Aranjuez and Toledo

Toledo can be reached by bus or car from Madrid on N401 in just under an hour. With a slightly longer drive by way of N IV/A4, you can
43 break your journey at **Aranjuez,** an oasis in the middle of the parched Castilian plateau. Once the site of a Habsburg hunting lodge on the banks of the Tajo, Aranjuez became in the 18th century a favorite summer residence of the Bourbons, who constructed a large palace and other buildings, created extensive gardens, and planted woods; in the following century, it developed into a popular retreat for the people of Madrid. Today, the spaciously and regularly laid-out small town that grew up in the vicinity of the palace retains a faded elegance. The **Palacio Real** (Royal Palace) itself reflects French grandeur. The high point of the sumptuous interior is a room covered entirely with porcelain; there are also numerous elaborate clocks and a good museum of costume. Shaded riverside gardens, full of statuary and fountains, afford pleasant relaxation after the palace tour. *Tel. 91/891–0740. Admission: 500 pesetas. Open May–Sept., Tues.–Sun. 10–6:30; Oct.–Apr., Tues.–Sun. 10–5:30. Admission to gardens free. Open May–Sept., daily 8–6:30; Oct.–Apr., daily 8–8:30.*

The charming **Casa del Labrador** (Farmer's Cottage), a small and intimate palace at the eastern end of Aranjuez, built by Carlos IV in 1804, has a jewellike interior bursting with color and crowded with delicate objects. Between the Royal Palace and the Casa del Labrador is the **Casa de Marinos:** (Sailors' House), where you will see a gondola that belonged to Felipe V and other plushly decorated pleasure boats that once plied the river. *Admission to Casa del Labrador and Casa de Marinos: 500 pesetas. Open May–Sept., Tues.–Sun. 10–6:30; Oct.– Apr., Tues.–Sun. 10–5:30; closed Mon.*

44 The contrast between Aranjuez and nearby **Toledo** could hardly be more marked. From the sensuous surroundings and French-style elegance of the former, you move to a place of drama and austerity, tinged with mysticism, that was long the spiritual and intellectual capital of Spain. No matter which route you take from Madrid, your first glimpse of Toledo will be of its northern gates and battlements rising up on a massive granite escarpment. The flat countryside comes to an end, and a steep range of ocher-colored hills rises on each side of the city.

Numbers in the margin correspond to points of interest on the Toledo map.

At the main northern gate of Toledo—the sturdy, freestanding **45** **Puerta de Bisagra**—turn right to the large traffic circle called the Plaza de Alfonso VI. Follow the walls around to the west, cross a modern bridge, and then turn left onto the Carretera de Circunvalación. It slowly climbs up the brush-covered southern slopes of the gorge, passing the occasional villa. Almost immediate- **46** ly to your left is the **Puente de San Martín**, a pedestrian bridge dating to 1203 and featuring splendid horseshoe arches. High above this, and the most prominent monument in western Toledo, is the late-15th-century church of **San Juan de los Reyes**. A much better and more extensive view of Toledo is to be had from the eastern end of the gorge. Continue driving along the Circunvalación, passing below the modern parador (*see* Dining and Lodging, *below*), and you will eventually come to a belvedere where you can park your car (except in the middle of the day, when buses line up) and look down over almost all the main monuments of Toledo.

The rock on which Toledo stands was inhabited as far back as prehistoric times, and there was already an important Iberian settlement here when the Romans came in 192 BC. On the highest point of the rock—on which now stands the Alcázar, the dominant building on the Toledo skyline—the Romans built a large fort, and this was later remodeled by the Visigoths, who had, by the middle of the 6th century AD, transformed the town into their capital. In the early 8th century, the Moors arrived.

During their occupation of Toledo, the Moors furthered its reputation as a great center of learning and religion. Enormous tolerance was shown toward those who continued to practice Christianity (the so-called Mozarabs), as well as to the town's exceptionally large Jewish population. Today, the Moorish legacy is evident in the strong crafts tradition here, in the mazelike arrangement of the streets, and in the predominance of brick rather than stone. To the Moors, beauty was a quality to be found within and not to be shown on the surface, and it is significant that even the cathedral of Toledo—one of the most richly endowed in the whole of Spain—is difficult to see from the outside, being largely obscured by the warren of houses that surrounds it. Long after the departure of the Moors, Toledo remained secretive, its life and treasures hidden behind closed doors and austere facades.

Alfonso VI, aided by El Cid, captured Toledo in 1085 and styled himself "Emperor of Toledo." Under the Christians, the strong intellectual life of the town was maintained, and Toledo became famous for its school of translators, who spread to the West a knowledge of Arab medicine, law, culture, and philosophy. Religious tolerance continued, and during the rule of Peter the Cruel (so named because he allegedly had members of his own family murdered to advance himself), a Jewish banker, Samuel Levi, became royal treasurer and

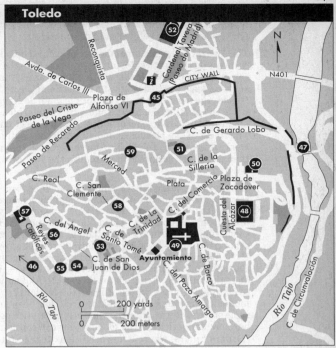

one of the wealthiest and most important men in town. By the early 15th century, however, hostility toward both Jews and Arabs grew as Toledo developed more and more into a bastion of the Catholic Church.

As Florence had the Medici and Rome the papacy, so Toledo had its long and distinguished line of cardinals, most notably Mendoza, Tavera, and Cisneros. Under these great patrons of the arts, Renaissance Toledo emerged as a center of humanism. Economically and politically, however, Toledo had already begun to decline in the 16th century. The expulsion of the Jews from Spain in 1492 had particularly serious economic consequences for Toledo, the decision in 1561 to make Madrid the permanent center of the Spanish court led to the town's loss of political importance, and the expulsion from Spain of the converted Arabs (Moriscos) in 1601 resulted in the departure of most of Toledo's celebrated artisan community. The years the painter El Greco spent in Toledo—from 1572 to his death in 1614—were those of the town's decline. Its transformation into a major tourist center started in the late 19th century, when the works of El Greco came to be widely appreciated after years of neglect. Today, Toledo is prosperous and conservative, high priced, silent at night, and closed in atmosphere. Yet Spain has no other town of this size with such a concentration of major monuments and works of art.

Leaving the belvedere and continuing around the gorge in a counterclockwise direction, you pass on your left the **Puente de Alcántara,** the oldest of the town's bridges, of Roman origin. On your right is a heavily restored castle built after the Christian capture of 1085, and above this stands a vast and depressingly austere military academy, a typical example of Fascist architecture under

Franco. The Circunvalación will deposit you back at the Puerta de Bisagra. Toledo's maze of narrow streets was not made for cars; park either at your hotel or outside the walls.

48 The **Alcázar** is the monument with the earliest opening time. The entrance is on the north side, but to get there from the Cuesta del Alcázar (the street that leads up to the Alcázar from Toledo's main square), you have to do almost a full circle of the building. The south facade, the most severe, is the work of Juan de Herrera, of Escorial fame; the east facade, meanwhile, gives a good idea of the building's medieval appearance, incorporating a large section of battlements. The finest of the facades is undoubtedly the northern, one of many works executed in Toledo by Alonso de Covarrubias, who did more than any other architect to introduce the Renaissance style to this town.

Within the building is both a military headquarters and a large military museum—one of Spain's few remaining homages to Francoism, hung with tributes from various right-wing military groups and figures from around the world. Architecturally, its highlight is Covarrubias's harmonious Italianate courtyard, which, like most other parts of the building, was largely rebuilt after the civil war of 1936–39, when the Alcázar was besieged by the Republicans. Though the Nationalists' ranks were depleted, they managed to hold on to the building. Franco later turned the Alcázar into a monument to Nationalist bravery; the office of the Nationalist general who defended the building, General Moscardó, has been left in exactly the same state as it was after the war, complete with peeling ceiling paper and mortar holes. The gloomy tour can continue with a visit to the dark cellars, where living conditions at the time of the siege are evoked.

More cheerful is a ground-floor room full of beautifully crafted swords, a Toledan specialty introduced by the Moorish silver workers. At the top of the grand staircase, which apparently made even Carlos V "feel like an emperor," are rooms displaying a vast collection of toy soldiers. *Tel. 925/22–30–38. Admission: 125 pesetas. May–Sept., Tues.–Sun. 9:30–1:30 and 4–6:30; Oct.–Apr., Tues.–Sun. 9:30–1:30 and 4–5:30.*

49 From opposite the southwestern corner of the Alcázar, a series of alleys descends to the east end of the **catedral** (cathedral), affording good views of the cathedral tower. Make your way around the southern side of the building, passing the mid-15th-century **Puerta de los Leones,** with magnificently detailed and realistic carvings by artists of northern descent. Emerging into the small square in front of the cathedral's west facade, you will see to your right the elegant **Ayuntamiento,** begun by the young Herrera and completed by El Greco's son, Jorge Manuel Theotokópoulos. Jorge Manuel was also responsible for the cathedral's Mozarabic chapel, the elongated dome of which crowns the right-hand side of the west facade; the rest of this facade is mainly of the early 15th century and features as its centerpiece a representation of the Virgin presenting her robe to Toledo's patron saint, the Visigothic Ildefonsus.

Enter the cathedral from the 14th-century cloisters to the left of the west facade. The primarily 13th-century architecture is inspired by the great Gothic cathedrals of France, such as Chartres; the squat proportions, however, give it a Spanish feel, as do the wealth and heaviness of the furnishings and the location of the elaborate choir in the center of the nave. Immediately to your right as you enter the building is a beautifully carved Plateresque doorway by Covarrubias, marking the entrance to the Treasury. The latter houses a small Crucifixion by the Italian painter Cimabue and an extraordinarily intricate late-15th-century monstrance by Juan del Arfe, a silversmith of German descent; the ceiling is an excellent example of Mudéjar workmanship.

From here, walk around to the ambulatory, off the right-hand side of which is a chapter house featuring a strange and quintessentially Spanish mixture of Italianate frescoes by Juan de Borgoña. In the middle of the ambulatory is a dazzling and famous example of Baroque illusionism by Narciso Tomé, known as the *Transparente*, a blend of painting, stucco, and sculpture.

Finally, off the northern end of the ambulatory, you will come to the sacristy, where a number of El Grecos are to be found, most notably the work known as *El Espolio* (Christ being stripped of his raiment). One of El Greco's earliest works in Toledo, it fell foul of the pedantic Inquisition, which accused the artist of putting Christ on a lower level than some of the onlookers. El Greco was thrown into prison, and there his career might have ended had he not by this stage formed friendships with some of the more enlightened clergy of the town. Before leaving the sacristy, look up at the colorful and spirited Late Baroque ceiling painting by the Italian Luca Giordano. *Admission: 350 pesetas. Open Tues.–Sat. 10:30–1 and 3:30–6 (until 7 in summer), Sun. 10:30–1:30 and 4–6.*

On leaving the cathedral, turn right outside the cloister's entrance and then turn right again. You will find yourself on the Calle del Comercio, the town's narrow and lively pedestrian thoroughfare, lined with bars and shops and shaded in the summer months by awnings suspended from the roofs of tall houses. The street ends in the Plaza Zocodover, the town's main square, built in the early 17th century as part of an unsuccessful attempt to impose a rigid geometry on the town's chaotic Moorish ground plan.

Time Out On the south side of the square, and on the narrow street leading off the middle of it, are numerous bars, cafés, and modest restaurants. Those on the square—one of which features in Luis Buñuel's movie *Tristana*—have chairs and tables outside.

⑤⓪ Next, you can visit the **Museo de la Santa Cruz,** which can be reached from Plaza de Zocodover by going through the Moorish arch on the square's eastern side and descending a few steps. One of the joys of this museum is that it is housed in a beautiful Renaissance hospital with a stunning classical Plateresque facade. Unlike the other monuments in town, the museum is open all day without a break and in the early hours of the afternoon is delightfully quiet. The light and elegant interior has changed little since the 16th century, the main difference being that works of art have replaced the hospital beds. Look for the paintings by El Greco on the upper floor—in particular, the *Assumption* of 1613, the artist's last known work. A small **Museo de Arqueología** has been arranged in and around the hospital's delightful cloister, off which a beautifully decorated staircase by Alonso de Covarrubias can also be found. *Tel. 925/22–10–36. Admission: 200 pesetas. Open Tues.–Sat. 10–6:30, Sun. 10–2, Mon. 10–2 and 4:30–6:30.*

Back on the Plaza de Zocodover, cross to the western side of the square and enter the Calle de la Sillería. The third main turn to your **⑤①** right, the Cuesta del Cristo de la Luz, will take you to the **Capilla del Cristo de la Luz** (Chapel of Christ of the Light), which lies behind railings in a small park above the town's northern ramparts. The gardener will open the gate for you and show you around, but in case he is not there, inquire at the house opposite. The exposed chapel was originally a tiny Visigothic church, transformed into a mosque during the Moorish occupation; the arches and vaulting of the mosque survive, making this the most important relic of Moorish Toledo. The story behind the chapel's name is that the horse of Alfonso VI, who was riding in triumph into Toledo in 1085, knelt in front of the building; it was then discovered that behind the masonry was a candle that had burned continuously throughout the time that the Infidels had been in power. The first Mass of the Reconquest was said here, and later a Mudéjar apse was added (now shielded by glass). After you have looked at the chapel, the gardener will take you across the ramparts to climb to the top of the Puerta del Sol, a 12th-century Mudéjar gatehouse. *Admission: tip to gardener. Open any reasonable hour.*

Walking outside the walls and passing through Covarrubias's imposing Puerta de Bisagra, you will come to a long and slightly decayed square, the Paseo de Merchán, dominated at its northern end

52 by the **Hospital de Tavera,** Covarrubias's last work. Unlike the Hospital of Santa Cruz, this complex is unfinished and slightly dilapidated. It is nonetheless full of character and has an evocatively ramshackle museum in its southern wing, looked after by two exceptionally friendly and eccentric women. The most important work in the museum's miscellaneous collection is a painting by the 17th-century artist José Ribera. In the hospital's monumental chapel is the *Baptism of Christ* by El Greco and the exquisitely carved marble tomb of Cardinal Tavera, the last work of Alonso de Berruguete. Descend into the crypt to experience some bizarre acoustical effects. *Tel. 925/22–04–51. Admission to hospital: 300 pesetas; admission to adjoining church: 500 pesetas. Open daily 10:30–1:30 and 3:30–6.*

53 El Greco's most famous painting can be found in the church of **Santo Tomé;** ideally, you should get here as soon as it opens in the morning, for later on in the day, especially in the summer months, you may well have to wait in line to get inside. To walk to the chapel from the cathedral, head west along the Calle de la Trinidad and join the Calle de Santo Tomé. The church is on the left-hand side, adorned by an elegant Mudéjar tower. The entrance to the specially built chapel housing El Greco's *Burial of Count Orgaz* is on the other side of the building and can be reached by turning left down the Travesía de Santo José, and then left again. The painting—the only one by the artist to have been consistently admired over the centuries—portrays the benefactor of the church being buried with the posthumous assistance of St. Augustine and St. Stephen, who miraculously appeared at the funeral to thank him for all the money he had given to religious institutions named after them. Though the count's burial took place in the 14th century, El Greco painted the onlookers in contemporary costumes and included people he knew; the boy in the foreground is one of El Greco's sons, while the sixth figure on the left is said to be the artist himself. *Admission: 100 pesetas. Open Oct.–Apr., daily 10–1:45 and 3:30–5:45; May–Sept., daily 10–1:45 and 3:30–6:45.*

You are now in the tourist heart of Toledo, and from Santo Tomé all the way to San Juan de los Reyes stretches a succession of souvenir

54 shops. **Casa de El Greco** (El Greco's House), another tourist magnet, is farther down the hill from Santo Tomé, off the Calle de San Juan de Dios. The property belonged to Peter the Cruel's Jewish treasurer, Samuel Levi, and it is known that the artist once lived in a house owned by this man; whether he lived in this one, however, is pure conjecture. The interior, done up in the late 19th century to resemble a "typical" house of El Greco's time, is a pure fake, albeit quite a pleasant one. The once-drab museum attached to it is currently being restored and remodeled; one of the few works to be seen at present is a large panorama of Toledo by El Greco, featuring in the foreground the Hospital of Tavera. *Tel. 925/22–40–46. Admission: 200 pesetas. Open Tues.–Sat. 10–2 and 4–6, Sun. 10–2.*

55 The **Sinagoga del Tránsito** (Tránsito Synagogue), at the bottom of the street, is a 14th-century structure financed by Samuel Levi. Plain on the outside, the walls of this simple rectangular structure are sumptuously covered inside with intricate Mudéjar decoration, as well as Hebraic inscriptions glorifying God, Peter the Cruel, and Levi himself. The upper, women's gallery has recently been opened to the public for the first time following loving restoration; the rooms adjoining the main hall reopened in 1991 as a small museum of Jewish culture in Spain. *Admission: 200 pesetas. Open Tues.–Sat. 10–2 and 4–6, Sun. 10–2.*

Turn right onto the wide Calle de Los Reyes Católicos and you will
56 come shortly to the town's other synagogue, **Santa María la Blanca.** Nearly two centuries older than the Tránsito Synagogue, it has a white interior featuring a forest of columns supporting capitals of the most enchanting filigree workmanship. Stormed in the early 15th century by a Christian mob led by St. Vincent Ferrer, the synagogue was later put to a variety of uses—as a carpenter's workshop, a store, a barracks, and a refuge for reformed prostitutes. *Admission: 100 pesetas. Open Oct.–Apr., daily 10–2 and 3:30–6; May–Sept., daily 10–2 and 3:30–7.*

A few steps from Santa María la Blanca, at the western end of town,
57 is the convent church of **San Juan de los Reyes,** erected by Ferdinand and Isabella to commemorate their victory at the battle of Toro in 1476 and intended originally to be their burial place. The building is largely the work of Juan Guas, who considered it his masterpiece and asked to be buried here himself. Guas, one of the greatest exponents of the Gothic, or Isabelline, was an architect of prolific imagination and great decorative exuberance. The white interior, in true Plateresque fashion, is covered with inscriptions and heraldic motifs. *Admission: 100 pesetas. Open Oct.–Apr., daily 10–1:30 and 3:30–5:45; May–Sept., daily 10–1:45 and 3:30–6:45.*

Walk uphill from San Juan de Los Reyes on the Calle del Ángel and you will rejoin the Calle de Santo Tomé; from there, it is a short walk back to the cathedral. For a diversion into a virtually unspoiled part of town, turn left by the church of Santo Tomé onto the Plaza Valdecaleros. At the top of this square, turn left again and then immediately right onto the Calle San Clemente; the **Convento de San Clemente** (on the left-hand side) has a richly sculpted portal by Covarrubias.

58 **San Román,** at the top of the street, is an early 13th-century Mudéjar church, with extensive remains of frescoes inside; it has been deconsecrated and now serves as a **Museo de los Concilios y de la Cultura Visigoda** (Museum of Visigothic Art), featuring statuary, manuscript illustrations, and delicate jewelry. *Admission: 100 pesetas. Open Tues.–Sat. 10–2 and 4–6:30, Sun. 10–2.*

Almost every wall in this exceptionally quiet part of town belongs to a convent, and the empty streets here make for contemplative walks. This was a district much loved by the Romantic poet Gustavo Adolfo Bécquer, author of *Rime,* the most popular book of Spanish verse before García Lorca's *Romancero Gitano*. His favorite corner was the tiny square in front of the 16th-century convent church of **Santo Domingo,** a few minutes' walk to the north of San Román, below the Plazuela de Padilla. You will find here not only the earliest of El Greco's Toledo paintings, but also the artist's coffin. The friendly nuns at the convent will show you around an eccentric little museum, which includes documents bearing El Greco's signature. *Admission: 150 pesetas. Open Mon.–Sat. 11–2 and 4–7, Sun. 4–7.*

What to See and Do with Children

Unquestionably, the greatest treat that you could give your children, and probably yourself, is to take them to see the **fountains at La Granja,** 6 km (4 mi) south of Segovia (*see* Tour 1, *above*). Installed in the late 18th century, they were immediately hailed as among the great artistic and technological marvels of the age. Of exceptional intricacy and ingenuity, they benefit from the very strong water pressure provided by their location on the slopes of the Sierra de Guadarrama. Every Wednesday, Saturday, and Sunday evening at 6, from May 1 to September 30, crowds of noisy Spanish children gather at the gates of La Granja as a man turns on the water with a large key. The jets shoot up from unpredictable places and angles, so be prepared for a good soaking.

Shopping

Salamanca   **Salamanca** has a reputation for **leatherwork;** the most traditional shop in town where you can buy it is **Salón Campero** (Plaza Corrillo 5).

Segovia   After Toledo, **Segovia province** ranks next in importance for its crafts. **Glass** and **crystal** are a specialty of **La Granja,** while **ironwork, lace,** and **embroidery** are famous in Segovia itself. In search of the old, authentic article, go to **San Martín 4** (Plaza San Martín 4, Segovia), an excellent **antiques** shop. You can buy good **lace** from the Gypsies in Segovia's **Plaza del Alcázar,** but be prepared for a lot of strenuous bargaining and never offer more than half the opening price.

Toledo   The most renowned center for crafts in Castile, if not in the whole of Spain, is **Toledo province.** Here, the Moors established **silverwork, damascene** (metalwork inlaid with gold or silver), **embroidery,** and **pottery** traditions that are still very much alive. Next to the church of San Juan de los Reyes in Toledo is a turn-of-the-century art school that teaches these various crafts and helps to maintain standards. For much cheaper pottery, you would be better off stopping at the large roadside emporia on the outskirts of the town, on the main road to Madrid. Better still, go to **Talavera la Reina,** 76 km (47 mi) west of Toledo, where most of this pottery is made. The finest embroidery in the province is from **Oropesa** and **Lagartera.**

Sports

Golf   There are golf courses at Alcalá de Henares, Salamanca, and numerous smaller places in the immediate surroundings of Madrid. For further information, contact the **Real Federación Española de Golf** (Capitán Haya 9, 28020 Madrid, tel. 91/555–2682).

Hiking and Mountaineering   The best area for both hiking and mountaineering is the Sierra de Gredos, and you could base yourself here at the Gredos Parador (*see*

Dining and Lodging, *below*). The range has six mountain huts with limited accommodations and facilities; for information on these and on mountaineering in general, contact the **Federación Española de Montañismo** (Alberto Aguilera 3, 28015 Madrid, tel. 91/445–1382).

Hunting and Fishing These are the most traditional Castilian leisure activities. Most of the private game reserves are in the provinces of Toledo and Guadalajara, where the red-legged partridge is one of the most sought-after species. The Spanish ibex can be hunted in the Sierra de Gredos. Information can be obtained from **ICONA** (Gran Vía de San Francisco 4, tel. 91/347–6000) and **Federación Española de Caza** (Av. Reina Victoria 72, 28006 Madrid, tel. 91/553–9017). Hunting and fishing permits must be obtained locally (not in Madrid); inquire at local tourist offices.

The most common fish in Castile's rivers are trout, pike, black bass, and blue carp; among the main trout rivers are the Eresma, Alto Duero, Júcar, Jarama, Manzanares, Tajo, and Tormes. Obtain permits and information from ICONA (*see above*) and from the **Federación Española de Pesca** (Navas de Tolosa 3, 28013 Madrid, tel. 91/532–8353).

Skiing Skiing is popular in the Sierra de Gredos and in the Guadarrama resorts of La Pinilla (Segovia), Navacerrada (Madrid), Valdesqui (Madrid), and Valcotos (Madrid). Current information on skiing conditions can be obtained from **ATUDEM** (tel. 91/458–1557), although you'll do better to call the slope you're planning on visiting; general information is available from **Federación Española de Deportes de Invierno** (Claudio Coello 32, 28001 Madrid, tel. 91/575–0576).

Dining and Lodging

Dining

The classic dishes of Castile are *cordero* (lamb) and *cochinillo* (suckling pig) roasted in a wood oven. These are the particular specialties of Segovia, which is widely thought of as the gastronomic capital of Castile, thanks largely to the international reputation of such long-established restaurants as the Mesón de Cándido and the Mesón Duque. In the Segovian village of Pedraza, superb roast lamb is served with hearty red wine.

The mountainous districts of Salamanca are renowned for their hams and sausage products—in particular, the villages of Guijuelo and Candelario. Bean dishes are a specialty of El Barco (Ávila) and La Granja (Segovia), while *trucha* (trout) and *cangrejos de río* (river crab) are common to Guadalajara province. Game is abundant throughout Castile, two famous dishes being *perdiz en escabeche* (the marinated partridges of Soria) and *perdiz estofada a la Toledana* (the stewed partridges of Toledo). The most exotic and complex cuisine in Castile is perhaps that of Cuenca, where you will find two outstanding restaurants, Figon de Pedro and Los Claveles. A strong Moorish influence prevails here—for instance, in *gazpacho pastor* (a hot terrine made with a variety of game, topped with grapes).

Among the region's sweets are the *yemas* (sugared egg yolks) of Ávila, *almendras garrapiñadas* (candied almonds) of Alcalá de Henares, *mazapan* (marzipans) of Toledo, and *ponche Segovia* (egg toddy of Segovia). La Mancha is the main area for cheeses, while Aranjuez is famous for its strawberries and asparagus.

Much of the cheap wine in Spain comes from La Mancha, south of Toledo. Far better in quality, and indeed among the most superior Spanish wines, are those from the Duero Valley, around Valladolid. Look, in particular, for the Marqués de Riscal whites from Rueda and the Vega Sicilia reds from Valbuena; Peñafiel is the most common of the Duero wines. An excellent, if extremely sweet, Castilian liqueur is the *resolí* from Cuenca made from aquavit, coffee, vanilla, orange peel, and sugar and often sold in bottles in the shape of Cuenca's Casas Colgadas.

Dress in restaurants of this region is usually casual, unless otherwise indicated. Reservations are not necessary unless so specified.

Highly recommended restaurants are indicated by a star ★.

Category	Cost*
$$$$	over 6,500 ptas
$$$	4,000–6,500 ptas
$$	2,500–4,000 ptas
$	under 2,500 ptas

* *per person for a three-course meal, including wine, excluding tax*

Lodging

The most stylish of Spain's hotels are usually the paradors. Though this holds true in the region around Madrid, the oldest and most beautiful of the paradors here are generally to be found in the lesser towns, such as Ciudad Real and Sigüenza, rather than in the major tourist centers. The paradors at Salamanca, Toledo, Segovia, and Soria are all in ugly or nondescript modern buildings, albeit with magnificent views. Fortunately, the region has many other memorable alternatives to paradors, such as the beautifully and centrally situated Los Linajes in Segovia, the Palacio de Valderrábanos in Ávila (a 15th-century palace next to the cathedral), and Cuenca's Posada San José, a 16th-century convent in a spectacular situation.

Highly recommended hotels are indicated by a star ★.

Category	Cost*
$$$$	over 13,000 ptas
$$$	8,000–13,000 ptas
$$	4,000–8,000 ptas
$	under 4,000 ptas

* *All prices are for a standard double room, excluding tax.*

Alarcón
Lodging

Parador Nacional Marqués de Villena. For indulging in medieval fantasies, this parador is virtually unrivaled. Set in a 14th-century castle with a spectacular position above a gorge, the hotel has only 13 small rooms, some of which are in the corner towers and have as windows the narrow slots once used to shoot arrows out of; other rooms have window niches where the women of the household would sit to do needlework. Dinners are served in a high-arched baronial hall adorned with shields, armor, and a gigantic fireplace recalling medieval banquets. *Av. Amigos de los Castillos 3, 16213, tel. 966/33–13–50, fax 966/33–11–07. 13 rooms. Facilities: restaurant, garden. AE, DC, MC, V. $$$$*

Alcalá de Henares
Dining

Hostería del Estudiante. One of the original buildings acquired by Spain's parador chain, this restaurant is magnificently set around a 15th-century cloister and features wood-beam ceilings, a large and splendid fireplace, and glass-and-tin lanterns. Appropriate to such a traditional setting is the good and simple Castilian food, a particular specialty being roast lamb. *Los Colegios 3, tel. 91/888–0330. AE, DC, MC, V. No dinner July and Aug. Closed Mon. $$*

Ávila
Dining
★

El Molino de la Losa. Few restaurants could have a better or more exciting situation than this one. Standing in the middle of the River Adaja, with one of the best views of the town's walls, it occupies a 15th-century mill, the working mechanism of which has been well preserved and provides much distraction for those seated in the animated bar. Lamb here is roasted in a medieval wood oven, and there is fish freshly caught from the river; this is also a good place to try the beans from nearby El Barco (*judías de El Barco*). In the beautiful garden outside is a small playground for children. *Bajada de la Losa 12, tel. 918/21–11–01 or 918/21–11–02. AE, MC, V. Closed Mon. in winter. $$*

Mesón del Rastro. The best alternative after El Molino de la Losa, this restaurant occupies a wing of the medieval Abrantes Palace and has an attractive old-style interior. Once again, try the lamb and the El Barco beans; also good is the *caldereta de cabrito* (goat stew). The place suffers somewhat from its popularity with tour buses, and service is slow and impersonal. *Plaza Rastro 1, tel. 918/21–12–18. AE, DC, MC, V. $$*

Lodging
★

Palacio de Valderrábanos. The hotel stands right in front of the cathedral and occupies a 15th-century palace that originally belonged to the first bishop of Ávila. The medieval splendor of the sculpted granite exterior shields a luxury hotel of distinctly old-fashioned character. The spacious rooms retain a 1920s-style decor. *Plaza de la Catedral 9, 05001, tel. 918/21–10–23, fax 918/25–16–91. 73 rooms with bath. Facilities: restaurant, conference room. AE, DC, MC, V. $$$*

Parador Nacional Raimundo de Borgoña. This largely rebuilt medieval castle attached to the town walls has none of the character or architectural interest of the Palacio de Valderrábanos, but it does have slightly more sophisticated furnishings. It also has the advantage of a beautiful garden, from which you can climb up onto the town's ramparts. *Marqués de Canales y Chozas 16, 05001, tel. 918/21–13–40, fax 918/22–61–66. 62 rooms with bath. Facilities: restaurant, parking, garage, garden, conference room. AE, DC, MC, V. $$$*

Ciudad Rodrigo
Dining

Mayton. This restaurant has a most engaging wood-beamed interior, bursting with a wonderful and eccentric collection of antiques, ranging from pestles and mortars to Portuguese yokes and old typewriters. In contrast to the decor, the emphasis of the cooking is on simple preparation; the specialties are fish, seafood, goat, and lamb. *La Colada 9, tel. 923/46–07–20. AE, DC, MC, V. $$*

Lodging

Parador Nacional Enrique II. Occupying part of the magnificent castle built by Enrique II of Trastamara to guard over the Agueda Valley, this parador is a series of small white rooms along the sturdy and gently sloping outer walls of the building; ask for room No. 10 if you want one that has kept its original vaulting. A special feature throughout the hotel is the under-floor heating in the bathrooms.

Some of the rooms, as well as the restaurant, overlook a beautiful garden that runs down to the River Agueda; beyond the river the view surveys fertile plains. *Plaza Castillo 1, 37500, tel. 923/46–01–50, fax 923/46–04–04. 27 rooms. Facilities: parking, garden, conference room. AE, DC, MC, V. $$$*

Conde Rodrigo. A good and cheaper alternative to the parador, this hotel is situated in a dignified old building on the town's cathedral square. The clean and simply furnished rooms are modern and lack character, but those on the front have balconies with excellent views of the cathedral. *Plaza del Salvador 7, 37500, tel. 923/46–14–04, fax 923/46–14–08. 35 rooms. Facilities: restaurant, parking, conference hall. AE, MC, V. $$*

Cuenca
Dining
★

Figón de Pedro. The owner of this restaurant, Pedro Torres Pacheco, is one of the famed restaurateurs of Spain and has done much to promote the excellence of Cuenca cuisine. In this pleasantly low-key and modest-looking establishment in the lively heart of the modern town, you can try such unusual local specialties as *gazpacho pastor* (a hot terrine made here with partridge, hare, and rabbit), *ajo arriero* (a paste made with pounded salt cod), and *alaju* (a sweet of obvious Moorish origin and consisting of honey, bread crumbs, almonds, and orange water). You can finish off your meal with resolí, the Cuenca liqueur. *Cervantes 13, tel. 966/22–45–11. Weekend reservations advised. AE, DC, MC, V. Closed Sun. evening and Mon. $$$*

Mesón Casas Colgadas. Run by the management of the Figón de Pedro, it offers much the same fare, but more pretentiously, in an ultramodern white dining room in the spectacularly sited Casas Colgadas, next to the Museum of Abstract Art. *Canónigos s/n, tel. 966/22–35–09. Weekend and holiday reservations required. AE, DC, MC, V. Closed Tues. evening. $$$*

★ **Los Claveles.** In a quiet and attractive part of the new town, with a colorful, homey interior filled with curiosities and posters (even on the ceiling), this is, in many ways, one of the most agreeable restaurants in Castile. The present owner's father bought the establishment in 1950, following a drunken spree after a bullfight; he realized what he had done only the next day, but fortunately persevered with the place and soon helped win for it a great local popularity. His widow still does the cooking, which is every bit as good as that of El Figón, with perhaps a more authentic character: You feel that she is perpetuating family traditions that go back centuries. All the Cuenca specialties can be found here, including *morteruelo* (an even richer and more elaborate version of gazpacho pastor, containing liver and ham). The gazpacho pastor here is served with the traditional grapes, a truly Moorish touch. *Torres 34, tel. 966/21–38–24. Closed Thurs. and Sept. MC, V. $$*

Lodging
Cueva del Fraile. This luxurious hotel, 7 km (4½ mi) out of town on the Buenache road, occupies a 16th-century building in dramatic surroundings. The white rooms have reproduction traditional furniture, stone floors, and some wood ceilings. *Ctra. Cuenca-Buenache, 16001, tel. 966/21–15–71, fax 966/21–15–73. 54 rooms with bath. Facilities: garden, pool, parking, garage, tennis courts, conference room. Closed Jan. 10–Mar. 2. $$$*

Parador de Cuenca. Spain's newest parador (opened in 1993) is in an exquisitely restored 16th-century monastery situated in the gorge below Cuenca's famous hanging houses. The guest rooms are furnished in a lighter and more luxurious style than one usually finds in Castilian houses of the same vintage. *Paseo Hoz de Huecar s/n, 16001, tel. 969/23–23–20, fax 969/23–25–34. 124 rooms with bath. Facilities: restaurant, bar, indoor pool, tennis. AE, DC, MC, V. $$$*

★ **Posada San José.** This is still the only hotel in the Old Town, and it's just as good, if somewhat more modest, than the nearby parador. Tastefully installed in a 16th-century convent, it clings to the top of the Huécar gorge, which most of its rooms overlook. The furnishings are traditional and in the spirit of the building. The atmosphere is friendly and intimate. Reservations are essential, preferably well ahead. *Julián Romero 4, 16001, tel. 966/21–13–00. 16 rooms with bath, 9 without. MC, V. $$*

El Burgo de Osma
Dining

Virrey Palafox. One of Castile's famed restaurants, this is a family-run establishment set in a modern building. Inside, decor is traditional Castilian style, complete with white walls and a timber-beamed ceiling. The long dining room, adorned with old furnishings, is divided into smoking and nonsmoking sections. The emphasis is on fresh, seasonal produce. Vegetables are home-grown, and there is excellent local game throughout the year. The specialty of the house is fish, in particular *merluza Virrey* (hake stuffed with eels and salmon). On February and March weekends, a pig is slaughtered and a marvelous and very popular banquet is held (about 4,500 pesetas). *Universidad 7, tel. 975/34–02–22. AE, DC, MC, V. Closed Sun. evening in winter and Dec. 15–Jan. 15. $$–$$$*

Lodging

Virrey II. Twenty clean, modest, and inexpensive rooms are to be found above the famous restaurant of this name. For more stylish accommodation, try this new hotel, opened by the same management in 1990 a few hundred yards away. Situated on the village's beautiful main square, it adjoins the 16th-century Convent of San Agustín and appears to form part of it. Though of recent construction, the hotel is built with traditional materials and has an Old World look. The rooms, most of which overlook the square, have marble floors, stone walls, and tastefully simple decoration. *Calle Mayor 2, 42300, tel. 975/34–13–11, fax 975/34–08–55. 52 rooms. Facilities: conference room, small dining room. AE, DC, MC, V. $$$*

Navarredonda de Gredos
Lodging

Parador Nacional de Gredos. Built in 1926 on a site chosen by Alfonso XIII, this was the first of the parador chain; it was enlarged in 1941 and again in 1975. Though modern, the stone architecture has a sturdy, traditional look and blends well with the magnificent surroundings. The rooms are standard parador, with heavy dark furniture and light walls. It has excellent views of the Gredos range and is the ideal base for a hiking or climbing holiday. *Carretera Barraco–Béjar, 05001, tel. 918/34–80–48, fax 918/34–82–05. 77 rooms with bath. Facilities: restaurant, parking, garden, conference room, tennis courts, bookshop. AE, DC, MC, V. $$$*

Pedraza
Dining

El Yantar de Pedraza. This traditional establishment, with wooden tables and beamed ceilings on the village's enchanting main square, is famous for its roast meats. It is certainly the place to come to for that most celebrated of Pedraza's specialties—*corderito lechal en horno de leña* (baby lamb roasted in a wood oven). *Plaza Mayor, tel. 911/50–98–42. Reservations advised on weekends. AE, MC, V. Closed evenings Sept. 15–July 15, and Mon. $$$*

Lodging

La Posada de Don Mariano. Opened in 1989, this hotel was originally a farmer's home. Each of the rooms in the picturesque old building has been carefully decorated in a different style with rustic furniture and antiques. The atmosphere is intimate, but the prices are grand. *Plaza Mayor 14, 40172, tel. 911/50–98–86/87. 18 rooms with bath. AE, DC, MC, V. $$$*

Salamanca
Dining

Chez Victor. If you are tired of traditional Castilian cuisine, this chic, modern restaurant is the place to come to. The owner and cook, Victoriano Salvador, learned his trade in France and now adapts

French food to Spanish taste, with numerous whimsical touches quite his own—for instance, *sesos de cordero al vinagre de frambuesa* (lamb brains in raspberry vinegar) and *raviolis rellenos de marisco* (ravioli stuffed with shellfish). The desserts are outstanding—in particular, the chocolate ones. *Espoz y Mina 26, tel. 923/21–31–23. AE, DC, MC, V. Closed Sun. evening, Mon., and Aug. $$$*

Río de la Plata. This tiny basement restaurant, dating back to 1958, has a friendly, old-fashioned character; the elegant, gilded decor is a pleasant change from the ubiquitous Castilian-style interiors typical of this region. The food is simple but carefully prepared, with good-quality fish and meat. *Plaza Peso 1, tel. 923/21–90–05. AE, MC, V. Closed Mon. and July. $$*

Lodging **Gran Hotel.** The *grande dame* of Salamanca's hotels got a facelift in 1994 and now offers stylishly baroque lounges and refurbished yet old-fashioned oversize rooms just steps from the Plaza Mayor. *Plaza Poeta Iglesias 3, 37001, tel. 923/21–35–00, fax 923/21–35–01. 109 rooms with bath. Facilities: restaurant, bar, garage. AE, DC, MC, V. $$$*

Palacio del Castellanos. Opened in 1992 in an immaculately restored 15th-century palace, this hotel offers a much needed altenative to Salamanca's national parador (probably the ugliest in the chain). This palacio has an exquisite interior patio and an equally beautiful restaurant. *San Pablo 58, tel. 923/26–18–18, fax 923/26–18–19. 69 rooms. AE, DC, MC, V. $$$*

Las Torres. Situated on the Plaza Mayor above the lively café of this name (*see* Tour 3 in Exploring Around Madrid, *above*), this slightly seedy and depressing place with pale green rooms may well be where you choose to end up in Salamanca. Its position could not be bettered, and if you are given a room overlooking the square, the view will make up for everything else. *Plaza Mayor 26, 37001, tel. 923/21–21–00 or 923/21–21–01. 26 rooms. No credit cards. $$*

Segovia **Casa Duque.** Founded by Dionisio Duque in 1895 and still in the fami-
Dining ly, this is the second most famous restaurant in town. The intimate interior, homey wood-beam decoration, and plethora of beautiful and fascinating objects hanging everywhere give it a look similar to Cándido's. It is smaller and friendlier, though, and benefits greatly from the charismatic presence of Julian Duque, the owner. Never still for a moment, Duque attends to all his clients with eccentric but not obsequious charm. Roasts are the specialty, but you should also try the *judiones de La Granja Duque*—the excellent kidney beans from nearby La Granja, served with sausages. *Cervantes 12, tel. 911/43–05–37. Reservations required weekends, advised other times. AE, DC, MC, V. $$$*

Mesón de Cándido. More than a restaurant, this is a national monument; it was declared such in 1941. Situated under the aqueduct and comprising a quaint medley of small, irregular dining rooms covered with memorabilia, it has served as an inn since at least the 18th century. Cándido took over the running in 1931 and, with his energy and flair for publicity, managed to make it the Spanish restaurant best known abroad: Hung everywhere are photographs of the countless celebrities who have been here, ranging from Salvador Dalí to Princess Grace of Monaco. The place is now run by Cándido's son, but Cándido regularly pokes in his famous bald head to see how things are going. All first-time visitors are virtually obliged to eat the *cochinillo* (suckling pig), the delicacy of which used to be attested by Cándido's slicing it with the edge of a plate; the trout here is also renowned. *Plaza de Azoguejo 5, tel. 911/42–59–11. Reservations required weekends, advised other times. AE, DC, MC, V. $$$*

★ **Mesón de José María.** The exceptionally lively bar through which you must pass to reach the restaurant augurs well for the rest of the establishment. Though of relatively recent date in Segovian terms, this place has already surpassed its formidable rivals and deserves to be considered one of Spain's finest restaurants. The hospitable and passionately dedicated owner is devoted to maintaining the traditional specialties of his region while making innovations of his own. The emphasis is on freshness and quality of produce, and the menu changes constantly. The large old-style dining room is always packed, and the waiters are uncommonly friendly. *Cronista Lecea 11, tel. 911/43–44–84. AE, DC, MC, V. $$$*

Dining and Lodging **Parador Nacional de Segovia.** Architecturally one of the most interesting and beautiful of the modern paradors, this low building, which was recently expanded substantially, is spaciously arranged amid greenery on a hillside. The rooms are light, with generous amounts of glass. The panorama of Segovia and its aqueduct is unbeatable, but there are disadvantages in staying so far from the town center. The restaurant serves traditional Segovian and international dishes—for instance, *lomo de merluza al aroma de estragón* (hake fillet with tarragon and shrimp). *Carretera de Valladolid s/n, 40003, tel. 911/44–37–37, fax 911/43–73–62. 103 rooms with bath. Facilities: restaurant, garage, garden, indoor and outdoor pools, conference hall with simultaneous translation facilities. AE, DC, MC, V. $$$$*

Lodging **Los Linajes.** The only luxury hotel within the old walls of Segovia,
★ this is also by far the best hotel in town. Part of the well-modernized building belongs to a medieval palace; there are wonderful views over the town's northern ramparts and out into the countryside. *Doctor Velasco 9, 40003, tel. 911/43–12–01, fax 911/43–15–01. 53 rooms. Facilities: restaurant, bar, conference room, parking. AE, MC, V. $$$*

Infanta Isabel. A recently restored building with a Victorian feel houses this small and central hotel. It's just two steps off the Plaza Mayor and offers great views of Segovia's cathedral. The rooms are feminine and light with painted white furnishings. *Plaza Mayor s/n, 40001, tel. 911/44–31–05, fax 911/43–32–40. 29 rooms. Facilities: coffee shop, garage. AE, MC, V. $$*

Sigüenza **Parador Nacional Castillo de Sigüenza.** Of the many castles belong-
Lodging ing to the parador chain, this is one of the most impressive and his-
★ torically important. At the very top of the beautiful town of Sigüenza, this mighty, crenellated structure has hosted royalty over the centuries, from Ferdinand and Isabella right up to the present king, Juan Carlos. Some of the rooms have four-poster beds and balconies perched over the wild landscape. *Subida al Castillo s/n, 19250, tel. 911/39–01–00, fax 911/39–13–64. 77 rooms with bath. Facilities: restaurant, parking, garden, conference room. AE, DC, MC, V. $$$*

Soria **Mesón Castellano.** The most traditional restaurant in town, this cozy
Dining establishment has a large open fire over which succulent *chuletón de ternera* (veal chops) are cooked. Another specialty is its *migas pastoriles* (soaked bread crumbs fried with peppers and bacon), a local dish. *Plaza Mayor 2, tel. 911/21–30–45. AE, MC, V. $$*

Lodging **Parador Nacional Antonio Machado.** This modern building has a superb hilltop setting, surrounded by trees and parkland, and excellent views of the hilly Duero Valley. It is named after the poet who came often to this site for inspiration. *Parque del Castillo, 42005,* *tel. 911/21–34–45, fax 911/21–28–49. 34 rooms with bath. Facilities: restaurant, parking, garden. AE, MC, V. $$$*

Toledo
Dining
★

Asador Adolfo. Only a few steps from the cathedral, but discreetly hidden away and making no attempt to attract the passing tourist trade, this is unquestionably the best and most dignified restaurant in town. The modern main entrance shields an old and intimate interior featuring in its principal dining room a wood-beam ceiling with extensive painted decoration from the 14th century. The emphasis is on freshness of produce and traditional Toledan dishes, but there is also much innovation. Especially good starters are the *pimientos rellenos* (stuffed peppers). For a main course, try the *merluza al azafrán* (hake subtly flavored with saffron from the area). You should finish with another Toledan specialty, *delicias de mazapan* (marzipan), which is cooked here in a wooden oven and is the finest and lightest to be found in the whole town. *Granada 6 and Hombre de Palo 7, tel. 925/22–73–21. Reservations required on weekends. AE, DC, MC, V. Closed Sun. evening. $$$*

Hierbabuena. Dine on an enclosed Moorish patio with plenty of natural light, at tables covered with crocheted cloths. The food here is just as inviting as the setting, and it is surprisingly reasonably priced; try artichokes stuffed with seafood or steak with bluecheese sauce. *Cristo de la Luz 9, tel. 925/22–34–63. Reservations advised. MC, V. $$*

Hostal del Cardenal. The restaurant of this famous hotel adjoining the northern walls of the town has a long-standing reputation and is very popular with tourists. The setting is beautiful (*see* Lodging, *below*), but the food is not quite what it used to be. The dishes are mainly local, and in season you will find delicious asparagus and strawberries from Aranjuez. *Paseo Recaredo 24, tel. 925/22–08–62. AE, DC, MC, V. $$*

Lodging

Parador Nacional Conde de Orgaz. This modern building on the outskirts of Toledo blends well with its rural surroundings and has an unbeatable panorama of the town. The architecture and furnishings, emphasizing brick and wood, make concessions to the traditional Toledan style. *Paseo Emperador s/n, 45001, tel. 925/22–18–50, fax 925/22–51–66. 77 rooms with bath. Facilities: garden, pool. AE, DC, MC, V. $$$$*

Hostal del Cardenal. Built in the 18th century as a summer palace for Cardinal Lorenzana, this is a quiet and beautiful hotel with light-colored rooms decorated with old furniture; some rooms overlook the hotel's enchanting wooded garden, which lies at the foot of the town's walls. It is difficult to believe that the main Madrid road is only a short distance away. *Paseo de Recaredo 24, 45004, tel. 925/22–49–00, fax 925/22–29–91. 27 rooms. Facilities: restaurant, garden. AE. $$$*

Pintor El Greco. Next door to the famous painter's house-museum (closed for restoration until 1996), this friendly hotel is in what was once a 17th-century bakery. Extensive renovation has resulted in a light and modern interior, with some antique touches such as exposed brick vaulting. *Alamillos del Transito 13, 45002, tel. 925/21–42–50, fax 925/21–58–19. 35 rooms. AE, DC, MC, V. $$*

Valladolid
Dining

La Fragua. In a modern building with a traditional Castilian interior of white walls and wood-beam ceilings, Valladolid's most famous and stylish restaurant counts members of the Spanish royal family among its patrons. Specialties include meat roasted in a wood oven and dishes more imaginative than those of the standard Castilian table, such as *rape Castellano Gran Mesón* (breaded skate served with clams and peppers) and *lengua empiñonada* (tongue coated in pine nuts). *Paseo Zorrilla 10, tel. 983/33–71–02. AE, DC, MC, V. Closed Sun. evening in winter, all Sun. in summer. $$$*

Lodging **Olid Melia.** A characterless modern block, the Hotel Olid Melia is situated in the middle of one of Valladolid's most attractive old districts. The building was erected in the early 1970s, and its pale green curtains and dark, heavy furniture have a somewhat dated look. The ground and first floors, however, have recently been dramatically remodeled and given a marbled, pristine elegance. *Plaza de San Miguel 10, 47003, tel. 983/35–72–00, fax 983/33–68–28. 226 rooms with bath. Facilities: garage, conference hall, hairdresser. AE, DC, MC, V. $$$*

Zamora **Parador Nacional Condes de Alba y Aliste.** This pleasing establish-
Lodging ment offers a central but quiet location, a historic building with a distinctive Renaissance patio, good landscape views, and a friendly and intelligent staff. *Plaza Viriato 5, 49014, tel. 988/51–44–97, fax 988/53–00–63. 27 rooms with bath. Facilities: garage, garden, pool. AE, DC, MC, V. Expensive.*

The Arts and Nightlife

The Arts

Outside Madrid, the arts do not flourish in Castile. A renowned **annual theater festival** does take place in the La Mancha town of **Almagro.** Information on performances is available from the tourist office at Almagro (Carnicería 11, tel. 926/86–07–17).

Nightlife

Nightlife, though provincial in comparison to Madrid, flourishes in a number of Castilian towns. The liveliest places are the university towns of Salamanca and Valladolid.

Ávila For a fashionable bar in Ávila—almost a contradiction in terms—you should try the unappealingly named **El Rincón del Jamón** (Ham Corner) at Calle Vicente Manzaredo 11.

Salamanca The main area in Salamanca (*see* Tour 3 in Exploring Around Madrid, *above*) is around the Calle Bermejeros, but for a stylish and fashionable bar/discothèque, try **Camelot,** on the Calle Bordadores.

Segovia Segovia's main nocturnal district is around the Plaza San Martín, where the activity is concentrated in three loud and exceptionally lively bars: **El Gimnasio, El Ojo,** and **El Narziotas.**

Toledo Toledo's nightlife is concentrated around the Plaza Zocodover. Some of the best night bars are to the west of this square, lining the Calle Sillería and its continuation, Alfileritos. Just to the south of the square is the recently reopened **Amsterdam,** a lively and friendly bar filled mainly with young people. For discothèques you should go to the underground complex known as the Miradero, to the north of the plaza; try the newly revamped **La Máscara.**

Valladolid Valladolid has a wide choice of places to go to at night. The Zona Francisco Suarez and the Zona Iglesia La Antigua are the two districts that are popular with students. Livelier and more fashionable still are the Zona Cantarranas (in particular, the **Inoxidable**) and around the Plaza Mayor.

5 León, Galicia, and Asturias

By Deborah Luhrman

Updated by Mary Ellen Schultz

Diverse and far-flung, this region includes Spain's wildest mountain scenery in the Picos de Europa and most pristine beaches in the remote coves of the Lugo coast. It also includes the ramshackle countryside of Galicia, coal mines, heavy industry, and the lonesome high plains of Castile, near León.

Green, rain-swept landscapes are what northwestern Spain is all about. Ancient granite buildings wear a blanket of moss, and even the *horreos* (granaries) are built on stilts above the damp ground. Bagpipes replace flamenco guitar in this part of Spain, evidence of ancient Celtic ties, and even a local folk dance, the *muñeira*, resembles a combination highland fling and Irish jig.

While Galicia, Asturias, and León are off the beaten track for foreign visitors to Spain, they are not untouristed. Hordes of Spanish families flock to the cool northern beaches and mountains each summer. The city of Santiago de Compostela, whose cathedral is said to house the remains of the apostle St. James, has been attracting tourists for more than 900 years, and, in fact, the first guidebook ever published, the Calixtus Codex of 1130, describes the route to Santiago that you can follow now. Because of those medieval pilgrims who made the journey to Santiago, the region is dotted with rich churches, shrines, and hospitals. Most of the monuments you will see in the province of León and the region of Galicia owe their existence to the pilgrimage route.

Asturias, north of the main pilgrimage trail, has always been slightly separate from the rest of the country because of a barrier of high mountains. This is the only region of Spain that was not conquered by the Moors and shows little Arabic influence in its architecture. It was from their mountain base at Covadonga that the Christians won their first decisive battle against the Moors and launched the reconquest of Spain. Though it took some 700 years, the Reconquest made Spain one of the world's most Roman Catholic countries, a legacy that remains today.

Essential Information

Important Addresses and Numbers

Tourist Information

For information about the city and province of **León**, contact the **Oficina de Turismo de León** (Plaza de Regla 3, 24003 León, tel. 987/23–70–82); for information about **Galicia** and the city of Santiago de Compostela, contact the **Oficina de Turismo** (Rua de Villar 43, 15705 Santiago de Compostela, tel. 981/58–40–81), and about the principality of **Asturias**, contact the **Oficina de Turismo** (Plaza de la Catedral 6, 33007 Oviedo, tel. 98/521–3385).

Other tourist offices in towns covered in this chapter are **Astorga** (kiosk in Plaza de España), **Cangas de Onis** (Emilio Laria 2, tel. 98/584–8005), **El Grove** (Plaza Corgo, tel. 986/73–09–75), **Gijón** (Marqués de San Esteban 1, tel. 98/534–6046), **La Coruña** (Dársena de la Marina, tel. 981/22–18–22), **Ponferrada** (next to castle, tel. 987/42–42–36), **Pontevedra** (General Mola 2, tel. 986/85–08–14), **Ribadeo** (Plaza de España, tel. 982/11–06–89), **Ribadesella** (Carretera Piconera, tel. 98/586–0038), **Tuy** (Puente Tripes, tel. 986/60–17–85), and **Vigo** (Jardines de las Avenidas, tel. 986/43–05–77).

Arriving and Departing by Plane

Galicia is served by an international airport 12 km (7 mi) east of **Santiago de Compostela** at Labacolla (tel. 981/59–74–00), with daily flights on Iberia to London, Paris, Zurich, Geneva, and Frankfurt. Regular domestic flights connect Santiago with the rest of Spain, including daily service to Madrid and Barcelona. The region's other two domestic airports are in **La Coruña** (tel. 981/23–22–40) and in Asturias, near **San Esteban de Pravia,** 47 km (28 mi) north of Oviedo (tel. 98/554–7733).

Iberia has ticket offices in **Gijón** (Alfredo Truán 8, tel. 98/535–1846), **La Coruña** (Plaza de Galicia 6, tel. 981/22–87–30), **Oviedo** (Uria 21, tel. 98/524–0250), and **Santiago de Compostela** (Calvo Sotelo 25, tel. 981/57–20–28).

Airport buses leave from in front of the Iberia office and the bus station (*see below*) in Santiago. The Asturias airport can be reached by buses that leave from the Iberia office in Gijón and the Iberia terminal in Oviedo (Marqués de Pidal 20).

Arriving and Departing by Car, Train, and Bus

By Car N VI, also called the La Coruña Highway, links Spain's northwestern region with Madrid. Although it is a four-lane expressway for the first 90 km (54 mi) out of the capital, the rest of the road is two or three lanes. Be warned that it is heavily traveled by slow-moving trucks. Good highways connect Santiago and La Coruña, Ferrol and Vigo, Caraballo and La Coruña, and Vigo and Tuy (on the border with Portugal).

Although distances are great in Galicia and Asturias, travel by car is really the best way to appreciate the countryside.

By Train RENFE runs several trains a day from Madrid to León (4 hours), Oviedo (7 hours), and Gijón (8 hours), while a separate RENFE line serves Galicia (11 hours to Santiago). Daytime first-class and second-class cars are available, as is an overnight train with sleeping compartments. RENFE ticket windows are at the stations in **Gijón** (tel. 98/517–0202), **La Coruña** (tel. 981/15–02–02), **León** (tel. 987/27–02–44 or 987/27–02–02), **Oviedo** (tel. 98/524–3364), and **Santiago de Compostela** (tel. 981/52–02–02).

Narrow-gauge FEVE trains clatter across northern Spain, connecting Galicia and Asturias with Santander, Bilbao, and Irún, on the French border. Tickets can be purchased at the train stations or the main office in Oviedo (Av. Santander s/n, tel. 98/529–0104).

By Bus ALSA runs daily buses to Galicia and Asturias from Madrid and has weekly service from Paris, Brussels, Zurich, Nîmes, Toulouse, and Lyon. Several other companies operate between the region and major Spanish cities. Contact the bus stations for information in **León** (Cardenal Lorenzana s/n, tel. 987/21–10–00), **Oviedo** (Plaza Primo de Rivera 1, tel. 98/528–1200), and **Santiago** (San Cayetano, tel. 981/58–77–00).

Getting Around

By Car A four-lane divided highway links León with Oviedo and Gijón, providing the fastest way to cross the Cantabrian Mountains. A north–south Galician expressway was completed in 1992, shortening the travel time between La Coruña, Santiago, Pontevedra, and Vigo. Elsewhere the roads either wind along the coast or climb over the hills, always slow-going and seldom direct. Be sure to allow more time than you think it will take.

By Train Local trains connect all the small towns with the major cities of Galicia and Asturias, but be prepared for dozens of stops.

By Bus For information on the numerous local bus routes, contact the tourist offices or bus stations (*see* Arriving and Departing by Bus, *above*).

Guided Tours

Orientation The **Transcantabrico narrow-gauge train tour** offered by FEVE is an eight-day, 1,000-km (600-mi) journey through the Basque country, Galicia, and Asturias, with English-speaking guides and a private bus that takes the group from train stations to the regional artistic and natural attractions. Passengers sleep on the train and dine on local specialties at each stop. Trains run from June through September; the cost is approximately $1,500 per person, all-inclusive. For reservations, contact **Transcantabrico** (General Rodrigo 6, 28003 Madrid, tel. 91/553–7656), **E.C. Tours** (10153½ Riverside Dr., Toluca Lake, CA 91602, tel. 213/874–3848 or 800/388–0877), or **Marsans** (66 Whitmore St., London W1H 9LG, tel. 071/224–0504).

RENFE also offers a luxury train tour called "The Way of St. James" in the vintage *Al Andalus Express* (*see* Getting Around by Train in Chapter 1). The two-day trip includes visits to Burgos, León, and Santiago de Compostela. Gourmet menus are prepared, and passengers sleep in elegantly restored turn-of-the-century coaches. Trains run in July and August; the cost is approximately $1,500 per person, not including city tours.

Special-Interest **Trastur** (in Oviedo, tel. 98/580–6036) offers wilderness trips on horseback through the remote valleys of western Asturias. The five- to 10-day trips are designed for beginners and experienced cowboys; mountain cabins provide shelter along the trail. Tours begin and end in Oviedo and cost approximately $75 a day, all-inclusive. In Galicia, try **Galiciaventura** (Calle Manuel Pereira 10–Bajo, 32003 Orense, tel. 986/23–53–74). The **Centro Hípico de Turismo Ecuestre y de Aventuras "Granjo O Castelo"** in Galicia (Rúa Urzaiz 91–5A, 36201 Vigo, tel. 986/42–59–37) conducts horseback-riding excursions along the pilgrimage routes to Santiago from Pedrafita do Cebreiro and from Braga (in Portugal). **Reatur** (Rúa Castelao 11–1, 3266 Allariz, Orense, tel. 988/44–20–66) offers guided historical and cultural walks, some of which include hiking, horseback riding, mountain biking, and canoeing in the surrounding areas.

Walking Tours In Santiago, walking tours with multilingual guides are organized by the tourist office during peak travel periods. The three-hour tour covers all the major monuments and costs approximately $10.

Exploring León, Galicia, and Asturias

Orientation

Our first tour starts with the attractions of León before heading west toward Galicia along the ancient Way of St. James. Our second tour includes the pilgrims' destination, Santiago de Compostela, then travels west to the beach resort of Muros, then south to

Pontevedra and the fishing towns of the Rías Bajas before taking us north again to the thriving port of La Coruña. Last, moving east, we come to Oviedo and the natural beauty of Asturias, taking in the apple orchards and cider bars of Villaviciosa and heading on to Spain's most jagged mountains, the Picos de Europa.

Highlights for First-time Visitors

Archbishop's Palace in Astorga (*see* Tour 1)
Gothic cathedral of León (*see* Tour 1)
Prehistoric cave paintings near Ribadesella (*see* Tour 3)
Pre-Romanesque churches of Asturias (*see* Tour 3)
San Isidoro's 12th-century frescoes (*see* Tour 1)
Santiago de Compostela cathedral and old town (*see* Tour 2)
Shrine and National Park of Covadonga (*see* Tour 3)

Tour 1: León and the Way of St. James

Numbers in the margin correspond to points of interest on the León, Galicia, and Asturias map.

❶ León sits on the banks of the Bernesga River in the high plains of Old Castile. It was founded as a permanent camp for the Roman legions in AD 70. Historians say the city's name has nothing to do with the proud lion that has been its emblem for centuries, but is instead a corruption of the Roman word *legio* (legion).

The capital of Christian Spain was moved south to León from Oviedo in 914 as the Reconquest spread, launching the city's richest era. Walls were built around the old Roman town, and parts of the 2-meter- (6-ft-) thick medieval ramparts are still visible in the middle of the modern city.

Today, León is a wealthy provincial capital. The wide avenues are lined with shops, while a half-timbered old town remains to give visitors a glimpse of what life was like until this century.

León is proudest of its soaring Gothic **catedral** (cathedral), on the Plaza de Regla. From outside the cathedral notice the flying buttresses used to support walls that are built with more windows than stone. The front of the cathedral is decorated with three weatherworn, arched doorways, the center one adorned with slender statues of the apostles.

The cathedral, begun in 1205, contains 125 stained-glass windows plus three giant rose windows. The glass casts bejeweled shafts of light throughout the lofty interior. This ethereal feeling is enhanced by a clear glass door on the choir that permits an unobstructed view to the altar and apse windows. Take a good look at the lower-level windows. You'll see little 13th-century faces looking at you from amid a kaleidoscope of stunning colors. The cathedral also contains the sculptured tomb of King Ordoño II, who moved the capital of Christian Spain to León. Inside the cathedral museum, look for the carved wood Mudéjar archives, with a letter of the alphabet above each door. It's one of the world's oldest file cabinets. *Plaza de Regla, tel. 987/23–00–60. Admission to museums: 250 pesetas. Open July–Aug., weekdays 10–1:30 and 4–6, Sat. 10–1:30; Sept.–June, weekdays 9:30–1:30 and 4–7, Sat. 9:30–1:30; closed Sun.*

Head west on Avenida Generalísimo Franco and take a peek inside the **Farmacia Merino.** Only the medicines have changed since it opened in 1827. The ceiling is richly carved, as are the walls, which include a niche for each apothecary jar.

León, Galicia, and Asturias

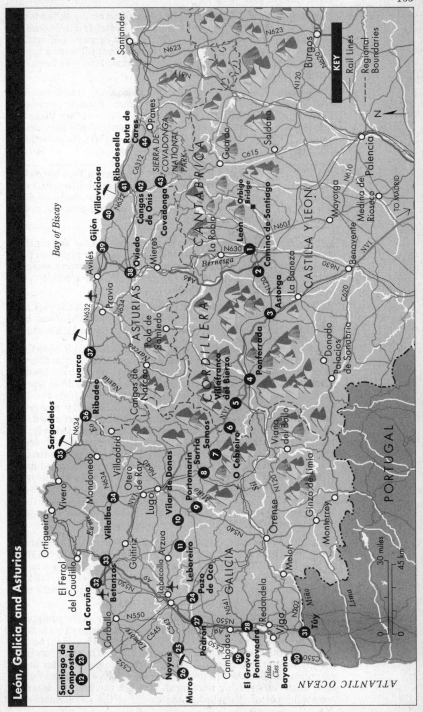

Santiago de
Compostela
12—23

KEY

— Rail lines
--- Regional
Boundaries

N

Bay of Biscay

ATLANTIC OCEAN

PORTUGAL

GALICIA

ASTURIAS

CASTILLA Y LEON

CANTABRICA

CORDILLERA

30 miles

45 km

Now take a left and head south on Calle Paloma and walk two blocks to the **Plaza Mayor** in the heart of León's old town. If it is Wednesday or Saturday, the plaza will be bustling with farmers selling their produce and cheeses. Look at their feet; many still wear a type of wooden shoes called *madreñas*, which are raised on three heels, two in the front and one in the back.

The arcaded Plaza Mayor is surrounded by many simple half-timbered houses, just the sort you'd expect Sancho Panza to come stumbling out of. Head half a block uphill to the 12th-century **Plaza San Martín**, where most of León's *tapas* (savory tidbits) bars are located. This area is called the Barrio Húmedo (Wet Neighborhood) because of all the wine poured every evening.

Time Out In a corner of Plaza San Martín is the cozy **Prada a Tope** bar, which serves the region's Bierzo wine out of a big barrel. The locale doubles as a gourmet food shop showcasing local products, and the friendly staff may offer you samples of roast red peppers, potent brandy-soaked cherries, or candied chestnuts.

Wind your way back to Avenida Generalísimo Franco and continue west toward the center of the modern city. On your right you'll see the **Casa de Botines,** a multigabled and turreted behemoth designed at the end of the 19th century by controversial Catalan architect Antonio Gaudí. It now houses a bank.

Backtrack one block and head north on Calle Cid, pass the park, and you'll arrive at the basilica of **San Isidoro el Real,** which was built into the side of the city wall in 1063 and rebuilt in the 12th century.

The adjoining **Panteón de los Reyes** (Royal Pantheon) is sometimes called the Sistine Chapel of Romanesque art. The vibrant frescoes painted in the 12th century on the pillars and ceiling have been remarkably preserved in the cool, dry building. The pantheon was the first building in Spain to be decorated with scenes from the New Testament. Be sure to look for the agricultural calendar painted on one archway, showing which farming task should be performed each month. Twenty-three kings and queens were once buried here, but their tombs were destroyed by French troops during the Napoleonic Wars. The museum tastefully displays San Isidoro's treasures, including a jewel-encrusted agate chalice, a richly illustrated handwritten Bible, and an enormous collection of polychrome wood statues of the Virgin Mary. *Plaza de San Isidoro, tel. 987/22–96–08. Admission to Royal Pantheon: 250 pesetas. Open July and Aug., Mon.–Sat. 10–1:30 and 3–8:30, Sun. 9–2; Sept.–June, Tues.–Sat. 10–1:30 and 4–6:30, Sun. 10–1:30; closed Mon.*

Walk around the back of the basilica for a closer look at the old city walls, then head down Avenida Suero de Quiñones toward the **Hostal San Marcos.** Legend has it that the knight Quiñones was the toughest hombre on the Way of St. James. In the year 1434, he staked out his turf on a bridge outside town and for a month challenged all the other knights who policed the route.

At the end of the street, along the Bernesga River, is the sumptuous **Antiguo Monasterio de San Marcos,** a former monastery that is now a five-star hotel in the parador chain (*see* Dining and Lodging, *below*). Originally the site was a home for knights of the Order of Santiago, who patrolled the Way of St. James, and a stopping place for weary pilgrims. In 1513 the monastery you see today was begun by the head of the order, King Ferdinand, who felt the knights deserved something better. Finished at the height of the Renaissance, the building's Plateresque facade is a sea of small sculptures, many of knights and lords. Inside is an elegant manorial staircase and a splendid cloister full of medieval statues. Enjoy a drink in the bar; the tiny windows are the original defensive slits. The building also houses the **Museo Arqueológico** (Provincial Archaeology Museum) famous for the haunting 11th-century ivory Carrizo crucifix. *Plaza de San Marcos, tel. 987/24–50–61 or 987/23–64–05. Admission to museum: 200 pesetas. Open July–Aug., Tues.–Sat. 10–2 and 4:30–8, Sun. 10–2; Sept.–June, Tues.–Sat. 10–2 and 4–7:30, Sun. 10–2; closed Mon.*

Leaving León, follow signs to the N120 and head southwest; stop to admire the 13th-century Orbigo Bridge, 23 km (14 mi) outside the city, where Quiñones made his stand. We are now on the **Camino de Santiago** (Way of St. James), marked by the Spanish government with large signs for motorists and small signs for the 2,000 or so pilgrims who make the journey each year on foot.

In the Middle Ages Santiago de Compostela, where the apostle St. James is said to be buried, was considered the third most important shrine in the Christian world, after Jerusalem and Rome. Making the difficult pilgrimage all but ensured the faithful a spot in heaven. At peak periods in the 12th century, as many as 2 million people a year traveled the road to Santiago from all over Europe.

It was crowded with thieves and knights to protect the travelers from them, innkeepers who grew wealthy on the tourist trade, and even souvenir sellers who provided the scallop shells worn by the pilgrims as a symbol of St. James, the fisherman.

The main pilgrimage route traverses the Pyrenees at Roncesvalles and extends across northern Spain to Santiago. Picking up the road in León will give you two full days on the Way of St. James with plenty to see.

Astorga is 46 km (27 mi) southwest of León, as you continue on N120. The drabness of the town is relieved by the fairy-tale Neo-Gothic **Palacio Episcopal** (Archbishop's Palace), designed for a Catalan cleric by Gaudí just before the turn of the century. No expense was spared in creating this fanciful building, which today houses the **Museo del Camino** (Museum of the Way). Be sure to note the standard pilgrim costume: a heavy black cloak, a staff hung with gourds, and a wide-brimmed hat bedecked with scallop shells. *Adjacent to cathedral. Admission: 150 pesetas. Open Apr.–Sept., daily 10–1 and 4–8; Oct.–Mar., Tues.–Sun. 11–1 and 3:30–6:30; closed Mon.*

Astorga, where the pilgrimage roads from France and Portugal merged, once boasted 22 hospitals to lodge and care for the travelers. Today, the only one left is the Hospital of Astorga, also adjacent to the cathedral. The **cathedral** itself is a huge 15th-century building with Baroque decorations, containing no fewer than four statues of St. James.

Time Out Before you leave, you might want to buy a box of the pastries that every Spaniard associates with Astorga. The rich tea cakes (*mantecadas*) are sold in shops near the cathedral.

Joining the Madrid–La Coruña highway, N VI, head west again for 64 km (40 mi) to **Ponferrada.** This is the start of a hilly region with beautiful fertile valleys. Ponferrada itself is a mining and industrial center and gets its name from an iron toll bridge built by a local bishop in the 1100s. The tall, slim turrets of the 13th-century **Castillo de los Templarios** (Templars' Castle) on the western edge of town command sweeping views of the countryside and may have once been used by the knights of the Order of St. James to police the route. *Florez Osorio 4. Admission free. Open Apr.–Sept., Wed.–Mon. 9–1 and 4–7; Oct.–Mar., Wed.–Mon. 9–1 and 3–6; closed Tues.*

Crossing the grape-growing region of León, where the slightly acidic Bierzo wine is produced, stay on N VI from Ponferrada for about **⑤** 20 km (12 mi) and you will arrive in **Villafranca del Bierzo.** The medieval village is dominated by a massive feudal fortress, still inhabited. Stroll the streets and look for the crests on the old manor houses. Wine can be purchased at the **Cooperativo Villafranquina** on the highway. Villafranca was an important stopping place for pilgrims because the next stretch of the road heads over a high mountain pass. In fact, you can visit the Romanesque church of **Santiago** and see the door of pardon, a sort of spiritual consolation prize for weak pilgrims who couldn't make it over the mountains.

The Way of St. James veers left, to the south, from N VI in about 25 km (15 mi) at the pass of Pedrahita. Climb the steep, narrow road **⑥** and you'll arrive at one of the most unusual hamlets in Spain, **O Cebreiro.** Round, thatched-roof stone huts called *pallozas* have been preserved in a sort of monument to the way the people in these windswept Galician mountains lived until just a few decades ago. One hut is now a **museum** of the region's Celtic heritage. The village, at 1,109 m (3,648 ft), also contains a rustic **sanctuary** from the 9th century, the oldest church on the route.

⑦ Continue along this mountain road to the town of **Samos,** with its **⑧** Benedictine monastery, and then **Sarria,** a medieval village with the **⑨** pilgrim's hospital of La Magdalena. In **Portomarin,** on the banks of the Miño River, the Romanesque church was moved uphill, stone by stone, before the town was flooded by a new dam. Farther on, stop at **⑩** the church in **Vilar de Donas** to pay tribute to the knights of St. James, whose tombs line the inside walls. Portraits of the two medieval noblewomen who built the church are included among those of the apostles in 15th-century frescoes adorning the apse.

From here, the countryside flattens out and you can stop at **⑪** **Leboreiro,** a village with simple medieval stone houses surrounding a Romanesque church. A stretch of the ancient road, paved with granite boulders, is still surprisingly intact.

Tour 2: Santiago de Compostela and the Galician Coast

Numbers in the margin correspond to points of interest on the León, Galicia, and Asturias and Santiago de Compostela maps.

⑫ **Santiago de Compostela** was built to impress. Imagine the pilgrims walking across Spain for 30 days and finally arriving at the foot of the great cathedral. The sheer size of the opulent building is awe-inspiring, with its main entrance raised two stories above the spacious **Plaza del Obradoiro.** Its soaring twin towers give a sense of harmony, and a benign St. James, dressed in pilgrim's costume, smiles down from his lofty perch.

One starry night in the year 813, a hermit was directed by a divine light to a field just outside present-day Santiago de Compostela. Digging began, and religious leaders unearthed a sarcophagus said to contain the remains of St. James. The name Compostela is believed to have come from the Latin *campus stellae* (field of the star). How the apostle's remains got to Galicia is somewhat of a mystery. One legend says that after St. James was beheaded by King Herod

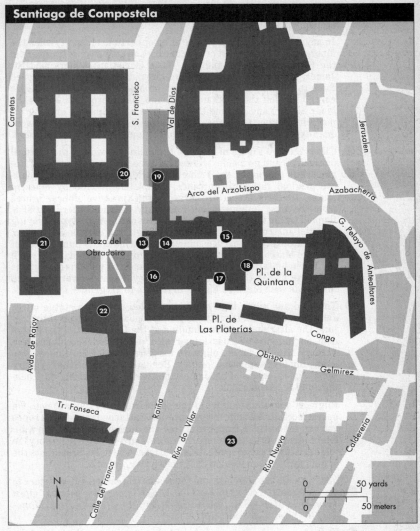

Santiago de Compostela

Carretas

S. Francisco

Val de Dios

Jerusalen

Arco del Arzobispo

Azabachería

G. Pelayo de Antealtares

Plaza del
Obradoiro

Pl. de la
Quintana

Pl. de
Las Platerías

Conga

Obispo

Gelmirez

Avda. de Rajoy

Tr. Fonseca

Raiña

Rúa do Vilar

Rúa Nueva

Caldereria

Calle del Franco

N

0   50 yards

0   50 meters

Catedral, **13**

Colegio de
San Jerónimo, **22**

High altar, **15**

Hostal de los Reyes
Católicos, **20**

Museums, **16**

Old town, **23**

Palacio Gelmírez, **19**

Palacio de Rajoy, **21**

Pórtico de la Gloria, **14**

Puerta de las
Platerías, **17**

Puerta Santa, **18**

in Jerusalem, his headless body was smuggled to Spain, where it lay hidden for centuries.

In any case, the discovery came at an opportune moment, when the Moors had overrun most of the country and only a weak fragment of the Christian army remained. Those Christian soldiers said St. James, armed with a great sword and riding a white charger, led them to their first victory against the Moors in Clavijo in 844. He earned himself the nickname Santiago Matamoros (St. James the Moor Slayer) and became the patron saint of Spain. Carrying his powerful banner throughout the Reconquest, the Christians went on to expel the Moors from Spain and conquer much of the Americas.

⑬ Climb the two flights of steps to the main doorway of the **catedral** (cathedral) and go inside, where you'll see the finest creation of Ro-
⑭ manesque sculpture, the 12th-century **Pórtico de la Gloria.** This is the original cathedral entrance, completed in 1188 by Maestro Mateo. Its three arches are carved with expressive biblical figures from the Last Judgment and Purgatory. In the center, Christ is flanked by his apostles and the 24 Elders of the Apocalypse playing celestial instruments. Just below Christ is a serene St. James, poised atop a richly carved column that includes the humble face of Maestro Mateo at the bottom. Look carefully at this pillar and you'll see five indentations made over the centuries by millions of pilgrims who have placed their hands here as they leaned forward to touch foreheads with Maestro Mateo, in tribute to his genius.

⑮ The gold and silver **high altar** is presided over by a statue of St. James dressed in a sumptuous jeweled cloak. Climb the stairs behind the altar and you are standing at the focal point of the cathedral, surrounded by a dazzling array of decoration, sculptures, and drapery. At this point, pilgrims kiss the cloak of St. James—the grand finale of a spiritual journey. Beneath the altar in the crypt are the alleged remains of St. James and two of his disciples, St. Theodore and St. Athanasius.

Pilgrims' masses are sung in the cathedral every day at noon. On special occasions a huge incense burner is attached to the thick ropes you can see hanging from the ceiling and anchored against the wall. Eight strong priests swing the *botafumeiro* (a large incensory) in wide arcs over the congregation. National television broadcasts the ceremony live each year on St. James's Day, July 25.

⑯ You can see a botafumeira and the rest of the cathedral's treasure in the **museums.** *Tel. 981/57-23-00. Admission: 300 pesetas. Open July–Oct., Mon.–Sat. 10–1 and 4–7, Sun. 10–1; Nov.–June, Mon.–Sat. 10–1 and 4–6, Sun. 10–1.*

⑰ Exit through the **Puerta de las Platerías,** on the right side of the nave. The so-called silversmith's door is named for the intricate style of stone carving that completely covers the entryway. The double doorway is the only purely Romanesque part of the cathedral's exterior and opens onto the Plaza de las Platerías, with its graceful fountain, a favorite photo spot.

Continuing counterclockwise around the cathedral, we come to the wide **Plaza de la Quintana,** the haunt of young travelers and musi-
⑱ cians during the warm summer months. The **Puerta Santa** on this plaza is only opened in years in which St. James's Day falls on a Sunday.

Walk around the rest of the cathedral and take in the handsome complex of buildings. As you pass under the Arco del Arzobispo (Bishop's Arch) and arrive back at the Plaza del Obradoiro, you can visit

⑲ the rich 12th-century **Palacio Gelmírez** (Palace of Archbishop Gelmírez) with its Baroque apartments and a lavish 30-meter-long meeting room crowned by a carved ceiling depicting the marriage of King Alfonso IX. *Tel. 981/57–23–00. Admission: 100 pesetas. Open May–Oct., Mon.–Sat. 10–1 and 4–7, Sun 10–1.*

⑳ The **Hostal de los Reyes Católicos** is Santiago's other eye-catching building, constructed in 1499 by Ferdinand and Isabella, the Catholic Monarchs, in gratitude to Santiago for having finally expelled the Moors. Now a parador (*see* Dining and Lodging, *below*), the magnificent building began as a hospice to house pilgrims, but it was quickly converted into a hospital to care for those who fell ill along the road. It remained a hospital until 1953, when it was converted to shameless luxury. There are four arcaded patios with murmuring fountains and gargoyle rainspouts said to be caricatures of the 16th-century townsfolk. The public is allowed to visit in the company of an official city guide. *Admission free. Open daily 10–1 and 4–6.*

As you stand in the middle of the Plaza del Obradoiro, the building
㉑ directly opposite the cathedral is the **Palacio de Rajoy** (Rajoy Pal-
㉒ ace), now the city hall, and the fourth side is enclosed by the **Colegio de San Jerónimo** (San Jerónimo College).

Santiago de Compostela has many other old manor houses, convents, and churches that in most towns would receive headline attention. But the best way to spend your remaining time here is to
㉓ walk around the **old town,** losing yourself in the maze of plazas and narrow streets. The most beautiful Santiago streets are the arcaded Rúa do Vilar, Calle del Franco, and Rúa Nueva. You'll notice that all the streets, archways, and buildings are constructed with big granite blocks, tinted green with the moss that flourishes in this rainy climate. The people of Santiago have learned to accept the wet weather; they never go anywhere without an umbrella and proudly point out that a glazing of rain adds beauty to their streets and buildings.

Time Out | When it's time for a break, head for Santiago's most unusual wine bar, **Bodega Abrigadoiro** (Carrera del Conde 5, tel. 981/56–31–63), in the old town. It's decorated with a working waterwheel, to cool the bottles of young local Ribeiro wine. Your order of *tetilla* (the creamy regional cheese) or a plate of *chorizo* (sausage) comes with a basket of country bread, perfect for a snack.

Numbers in the margin correspond to points of interest on the León, Galicia, and Asturias map.

A 27-km (16-mi) drive southeast of Santiago on N525 allows you to
㉔ visit **Pazo de Oca,** a Galician-style country manor house. The feudal barons who controlled the peasant society of the kingdom of Galicia lived in *pazos*, or homes like this, once sprinkled throughout the region. Walk through the lovely gardens to the lily pond and lake, where a stone boat stays miraculously afloat. *Tel. 981–/57–07–61. Admission: 125 pesetas. Open Apr.–Sept., daily 9–1 and 4–8; Oct.–Mar., daily 10–1 and 3–6.*

If you love beaches, head due west from Santiago along scenic C543 toward the Galician coast, which is sliced by a series of wide estuaries called the *Rías Altas* and *Rías Bajas*. The hilly drive takes you through countryside dotted with tiny farms and *horreos* (grain storage sheds raised 5 feet (1½ meters) off the ground on granite pillars). Notice how even the vineyards are staked with granite posts.

You are likely to see stout black-clad peasant women gracefully carrying heavy loads on their heads.

㉕ A 45-minute drive brings you to **Noyas,** a historic town with the Gothic church of San Martín facing resolutely out to sea and mysterious Celtic inscriptions on the gravestones in the medieval cemetery. The best places to swim and sun are **Testal** and **Boa** beaches.

㉖ Cross the narrow neck of the Tambre River and head up the other side of the *ría* (estuary) to the cheerful harbor town of **Muros,** a popular summer resort with good beaches on Point Louro. Try **Praia de San Francisco** or **Praia de Area.**

㉗ Back on N550, the main north–south highway, the town of **Padrón** is 18 km (11 mi) south of Santiago. This is the town that grew up beside the Roman port of Iria Flavia and the birthplace of Galicia's heroine, the 19th-century poet, Rosalia de Castro. But probably more famous are the delicious *pimientos de Padrón* (tiny green peppers fried and sprinkled with sea salt). The fun in eating them is that one in five or so is hot.

㉘ **Pontevedra** is the next city south along N550. You've probably noticed by now that road signs are difficult to read in Galicia because most have been spray-painted over with place names in the regional language, Gallego, which is actually an offshoot of Portuguese and sounds very different from Spanish.

A charming old town is preserved in Pontevedra, similar in style to Santiago but practically undiscovered by tourists. On the edge of the maze of granite block streets and plazas is the seaman's 16th-century **Santa María Mayor** church, which has a beautifully carved facade in the intricate Plateresque style. The **Museo Provincial** (Provincial Museum) (Sarmiento 51, tel. 986/84–19–27; admission: 175 pesetas; open daily 11–1:30 and 5–8) is housed in two 18th-century mansions. Be sure to see the medieval statues, which were removed from the Door of Glory in Santiago's cathedral when the new facade was built.

㉙ Driving west on C550, you see the *albariño* vineyards, which produce the region's best and rarest wine. The village of **El Grove** (pronounced *GROW-bay*) is on the peninsula, and nearby is the wooded island of **La Toja,** with its luxury spa hotel and golf course (*see* Dining and Lodging, *below*). The gourmet paradise of El Grove throws a shellfish festival each year during the second week of October. But don't wait; you can enjoy the day's catch cooked to order in taverns and restaurants year-round.

㉚ The A9 expressway takes you from Pontevedra to the industrial center of Vigo in about half an hour. From here, head along the southern bank of the Ría Vigo on C550 to **Bayona** on the cape. This was the first town to receive news of the discovery of the New World when one of Columbus's ships landed here in 1493. The main attraction is the **Monte Real,** a hilltop castle-fortress now turned into one of Spain's most popular parador hotels. Walk around the battlements for superb views.

㉛ Follow the coastal road C550 around the peninsula and up the banks of the Miño River, which separates Spain from Portugal, and you come to the town of **Túy.** It was an important defensive position during the seemingly endless medieval wars between Castile and Portugal—which explains why the 13th-century **cathedral** has the look of a fortress. The steep, narrow streets are rich with ancient crested mansions, evidence of Túy's former stature as one of the seven capitals of the Galician kingdom. Today it is important as a border town with Portugal.

To reach northern Galicia and the road to Asturias, take N550 and
② A9 north to **La Coruña,** one of Spain's busiest ports. The weather here can be fierce, wet, and windy, giving this stretch of the Galician seaboard the nickname "Coast of Death." Climate explains the enclosed wood balconies on the tall harbor houses: small panes of glass provide protection from the gales and capture the warmth of the sun when it shines.

La Coruña is built on a narrow strip of land jutting out to sea. Out on the tip of the peninsula is the **Torre de Hercules** lighthouse (renovations and a small museum were due to be completed by late 1994; inquire at the tourist office). The lighthouse was originally built during the reign of Trajan, the Roman emperor born in Spain in AD 98. The whole structure was rebuilt in the 18th century, and all that remain from Roman times are inscribed foundation stones. Huff and puff your way up the 242 steps, and you'll be rewarded with superb views of the city and coastline. Imagine what it must have been like on July 11, 1544, when Spain's Prince Philip set sail with a fleet of 78 vessels for his wedding to Mary Tudor, the daughter of Henry VIII and Catherine of Aragón. In June 1588, the by now King Felipe II assembled another fleet at La Coruña for a different type of voyage. The "invincible" Spanish Armada sailed from here to conquer England. It might have succeeded if not for a ferocious storm that scattered the fleet. The surviving ships limped back into La Coruña a month later. The spirit of Spain had been badly shaken, and to make matters worse, England's notorious Sir Francis Drake sacked the town the following year. The damage done by the English would have been much worse if not for the heroism of a local housewife, María Pita. She saw Drake's men climb the hill into the old town and at great risk fired a cannon to warn the residents. The **Plaza de María Pita** at the edge of the old town is named after her.

Time Out   The Plaza de María Pita is a beautiful square with many open-air bars and restaurants in the summer. City Hall dominates one side of the square. The cafés **Plaza** or **Río Tinto** are fine for a drink or snack before exploring the old town.

At the northeastern tip of the old town is the **Castle of San Antón,** formerly a 16th-century fort. It now houses the Archaeology Museum (tel. 981/20–59–94; admission 150 pesetas; open daily June–Sept., 10–2 and 4:30–7:30; Oct.–May, 10–2 and 4:30–7), where you can see remnants of the prehistoric Celtic culture that once thrived in this region. There are silver artifacts and pieces of the Celtic stone forts called *castros*. On the edge of the old town is the **Museo de Bellas Artes** (Plaza del Pintor Sotomayor, tel. 981/20–56–30; admission 200 pesetas; open Tues.–Sun. 10–3; closed Mon.), which houses paintings and a good collection of Goya etchings. Up on a hill overlooking the city is the **Casa de las Ciencias** (Science Museum; Parque Santa Margarita, tel. 981/27–91–56; admission 150 pesetas; admission to planetarium: 150 pesetas; open June–Sept., Tues.–Sat. 11–9, Sun. 11–2:30; Oct.–May, Tues.–Sat. 10–7, Sun. 11–2:30; closed Mon.). It's a hands-on place in which children can learn the principles of physics and technology.

Heading east 25 km (18 mi) on N VI, you come to the medieval town
③ of **Betanzos.** Parts of the old walls still stand, and you enter through one of the old gateways. The 12th-century **San Francisco** church contains the remains of Fernán Perez de Andrade, one of Galicia's feudal

nobles. The 15th-century **Santa María de Azogue Church** was built by the mariners' guild, while the tailors' guild put up the Gothic-style **Santiago Church,** which includes a Door of Glory inspired by the original in Santiago Cathedral.

Another 46 km (27 mi) farther east on N VI, turn north on N634 toward **Villalba,** which has a tiny parador in a castle associated with the same Andrade family. Continue a winding 81 km (48 mi) past Villalba on N634 and you're back to the coast. Spain's cleanest and least crowded beaches are north of here. If the weather is good, you may want to do some beach exploring or visit the town of **Sargadelos,** where Spain's most distinctive modern-design ceramics are made.

Ribadeo, on the broad ría of the same name, is about 20 km (12 mi) east. Make the bracing walk out to the estuary lighthouse, where you can watch the waves crash against the rocks and study the fishermen hauling in their catch. Upriver is a favorite haunt for salmon and trout fishermen. Just 2 km (1 mi) outside town is the Santa Cruz hill, with more sweeping views and a monument to the bagpipe, the most common folk instrument in Galicia and Asturias.

Tour 3: Oviedo and the Principality of Asturias

Our third tour takes us through the far western reaches of Asturias along N634 into Oviedo. On the way, stop at the village of **Luarca,** tucked into a cove with a sparkling bay and a fishing port. It's a maze of cobbled streets, stone stairways, and whitewashed houses, with painted flowerpots decorating the edge of the harbor.

Back on N634, you'll notice that the countryside is beginning to look a bit more prosperous. Wooden thatched-roof horreos strung with golden bundles of drying corn replace the stark granite sheds of Galicia. Another 100 km (60 mi) through rolling hills and industrialized valleys and you arrive in **Oviedo,** the Asturian capital.

Start your visit to Oviedo just outside the city on the slopes of Mt. Naranco, with two exquisite 9th-century chapels that are unique in all the world and add insight to the rest of the city's monuments. The church of **Santa María del Naranco,** with its superb views, and its plainer sister, **San Miguel de Lillo,** 300 yards uphill, are the jewels of an early architectural style called Asturian Pre-Romanesque, which was centuries ahead of its time. Notice the carved hunting scenes and ceiling vaulting, art and architecture that didn't show up in the rest of Europe for another 200 years. These masterpieces were commissioned as part of a summer palace by King Ramiro I when Oviedo was the capital of Christian Spain. They have survived more than 1,000 years, and, what's more unusual, you can still enjoy them today in the same natural setting that they were designed for. From the arched porches of Santa María, the valley of Oviedo is spread out at your feet. On a clear day the mighty snowcapped Picos de Europa gleam in the distance. *Carretera de los Monumentos, 2 km (1¼ mi) outside town, tel. 98/529–6755. Admission: 200 pesetas (free on Mon.). Open Apr.–Sept., Mon.–Sat. 10–1 and 3–7, Sun. 10–1; Oct.–Mar., Mon.–Sat. 10–1 and 3–5, Sun. 10–1.*

Head for the tallest building in the panorama and you'll arrive at the Gothic **cathedral,** built from the 14th to the 16th century around Oviedo's most cherished monument, the **Cámara Santa** (Holy Chamber). King Ramiro's predecessor, Alfonso the Chaste (792–842), erected the Cámara Santa to hide the treasures of Christian Spain during the long struggle with the Moors. The chamber was heavily damaged during the Spanish civil war but has now been rebuilt. Inside, in the center, is the gold-leaf **Cross of the Angels,** encrusted with pearls and jewels. It was commissioned by Alfonso the Chaste in 808 and is inscribed with the warning: "May anyone who dares to remove me from the place I have been willingly donated be struck down by a bolt of divine lightning." On the left is the more elegant **Victory Cross,** actually a jeweled sheath crafted in 908 to cover the oak cross used by Pelayo in the battle of Covadonga (*see below*). Despite the warning, the crosses and other treasures were stolen from the cathedral in 1977 but were recovered relatively intact as thieves tried to spirit them out of Europe through Portugal. *Plaza Alfonso II El Casto, tel. 98/522–1033. Admission: 250 pesetas. Open May–Oct., Mon.–Sat. 10–1 and 4–7; Nov.–Apr., Mon.–Sat. 10–1 and 4–6; closed Sun.*

Time Out Oviedo has **Cabo Peñas** (Melquiades Alvarez 24), an outstanding tapas bar that shouldn't be missed. It's a huge brick place, bedecked with hams and corn and stacked to the ceiling with wine barrels. You sit on stools at high tables and order plates of salad, sausage, cheese, and seafood from high-speed waiters.

Look directly across the plaza from the cathedral for the 15th-century **Palacio de la Rúa;** it is the oldest in town and still inhabited. Nearby are the beautifully cleaned 16th-century **Antigua Universidad de Oviedo** and, behind the cathedral, the **Museo Arqueológico** (San Vicente 3, tel. 98/512–5405; admission free; open Tues.–Sat. 10–1:30 and 4–6, Sun. 11–1; closed Mon.), housed in the splendid Monastery of San Vicente and containing fragments of Pre-Romanesque buildings. If you've got a taste for Asturian art, visit the **Santullano Church** (Plaza Santullano; admission free; open May–Oct., Tues.–Sun. 11–1 and 4:30–6; Nov.–Apr., Tues.–Sun. 12–1 and 4–5; closed Mon.), built in the 9th century.

If you are a fan of exquisite hotels, take a peek at the **Hotel de la Reconquista** (*see* Dining and Lodging, *below*), a former 18th-century hospice with an imposing Baroque shield on the front. The Spanish crown prince, who carries the title Prince of Asturias, presents an award for world achievement each year from the ornate hotel chapel.

㊴ The lively city of **Gijón** (pronounced *he-HONE*), 28 km (17 mi) north, can be reached on A66. Gijón is part fishing port and part summer holiday resort. It is also a university town and jam-packed with inviting cafés and noisy night spots. Get your bearings by walking the promenade along **San Lorenzo Beach,** which extends from one end of town to the other. It's beautiful in the off-season, but summer swimming is often prohibited because of pollution. Cross the narrow peninsula and you'll be at the harbor, where the fishing fleet comes in with the day's catch. On the hill at the tip of the peninsula is the old fishermen's quarter, **Cimadevilla.** This is also the hub of the city's nightlife. The **Roman Baths** (Campo Valdez), dating back to the time of Emperor Augustus, are closed for excavations and can no longer be visited. However, on the other side of the **Parque Isabel la Católica** at the eastern edge of town, stop in at the **Museo de la Gaita** (Bagpipe Museum, tel. 98/537–3335; admission free; open weekdays 10–7; closed weekends), which has a collection of bagpipes from all over the world and a number of craft workshops. The museum is in a park called the **Pueblo de Asturias,** containing interesting examples of typical Asturian country houses and horreos, desperately in need of better care.

Eastward from Gijón on N632 is the apple orchard country that produces the famous hard cider of Asturias. Green rolling hills, cows,

and wood-shuttered white chalets make this place look more like
Switzerland than Spain. The cider capital of **Villaviciosa** is 32 km (19
mi) down the road. It has a big dairy and several cider-bottling
plants, as well as a picturesque old quarter. Emperor Charles V first
set foot in Spain just down the road from here.

Time Out The real reason to stop in Villaviciosa is to sample the cider. The
main square is lined with cider bars, but one of the best is **El Furacu**
(Plaza Generalísimo 26). The waiter will bring you a full bottle of cider, raise it high above his head, and hold your glass down by his
knees. Then he'll pour, looking straight ahead; it's more macho that
way. Of course, some of the cider splashes on the sawdust-covered
floor. This is not a show for the tourists; the locals claim their flat
cider is aerated this way and tastes better.

Continuing another 38 km (22 mi) east, you reach the fishing village-
cum-beach resort of **Ribadesella,** famous for international canoe
races held on the Sella River the first Saturday of every August.
Aside from plentiful fresh seafood, the town's other attraction is the
Tito Bustillo Cave. The cave was discovered in 1968 by Señor
Bustillo, and within two years it was announced that the 20,000-
year-old paintings in the caves were on a par with those in Lascaux,
France, and Altamira. Giant horses and deer prance about the walls
of the three-chamber cavern. To protect the paintings, no more than
400 visitors a day are allowed inside. *Guided tours in Spanish. Tel.
98/586–1118 or 98/586–1120. Admission: 235 pesetas adults, 70 pesetas children, free on Tues. Open daily 10–1 and 3:30–5:15 except
Sun. in July and Aug.*

Head south about 25 km (18 mi) along the narrow valley carved by
the Sella River to arrive at **Cangas de Onís.** This town was the first
capital of Christian Spain, before the court was moved to Oviedo,
and has the feel of a bracing mountain village. Cangas has a hump-
backed, ivy-covered **Roman bridge** that spans the Sella River Gorge
and is a favorite spot for picture taking.

About 2 km (1¼ mi) east of town on C6312, turn south and head directly for the imposing Peña Santa peak (2,596 m/8,488 ft). At the
end of the winding road is the famous shrine of **Covadonga,** considered the birthplace of Spain. Here, in 718, a handful of sturdy Asturian Christians, led by Don Pelayo, took refuge in the Cave of St.
Mary, about halfway up a cliff, where they prayed to the Virgin
Mary to give them strength to turn back the Moors. They did resist
the superior Moorish forces and set up a Christian kingdom that
eventually led to the Reconquest. Covadonga itself has a basilica in a
magnificent mountain setting and a shrine in the legdendary cave,
which includes an 18th-century statue of the Virgin and Don
Pelayo's grave. The museum displays the treasures donated to the
Virgin of the Cave, including a crown studded with more than 1,000
diamonds. *Tel. 98/584–6077 or 98/524–1412. Suggested admission:
50 pesetas adults, 25 pesetas children. Open Mar.–June, daily 11–2
and 4–6; July–Sept., daily 10:30–2 and 4–7:30; Oct., daily 11:30–2
and 4–6; Nov.–Mar., weekends 11:30–2 and 4–6; closed weekdays.*

A narrow lane connects Covadonga with two alpine lakes in the
heart of the **Sierra de Covadonga National Park.** Toss your fears
aside and head uphill for a spectacular view all the way to the ocean
from the **Mirador de la Reina.** Above the tree line at the top of the
road are **Lake Enol** and **Lake Ercina;** wild horses graze nearby.
Pope John Paul II was brought up here to picnic during his tour of
Galicia and Asturias in 1989.

Wind your way back toward Cangas de Onís, but when you reach C6312, turn east toward Panes. This 55-km (33-mi) drive between **44** Cangas de Onís and Panes, called the **Ruta de Cares** (Cares Route), is the most beautiful in Asturias. The road passes through the towns of Benia and Carreña, with their crested houses, to arrive in **Arenas de Cabrales.** This is the area where the popular Cabrales blue cheese is made. From here, a branch of the road heads into the mountains, and you can follow the Cares River toward the toothlike **Naranjo de Bulnes** (2,519 m/8,264 ft). A number of hiking trails begin here for treks to the villages of Carmarmeña and Bulnes and the spectacular Cares Gorge. Back in Arenas, follow the road east to Panes, and from there you can head for the coast.

What to See and Do with Children

León has a long **park** strung out on the banks of the **Bernesga River,** with playground equipment every 31 meters (100 ft) or so. It's a perfect place to let the little ones run off some steam while Mom and Dad study the map and relax.

Right in the center of Oviedo is **Campo de San Francisco park,** with swans and ducks to feed, as well as plenty of ice cream vendors on hot summer days.

Off the Beaten Track

The **Islas Cies** (pronounced *SEE-ace*), or Cies Islands, lie in the Atlantic Ocean about 35 km (21 mi) out from Vigo. For a glimpse of one of the last unspoiled refuges on the Spanish coast, don't pass up the opportunity to make a trip to the islands. During July, August, and September, about eight boats a day leave from Vigo harbor for the Cies Islands, returning later in the day. Round-trip fare is about $15. The 45-minute ride will bring you to fine white-sand beaches with water that's deep blue-green. This is a nature reserve; birds abound, and the only land transportation is your own two feet. It takes about an hour to hike across the main island. For camping reservations (required), call Camping Islas Cies (tel. 986/43–83–58).

Shopping

Arts and Crafts Galicia is famous throughout Spain for distinctive blue-and-white **ceramics** with bold modern designs. The pieces are made in Sargadelos and O Castro. There is a factory museum and showroom nearby in Cervo on the Lugo coast (**Cerámica de Sargadelos,** Carretera Paraña s/n, tel. 982/55–78–41 or 982/55–76–00; open weekdays 8:30–1 and 4:30–6). A wide choice is also available in Santiago at **Sargadelos** (Rua Nueva 16, tel. 981/58–19–05) and in Sada, near La Coruña, at the combination factory and museum **Cerámicas del Castro** (Carretera Sada–La Coruña s/n, tel. 981/62–02–25). In León, **Artesanías el Grano** (Plaza del Grano) makes **ceramic tile** reproductions of the frescoes found in the San Isidoro Pantheon. **Glazed terracotta ceramics** from Buño (40 km/25mi west of La Coruña on C552) are highly prized. Stop by **Alfaería y Cerámica de Buño** (Calle Barreiros s/n, Buño, tel. 981/71–12–51) for a selection of vases, plates, and wine jugs based on traditional designs. Beautifully crafted black stone **jewelry,** called *azabache* (jet), is found in Santiago at **Fernando Mayer** (Plaza de las Platerías 6, tel. 981/58–50–77) and in Villaviciosa at **Adolfo Cayado Alonso** (Calle Vedriñana) or **José Ordieres Rodriguez** (Calle Arguero). In Betanzos, outside La Coruña, you can visit a **bagpipe workshop** and buy the real thing at **Sellas y Gaitas** (Cerca s/n; open weekdays 10–1 and 5–8).

Clothing Galicia boasts some of Spain's top fashion designers, notably **Adolfo Dominguez,** whose headquarters is in Orense (Av. de la Habana 56, tel. 988/23–45–11). He has stores in Santiago (General Pardiñas 8, tel. 981/56–29–52) and La Coruña (Finisterre 3, tel. 981/25–15–39). Another popular designer, **Teodoro,** has set up shop in Pontevedra (Nuevas Galerías de la Oliva), offering moderately priced ensembles in cotton, linen, and other natural fibers. For unique Spanish-designed children's outfits, try **Oliver** (Sanjurjo 21, León).

For **berets,** the traditional male headgear of the region, try **Luis Tomé Pérez Fábrica de Gorras y Boinas** (Linares Rivas 52, tel. 981/23–20–14) in Coruña. The women of the fishing town of Camariñas fashion exquisite handmade **lace** collars and scarves, as well as table linens. Some of the best places to buy their work are **Vainica** (Rúa do Vilar 58, Santiago, tel. 981/56–67–22), **Dosel** (Rúa Nova 26, Santiago, tel. 981/56–60–78), and **Carmina Touriña** (Panaderas 19, La Coruña, tel. 981/20–62–90).

Food Items If you liked *fabada* (butter beans and sausage), you can take home a do-it-yourself kit complete with beans and meat conserved in a vacuum pack from **Casa Veneranda** (Melquiades Alvarez 23, Oviedo, tel. 98/521–2454). Individual-size Santiago **almond cakes** are sold at **Confitería Vilas** (Rosalia de Castro 70, Santiago, tel. 981/59–68–58), the same ones served at Anexo Vilas Restaurant. Also in Santiago, try **Confitería Mora** (Rua do Vilar 60, tel. 981/58–10–14). In León, regional **cherries in brandy, roasted red peppers,** and **candied chestnuts** are packaged by **Prada a Tope** (Plaza San Martín 1).

Sports

Beaches After allowing unbridled development to spoil the beaches of the Costa del Sol, the Spanish government is now promoting the attractions of northern beaches. Here, though, the weather is not reliable. If a day is hot and sunny, a beautiful beach should be nearby in most of this region. Recommended strands include Llanes, Ribadesella, Cudillero, Santa Ana at Cadavedo, Luarca, Tapia de Casariego, Muros, Noya, El Grove, Islas Cies, Boa, and Testal. Not recommended because of industrial pollution are San Lorenzo, in Gijón, and beaches near Avilés. Unfortunately, the beaches of the Rías Bajas also have some pollution problems.

Canoes and Kayaking Ribadesella, in Asturias, is the white-water capital of Spain. An international race in August is the highlight of the season; the race starts at Arriondas and finishes in Ribadesella. There are several other navigable waterways as well; the tourist office can help you map out a route to match your abilities.

Golf Asturias has two good golf courses, the **Club de Golf de Castiello** in Gijón (tel. 98/536–6313) and **La Barganiza** in Siero (tel. 98/522–4965). Gallegos are fast becoming enamored of teeing off. Courses throughout Galicia include **Monte la Zapateira** (Calle Zapateira s/n, 15310 La Coruña, tel. 981/28–52–00), 11 km (6 mi) from the city; **Domaio** (Domaio, Pontevedra, tel. 986/33–03–86); **La Toja** (Isla La Toja, Pontevedra, tel. 986/73–08–18); and **Padrón** (Padrón, La Coruña, tel. 981/59–88–91). Santiago's links—a private club—are near the airport, **Campo de Golf del Aero Club Labacolla** (tel. 981/59–20–92).

Hiking and Climbing The Picos de Europa and the Covadonga National Park are excellent hiking areas. One of the most popular walks is the **Cares Gorge** (*see* Tour 3, *above*). The tourist offices in Oviedo and Cangas de Onís can help you organize your trek, but for more technical climbing, contact **Servicio de Guías de Montaña** (Cangas de Onís, tel. 98/584–8916). **Mazaneda Estación de Montaña** in Orense (31875 Pobra de Trives, tel. 988/30–87–67) is a full-service resort with mountaineering, biking, and skiing programs. **Nortrak** in La Coruña (Rúa Inés de Castro 7-B, 15005, tel. 981/15–16–74) offers diverse activities ranging from mountain excursions and trekking to paragliding and bungee jumping.

Skiing The three small ski areas in this region cater mostly to families and local residents. The largest is **San Isidro** (tel. 987/73–11–15 or 987/72–11–18), in the Cantabrian Mountains, with one chair lift and 12 slopes. Just east of there is **Valgrande Pajares** (tel. 98/549–6123; two chair lifts, eight slopes). West of Orense, in Galicia, **Manzaneda** (tel. 988/31–08–75) has one chair lift and seven slopes. Valgrande Pajares and Manzaneda also have cross-country skiing.

Dining and Lodging

Dining

Galicia and Asturias are famous throughout Spain for seafood. Specialties include *merluza a la Gallega* (steamed hake in Galician paprika sauce) and *merluza a la sidra* (steamed hake in a tangy Asturian cider sauce). Scallops *(vieira)*, the symbol of the pilgrim to Santiago, are popular in Galicia, where there are also entire bars that serve nothing but wine and *pulpo* (fried octopus). In Asturias salmon and trout from local rivers are a treat. The region is also famous for hearty stews that warm you on a wet, chilly day. In Asturias try *fabada* (butter beans and sausage), and in Galicia sample *caldo Gallego* (stew of potatoes, cabbage, chickpeas, and meat broth). Savory fish or meat pies called *empanadas* are native to Galicia and can be eaten out of the hand like a sandwich. The province of León specializes in roast lamb and suckling pig and produces a sparkling rosé wine called *bierzo*, similar to the acidic Galician *ribeiro*. The best Galician wine is the smooth, crisp white *albariño*, while Asturias is famous for its *sidra* (hard cider), served either carbonated or still. While much of this region is rural and remote, restaurant prices are not substantially lower than those in the rest of the country—especially those in Santiago de Compostela, which has been making a living from tourism for 900 years. Expect to pay a lot for fine food.

Informal dress is acceptable at all restaurants in León, Galicia, and Asturias, but shorts and beach garb are not. Regional restaurants are not likely to turn away tourists, no matter how they are dressed, but women will probably feel more comfortable in skirts or dressy pants, and men should wear slacks with sports shirts. Jackets are not required.

Highly recommended restaurants are indicated by a star ★.

Category	Cost*
$$$$	over 6,000 ptas
$$$	4,500–6,000 ptas
$$	2,800–4,500 ptas
$	under 2,800 ptas

*per person, excluding drinks, service, and tax

Lodging

The government-run parador hotel chain has cornered the market on charming places for tourists to stay. Galicia has nine parador hotels, three in elegant manor houses and two in old fortresses. León boasts one of the finest paradors in the system, in a stunning converted convent. The parador in Asturias is in the Gijón city park. Check descriptions carefully before making your choices because some paradors are in modern buildings. Most of the good-quality hotels are high rises geared to business travelers or package tour groups. It may be a good idea to inspect your room before settling in, for some rooms, even in the fine hotels, can be suffocatingly small. Reservations are important through the busy summer season, May–October, but not essential the rest of the year.

Highly recommended lodgings are indicated by a star ★.

Category	Cost*
$$$$	over 16,000 ptas
$$$	12,000–16,000 ptas
$$	8,000–12,000 ptas
$	under 8,000 ptas

*All prices are for a standard double room for two, excluding tax and breakfast.

Bayona
Dining and Lodging
★

Parador Conde de Gondomar. A modern hotel has been constructed inside the walls of a medieval castle. All rooms are furnished with period reproductions, and some have balconies, with views of the sea from a hilltop fortified since 200 BC. The dining room serves regional specialties; try the *entremeses variados* (mixed appetizers) for a sampler of typical seafoods. *Carretera de Bayona, 36300, tel. 986/35-50-00. 124 rooms with bath. Facilities: restaurant, bar, beach, pool, gym, tennis court, sauna, playground, garden. AE, DC, MC, V. $$$*

Cambados
Dining and Lodging

Parador El Albariño. Built in 1966 in the style of an old manor house, this parador faces the Atlantic. The lobby has heavy leather furniture and beamed ceilings. The rooms are simply furnished with wrought-iron lamps, handmade rugs, and ceiling-high wood shutters over small-paned windows. The dining room serves such Galician dishes as *lacon con grelos* (ham with turnip tops). Be sure to order a bottle of local albariño wine. *Paseo de Cervantes s/n, 36630, tel. 986/54-22-50. 63 rooms with bath. Facilities: restaurant, bar, garden, tennis. AE, DC, MC, V. $$*

Cangas de **La Tiendona.** This handsomely restored roadhouse is strategically
Onís located halfway between the mountains of Cangas de Onís and the
Dining and beaches of Ribadesella. Rooms feature country-style furnishings
Lodging and beamed ceilings. The dining room emphasizes regional special-
ties such as smoked salmon, fabada, and cider. *Ctra. Nac.*
Arriondas–Ribadesella, tel. 98/584–0474. 18 rooms. Facilities: res-
taurant, bar. AE, V. $$

La Coruña **El Coral.** The front window is a high altar of shellfish, with varieties
Dining of mollusks and crustaceans you've probably never seen before. In-
side, wood-paneled walls, crystal chandeliers, and 12 white-clothed
tables provide the setting for an intimate, elegant yet casual meal.
Diners here are encouraged to take time to enjoy the food and con-
versation. Specialties include traditional regional dishes such as
hake and *cachelos* (potatoes) drizzled with garlicky, paprika-in-
fused oil, or a mind-boggling, stomach-satisfying *turbante de*
mariscos, a platter (literally a "turban") of steamed and boiled shell-
fish. *Estrella 2–4, tel. 981/22–10–82. Reservations required. AE,*
DC, MC, V. Closed Sun. except June–Sept. $$–$$$

Lodging **Finisterre.** Fitness was on the minds of the designers of this hotel, a
superbly located high rise where the old town joins the bay. It has
its own sports complex and four pools. Long a favorite with busi-
nessmen visiting La Coruña, Finisterre has comfortable, carpeted
rooms with modern wood furnishings and brightly colored uphol-
stery. Many rooms overlook the bay. *Paseo del Parrote, 15314, tel.*
981/20–54–00. 127 rooms with bath. Facilities: restaurant; bar; 4
pools, 2 heated all year; tennis; gym; sauna; children's playground;
garden. AE, DC, MC, V. $$$

Gijón **Casa Victor.** Owner Victor Bango runs an inventive seafood restau-
Dining rant that adds a touch of new cuisine to many traditional Asturian
dishes. The bright and noisy dining room is always packed. Service
is friendly. Try the hake in leek sauce or clams with asparagus.
Carmen 11, tel. 98/535–0093. Reservations advised. AE, DC, MC,
V. Closed Sun. evening, Thurs., Nov. $$

Dining and **Parador Molino Viejo.** The only parador in Asturias is one of the sim-
Lodging plest and friendliest in the chain. The modern rooms are small, with
bleached wood floors and thick pine shutters. Be sure to ask for a
view of the city park, a favorite with joggers or families with chil-
dren. The dining room is popular with locals. Try the *tigres* (spicy
stuffed mussels), *pimientos de piquillos rellenos de champiñones*
(green peppers stuffed with squid and rice), or the *oricios* (sea ur-
chins), eaten raw or served steamed with lemon juice or a spicy hot
sauce. The garden cider bar is often crowded with locals. *Parque de*
Isabel la Católica, 36980, tel. 98/537–0511. 40 rooms with bath. Fa-
cilities: restaurant, garden. AE, DC, MC, V. $$

El Grove **Posada del Mar.** Overlooking the channel that separates El Grove
Dining from the island of La Toja, the dining room is decorated with a collection of country ceramics from all parts of Spain. Expertly prepared seafood is king here. Try the monkfish in garlic butter and the
caldo Gallego. *Castelao 202, tel. 986/73–01–06. Reservations ad-*
vised for weekend lunches. AE, MC, V. Closed mid-Dec.–Jan. $$

Lodging **Gran Hotel de la Toja.** This sybaritic Spanish version of Belle
Epoque elegance is surrounded by a pine forest. Rooms are simple
and slightly dowdy compared to the grandiose formality of the spa
hotel's public salons and foyers. Dining areas have expansive sea
views, and special diet menus are available. *36991 Isla de la Toja,*
tel. 986/73–00–25. 201 rooms with bath. Facilities: restaurant, min-
eral-springs therapy, beach, pool, 9-hole golf course, tennis court,

shooting, riding, gym, sauna, discothèque, casino. AE, DC, MC, V. $$$$

León **Adonias.** Enter through the ground-floor bar and climb one flight up
Dining to the softly lit green dining room, furnished with rustic tables and
colorful ceramics. The cuisine is based on regional products such as
cured hams, roast peppers, and chorizo. Try the grilled sea bream
and the homemade lemon pudding. *Santa Nonia 16, tel. 987/20–67–
68. Reservations advised. AE, DC, MC, V. Closed second half of
July. $$*

Casa Pozo. This longtime favorite is located right across from city
hall on the historic Plaza de San Marcelo. A display case of meats
and fish adorns the entrance, while the bright dining rooms are sim-
ply furnished with heavy Castilian tables and chairs. Owner Gabriel
del Pozo Alvarez, called Pin by his loyal customers, supervises the
busy kitchen and attentive service. Specialties include fresh peas
with ham, roast lamb, and deep-fried breaded hake. *Plaza de San
Marcelo 15, tel. 987/22–30–39 or 987/23–71–03. AE, DC, V. Closed
Sun., first half of July, and 2 weeks at Christmas. $$*

Nuevo Racimo de Oro. Set on the second floor of a ramshackle 12th-
century tavern in the heart of the old town, the restaurant specializes in roast suckling lamb cooked in a wood-fired clay oven. Try the
spicy Castilian garlic soup served in a wooden bowl with a wooden
spoon, or medieval-style spinach with raisins and pine nuts. *Plaza
San Martín 8, tel. 987/21–47–67. No reservations. MC, V. Closed
Sun. evening, Tues. $$*

Dining and **Hotel San Marcos.** This magnificent parador is a restored 16th-cen-
Lodging tury monastery built by King Ferdinand to shelter pilgrims walking
★ the route of Santiago. The Plateresque facade is longer than a foot-
ball field. A church and an archaeology museum are housed in the
same building. The rooms are furnished with valuable antiques and
high-quality reproductions. A modern addition with a pool has been
built on the back of the hotel. If you enjoy medieval luxury, ask for a
room in the old section. The elegant dining room overlooks the
Bernesga River. Try the braised baby lamb chops, *cecina* (smoked
beef), or the sole with raisin and pine-nut sauce. Top off the meal
with *leche quemada*, a light egg custard with a carmelized crust.
*Plaza de San Marcos 7, 24001, tel. 987/23–73–00. 258 rooms with
bath. Facilities: restaurant, bar, gardens, beauty parlor. AE, DC,
MC, V. $$$*

Lodging **Hotel Riosol.** This modern high rise is across the river from town and
not far from the train station. The comfortable carpeted rooms, decorated with black-lacquer furniture and gold wallpaper, are a frequent choice of business travelers. *Av. de Palencia 3, 24001, tel. 987/
21–66–50. 141 rooms with bath. Facilities: restaurant, coffee shop.
AE, DC, MC, V. $*

Llanes **La Pousada de Babel.** This is one of several exquisite family-run inns
Lodging that have sprung up to cater to Asturias's growing fame as a center
for rural tourism. The tiny hotel offers plenty of personal attention
and roaring fires in the public rooms. One of the bedrooms is in a converted granary. *La Pereda, 33509, tel. 98/540–2525. 8 rooms with
bath. Facilities: restaurant, bar, library, gardens, mountain bikes,
horseback riding. MC, V. $$*

Luarca **Leonés.** Medieval images are evoked by the large iron chandeliers
Dining and rural antiques that line the walls. Try peppers stuffed with
shellfish or fabada, and for dessert, apple sherbet. If you don't use a
credit card, you can order from a substantially cheaper menu. *Paseo*

Alfonso X el Sabio, tel. 98/564–0995. No reservations. AE, DC, MC, V. $$

Lodging **Gayoso.** This comfortable old and charming hotel has been run by the same family for 120 years. It has spacious rooms and wooden balconies with views of the Black River. Five of the hotel's 30 rooms have been upgraded to three-star status, and cost almost twice as much as the others. *Paseo de Gómez 4, 33700, tel. 98/564–0050. AE, DC, MC, V. $$*

Oviedo **Casa Fermin.** This sophisticated pink-and-granite restaurant, with
Dining its plants and skylights, has an air of modernity that belies more
★ than 50 years of experience in the kitchen. Founder Luis Gil has introduced traditional Asturian cuisine in seminars around the world and frequently holds week-long festivals at Casa Fermin featuring visiting chefs. The wine cellar is extensive. Specialties include fabada; wild game in season; and hake in cider, decorated with rounds of fresh apple. *San Francisco 8, tel. 98/521–6452. Reservations advised on weekends. AE, DC, MC, V. Closed Sun. evening. $$$*

★ **Trascorrales.** Nouvelle Spanish cuisine is presented with flair at this unusual restaurant. Tucked into a vine-covered building in the corner of the plaza that houses Oviedo's fish market, Trascorrales is a jumble of cozy wooden booths decorated with copper on the walls and wicker lampshades. Recommended dishes include crab mousse, filet mignon with sweet mustard, and fresh strawberries in a sugar-and-spice pepper sauce. *Plaza Trascorrales 19, tel. 98/522–2441. Reservations advised. AE, DC, MC, V. Closed Sun. $$$*

El Raitan. Owned by the same family as Trascorrales, and just across the plaza from it, El Raitan is perfect if you have a big appetite. The restaurant is styled like an old-fashioned kitchen, with an antique cookstove in the entrance. At lunch, there's no menu; everyone is served the same nine dishes, all Asturian specialties: seafood soup, crab bisque, vegetable and bean stew, fabada, potatoes stuffed with meat, onions filled with tomatoes, rice pudding, crepes, and nut pastries. *Plaza Trascorrales 6, tel. 98/521–4218. Reservations advised. AE, DC, MC, V. Closed Sun. evening. $$*

★ **La Maquina.** To sample the best fabada in Asturias, head 6 km (4 mi) outside Oviedo on the road to Avilés. Stop when you see the farmhouse with the miniature locomotive out front; there's no other sign. The only decoration in the *L*-shape whitewashed dining room is a wooden hat rack, but the kitchen has been cooking fabada for 50 years and attracts customers from all over Spain. Leave room for the memorable rice pudding topped by a crisp layer of hot caramel. *Av. de Santa Barbara 59, tel. 98/526–0019. Reservations advised. AE, MC. Lunch only, closed Sun. $*

Lodging **Hotel de la Reconquista.** Housed in an 18th-century hospice embla-
★ zoned with a huge stone coat of arms, the Reconquista is run by the Italian Ciga chain. The wide lobby is circled by a balcony supported on granite pillars. It is decorated with 18th-century paintings, velvet upholstery, and the same type of carpet the king has in the Royal Palace. A pianist entertains nightly. The rooms are large and modern, with comfortable beds and a big armchair for collapsing into after a day of sightseeing. *Gil de Jaz 16, 33004, tel. 98/524–1100. 142 rooms with bath. Facilities: restaurant, coffee shop, bar, beauty parlor, men's sauna. AE, DC, MC, V. $$$$*

Hotel Principado. If you value friendliness over flash, you might enjoy a stay at the Principado, located between the old town and the park. The rooms were renovated in 1989, but the public lobby is still like a comfortable living room. *San Francisco 6, 33003, tel. 98/521–7792. 70 rooms with bath. Facilities: restaurant, bar. AE, MC, V. $$*

Pontevedra **Casa Solla.** Owner Pepe Solla makes the most of the bountiful har-
Dining vest from local coasts and vineyards at his terraced garden restau-
★ rant, 2 km (1¼ mi) outside town on the highway to El Grove. Try the
sole in albariño wine sauce, filet mignon in red wine, and the mandarin oranges with hot caramel sauce. *Carretera El Grove, Km 2, tel.
986/85–26–78. Reservations advised. MC, V. Closed Thurs. and
Sun. evening. $$*

Lodging **Casa del Barón.** An understated 18th-century manor house in the
heart of Pontevedra, this parador hotel has a baronial stone stair-
way that winds into the front lobby. The rooms are furnished with
antique reproductions and face a rose garden. *Maceda s/n, 36002,
tel. 986/85–58–00. 47 rooms with bath. Facilities: restaurant, li-
brary, garden. AE, DC, MC, V. $$*

Ribadeo **O Xardin.** Recent renovations have not destroyed the charm of this
Dining old-fashioned garden restaurant. Specialties include mint-scented
vegetable pudding, casserole of monkfish and scallops, and sole with
wild mushroom and albariño wine sauce. *Reinante 20, tel. 982/11–
02–22. No reservations. DC, MC, V. Closed Mon. except in sum-
mer. $$*

Lodging **Parador de Ribadeo.** A modern parador built on the banks of the Eo
River, it has views across to Asturias. Gleaming hardwood floors
and hefty rafters convey a feeling of warmth in this whitewashed ho-
tel. Rooms have Castilian-style furniture, artisan rugs, and large
baths. The estuary provides a cornucopia of shellfish for the dining
room, including cockles, clams, and oysters. *Amador Fernández,
27700, tel. 982/11–08–25. 47 rooms with bath. Facilities: restaurant,
garden. AE, DC, MC, V. $$*

Ribadesella **El Repollu.** This small, simple, and homey grill specializes in fish
Dining dishes. There's not even a foyer; once you enter, you are standing
next to people dining. Try the fresh-grilled turbot. The house
Cabrales cheese is explosive! *Santa Marina 2, tel. 98/586–0734. No
reservations. AE, DC, MC, V. Closed Oct. $*

Santiago de **Anexo Vilas.** Owner Moncho Vilas likes to mingle with his happy cus-
Compostela tomers and loves to promote Galician cuisine. His expertise in the
Dining kitchen has won acclaim from Spanish gourmets, and he even pre-
★ pared the banquet when Pope John Paul II visited Santiago in 1989.
The pope's menu included seafood empanada, mussels, deep-fried
hake, and Santiago almond cake. Other specialties are salmon with
clams and hake a la Gallega (with paprika sauce). Anexo Vilas is a
little outside town but worth the walk. *Av. Villagarcia 21, tel. 981/
59–83–87. Reservations advised. AE, MC, V. Closed Mon. $$$*

Don Gaiferos. Named for a mythical medieval minstrel who used to
roam the trail to Santiago, Don Gaiferos is in the old section of town.
Stone walls, modern furnishings, and indirect lighting enhance the
international cuisine. Selections include pepper steak and sole
cooked in wine with béchamel sauce and Parmesan cheese. *Rua
Nova 23, tel. 981/59–38–94. Reservations advised. AE, MC, V.
Closed Sun. $$$*

San Clemente. On a tiny square off the Plaza del Obradoiro, this restaurant offers high-quality seafood just about any time of the day or
night (closed 2–8 AM). Don't be put off by the long bar in the front
room; let them lead you to the large, comfortable dining room in back
and feast on scallops, shrimp, sole, hake, or the famous Galician *pulpo*
(fried octopus). *San Clemente 6, tel. 981/56–54–26. AE, DC, MC, V.
$$*

Lodging **Araguaney.** If you prefer modern luxuries, book into the Araguaney. It's a glass-and-chrome palace built by an Arab who came to Santiago as a medical student and fell in love with the daughter of a wealthy Galician family. The rooms are spacious. The discothèque, built underneath the glass-bottom pool, is one of the trendiest night spots in town. *Alfredo Brañas 5, 15701, tel. 981/59–59–00. 65 rooms with bath. Facilities: restaurant, bar, heated pool, sauna, discothèque, hairdresser. AE, DC, MC, V. $$$$*

★ **Hostal de los Reyes Católicos.** A converted 15th-century hospital, one of Santiago's main tourist attractions, houses a legendary parador hotel. The hospital was built as a tribute to St. James by King Ferdinand and Queen Isabella after the Moors were expelled from Spain. Behind a two-story-high Plateresque facade are four interior patios with formal gardens, murmuring fountains, carved stone arcades, and amusing gargoyles. The rooms are very large and furnished with a collection of antiques that spans five centuries and includes some regal canopy beds. *Plaza del Obradoiro, 15705, tel. 981/58–22–00. 136 rooms with bath. Facilities: restaurant, bar, hairdresser. AE, DC, MC, V. $$$$*

Peregrino. The best of the moderately priced lodgings in Santiago is a relatively new motel-style inn about a 15-minute walk from the center of town and not far from Anexo Vilas (*see above*). The airy, modern rooms are furnished in unobtrusive earth tones with bright accents and have large new baths. *Rosalia de Castro s/n, 15706, tel. 981/52–18–50. 148 rooms with bath. Facilities: garden, heated pool, discothèque. AE, DC, MC, V. $$*

Túy
Dining and Lodging

Parador San Telmo. Located on the bluffs overlooking the Miño River, which divides Spain from Portugal, the hotel is modeled after a *pazo* (Galician country manor house). Paintings by local artists and rural antiques decorate the lobbies. The rooms are furnished with convincing reproductions. Good views of the surrounding woods can be had from the windows of the dining room, where regional specialties include river salmon and trout. *36700 Túy, tel. 986/60–03–09. 22 rooms with bath. Facilities: restaurant, bar, garden, pool. AE, DC, MC, V. $$*

Villafranca del Bierzo
Dining and Lodging

Parador de Villafranca del Bierzo. This modern two-story hotel, built in 1975, sits on a hilltop overlooking the fertile Bierzo valley. The ample rooms have heavy wood furniture and window shutters, comfortable beds, and large baths. The brick and wrought-iron dining room offers meals that include fresh Bierzo trout and *chanfaina barciana* (fried liver and bread crumbs). Also try the local Bierzo wine. *Calvo Sotelo s/n, 24500, tel. 987/54–01–75. 30 rooms with bath. Facilities: restaurant, bar, garden. AE, DC, MC, V. $–$$*

Villalba
Dining and Lodging

Parador Condes de Villalba. This tiny parador is housed in a medieval tower that was once a fortress. A drawbridge leads to the two-story lobby, hung with medieval-style tapestries. Three large octagonal rooms are stacked on top of one another in the massive tower, and three more are in a lower building. They have beamed ceilings and hardwood floors, hand-carved Spanish-style furniture, and wood chandeliers. The dining room offers regional seafood and specializes in empanadas. *Valeriano Valdesuso, 27800, tel. 982/51–00–11. 6 rooms with bath. Facilities: restaurant, bar, garden. AE, DC, MC, V. $$$*

The Arts and Nightlife

The Arts

Concerts by internationally known orchestras and solo artists take place in Santiago de Compostela at the Auditorium of Galicia. A schedule of events is available at the tourist office.

The Hostal de los Reyes Católicos, in Santiago, holds a classical music course from July 20 to August 10 each summer. Some 150 musicians from many countries participate, and free **concerts** are given in the beautiful hotel performance hall every night.

Plays and concerts are also presented at the Municipal Theater in Oviedo; check newspapers for schedules.

Fiestas Northwestern Spain abounds in folklore and popular fiestas. Some of the major ones include:

Festa do Chrouizo en Sant Anton de Abedes, January 17, Verin (Orense); parade and sausage festival in honor of the local saint.
Procesión dos Fachos, night of January 20, Castro Caldelas in Orense; torchlight procession commemorating the village's survival of a cholera outbreak in 1753.
Fiesta del Cocido, second Sunday in February, Lalin (Pontevedra); celebrates Galicia's version of the hearty national meat, potato, and vegetable stew.
Fiesta del Queso, first week in March, Arzua (La Coruña); folklore and food, with a contest for outstanding cheeses of the region.
Semana Santa, Easter week, Viveiro; barefoot procession of flagellants, illuminated by hundreds of candles held by spectators and participants.
Fiesta de los Huevos Pintados, Easter week, Pola de Siero; decorative, intricately painted Easter eggs.
Rapa das Bestas, July 7–8, Pontevedra; roundup of wild horses.
Cider Festival, Mid-July, Nava, Asturias.
Día de Santiago, July 25, Santiago de Compostela; fireworks and mass celebrated with botafumeiro incense burner.
Shepherds' Festival, July 25, Cangas de Onís and Covadonga National Park; regional dances and bagpipe music.
Albariño Wine Festival, first Sunday in August, Cambados.
Día de América, September 19, Oviedo; Latin American costumes, parades, and street dances.

Nightlife

León's nightlife centers on the **Barrio Húmedo,** near the cathedral in the old part of town; try the popular **El Gaucho** bar, where they serve a cup of spicy garlic soup or an order of peppery potatoes with every drink. In Santiago, bars line the streets of the old town, and the most popular discothèque in town is at the **Araguaney Hotel** (*see* Dining and Lodging, *above*). In Oviedo you can get a nightcap at the plant-filled **Sidreria Venicia** (Doctor Casal 13), while the younger crowd will enjoy the loud rock music at the brass-and-glass **La Loggia** across the street from the cathedral. In La Coruña, wander along Calle Estrella, Calle de los Olmos, and La Galera for traditional cheese, ham, and octopus tapas and local ribeiro wine served in *tazas* (white ceramic cups). For more expensive shellfish tidbits, try the Calle Troncoso, behind the Plaza María Pita. Serious night owls head for the area around Orzan beach, the Marina, or the streets of old town. In picturesque Betanzos, locals head for the bars along Calle del Progreso.

There are two casinos in the region—the **Casino del Atlántico,** in La Coruña (Jardines de Médez Nuñez, tel. 981/22–16–00), and **Casino La Toja** (La Toja, tel. 986/73–10–00).

6 Burgos, Santander, and the Basque Country

*By Mark
Potok*

This chapter explores three very different destinations in northern
Spain. Burgos, at the edge of the central meseta, is one of the most
quintessentially Castilian cities; Santander (Cantabria), once the
seaport for Old Castile on the Bay of Biscay, is a very Spanish beach
resort and mountainous zone wedged between the Basques to the
east and the Asturians to the west; and the Basque country
(Euskadi in its own mysterious non-Indo-European language), with
its moist green hills and rugged coastline, is a distinct and semi-au-
tonomous national and cultural entity within the Spanish state.

Burgos was the 11th-century capital of Castile and the native city of
El Cid, or "lord conqueror," Spain's legendary hero of the Christian
reconquest of the Iberian Peninsula from Moorish domination.
Franco's wartime headquarters were established at Burgos during
the 1936–39 Spanish Civil War, possibly as much for symbolic as for
strategic reasons. Even today the army and the clergy seem to set
the tone in this somber city, which sprawls in the shadow of one of
Europe's finest Gothic cathedrals.

Santander is a traditionally Castilian and conservative stronghold
with sandy beaches, the peaks of the Cantabrian mountains, tiny
mountain towns, and colorful fishing villages.

The Basque country is a country within a country, or a nation within
a state (the semantics are much debated, even today) with a language of its own: Euskera. In contrast to the individualistic, anar-
chic, and passionate Latin peoples who have been their neighbors,
the Basques have most often been regarded as collective-minded,
democratic, and practical. They are also known to love competition—it's been said that Basques will bet on anything that has numbers on it and moves. Such traditional rural sports as chopping
mammoth tree trunks, lifting boulders, or scything grass reflect the
Basques' traditional attachment to the land and farm life as well as
an ingrained admiration for feats of strength and endurance. Even
poetry and gastronomy become contests in Euskadi, as *bersolaris*
(amateur poets) improvise duels of (often very witty) verse, and
men-only *sociedades gastronómicas* compete in cooking contests to
see who can make the best *marmitako* (tuna stew).

The much-reported Basque independence movement is made up of a
small but radical sector of the political spectrum. The underground
organization known as ETA, or Euskadi Ta Askatasuna (Basque
Homeland and Liberty), has claimed over 700 victims in 25 years of
terrorist activity. While this continuing problem is extremely unlikely to affect or endanger the visitor, it will be inescapably apparent in the political graffiti—of an unusually colorful and photogenic
variety—that adorn nearly every free inch of wall space from San
Sebastián to Bilbao to Pamplona.

The Basque country also has longtime connections with both Britain
and the United States. Bilbao and its province of Vizcaya, in particular, were the source of most of the iron used by the English during
the Industrial Revolution. The region as a whole, poor before industry made it a center of productivity on the peninsula, has long sent
out wave upon wave of immigrants to the New World. Consequently, the Basques are unusually friendly to both Americans and the
British—often friendlier, in fact, than they are to Spaniards of the
south, who are still widely seen as unwelcome interlopers.

Essential Information

Important Addresses and Numbers

Tourist Information General information and pamphlets on the Basque provinces (Alava, Vizcaya, and Guipúzcoa) are available in the regional government building (Parque de la Florida, Vitoria, tel. 945/13–13–21) and at Calle Fueros 1, San Sebastián, tel. 943/42–62–82).

Bilbao: The official city tourism office is on the ground floor of the Teatro Arriaga downtown (Plaza Arriaga, tel. 94/416–0022 or 94/416–0288), the regional tourism office is at Gran Via 44–1 Izq. (tel. 94/424–2277). **Burgos:** Plaza Alonso Martínez 7, tel. 947/20–31–25. **Guernica:** Akertale 8, tel. 94/625–5892. **Pamplona:** Calle Duque de Ahumada 3, tel. 948/22–07–41. **San Sebastián:** Calle Reina Regente s/n, tel. 943/48–11–66. **Santander:** Plaza Porticada 1, tel. 942/31–07–08. **Vitoria:** Edificio Europa, Av. Gasteiz, tel. 945/16–15–98.

Emergencies **Police:** tel. 091.

Consulates **Bilbao:** *Great Britain*, Calle Alameda Urquijo 2, 8th floor, tel. 94/415–7600 or 94/415–7722. *United States*, Avenida Lehendakari Aguirre 11, 3rd floor, tel. 94/475–8300 or 94/475–8308.

Arriving and Departing by Plane

The major airport serving the region is 11 km (7 mi) outside Bilbao, and Iberia has regular connections between there and England, France, Madrid, and Barcelona. Smaller, less convenient airports serve Santander, San Sebastián, and Pamplona, each with less frequent service to Madrid and Barcelona.

Arriving and Departing by Car, Train, Bus, and Boat

By Car Traveling by car is the best way to see Burgos, Santander, and the Basque country, the remotest point of which is an easy one-day drive from Madrid. From the capital, the logical starting point for such a visit to the north, it's 242 km (150 mi) on the N I (or the A1 toll road) to Burgos, and 396 km (246 mi) if you continue on the N623 to Santander. Driving direct from Madrid to Bilbao will take you 401 km (247 mi): Follow the N I or A1 past Burgos to Miranda del Ebro, where you pick up the A68 into Bilbao. From Madrid, San Sebastián is 472 km (293 mi) if you travel the fastest route, via Bilbao, and take the A8 toll road from there.

By Train Burgos, Santander, Bilbao, and San Sebastián are all well served by trains direct from the Chamartín Station in Madrid or, with some changes, from virtually every major city in Spain. If you're leaving from Madrid, call the RENFE train company for information (tel. 91/530–0202).

By Bus Daily bus service connects all the major cities of the region to Madrid, with several departures a day in some cases. San Sebastián and Bilbao are especially well connected with the capital. In Madrid, try getting through to Continental Auto bus company for information (tel. 91/533–0400), or go right to the station at Calle Alenza 20.

By Boat Santander is linked to Plymouth, England, by a twice-weekly car ferry that operates year-round. For information, contact Brittany Ferries (Paseo de Pereda 27, Santander, tel. 942/22–00–00, main office, or 942/21–45–00, port); or Brittany's offices in England

(Millbay Docks, Plymouth, PL1 3EW, tel. 0752/22–13–21); or go through travel agencies in Spain or Britain. Be sure to book at least six weeks in advance in summer because the 24-hour passages are often sold out. Another option is the ferry that travels between Bilbao and Portsmouth, England; there are two sailings each week. Contact Ferries Golfo de Vizcaya (Cosme Etxevarrieta 1, 48009 Bilbao, tel. 94/423–4477 or fax 94/423–5496).

Getting Around

By Car Because so many of the north's attractions are rural landscapes and relatively small towns, a car is the ideal mode of transportation. Some distances within this relatively small area are Burgos–Bilbao, 159 km (99 mi); Santander–Bilbao, 107 km (66 mi); Bilbao–San Sebastián, 99 km (61 mi); and San Sebastián–Pamplona, 91 km (56 mi). The region offers the best road system in Spain, with several excellent toll roads and most of the smaller roads paved and in very good shape. The N 1 from the French border to San Sebastián and Vitoria is packed with tourists in July and August, however, and should be avoided at all costs during those months. In addition, the N634 from Santander to Bilbao snakes through mountainous country and can be very slow going because of trucks, however, a new four-lane highway, due to be completed in 1993, will dramatically improve that trip.

By Train Trains are not the ideal way to travel the region, although many major cities are connected by rail. The main train stations in the region belong to the RENFE system. They are **Burgos** (end of Avenida Conde de Guadalhorce, tel. 947/20–35–60; RENFE agent, Calle La Moneda 21, tel. 947/20–91–31); **Santander** (Calle Rodríguez near the center of town, tel. 942/21–02–11; RENFE office, Paseo de Pereda 25, tel. 942/21–23–87 or 942/21–85–67); **Bilbao** (Estación del Abando, Calle Hurtado de Amezaga, tel. 94/423–8623 and 94/423–8636); **San Sebastián** (Estación del Norte, Avenida de Francia, tel. 943/28–30–89 and 943/28–35–99; RENFE's main offices, Calle Camino 1, tel. 943/42–64–30); and **Pamplona** (on the road to San Sebastián, tel. 948/13–02–02). In addition, the regional FEVE train company (Estación de FEVE, next to the Estación de Abando, Bilbao, tel. 94/423–2266) runs a delightful narrow-gauge train that winds through stunning alpine and coastal landscapes. From San Sebastián, lines west to Bilbao and east to Hendaye depart from the Estación de Amara (Plaza Easo 9, tel. 943/45–01–31 or 943/47–18–52).

By Bus Bus service among the main cities and most smaller towns is comprehensive, but few cities have main bus stations where information can be obtained; most have numerous bus companies serving different routes and leaving from different points. Ask at travel agencies or local tourist offices. The following do have central bus stations: **Burgos** (Calle Miranda 4, tel. 947/26–55–65); **Santander** (Calle Navas de Tolosa s/n, tel. 942/21–19–95); **Pamplona** (Calle Conde Oliveto 8, tel. 948/22–38–54); and **San Sebastián** (Calle Sancho el Sabio 33, tel. 943/46–39–74); each of the local bus companies runs a booth in the station.

Guided Tours

There are no regularly organized tours in the region, but travel agencies in the major cities discussed can tell you about occasional possibilities offered by local firms, usually during the summer. In

Pamplona, the tourist office keeps a list of private guides and interpreters for hire.

Exploring Burgos, Santander, and the Basque Country

Orientation

All parts of the region will not appeal equally to all visitors. If your taste is for traditional Spain, a parched land of whitewashed villages and brilliant light, you will want to concentrate on Burgos, at the beginning of the tour. But if your tastes run to misty, romantic hills; landscapes dotted with grazing sheep and horses; and picturesque fishing villages, you will want to spend most of your time on the north coast and its provinces and in Navarra, an extremely rustic province that runs right up into the western end of the Pyrenees.

Highlights for First-time Visitors

Bay of Santander (*see* Tour 2)
Bermeo Harbor (*see* Tour 4)
Burgos Cathedral (*see* Tour 1)
La Concha Beach in San Sebastián (*see* Tour 5)
Fine Arts Museum in Bilbao (*see* Tour 3)
Guernica's ancient oak (*see* Tour 4)
Olite Castle (*see* Tour 6)
Pamplona City Hall (*see* Tour 6)
Roncesvalles Pass (*see* Tour 6)
Sanctuary of St. Ignatius of Loyola (*see* Tour 4)

Tour 1: Burgos

Numbers in the margin correspond to points of interest on the Basque Country and Burgos maps.

① Set on the banks of the Arlanzón River, **Burgos** is a small city that boasts some of the most outstanding Spanish architecture of the Middle Ages. Reached by a relatively good road from Madrid, the city first presents the twin spires of its magnificent cathedral, which rises headily above the main bridge and gate into the old city center. The second glory of Burgos lies in its heritage as the city of El Cid, the part historical, part mythical hero of the Christian Reconquest of Spain.

Burgos has been known for centuries as a center of militarism and religion, and even today you will see more nuns and military officers on the streets than almost anywhere else in Spain. The city was born as a military camp in 884, a fortress built on the orders of the Christian king Alfonso III, who was having a hard time defending the upper reaches of Old Castile from the constant forays of the Arabs. It quickly became a key in the defense of Christian Spain. The ruins of the castle erected then still overlook Burgos.

Burgos's religious identity as an early outpost of Christianity was consolidated with the founding of the Royal Convent of Las Huelgas in 1187. The city also became an important station on the Way of St.

James, a place where religious pilgrims stopped for rest and suste-
nance throughout the Middle Ages.

❷ The **catedral** (cathedral) is the city's high point and contains such a
wealth of art and other treasures that jealous Burgos residents actually lynched their civil governor on the morning of January 25, 1869,
for trying to follow instructions from Madrid to make an inventory.
The proud Burgalese apparently feared the poor man was preparing
to remove the treasures.

Most of the outside of the cathedral is sculpted in flamboyant Gothic
style. The cornerstone of the building was laid in 1221, and by the
middle of the 14th century, the cathedral's twin 84-m (275-ft) towers
were completed; the final chapel was not finished until 1731. The interior boasts 13 chapels, the most elaborate of which is the hexagonal Condestable Chapel. You will also find the tomb of El Cid (1026–
99) and his wife, Ximena, under the transept. El Cid, whose real
name was Rodrigo Díaz de Vivar, was a mercenary warrior whose
victories over the Moors made him famous; the medieval *Song of My
Cid* transformed him into a Spanish national hero.

At the other end of the cathedral, high above the West Door, is the
Papamoscas (Flycatcher) clock, so named for the sculptured bird
that opens its mouth as the mechanism marks every hour. Some of
the finest wrought-iron work in central Spain is to be seen in the
grilles, and the choir features 103 delicately carved walnut stalls, no
two alike. The 13th-century stained-glass windows that once shed a
beautiful filtered light in the cathedral were destroyed in 1813—yet
another Spanish treasure destroyed by Napoleon's retreating
troops, this time when they blew up the Burgos castle. *Plaza del Rey
San Fernando, tel. 947/20–47–12. Admission to cathedral museum
and cloister: 400 pesetas or, in groups, 250 pesetas each. Open daily
9:30–1 and 4–7.*

❸ Across the Plaza del Rey San Fernando from the cathedral is the
city's main gate, the **Arco de Santa María.** Walk through it toward
the river and look up above the arch—the 16th-century statues are
of the first Castilian judges, El Cid, Spain's patron saint James, and
King Charles I of Spain. This gate fronts on the city's loveliest
❹ promenade, the **Espolón.** The walkway follows the riverbank and is
shaded with sycamores.

Time Out Take in the city's most pleasant aspects at any of the cool outdoor
terrazas that line the Espolón.

❺ On the western edge of town—a rather long walk if you're not driving—is the **Monasterio de Las Huelgas Reales** (Royal Convent of Las
Huelgas), still run by nuns who live much of their lives hidden away
behind a double iron grille. Founded in 1187 by King Alfonso VIII
and his wife, Eleanor, daughter of Henry II of England, this convent for noble ladies was unprecedented in the 12th century for the
remarkable powers it gave to the women running it. The present
building was originally a summer palace for the kings of Castile and
in 1988 underwent major renovations in connection with its 800th
anniversary. The convent was conceived in Romanesque style, as
can be seen in the military lines of its tower, and housed a royal mausoleum; the tombs of its founders are still there. All but one of the
royal coffins kept at Las Huelgas were desecrated by Napoleon's soldiers, but this last contained clothes that form the basis of the medieval textile museum housed in part of the elaborately endowed
convent complex. Don't miss the Chapel of St. James, where Castilian noblemen came to be knighted by the articulated statue of

The Basque Country

N

Bay of Biscay

Bay of Santander

Santander

8

Ajo

Santillana del Mar

9

Altamira Caves

Camargo

N634

Bay of Santoña

Mundac

Berme

14

15

CANTABRIA

Colindres

Laredo

10

11

Plencia

Algorta

C6320

Elanchave

16

Arenas de Iguña

Castro-Urdiales

N634

Baracaldo

Bilbao

13

Gu

12

N634

A8

Ontaneda

N623

C6318

Llodio

Durango

N611

Villasante

Amurrio

N240

Reinosa

P. del Ebro

Cilleruelo

N625

Berberana

Vitori Gaste

Villarcayo

Valdenoceda

C32

Oña

Miranda de Ebro

(CASTILLA)

Villadiego

Masa

N623

Briviesca

A

Haro

Río Ebro

A68

N1

Melgar

N120

Belorado

N120

Fuenmayor

Rubena

Nájera

N620

Burgos

1 — **7**

CASTILLA Y LEON

Cuevas de S. Clemente

Canales de la Sierra

N111

N1

N234

C110

Arlanza

Salas de los Infantes

Lerma

N1

TO MADRID

Navaleno

N234

Abejar

Cidnes

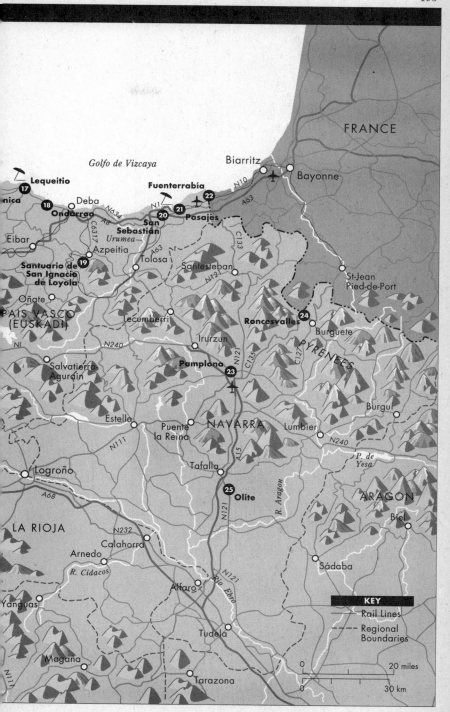

FRANCE

Golfo de Vizcaya

Biarritz

Bayonne

Lequeitio
17

nica

Deba

18

Ondarroa

N634

Fuenterrabia

22

N1

21

20

Pasajes

San
Sebastián

St-Jean
Pied-de-Port

A63

Eibar

C6317

Urumea

Azpeitia

A63

Tolosa

Santesteban

Santuario de
San Ignacio
de Loyola

19

N121

PAIS VASCO
(EUSKADI)

Oñate

Lecumberri

Roncesvalles

24

Burguete

NI

N240

Irurzun

PYRENEES

Salvatierra-
Aguráin

N121

C135

C127

Pamplona

23

Burgui

Estella

NAVARRA

Lumbier

N240

N111

Puente
la Reina

A15

P. de
Yesa

Logroño

Tafalla

ARAGON

A68

25

Olite

Biel

LA RIOJA

N232

Calahorra

N121

R. Aragon

Sádaba

Arnedo

R. Cidacos

N121

Alfaro

Rio Ebro

Yanguas

Tudela

NIII

Magaña

Tarazona

KEY	
——	Rail Lines
- - -	Regional Boundaries

0 _____ 20 miles

0 _____ 30 km

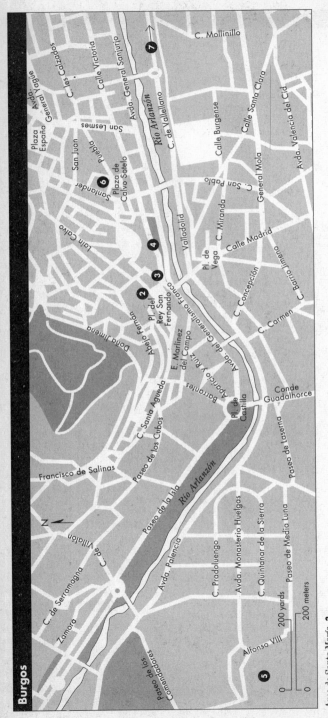

Burgos

Arco de Santa María, **3**
Cartuja de
Miraflores, **7**
Casa del Cordón, **6**
Catedral, **2**
Espolón, **4**
Monasterio de Las
Huelgas Reales, **5**

Spain's patron saint—the figure lowered its sword arm, dubbing the candidates knights with a tap on the shoulder. *1.6 km (1 mi) south-west of town, along the Paseo de la Isla and left across the Malatos Bridge, tel. 947/20–16–30. Admission: 450 pesetas; in groups, 300 pesetas; free Wed. Open Tues.–Sat. 11–1:15 and 4–5:15, Sun. 11–1:15. Closed Mon.*

❻ The **Casa del Cordón** (Plaza de Calvo Sotelo) is the 15th-century palace where the Catholic Monarchs received Columbus after his second voyage to the New World. Today it is a bank building and can only be viewed from the outside.

Three km (1¾ mi) east of town, at the end of a poplar- and elm-lined
❼ drive, is the **Cartuja de Miraflores,** with an even more unusual link to the Americas. Founded in 1441, this florid Gothic charterhouse has an Isabelline church boasting an altarpiece by Gil de Siloe, which is said to be gilded with the first gold brought back from the New World. *Follow signs from the city's main gate. Admission free. Church open for mass Mon.–Sat. at 9, Sun. and holidays 7:30 and 10:15 AM; main building open Mon.–Sat. 10:15–3 and 4–6, Sun. and holidays 11:20–12:30, 1–3, and 4–6.*

After a day in Burgos, or just lunch and a look at the cathedral, you have a choice: Take the relatively poor and slow N623 through the Cantabrian Mountains to Santander (156 km/97 mi), or skip Cantabria and head straight for Bilbao (159 km/99 mi) on the A1 and A68 toll roads.

Tour 2: Santander, Laredo, and Castro-Urdiales

Numbers in the margin correspond to points of interest on the Basque Country map.

❽ **Santander** is one of the great Bay of Biscay ports, and the first thing that will strike you about it is its situation on the western edge of the Bay of Santander. A major northern beach resort—especially for Spanish tourists from the south—the city is surrounded by beaches that happily lack the package-tour feel of most Mediterranean resorts. A huge fire in 1941 destroyed most of the old town; the city now may be the most modern in Spain. It is a lively place, but unusually conservative, especially next to its liberal neighbor, the Basque country. It is one of the few places in Spain that didn't topple its statue of General Franco after he died in 1975. The province, renamed Cantabria from Santander in 1984, when it became an official autonomous region, is historically part of Old Castile.

The origins of Santander are obscure, but it was already a busy port in the 11th century and enjoyed a thriving commercial life between the 13th and 16th centuries. The waning of Spain's naval power and a series of deadly plagues during the reign of Felipe II, however, caused the city's fortunes to plummet. It came back to life commercially only in the 18th century, when it was finally allowed by Madrid to engage in trading with the Americas. In 1910, a summer residence, the **Palacio de la Magdalena,** was built by popular subscription as a gift to Alfonso XIII and his queen, Victoria Eugenia. Thus the city gained status as one of the royal residences of Spain, but even this failed to make it thrive like San Sebastián. Today, it still suffers from second-best status among northern cities.

Apart from beaches (*see* Beaches, *below*), Santander benefits from a number of promenades and gardens, most of them facing the bay. Walk east along the **Paseo de Pereda,** the main boulevard, to the **Puerto Chico,** a small yacht harbor. Farther on, following the

Avenida Reina Victoria, you come to the panoramic tree-lined park paths above the first of the city's beaches, the **Playa de la Magdalena.** Walk onto the Magdalena Peninsula to the Magdalena Palace, today used as the summer seat of the University of Menéndez y Pelayo, which offers Spanish-language and culture courses for foreigners. The grounds offer dramatic views of the bay.

Beyond the Magdalena Peninsula, wealthy locals have built mansions facing the long stretch of shoreline known as **El Sardinero,** today the city's best beach. The heart of the neighborhood is the Belle Epoque **Gran Casino del Sardinero,** an elegant, twin-tower casino and restaurant that is worth a quick visit, even if the gaming tables hold no charms for you. A white building fronted with attractive red awnings in a small park set with sycamores, it lies at the center of the vacationer's Santander, surrounded by expensive hotels and some of the finest restaurants in the area. These universally specialize in the fresh seafood for which Cantabria is famous.

Back in the old city, the center of life is the **Plaza Porticada,** officially called the Plaza Velarde. This rather unassuming little square is the seat of Santander's annual star event, the International Festival of Music and Dance, a series of outdoor performances in August. A few steps away, across the Avenida de Calvo Sotelo, is the blockish **Buen Pastor Cathedral** (Somorrostro s/n), a building marking the transition between Romanesque and Gothic. It was badly damaged in the 1941 fire and then largely rebuilt. The chief item of interest here is the tomb of Marcelino Menéndez y Pelayo (1856–1912), the city's most famous literary figure. Walk west on the Avenida de Calvo Sotelo to the **Museo Municipal de Bellas Artes** (City Fine Arts Museum, Calle Rubio s/n, tel. 942/23–94–85; admission free; open Tues.– Fri. 10–1 and 5–8, Sat. 10–1, closed Sun.) for a look at a rich collection of works by Flemish, Italian, and Spanish artists. Noteworthy in this collection is Goya's ironic portrait of the absolutist King Fernando VII; the smirking face of the lion at the king's feet gives you a clue to the feelings Goya had toward his patron. The same building holds the **Biblioteca Menéndez y Pelayo,** a wood-paneled library housing some 50,000 volumes and the study of the writer, kept as it was in his day (tel. 942/23–45–34; admission free; open Mon.–Fri. 9–2 and 4–9:30, Sat. 9–1:30; closed Sun.).

9 The world-famed **Altamira Caves,** known as the "Sistine Chapel of Rupestrian Art" for the beauty of the drawings, which are judged to be some 13,000 years old, are 29 km (18 mi) west of Santander and 3 km (2 mi) from the delightfully medieval town of Santillana del Mar. The caves, first uncovered in 1875, are testimony to early man's love of beauty and to his skill—especially in the use of the forms of the rock to accentuate perspective in these drawings. The floods of tourists who once visited this site led to serious deterioration of the treasure, and visitors must now apply some eight months in advance to have a hope of being among the 25 people allowed in daily. There is an adjoining museum and a cave with interesting rock formations that can be visited freely. *To see the drawings, write for permission, including the names and number of people in your group, and what date you hope to visit: Centro de Investigación de Altamira, 39330 Santillana del Mar; tel. 942/81–80–05. A waiting list of about 8–10 months is normal, so you'll want to write at least that long in advance.*

Leaving Santander en route to the Basque country, take the N635 southeast and then the N634 east, stopping first at Laredo (49 km/30 **10** mi). Although you would hardly know it today, **Laredo** was an early home port of the Spanish Armada and remained the chief harbor in the north until the French sacked it in the 18th century and Santander became the regional capital. This little town witnessed the visits of the most powerful of Spanish royalty, including Isabella the Catholic (Isabel la Católica) and Charles I of Spain, better known as the Holy Roman Emperor Charles V (Carlos V). When Charles, the most powerful monarch in European history, stopped by in 1556, he donated two brass choir desks in the shape of eagles that can still be seen today in the parish **Iglesia de Asunción** (Church of the Assumption) in the center of the town's tiny Old Quarter. Take an hour to walk through the Old Quarter; ancient mansions with heraldic coats of arms are commonplace.

The N634 now winds up into the green hills behind Laredo, with views of the **Bay of Santoña** over your shoulder. A short drive, parts of it within sight of the coast, takes you into the fishing village of **Castro-Urdiales,** believed to be the oldest settlement on the Cantabrian coast. Called Flaviobriga by the Romans, it became the region's leading whaling port in the 13th and 14th centuries, with almost three times today's 13,000 residents. Overlooking the town is the Santa María Church, revered locally as a Gothic work of art; just behind the church is an ancient castle to which has been added a modern lighthouse. Aside from its arcaded main plaza and the narrow streets of its Old Quarter (much of which burned on May 11, 1813), Castro-Urdiales is famous for the seafood caught by its fishermen and prepared in its excellent taverns and restaurants.

The 45-minute drive from Castro-Urdiales on the N634 to Bilbao takes you through some of the sprawling industrial development that mars much of Vizcaya, the westernmost of the Basque provinces.

Tour 3: Bilbao

Bilbao (Bilbo, in Euskera), Spain's sixth-largest city and the commercial capital of the Basque country, with its surrounding industrial suburbs, takes in some 430,000 people. The Vizcaya province now has nearly 1.2 million inhabitants, just over half of the Basque country's total population of 2,150,000. The River Nervion, on which it is built, is lined with huge industrial cranes, steel mills, shipyards, and a plethora of smaller heavy industries, many of which are in grave decline, contributing to the political and social malaise of the region. Water and air pollution is a problem. Signposts are in the Basque language, as well as in Spanish (very often with the Spanish blotted out by nationalist spray painters).

The highlights of Bilbao, which climbs giddily up the steep hills rising from the river, include a Casco Viejo (Old Quarter), also known as **Siete Calles** and a number of wide boulevards that date from the late 19th century (see especially **Gran Vía,** the main shopping artery). The city is also rich in cultural institutions, including a major fine arts museum. It is certainly one of the best cities for eating on the Spanish peninsula.

Founded in 1300 by a Vizcayan noble, Diego López de Haro, Bilbao was predated by settlements of primitive tribes. Only in the mid-19th century did the city become an important industrial center, thanks mainly to the wealth of minerals in the surrounding hills. A wealthy industrial class grew up here—as did the tough working-class suburbs of Portugalete, Baracaldo, and others that line the Margen Izquierda (Left Bank) of the Nervión estuary. Many of the wealthy have left in the last 25 years—the fear of kidnapping and the extortion of ETA's so-called revolutionary tax has driven them away to Madrid. The right-bank suburb of Getxo, for instance, is remarkable for its abandoned mansions, many of them in ruins and presently being restored.

In Siete Calles, on the river's right bank, by the Arenal Bridge, you will see Bilbao's most typical panorama: the rust-colored river, the beautifully refurbished **Teatro Arriaga** (built in 1890), and the train that runs along the riverbank. The Old Quarter, walled until the 19th century, lies around the **Santiago Cathedral** (open during the celebration of Mass). This church was a stop for pilgrims on one of the routes to Santiago; work on the structure began in 1379, but fire destroyed most of it in 1571. It has a notable outdoor arcade. Continue through the Old Quarter, where you will see ancient mansions and fine ironwork on many balconies. The quarter received a major face-lift after the devastating floods of August 1983 and is now an upscale shopping district, replete with bars, restaurants, and a bustling nightlife. The most interesting square is the 64-arch **Plaza Nueva,** where a street market is pitched every Sunday morning.

Nearby, at the Ayuntamiento Bridge, is the riverside **Ayuntamiento** (City Hall), built in 1892 and floodlit at night. Stop before reaching this neoclassical building and take the elevator at Calle Esperanza 6. This will lift you up to the **Basílica de Begoña,** the huge church from which you have a stunning view of Bilbao, with the Nervión winding through it. Its clean Gothic hulk was begun in 1519 on the spot where the Virgin Mary had supposedly appeared long before.

Time Out   In the modern district, a 20-minute walk from the Old Quarter, the **Café Gran Vía** (Gran Vía 40) is a good place for a tapa and something to drink. Near the Carlton Hotel, it has long been a favorite watering hole for the city's movers and shakers.

Don't miss the nearby **Museo de Bellas Artes** (Fine Arts Museum), in the Doña Casilda Iturriza Park, a half-hour walk west of the Old Quarter. The museum's treasures are displayed exceptionally well. It offers a large collection of the works of Flemish, French, Italian, and Spanish painters, including El Greco, Goya, Velázquez, Zurbarán, and Rivera, as well as modern Basque artists (tel. 94/441–0154 and 94/441–9536; admission free; open Tues.–Sat. 10–1:30 and 4–7:30, Sun. 10–2; closed Mon.). If you're interested in local history, stop by the **Museo Arqueológico** (Museum of Basque Archaeology, Ethnology, and History; Calle Cruz 4; tel. 94/415–5423; admission free; open Tues.–Sat. 10:30–1:30 and 4–7, Sun. 10:30–1; closed Mon.). It houses items related to Basque crafts, fishing, and agriculture.

From Bilbao, pick up the A8 toll road and follow signs to the Guernica (Gernika, in Euskera) exit; from there, the C6313, a good road through the pine-clad coastal hills of Vizcaya, takes you north to Guernica (33 km/20 mi).

Tour 4: Guernica, the Basque Fishing Coast, and the Sanctuary of St. Ignatius of Loyola

⑬ On Monday, April 26, 1937, market day, **Guernica** suffered history's second terror bombing against a civilian population (the first, much less famous, was against neighboring Durango, about a month earlier). The planes of the Nazi Luftwaffe were sent with the blessings of General Franco to subjugate the traditional seat of Basque independence. Since the Middle Ages, Spanish sovereigns had sworn under the ancient oak tree of Guernica to respect Basque fueros, or special local rights—just the kind of local independence inimical to the authoritarian general. More than a thousand people were killed in the bombing, and today Guernica remains a symbol of independence in the heart of every Basque, known to the world through Picasso's painting (now in Madrid's Centro de Arte Reina Sofía).

The city was destroyed—though miraculously the tree emerged unscathed—and has been rebuilt as a modern and largely unattractive place. One point of interest, however, is the stump of the sacred oak, which finally died several decades ago, in the courtyard of the Casa de Juntas (a new oak has been planted alongside the old one); it is the object of many pilgrimages. Nearby is the stunning Ría de Guernica estuary, a stone's throw from some of the most colorful fishing towns in Spain. Follow signs for Bermeo, but before you get there, be sure to stop at the Mirador de Portuondo, a roadside lookout with an excellent view of the estuary (at kilometer post 43 on B635). A little

⑭ farther on is **Mundaca** (Mundaka, in Euskera), a tiny town that draws surfers from all over the world, especially in the November-to-February season. Just beyond is Bermeo, to many the quintessential northern Spanish fishing town.

⑮ **Bermeo** claims the largest fishing fleet in Spain, 62 long-distance boats of more than 150 tons and 121 smaller craft that specialize in hake, preeminent fish of the Basque country and a favorite among all Spaniards. Bermeo was long a whaling port; in the 16th century, local whalers had to donate the tongue of every whale to help raise money for the church. Bermeo still has one of only two wooden shipyards on the northern coast, and the boats that fill its harbor form a cheerful picture. Drive to the top of the town's windswept hill, where the cemetery overlooks the crashing waves of the coast below, and where at sunset townspeople tend family tombs.

You can now head back on the B635, passing Guernica, toward Lequeitio (Lekeitio, in Euskera). For a rewarding side trip, turn left

⑯ at Muretagana and follow the signs to the road's end in **Elanchove** (Elantxobe, in Euskera). This tiny fishing village is nestled amid huge, steep cliffs, with a small breakwater protecting its fleet from the storms of the Bay of Biscay. The view of the port from the upper village, which is quite unused to tourists, is breathtaking; if you take the lower fork in the road, you will drive into the port itself.

Time Out In the upper town, stop in at the rustic **Bar Itxasmin,** which has a small restaurant just off the plaza where the road ends.

⑰ Make your way from here to **Lequeitio.** This bright little town is similar to Bermeo but has two wide, sandy beaches for windsurfing and swimming right by the harbor. Soaring over the Gothic Santa María church (open for Mass only) is a graceful set of flying buttresses. Lequeitio is famous for its September 1–18 fiestas, which include a gruesome event in which men dangle for as long as they can from the necks of dead geese tied to a cable over the inlet while the cable is whipped in and out of the water by crowds of burly men at either end.

⑱ **Ondárroa,** farther east along the coast, is another gem of a fishing town; like its neighbors, it boasts a major fishing fleet painted in red, green, and white—the colors of the *Ikurriña*, the Basque national flag. A slowly curving inlet, the laundry hanging from the typical five-story buildings, the stone bridges over the inlet, and the busy port itself all contribute to an atmosphere that has drawn numerous filmmakers.

After a short drive east, you can pick up the A8 toll road and drive straight on to San Sebastián, a trip of about half an hour. Or you may prefer to make a stop near Azpeitia, at the birthplace of one of Spain's greatest religious figures, St. Ignatius of Loyola, founder of the Jesuits and spiritual architect of the Catholic Reformation. Take the exit marked for Azpeitia and Loyola, south on the G6317 road; it is a half-hour trip.

⑲ The shrine **Santuario de San Ignacio de Loyola** (Sanctuary of St. Ignatius of Loyola) was erected in honor of Iñigo Lopez (1491–1556) after he was sainted in 1622 as Ignacio de Loyola for his defense of the Catholic Church against the tides of Luther's Reformation. Iñigo for many years sought earthly glory in the fratricidal struggles that characterized the Basque country at the time. But after being badly wounded at Pamplona and returning to his family's ancestral home to recover, he abandoned war and took up religion. Almost two centuries later, the Roman architect Carlos Fontana designed the basilica that was to memorialize the saint, after whom five major universities in the United States and Canada and many others worldwide have been named. The basilica is Baroque in style, but a severe Baroque that does justice to the austere saint's memory. Inside, however, it is rich with polychrome marble, ornate altarwork, and a huge but delicate dome. The old family tower house, a fortresslike structure adjoining the basilica, contains the room where Iñigo gave himself to religion. The massive chest was carved by Indians in Spain's Paraguayan missions.

Heading east again toward San Sebastián, you have a choice of the toll road or the coastal N634 highway. The former is quick and scenic (44 km/27 mi); the latter will take you through three of the prettiest towns on the Basque coast: Zumaya, Guetaria, and Zaraúz.

Tour 5: San Sebastián to Fuenterrabía

⑳ **San Sebastián** is a sophisticated city that arcs around one of the finest urban beaches in the world, **La Concha** (The Shell), so named for its almost perfect resemblance to the shape of a scallop shell. The elegant turn-of-the-century buildings and promenade that line the wide, sandy beach evoke images of Rio de Janeiro. In the middle of the entrance to the bay, tiny Santa Clara Island protects the city from Bay of Biscay storms, making La Concha one of the calmest beaches on the entire northern coast of Spain. A large hill dominates each side of the cove's entrance, and a visit to **Monte Igueldo,** on the southwest side, is a must. (You can drive up for a toll of 90 pesetas per person or take the cable car—funicular—for 130 pesetas roundtrip; open 10–8 in summer, 11–6 in winter; departures every 15 minutes.) From here, you see the remarkable panorama for which San Sebastián is famous, a view of gardens, parks, wide tree-lined boulevards, and Belle Epoque buildings.

The first records of San Sebastián date to the 11th century, though there were certainly small fishing settlements here long before that time. For centuries a backwater, the city had the good fortune in 1845 to attract Queen Isabella II, who was seeking relief from a skin ailment in its balmy waters. Her arrival was followed by that of much of the aristocracy of the time, and the city became a favored spot for the wealthy. San Sebastián is laid out in a remarkably modern way, with wide streets on a grid pattern, thanks mainly to the 12 different times it has been largely destroyed by fire. The latest occurred after the French were expelled in 1813; English-Portuguese forces occupied the city, badly abused the population, and then proceeded to torch it. Today, San Sebastián is a seaside resort in a class with Nice and Monte Carlo.

Every Spaniard will tell you that his or her native town is where you will eat best in Spain; but after that, most will agree that San Sebastián is second best. Many of the city's restaurants—along with scores of private, all-male eating societies—are in the **Parte Vieja** (Old Section), just beyond the elegant **Casa Consistorial** (City Hall). This building, next to the formal **Alderdi Eder** gardens, began life in 1887 as a casino. After gambling was outlawed early in this century, the town council decided to move there from the Plaza de la Constitución, the main square in the Old Quarter. The city is probably the most expensive in Spain in summer, when it is a favorite destination for French tourists (and the seasonal seat of the Spanish government); accommodations are scarce.

San Sebastián is divided by the Urumea River, which is crossed by three bridges inspired by French architecture of the late 19th century. At the mouth of the Urumea, especially in September, the incoming surf smashes the rocks with such force that waves erupt to heights of as much as five stories.

Two monumental buildings, apart from the City Hall, stand out: the **Buen Pastor** (Good Shepherd) **Cathedral,** near the beachfront, and the **Basílica de Santa María,** considered the first church of the city and located in the Old Quarter (both churches are open for Mass). The best way to see this city, another center of Basque nationalism, is simply to walk around, not confining yourself to the Old Quarter. San Sebastián is full of promenades and pathways, several leading up the hills that surround it; it is a metropolis built for the enjoyment of the eye and spirit.

㉑ Ten km (6 mi) east of San Sebastián is the historic port of **Pasajes** (Pasaia, in Euskera), whence Lafayette set out to aid the rebels of the American Revolution. It is actually three towns in one large bay: Pasajes Ancho, an industrial port; Pasajes de San Pedro, a large fishing harbor; and Pasajes de San Juan. This last is a tiny settlement of 18th- and 19th-century buildings along a single street that fronts the bay's outlet to the sea. It is best reached by driving into Pasajes de San Pedro and catching a launch that takes you across the mouth of the harbor (around 50 pesetas, depending on the time of day). The town is famous for its fine restaurants.

㉒ A final fishing port before you reach the French border is **Fuenterrabía** (Hondarribia, in Euskera). The harbor, lined with three- and four-story fishermen's homes and small fishing boats, is a beautiful but rather touristy spot. If you have a taste for history, follow signs up the hill to the medieval bastion and onetime castle of Charles V, today a national parador.

Either of two routes from the northeast corner of the Basque country to Pamplona is a dramatic drive, taking you through spectacular mountains that are snowcapped and often impassable in the winter months. The fastest way is by the major highway from San Sebastián to Tolosa, a busy industrial stretch, and then on N240 into the mountains, finally descending into Pamplona (91 km/56 mi). A somewhat prettier drive (134 km/83 mi), if slower and more tortuous, is by C133, which starts out near the French border (and Fuenterrabía); catch the N121 about halfway, and continue on to Pamplona, the ancient capital of Navarra (Navarre).

Tour 6: Pamplona, Roncesvalles, and Olite

㉓ **Pamplona** is known the world over for the event made famous by Ernest Hemingway in *The Sun Also Rises* (also called *Fiesta*)—the running of the bulls during the festival of San Fermín, July 6–14. The population of this ancient kingdom's seat triples during the fiesta, and rooms must be reserved many months in advance (hotel prices also almost triple for the event), though some 700 private rooms are also rented out; tickets to the actual bullfights, as opposed to the running (to which access is free), can be difficult to obtain. Every morning at 7 o'clock sharp a skyrocket is shot off, and the bulls kept overnight in the corral are loosed through a series of closed-off streets leading to the bullring, an 825-m (902-yd) dash. Running before them are Spaniards and foreigners feeling festive enough to risk a goring, wearing the traditional white shirts and trousers with red neckerchiefs and carrying rolled-up newspapers to swat the bulls with. If all goes well—no serious gorings, or even deaths—the bulls arrive in the ring in just 2½ minutes.

Pamplona was founded by the Roman emperor Pompey as Pompaelo or Pameiopolis and was successively taken by the Franks, the Goths, and the Moors. The Pamplonans managed to expel the Arabs temporarily in 750, putting themselves under the protection of Charlemagne. But the foreign commander took advantage of this trust to destroy the city walls, so that when he was driven again from the area by the Moors, the Navarrese took their revenge, ambushing and savagely slaughtering the retreating Frankish army as it fled over the Pyrenees through the mountain pass of Roncesvalles in 778. This is the episode depicted in the *Song of Roland*, although the author of that work chose to cast the aggressors as Moors. For centuries after that event, Pamplona remained as three argumentative towns, until they were forcibly incorporated into one city by Carlos III (the Noble, 1387–1425) of Navarra.

The **Pamplona Cathedral,** set near the portion of the ancient walls rebuilt in the 17th century, is one of the most important religious buildings in Spain because of its fine Gothic cloister. Inside are the tombs of Charles III and his wife, marked by an alabaster sculpture. The **Museo Diocesano** houses a collection of religious art spanning the period from the Middle Ages to the Renaissance. *Calle Curia s/n. Admission free.*

On the nearby Calle Santo Domingo, in a 16th-century building that once served as a hospital for pilgrims on their way to Santiago, is the **Museo de Navarra** (Calle Jaranta s/n, tel. 948/22–78–31; admission: 200 pesetas; open Tues.–Sat. 9–2 and 5–7, Sun. 9–2; closed Mon.), with a collection of local archaeological artifacts and historical costumes. The most remarkable civil architecture in the city is the ornate **ayuntamiento** (city hall), on the Plaza Consistorial; this 18th-century structure is unusual for the blackish color it has acquired over the years, set off against its gilded balconies. Stop for a look at its wood-and-marble interior.

Time Out In the central Plaza del Castillo, the gentry of Pamplona have been flocking to the ornate, French-style **Café Iruña** since 1888. The bar and salons are sumptuously paneled in dark woods; if you walk through, past the stand-up bar, you reach the attached bingo hall, another classic (you must be 18 to play; Plaza del Castillo 44; open daily 5 PM–3 AM).

One of Pamplona's main charms is the warren of small streets near the Plaza del Castillo, which are filled with restaurants, taverns, and bars. Pamplonans, a hardy sort, historically given to smuggling over the nearby Pyrenees, are known far and wide for their capacity to eat and drink.

The central **Ciudadela,** the ancient fortress, which today is a parkland of promenades and pools, is also worth a visit; walk through in the late afternoon, the time of the *paseo* (traditional stroll), for a taste of city life.

㉔ Forty-eight km (30 mi) north of Pamplona is the 1,057-m- (3,468-ft-) high mountain pass of **Roncesvalles,** one of the most beautiful routes into France. A simple cross marks the site of the legendary battle where Roland fell after vainly calling for help on his Sicilian ivory battle horn. In the tiny town a short drive down the mountain (population, about 100), you'll find the chapel of Santiago, the first church on the Spanish section of the Way of St. James. Walk into the Colegiata (Royal Collegiate Church), built at the orders of King Sancho the Strong (open irregular hours); inside is the king's tomb, measuring 2¼ m (7 ft, 4 in), for the monarch was a giant, as well as two thorns that are said to have come from the crown worn by Christ.

Return to Pamplona to catch the A15 toll road to Olite, 41 km (25 mi) south. The route, largely through wine country, is a stark contrast to any area yet seen on this itinerary; in spring it is particularly beautiful, with fields full of wildflowers.

㉕ **Olite's** national parador is part of a castle restored by Carlos III in the French style, a fantasy structure of ramparts, crenel-lated walls, and watchtowers. You can walk the ramparts in the part not occupied by the parador (admission: 200 pesetas; open daily 10–2 and 4–5). Much of the town is ancient and a pleasure to walk through. The 11th-century San Pedro church is interesting for its finely worked Romanesque cloisters and portal.

What to See and Do with Children

The principal attractions of the north for children are the area's natural splendors: the **beaches** of Santander and San Sebastián, the many **parks and promenades** of both these cities, and **hiking** in the hills. During the high season at these beaches, and to a lesser extent in Zarauz (*see* Beaches, *below*), you can rent **pedal boats, windsurfing** equipment, and so on.

Take the **funicular** (*see* Tour 5, *above*) to the top of Monte Igueldo, overlooking San Sebastián, for the **amusement park.** *Open Easter–Aug., daily 10–10; early spring and late fall, daily 10–8; winter, Mon.–Sat. 11–6, Sun. and holidays 10–8.*

Off the Beaten Track

Almost any side road in northern Spain will take you to some undiscovered little town that will stay in your memory. One particularly idyllic spot, a mountain village of rugged farmers and shepherds, *caseríos* (farmhouses), and dewy meadows, is **Alto Ceanuri** (Upper Ceanuri). Bajo Ceanuri (Lower Ceanuri) is easy to find, on N240, a half-hour south of Bilbao; from there, follow the poorly marked road into the mountains. Another choice is **Leiza,** between San Sebastián and Pamplona (turn off the main road at Lecumberri). This stone farming town, just over the spectacular Huici Pass, evokes visions of ancient Basque mythology, which included such beings as *sorquinas* (witches) and *lamias* (female spirits). It is also home to Iñaki Perurena, the long-reigning champion stone-lifter and local butcher. **Mondragón,** on C6213, northeast of Vitoria in the beautiful Leniz Valley, is where the very large and successful workers' cooperative, known as Fagor, is based and has most of its factories. The number-one producer of kitchen appliances in Spain, Fagor was begun by a socially conscious priest in the 1940s and remains the object of pilgrimages by labor and other groups today. Some prehistoric cave paintings you can see without the hassle of Altamira are in the **Santimamiñe caverns** (conducted visits, Tues.–Sun. 10:30, noon, 4, and 5:30) on the road to Elanchove (*see* Tour 4, *above*).

If a trip to the heart of the urban Basque country intrigues you, go to what's marked on most maps as the **Puente de Vizcaya** but known as the Puente Colgante (Hanging Bridge)—an 85-year-old symbol of Bilbao industry. The bridge, a transporter hung from cables, ferries cars and passengers across the Nervion, uniting two distinct worlds: exclusive, quiet Las Arenas and Portugalete, a much older working-class town, now filled largely with jobless steelworkers (Dolores Ibarruri, the famous Republican orator of the Spanish civil war known as *La Pasionaria*, was born here).

Shopping

The **txapelas** (berets) of the Basque country are famous worldwide and make fine gifts: They are best when waterproofed and keep you remarkably warm in the rain and mist so typical of the north. In the Old Quarter of Bilbao, try Sombreros Gorostiaga on Calle Victor, a shop that sells the most famous line of all—Boinas (berets) Elosegui. In San Sebastián, Ponsol (Calle Narrica 4, tel. 943/42–08–76) is the best place to buy Boinas and men's hats of all kinds.

Botas are the wineskins from which Basques typically drink while at bullfights or during fiestas. The art is in drinking a stream of wine while the bota is held at arm's length—but without spilling a drop, please, if you intend to maintain your honor before hypercritical Basque onlookers. Botas can be bought in any Basque town of any size, but for an especially fine brand, try the ZZZ line, sold at Anel (Calle Comedías 7) in Pamplona. The **neckerchiefs** worn during the running of the bulls are available in Pamplona shops; the same shops sell **gerrikos,** the wide belts worn by Basque sportsmen during contests of strength to hold in overstressed organs.

Burgos is famous all over Spain for its wide variety of bland **cheeses,** known simply as Burgos cheeses. Try the Casa Quintanilla (Calle Paloma 17). Santander, for its part, is known as a **ceramics** center. There are several touristy retailers on the Calle Arrabal downtown, but La Muralla, at No. 17, is known locally as the best bet. Every Spanish town has its favorite **sweet:** In San Sebastián, stop in at Juncal (Avenida Libertad 32) for a fabulous selection of chocolates. In Pamplona, try Salcedo (Calle Estafeta 37), open since 1800, which invented, and still sells, almond-based *mantecadas* (powder cakes), as well as *coronillas* (a delightful almond and cream concoction). In the same city, at Calle Zapateria 11, stop in at Hijas de C. Lozano, which offers the *café y leche* (coffee and milk) toffees that are prized all over Spain.

Sports

Fishing The brooks and streams flowing out of the Pyrenees toward Pamplona, or westward toward the Atlantic Ocean, are a trout and salmon fisherman's paradise. Ask at the local tourist office for permit information.

Horse Racing San Sebastián has a scenically located first-class track, or *hipódromo*, with a busy summer season and a recently inaugurated winter season as well. Information is available at Plaza de Zaragoza 2 (tel. 943/42–54–65 or 943/42–61–44, or at the track, tel. 943/37–16–90).

Pelota and Other Basque Sports Pelota is the Basque national sport, and most towns of any size have a local *frontón* (arena). The best local frontón, from which the finest players depart for Miami and other U.S. *jai-alai* frontóns, is Guernica Jai-Alai (Calle Carlos Gongoiti 14, **Guernica,** no phone; about 600 pesetas; games on weekends and Mon.). In **Pamplona,** try Euskal-Jai Berri (6 km/3.7 mi out in Huarte, tel. 948/33–11–59 or 943/33–11–60; games Thurs. and weekends). In **San Sebastián,** the main frontón is Galarreta Jai-Alai (on the highway to Hernani, tel. 943/55–10–23; games Thurs. and weekends). Games normally start at 4 or 4:30. Other traditional Basque sports *(herri-kirolak)* include *sokatiri* (tugs-of-war), *aizkolaris* (contests by woodchoppers), rambutting, scything competitions, and more. But the most bizarre, and interesting, of the local competitions has to be the *harrijasotazailes* (the raising of huge rocks by stone lifters). Events are posted locally, or ask at the tourist office. If you are lucky, you may arrive in a town when one is taking place.

Soccer By far the best team in the area is the Athletic Club Bilbao in Bilbao. For information check local publications, inquire at the tourist office, or call the club (Mazaredo 23, tel. 94/424–0877). To buy tickets, go to the Estadio San Mamés (Calle Luis Briñas).

Water Sports All manner of nautical equipment may be rented at both beaches in **San Sebastián** and at El Sardinero beach in **Santander.** Information on sailing and yachting may be obtained in Santander through the Royal Nautical Club (in the Puerto Chico on the city waterfront, tel. 942/21–40–50).

Beaches

In **Santander** there are three excellent sandy beaches: Magdalena, nearest to town; El Sardinero, the most elegant and well equipped, with all kinds of nautical sports equipment for rent and for sale; and Matalenas, near the camping site of Bellavista. In **San Sebastián,** the La Concha and Ondarreta beaches, directly in front of the city, are beautiful and clean, but packed wall to wall for the entire summer holiday season. Another, less crowded choice is the town of **Zaraúz,** 22 km (14 mi) west of San Sebastián. Smaller beaches can be found in coves all along the Cantabrian and Basque fishing coast, most notably in **Lequeitio.** Bathing around Bilbao is not advised because of industrial pollution.

Dining and Lodging

Dining

Northern cuisine, especially the cooking of the Basques, is arguably the best in Spain. It combines the use of the marvelous fresh fish of the Atlantic with a love of sauces that is rare in the south—a product, no doubt, of the region's proximity to France. In recent years, *nueva cocina vasca* (new Basque cooking) has introduced exciting new elements to an already superb fare. Wines are not the strong point of the north, though Navarra produces some fine vintages (and in such quantity that churches in Allo, Peralta, and other towns were built with lime-thickened wine); more important, the Basques and Cantabrians are perfectly willing to import the excellent Riojas from the wine belt just to their south.

Food is not cheap in the Basque country—indeed, few things are. But for your money, you'll taste some of the most superb creations in Europe, in an ambience that ranges from the traditional hewn beams and stone walls of old farmhouses and Castilian *mesones* (inns) to the most international settings.

Casual dress is acceptable in most restaurants of the region. However, some of the more expensive ones will expect somewhat more formal wear. A jacket and tie will always suffice for men, a reasonably dressy outfit for women.

Highly recommended restaurants are indicated by a star ★.

Category	Cost (major cities)*	Cost (other areas)*
$$$$	over 8,500 ptas	over 6,000 ptas
$$$	5,000–8,500 ptas	4,000–6,000 ptas
$$	2,500–5,000 ptas	2,000–4,000 ptas
$	under 2,500 ptas	under 2,000 ptas

per person, including three courses and excluding drinks, service, and tax

Lodging

The largely industrial and well-to-do north is a relatively expensive region of Spain, and this is nowhere more apparent than in lodging prices. Touristy San Sebastián is particularly pricey, especially in the summer, and Pamplona rates double or triple during the San Fermín fiesta in July. However, the quality of hotels, service, and connected restaurants is generally quite high. You need to reserve ahead in Bilbao, which fills up year-round with business conventions, and in all other cities during the summer.

Highly recommended hotels are indicated by a star ★.

Category	Cost (major cities)*	Cost (other areas)*
$$$$	over 20,000 ptas	over 15,000 ptas
$$$	12,000–20,000 ptas	9,000–15,000 ptas

$$	7,500–12,000 ptas	6,000–9,000 ptas
$	under 7,500 ptas	under 6,000 ptas

All prices are for a standard double room, excluding breakfast and tax.

Bermeo
Dining

Jokin. There's a good view of the Puerto Viejo (Old Port) from this cheerful, strategically located restaurant. Fish comes directly off the boats you see in the harbor below. Try the *rape Jokin* (angler in a clam and crayfish sauce) or *chipirones en su tinta* (small squid in its own ink); for dessert, the *tarta de naranja* (orange cake) is recommended. *Eupeme Duna 13, tel. 94/688–4089. Weekend reservations advised. AE, DC, MC, V. Closed Sun. evening. $$*

Bilbao
Dining

Goizeko Kabi. At one of Bilbao's *crème de la crème* restaurants—no mean distinction—you can choose your own crab or crayfish from an aquarium. The dining rooms are elegant, of brick and wood paneling, and set off with Persian rugs and tapestry-upholstered chairs. Chef Fernando Canales's creations include *alcachofas rellenos de verdura, salpicón de mollejitas* (artichokes stuffed with vegetables, sweetbreads, and goose liver), and *capricho de bacalao y caracoles* (cod fried in garlic with snails and served in pastry). *Particular de Estraunza 4 y 6, tel. 94/442–1129. Reservations required. AE, DC, MC, V. Closed Sun. $$$*

★ **Ariatza.** The upstairs dining room, all wallpaper and dark wood flooring, is homey yet elegant. There's an intriguing and delicious selection of traditional and nouvelle elements here: In the former category, try *merluza a la koskera* (hake in a green sauce of clams and asparagus); in the latter, *pastel de verduras* (an aspiclike vegetable delight that looks like a painting and tastes better). One imaginative dessert is *gratinado de frutas* (fruits in a sweet white sauce). *Somera 1, tel. 94/415–9674. Weekend reservations advised. AE, DC, MC, V. Closed Sun. evening and Mon. $$*

★ **Retolaza.** Bilbao's movers and shakers have been coming to this restaurant since 1906. Now operated by the third generation of the founding family, it is a typical mesón, with wood beams and low ceilings. Classic Vizcayan fare includes *sopa de aluvias* (red beans and sausage) or *bacalao pil-pil* (cod fried with garlic and served in a white sauce). *Tendería 1, tel. 94/415–0643. No reservations. MC, V. Closed holiday evenings, Sun., Mon.; July 24–Aug. 23; Easter week. $$*

Lodging

Carlton. The luminaries who have trod the halls of this grand old but recently refurbished hotel include Orson Welles, Ava Gardner, Ernest Hemingway, Lauren Bacall, and most of Spain's great bullfighters. During the Spanish civil war, it was the seat of the Republican Basque government; later, it housed many Nationalist generals. It is still elegant and well attended. *Federico Moyúa 2, 48009, tel. 94/416–2200, fax 94/416–4628. 142 rooms with bath. Facilities: restaurant, bar, conference halls. AE, DC, MC, V. $$$*

Hotel Ercilla. This modern hot spot fills with the taurine crowd during Bilbao's *semana grande* in early August, partly because of its location convenient to the bullring and partly because it has taken over from the Carlton as the place to see and be seen in Bilbao. Its impeccable rooms, facilities, and services have also helped its reputation. The Ercilla definitely generates a certain buzz of excitement, so this might not be the place to stay if you're looking for a quiet getaway. *Calle Ercilla 37–39, 48009, tel. 94/410–2020, fax 94/443–9335. 346 rooms. AE, DC, MC, V. $$$*

★ **Arana.** Hidden away in the Old Quarter behind an unassuming entrance, this hotel is cheery but tranquil. The second-floor lobby is particularly warm, with the dark, woody feel of the Basque country. Old rooms have dark furnishings, while newer rooms have lighter, blond wood decoration; both are appealing. The dining room is for breakfast only. *Bidebarrieta 2, 48005, tel. 94/415–6411, fax 94/416–1205. 69 rooms, 34 with bath. AE, DC, MC, V. Closed Dec. 24–Jan. 7. $*

Burgos
Dining and
Lodging
★

Mesón del Cid. In a 15th-century building that once housed one of the first printing presses in Spain, this family-run restaurant has been offering traditional Burgalese cooking for four generations. The second- and third-floor dining rooms are framed with hand-hewn beams, and many tables have a spectacular view of the cathedral. The *pimientos rellenos* (peppers stuffed with meat) are succulent, as are the *pisto Don Diego* (vegetable stew with egg) and the Doña Jimenez soup (a garlic soup with bread and egg). A very comfortable hotel is attached. *Plaza Santa María 8, 48383, restaurant, tel. 947/20–59–71; No reservations. Closed Sun. evening; tel. 947/20–87–15, fax 947/26–94–60. 29 rooms. AE, DC, MC, V. $$$*

Lodging

España. Centrally located on the sycamore-shaded Espolón, this hotel offers a bird's-eye view of Burgos's main promenade and the Arlanzón River. Rooms are modern, and service is attentive. *Paseo de Espolón 32, 09003, tel. 947/20–63–40, fax 947/20–13–30. 69 rooms with bath. Facilities: restaurant. MC, V. Closed Dec. 20–Jan. 20. $*

Castro-Urdiales
Dining
★

Mesón Marinero. This pearl of a tavern and restaurant is a gastronomic delight, where local fishermen rub elbows with the visiting elites. The array of tapas spread out on the bar will tempt you to forgo the main meal and *tapear* away your dinner hour; but if you don't succumb, you'll be in for a treat in the elegant second-floor dining room overlooking Castro's weathered fishing port, whence come the fish and shellfish served. An unbeatable dessert is the *tostada de leche frita* (a milk-based custard concoction). *Correría 23, 09003, tel. 942/86–00–05. Weekend reservations advised. AE, DC, MC, V. $$*

Elanchove
Lodging

Arboliz Jatetxea. Set on a bluff dramatically overlooking the coast, about a mile outside Elanchove on the road to Lequeitio, this rustic little inn is isolated yet pleasant. The rooms are simple, modern, and well kept, and several have balconies. *48311 Arboliz 12, 48311 Ibarranguelua, tel. 94/627–6283. 9 rooms, 3 with bath. Facilities: restaurant. AE, MC, V. Reservations advised July–Sept. $*

Fuenterrabía
Dining

Ramón Roteta. Set in a beautiful old villa with an informal garden, this restaurant offers excellent food, making it *the* choice for anyone staying at the local parador. Sample the garlic and shrimp pastries, the fresh pasta with wild mushrooms, or the rice with vegetables and clams. The pastry is all homemade. *Villa Ainara, Calle Irún 2, tel. 943/64–16–93. Reservations advised. AE, DC, MC, V. Closed Sun. evening and Thurs., except in summer. $$$*

La Hermandad de Pescadores. This centrally located "brotherhood" is owned by the local fishermen's guild and serves simple and hearty fare at reasonable prices. Try the *sopa de pescado* (fish soup) or the *almejas a la marinera* (clams in a creamy sauce). If you come outside of peak hours (2–4 and 9–11), you'll find room at the long communal boards. *Calle Zuloaga s/n, tel. 943/64–27–38. Reservations advised. AE, DC, MC, V. Closed Tues. evening and Wed. $*

Lodging

Parador El Emperador. This parador, replete with suits of armor and other chivalric bric-a-brac, was completely renovated in 1993. It's a superb medieval bastion that dates back to the 10th century, and was the residence of Carlos V in the 16th century. Many rooms have gorgeous views of the Bidasoa River and estuary, which is dotted with colorful fishing boats. Be sure to reserve ahead. Ask for one of the three "special" rooms; they're worth the extra $30. *Plaza Armas de Castillo, 20005, tel. 943/64–55–00, fax 943/64–21–53. 36 rooms with bath. Facilities: bar. AE, DC, MC, V. $$$*

Guernica
Dining
★

Baserri Maitea. This is your chance to see the inside of one of the traditional *caseríos* (farmhouses) that are scattered over the hills of the Basque country. Strings of red peppers and garlic hang from wooden beams in the cathedral-like interior of this 300-year-old building. It is set in the hills above the Guernica estuary; the driveway leading to it from the Guernica–Bermeo road is well marked. Entrées include the *pescado del día* and *cordero de leche asado al horno de leña* (milk-fed lamb roasted in wood-burning ovens). The pastries are homemade. *B635 road to Bermeo, Km 2, tel. 94/625–3408. Reservations required. AE, DC, MC, V. Closed Sun. evening, except in summer. $$*

Lodging
★

Boliña. Not far from the famous oak in downtown Guernica, the Boliña is pleasant, friendly, and modern—a good base for exploring the Vizcayan coast. Rooms are smallish but comfortable. *Barrenkale 3, 48300, tel. and fax 94/625–0300. 16 rooms with bath. Facilities: bar, restaurant. AE, DC, MC, V. $*

Laredo
Dining and Lodging

Risco. *Risco* means "cliff" in Spanish, an appropriate name for this hotel-restaurant built into the craggy slope overlooking the historic port of Laredo. The food is renowned as an ingenious mixture of classical and more nouvelle Cantabrian cuisine. Try the *pimientos rellenos de cangrejo y de buey de mar* (peppers stuffed with crab and fish). Every room has a spectacular view of the town and cove below. *La Arenosa 2, 39770, tel. 942/60–50–30. 25 rooms with bath. Hotel reservations required July and Aug. AE, DC, MC, V. Restaurant closed Wed., except July and Aug. $$*

Loyola
Lodging
★

Arocena. One of the European spa hotels so popular around the turn of the century, the Arocena was completely refurbished in 1987. It has free bus service to the nearby springs, whose medicinal waters are still used to treat liver-related diseases. The rooms facing away from the road have especially fine views of the mountains behind. The common rooms, including an elegant restaurant and the lobby, faithfully retain the hotel's Belle Epoque flavor. *San Juan 12, 20740, Cestona (10 min. from Loyola), tel. 943/14–70–40, fax 943/14–79–78. 109 rooms with bath. Facilities: restaurant, bar, pool, parking, tennis, children's playground, chapel. AE, DC, MC, V. $$*

Mundaca
Dining

Casino José Mari. Constructed in 1818 as the local fishermen's guild auction house, this building, with wonderful views of Mundaca's beach, is now a local eating club, but the public is welcome. It is a super lunch stop in summer, when you can sit in the glassed-in upper-floor porch. Very much a local haunt, the club serves excellent fish caught, more often than not, by members. *In the park at the center of town, tel. 94/687–6005. No reservations. AE, MC, V. $$*

Lodging

Atalaya. This historic 1911 landmark is a private house tastefully redone as a hotel. The rooms are charming and comfortable, and those upstairs offer balconies with marvelous views. Ask for Room No. 12, the best in the house. The breakfast room is cheerful and light. *Itxaropen Kalea 1, Villa María Luisa Esperanza, 48360, tel. 94/687–6888, fax 94/687–6899. 15 rooms. Facilities: bar. AE, DC, MC, V. $$*

Olite
Lodging
★

Parador Príncipe de Viana. This is a fantasy palace-castle, named for the grandson of Carlos III, who spent his life here. The parador is part of the castle complex for which Olite is famous. The chivalric atmosphere is well preserved, with grand salons, secret stairways, heraldic tapestries, and the odd suit of armor. *Plaza de los Teobaldos 2, 31390, tel. 948/74–00–00, fax 948/74–02–01. 43 rooms with bath. Facilities: restaurant, bar. AE, DC, MC, V. $$*

Pamplona
Dining

Josetxo. Pamplonans consider this their city's finest restaurant. It's a homey, warm place, run by a family whose specialties include, for starters, *hojaldre de marisco* (shellfish pastry) and, for an entrée, *ensalada de langosta* (spiny lobster salad). *Príncipe de Viana 1, tel. 948/22–20–97. Weekend reservations advised. AE, DC, V. Closed Aug. and Sun., except in May and during San Fermín. $$$*

★ **Erburu.** In the heart of the nightlife district, this dark wood-beamed restaurant is frequented by Pamplonans in the know—a true "find." Come here to eat or just to sample tapas at the bar. Try the *merluza con salsa verde* (hake in green sauce), a Basque classic, or any of a whole range of dishes made with *alcochofas* (artichokes). *San Lorenzo 19–21, tel. 948/22–51–69. No reservations. AE, DC, MC, V. Closed Mon. and 2nd half of July. $$*

Lodging

La Perla. Hemingway and Henry Cabot Lodge slept here, but then so did many other famous people who happened to be passing through. At 125, La Perla is the oldest hotel in town. The founder's son was a bullfighter, and two of the beasts he slew preside over the salon. It's a bit faded but very charming, right on the main plaza. *Plaza del Castillo 1, 31001, tel. 948/22–77–06. 67 rooms, 45 with bath. AE, DC, MC, V. $$ (except July 1–20, when it is $$$$)*

Casa Otano. This lovely, ramshackle hotel is simple and well placed, right in the middle of the tapas and wine circuit and just a few paces from Pamplona's central square. The restaurant downstairs will keep you well fed. The general atmosphere of the Otano is compatible with the San Fermín madness that will be raging in the street if you are there during fiestas (July 6–15). *San Nicolas 5, 31001, tel. 948/22–50–95. AE, DC, MC, V. Closed July 16–31. $*

Pasajes de San Juan
Dining
★

Casa Cámara. Four generations ago, Pablo Camara turned this old fishing wharf into a first-class restaurant projecting into the entrance to the Pasajes Bay. The dining room has dramatic views and a pit from which crayfish are hauled up for inspection by diners. Try *cangrejo del mar* (spider crab with vegetable sauce) or the superb hake in green sauce. *Pasajes de San Juan, tel. 943/52–36–99 or 943/51–78–74. Reservations required. V. Closed Sun. evening and Mon. $$*

San Sebastián
Dining

Akelarre. This restaurant is set on the slopes of Monte Igueldo, with spectacular views of La Concha Bay and San Sebastián. Chef Pedro Subijana is known for, among other things, his *lubina a la pimienta verde* (sea bass with green pepper) and Basque classics like squid in a sauce of its own ink. *Barrio de Igueldo, tel. 943/21–20–52 or 943/21–40–86. Reservations required. AE, DC, MC, V. Closed Sun. evening, Mon., first 2 weeks of June, and Dec. $$$$*

★ **Arzak.** Renowned chef Juan Marí Arzak's restaurant, on the city's outskirts on the road to Fuenterrabía, is in an intimate cottage setting. But the place is internationally famous, so reserve well ahead. The entire menu is a wonder, with traditional Basque preparations and more recent creations such as the birds in fruit and vegetable sauce. The pastries are extremely light and wonderful. Prices are very fair. *Alto de Miracruz 2, tel. 943/28–55–93 or 943/27–84–65. AE, DC, MC, V. Closed Mon., Sun. evening; last 2 weeks in June and 2 in Nov. $$$*

Panier Fleuri. One of the most select wine lists in Spain complements the food here, served in a sober dining room overlooking the crashing surf at the mouth of the Urumea River. Chef Tatus

Fombellida is a winner of Spain's national gastronomy prize, no mean feat. Try his *faisan* (pheasant) or the *supremas de lenguado a la florentina* (sole baked with spinach and served with hollandaise sauce) and for dessert, the lemon sorbet with champagne. *Paseo de Salamanca 1, tel. 943/42–42–05. Reservations required. AE, DC, MC, V. Closed Sun. evening and Wed.; last 2 weeks of Dec., 3 weeks in June, Christmas week. $$$*

Mari Galant. Part of the pleasure of this restaurant is its location, right on the beach in the Hotel Londres y Inglaterra. Chef Juan Antonio Alcorta offers an array of traditional Basque foods; one good choice is the *rape con hongos* (angler with forest mushrooms). *Zubieta 2, tel. 943/42–69–89. Reservations advised in summer. AE, DC, MC, V. $$*

Casa Vallés. Just a two-minute walk from the back of San Sebastián's cathedral, this fine little tapas bar/restaurant displays some 30 to 40 different, freshly prepared, and uniformly irresistible creations on the bar at midday and again in the early evening. Famous among locals, Casa Vallés combines excellent offerings with top value. *Reyes Católicos 10, tel. 943/45–22–10. AE, DC, MC, V. Closed Wed. and June 15–30. $*

Lodging **María Cristina.** The graceful beauty of the Belle Epoque is evoked by San Sebastián's top luxury hotel, which sits like the queen it's named after on the elegant west bank of the Urumea River. The grandeur continues inside the entrance; in salons filled with Oriental rugs, potted palms, and Carrara marble columns; and in bedrooms to match. *Paseo República Argentina s/n, 20004, tel. 943/42–49–00, fax 943/42–39–14. 139 rooms with bath. Facilities: restaurant, bar, parking, lounges, hairdresser, boutiques, conference and banquet halls. AE, DC, MC, V. $$$$*

Londres y Inglaterra. This stately hotel has a privileged position on the promenade above the main La Concha beach. It also offers a quiet lobby with chandeliers, fine rooms, and attentive, warm service. Its bar faces the bay. *Zubieta 2, 20007, tel. 943/42–69–89, fax 943/42–00–31. 130 rooms with bath. Facilities: restaurant, bar, casino. AE, DC, MC, V. $$$*

Bahía. Just a two-minute walk from the beach, this hotel is small but appealing. It has a warm, welcoming lobby, with an odd but cute minibar and salon, and its rooms are comfortable and modern. *San Martín 54 Bis, 20007, tel. 943/46–92–11. 59 rooms with bath. MC, V. $$*

Santander **Bodega del Riojano.** The paintings on wine barrel ends that decorate
Dining this restaurant have given it the sobriquet Museo Redondo (Round
★ Museum), but this is not its only charm. The building dates back to the 16th century, when it was a wine cellar, and the atmosphere is carried on in dark wood beams and tables. The menu changes daily and seasonally, but try the fish of the day, always a sure bet on the Cantabrian coast. Desserts are homemade. *Río de la Pila 5, tel. 942/21–67–50. Reservations advised in summer. AE, DC, MC, V. Closed Sun. evening in winter. $$*

Rhin. On the El Sardinero Beach, next to the casino, this restaurant offers views from every seat and dining on a large terrace in summer. The Rhin is somewhat touristy, however, and the food is not the best in town. Among the better dishes are *lomos de merluza con cocochas y setas* (hake fillets with wild mushrooms and hake barbels) or, if you miss meat, the *lomo de añojo al queso de Tresviso* (steak with Tresviso cheese). *Plaza de Italia, tel. 942/27–30–34. Reservations advised in summer. AE, DC, MC, V. $$*

Lodging **Las Brisas.** Jesús García and his wife, Teresa, have managed to turn
★ this 75-year-old mansion into a ritzy, cottage-style hotel by the sea.
If you value homey atmosphere and personality, this is the place for
you. Each room is different, from dollhouse alcoves to an odd but attractive two-story family room. The basement bar and breakfast
room is especially cozy. Just a few hundred feet from the beach, the
house offers many rooms with fine views. *Travesía de los Castros 14,
39005, tel. 942/27–09–91 or 942/27–50–11. 14 rooms with bath. AE,
DC, MC, V. Reserve for summer by Easter. $$–$$$*

★ **México.** Don't be put off by the modest exterior. The personal touch
still counts in this family-run establishment, and the breakfast room
is very elegant, with Queen Anne chairs, inlaid porcelain rosettes,
and oak wainscoting. The rooms are very pleasant, with high ceilings and the glassed-in balconies typical of the region. Reserve in
advance because word of this good deal has gotten around. *Calderón
de la Barca 3, 39002, tel. 942/21–24–50, fax 942/22–92–38. 36 rooms
with bath or shower. MC, V. $*

The Arts and Nightlife

The Arts

The easiest way to find out about local cultural events, particularly
if you don't read Spanish, is through local tourist offices.

San Sebastián's film festival is held in the second half of September,
although exact dates vary; ask at the tourist office or read the local
press for details and ticket information. The same is true of the jazz
festival in late July, an event that draws many of the world's top performers year after year. A varied program of theater, dance, and
other events is offered year-round at the beautiful Teatro Victoria
Eugenia (Reina Regente s/n, tel. 943/48–11–55 for information, 943/
48–11–60 for tickets). Another leading theater is the Principal
(Mayor 3, tel. 943/42–61–12).

Bilbao hosts an August music festival; again, ask at the tourist office, as venues change. The city's pride and joy, a magnificently restored building on the Nervion River, is the Teatro Arriaga (Plaza
Arriaga s/n, 94/416–3244). The theater consistently draws world-
class ballet, theater, concerts, opera, and *zarzuela* (comic opera).
Opera and *zarzuela* also is frequently on offer at the Teatro Coliseo
Alvia (Alameda Urquijo 13, tel. 94/415–3954; information on opera is
available at Rodriguez Arias 3, tel. 94/415–5490).

Santander's big event is the International Music and Dance Festival,
which attracts leading international artists throughout August.
Many of the events are in the city's comely main square, Plaza
Porticada. The backdrops for many other performances are even
more extraordinary: local monasteries, palaces, churches. You'll
find information at the tourist office and at seasonal box offices in
the Plaza Porticada and the Jardínes de Pereda park. The city's
Teatro Coliseum (Plaza de los Remedios 1, tel. 942/21–14–60) is normally a movie theater, but hosts a summer theater.

Although smaller, **Pamplona** also offers a varied summer program
of theater, zarzuela, ballet, and concerts. For information, contact
the Teatro Gayarre (Avenida Carlos III Noble 1, tel. 948/22–01–39).
In August, the Festivales de Navarra includes theater and other
events.

Nightlife

Nightlife barely exists in some of the smaller towns and villages, but the larger cities offer lively bar and tapa-hopping scenes. In **Bilbao,** head for the Casco Viejo, where scores of small bars stay open into the wee hours on weekends. **San Sebastián's** Parte Vieja is known for its tapas and the river of people who crowd its streets nightly. **Pamplona's** nightlife is concentrated in and around the Plaza del Castillo and down Calle San Nicolas, while **Burgos,** in keeping with its overall sober quality, offers little in the way of evening fun.

7 The Pyrenees

*By George
Semler*

*Born and
educated in
the United
States, writer,
journalist,
and
translator
George Semler
has lived in
Spain,
playing
hockey,
skiing, and
fly-fishing the
streams of the
Pyrenees, for
the past 20
years.*

For better or for worse, the Pyrenees have historically sealed off the Iberian Peninsula from the rest of Western Europe, helping to shape a trans-Pyrenean culture distinct from that of neighboring France. The tribes inhabiting the prehistoric Pyrenees—originally cave dwellers, later shepherds and farmers—saw the first invaders arrive by ship across the Mediterranean when the Greeks landed at Empúries in the 6th century BC. The seagoing Carthaginians colonized Spain in the 3rd century BC, and their great general Hannibal surprised the Romans by crossing the Oriental Pyrenees in 218 BC. After defeating the Carthaginians, the astute, empire-building Romans constructed roads through the mountains: Via Augusta at Portus, Strata Ceretana through Llivia and Seu d'Urgell to Lleida, Summus Pyrenaecus at Somport to Jaca and Zaragoza, and the route through Roncesvalles to Pamplona in the western Pyrenees.

After the fall of Rome, the Iberian Peninsula was the last part of the empire the Visigoths took over, finally crossing the Pyrenees in AD 409. Those northern tribes were eventually met by invaders from the south—the Moors in the 8th century. The Moorish influence was always weaker in the Pyrenees and was only briefly and unsuccessfully able to push past the mountains into the rest of Europe. In fact, Christianity survived the Islamic encroachment by fleeing to the hills, dotting the Pyrenees with Romanesque art and architecture. When Christian crusaders reconquered Spain, the Pyrenees was divided among three feudal kingdoms: Catalunya, Aragón, and Navarra, proud and independent entities with their respective spiritual "cradles" up in the mountains at the Romanesque monasteries of Ripoll, San Juan de la Peña, and San Salvador de Leyre.

Down through the centuries, the barrier of the Pyrenees remained a force to reckon with. Napoleon never completed his conquest of the Iberian Peninsula, and the German Third Reich chose not to attempt to occupy post–civil war Spain.

The Pyrenees stretch 435 km (270 mi) along Spain's border with France. There are three main ranges: the Catalan Pyrenees, the central Pyrenees (in Aragón), and the Pyrenees of Navarra, which fall gently westward through the Basque country to the Bay of Biscay. The highest peaks are in Aragón—Aneto in the Maladeta ridge, Posets, and Monte Perdido, all of which are around 3,400 meters or 11,000 feet above sea level.

These snowcapped mountains looming over Spain have always been a magical realm apart, the source of legend and superstition, of myth and mystical religious significance. They have protected within their own meadows and valleys the last vestiges of several ancient cultures. Each mountain system is drained by rivers forming a series of valleys that, especially until the 10th century, were all but completely isolated from one another, as well as from the world beyond. The local languages range from Castilian Spanish to Euskera (Basque) in upper Navarra; to dialects such as Grausín, Chistavino, Cheso, Patués, or Benasqués in Aragón; to Aranés, a dialect of Gascon French, in the Vall d'Aran; to Catalan in the Cerdanya, the Vall de Camprodón, and eastward.

Thoroughly exploring any one of these valleys—the flora and fauna, the local gastronomy and architecture, the peaks and upper meadows, the remote glacial lakes and streams, the Romanesque art hidden in a thousand chapels and hermitages—is a lifetime project. The five tours suggested here are introductions to some of the richest and most remote combinations of geography and civilization Spain has to offer.

Essential Information

Important Addresses and Numbers

Tourist Information The regional tourist offices for the areas covered in this chapter are **Oficina de Turismo de Barcelona** (Gran Via de les Corts Catalanes 658, Barcelona, tel. 93/301–7443) for Catalunya; **Oficina de Información y Turismo** (Coso Alto 23, Huesca, tel. 974/21–25–83) for Aragón; and **Oficina de Información Turística** (Duque de Ahumada 3, Pamplona, Navarra, tel. 948/21–12–87) for Navarra.

Local tourist offices in major towns covered in this chapter are **Aínsa** (Avenida Pirenaica 1, Aínsa, Huesca, tel. 974/50–07–67); **Benasque** (Plaza Mayor 5, Benasque, Huesca, tel. 974/55–12–89); **Camprodón** (Plaça Espanya 1, Camprodón, Gerona, tel. 972/74–00–10); **Jaca** (Avenida Rgto. Galicia, Jaca, Huesca, tel. 974/36–00–98); **Puigcerdà** (Carrer Querol 1, Puigcerdà, Gerona, tel. 972/88–05–42); **Seu d'Urgell** (Avinguda Valira s/n, Seu d'Urgell, Lleida, tel. 973/35–15–11); and **Viella** (Avenida Castiero 15, Viella, Lleida, tel. 973/64–09–79).

Emergencies **Barcelona:** Red Cross (tel. 93/205–1414). **Province of Gerona:** Red Cross (tel. 972/20–04–15); Guardia Civil (tel. 972/20–13–81). **Province of Huesca:** Red Cross (tel. 974/22–11–86); Guardia Civil (tel. 974/24–47–11). **Province of Lleida:** Red Cross (tel. 973/26–70–11); Guardia Civil (tel. 973/24–50–12). **Province of Navarra:** Red Cross (tel. 948/22–64–04); Guardia Civil (tel. 948/23–70–00).

Arriving and Departing by Plane

El Prat International Airport at Barcelona is the major center for transportation to and from the Pyrenees region. El Prat is 15 minutes and a 2,500-peseta taxi ride from the center of Barcelona, 30 minutes and considerably cheaper (400 pesetas) by train or bus.

To travel from Madrid to a jumping-off point for the Pyrenees, take the shuttle (Puente Aereo) to Barcelona or go by a scheduled flight to the Hondarribia airport at Fuenterrabía, 20 minutes from San Sebastián.

Arriving and Departing by Train

The overnight train from Madrid's Chamartín Station to Barcelona or San Sebastián offers several advantages: You leave late (9:15 PM–11 PM) and arrive early (7:30 AM–8:30 AM), thus losing no day-time activities at either end; you may sleep wonderfully; and you save the difference between the air and the train fare.

Getting Around

By Car The only practical way to tour the Pyrenees—short of hiking—is by car. The most difficult road into the Oriental Pyrenees is over the Toses Pass to Puigcerdà. The wide two-lane roads of the Cerdanya are new and well paved. Moving west, roads may be more difficult to navigate. Car rentals are available at airports at both ends of the Pyrenees (*see* Chapter 6, Burgos, Santander, and the Basque Country, or Chapter 8, Barcelona).

By Train Three railheads have been established in the Pyrenees, at Puigcerdà in the Cerdanya, Pobla de Segur in the Noguera Pallaresa valley, and Canfranc north of Jaca below the ski resorts of Candanchú and Astún.

Exploring the Pyrenees

Orientation

Traversing the Pyrenees from the Mediterranean Sea to the Atlantic Coast is a pilgrimage of deep cultural and telluric significance for many local mountain lovers. A six- to seven-week hike on foot, the crossing can be accomplished in 10 days to two weeks by automobile.

You can begin by wading in the Mediterranean at Cap de Creus (*see* Barcelona Excursions in Chapter 8), peninsular Spain's easternmost point, just north of Cadaqués, and then cross westward to Fuenterrabía (*see* Tour 5 in Chapter 6) to do the same in the Bay of Biscay; or you can travel in the opposite direction, reversing the order of this chapter. On the westbound trip, a day's drive through Figueres and Olot (*see* Barcelona Excursions in Chapter 8) will bring you to the start of Tour 1: the Vall de Camprodón, where you will find unspoiled mountain towns, skiing, and wildlife. The second tour takes you through the widest and sunniest valley in the Pyrenees, La Cerdanya. From there you can move westward in Tour 3 through the Vall d'Aran, Aigües Tortes National Park, and the winter-sports center of Baqueira-Beret and visit the Romanesque churches of the Noguera de Tor Valley. In the fourth tour, you can explore the remote valleys of Alto Aragón, the Ordesa and Monte Perdido National Park, and Jaca, the region's most important town. On the fifth tour you move through western Aragón into the Pyrenees of Navarra to visit the Irati Forest, climb over the Velate Pass, and follow the Bidasoa River down to the Atlantic at Fuenterrabía.

Highlights for First-time Visitors

Aigües Tortes National Park (*see* Tour 3)
Beget's church and bell tower (*see* Tour 1)
Benasque (*see* Tour 4)
Ordesa and Monte Perdido National Park (*see* Tour 4)
San Juan de la Peña (*see* Tour 5)
Sant Climent Church in Taüll (*see* Tour 3)
Seu d'Urgell: rose window, Santa Maria Cathedral (*see* Tour 2)
Vall d'Aran (*see* Tour 3)

Tour 1: Vall de Camprodón

Numbers in the margin correspond to points of interest on the Catalan Pyrenees map.

Catalunya's easternmost Pyrenean valley, the **Vall de Camprodón,** can be reached from Barcelona by way of N152 through Vic and Ripoll; from the Costa Brava by way of Figueres and Olot; or from France through the Ares Pass, which enters the head of the valley at an altitude of 1,610 m (5,280 ft) from the French Vallespir and Amélie-les-Bains. The Vall de Camprodón includes several exquisite towns and churches; a ski area; and peaks and bowls, such as the Sierra de Catllar, where mountain goats, snow partridge, and wild boar abound. One of the least commercially developed valleys in the Catalan Pyrenees, it has conserved much of its ecological and agricultural integrity.

❶ Camprodón, the capital of the *comarca* (county), lies at the junction of the Rivers Ter and Ritort, both excellent trout streams. The two rivers flow by, through, and under much of the town, giving Camprodón a certain waterfront character, as well as a long history of recurrent flooding. The town owes much of its opulence to the summer residents from Barcelona who constructed important mansions, beginning at the turn of the century, along the leafy, tree-lined promenade, Passeig Maristany, at the northern edge of town. Camprodón's best-known symbol is the elegant 12th-century stone bridge that broadly spans the River Ter in the center of town. It consists of a single wide arch with a graceful angle descending outward from a central peak. Camprodón is also known for its sausages of every imaginable size, shape, and consistency and for its two cookie factories, locked in competition, Birbas and Pujol. (Birbas are better and have a picture of the bridge on the box.)

From Camprodón you can take C151 north toward the French border at Coll D'Ares and turn east toward **Rocabruna,** a tight village of crisp, clean Pyrenean stone at the source of the crystalline River Beget.

❷ The village of **Beget,** widely considered Catalunya's *més bufó* (cutest), was connected to the rest of the world by asphalt roadway in 1980 and until the mid-'60s was completely cut off from motorized transportation of all kinds. Beget's 30 houses are eccentric stone structures with heavy wood doors and an unusual golden tone peculiar to the Camprodón Valley. Graceful stone bridges span the stream, while protected trout feast below. The 11th-century **Sant Cristófol Church** has a diminutive bell tower and a six-foot Majestat, a polychrome wood carving of Christ robed in a head-to-foot tunic, dating from the 12th or early 13th century. The church is usually closed, but anyone in town can direct you to the keeper of the key.

❸ Back on C151, a right turn north leads to the village of **Molló,** farther up the River Ritort toward Coll D'Ares. Molló is the site of one of the valley's best Romanesque churches, a 12th-century structure of exceptional architectural balance and simplicity, with a delicate Romanesque bell tower that seems set into the building and the surrounding countryside as naturally and perfectly as some half-hidden Pyrenean mushroom.

❹ The other road out of Camprodón follows the River Ter to **Setcases,** a tiny village nestled at the head of the valley. Although Setcases (literally, "seven houses") is somewhat larger than its name would imply, the town retains a distinct mountain spirit, a special gravelly roughness perhaps a product of the *torrents* constantly flowing through and over the streets of town on their way to the River Ter.

The Vallter ski area, above Setcases, built into a glacial cirque reaching a height of 2,505 m (8,216 ft), has a dozen lifts and views east from the top all the way out to the Bay of Roses and Cap de Creus on the Costa Brava.

On the road back down the valley from Setcases, Llanars, just short of Camprodón, has an exceptional 12th-century church of a rare shade of ocher. The wood-and-ironwork portal carries a depiction of the martyrdom of St. Steven.

South of Camprodón, **Sant Joan de les Abadesses**—named for the 9th-century abbess Emma, daughter of Guifré el Pilós, the founder of the Catalonian nation and medieval hero of the Christian reconquest of Ripoll—is the site of the important 12th-century church of Sant Joan. The altarpiece is a 13th-century polychrome wood sculp-

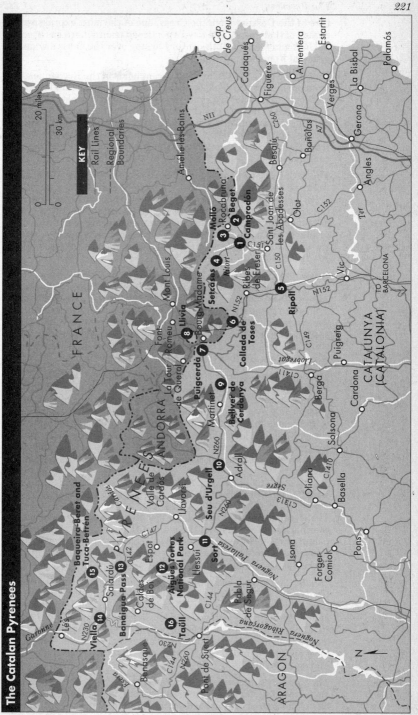

The Catalan Pyrenees

KEY

Rail Lines

Regional Boundaries

20 miles

30 km

FRANCE

Cap de Creus

Cadaqués

Estartit

Palamós

Armentera

La Bisbal

Verges

Gerona

Figueres

Anglès

Bañolas

NII

Amélie-les-Bains

Besalú

C260

Olot

C152

Ter

Rocabruna

Molló

Beget

Camprodón

2

3

1

Sant Joan de les Abadesses

Vic

Mont Louis

Setcases

Mlort

Ribes de Freser

C151

C150

4

N152

5

Ripoll

N152

TO BARCELONA

Bourg-Madame

Llívia

6

Collada de Toses

8

La Tour de Querol

Font-Romeu

Puigcerdà

7

Llobregat

Puigreig

CATALUNYA (CATALONIA)

9

Bellver de Cerdanya

Martinet

C149

Berga

C1141

Cardona

Solsona

ANDORRA

P Y R E N E E S

Valle de Cardós

N260

Adrall

10

Seu d'Urgell

Adrall

Segre

Oliana

C410

Basella

C1313

Llavorsí

N260

Isona

Forget-Comiol

Pons

Baqueira-Beret and Tuca-Betren

C147

Espot

Aigües Tortes National Park

12

Llessui

11

Sort

C144

Pobla de Segur

Noguera Pallaresa

Salardú

15

Caldes de Boí

C142

13

Bandaigua Pass

16

Taüll

Les

N230

14

Viella

Garonne

Benasque

C144

N230

Pont de Suert

Noguera Ribagorçana

ARAGON

N

ture of the Descent from the Cross, one of the most expressive and human of that epoch. The town's porticoed main square has a medieval look and feel; the 12th-century bridge over the Ter is a wide and graceful Romanesque design.

❺ Ripoll, one of the first Christian strongholds of the Reconquest and an important center of religious erudition during the Middle Ages, has come to be known as the *bressol* (cradle) of Catalonian nationhood. A dark and mysterious country town built around a 9th-century Benedictine monastery, Ripoll was a focal point of culture throughout the Rousillon—French Catalonia and the Pyrenees—from the monastery's founding in 888 until the middle of the 19th century.

The 12th-century **Santa Maria Church** doorway is one of the great works of Romanesque art in Catalunya. Designed as a triumphal arch, its sculptures portray the glory of God and his creatures from the creation onward. A guide to the figures on the portal, the work of stonemasons and sculptors of the medieval Rousillon school, is available at the church or at the information kiosk nearby. *Admission: to cloister, 200 pesetas; to museum, 300 pesetas. Open daily 10–2 and 3–7; closed Mon.*

It is a 63-km (39-mi) drive on Rte. N152 from Ripoll through Ribes **❻** de Freser and over the **Collada de Toses** (Toses Pass) to Puigcerdà. Above Ribes, the road winds up to the top of the pass over a sheer drop down to the Freser stream. From here you can see, even during the driest months, emerald-green pastures glowing moistly in shaded corners, while, above the tree line, shale and brown peaks stand in sharp relief. In early spring the climate can change from April showers at Ribes to a sweeping blizzard at Toses.

This traditional approach to the Cerdanya has been all but replaced by the road through Manresa, Berga, and the Túnel del Cadí (Cadí tunnel) since 1984. Toses was a natural barrier for centuries, crossed only by stagecoaches until the railroad connected Puigcerdà to Barcelona in 1924. The 32 km (20 mi) of switchback curves between Ribes and La Molina were enough to keep many would-be visitors safely in Barcelona until the tunnel cut the driving time from over three hours to under two and all but eliminated the danger factor.

Tour 2: La Cerdanya

The Pyrenees' widest and sunniest valley—popularly said to be in the shape of the imprint of the hand of God—is La Cerdanya. High pastureland bordered to the north and south by snow-covered mountains, the valley starts in France at Mont Louis and ends at Martinet in the Spanish province of Lleida.

"Meitat de França, meitat d'Espanya, no hi ha altra terra com la Cerdanya" ("Half France, half Spain, there's no country like the Cerdanya"): The Cerdanya Valley straddles the border, which meanders through the rich valley floor no more purposefully than the River Segre itself. Inhabitants of both sides of the border speak Catalan, a Romance language derived from early Provençal French, and have always regarded the international division of the valley with undisguised hilarity.

The Cerdanya, unlike any other valley in the upper Pyrenees, runs east–west and, for this reason, has a record annual number of hours of sun. Two solar stations collect and store energy at Font Romeu, while in Mont Louis, also on the French side of the valley, there is a medieval solar oven that was once used for baking bread.

7 **Puigcerdà** (*puig* means "hill"; *cerdà* derives from "Cerdanya") is the valley's largest town. From the small piece of high ground upon which it stands, the views down across the meadows and up into the surrounding Pyrenees inspire simultaneous sensations of height and humility. The Romanesque bell tower and the sunny sidewalk café beside it are among Puigcerdà's prettiest spots, along with the Gothic **Santa Maria Church** and its long square, the Plaça del Cuartel, where Sunday markets attract shoppers from both sides of the border to browse through clothes, cheeses, fruits, vegetables, wild mushrooms, and produce of all kinds.

The Plaça Cabrinetty, with its porticoes and covered walks, has a sunny northeast corner where farmers in for the Sunday market gather to discuss their lives and times. This square is protected from the wind and ringed by two- and three-story houses of various pastel colors, some with engraved decorative designs, all with balconies. Leaving the lower end of Plaça Cabrinetty, Carrer Font d'en Llanas winds down to the *font* (spring) where *Voldria,* a haunting verse by the Cerdanya's greatest poet, Magdalena Masip (c. 1890–1970), is inscribed on a plaque over the fountain.

From the font, a 300-yard walk around to the right will bring you to the stairs leading up from the train station to the balcony in front of the town hall. From this *mirador,* an ample view of the Cerdanya Valley stretches all the way past Bellver de Cerdanya down to the rock walls of the Sierra del Cadí above Martinet and the end of the valley itself.

Time Out The **Madrigal** (Alfons I 1), the best *tapas* (hors d'oeuvres) restaurant in Puigcerdà, is located next to the town hall square. Pere Compte, owner and manager, can serve up delicacies ranging from hot mushrooms to squid to Serrano ham on *pa amb tomaquet* (toasted country bread with oil, garlic, and fresh tomato paste) from 9 AM to well after midnight.

A good way to explore the Cerdanya valley floor is by walking from Puigcerdà north to **La Tour de Querol** in France or out to Aja and Vilallovent to the southeast on roads that wind through green fields filled in spring with foals and calves. Another scheme is to take the train out to Alp or Urtg or up to La Tour de Querol and walk back to Puigcerdà.

8 **Llívia,** 6 km (4 mi) away, is a Spanish enclave surrounded by French territory. Marooned by the semantics of the 1659 Peace of the Pyrenees treaty that ceded 33 villages to France, Llívia, incorporated as a *vila* (town) by royal decree of Carlos V—who spent a night there in 1528 and was impressed by its beauty and the hospitality of its inhabitants—remained Spanish. Llívia's fortified church is an acoustical gem. The ancient pharmacy, now a museum, was founded in 1415 and is considered Europe's oldest.

9 **Bellver de Cerdanya,** 20 minutes west of Puigcerdà on N260, has conserved its slate-roofed fieldstone Pyrenean architecture more successfully than have many of the larger towns in the Cerdanya. Perched on a promontory over the River Segre, which folds neatly around the town, Bellver is, in many ways, a fishing village. The river is the town's main event, day after day, and discussions about how much water is coming down and whether it is low or high, muddy or clear, warm or cold, virtually replace the weather as a topic of conversation. Bellver's Gothic church and porticoed square in the upper part of the town are lovely examples of traditional Pyrenean mountain village design.

⑩ Seu d'Urgell, a 45-minute drive from Puigcerdà past Bellver and Martinet along the Segre River, is an ancient town tucked under the Sierra del Cadí. Seu d'Urgell's historical importance as the seat of the regional archbishopric since the Middle Ages has left the city with a rich legacy of art and architecture.

The 12th-century **Santa Maria Cathedral,** smaller than Barcelona's Santa Maria del Mar, is similarly graceful in line and proportion. Sunlight gleaming through the rich reds and blues of Santa Maria's southeast-facing rose window over the deep gloom of the transept is among the most moving sights in the Pyrenees. The 13th-century cloister, with its 50 columns and their individually carved capitals—sculpted by the same Rousillon school of masons who carved the Santa Maria monastery doorway in Ripoll—is an elaborate and intricate work of art, as is the elegant 11th-century Sant Miquel Chapel. *Admission: 250 pesetas. Open daily 9–1 and 4–8.*

The special mountain *ambiente* of the streets, the dark balconies and porticoes, overhanging galleries, and colonnaded porches of town, make Seu d'Urgell a memorable discovery as well as a convenient link between the Cerdanya and points beyond.

Tour 3: The Western Catalan Pyrenees

From Seu d'Urgell, the Vall d'Aran can be reached by taking N260 toward Lleida, turning west at Adrall, and driving 53 km (33 mi) **⑪** over the Cantó Pass to Sort. **Sort,** the capital of the Pallars Sobirà (Upper Pallars Valley), is a sports center offering skiing, fishing, and white-water kayaking. Don't be content with the Sort you see from the main road; a block back there is a mountain town honeycombed with tiny streets and protected corners built against heavy winter weather. Sort is also the origin of the road into the unspoiled world of the Assua Valley, a hidden pocket of untouched and unexploited mountain villages, such as Saury and Olp. The Romanesque church of Sant Pere, in the village of **Llessui** at the head of the valley, is topped with a bell tower resembling a pointed witch's hat, characteristic of the Vall d'Aran and its environs. The ski area at Llessui presides over the valley, along the slopes of the Altars peak above.

From **Llavorsí,** 14 km (9 mi) on C147 from Sort, at the junction of the Noguera Pallaresa and the Cardós rivers, the road up to the valleys of Cardós and Vallferrera branches off to the northeast. A trip up the **Vallferrera Valley** is a good way to get into some unfrequented countryside, explore icy trout streams, or browse through the Romanesque and pre-Romanesque buildings scattered in and around the village of **Alins** under Catalunya's highest mountain, the Pica d'Estats. In the neighboring **Cardós Valley,** the svelte Romanesque bell tower of the Santa Maria Church rises amid the greens of alfalfa and early wheat and the bright red splashes of poppies in May.

After Escaló, 12 km (8 mi) from Llavorsí, the road to Espot and the **⑫ Aigües Tortes National Park** branches off to the west. This wild domain of meadows and woods in the shadow of the twin peaks of Els Encantats includes a maze of more than 50 lakes (the beautiful **Sant Maurici** among them) in addition to streams, waterfalls, and marshes. Forested by pines, firs, beech, and silver birches, it has ample pastureland inhabited by Pyrenean chamois, capercaillie, golden eagle, and ptarmigan. The park has strict rules: no camping, no fires, no vehicles beyond certain points, no loose pets. Access to the park is free, however, and shelters equipped with bunks and mattresses provide overnight accommodations. The Ernest Mallafré *refugio*, or shelter (tel. 973/62–40–09; closed Jan.; sleeps 36), at the foot of Els Encantats near lake Sant Maurici and the L'Estany Llong shelter (tel. 973/69–02–84; open mid-June–mid-Oct.; sleeps 57), in the Sant Nicolau Valley are typical. General information and reservations may be obtained from the park administration in Lleida (Camp de Mart, 35, 25004, tel. 973/24–66–50).

Espot, which has a ski area (Super-Espot), nestles at the floor of the valley along a clear, aquamarine stream. La Capella Bridge, a perfect, mossy arch over the flow, seems to have sprouted directly from the Pyrenean slate itself.

From Esterri d'Aneu, C142 reaches the **Mare de Deu de Ares** sanctuary, a hermitage and refugio at an altitude of 1,403 m (4,600 ft), and, finally, the 1,158-m (6,798-ft) **Bonaigua Pass,** offering a dizzying look back at the Pallars Mountains and ahead to the Vall d'Aran with the Maladeta massif towering above, shimmering in its white glacial frosting.

The **Vall d'Aran** is at the western edge of the Catalan Pyrenees and the northwestern corner of Catalunya. Located north of the main Pyrenean axis, it is the Catalan Pyrenees' only Atlantic valley, opening into the plains of Aquitania and drained by the Garonne, which flows into the Atlantic Ocean north of Bordeaux. The 48-km (30-mi) drive from the Bonaigua Pass to the Pont del Rei border with France faithfully follows the riverbed through the valley.

The Atlantic personality of the valley is manifested in its climate— wetter, colder, and more dependent on weather systems originating in the North Atlantic—and in its language: The 6,000 inhabitants speak Aranés, a dialect of Gascon French that can, with some difficulty, be understood by speakers of Catalan and French.

Originally part of the Aquitanian county of Comenge, the Vall d'Aran maintained feudal ties with the Pyrenees of Spanish Aragón and, from the 12th century, became part of the Catalonia–Aragón realm. In 1389 the valley was officially assigned to Catalunya.

The Vall d'Aran, neither as wide as the Cerdanya nor as oppressively narrow and vertical as Andorra, has a special tone, a sense of well-being and order, an architectural consonance unique within Catalunya. The iron-gray slate roofs clustered on the mountainsides, the lush green vegetation, the dormer windows—a clear manifestation of French influence—all make the Vall d'Aran instantly recognizable as another country, a geographic and cultural pocket that happens to have washed up on the Spanish side of the border.

Viella, the capital, is a lively crossroads vitally involved in the Aranese movement to defend and reconstruct the valley's architectural, institutional, and linguistic patrimony. The Romanesque **Sant Miquel** parish church's octagonal 14th-century bell tower is one of the town's trademarks, as is the 15th-century Gothic altar. The partly damaged 12th-century *Cristo de Mig Aran* wood carving is one of the medieval Pyrenees' most admired works. Displayed under glass at Sant Miquel Church, this polychrome wooden bust evokes a level of emotion and a sense of mortality and humanity rarely achieved by medieval sculptors.

From Viella you can visit **Salardú,** with its porticoed central *plaça* and an especially tall, graceful bell tower. The village of **Tredós,** site of the **Church of Santa Maria de Cap d'Aran,** symbol of the Aranese independence movement and, until 1827, meeting place for the valley's governing body, the Consell General, lies just east of Salardú.

Due north of Salardú, the town of **Baguergue** is 12 km (7½ mi) below the sanctuary of **Santa Maria de Montgarri.** This partly ruined 11th-century structure was once an important way station on the route into the Vall d'Aran from France. The beveled hexagonal bell tower's spire and the rounded brook-bottom stones give the structure a speckled sharpness not unlike the coloring of the Pyrenean *truite de riu* (native trout).

Elsewhere in the Vall d'Aran is Lés, the village that shows the greatest French influence. **Gessa's** church is a well-preserved Aranese specimen, including its pointed tower, slate roof, and cobblestone walls. **Bossost's** Romanesque church has a simple carving on its northern door portraying the Supreme Being at the center of the universe.

The Vall d'Aran abounds with hiking and climbing excursions. Guides are available year-round and have an office in Viella.

The **Joeu Valley,** above the town of Les Bordes, 9 km (6 mi) west of Viella, provides a surprising look into the Vall d'Aran's water system. One of the two main sources of the Garonne, the Joeu River at Artiga de Lin cascades down the Barrancs waterfalls, disappears underground into the Aigualluts tunnel, and reappears 4 km (2½ mi) later at Guell d'Et Joeu, flowing north toward the Garonne and, eventually, the Atlantic.

⑮ The nearby **Baqueira-Beret** and **Tuca-Betrén** winter-sport centers, visited annually by King Juan Carlos I and the royal family, provide Catalunya's most varied and reliable skiing.

The 6-km (4-mi) Viella tunnel under the Maladeta peak connects the Vall d'Aran with the Alta Ribagorça Oriental. This valley includes the east bank of the Noguera Ribagorçana River and the Llevata and Noguera de Tor valleys. The Romanesque churches of the latter offer the richest concentration of medieval art and architecture in the Pyrenees.

Rte. N230 runs south from Viella, 33 km (20 mi) to the intersection with N260, which goes west to the Fadas Pass. Four km (2½ mi) farther, the road up the **Noguera de Tor Valley** turns to the northeast, 2 km (1½ mi) short of Pont de Suert.

The quality and unity of design apparent in each of the churches in the villages scattered along the Noguera de Tor came about as a result of the protection of the counts of Erill. The Erill knights, away fighting the Moors in distant theaters of the Reconquest, left their women behind to support the creation of the religious structures in the area. They brought in the leading masters—architects, masons, sculptors, painters—to build and decorate the valley's churches. To what extent a single eye may have been responsible for the extraordinarily harmonious and coherent set of churches along the Noguera de Tor River may never be known, but what is certain is that they all share definite characteristics: a certain miniaturistic tightness; an eccentric or irregular design; and square and slender bell towers at once light and forceful, perfectly balanced against the rocky background.

⑯ One such church, located at the edge of **Taüll,** is **Sant Climent,** built in 1123. This three-naved basilica has a six-story belfry that is visible from a distance. The proportions, the Pyrenean stone changing hues in the light, the close and intimate feel of the place, all create an exceptional balance and harmony. The church's murals, including the famous *Pantocrator*, the work of the "Master of Taüll," were moved to Barcelona's Museum of Catalan Art in 1922; reproductions of the murals have been installed in Sant Climent. *Admission: 250 pesetas. Open daily 9–2 and 4–8.*

Although Sant Climent is the best known of these Romanesque gems, other important churches include Sant Feliu, at Barruera; Sant Joan Baptista, at Boí; Santa Maria, at Cardet; Santa Maria, at Coll; Santa Eulàlia, at Erill-la-vall; La Nativitat de la Mare de Deu and Sant Quirze, at Durro; Sant Llorenç, at Sarais; and Sant Nicolau, in the Sant Nicolau Valley, at the entrance to the Aigües Tortes National Park.

Taüll, a town of narrow streets and tight mountain design—wooden balconies, steep slate roofs—now has a ski resort, Boí-Taüll, at the head of the Sant Nicolau Valley.

The thermal baths at **Caldes de Boí,** 6 km (4 mi) north of Taüll, include, between hot and cold sources, 40 springs. The caves inside the area of the baths, with thermal steam seeping through the cracks in the rock, are a singular natural phenomenon. You can take advantage of the therapeutic qualities of these baths at either the Hotel Caldes or the Hotel Manantial. Services range from a thermal bath costing 1,000–1,500 pesetas to a 3,000-peseta underwater body massage; arthritic patients are frequent visitors. *Tel. (Barcelona) 93/302–4088, fax 93/301–1856, or Hotel Caldes, tel. 973/69–62–30, or Hotel Manantial, tel. 973/69–01–91. Open June 24–Sept. 30.*

The western end of the Aigües Tortes National Park (*see* entrance at Espot, *above*) can be reached through the Sant Nicolau Valley to the east; to the west, 7 km (4½ mi) north of Pont de Suert, N260 turns toward the Benasque Valley and the Central Pyrenees of Aragón.

Tour 4: The Central Pyrenees—Aragón

Numbers in the margin correspond to points of interest on the Central and Western Pyrenees map.

In **Alto Aragón** (Upper Aragón), the northern part of the province of Huesca, the Maladeta (3,404 m/11,165 ft), Posets (3,375 m/11,070 ft), and Monte Perdido (3,355 m/11,004 ft) massifs are the highest points in the Pyrenean chain. The north–south valleys were originally formed by glaciers at their headlands, and the lower deep canyons and gorges were cut by rivers swollen by torrential rainfalls and heavy snow runoff.

Communications in this part of the Pyrenees were all but nonexistent until recently. Four-fifths of the area had never seen a vehicle of any kind until the beginning of the century, while the 150 km (93 mi) of border with France between Portalet de Aneu and Vall d'Aran never had an international crossing. The combination of high peaks, deep defiles, and lack of communication has produced some of the Iberian Peninsula's most isolated towns and valleys. The inhabitants of much of Alto Aragón have local dialects, such as Grausín or Benasqués; regional variations on the typical Aragonese folk dance, the *jota;* and different kinds of folkloric costumes from valley to valley. The unspoiled natural setting, primarily vertical rock formations, provides a habitat for a wide variety of Pyrenean wildlife, including several strains of mountain goat; deer; and, in Ordesa and Monte Perdido National Park, the Pyrenean brown bear.

The Noguera Ribagorçana River is the border between Catalunya and Aragón, everything west of the river forming part of the Aragonese Ribagorza. Seventy km (43 mi) west on N260 off the road from Viella to Pont de Suert is Castejón de Sos and the Esera River, leading north beside C139 up into the islandlike Benasque Valley. It shares the Maladeta massif with the Vall d'Aran.

17 **Benasque,** as Aragón's easternmost township, has always been an important link between Catalunya and Aragón. The 13th-century **Santa María Mayor Church** and the ancient manor houses of the old families of Benasque, such as the palace of the counts of Ribagorza on Calle Mayor, all of a uniform aristocratic dignity, are among the most notable structures in this town of 1,000 inhabitants. From Benasque you can make excursions to the Maladeta massif, the Refugio de la Renclusa, and the Pico de Aneto. The stone farmhouses of **Anciles,** 2 km (1¼ mi) south of Benasque, are sturdy examples of mountain design.

The nearby **Cerler** ski area (tel. 974/55–10–12), 6 km (3¾ mi) from Benasque, has lifts on the slopes of the Cogulla peak east of town. Built on a high shelf over the valley at an altitude of 1,540 m (5,051 ft), Cerler has 26 ski runs, 3 lifts, and a helicopter service, with guides, to drop you at the highest peaks.

18 South of **Castejón de Sos,** down the Esera Valley, through the Congosto de Ventamillo—a sheer slice through the rock made by the Esera River—a turn west on N260 cuts over to **La Aínsa** at the junction of the Rivers Cinca and Ara. La Aínsa's arcaded central plaza and old part of town are pure medieval village design, with heavy stone archways and tiny windows, while the 12th-century Romanesque church has a quadruple-vaulted door. *Admission free. Open daily 9–2 and 4–8.*

You can explore the **Cinca Valley** from the river's source at the head of the valley above Bielsa, at the Parador Nacional Monte Perdido (*see* Dining and Lodging, *below*) overlooking the Pineta Reservoir and the Ordesa and Monte Perdido National Park.

19 Northwest of Bielsa the **Monte Perdido glacier** and the icy **Marbore Lake** drain into the **Pineta Valley** and the Pineta Reservoir. You can take three- or four-hour walks from the parador up to the Larri, Munia, or Marbore lakes among remote peaks.

North of Bielsa, the road leading to the French border reaches **Parzán,** in the Barrosa Valley, with trails up to Chisagües and Urdiceto. Looking back down the valley is like seeing a detailed relief map of the terrain you are about to cover on your way back down to La Aínsa.

20 The town of **Bielsa** itself, located at the confluence of the Cinca and Barrosa rivers, is a busy summer resort with archaic porticoed plazas and medieval mountain architecture.

A rewarding detour is the **Gistáin Valley,** rising to the east of **Salinas** 7 km (4½ mi) back toward La Aínsa. The Cinqueta River drains the Gistáin Valley, flowing through the mountain villages of Sin, Senes, and Serveta. The towns of Plan and San Juan de Plan preside from the head of the valley. San Juan de Plan has become a guardian of local folklore. An **Ethnographic Museum** (admission: 300 pesetas; open daily 9–2 and 4–8) and a dance ensemble have been founded.

21 Back on the road to La Aínsa, the **Añisclo Canyon** lies 5 km (3 mi) above the town of Escalona. An asphalt road off to the right runs 14 km (8½ mi) along the edge of the sheer rock divide to the ancient

The Central and Western Pyrenees

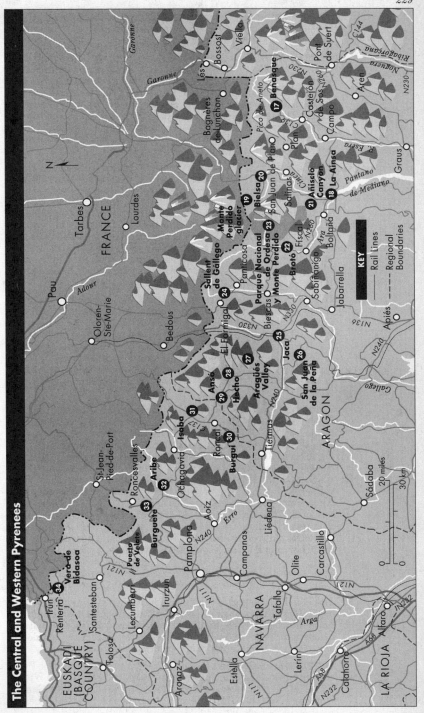

EUSKADI (BASQUE COUNTRY)

FRANCE

ARAGON

NAVARRA

LA RIOJA

KEY
Rail Lines
Regional Boundaries

stone bridge at **San Urbez.** On the far bank of the river is the cave chapel named for San Urbez, a hermit monk from Bordeaux, who lived there in the 8th century.

From La Aínsa, turn west on Rte. N260 for the 48-km (30-mi) drive through Boltaña to **Brotó,** an exemplary Aragonese mountain town with a 16th-century Gothic church and satellite villages such as **Oto,** which has several stately manor houses with classical local features: oversize windows and entryways, conical chimneys, and wooden galleries. The entrance to Ordesa national park, next to the town of Torla, lies to the north under the vertical walls of the Mondarruego Mountain, source of the Ara River and its tributary, the Arazas, which forms the famous Ordesa Valley.

The **Parque Nacional de Ordesa y Monte Perdido** (Ordesa and Monte Perdido National Park), founded by royal decree in 1918 for the purpose of protecting the natural integrity of the Central Pyrenees, has subsequently increased more than 10 times in size, from 4,940 to 56,810 acres, as provincial and national authorities have added the Monte Perdido massif, the head of the Pineta Valley, and Escuain and Añisclo canyons. Defined by the Ara and Arazas rivers, the Ordesa Valley is a natural cornucopia, richly endowed with pine, fir, larch, beech, and poplar forests; lakes, waterfalls, and high mountain meadows; and protected wildlife, including boar, chamois, and the famous *Capra Pyrenaica* mountain goat.

Hikes through the park on well-marked and -maintained mountain trails lead to waterfalls, cirques, caves, and vantage points. There are a few spots that, while not physically difficult, are precarious. Information and guidebooks are available at the booth on the way into the park. The park should be visited from the beginning of May to the middle of November during normal years, but check conditions in regional tourist offices before either driving into a blizzard in May or missing *el veranillo de San Martín* (Indian summer) in the fall.

Follow N260 over the Cotefablo Pass from Torla to **Biescas.** The Tena Valley, a north–south-oriented hexagon of 400 sq km (248 sq mi), is formed by the Gállego River and its two tributaries, the Aguaslimpias and the Caldares. A glacial valley surrounded by peaks rising to over 3,000 m (such as the 3,298-m-high Vignemale), Tena has become a busy winter-sport and hiking center over the past 20 years. Starting from the top, **Sallent de Gállego,** at the head of the valley, has long been a jumping-off point for excursions to Aguaslimpias, Piedrafita, and the meadows of the Gállego headwaters at **El Formigal** (a major ski area) and Portalet. The Pyrenean *ibon* (glacial lake) of **Respumoso,** accessible by walking 2½ hours above the old road from Sallent to Formigal, is a peaceful and perfectly horizontal expanse amid all that vertical Pyrenean landscape.

Back down the valley through Biescas, a westward turn at Sabiñánigo onto N330 leaves a 14-km (9-mi) drive to Jaca.

Jaca, the most important municipal center in Alto Aragón, with a population of more than 15,000, is anything but a sleepy mountain town. Bursting with ambition and blessed with the natural resources to exploit their relentless drive, Jacetanos are determined to host a Winter Olympics before the end of the century.

Jaca hosts or has hosted a Summer University, the Center for Pyrenean Studies, the biannual Pyrenean Folklore Festival, the Winter Games of the Pyrenees, and the World University Winter Games. World and National Figure Skating Championships are held nearly every year, and the national ice hockey King's Cup is often played on Jaca's Olympic-size ice rink. Jaca's ice hockey program, which has been developed since the opening of the rink in 1972, is today one of Spain's best, along with San Sebastián's Txuri Urdiñ and another Pyrenees club, Puigcerdà in the Catalan Cerdanya.

Time Out   One of Jaca's simplest restaurants is **La Campanilla** (Escuelas Pías 6), behind the Town Hall. La Campanilla's baked potatoes with garlic and olive oil are an institution in Jaca, unchanged for as far back as anyone can remember.

Once the capital of the 11th-century kingdom of Jacetania and an important stop on the pilgrimage to Santiago de Compostela, Jaca has an 11th-century **cathedral** that is one of Spain's oldest. The Museo Episcopal (admission: 300 pesetas; open daily 11–1:30 and 4:30–6:30) is filled with excellent Romanesque and Gothic mural paintings. The **Ciutadella** (Fortress; admission free; open Oct.–Mar., daily 11–2 and 4–5; Apr.–Sept., daily 5–6) in town and the **Rapitán** garrison (admission free; open July and Aug., Mon.–Sat. 5–8, Sun. and holidays 11–1) outside town are both good examples of 17th-century military architecture. The **Ayuntamiento** door is a notable Renaissance design.

The ski areas of **Candanchú** and **Astún** are 32 km (20 mi) north on the road to Somport and the French border.

Tour 5: West of Jaca

Before starting west through the Aragonese valleys of Hecho and Ansó, you might want to take a loop south to visit the monastery of **San Juan de la Peña,** a site connected to the legend of the Holy Grail as well as a symbol of Christian resistance during the Moorish invasion of Spain between the 8th and 15th centuries. It can be reached by driving south to the town of Bernués (16 km/10 mi), where a right turn leads 12 km (7 mi) to the monastery. Its origin is traced to the 9th century, when a hermit monk named Juan settled on the *peña* (cliff) on the Pano Mountain. A monastery was founded at that spot in 920. In 1071, Sancho Ramirez, son of King Ramiro I, founded the Benedictine monastery of San Juan de la Peña, making use of the previous monastery built into the rock wall of the mountain. The cloister, tucked under the cliff, was constructed during the 12th century and features carved capitals depicting biblical scenes. *Open Oct.–Mar., Wed.–Sun. 11–1:30 and 4–6; Apr.–Sept., Tues.–Sun. 10–1:30 and 4–7.*

The Aragüés, Hecho, and Ansó are the last three Aragonese valleys. From Jaca, head west on N240 and take a hard right at Puente de la Reina, after turning right to cross the bridge, and continue north along the Aragón-Subordán River.

The first right after 15 km (9 mi) leads into the **Aragüés Valley** along the Osia River to Aisa and then Jasa. Two km (1¼ mi) from Jasa is Aragüés del Puerto, and above is the Bisaurín Peak, at 2,658 m (8,638 ft), one of the highest in the area. **Aragüés del Puerto** is a tidy mountain village with stone houses and diminutive nooks and crannies. The distinctive folk dance in Aragüés is the *Palotiau*, a special variation of the *jota* performed only in this village. At the source of the River Osia, the **Lizara** cross-country ski area is located in a flat between the Aragüés and Jasa valleys where you can find dolmens left from the megalithic period.

The **Hecho Valley** can be reached by returning to the valley of the Aragón-Subordan and turning north again. The **Siresa Monastery,** above the town of **Hecho,** is the area's most important monument, a 9th-century retreat of which only the 11th-century church remains. The Cheso dialect is still alive in the Hecho Valley and continues to be used by some writers and poets. The **Selva de Oza** (Oza Forest), at the head of the valley, is the natural pièce de résistance, reachable only after passing through the Boca del Infierno (Mouth of Hell), a tight draw where both the road and the river pass. On the other side of the Selva de Oza is a Roman road that, before the 4th century, was used to reach France through the El Palo Pass and became one of the first routes used to cross the border and the Pyrenees on the pilgrimage to Santiago de Compostela in northwestern Spain.

The **Ansó Valley** is Aragón's western limit. Rich in fauna (mountain goats, wild boar, even bear) the Ansó Valley follows the Veral River up to Zuriza. Above Zuriza there are three cross-country ski areas known as the Pistas de Linza. Near Fago is the sanctuary of Virgen de Puyeta, patron saint of the valley. From the town of **Ansó,** you can travel west to Roncal on a difficult but beautiful road through the Sierra de San Miguel.

The Pyrenees of **Navarre** extend west from Roncal, at the border with Aragón, to Vera de Bidasoa, where the Bidasoa River, the border between France and Spain, flows down through the western Pyrenean foothills to the Bay of Biscay. From the peaks of Anie (2,504 m/8,213 ft) and Ori (2,017 m/6,616 ft) and the plateau of the Tres Reyes (2,434 m/7,984 ft), the mountains gradually descend to Larrún (900 m/2,952 ft) in the west.

Take N240 from Jaca west along the Aragón River; a right turn north on NA137 follows the Esca River from the head of the Yesa Reservoir up the **Roncal Valley,** famous for its sheep's milk cheese and as the birthplace of Julián Gayarre (1844–1890), the leading tenor of his time. The 34-km (21-mi) drive through the towns of **Burgui** and Roncal to the valley's capital at **Isaba** winds through green hillsides and Basque *caseríos* housing families of farmers and their livestock. Burgui's red-tile roofs backed by soft, rolling pastures contrast with the vertical rock and steep slate roofs of the Aragonese and Catalan Pyrenees, while Isaba's wide-arched bridge across the Esca is a reminder of Roman engineering influence on later construction. If you can, try to be in the Roncal Valley for the celebration of the Tribute of the Three Cows, held every July 13 since 1375. The mayors of the valley's villages, dressed in their distinctive traditional gowns, gather at the San Martín peak to receive the symbolic payment of three cows from their French counterparts, in memory of the settlement of ancient border disputes over rights to high pastures and water sources. The road west (NA140) to Ochagavia through the Lazar Pass offers views of the peaks of Anie and Ori towering just over the French border.

Two km (1¼ mi) south of Ochagavia, at Escároz, a small secondary roadway winds 22 km (14 mi) over the Abaurrea heights to **Aribe.** From there, a 15-km (9-mi) detour through the town of Orbaiceta up to the headwaters of the Irati River at the Irabia Reservoir is a good chance to have a look at the **Selva de Irati** (Irati Forest), one of the few forests in the Pyrenees and the most trees you will have seen in a long time. It is said, though not widely believed, that before the construction of the 16th-century Spanish Armada depleted Spain's forests beyond repair, a squirrel could cross the Iberian Peninsula without touching the ground.

③③ South of Roncesvalles (*see* Chapter 6, *above*), **Burguete** lies between two mountain streams forming the headwaters of the Urobi River. The town became famous in 1926 when Ernest Hemingway published *The Sun Also Rises*, with its evocative description of trout fishing in an ice-cold stream above a moist Navarran village called Burguete. Since then, many travelers to Burguete and to Roncesvalles have attempted to re-create the mood of this happy parenthesis in the novel.

From Burguete you can continue southeast on C135 until you reach a small road on the right to Egozcue, which connects with the N121, where you turn north and climb over the **Puerto de Velate** (Velate Pass) to **Vera de Bidasoa** and the sea.

③④

What to See and Do with Children

Le petit train jaune (the little yellow train) leaves daily from La Tour de Querol or from Bourg-Madame, a short walk from Puigcerdà (*see* Tour 2), winding through the Cerdanya to the walled city of Vilafranca de Conflent. The *carrilet* (**narrow-gauge railway**) is the last in the Pyrenees and is now used for tours as well as for getting around the valley. The 63-km (39-mi) tour can take most of a day, especially if you get off to browse through Mont Louis or Vilafranca. The train, which resembles an illustration from a Dr. Seuss story, is a great favorite with children and adults alike. *Cost: 2,000 pesetas (100 francs) per person in groups of 10 or more, 3,000 pesetas (150 francs) singly. Boarding at SNCF stations at Bourg-Madame or LaTour de Querol, payable in French francs only. Schedules at Touring travel agency or Turismo Office, Puigcerdà; or at RENFE station below Puigcerdà.*

Off the Beaten Track

Nuria The cogwheel train from Ribes (*see* Tour 1) up to Nuria is one of the most spectacular and unusual excursions Catalunya has to offer. Known as the *cremallera* (zipper), the cogwheel line was constructed in 1917 to connect Ribes with the sanctuary of La Mare de Deu de Nuria (The Mother of God of Nuria). (The ride takes 45 minutes and costs 1,500 pesetas round-trip.) Nuria, located at an altitude of 2,001 m (6,562 ft) at the foot of Puigmal, is a ski area as well as the site of some of Spain's earliest ice hockey activity, starting in the early 1950s.

The legend of Nuria, a Marian religious retreat, is based on the story of Sant Gil of Nîmes, who did penance in the valley of Nuria during the 7th century, leaving behind a wooden statue of the Virgin Mary, a bell he used to call local shepherds to prayer, and a cooking pot. Three centuries later, a pilgrim found these treasures, still kept in the sanctuary at Nuria. The bell and the pot came to have special importance to barren women, who were enabled to bear as many children as they wished by placing their heads in the pot and ringing the bell, each peal of the bell meaning another child. *Admission free. Closed only during religious celebrations.*

The Upper Cerdanya Excursions to the upper reaches of the Cerdanya (*see* Tour 2) require some organization but are always unforgettable successes. The Touring travel agency (tel. 972/88–06–02 or 972/88–14–50; fax 972/88–19–39) in Puigcerdà can be of assistance in arranging routes, guides, horses, or jeeps for treks to upper lakes, peaks, and meadows.

Prat d'Aguiló (Eagle's Meadow) is a spectacular high meadow, perfect for a cookout overlooking the valley. An hour's drive above Martinet up a dirt road that is rough but navigable by normal automobile, Prat d'Aguiló is one of the highest points in the Cerdanya accessible without recourse to a jeep or a hike. Another seemingly short climb (which will end up taking about three hours), to the top of the sheer rock wall of the Cadí range, reaches an altitude of nearly 2,440 m (8,000 ft). On a clear day the view includes Puigcerdà and beyond, and the River Segre is no more than a thin silver ribbon on the valley floor.

The Baztán Valley
Tucked neatly over the headwaters of the Bidasoa River (*see* Tour 5), north of the Velate Pass, and under the peak of Garramendi looming over the border with France, the Baztán Valley's rounded green hills are an ideal halfway stop between the rocky crags of the central Pyrenees and the Atlantic Ocean below. Each village in this enchanted valley seems smaller and simpler than the next, tiny clusters of red-tile-roofed, whitewashed mortar and stone grouped around the town *frontón* (handball court).

Shopping

Shopping in the Pyrenees features local specialties, such as herbs, goat cheese, wild mushrooms, honey, and basketry, found in the Sunday markets held in most towns.

Sports

Participant Sports

Fishing
Well-populated with trout, the mountain streams of the Pyrenees provide excellent angling from the third Sunday in March until the end of August. The River Segre has fine trout fishing down as far as Ponts. Although virtually all the rivers and streams flowing out of the Pyrenees provide good habitats for fish and fisherman alike, the Garonne, Aragón, Gállego, Noguera Pallaresa, Arga, and Esca are notable. Season licenses for fishing for each autonomous region (Catalunya, Aragón, Navarra) can be purchased at local Rod & Gun Clubs *(Asociaciones de Pesca, Caza)*, at the Federació Catalana de Pesca (Av. Madrid 118, Barcelona, tel. 93/330–4818), or from the regional fishing authorities: Servei Territorial d'Agricultura, Ramaderia, i Pesca de Barcelona (Carrer Sabí d'Arana 22–24, Barcelona, tel. 93/330–6451).

Golf
The Cerdanya has two golf courses, at **Puigcerdà** (tel. 972/88–09–50) and at **Font Romeu** (tel. 968/30–38–09) in France. Greens fees are 6,500 pesetas at Puigcerdà and 250 francs at Font Romeu.

Hiking
Mountain climbing and hiking are fundamental Pyrenean activities during the summer months. Walking the crest of the Sierra Catllar above Setcases, scaling the Cadí over the Cerdanya, or climbing from Benasque to the highest peaks in the Pyrenees, Aneto and Posets, are some of the most popular excursions. The GR11 and the HRP (Haute Route Pyrénées) are well marked the entire length of the Pyrenees chain. Local *excursionista* clubs and, especially, the Centro Excursionista de Catalunya in Barcelona (Carrer Paradís 10, tel. 93/315–2311) can advise climbers and hikers.

Hunting
Red-leg partridge, rabbit, wild boar, and chamois inhabit the Pyrenees. Visitors are welcome to bring and use firearms legally registered and accompanied by the appropriate permits from their home

countries. The only difficulty in hunting in Spain, a major one, is arranging a place to shoot, as nearly all land with game on it is leased to private groups of hunters. The Federació Catalana de Caça (Via Laietana 9, 4–2, Barcelona, tel. 93/310–2307) or local hunting associations and tourist offices can be helpful in solving this problem.

Ice Skating **Jaca** (tel. 974/36–10–32) and **Puigcerdà** (tel. 972/88–02–43) have excellent ice rinks, as does Vielha, where a spectacular ice rink, gymnasium, and swimming pool were opened in 1994.

Kayaking **Seu d'Urgell** is known for kayaking (Federación Catalana de Piraguismo, Avinguda Madrid 118, Barcelona, tel. 93/330–4448), as is **Sort** in the Noguera Pallaresa Valley.

Skiing The Pyrenees can provide fine skiing from December through March at more than 20 ski resorts, ranging from Vallter 2000 at **Setcases** in the Camprodón Valley, west to **Isaba** and **Burguete** in the province of Navarra. Although weekend skiing can be crowded in the eastern valleys, Catalunya's western Pyrenees, especially **Baqueira-Beret,** in the Vall d'Aran, rank among Spain's best wintersports centers. **Cerler-Benasque** (*see* Tour 4, *above*), **Panticosa, Formigal, Astun,** and **Candanchú** are the major ski areas in Huesca. Aercombi (Viella, tel. 973/64–57–97) offers off-piste helicopter skiing.

Cross-country skiing is becoming increasingly popular in the Pyrenees. **Lles** in the Cerdanya; **Salardú** and **Beret** in the Vall d'Aran; and **Panticosa, Benasque,** and **Candanchú** in Aragón are among the leading Nordic ski areas.

El País, Spain's daily newspaper, distributed nationally, prints complete ski information every Friday during the winter-sports season. For up-to-the-minute information, contact the hot line in Barcelona (tel. 93/416–0194). For further information, contact the Federació Catalana Esports d'Hivern (Carrer Casp 38, Barcelona, tel. 93/302–7040).

Spectator Sports

The Vall d'Aran's most extraordinary winter-sports event is the annual horse race on ice, the **Rally Hipic Internacional Sobre Neu,** held every February over a 16-km (10-mi) course of packed snow. Contact the Centro Internacional Turístico del Val d'Aran (tel. 973/64–09–79) for information.

Dining and Lodging

Dining

Pyrenean cuisine is characterized by a rich variety of local ingredients. Trout, often from mountain streams and lakes, mountain goat, deer, wild boar, partridge, rabbit, duck, woodcock, and quail are roasted over coals or slowly cooked in aromatic stews called *civets* in Catalonia and *estofadas* in Aragón and Navarra. Fish and meat alike are often seared on slabs of slate (*a la llosa* in Catalan, *a la piedra* in Castilian). Wild mushrooms are another important local specialty when in season (usually in the fall). A guidebook to edible mushrooms and a visit to a village market will help you learn to identify these culinary gems, but always rely on expert opinion before eating one. Dress in restaurants throughout the Pyrenees tends to be casual.

Highly recommended restaurants are indicated by a star ★ .

Category	Cost*
$$$$	over 5,000 ptas
$$$	4,000–5,000 ptas
$$	2,500–4,000 ptas
$	1,000–2,500 ptas

per person for a three-course meal, including tax, drinks, and service

Lodging

Hotels in the Pyrenees tend to be informal and outdoorsy in feeling, usually with a friendly open fireplace in the public rooms. In design they blend with the mountains that surround them and are built of wood and slate, typically with steep roofs. The comfortable, protected but not luxurious atmosphere found in most hotels here reflects the tastes of the visitors—mostly skiers and hikers.

Highly recommended lodgings are indicated by a star ★ .

Category	Cost*
$$$$	over 12,000 ptas
$$$	9,000–12,000 ptas
$$	5,000–9,000 ptas
$	under 5,000 ptas

All prices are for two people sharing a double room and include service and tax.

Arizcun
Dining and Lodging
★

Fonda Etxeberria. This tiny inn is an old farmhouse with creaky floorboards and oak doors. The rooms are small but handsomely decorated, and not all have private baths. The restaurant specializes in simple country dishes, such as bean stew and roast lamb. *Next to the frontón, tel. 948/45–30–13. 16 rooms. Facilities: restaurant. MC, V. $*

Bellver de Cerdanya
Dining

Grau de l'Os. This cozy mountain retreat—"Bear Cave" is the translation—is decorated in wood brightwork and simple, rough-hewn carpentry. The typical Catalan cuisine features combinations such as roast rabbit with *all i oli* (olive oil and garlic sauce), *civet de jabalí* (stewed wild boar), and quail, partridge, trout, and lamb. *Jaume II de Mallorca 5, tel. 973/51–00–46. Reservations recommended on weekends. AE, DC, MC, V. Closed Wed. $$*

Benasque
Dining and Lodging

Benasque. This solid stone structure , surrounded by the highest crests in the Pyrenees, makes an excellent base camp. The decor and the ambience are distinctly Castilian, with a predominantly wood interior and traditional furniture. The restaurant's Aragonese mountain cuisine features such specialties as the *sopa Benasquesa* (a hearty highland soup) and *crepas Aneto* (crêpe filled with ham, mushrooms, and béchamel sauce). *Carretera de Anciles, 22440, tel. 974/55–10–11, fax 974/55–15–09. 38 rooms. Facilities: restaurant (reservations recommended). V. $*

Bolvir de Cerdanya
Dining and Lodging
★

La Torre del Remei. Two miles west of Puigcerdà, this splendid family mansion built in 1910 has been brilliantly restored by José María and Loles Boix of Can Boix in Martinet (*see below*). Can Boix is still impeccable, but La Torre del Remei is even better, having gone so far as to expropriate the Boix's coveted Michelin star. Everything about the Torre del Remei, from the *belle epoque* luxury of the manor house itself to the redesigned bathroom floors, heated bathroom floors, huge bathtubs, the bottle of Moët et Chandon on ice upon arrival, and, of course, the cuisine, is superb. Loles will advise you what's best on the menu that day. Reserve well in advance. *Camí Reial s/n, 17463, tel. 972/14-01-82, fax 972/14-04-49. 11 rooms. Facilities: restaurant, pool, 2 putting greens. AE, DC, MC, V. $$$$*

Camprodón
Lodging

Hotel Güell. Owned and managed by the charming Güell family, this elegant structure of glass, wood, and stone is home to skiers and enthusiasts of the Camprodón Valley. The rooms are decorated simply but tastefully with heavy Pyrenean wood furniture. *Plaça d'Espanya 8, 17867, tel. 972/74-00-11, fax 972/74-11-12. 38 rooms. AE, DC, MC, V. $$*

Elizondo
Dining
★

Galarza. This stone town house overlooks the Baztán River and serves excellent Basque fare, with a Navarran emphasis on vegetables. Recommended dishes include *Txuritabel* (roast lamb in season with a special stuffing of egg and vegetables) and *txuleta de ternera* (veal raised in the valley). *Calle Santiago 1, tel. 948/58-01-01. Reservations accepted. MC, V. $$*

Gessa
Dining

Casa Rufus. In the tiny gray-stone village of Gessa, between Viella and Salardú, Casa Rufus is cozily furnished with pine and checked tablecloths. Rufus himself, who also runs the ski school at Baqueira, specializes in local country cooking; try the *conejo relleno de ternera* (rabbit stuffed with veal). *Sant Jaume 8, tel. 973/64-52-46 or 973/64-58-72. MC, V. Open only during ski season (Dec.–Apr.) and in Aug. Closed Sun. $*

Jaca
Dining

Casa Paco. Miguel Alegre and his British wife, Allison Smith, have made the cozy Casa Paco, furnished with bright wood and checked tablecloths, one of Jaca's best restaurants. Their seasonally fresh and innovative cuisine features game of all kinds: venison, wild boar, partridge, and woodcock. The current chef is a specialist in Basque cuisine, giving Casa Paco an extra international dimension to accompany local Aragonese home cooking. *La Salud 10, tel. 974/36-16-18. Reservations recommended on weekends. AE, DC, MC, V. $$*

Lodging

Gran Hotel. This rambling wood, stone, and glass structure has a garden and a separate dining room wing. It is central to life and tourism in Jaca. The rooms are comfortable, decorated in rich colors, with practical wood furniture. *Paseo de la Constitución 1, 22700, tel. 974/36-09-00, fax 974/36-40-61. 166 rooms. Facilities: restaurant, pool, garden, conference rooms. AE, DC, MC, V. $$*

Llívia
Dining
★

Can Ventura. Built into a 17th-century farmhouse, this superb restaurant is certainly the best around Puigcerdà for decor, cuisine, and value. Trout or beef cooked on Pyrenean slate (*a la llosa*) is one of the specialties of the house, while the *entretenimientos*, a wide selection of hors d'oeuvres, is a delicious way to begin a meal. *Plaça Major 1, tel. 972/89-61-78. Reservations necessary weekends and holidays. Closed Tues. and Oct. MC, V. $$*

Dining and Lodging

Hotel Llívia. An ideal clubhouse/base of operations for skiing in France, Andorra, or Spain, the Hotel Llívia is owned and operated by the warm and generous Pous family, the proprietors of Can Ventura (*see above*). A spacious structure with large fireplaces and a glass-wall dining room nearly as scenic as a picnic in a Pyrenean meadow, the hotel runs transports to nearby ski resorts and can organize tours, excursions, riding, or trout fishing. *Av. de Catalunya s/n, 17527, tel. 972/89–60–00, fax 972/14–60–00. 55 rooms. Facilities: restaurant. DC, MC, V. $$*

Martinet
Dining and Lodging
★

Can Boix. Although this blocky modern building doesn't look like much from the outside, this hotel and restaurant is one of the Cerdanya's premier gastronomical establishments. (The premier prize goes to Can Boix owners' La Torre del Remei, *see above.*) José María Boix and his wife, Loles, prepare a mix of Catalan and French cuisine, featuring *setas* (wild mushrooms) in season and surprising specialties such as *canard magret amb mel* (duck breasts with honey) or *trinxat rostit* (chopped potato and cauliflower prepared with bacon). *Carretera Puigcerdà–Seu d'Urgell, tel. 973/51–50–50, fax 973/51–52–68. 34 rooms. Weekend reservations recommended. AE, DC, MC, V. $$$*

Ordesa and Monte Perdido National Park
Dining and Lodging

Parador Nacional Monte Perdido. This modern structure of glass, steel, and stone overlooks the spectacular national park, the peak of Monte Perdido, and the source of the Cinca River. The rooms are decorated in bright wood, but the best part is the proximity to the park and the views. The restaurant specializes in Aragonese mountain dishes such as *pucherete deParzán* (a stew with beans, sausage, and an assortment of vegetables). *Migas Aragonesas* (a combination of bread, grapes, and sausage) is another typical local dish. *Bielsa, 22350, tel. 974/50–10–11, fax 974/50–11–88. 24 rooms. Facilities: restaurant (reservations required). AE, DC, MC, V. $$$*

Panticosa
Dining and Lodging

Morlans. In an Aragonese mountain structure of stone and wood, the rooms here are warm and well equipped with views south over Panticosa's ski area and mountains beyond. The barbecue restaurant on the ground floor specializes in roast meats, especially lamb, goat, and suckling pig. The upper restaurant serves *civets* (stews) of deer, boar, and mountain goat, along with other Upper Aragonese favorites, such as *pochas* (bean soup with sausage). *Calle de San Miguel, Barriada de la Cruz, 22066, tel. 974/48–70–57, fax 974/48–73–86. 25 rooms. Room reservations required. Facilities: 2 restaurants ($). MC, V. $$*

Puigcerdà
Dining and Lodging

Hotel Maria Victoria. This comfortable and central perch overlooking the Cerdanya Valley is a relaxed and convenient in-town base. The staff is impeccably friendly and helpful; the rooms, charmingly lived-in, have creaky wooden floors, flowered wallpaper, and panoramic views down the wide valley to the Sierra del Cadí. The restaurant is a glassed-in room warmed by the sun in winter, breezy and open in summer. House specialties include grilled rabbit or lamb chops with *all i oli* sauce and *escudella* (a country stew including assorted meats and vegetables). *Querol 9, 17520, tel. 972/88–03–00. 50 rooms. Facilities: restaurant. AE, MC, V. $$*

Dining

Madrigal. This popular bar and restaurant is near the Puigcerdà town hall and the balcony overlooking the valley. The low-ceilinged wood-trimmed dining room upstairs is filled with tables and benches. Selections include tapas or a meal of assorted specialties such as *calamares a la romana* (squid rings), quail, Serrano ham, *albóndigas* (meatballs), *caracoles* (snails), *esqueixada* (raw codfish with peppers and onion), or wild mushrooms in season. Pere Compte, proprietor and host, is always helpful in suggesting selections. *Alfons I 1, tel. 972/88–08–60. No credit cards. $*

Rocabruna
Dining

Can Po. Perched over a deep gulley where ducks and rabbits soon to be invited into the kitchen roam happily, Can Po serves first-rate cuisine in an ancient ivy-covered stone and mortar farmhouse. House specialties include *peu de porc* (pigs' feet) and *anec amb peras* (duck prepared with stewed pears). *Carretera de Beget s/n, 17867, tel. 972/74–10–45. Open daily July–Sept.; Fri.–Sun., Oct.–June. MC, V. $$*

Seu d'Urgell
Dining and Lodging

El Castell. This wood-and-slate structure is well known as one of the area's finest dining and lodging spots. There are three types of rooms: Those on the second floor are decorated primarily with wood and have balconies overlooking the river; third-floor rooms are constructed in a mountain-hideaway style with slanted ceilings and dormer windows; suites consist of room and salon. The restaurant specializes in mountain cuisine, such as civet de jabalí and *llom de cordet* (lamb cooked over coals). Reservations are required for lodging. *Ctra. de Lleida, K129, Aptdo. 53, 25700, tel. 973/35–07–04, fax 973/35–15–74. 38 rooms, 4 suites. Facilities: restaurant (weekend reservations required). AE, DC, MC, V. $$*

Viella
Dining
★

Era Mola. A restored stable with wood beams and whitewashed walls, this intimate spot specializes in Aranese cuisine with a definite French flair. The *confite de pato* (duck stewed with apple) and *magret de pato* (breast of duck served rare with *carradetas*, wild mushrooms from the valley) are two house favorites. *Carrer Marrec s/n, tel. 973/64–08–68. Weekend reservations required. MC, V. $$*

Dining and Lodging

Parador Nacional Valle de Aran. This solid granite structure, a modern design with large windows overlooking the Maladeta peaks, has an interior decorated in wood. The rooms are furnished with traditional carved Spanish furniture and floor-to-ceiling curtains. The restaurant serves Catalan cuisine, such as *entremeses Parador* (a selection of hors d'oeuvres, including sausage, asparagus, pâtés, hams, and assorted vegetables) and *espinacas a la catalana* (spinach cooked in olive oil with pine nuts, raisins, and garlic). *Ctra. del Tunel s/n, 25530, tel. 973/64–01–00, fax 973/64–11–00. 135 rooms. Facilities: restaurant (reservations recommended). AE, MC, V. $$$*

Lodging

Residencia d'Aran. On the left side of the road entering Viella, this modern hotel commands some of the best views in town. Bedrooms are bright and simply furnished. The cozy sitting room and the charming family who manage the hotel make your stay there delightful. Book ahead during ski season; you are 15 minutes from the slopes. *Ctra. del Tunel s/n, 25530, tel. 973/64–00–75. 40 rooms with bath. AE, DC, MC, V. $$*

Nightlife

Both Puigcerdà and Jaca have disco scenes so torrid that a moment in the embrace of all that sound and fury may render sleep impossible until well after sunrise.

Puigcerdà

Clubs such as **Patrick's** (by the Park Hotel below town), **Gatzara** (tel. 972/88–07–57), and **De Nit** (5 km from Puigcerdà near Caixans on the road to Alp) are filled with young people from both sides of the border until dawn on weekends and holidays.

Jaca

Jet (tel. 974/36–39–15) and **Crestas** (tel. 974/36–33–28) are thronged with skiers and hockey players in season (Oct.–Apr.).

8 Barcelona

By Philip Eade

Updated by George Semler

Capital of Catalunya (Catalonia) and Spain's second-largest city, Barcelona has long rivaled, even surpassed, Madrid in industrial muscle and business acumen. Though Madrid has now finally well and truly taken up the mantle of capital city, Barcelona has relinquished none of its former prowess. The city witnessed a massive building program in anticipation of the big event of 1992, the long-cherished goal of hosting the Olympics, during which world attention focused on Barcelona. It ranks as one of Europe's most beautiful cities: Few places can rival the narrow alleys of the Gothic Quarter for medieval atmosphere or the elegance and distinction of the boulevards in its Moderniste Eixample.

Barcelona enjoys an active cultural life and heritage. It was the home of the architect Antoni Gaudí i Cornet (1852–1926), whose buildings form the most startling statements of Modernisme, a Spanish and mainly Catalan offshoot of Art Nouveau, whose other leading exponents were the architects Lluís Domènech i Montaner and Josep Puig i Cadafalch. The painters Joan Miró (1893–1983) and Antoni Tàpies (born 1923) also began their careers here. It is the place where Pablo Picasso spent his formative years, and it has a museum devoted to his works. It can claim Spain's oldest and best opera house, the Liceu, and acknowledges with pride contributions to the arts of such native Catalans as cellist Pablo (Pau, in Catalán) Casals (1876–1973), surrealist Salvador Dalí (1904–1989), and opera singers Montserrat Caballé and Josep (José) Carreras. It flaunts a fashion industry hard on the heels of those of Paris and Milan, as well as one of the world's most glamorous soccer clubs.

In 133 BC the Romans conquered the city built by the Iberian tribe known as the Laietans and founded a colony they called Colonia Favencia Julia Augusta Paterna Barcino. In the 5th century, Barcelona was established as the Visigothic capital, the Moors invaded during the 8th century, and in 801 the Franks under Charlemagne captured Barcelona and made it their frontier with the Moorish empire on the Iberian Peninsula. By 988, the autonomous Catalonian counties had gained independence from the Franks, and in 1137 they were united through marriage with the House of Aragón. In 1474 the marriage of Ferdinand of Aragón and Isabella of Castile brought Aragón and Catalonia into a united Spain. As the capital of Aragón's Mediterranean empire, Barcelona had grown in importance between the 12th and the 14th centuries, and began to falter only when maritime emphasis shifted to the Atlantic after 1492. Despite Madrid's becoming the permanent seat of government in 1562, Catalonia continued to enjoy autonomous rights and privileges until 1714 when, in reprisal for having backed the pretender to the Spanish throne, all institutions and expressions of Catalonian nationalism were suppressed by the triumphant Felip V. Not until the 19th century would Barcelona's industrial growth bring about a *Renaixença* (renaissance) of nationalism and a cultural flowering redolent of the city's former opulence.

The tradition of independence nevertheless survived intact, and on numerous occasions Catalonia has revolted against the central authority of Madrid. During the civil war, Barcelona was a Republican stronghold and base for many anarchists and Communists. As a result, during the Franco dictatorship, Catalan identity and language were both suppressed, through such devices as book burning, the renaming of streets and towns, and the banning of the use of Catalan in schools and the media. But this repression had little lasting effect, for the Catalans have jealously guarded their language and culture and still only reluctantly think of themselves as Spaniards.

Catalonian home rule was granted after Franco's death in 1975, and in 1980 the ancient Generalitat, Catalunya's autonomous parliament, was reinstated. Catalan is now heard on every street, eagerly promoted through free classes funded by the Generalitat. Street names are now in Catalan, and newspapers, radio stations, and a TV channel publish and broadcast in Catalan. The circular Catalan *sardana* is danced regularly all over town. The triumphant culmination of this rebirth has, of course, been the staging of the Olympics in 1992. Stadia and pools were renovated, new harborside promenades created, and an entire set of railway tracks moved to make way for the Olympic Village. Not content to limit themselves to Olympics building projects, Barcelona's last two mayors have presided over the creation of an architecture student's paradise.

It's best not to visit in summer, when Barcelona swelters. Winters are characterized by clear blue skies and relatively mild temperatures. Rains tend to come only during the change of seasons in early November and late February.

Essential Information

Arriving and Departing by Plane

All international and domestic flights arrive at the stunning glass, steel, and marble **El Prat de Llobregat Airport,** 14 km (8½ mi) south of Barcelona, just off the main highway to Castelldefels and Sitges. For information on arrival and departure times, call Iberia at the airport (tel. 93/401–3131, 401–3535 at night; for general information, tel. 93/301–3993 for InforIberia, or 93/302–7656 for Iberia international reservations and reconfirmations). The only airlines with direct flights from the United States to Barcelona are TWA and Delta.

Between the Airport and Downtown Check first to see if your hotel provides a free shuttle service. Otherwise, you have the option of train, bus, taxi, or renting a car to drive yourself in.

By Train The train from the airport to Sants Station in the city leaves every 30 minutes between 6:12 AM and 10:42 PM (Sants–airport 5:40 AM–10:12 PM) and takes 20 minutes. There are also trains every 30 minutes to and from Plaça de Catalunya Station: airport–Plaça de Catalunya 6:12 AM–10:12 PM and Plaça de Catalunya–airport 6:05 AM–10:05 PM. The fare is 400 pesetas.

By Bus The Aerobus leaves the airport for Plaça de Catalunya every 15 minutes (6:25 AM–11 PM) on weekdays and every 30 minutes (6:45 AM–10:45 PM) on weekends. From Plaça de Catalunya to the airport, it leaves every 15 minutes (5:30 AM–10 PM) on weekdays and every 30 minutes (6:00 AM–10 PM) on weekends. The fare is 450 pesetas.

By Taxi A cab from the airport to downtown costs from 2,500 to 3,000 pesetas.

By Car By following signs to the Centre Ciutat, you will enter the city along Gran Via. The journey to the center of town can take anywhere from 15 to 45 minutes depending on traffic conditions.

Arriving and Departing by Car, Train, and Bus

By Car Barcelona is notorious for its parking difficulties, so there is a lot to be said for not coming by car. However, if you are prepared to pay 3,000 pesetas per day for a parking lot, of which there are plenty, and brave the hectic driving conditions, a car can be a convenient and independent way of seeing the city.

By Train Almost all long-distance and international trains arrive and depart from **Estació de Sants** (Sants Station; Plaça Països Catalans, tel. 93/490–0202). There is another station on Passeig de Gràcia (corner of Aragó, tel. 93/490–0202), where some trains stop before going on to, or after leaving, Sants. The **Estació de França,** near the port, handles long-distance trains to and from France.

By Bus Barcelona has no central bus station, but most buses to Spanish destinations operate from the **Estació Norte–Vilanova** (at the end of Av. Vilanova, a couple of blocks east of the Arc de Triomf, tel. 93/245–2528). Most international buses arrive at and depart from **Estació Autobuses de Sants** (Carrer Viriato, next to Sants train station, tel. 93/490–4000). Scores of independent companies operate from depots dispersed about town (*see* Barcelona Excursions, *below*).

Getting Around

Modern Barcelona, above the Plaça de Catalunya, is built on a grid system, though there's no helpful coordinated numbering system. The old town, from the Plaça de Catalunya to the port, is a labyrinth of narrow streets, and you'll need a good street map to get around. Most sightseeing can be done on foot—you won't have any choice in the Gothic Quarter—but you'll need to use the metro or buses to link sightseeing areas. If you're using an old map, you'll find that all the street names are now written in Catalan. For general information on the city's public transport, call 93/412–0000. Public-transport maps showing bus and metro routes are available free from booths in Plaça de Catalunya.

By Metro The subway is the fastest and cheapest way of getting around, as well as the easiest to use. You pay a flat fare of 125 pesetas, no matter how far you travel, but it is more economical to buy a Targeta T-2 (valid for metro and FF. CC. Generalitat trains, Tramvía Blau [blue tram], and Montjuïc Funicular; *see below*) costing 650 pesetas for 10 rides. It runs 5 AM–11 PM (until 1 AM on weekends and holidays).

By Bus City buses run daily from 5:30 AM to 11:30 PM. Fares are 125 pesetas (140 pesetas Sundays and holidays); for multiple journeys purchase a Targeta T-1, costing 700 pesetas and good for 10 rides (valid for the same as T-2 plus buses). Route maps are displayed at bus stops. Note that those with a red band always have a stop at a central square—Catalunya, Universitat, or Urquinaona—and blue indicates a night bus. From June 23 to September 17, 10 AM–7 PM, bus No. 100 operates on a circuit that takes in all the important sights. A day's ticket, which you can buy on the bus, costs 1,000 pesetas (750 pesetas half-day) and also covers the fare for the Tramvía Blau, funicular, and Montjuïc cable car across the port.

By Taxi Taxis are black and yellow and, when available for hire, show a green light. The meter starts at 350 pesetas (lasts for 6 minutes), and there are supplements for luggage, night travel, Sundays and fiestas, rides from a station or to the airport, and for going to or from the bullring or a soccer match. There are cab stands all over town; cabs may also be flagged down on the street. Make sure the driver puts on his meter. To phone a cab, try 93/387–1000, 93/490–2222, or 93/357–7755.

By Cable Car and Funicular Montjuïc Funicular is a cog railroad that runs from the junction of Avinguda Paral.lel and Nou de la Rambla to the Miramar Amusement Park on Montjuïc (Paral.lel metro). It operates weekends and

Barcelona Metro

Mediterranean Sea

KEY

L1 Metro Terminals
○ Metro Stations
▭ Transfer Stations
— Railway Lines
••• Funicular
••• Teleféric
┼┼┼ Tramvia Blau
▭▭▭ FF.CC. Generalitat

↓ TO AIRPORT ✈

fiestas 11 AM–8 PM in winter, and daily 11 AM–9:30 PM in summer; the fare is 125 pesetas. A cable car (*teleféric*) then takes you from the amusement park up to Montjuïc Castle (in winter, operates weekends and fiestas 11–2:45 and 4–7:30; in summer, daily 11:30 AM–9 PM; fare: 350 pesetas).

A Transbordador Aeri Harbor Cable Car runs between Miramar and Montjuïc across the harbor to Torre de Jaume I on Barcelona *moll* (jetty), and on to Torre de Sant Sebastià at the end of Passeig Nacional in Barceloneta. You can board at either stage. Fare: 700 pesetas (850 pesetas round-trip). Operates Oct.–June, weekdays noon–5:45, weekends noon–6:15; June–Oct., daily 11–9.

To reach Tibidabo summit, take the metro to Avinguda de Tibidabo, then the Tramvía Blau (single fare: 150 pesetas) to Peu del Funicular, and the Tibidabo Funicular (single fare: 300 pesetas) from there to the Tibidabo fairground. It runs every 30 minutes, 7:05 AM–9:35 PM ascending, 7:25 AM–9:55 PM descending.

By Boat   Golondrinas harbor boats operate short harbor trips from the Portal de la Pau, near the Columbus Monument. Fare: 350 pesetas for a half-hour trip. Depart fall and winter, daily 11–5 (6 on weekends); spring, daily 11–6 (7 on weekends); summer, daily 11–9.

Important Addresses and Numbers

Tourist Information   Tourist offices dealing with Barcelona itself are at **Sants Estació** (open daily 8–8), **Estació França** (open daily 8–8), **Palau de Congressos** (Av. María Cristina s/n, open 10–8 during trade fares and congresses only), **Ajuntament** (Plaça Sant Jaume, open June 24–Sept., Mon.–Fri. 9–8; Sat. 8:30–2:30), and **Palau de la Virreina** (La Rambla 99, open June 24–Sept., Mon.–Sat. 9–9; Sun. 10–2). Those with information about Catalunya and Spain are at **El Prat Airport** (tel. 93/478–4704, open Mon.–Sat. 9:30–8; Sun. 9:30–3) and **Gran Via de les Corts Catalanes 658**, near the Ritz Hotel (tel. 93/301–7443, open weekdays and Sun. 9–7; Sat. 9–2).

In summer (July 24–September 15), **tourist information aides** patrol the Gothic Quarter and Ramblas area 9 AM–9 PM; they travel in pairs (one of each sex), and you can recognize them by their uniforms of red shirts, white trousers or skirts, and *i* badges.

American Visitors' Bureau: Gran Via 591, between Rambla de Catalunya and Balmes, 3rd floor (tel. 93/301–0150/0032).

Consulates   **U.S.:** Pg. Reina Elisenda 23, tel. 93/280–2227; **Canadian:** Via Augusta 125, tel. 93/209–0634; **U.K.:** Diagonal 477, tel. 93/419–9044.

Emergencies   **Tourist Attention,** a service provided by the local police department (Guardia Urbana; Ramblas 43, tel. 93/317–7016; open 24 hours), will provide assistance if you've been the victim of a crime, need medical or psychological help, or need temporary documents in the event of loss of the originals. It has English interpreters.

Other emergency services are as follows. **Police:** National Police, tel. 091; Municipal Police, tel. 092; main police station, Via Laietana 43, tel. 93/301–6666. **Ambulance:** Creu Roja, tel. 93/300–2020. **Hospital:** Hospital Clinic (metro: Hospital Clinic, blue line), Villarroel 170, tel. 93/454–6000/7000. **Emergency Doctors:** tel. 061.

English-language Bookstores   **El Corte Inglés** in Plaça Catalunya sells a few English guidebooks and novels, but the selection is very limited. For more variety, try **English Bookshop** (Calaf 52, tel. 93/239–9908), **Jaimes Bookshop** (Passeig de Gràcia 64, tel. 93/215–3626), **Laie** (Pau Claris 85, tel. 93/

318–1357), **Llibreria Francesa** (Passeig de Gràcia 91, tel. 93/215–1417), **Come In** (Provença 203, tel. 93/253–1204), or **Llibreria Bosch** (Ronda Universitat 11, tel. 93/317–5308, and Roselló 24, tel. 93/321–3341). The bookstore at the **Palau de la Virreina** at La Rambla 99 also offers a selection of some of the better books on Barcelona in English.

Late-night Pharmacies   Look in any of the local newspapers under "Farmacias de Guardia" for addresses of those whose turn it is to be open late night and 24 hours.

Travel Agencies   **American Express** (Roselló 257, on the corner of Passeig de Gràcia, tel. 93/217–0070), **Iberia's** central office (Passeig de Gràcia 30, Diputació 258, tel. 93/410–3382), **Wagons-Lits Cook** (Passeig de Gràcia 8, tel. 93/317–5500), and **Bestours** (Diputación 241, tel. 93/487–8580).

Car and Motorcycle Rental   **Atesa** (Balmes 141, tel. 93/237–8140), **Avis** (Casanova 209, tel. 93/209–9533), **Hertz** (Tuset 10, tel. 93/217–3248), and **Vanguard** (cars and motorcycles, Londres 31, tel. 93/439–3880).

Bicycle Rental   **Bicitram** (Marquès de l'Argentera 15, tel. 93/792–2841) and **Los Filicletos** (Passeig de Picasso 38, tel. 93/319–7811).

Guided Tours

Orientation Tours   City sightseeing tours are run by **Julià Tours** (Ronda Universitat 5, tel. 93/317–6454) and **Pullmantur** (Gran Via 635, tel. 93/318–5195). Tours leave from these terminals, though it may be possible to be picked up from your hotel. Prices are 3,300 pesetas (a half day) and 8,000 pesetas (a full day).

Special-Interest and Walking Tours   The main organization for walking tours is **Terra Endins** (Ausias Marc 49, tel. 93/232–2413). Every month this excellent group produces a new agenda of cultural visits. There's usually one visit per day (but not every day), and the cost for nonmembers is 350 pesetas. If you are a serious Gaudí enthusiast, contact **Amics de Gaudí** (Friends of Gaudí; Av. Pedralbes 7, tel. 93/204–5250) well ahead of your visit. The Tourist Information office in the Palau de la Virreina at La Rambla 99 also rents cassettes with walking tours that follow footprints painted—different colors for different tours—on sidewalks through Barcelona's most interesting spots. The do-it-yourself method is to pick up the guides produced by the Tourist Office, *Discovering Romanesque Art* and *Discovering Modernist Art*, which outline itineraries for all of Catalunya.

Personal Guides   Contact the **Barcelona Tourist Guide Association** (tel. 93/345–4221) or the **Barcelona Guide Bureau** (tel. 93/268–2422) for a list of English-speaking guides.

Excursions   These are run by **Julià Tours** and **Pullmantur** and are booked as above. The principal trips are either full- or half-day tours to Montserrat to visit the monastery and shrine of the famous Moreneta, Catalonia's beloved Black Virgin; or a full-day trip to the Costa Brava resorts, including a boat cruise to Lloret de Mar.

Exploring Barcelona

Orientation

Barcelona is made up of two distinct and contrasting parts. The old city lies between Plaça de Catalunya and the port. Above it is the grid-patterned extension built after the city's third set of walls were torn down in 1860, known as Eixample, where most of the Moderniste architecture is to be found.

Tour 1 explores the Gothic Quarter, with its wealth of medieval buildings, among them the cathedral and the Picasso Museum. Tour 2 leads you along the Ramblas, Barcelona's most famous street, taking in such highlights as the Columbus Monument and Gaudí's Palau Güell. Tour 3 works its way up Passeig de Gràcia, past numerous Moderniste buildings, and ends with a visit to Gaudí's famous cathedral of the Sagrada Família. Tour 4 starts with Gaudí's Parc Güell and continues to Tibidabo and then Pedralbes. Our final two circuits take you to the city's two downtown parks, Ciutadella and Montjuïc, flanking the old city and linked by a cable-car ride high across the port. Montjuïc was the hub of Olympic activity in 1992.

Highlights for First-time Visitors

Casa Milà (*see* Tour 3)
Cathedral (*see* Tour 1)
Miró Foundation (*see* Tour 6)
National Museum of Catalan Art (*see* Tour 6)
Olympic Stadium (*see* Tour 6)
Palau Güell (*see* Tour 2)
Palau de la Música (*see* Tour 5)
Parc Güell (*see* Tour 4)
Picasso Museum (*see* Tour 1)
The Ramblas (*see* Tour 2)
Sagrada Família (*see* Tour 3)
Santa Maria del Mar (*see* Tour 1)
Tibidabo, on a clear day (*see* Tour 4)

Tour 1: The Barri Gòtic (Gothic Quarter)

Numbers in the margin correspond to points of interest on the Tour 1: The Barri Gòtic map.

Parts of the Barri Gòtic and the Barri Xines (*see* Tour 2) received a spectacular sprucing up as part of the Olympic preparations. Wandering off into the heart of the quarter, you will come across squares freshly begot by the demolition of whole blocks and the planting of fully grown palms. Bag-snatching, alas, is common in these parts, so exercise caution at all times.

We begin on **Plaça de la Seu,** where on Saturday afternoon and Sunday morning the citizens of Barcelona gather to dance the *sardana*, a somewhat demure circular dance, though a great symbol of Catalan pride. Climb the steps to the magnificent Gothic **catedral** (cathedral), built from 1298 to 1450 (the spire and neo-Gothic facade were added in 1892). Architects of Catalan Gothic churches strove to make the high altar visible to the entire congregation—hence, the unusually wide central nave and slender side columns. Highlights are the beautifully carved choir stalls, Santa Eulàlia's tomb in the crypt, the battle-scarred crucifix in the Lepanto Chapel, and the tall cloisters surrounding a tropical garden. *Open daily 7:45–1:30 and 4–7:45.*

Around the corner is the **Museu Frederic Marès** (Frederic Marès Museum), where you can browse for hours among the miscellany assembled by sculptor-collector Frederic Marés. Displayed here are everything from paintings and polychrome crucifixes to pipes and

Barcelona Exploring *(Boxes Refer to Detail Maps)*

Tour 4

Avda. Diagonal

Avda. de Pedralbes

Passeig de Manuel Girona

Plaça Prat de la Riba

Plaça Pius XII

Plaça de la Reina Maria Cristina

Via de Carles III

C. de Numància

Avda. de Sarrià

C. d'Entença

C. de les Escoles

Ronda del General Mitre

C. de Modolell

Via Augusta

C. de Calvet

C. de Muntaner

Travessera de les Corts

Gran

Pl. de Francesc Macià

Avda. de Madrid

C. del Brasil

C. de Joan Güell

C. del Vallespir

C. de Berlín

Avda. de Josep Tarradellas

C. de París

C. de Corsega

Avda.

C. de Villarroel

C. de Muntaner

C. d'Aribau

C. de Sants

Estació Sants

C. del Rossello

C. de Provença

C. del Comte d'Urgell

C. de Casanova

C. de

C. d'Antoni de Capmany

C. de la Creu Coberta

Pl. Països Catalans

Avda. de Roma

C. de Villarroel

C. de Mallor

C. de Valencia

Entença

Rocafort

de Calàbria

C. de Viladomat

C. del Comte Borrell

C. d'Aragó

Tour 6

Gran Via de les Corts Catalanes

Plaça d'Espanya

C. de Vilamarí

C. de

C. de la Diputació

Plaça Universitat

Plaça de Sant Jordi

Pl. de les Cascades

Avda. Reina M. Cristina

Avda. de Mistral

Avda. del Parallel

C. de Sepulveda

C. de Floridablanca

C. de Tamarit

C. de Manso

Tour 2

Joaquin Costa

C. del

Pg. de les Cascades

Palau Nacional

C. de Lleida

C. de Hospital

Jardins de Joan Maragall

C. de Blai

C. de Magalhaes

Rda. de Sant Pau

Carretes

C. de Sant Pau

C. la Unió de la Rambla

Estadi Olímpic

Avda. de Miramar

Camí dels Tres Pins

Les Flores

C. Nou

KEY

◇ Metro Stations
— Railway Lines
✦✦✦ Funicular
⋯⋯⋯ Telefèric

Parc de Montjuïc

C. dels Mondials

Pg. de Montjuïc

Plaça Portal de la Pau

Jardins de Miramar

Castell de Montjuïc

Moll de Sant Bertràn

TORRE DE JAUME

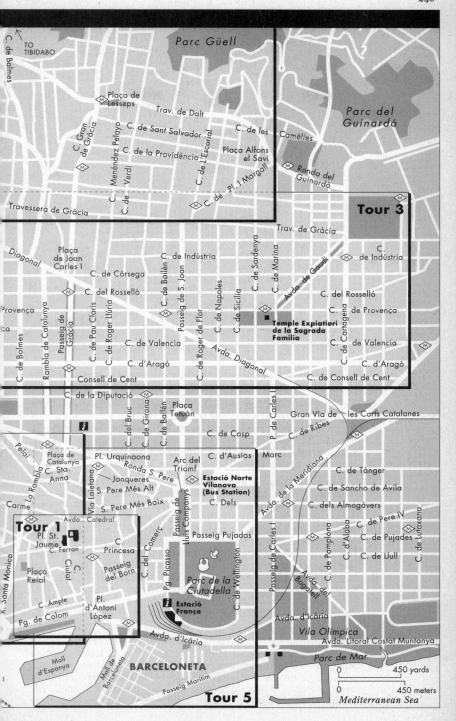

Parc Güell

TO TIBIDABO

C. de Balmes

Plaça de Lesseps

Trav. de Dalt

C. Gran de Gràcia

C. de Sant Salvador

Menéndez Pelayo

Verdi

C. de la Providència

C. de l'Escorial

C. de les Camèlies

Plaça Alfons el Savi

Parc del Guinardó

Ronda del Guinardó

Travessera de Gràcia

C. de Pl. i Margall

Tour 3

Trav. de Gràcia

Diagonal

Plaça de Joan Carles I

C. de Còrsega

C. del Rosselló

Provença

C. de Balmes

Rambla de Catalunya

Passeig de Gràcia

C. de Pau Claris

C. de Roger Llúria

C. de Bailén

Passeig de S. Joan

C. de Indústria

C. de Nápoles

C. de Roger de Flor

C. de Sicília

C. de Sardenya

C. de Marina

Avda. de Gaudí

C. de Indústria

C. del Rosselló

C. de Cartagena

de Provença

Temple Expiatori de la Sagrada Família

C. de Valencia

C. d'Aragó

Avda. Diagonal

C. de Valencia

C. d'Aragó

Consell de Cent

C. de Consell de Cent

C. de la Diputació

C. del Bruc

C. de Girona

C. de Bailén

Plaça Tetuán

C. de Casp

C. de Carles I

Gran Via de les Corts Catalanes

P. de Carles I

C. de Ribes

Plaça de Catalunya

Pl. Urquinaona

C. d'Ausias Marc

Avda. de la Meridiana

C. de Tánger

C. de Sancho de Avila

C. dels Almogàvers

Pelai

La Rambla

C. Sta. Anna

Carme

Via Laietana

Ronda S. Pere

Jonqueres

S. Pere Més Alt

S. Pere Més Baix

Arc del Triomf

Estació Norte (Vilanova) (Bus Station)

C. Dels

Passeig de Lluís Companys

Passeig Pujades

Avda. del

Passeig de Carles I

Avda. del Bogatell

C. de Pamplona

C. d'Alaba

C. de Pere IV

C. de Pujades

C. de Llull

C. de Luraxana

Tour 1

Pl. St. Jaume

C. Ferran

C. Princesa

Passeig del Born

Pg. Picasso

C. del Comerç

Pl. d'Antoni López

Parc de la Ciutadella

C. de Wellington

Avda. d'Icària

Vila Olímpica

Avda. Litoral Costat Muntanya

v. Santa Mònica

Plaça Reial

C. Ample

Pg. de Colom

Moll d'Espanya

Moll de Barceloneta

BARCELONETA

Passeig Marítim

Estació França

Avda. d'Icària

Tour 5

Parc de Mar

Catedral

Avda. Catedral

C. Ciutat

0   450 yards

0   450 meters

Mediterranean Sea

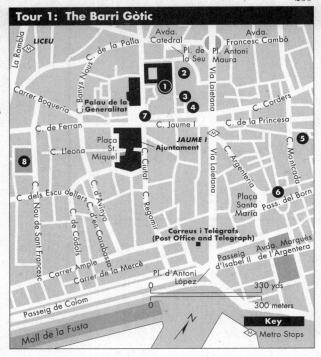

Tour 1: The Barri Gòtic

walking sticks. *Plaça Sant Iu 5. Admission: 350 pesetas, children under 18 and students free. Open Tues.–Sun. 10–7:30; closed Mon.*

❸ The neighboring **Plaça del Rei** embodies the very essence of the Gothic Quarter. After Columbus's first voyage to America, the Catholic Monarchs received him in the Saló del Tinell, a magnificent banquet hall built in 1362. Other ancient buildings around the square are the Palau Lloctinent (Lieutenant's Palace), the 14th-century chapel of Santa Àgata, and the Palau Padellàs.

❹ The latter houses the **Museu d'Història de la Ciutat** (City History Museum), which allows you to trace the evolution of the city. Founded by a Carthaginian, Hamilcar Barca, in about 230 BC, Barcelona shortly passed into the hands of the Romans during the Punic Wars. It didn't expand much until the Middle Ages, when trading links with Genoa and Venice began its long and illustrious mercantile tradition. Look for the plans submitted for the 19th-century extension, Eixample, to see how different the city would have looked had the radial plan of Antoni Rovira Trias not been blocked by cost-conscious bureaucrats in Madrid. Downstairs are some well-lighted Roman excavations. *Palau Padellàs, Carrer del Veguer 2. Admission: 350 pesetas. Open Tues.–Sat. 9–8, Sun. 9–1:30, Mon. 3:30–8.*

Cross Via Laietana, walk down Carrer de la Princesa, and turn right into Carrer Montcada. This narrow street contains one of **❺** Barcelona's most popular attractions, the **Museu Picasso** (Picasso Museum). Two 15th-century palaces provide a handsome, if somewhat inappropriate, setting for collections donated in 1963 and 1970, first by Picasso's secretary, and then by the artist himself. Although it contains very few of his major works, there is plenty here to warrant a visit, including childhood sketches, pictures from his Blue Period, and his famous 1950s Cubist variations on Velázquez's *Las Meninas. Carrer Montcada 15–19. Admission: 650 pesetas, children under 18 and students free. Open Tues.–Sat. 10–8, Sun. 10–3; closed Mon.*

Time Out   At the bottom of Carrer Montcada, a cluster of leather wineskins announces **Xampanyet,** a traditional tiled bar, popular for its house *cava* (sparkling white wine) and delicious Catalan *tapas* (savory tidbits). Opposite is **La Pizza Nostra,** a good place for a cup of coffee or a pizza and a glass of wine.

Carrer Montcada leads to Passeig del Born, an avenue lined with
❻ late-night cocktail bars. Adjoining the near end is the apse of **Santa Maria del Mar,** the most perfect of all Barcelona's Gothic churches. It was built from 1329 to 1383 in fulfillment of a vow made a century earlier by Jaume I to build a church for the Virgin of the Sailors. Its stark beauty is enhanced by a lovely rose window, soaring columns, and unusually wide vaulting. It is a fashionable place for weddings, and if you pass by on a Saturday afternoon, you are very likely to discover how Catalans perform this ceremony. *Open Mon.–Fri. 9– 12:30 and 5–8; closed weekends.*

Walk up Carrer Argentería to Via Laietana, recross it, and walk up
❼ Carrer de Ferran to **Plaça Sant Jaume,** a cobbled square in the heart of the Gothic Quarter, built in the 1840s. The two imposing buildings facing each other across the square are much older. The 15th-century **Ajuntament** (City Hall) to the left has an impressive black and burnished gold mural (1928) by Josep Maria Sert and the famous Saló de Cent, from which the Council of One Hundred ruled the city between 1372 and 1714. You can wander into the courtyard, but to visit the interior, you will need to ask permission in the office beforehand. The **Palau de la Generalitat,** opposite, seat of the autonomous Catalan government, is an elegant 15th-century palace with a lovely courtyard and first-floor patio with orange trees. The room whose windows you can see at the front is the Saló de Sant Jordi (St. George), dragon-slaying patron saint of Catalunya, as well as of England. For security reasons, you can visit the Generalitat only on the day of Sant Jordi, April 23.

Continue along Carrer de Ferran, with its attractive 19th-century shops and numerous Moderniste touches, and turn left at the end,
❽ through arches to the **Plaça Reial.** In this beautiful 19th-century arcaded square, newly repainted yellow houses overlook the wrought-iron Fountain of the Three Graces and lamp posts designed by a young Gaudí in 1879. Sidewalk cafés line the whole square. It has acquired quite a reputation for drug pushers, who form a lethargic barrier at the entrances to the square. They're easily avoided, and a heavy police presence discourages all but the most determined, so don't be put off. The most colorful time to come is on Sunday morning, when crowds gather at the stamp and coin stalls and listen to soapbox orators. At night it is the center for downtown nightlife. From here, you can saunter through to the Rambla.

Tour 2: La Rambla (Les Rambles)

Numbers in the margin correspond to points of interest on the Tour 2: La Rambla map.

Barcelona's most famous street is a snaking avenue of 24-hour newspaper kiosks, flower stalls, and bird sellers, along which traffic plays second fiddle to the endless *paseo* (stroll) of locals and visitors alike; it is the street that Federico García Lorca called the only one in the world he wished would never end. The whole avenue is referred to as Les Rambles (in Catalan) or **La Rambla** but each section has its own name: Rambla Santa Monica is at the southern end.

As you walk south from Plaça Reial toward the sea, Barri Xines (Chinatown), the notorious red-light district, is on your right. The Chinese never had much of a presence there, and the area is ill-famed for prostitutes, drug pushers, and street thieves.

❾ At the foot of the Rambla, take an elevator to the top of the **Monument a Colom** (Columbus Monument) for a breathtaking view over the city. The entrance is on the harbor side of the monument. *Admission: 350 pesetas adults, 150 pesetas children. Open June 24– Sept. 24, daily 9–9; Sept. 25–June 23, Tues.–Sat. 10–2 and 4–8, Sun. 10–7; closed Mon.*

Ahead on Moll de Barcelona you can see part of the redeveloped port area, comprising offices, fountains, shopping arcades, and new ferry terminals. You can also board the cable car that crosses the harbor to Montjuïc or board a Golondrina boat for a trip around the port (*see* Getting Around, *above*).

❿ Heading by land toward Montjuïc brings you to the **Museu Marítim** (Maritime Museum), housed in the 13th-century Drassanes Reials (Royal Dockyards). This superb museum is full of ships, including a spectacular life-size reconstructed galley, figureheads, nautical gear, and several early navigational charts. *Plaça Portal de la Pau 1. Admission: 350 pesetas. Open Tues.–Sat. 10–2 and 4–7, Sun. 10–2; closed Mon.*

⓫ Turn back up the Rambla, and a little way up turn left into Carrer Nou de la Rambla. At No. 3 is **Palau Güell.** Antoni Gaudí built this mansion in 1886–89 for his patron, a textile baron named Count Eusebi de Güell, and it projected the architect into the international limelight. The prominent Catalan emblem between the parabolic entrance gates attests to the nationalist leanings that Gaudí shared with Güell. The facade is a dramatic foil for the treasure house inside, where spear-shaped Art Nouveau columns frame the windows and prop up a series of minutely detailed wood ceilings. On the roof you can see good examples of Gaudí's decorative chimneys. *Admission: 350 pesetas. Temporarily open only at special hours due to renovations; afternoons 4–8 are a good time to try.*

⓬ Return to the Rambla and continue to the corner of Carrer de Sant Pau to view what remains of the **Gran Teatre del Liceu** (Opera House). Long considered one of Barcelona's most cherished jewels, the Liceu was gutted by fire in early 1994. Diva Montserrat Caballé stood on the Rambla in tears as this beloved venue was consumed by a mid-morning fire, the origins of which have been the subject of much speculation. The restoration of this landmark, one of world's oldest and most beautiful opera houses, will continue into 1996.

The next stretch of the Rambla is the most fascinating. The colorful paving stones on the Pla de la Boqueria were designed by Joan Miró. Turn right here to the adjoining squares, **Plaça del Pi** and **Plaça de Sant Josep Oriol,** among the Gothic Quarter's most tranquil. The **⓭** church of **Santa Maria del Pi** is another good example of Catalan Gothic.

Time Out   The **Bar del Pi** is a stylish and popular venue for better-heeled bohe-mians from the world over. The chairs outside move from one square

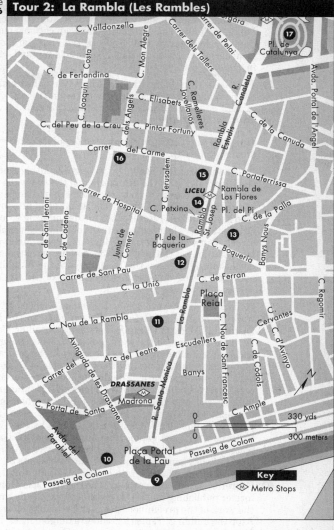

Tour 2: La Rambla (Les Rambles)

to another, following the sun, and are particularly popular on a Sunday morning.

⑭ Back on the Rambla, take a look inside the food market, **Mercat de Sant Josep o de la Boqueria** and at the **Antigua Casa Figueres**, a fine grocery and pastry store on the corner of Petxina, with a splendid mosaic facade and exquisite old fittings.

⑮ Farther on is the neoclassical **Palau de la Virreina**, built by a viceroy to Peru in 1778. It has recently been converted into a major exhibition center, and you should check out what's showing while you're here. *Rambla de les Flores 99, tel. 93/301–7775. Open Tues.–Sat. 10–2 and 4:30–9, Sun. 10–2, Mon. 4:30–9.*

16 Turn left down Carrer del Carme to the **Antic Hospital de la Santa Creu** (old hospital), surrounded by a cluster of other 15th-century buildings, today home to cultural and educational institutions. Particularly impressive and lovely is the courtyard of the Casa de Convalescència, with its Renaissance columns and scenes portrayed in *azulejos* (ceramic tiles).

17 The final stretch of the Rambla brings you to the **Plaça de Catalunya,** the banking and transport center of the city.

Tour 3: Eixample

Numbers in the margin correspond to points of interest on the Tour 3: Eixample map.

Above the Plaça de Catalunya, you come to an elegant area known as the Eixample. With the dismantling of the city walls in 1860, Barcelona embarked upon a vast expansion scheme, fueled by the return of rich colonials from America and an influx of provincial aristocrats who had sold their estates after the debilitating second Carlist War (1847–49); (*see* Chapter 2, Portraits of Spain, Chronology). The grid street plan was the work of Ildefons Cerdà. Much of the building here was done at the height of the Modernisme movement. The principal thoroughfares of the Eixample are the Rambla de Catalunya and the Passeig de Gràcia, where some of the city's most elegant shops and cafés are to be found.

Moderniste houses are among Barcelona's special drawing cards, so **18** walk up Passeig de Gràcia until you come to the **Manzana de la Discòrdia** (Block of Discord), between Consell de Cent and Aragó. Its name is a pun on the word *manzana,* which means both "block" and "apple," alluding to the discordant architectural styles on the block and to the classical myth of the Apple of Discord. The houses here are quite fantastic: The floral Casa Lleó Morera (No. 35) was extensively rebuilt (1902–6) by Domènech i Montaner, and with permission you can visit the ornate interior, which now houses the Patronat de Turisme (tel. 93/302–0608). The pseudo-Gothic, pseudo-Flemish Casa Amatller (No. 41) is by Puig i Cadafalch and features a terraced gable. Next door is Gaudí's Casa Batlló, with a mottled facade that resembles a breaking wave. Nationalist symbolism is at work here: The scaly roof line represents St. George's dragon with his cross stuck into its tail. Walking left 1½ blocks down **19** Carrer d' Aragó, you come to Domènech's **Casa Montaner i Simó,** a former publishing house that has been beautifully converted to hold the work of the preeminent postwar Catalan painter Antoni Tàpies. Atop the building, Tàpies has added a tangled metal hairdo, entitled *Núvol i cadira (Cloud and Chair).* The airy split-level Fundació Tàpies has temporary exhibitions and a library strong on Tàpies and Oriental art. *Admission: 450 pesetas. Open Tues.–Sun. 11–8; closed Mon.*

Back to Passeig de Gràcia, and our next stop—this time, on the **20** right—is Gaudí's **Casa Milà,** nicknamed La Pedrera (The Quarry), whose remarkable curving stone facade with ornamental balconies actually ripples its way around the corner of the block. In 1910 Barcelona's bourgeoisie were quite taken aback by the appearance of these cavelike apartments on their most fashionable street. From the roof, you have as good an opportunity as any of peering into the courtyards of Eixample blocks. *Passeig de Gràcia 92. Admission free. Open for guided visits Tues.–Sat. at 10, 11, noon, 1, and 4; closed Sun. and Mon.*

Tour 3: Eixample

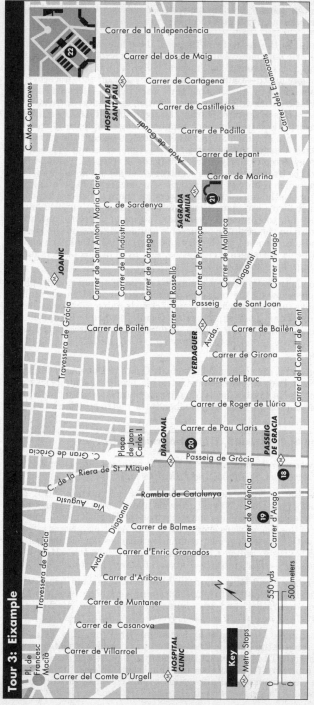

Pl. de Francesc Macià

Carrer de la Independència

Carrer del dos de Maig

Carrer de Cartagena

Carrer de Castillejos

Carrer de Padilla

Carrer de Lepant

Carrer de Marina

Carrer dels Enamorats

HOSPITAL DE SANT PAU

Avda. de Gaudí

C. Mas Casanoves

C. de Sardenya

SAGRADA FAMILIA

C. de Sant Antoni Maria Claret

JOANIC

Carrer de Sant Antoni Maria Claret

Carrer de la Indústria

Carrer de Còrsega

Carrer del Rosselló

Carrer de Provença

Carrer de Mallorca

Diagonal

Carrer d'Aragó

Travessera de Gràcia

Passeig   de Sant Joan

Carrer de Bailèn

VERDAGUER

Avda.

Carrer de Bailèn

Carrer de Girona

Carrer del Consell de Cent

Carrer del Bruc

Carrer de Roger de Llúria

DIAGONAL

Plaça de Joan Carles I

Carrer de Pau Claris

20

PASSEIG DE GRACIA

C. Gran de Gràcia

Passeig de Gràcia

C. de la Riera de St. Miquel

18

Via Augusta

Diagonal

Avda.

Rambla de Catalunya

Carrer de Balmes

Carrer de València

Carrer d'Aragó

19

Travessera de Gràcia

Carrer d'Enric Granados

Carrer d'Aribau

Carrer de Muntaner

Carrer de Casanova

HOSPITAL CLÍNIC

Carrer de Villarroel

Carrer del Comte D'Urgell

N

550 yds

500 meters

Key

Metro Stops

Casa Milà, **20**
Casa Montaner i Simó, **19**
Hospital de Sant Pau, **22**

Manzana de la Discòrdia, **18**
Temple Expiatori de la Sagrada Família, **21**

Time Out You can ponder the vagaries of Gaudí's work over a drink in **Amarcord,** a terrace café in La Pedrera.

㉑ Now, take the metro from Diagonal (blue line) to Barcelona's most eccentric landmark, Antoni Gaudí's **Temple Expiatori de la Sagrada Família** (Expiatory Church of the Holy Family). Unfinished at his untimely death—Gaudí was run over by a tram and, unrecognized for several days, died in a pauper's ward in 1926—this striking and surreal creation will cause consternation or wonder, shrieks of protest or cries of rapture. During the civil war, in 1936, the citizens of Barcelona loved their crazy temple enough to spare it from the flames that engulfed all the other churches (except the cathedral). Gaudí envisaged three facades: Faith, Hope, and Charity, each with four towers collectively representing the 12 apostles. These, in turn, would be dwarfed by a giant central tower some 155 meters (500 ft) high, which is not yet in existence. An elevator (100 pesetas) takes visitors to the top of the east towers (or there are steps) for a spectacular bird's-eye view. Construction began again in 1940 but faltered due to confusion over Gaudí's plans. Current controversy centers on the sculptor Subirach's angular figures on the western facade, condemned by the city's intellectual elite as kitsch and the antithesis of Gaudí's lyrical style, and by religious leaders for depicting Christ in the nude.

Also visit the crypt, with a museum of Gaudí's scale models, photographs showing the progress of construction, and photographs of Gaudí's funeral, which, in terms of crowds lining the streets, would have satisfied a senior statesman. Gaudí, 74 when he died, is buried here. *Admission: 500 pesetas, children under 10 free. Open Nov.– Mar., daily 9–6; Apr.–June and Sept.–Oct., daily 9–7; July–Aug., daily 8–9.*

㉒ From here, stroll down Avinguda de Gaudí to Domènech's **Hospital de Sant Pau,** which demonstrates his preference for bricks over stone and is notable for its Mudéjar motifs and wards set individually among the gardens. You can board the metro here back to Diagonal.

Tour 4: Parc Güell, Tibidabo, and Pedralbes

Numbers in the margin correspond to points of interest on the Tour 4: Parc Güell, Tibidabo, and Pedralbes map.

㉓ Take the metro to Lesseps, where you can catch bus No. 24 to Gaudí's **Parc Güell.** Named after his main patron, it was originally intended as a hillside garden suburb on the English model, but only two of the houses were ever built. It is an Art Nouveau extravaganza, with a mosaic pagoda, undulating benches, and large multicolored lizards guarding a Moderniste grotto. *Open Oct.–Mar., daily 10–6, Apr.–June, daily 10–7, and July–Sept., daily 10–9.*

There's a small museum in an Alice in Wonderland house where Gaudí lived from 1906 to 1926, containing some of his eccentric furniture, decoration, and drawings. *Admission: 300 pesetas. Open Apr.–Oct., daily 10–2 and 4–7, Nov.–Mar., daily 10–2 and 4–6:30.*

㉔ Next, make for **Tibidabo** by a combination of bus Nos. 24 and 22, changing at the Plaça de Lesseps, or by taxi, which is a lot easier. At Avinguda Tibidabo, catch the Tramvia Blau, which connects with the funicular (for details, *see* Getting Around, *above*) to the summit. The views from this hill are legendary, but clear days are few and far between. The shapes that distinguish Tibidabo from below turn out

Tour 4 : Parc Güell, Tibidabo, and Pedralbes

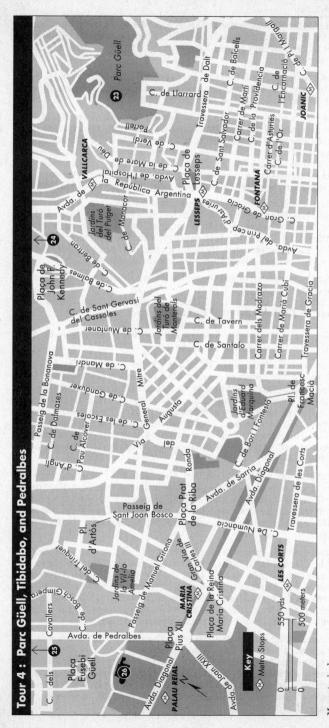

Key

◈ Metro Stops

0	550 yds
0	500 meters

Monasterio de
Pedralbes, **25**
Palau Reial de
Pedralbes, **26**
Parc Güell, **23**
Tibidabo, **24**

to be an ugly commercialized church, a vast radio mast, and the new 260-m (850-ft) communications tower. The misguided exploitation of this natural beauty spot is completed by a rather brash amusement park.

From Avinguda de Tibidabo (Plaça John F. Kennedy), take bus No. 22 to the end of the line. You pass through the picturesque suburb of Sarrià, at its heart an old village.

㉕ The bus drops you close to the **Monasterio de Pedralbes.** Founded by Reina (Queen) Elisenda for Clarist nuns in 1326, the convent has a triple-story Gothic cloister that is the finest in Barcelona. In the chapel are a beautiful stained-glass rose window and famous murals painted in 1346 by Ferrer Bassa, a Catalan much influenced by the Italian Renaissance. You can also visit the old living quarters. *Admission: 300 pesetas. Open Tues.–Sun. 9:30–2; closed Mon.*

Saunter down Avinguda de Pedralbes (or take bus No. 75) to the
㉖ **Palau Reial de Pedralbes,** built in the 1920s for King Alfonso XII and now home to the **Ceramics Museum,** a wide sweep of Spanish ceramic art from the 14th to the 18th century, with the influence of Moorish design techniques carefully documented. *Tel. 93/203–7501. Admission: 300 pesetas. Open Tues.–Sun. 9–2; closed Mon.*

From here you can board the metro (Palau Reial, green line) back to the center of town.

Tour 5: Ciutadella and Barceloneta

Numbers in the margin correspond to points of interest on the Tour 5: Ciutadella and Barceloneta map.

㉗ Start with the **Palau de la Música** on Carrer Amadeus Vives, just off the top of Via Laietana (metro: Urquinaona), a fantastic and flamboyant Moderniste building by Domènech i Montaner (1908) that rivals the best of Gaudí. The tiny ticket booths in the richly embellished columns are sadly now out of use. Try to get to a concert here, if only to see the interior, with its inverted stained-glass cupola (*see* The Arts and Nightlife, *below*). Otherwise you can make an appointment to see inside on Tuesday, Thursday, or Saturday (tel. 93/268–1000).

Continue along Carrer Sant Pere Més Alt to the Plaça Sant Pere and one of the oldest medieval churches in Barcelona, Sant Pere de les Puelles, which has beautiful stained glass and a stark interior. Make
㉘ your way out of this labyrinth to the **Arc del Triomf,** an imposing redbrick Moderniste arch built by Josep Vilaseca for the 1888 exhibition.

Stroll down the green center of Passeig Lluís Companys to the **Parc de la Ciutadella** (Citadel), Barcelona's main downtown park. The clearing dates from shortly after the War of the Spanish Succession, when Felipe V demolished some 2,000 houses to build a fortress and barracks for his soldiers, which, in turn, were pulled down in 1868 and replaced by gardens laid out by Josep Fontserè. In the park are a cluster of museums; the Catalan Parliament; and a zoo.

㉙ The arresting building as you enter the park is the **Castell dels Tres Dragons** (Castle of the Three Dragons), built by Domènech i Montaner as the café-restaurant for the 1888 exhibition. This became a workshop where Moderniste architects met to experiment with traditional crafts and exchange ideas. It is now home to the Zoological Museum. *Admission: 300 pesetas. Open Tues.–Sun. 9–2; closed Mon.*

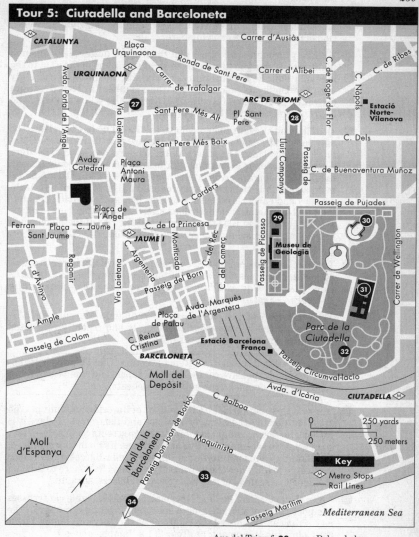

Tour 5: Ciutadella and Barceloneta

CATALUNYA

Plaça Urquinaona

Carrer d'Ausiàs

URQUINAONA

Ronda de Sant Pere

Carrer d'Alíbei

C. de Ribes

Avda. Portal de l'Angel

Carrer de Trafalgar

C. de Roger de Flor

C. Nápols

Estació Norte-Vilanova

Via Laietana

Sant Pere Més Alt

ARC DE TRIOMF

Pl. Sant Pere

C. Dels

Avda. Catedral

C. Sant Pere Més Baix

C. de Buenaventura Muñoz

Plaça Antoni Maura

Passeig de Pujades

Plaça de l'Angel

C. Carders

Museu de Geologia

Ferran

Plaça Sant Jaume

C. Jaume I

C. de la Princesa

Passeig de Picasso

Parc de la Ciutadella

Regomir

JAUME I

Montcada

C. del Rec

Carrer de Wellington

C. d'Avinyo

Via Laietana

C. Argenteria

Passeig del Born

C. del Comerç

Avda. Marquès de l'Argentera

Plaça de Palau

Estació Barcelona França

C. Ample

C. Reina Cristina

Passeig de Colom

BARCELONETA

Passeig Circumval·lacio

CIUTADELLA

Moll del Depòsit

Avda. d'Icària

C. Balboa

Moll de la Barceloneta

Passeig Don Joan de Borbó

Maquinista

250 yards

250 meters

Moll d'Espanya

N

Key

Metro Stops

Rail Lines

Passeig Marítim

Mediterranean Sea

Lluís Companys

Passeig de

Adjacent stand the Geology Museum and the beautiful Umbracle, whose black slats help create a jungle light for the valuable collection of tropical plants growing here.

Walk left through exotic trees and shrubs, not quite thickly enough planted to enable you to escape the sight and sound of the city, to the

30 lake and **Font de la Senyoreta del Paraïgua** (Fountain of the Lady with the Umbrella) and behind it the monumental **Font d' Aurora** (Fountain of Aurora), Gaudí's first work while still a student, and the centerpiece of the 1888 exhibition.

31 Heading to the right brings you to the **Palau de la Ciutadella,** the only surviving remnant of Felipe's fortress, now shared by the Catalan Parliament and the Museu d'Art Modern (Museum of Modern Art). The latter is something of a misnomer because only a small handful of rooms are given over to contemporary Catalan artists. Its main strength is the collection produced in Barcelona of late-19th-century and early 20th-century works. This golden period of painting and bohemianism in Barcelona saw Picasso living here, famous artistic tertulias in Els Quatre Gats, and the rise of the Modernista movement. *Admission: 500 pesetas. Open Mon. 3–7:30, Tues.–Sat. 9–7:30, Sun. 9–3.*

32 The excellent **zoo,** home to Snowflake, the world's only captive albino gorilla, occupies the whole bottom section of the park. *Admission: 1,000 pesetas, children under 3 free. Open Oct.–Mar., daily 10–5; Apr.–Sept., daily 9:30–7:30.*

The west gate of the park leads to Avinguda Marquès de l'Argentera, on the left of which is the lovely and recently renovated Estacío de França. Go left at Pla del Palau.

Time Out Across the Pla del Palau, on Reina Cristina, **Can Paixano** is legendary for its inexpensive cavas, delicious tapas, and rapid turnover of customers. It doubles as an expensive delicatessen.

33 Our next destination is the Old Quarter of **Barceloneta,** built in 1755 and traditionally the home of workers and fishermen. Today, it is rather run-down, and many of its interior streets have a deserted, somewhat threatening air. But at lunchtime its main thoroughfare, the Passeig Don Joan de Borbó, or Moll de la Barceloneta, comes strikingly to life when the citizens of Barcelona flock here to feast on the delicious seafood of its numerous no-frills restaurants.

34 From the end of the Passeig Nacional, a **teleféric** (cable car) crosses the port to Montjuïc, offering a spectacular bird's-eye view of the city. (You can also board the cable car at the Torre de Jaume I near the Columbus Monument; *see* Tour 2: La Rambla, *above*.)

Tour 6: Montjuïc

Numbers in the margin correspond to points of interest on the Tour 6: Montjuïc map.

Montjuïc, the hill to the south of town, was named for the Jewish cemetery once located on its slopes, although an alternate explanation has it being named for the Roman deity Jove or Jupiter. The most dramatic approach is by way of the cross-harbor teleféric, but you can reach it from the Paral.lel or Espanya metro stop.

The teleféric drops you at the Jardins de Miramar, a 10-minute walk, straight ahead, to the Plaça de Dante and the entrance to the amusement park. If you are nostalgic for the days of rock and roll,

you may want to look up Chus Martínez, onetime colleague of Bill
Haley and Eddie Cochrane, who runs the Bali restaurant here. It's
not unheard of for him to give an impromptu concert for his guests,
so check this out when you get here.

From here, another small cable car (fare: 300 pesetas; Oct.–June 21,
weekends 11–2:45 and 4–7:30; June 22–Sept., daily 11:30–9) takes
35 you up to the **Castell de Montjuïc.** Built in 1640 by rebels against
Felipe IV, the castle has been stormed several times, most famously
in 1705 by Lord Peterborough for Archduke Carlos of Austria. In
1808, during the Peninsular War, the castle was seized by the
French under General Dufresne. Later, during an 1842 civil distur-
bance, Barcelona was bombed by a Spanish artillery battery from
its heights. Today, it functions as a military museum housing the
weapon collection of Frederic Marés. *Admission: 100 pesetas. Open
Oct.–Mar., Tues.–Sat. 10–2 and 4–7, Sun. 10–2; Apr.–Sept.,
Tues.–Sat. 10–2 and 4–7, Sun. 10–8.*

The moat has been made into attractive gardens, with one side given
over to an archery range. From the various terraces, there are panoramic views over the city and out to sea.

Descend by the same cable car or walk and continue along the
36 Avinguda de Miramar to the **Fundació Miró** (Miró Foundation), a
gift from the artist Joan Miró to his native city and one of
Barcelona's most exciting contemporary art galleries. The white,
airy building was designed by Josep Lluís Sert and opened in 1975;
an extension was added by Sert's pupil, Jaume Freixa, in 1988. Miró
himself now rests in the cemetery on the southern slopes of
Montjuïc. During the Franco regime, which he strongly opposed,
Miró lived in self-imposed exile in Paris and in 1956 moved to Mallorca. When he died in 1983, the Catalans gave him a send-off amount-
ing to a state funeral. *Admission: 600 pesetas. Open Tues.–Sat.
11–7 (Thurs. 11–9:30), Sun. 10:30–2:30; closed Mon.*

37 Farther along this avenue you arrive at the **Estadi Olímpic** (Olympic
Stadium; tel. 93/424–0508: open weekdays 10–2 and 4–7, weekends
10–6). It was originally built for the Great Exhibition of 1929, with
the idea that Barcelona would then host the 1936 Olympics (ultimately staged in Hitler's Berlin). After twice failing to gain the
nomination, Barcelona celebrated the capture of its long-cherished
goal by renovating the semiderelict stadium in time for 1992 and giving it a seating capacity of 70,000 people. Next door stands the futuristic Palau Sant Jordi Sports Palace, designed by the Japanese
architect Arata Isozaki and built from the roof downward.

38 Descend now to the **Museu Nacional d'Art de Catalunya** (National
Museum of Catalan Art), in the imposing **Palau Nacional,** also built
in 1929 and recently renovated by Gae Aulenti, architect of the
Musée d'Orsay in Paris. The Romanesque and Gothic art treasures,
medieval frescoes, and altarpieces here are simply staggering.
Many were removed from small churches and chapels in the Pyrenees during the 1920s to ward off the threat of exportation by art
dealers. When possible, the works are being returned to their original homes or are being replicated, as with the famous *Pantocrator*
fresco, a copy of which is now back in the Church of Sant Climent de
Taüll (*see* Chapter 7, The Pyrenees). The museum also contains
works by El Greco, Velázquez, and Zurbarán. *Admission: 600 pesetas. Open Tues.–Sun. 9–2; closed Mon.*

Downhill, to the right of the Palau Nacional as you leave it, is the
39 **Museu Arqueològic** (Archaeological Museum), which contains many
important finds from the Greek ruins at Empúries, on the Costa

Tour 6: Montjuïc

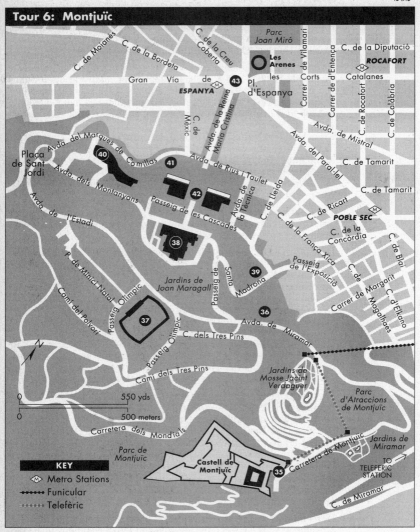

Castell de
Montjuïc, **35**

Estadi Olímpic, **37**

Fundació Miró, **36**

Mies van der Rohe
Pavilion, **41**

Museu
Arqueològic, **39**

Museu Nacional d'Art
de Catalunya **38**

Plaça de les
Cascades, **42**

Plaça d'Espanya, **43**

Poble Espanyol, **40**

Brava. These are exhibited, along with fascinating objects from, and explanations of, Megalithic Spain. *Admission: 300 pesetas. Open Tues.–Sat. 9:30–1 and 4–7; Sun. 9:30–1; closed Mon.*

④⓪ To the other side of the Palau Nacional is the **Poble Espanyol** (Spanish Village), created again for the 1929 Exhibition. It is a kind of Spain-in-a-bottle, with the local architectural styles of each province faithfully reproduced, enabling you to wander from the walls of Ávila to the wine cellars of Jerez. The most lively time to come is at night, for a concert or flamenco show. *Admission: 500 pesetas adults, 250 pesetas children under 14. Open daily 9 AM–3:30 AM.*

④① On the way down to Plaça d'Espanya, you pass the reconstructed **Mies van der Rohe pavilion** (open daily 10–6), the German contribution to the 1929 Exhibition: interlocking planes of white marble, green onyx, and glass. Next comes the multicolored fountain in the **④② Plaça de les Cascades.** Stroll down the wide esplanade past more ex-**④③** hibition halls to the large and somber **Plaça d'Espanya.** Across the square is Les Arenes bullring, now the venue for theater performances and political rallies rather than bullfights. From here, you can take the metro or bus No. 38 back to Plaça de Catalunya.

What to See and Do with Children

Take the children to the **zoo** in Ciutadella to visit the world's only captive albino gorilla (*see* Tour 5: Ciutadella and Barceloneta, *above*). They'll also enjoy taking a trip across the harbor in one of the **Golondrinas boats.** Ride the **cable car** across the harbor to the **Amusement Park** on Montjuïc (*see* Tour 6: Montjuïc, *above*) or the Tramvia Blau (tram) and **funicular** up to the **fun fair** on Tibidabo (*see* Tour 4: Parc Güell, Tibidabo, and Pedralbes, *above*).

Young scientific minds work overtime in the **Museu de la Ciència** (Science Museum), just below Tibidabo, many of whose displays and activities are designed for children (over age 7). *Teodor Roviralta 55 (metro: Avinguda de Tibidabo and Tramvia Blau halfway), tel. 93/212–6050. Admission: 400 pesetas. Open Tues.–Sun. 10–8; closed Mon.*

Children also appreciate the sightseeing time saved by a visit to **Catalunya en Miniature** (Catalunya in Miniature), which comprises 60,000 square meters of the province's most famous buildings, including the complete works of Gaudí, scaled down. *Torrelles de Llobregat (17 km/10½ mi west of Barcelona), tel. 93/689–0960. Admission: weekdays, 750 pesetas adults, 300 pesetas children; weekends, 1,000 pesetas adults, 500 pesetas children.*

Above all, don't miss the fairy-tale extravaganza of the **Parc Güell** (*see* Tour 4: Parc Güell, Tibidabo, and Pedralbes, *above*); it's a popular playground for Barcelona's children.

Off the Beaten Track

Go to see the soccer club **F.C. Barcelona** play, preferably against Real Madrid. The massive Camp Nou stadium seats 130,000 spectators, and crowds frequently number over 100,000. Look in the museum, with its impressive array of trophies and five-screen video showing memorable goals in the history of one of Europe's most glamorous soccer clubs. *Arístides Maillol, tel. 93/330–9411. Museum admission: 350 pesetas, 100 pesetas students. Open Oct.–Mar., Tues.–Fri. 10–1 and 4–6, weekends 10–1 and 3–6, closed Mon.; Apr.–Sept., Mon.–Sat. 10–1 and 3–6; closed Sun.*

The **Collserola Tower** that now dwarfs Tibidabo is an architectural triumph erected during the 1992 Olympics amid a certain amount of controversy. What is incontrovertible is the splendid panorama over the city that this lookout point provides. To reach the tower, take the funicular up to Tibidabo; there is free transport to the tower from Plaza Tibidabo. *Tel. 93/211–7942. Admission: 600 pesetas. Open weekdays 11–9; Sat., Sun., and holidays 11–7.*

Explore the **Gràcia** area, above Diagonal. This used to be a separate village, and it retains a distinctive air of independence.

Hunt out the tiny **Shoe Museum** (Museu del Calçat) in a hidden corner of the Gothic Quarter, between the cathedral and the Bishop's Palace. The collection includes a pair of clown's shoes and a pair worn by Pablo Casals. *Plaça de Sant Felip Neri. Admission: 250 pesetas. Open Tues.–Sun. 11–2; closed Mon.*

Shopping

Shopping Districts Elegant shopping districts are the Passeig de Gràcia, Rambla de Catalunya, and Avinguda Diagonal up as far as Carrer Ganduxer. Try Carrer Tuset, above Diagonal, for small boutiques. For more affordable, more old-fashioned, and typically Spanish-style shops, explore the area between the Ramblas and Via Laietana, especially around Carrer de Ferran. The area around Plaça del Pi, from the Boqueria to Carrer Portaferrissa and Carrer de la Canuda, has fashionable stores, jewelry, and gift shops. Most shops are open weekdays 9–1:30 and 5–8; Saturday hours are generally the same, but some don't open in the afternoon; on Sundays virtually all are closed.

Specialty Stores
Antiques Carrer de la Palla and Carrer Banys Nous in the Gothic Quarter are lined with antiques shops full of old maps, books, paintings, and furniture. An antiques market is held every Thursday, 10–8, in Plaça del Pi. The **Centre d'Antiquaris** (Passeig de Gràcia 57) contains 75 antiques stores. Try **Gothsland** (Consell de Cent 331) for Moderniste design.

Art The greatest concentration of prestigious galleries is along Carrer Consell de Cent, between Passeig de Gràcia and Carrer Balmes. The best known are **Sala Gaspar** at 323, and **Galeria Ciento** at 347. Carrer Petritxol, which leads down into Plaça del Pi (*see* Tour 2, La Rambla) is also lined with art galleries, as are the Carrer Montcada (*see* Tour 1, Barri Gòtic) and around the Passeig del Born (also *see* Tour 1).

Boutiques/Fashion If you are after fashion and jewelry, you've come to the right place, because Barcelona makes all the headlines on Spain's booming fashion front. Check out **El Bulevard Rosa** (Passeig de Gràcia 53–55), a collection of boutiques that stock the very latest outfits. Others are on Avinguda Diagonal between Passeig de Gràcia and Carrer Ganduxer. **Adolfo Domínguez,** Spain's top designer, is at Passeig de Gràcia 35 and Diagonal 570; **Joaquim Berao,** a top jewelry designer, is at Rosselló 277.

Design/Interiors At Passeig de Gràcia 102 is **Gimeno,** whose elegant displays range from unusual suitcases to the latest in furniture design. A couple of doors down, at 96, **Vinçon** is equally chic. Some 50 years old, it has steadily expanded through a rambling Moderniste house that was once the home of Moderniste poet/artist Santiago Rusiñol as well as the site of the studio of his colleague the painter Ramón Casas. It stocks everything from Filofaxes to handsome kitchenware. **Bd** (*Barcelona design*), at 291–293 Carrer Mallorca, located in another

Moderniste gem, Domènechi Muntaner's Casa Thomas, is another spectacular design store.

Department Stores The ubiquitous **El Corte Inglés** is at Plaça de Catalunya 14 and Diagonal 617 (metro: Maria Cristina). **Galerías Preciados,** now colonized by a host of English stores, from Dorothy Perkins to Marks and Spencer, is on Portal de L'Àngel and Plaça de Francesc Macià.

Food and Flea Markets The **Boqueria,** or Sant Josep Market, on the Rambla between Carrer del Carme and Carrer de Hospital, is a colorful and bustling food market, open Monday–Saturday. **Els Encants,** Barcelona's biggest flea market, is held Monday, Wednesday, Friday, and Saturday 8–7, at the end of Dos de Maig, on Plaça de les Glòries (metro: Glòries, red line). **Sant Antoni** market, at the end of Ronda Sant Antoni, is an old-fashioned food and clothes market, best on Sunday.

Sports

Participant Sports

Golf Barcelona is fortunate enough to be ringed by some excellent golf courses; be sure to call ahead to reserve tee times.

Around Barcelona **Reial Club de Golf El Prat** (08820 El Prat de Llobregat, tel. 93/379–0278), greens fees 6,000 pesetas and up. **Club de Golf de Sant Cugat** (08190 Sant Cugat del Vallès, tel. 93/674–3958), greens fees 5,000 pesetas. **Club de Golf Vallromanes** (08188 Vallromanes, tel. 93/568–0362), greens fees 3,500 pesetas weekdays, 6,000 pesetas weekends. **Club de Golf Terramar** (08870 Sitges, tel. 93/894–0580), greens fees 3,500–5,000 pesetas.

Farther Afield **Club de Golf Costa Brava.** La Masía, 17246 Santa Cristina d'Aro, tel. 972/83–71–50. Greens fees: 4,000–6,000 pesetas. **Club de Golf Pals.** Platja de Pals, 17256 Pals, tel. 972/63–70–09. Greens fees: 7,000 pesetas.

Gymnasiums Catalans are keen on fitness: You will see gymnasiums everywhere and in the Páginas Amarillas/Pàgines Grogues (Yellow Pages) under "Gimnasios/Gimnasis." Recommended is the new and exciting **Crack,** which has gym, sauna, pool, six squash courts, and paddle tennis. *Pasaje Domingo 7, tel. 93/215–2755. Admission: 2,000 pesetas for a day's membership plus small supplements for the courts.*

Swimming
Indoor Try the **Club Natació Barceloneta** (Passeig Marítim, tel. 93/309–3412; admission: 500 pesetas) or the **Piscines Pau Negre-Can Toda** (Ramiro de Maetzu, tel. 93/213–4344; admission: 500 pesetas).

Outdoor Uphill from Parc Güell is the **Parc de la Creueta del Coll** (Castellterçol, tel. 93/416–2625; admission: 300 pesetas), which has a huge outdoor swimming pool (*see also* Tennis, *below*).

Tennis The cheapest place to play tennis is the **Complejo Deportivo Can Caralleu** (Can Caralleu Sports Complex), above Pedralbes. The complex includes two pools, indoor and out (cost: 500 pesetas). *Tel. 93/203–7874. Admission: 700 pesetas per hour daytime, 1,000 pesetas per hour at night. Open daily 8 AM–11 PM.*

There is also the upscale **Club Vall Parc.** *Carretera de la Rabassada 79, tel. 93/212–6789. Admission: 2,750 pesetas per hour daytime, 3,250 pesetas per hour at night. Open daily 8 AM–midnight.*

Beaches

Barceloneta   This is the city's main beach and has become quite popular since being cleaned up for the Barcelona Olympics of 1992. There is now clean sand, surf, and perfectly decent swimming to be found just a 20-minute walk from the Rambla.

Others   As you go north, the first fine beaches you come to are Arenys, Sant Pol, and Calella, reached by train from Passeig de Gràcia. **Sant Pol** is the pick, with a sandy bathing beach and a lovely old town. Generally, the farther north you go toward the Costa Brava, the better the beaches become.

Ten km (6 mi) south is the popular day resort of **Castelldefels,** with a series of good beachside restaurants and bars and a long, sandy beach for sunning and bathing, though it's windy.

Topless bathing is fine on all these beaches, but nudists should head up the Costa Brava or down the Costa Dorada.

Dining

Combining many of the best elements of France and Spain, Catalan cuisine is wholesome and served in hearty portions. Spicy sauces are more prevalent here than elsewhere in Spain—for instance, you will come across garlicky *all i oli,* used to dress a wide variety of dishes. Typical entrées include *habas á la catalana* (a spicy broad-bean stew) and *bullabesa* (fish soup-stew similar to the French *bouillabaisse),* as well as macaroni: Pasta dishes are more popular here than in the rest of Spain. Bread is doused with olive oil and spread with tomato to make *pa amb tomaquet,* delicious on its own or as an accompaniment. Above all, *zarzuela de mariscos* (literally "operetta" of seafood) tastes better in Catalunya than anywhere else. You can accompany it with excellent wine from the Penedès region just to the south or the famous Catalan *cava* (champagne).

Menús del día offer good value, though they vary in quality and are generally served only at lunchtime. Restaurants usually serve lunch 1–4 and dinner 9–1. It is normal but by no means a requirement to tip; 10% is generous.

Highly recommended restaurants are indicated by a star ★.

Category	Cost*
$$$$	over 7,000 ptas
$$$	5,000–7,000 ptas
$$	2,400–5,000 ptas
$	under 2,400 ptas

per person, excluding drinks, service, and tax

$$$$ **Beltxenea.** Previously a smart Eixample apartment, Beltxenea, es-
   tablished in 1987, retains an atmosphere of privacy in its elegant dining rooms. In summer you can dine outside in the formal garden. Chef Miguel Ezcurra's outstanding cooking hails from the Basque country. His specialty is *merluza con kokotxas y almejas* (hake fried in garlic, simmered in stock, added to clams, and garnished with parsley). If the wine list defeats you, narrow it down to the Riojas. *Mallorca 275, tel. 93/215–3024. Reservations required.*

Dress: neat but casual. AE, DC, MC, V. Closed Sat. lunch, Sun., and July–Aug.

Botafumeiro. Up on Gràcia's main thoroughfare is Barcelona's finest shellfish restaurant, with dishes prepared according to traditional recipes. The waiters will impress you with their soldierly white outfits and superquick service. The tone set is maritime, with white tablecloths and pale varnished wood paneling. The obvious highlights are the *mariscos Botafumeiro* (myriad plates of shellfish that arrive one after the other). *Gran de Gràcia 81, tel. 93/218–42–30. Reservations advised. Dress: neat but casual. AE, DC, MC, V. Closed Sun. evening and Mon.*

★ **La Dama.** Manager-chef Josep Bullich, previously at Vía Veneto and Agut d'Avignon, has converted a Moderniste house into the chicest restaurant in town, with green walls, orange tablecloths, and a polished wood floor. The building was designed by the "amateur," Manuel Sayrach, who built only three buildings during his life. His Art Nouveau interior is perfect for Bullich, who likens his cooking to a movement in modern art. Try the *ensalada tibia de cigalas al vinagre de naranja* (langoustinesalad with orange vinegar). *Diagonal 423/425, tel. 93/202–0686. Reservations required. Jacket advised. AE, DC, MC, V.*

★ **Eldorado Petit.** In 1984 Luis Cruañas moved to Barcelona from the Costa Brava and opened this restaurant, which rapidly became known as the best in Barcelona and one of the top restaurants in Spain. The setting—a private villa in Sarrià, with an exotic garden for summer dining up in the hills—is simply beautiful, as is the diverse international cuisine. Try the *pichón relleno* (roast pigeon with truffles and foie gras). *Dolors Monserdà 51, tel. 93/204–5153. Reservations required. Dress: neat but casual. AE, MC, V. Closed Sun. and 2 weeks in Aug.*

Orotava. A 50th-anniversary painting by Miró and an acclaimed copy of Velázquez's *Los Borrachos (The Drunkards)* adorn this intimate baroque-style dining room. Game is the chef's special drawing card, and he is well supplied by clients who bring back the results of their sport from as far afield as Albacete. In season try the *faisán royal* (roast pheasant in a cream and truffle sauce).*Consell de Cent 335, tel. 93/302–3128. Reservations required. Jacket advised. AE, DC, MC, V. Closed Sun. year-round and Sat. June–Sept.*

Reno. Fish is smoked on the premises and meat is cooked on charcoal in this respected haute cuisine restaurant, just north of Diagonal. Game specialties are recommended in season; try the *perdiz a la moda Alcantara* (partridge in wine or port). The tasting (*de gustació*)menu allows you to sample several of the best dishes. Semicircular black sofas surround white-clothed tables, and dark paneling, interspersed with mirrors, extends to the ceiling. *Tuset 27, tel. 93/200–1390. Reservations strongly advised. Jacket and tie required. AE, DC, MC, V.*

Vía Veneto. A Baroque dining room with pink tablecloths, located just above Plaça de Francesc Macià, provides the setting for one of the city's more traditional restaurants. New and exciting Catalan recipes are forever forthcoming; try the *salmón marinado al vinagre de frambuesa* (salmon marinated in raspberry vinegar and aromatic herbs). *Ganduxer 10–12, tel. 93/200–7024. Reservations required. Jacket and tie required. AE, DC, MC, V. Closed Sat. lunch, Sun., and Aug. 1–20.*

$$$ Agut d'Avignon. This venerable Barcelona institution (since 1962) takes a bit of finding; head down Carrer Ferran from the Plaça de Sant Jaume, turn left down Carrer Avinyó, and Carrer Trinitat is the first alley off to the right. White walls, heavy wood tables, and

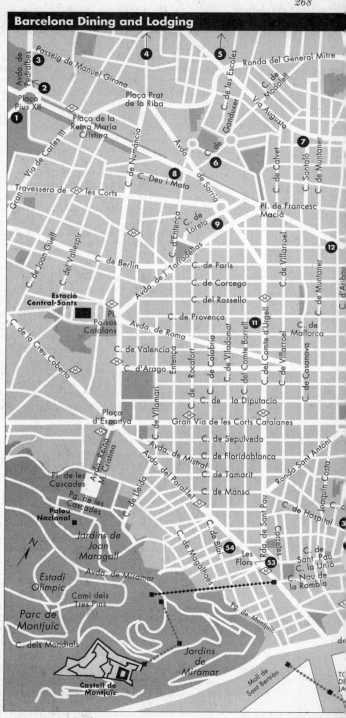

Barcelona Dining and Lodging

terra-cotta urns give the place a rustic air, and it's a favorite with businesspeople and politicians from across the road in the Generalitat. The cooking is traditional Catalan and specialties change with the season; from September to May, try the *pato con higos* (roast wild duck in a fig sauce). *Trinitat 3, tel. 93/317–3693. Reservations advised. Jacket advised. AE, DC, MC, V. Closed Holy Week and Christmas.*

Can Isidre. This small restaurant located just inside the Raval from Avinguda del Paral.lel has a long-standing tradition with Barcelona's artistic elite. Pictures and engravings by Dalí and other prominent artists line the walls. The traditional Catalan cooking with a slight French accent draws on the nearby Boqueria's fresh produce. The homemade foie gras is superb. Come and go by cab at night; the area's not the best. *Les Flors 12, tel. 93/441–1139. Reservations required. Dress: casual but stylish. AE, MC, V. Closed Sun., Holy Week, and mid-July–mid-Aug.*

La Cuineta. When the Madolell family converted their antiques business into a restaurant in the late 1960s, it soon gained respect for its neobaroque elegance, intimacy, and Catalan nouvelle cuisine. The clientele encompasses a wide range of foreigners and locals alike. Fish is the house specialty; try the *bacalao La Cuineta* (cod with spinach, raisins, pine nuts, and white sauce). The restaurant is located in two neighboring premises behind the cathedral's apse. *Paradís 4, tel. 93/315–0111 (closed Mon.), and Pietat 12, tel. 93/315–4156 (closed Tues.). No reservations. Dress: casual. AE, DC, MC, V.*

Jaume de Provença. People come here because of the very high reputation of the chef, Jaume Bargués. From his haute cuisine repertoire, try the *lenguado relleno de setas* (sole stuffed with mushrooms) or *lubina* (sea bass) soufflé. The restaurant, situated in the Hospital Clinic area of Eixample, has been recently redecorated in modern black and bottle green. *Provença 88, tel. 93/430–0029. Reservations required. Jacket advised. AE, DC, MC. Closed Sun. evening, Mon., and Aug.*

★ **Neichel.** Hailing from Alsace-Lorraine, chef Jean-Louis Neichel is not bashful about his reputation as he explains such French delicacies as the *ensalada de gambas al sésamo con puernas fritas* (shrimp in sesame-seed sauce with fried leeks). The prices fluctuate widely, depending on your choice. The setting is the ground floor of a Pedralbes apartment block, mundane modernity compared with the cooking. *Calle Bertran i Rozpide 16 bis (just off Av. Pedralbes), tel. 93/203–8408. Reservations required. Jacket advised. AE, DC, MC, V. Closed Sun., Christmas week, Holy Week, and Aug.*

★ **La Odisea.** The dark red walls of this small restaurant, near the cathedral front, are crowded with contemporary Catalan paintings, and a colorful portrait of the chef as you enter. The artistic sense translates to the cooking, adventurously concocted from myriad Mediterranean ingredients and brought to your table by friendly waiters. Try the *merluza al vapor con salsa de tomate fresco* (steamed sea bass with fresh tomato sauce) or *ensaladilla de higado* (liver salad served with mushrooms and Modena vinegar). *Copons 7, tel. 93/302–3692. Reservations required. Dress: neat but casual. AE, DC, MC, V. Closed Sat. lunch, Sun., Holy Week, and Aug.*

Quo Vadis. Just off the Ramblas, near the Boqueria market and Betlem Church, a shiny gray facade camouflages one of Barcelona's most respected restaurants. A succession of small dining rooms decorated in grays and greens provides an atmosphere of sleek intimacy. Its much-praised cuisine includes *pot pourri de setas* (mushrooms) and *higado de ganso con ciruelas* (fried goose liver with prunes). *Carme 7, tel. 93/317–7447. Reservations advised. Dress: neat but casual. AE, DC, MC, V. Closed Sun.*

★ **Tram-Tram.** At the end of the old tram line just uphill from the village of Sarrià, Isidre Soler and his stunning wife Reyes have put together one of the finest and most original of Barcelona's new culinary opportunities. Try the *menu de desgustació* and you might be lucky enough to get the marinated tuna salad, the cod medallions, and the venison filet mignons, among other tasty creations. Perfect-size portions, and the graceful setting—especially in or near the garden out back—make this a popular spot, and although having reservations is a good idea, Reyes can always invent a table on the spur of the moment, so don't pass up the chance to eat here because of lack of planning. *Major de Sarrià 121, tel. 93/204–8518. Reservations advised. Dress: as you wish. AE, MC, V. Closed Sun. and Dec. 24–Jan. 6.*

$$ **Arcs de Sant Gervasi.** Situated up the hill toward Muntaner, Arcs is a modern restaurant that has beige walls with frequently changed artwork, salmon pink tablecloths, and plentiful mirrors. The cooking is *cucina de mercat* (based upon what fresh produce is available in the market) and includes very good fish. Try the *lenguado a las almendras* (sole with almonds). *Santaló 103, tel. 93/201–9277. Reservations advised. Dress: neat but casual. AE, DC, MC, V.*

★ **El Asador de Aranda.** Few restaurants can compete with the setting here—a large, detached, redbrick castle above the Avenida Tibidabo metro. The dining room is large and airy, with a terra-cotta floor and traditional Castellano furnishings. The traditional Castilian cooking here has won high praise since the restaurant opened in 1988. Try *pimientos de piquillo* (hot spicy peppers) and then *chorizo de la olla* (chorizo sausage stew). *Av. Tibidabo 31, tel. 93/417–0115. Dinner reservations advised. Dress: casual. AE, DC, MC, V. Closed Sun. evening.*

Bilbao. Located at the corner of Venus and Perill (danger) this cozy bistro is indeed perilous to abstinence of all kinds. The overhanging balcony seems to place all diners on stage and it gets fun and foolish quickly. The Catalan cuisine is excellent and the value is among the best in Barcelona. A good place for earlyish dining at lunch or dinner. *Carrer de Perill 33, tel. 93/458–9624. Reservations held until nine o'clock only, after which it's first come, first served. Dress: casual. MC, V. Closed Sun. and holidays.*

Brasserie Flo. A block above the Palau de la Música, this used to be a textiles factory; you dine in a large, elegantly restored warehouse with arched vaulting, steel columns, and wood paneling. Opened in 1982 by a group of Frenchmen, the Brasserie serves an exciting combination of French and Catalan dishes. Try the freshly made foie gras and *choucroûte. Jonqueres 10, tel. 93/317–8037. Reservations advised. Dress: neat but casual. AE, DC, MC, V.*

Los Caracoles. Just below Plaça Reial, a wall of roasting chickens announces one of Barcelona's most famous tourist haunts, which, despite catering primarily to visitors, has great food and real atmosphere. At night you are likely to be serenaded at your table. The walls are hung thickly with azulejos and photos of bullfighters and visiting celebrities. House specialties are *suquillo de pescadores* (an assortment of fish fried in oil and butter and added to a sauce); paella; *mejillones* (mussels); and, of course, *caracoles* (snails). *Escudellers 14, tel. 93/302–3185. No reservations. Dress: casual. AE, DC, MC, V.*

Set Portes. A high-ceilinged dining room, black-and-white marble floor, and numerous mirrors hide behind these seven doors near the waterfront. Going strong since 1836, this restaurant fills up during the week with people from the Bolsa (Stock Exchange) across the way, but at night and on weekends it draws all sorts. The cooking is Catalan, the portions are enormous, and specialties are *paella de peix* (fish) and *sarsuela Set Portes* (seafood casserole). *Passeig Isabel II 14, tel. 93/319–3033. Reservations advised. Jacket advised. AE, DC, MC, V.*

La Vaqueria. This onetime cow shed has been wonderfully converted into an unusual eating place where tables for romantic couples and boisterous groups seem to coexist in perfect harmony. The feed bins and watering troughs have been left in place, and the country design has a certain urban elegance, along with a veneer of humor. The food is delicious and, for the most part, uncomplicated. The *solomillo de buey* (filet mignon) can be prepared with wild mushrooms, green peppers, or blue cheese and is always superb. *Deu i Mata 141, tel. 93/419–0346. Closed for lunch on Sat. and Sun. AE, DC, MC, V.*

$ **Agut.** Wood paneling surmounted by white walls on which hang
★ 1950s canvases forms the setting for the mostly Catalan diners in this homey restaurant in the lower reaches of the Gothic Quarter. It was founded in 1924, and its popularity has never waned, not least because the hearty Catalan fare offers fantastic value. In season (September–May), try the *pato silvestre agridulce* (sweet-and-sour wild duck). There's a good selection of wine but no frills such as coffee or liqueurs. *Gignas 16, tel. 93/315–1709. No reservations. Dress: casual. AE, MC, V. Closed Sun. evening, Mon., and July.*

Egipte. The Egipte, hidden away behind the Boqueria market, has become more and more popular over the last few years, especially with the young. The traditional Catalan home cooking (featuring such favorites as *habas a la catalana*—spicy broad-bean stew) emanates from an overstretched but resourceful kitchen, and the results can be uneven. Nevertheless, the many-tiered dining rooms with marble-top tables and Egyptian motifs continue to entice a lively and sophisticated crowd. The best time to come is lunchtime, when there is a good-value menú del día. There are sister branches at Jerusalem 3 and Rambla 79. *Jerusalem 12, tel. 93/317–7480. No reservations. Dress: casual. AE, DC, MC, V. Closed Sun.*

El Glop. Noisy, hectic, and full of jolly diners from all over Barcelona, El Glop's specialties are *calçotades* (giant spring onions baked in a clay oven) and *asados* (barbecued meats). House wine arrives in a porró (porrón in Spanish)—unless you're a practiced at pouring wine into your mouth from some distance, save your blushes by using the wider opening and a glass. Bright and simply furnished, this restaurant is located a few blocks north of Plaça del Sol in Gràcia. *Sant Lluís 24, tel. 93/213–7058. Reservations required. Dress: casual. MC, V. Closed Mon.*

★ **Sopeta Una.** Dining in this delightful, minuscule restaurant, with old-fashioned earthy decor and cozy ambience, is more like eating in a private house. The menu is in Catalan, all the dishes are Catalan, and everything is very genteel. Try the *cors de carxofes* (artichoke hearts with prawns and tomato and mayonnaise sauce) and for dessert, the traditional Catalan *música*—a plate of raisins, almonds, and dried fruit, served with a glass of Muscatel. *Verdaguer i Callis 6, tel. 93/319–6131. No reservations. Dress: neat but casual. AE, V. Closed Sun., Mon. AM, and Aug.*

La Tomaquera. Situated amid the fading glory of the Paral.lel theater district, this small and unpretentious restaurant is renowned across the city for its superb caracoles and *carns a la brasa* (charcoal-grilled meats), which arrive in giant portions and are accompanied by *all i oli* sauce. *Margarit 58, no tel. No reservations. Dress: casual. No credit cards. Closed Mon. and Aug.*

Bars and Cafés

Barcelona abounds in colorful old tapas bars; smart, trendy cafés; and a whole range of stylish in-vogue bars glorifying in the titles of *coctelerias* (cocktail bars), *whiskerias*, or *xampanyerias* (champagne bars). Below, we list just a few, but on the whole it is best to wander at will and try out any that take your fancy. Most stay open till 2:30 AM (*see* The Arts and Nightlife, *below*, for later spots).

Xampanyerias **La Cava del Palau.** Very handy for the Palau de la Música, this champagne bar serves a wide selection of cavas, wines, and cocktails, with cheeses, pâtés, smoked fish, or caviar on a series of stepped balconies adorned with shiny azulejos. *Verdaguer i Callis 10. Open Mon.–Sat. 7 PM–2:30 AM; closed Sun.*

El Xampanyet. Just down the street from the Picasso Museum, hanging *botas* (leather wineskins), but no sign, announce one of Barcelona's liveliest xampanyerias, packed full most of the time. The house cava, cider, and pan con tomate are served on marble-top tables surrounded by barrels and walls decorated with colored tiles (azulejos) and fading yellow paint. *Montcada 22. Open Tues.–Sun. 8:30 AM–4 PM and 6:30–midnight; closed Mon.*

Tapas Bars **Bar Rodrigo.** Next to the church of Santa Maria del Mar is this popular tapas bar of mirrors, marble-top tables, and steel columns. The specialty is the *vermut* (vermouth) cocktail. There is also a good-value menu for lunch. *L'Argenteria 67. Open 8 AM–1 AM; closed Wed. evening and Thurs.*

Cap Pep. This lively spot has an excellent selection of tapas served fresh and piping hot. *Plaça de les Olles 8. Closed Sun. and Mon. lunch.*

La Palma. Between the Ajuntament and Via Laietana, this has marble tables reminiscent of a Paris bistro, tapas to nibble, and newspapers to read. *Palma Sant Just 7. Open daily 7 AM–10 PM.*

Pla de la Garsa. Serving cheeses, pâtés, wines, and cava, this is a typically Catalan locale. If you just want a drink, come after midnight. *Assonadors 13 (off Montcada). Open daily 7 PM–1 AM.*

Cafés **Café de l'Acadèmia.** Said to serve the best *bocadillos* (French bread sandwiches) in town, this is a sophisto-rustic spot with wicker chairs and stone walls, frequented by politicians from the nearby Generalitat who come here to listen to classical music. *Lledó 1. Open daily 9 AM–4 PM and 9–11:30 PM.*

Café de l'Opera. Right opposite the Liceu, the high-ceilinged Art Nouveau interior plays host to opera goers and performers, but it's also right on the tourist trail, and you won't be the only visitor here. *Ramblas 74. Open Apr.–Sept., daily 24 hrs; Oct.–Mar., daily 10 AM–2 AM.*

Café Zurich. Few avoid a drink in Barcelona's best-known meeting place, a sea of alfresco tables perfectly placed to watch the world emerge from the top end of the Ramblas. *Corner of Pelai and Plaça Catalunya. Open daily 10 AM–midnight.*

Els Quatre Gats. This is the cafè where Picasso staged his first exhibition and met fellow Modernistes. Don't confuse it with the modern one next door. *Montsió 3. Open daily 8 PM–3 AM.*

Coctelerias **El Copetín.** On Barcelona's best-known cocktail avenue, this bar has exciting decor and good cocktails. *Passeig del Born 19. Open daily 7 PM–3 AM.*

Miramelindo. This bar offers a large selection of herbal liquors, fruit cocktails, pâtés, cheeses, and music, usually jazz. *Passeig del Born 15. Open daily 8 PM–3 AM.*

El Paraigua. Behind the Ajuntament, this rather pricey bar serves cocktails in a stylish setting with classical music. *Plaça Sant Miquel. Open daily 7 PM–1 AM.*

Lodging

The staging of the 1992 Olympic Games here caused a massive boom in hotel construction. New hotels shot up in the ferment, and existing ones underwent extensive renovations. The most spectacular new lodging place in Barcelona is the Hotel Rey Juan Carlos I, which now accompanies—and to some degree has replaced—the Princesa Sofía as the Barcelona luxury hotel closest to the airport. Room rates across the board have increased well above the rate of inflation in recent years, meaning that there are very few real bargains left. Don't give up too easily, however, as most receptionists will become flexible about rates if they suspect you might leave in search of cheaper accommodations. Write or fax ahead asking for a discount; you may be pleasantly surprised.

Generally speaking, hotels in the Gothic Quarter and Ramblas are convenient for sightseeing, have plenty of Old World charm, but, with some notable exceptions, are not as strong on creature comforts. Those in the Eixample are generally set in late-19th-century to 1950s town houses, often Moderniste in design; they all offer a choice between street and inner courtyard rooms, so be sure to specify when you book. The newest hotels, with the widest range of facilities, are out to the west along the Diagonal.

Reservations are a good idea, if only to make your bid for a good rate, but the pre-Olympics hotel-shortage days are over, and in the forseeable future there will be few times when lodging cannot be found with relative ease. Ask for weekend rates, which are often half-price.

Highly recommended hotels are indicated by a star ★.

Category	Cost*
$$$$	over 25,000 ptas
$$$	17,000–25,000 ptas
$$	9,000–17,000 ptas
$	under 9,000 ptas

All prices are for a standard double room, excluding tax.

$$$$ **Avenida Palace.** At the bottom of the Eixample, between the Rambla de Catalunya and Passeig de Gràcia, this hotel manages to convey a feeling of elegance and antiquated style despite dating only from 1952. The lobby is wonderfully ornate, with curving staircases leading off in many directions. Everything is patterned, from the carpets to the plasterwork, a style largely echoed in the bedrooms, although some have been modernized and the wallpaper subdued. Nevertheless, if you prefer contemporary simplicity, go elsewhere. *Gran Via 605–607, 08007, tel. 93/301–9600, fax 93/318–1234. 160 rooms with bath. Facilities: restaurant, bar, gym, health club, sauna. AE, DC, MC, V.*

★   **Condes de Barcelona.** Installed in the old Batlló house (the annex across the street is in the old Duarella house), this hotel is one of the city's most popular hotels—rooms need to be booked well in advance. The stunning pentagonal lobby features a marble floor and the columns and courtyard of the original 1891 building. The modern rooms have Jacuzzis and terraces over interior gardens. An affiliated fitness club around the corner offers facilities including squash courts and a pool. *Passeig de Gràcia 75, 08008, tel. 93/484-8600, fax 93/488-0614. 110 rooms with bath in the Batlló house and 73 in the newly opened Daurella house. Facilities: restaurant, bar, parking. AE, DC, MC, V.*

Le Meridien. Formerly the Manila and then Ramada Renaissance, the French-owned Le Meridien vies with the Colón and Rivoli Ramblas as the premier hotel in the Barri Gòtic. Bedrooms are light, spacious, and decorated in pastel shades. As well as hosting visiting rock stars such as Michael Jackson, the hotel is very popular with business people; facsimiles and computers in your room are available on request. A room overlooking the Ramblas is probably worth the extra noise. *Rambla 111, 08002, tel. 93/318-6200, fax 93/301-7776. 209 rooms with bath. Facilities: bar, restaurant, parking. AE, DC, MC, V.*

Princesa Sofía. Long regarded as the city's foremost modern hotel despite its slightly out-of-the-way location on Avda. Diagonal, this towering high rise offers a wide range of facilities and everything from shops to three different restaurants, including one of the city's finest, Le Gourmet, and the 19th-floor Top City, with breathtaking views. Modern bedrooms are ultracomfortable and decorated in soft colors. *Plaça Pius XII 4, 08028, tel. 93/330-7111, fax 93/411-2106. 505 rooms with bath. Facilities: 3 restaurants, bars, shops, hairdresser, gym, health club, sauna, 2 pools (indoor and outdoor), gardens, parking. AE, DC, MC, V.*

★ **Ritz.** Founded in 1919 by Caesar Ritz, this is the *grande dame* of Barcelona hotels. Extensive refurbishment has restored it to its former splendor. The imperial entrance lobby is awe-inspiring, the rooms contain Regency furniture, some have Roman baths and mosaics, and the service is impeccable. As for the price, you can almost double that of its nearest competitor. *Gran Via 668, 08010, tel. 93/318-5200, fax 93/318-0148. 158 rooms with bath. Facilities: restaurant, bar. AE, DC, MC, V.*

$$$ **Alexandra.** Behind a reconstructed Eixample facade, everything here is slick and contemporary. The rooms are spacious, attractively furnished with dark wood chairs and thatch screens on the balconies to give privacy to the inward-facing rooms. From the airy white marble hall up, the Alexandra is perfectly suited to modern Martini-sipping folk. *Mallorca 251, 08008, tel. 93/487-0505, fax 93/488-0258. 81 rooms with bath. Facilities: restaurant-grill and bar, parking. AE, DC, MC, V.*

Calderón. Ideally placed on the chic uptown extension of the Ramblas, this modern high rise possesses the range of facilities normally expected only of those farther out of town. Public rooms are huge, with cool white marble floors, a style continued in the bedrooms. Don't forgo one of the higher rooms, from which the views from sea to mountains and over the city are breathtaking. *Rambla de Catalunya 26, 08007, tel. 93/301-0000. 264 rooms with bath. Facilities: restaurant, piano bar, 2 pools (1 indoor, 1 outdoor on roof), 2 squash courts, gym, sauna, parking. AE, DC, MC, V.*

★ **Colón.** This cozy, older town-house hotel has a unique charm and intimacy reminiscent of an English country inn. It lays claim to the sightseer's ideal location, with many of the rooms overlooking the floodlit main facade of the cathedral. The rooms are comfortable and tastefully furnished; those to the back are quiet. The Colón was a great favorite of Joan Miró, and if you're not going to be disturbed by the cathedral bells, it's an excellent choice. *Av. Catedral 7,*

08002, tel. 93/301–1404, fax 93/317–2915. 147 rooms with bath. Facilities: restaurant, bar. AE, DC, MC, V.

Duques de Bergara. This hotel is set in a stately Moderniste mansion with high ceilings and the full range of art nouveau trappings. The public rooms successfully combine old and new, Persian rugs and glass tables. The bedrooms display restraint and elegance in their mingling of functional contemporary with antiques, though some are smaller and have thinner walls than one would wish. *Bergara 11, 08002, tel. 93/301–5151, fax 93/317–3442. 54 rooms with bath. Facilities: restaurant, bar. AE, DC, MC, V.*

Gran Derby. Every bedroom in this modern Eixample hotel has its own sitting room, and each is decorated with modern black-and-white tile floors, plain light walls, and coral bedspreads. Some have an extra bedroom, making this an ideal choice for a family. If it weren't for the location, some way out (for sightseeing purposes), just below Plaça Francesc Macià, it would be unreservedly recommended. *Loreto 28, 08029, tel. 93/322–3215, fax 93/419–6820. 44 rooms with sitting room and bath. Facilities: café, bar, parking. AE, DC, MC, V.*

Hotel Rey Juan Carlos I. This modern complex towering over the western end of Barcelona's Avinguda Diagonal is as much shopping mall as luxury hotel. Jewelry, furs, caviar, art, flowers and fashions, even limousines are for sale or hire at this giant concentration of hospitality and design. The lush garden, including a pond complete with swans, is the setting of an Olympic-sized swimming pool, and the green expanses of Barcelona's finest in-town country club, El Polo, spread luxuriantly out beyond. Hotel dining facilities include three restaurants, the luxurious French "Chez Vous," the Japanese Kokoro, and a buffet, as well as an American bar. Lecture halls and seminar rooms are abundant. *Avinguda Diagonal 661–671, 08028, tel. 93/448–0808, fax 93/448–0607. 375 rooms with bath, 37 suites, 2 presidential suites, 1 royal suite. Facilities: 3 restaurants, bar, parking, garden, swimming pool, hairdressers, boutiques. AE, DC, MC, V.*

★ **Majestic.** With an unbeatable location on the city's most stylish boulevard and a great rooftop pool, this is a near-perfect place to stay. The different combinations of wallpaper, pastels, and vintage furniture in the rooms and the leather sofas, marble, and mirrors in the reception area all suit the place rather well—and the jet set still comes here. The building is part Eixample town house and part modern extension, so bear this in mind when booking your room. *Passeig de Gràcia 70, 08008, tel. 93/488–1717, fax 93/488–1880. 335 rooms with bath. Facilities: restaurant, bar, health club, pool, parking. AE, DC, MC, V.*

Rivoli Ramblas. Behind the upper-Rambla facade lies imaginative slick, modern decor, marble floors, elegant pastel bedrooms, and a roof-terrace bar with panoramic views. *Ramblas 128, 08002, tel. 93/302–6643, fax 93/317–5053. 87 rooms with bath. Facilities: restaurant, cocktail bar, fitness center, spa, sauna, solarium. AE, DC, MC, V.*

$$ ★ **España.** They've completely modernized the large bedrooms here—the best and quietest overlook the bright interior patio—and now this erstwhile budget hotel, with already stunning public rooms, is a real winner. Its main attraction remains the Moderniste ground-floor decor, designed by Domènech i Montaner, and featuring a superbly sculpted hearth by Eusebi Arnau, elaborate woodwork, and a mermaid-populated Ramón Casas mural in the breakfast room. The restaurant is likewise beautiful. Don't miss this lovely concentration of Art Nouveau, even if you only stop in for lunch or dinner.

Sant Pau 9–11, 08001, tel. 93/318–1758, fax 93/317–1134. 76 rooms with bath. Facilities: restaurant, breakfast room, cafeteria. AE, DC, MC, V.

Gótico. Along with the neighboring Rialto and Suizo hotels, this now belongs to the Gargallo group, which has done a good job of renovating these three old favorites, popular with tour groups. Just off Plaça Sant Jaume, the Gótico is central for exploring the Gothic Quarter. The rooms have wood beams, white walls, heavy wood furniture, white tile floors, and walnut doors; ask for an exterior one. *Jaume I 14, 08002, tel. 93/315–2211, fax 93/315–3819. 80 rooms with bath. Facilities: cafeteria, bar. AE, DC, MC, V.*

★ **Gran Via.** Architectural features are the attraction of this grand 19th-century town house, close to the main tourist office. The original chapel has been preserved; also, you can have breakfast in a hall of mirrors, climb its elaborate Moderniste staircase, and call from the Belle Epoque phone booths. The rooms have plain alcoved walls, bottle green carpets, and Regency-style furniture; those overlooking Gran Via itself have better views but are quite noisy. *Gran Via 642, 08007, tel. 93/318–1900, fax 93/318–9997. 53 rooms with bath. Facilities: breakfast room, parking. AE, DC, MC, V.*

★ **Metropol.** Located between the lower reaches of the Rambla and Via Laietana, this town house offers easy access to the marina while being pleasantly off the tourist trail. Bedrooms are cozily decorated with plain orange carpets, green bedspreads, and modern prints. *Ample 31, 08002, tel. 93/315–4011, fax 93/319–1276. 68 rooms with bath. Facilities: cafeteria, bar. AE, DC, MC, V.*

Montecarlo. Entrance from the Rambla is through an enticing marble hall, and upstairs is a sumptuous large reception room with a dark wood Moderniste ceiling. The rooms are modern, bright, and functional; ask for a view of the Rambla if you don't mind the higher noise level. *Rambla 124, 08002, tel. 93/412–0404, fax 93/318–7323. 76 rooms with bath. Facilities: bar, cafeteria, buffet, parking. AE, DC, MC, V.*

Nouvel. Centrally located just below Plaça de Catalunya, this hotel blends white marble, etched glass, elaborate plasterwork, and carved dark woodwork in its handsome Art Nouveau interior. Renovated and upgraded to cash in on the recent Olympics, the bedrooms now have pristine marble floors, firm beds, and smart bathrooms. The narrow street is pedestrian-only and therefore quiet, but views are non-existent. *Santa Anna 18–20, 08002, tel. 93/301–8274, fax 93/301–8370. 74 rooms with bath. Facilities: breakfast room. AE, MC, V.*

Oriente. Down toward the seamier side of the city's action, Barcelona's oldest hotel has nevertheless retained all its style and charm. Its ornate public rooms and glowing chandeliers recall a bygone era. The only drawback is the somewhat functional decor of the rooms, some of which have an extra bed for families. It is popular with businesspeople, though, and located just below the Liceu Opera House. *Rambla 45–47, 08002, tel. 93/302–2558, fax 93/412–3819. 142 rooms with bath. Facilities: restaurant, bar. AE, DC, MC, V.*

Regente. The Moderniste decor and plentiful stained glass lend style and charm to this smallish hotel. The public rooms have been renovated over the last two years and are carpeted with many different patterns. The bedrooms, fortunately, are elegantly restrained; the verdant roof-terrace with a pool and the prime position on the Rambla de Catalunya complete the positive verdict. *Rambla de Catalunya 76, 08008, tel. 93/487–5989, fax 93/487–3227. 78 rooms with bath. Facilities: 2 restaurants, bar, pool. AE, DC, MC, V.*

Rialto. This hotel seems to have taken a leaf from the paradors' book with its subdued and classy decor of pine floors, white walls, and walnut doors. The rooms (ask for an exterior one) echo this look, with heavy furniture set against light walls, and they have all the same fittings as the Gótico. There is a vaulted bar in the basement and a modern mirrored *salón* by the lobby. *Ferran 42, 08002, tel. 93/ 318–5212, fax 93/315–3819. 132 rooms with bath. Facilities: cafeteria, bar. AE, DC, MC, V.*

Suizo. The last of the Gargallo hotels lacks the spacious corridors of the Rialto, but its public rooms are preferable, with elegant modern seating at the front of the hotel, either near the reception area or one floor up, with good views over the noisy square. The bedrooms have bright walls and either wood or tile floors. *Plaça del Àngel 12, 08002, tel. 93/315–4111, fax 93/315–3819. 48 rooms with bath. Facilities: restaurant, bar, cafeteria. AE, DC, MC, V.*

$ **Continental.** Something of a legend among cost-conscious travelers, this comfortable hotel with canopied balconies stands at the top of the Rambla, just below Plaça de Catalunya. Everything is cramped, but the bedrooms manage to accommodate large, firm beds. The green swirly patterns on the walls match those on the fast-fading carpets. Ask for a room on the Rambla side. A good breakfast is served overlooking the famous street. *Rambla 138, 08002, tel. 93/ 301–2508, fax 93/302–7360. 35 rooms with bath. Facilities: breakfast room. AE, DC, MC, V.*

★ **Jardí.** With views over the adjoining traffic-free and charming squares, Plaça del Pi and Plaça Sant Josep Oriol, this hotel's newly renovated bedrooms have immaculate white-tile floors, modern pine furniture, white walls, and powerful, hot showers. Be sure to get an exterior room—they're quiet and represent excellent value. The alfresco tables of the Bar del Pi downstairs are ideal for breakfasting. *Plaça Sant Josep Oriol 1, 08002, tel. 93/301–5900, fax 93/318–3664. 40 rooms with bath. Facilities: breakfast room. AE, DC, MC, V.*

Paseo de Gràcia. Formerly a hostel, this hotel has good-quality plain carpets and sturdy wooden furniture adorning the soft-color bedrooms. Add to this the location on the handsomest of Eixample's boulevards and this is an excellent budget option if you want to stay uptown. Half the rooms have superb rooftop terraces, with great views up to Tibidabo. *Passeig de Gràcia 102, 08008, tel. 93/215–5828, fax 93/215–3724. 33 rooms with bath. Facilities: breakfast room, bar. AE, DC, MC, V.*

★ **Peninsular.** Built for the 1890 Exposition, this hotel in the Barri Xines features an impressive coral marble lobby and an appealing interior courtyard, painted white and pale green and adorned with numerous hanging plants. The bedrooms have tile floors, good showers, and firm beds. Look at a few before choosing because all are different; some have views, others give onto the courtyard. *Sant Pau 34, 08001, tel. 93/302–3138, fax 93/302–3138. 80 rooms with bath, 20 rooms without bath. Facilities: breakfast room. MC, V.*

The Arts and Nightlife

With music halls, theaters, and some of Europe's trendiest night-clubs, Barcelona has a wide-ranging arts and nightlife scene. To find out what's on, look in newspapers or the weekly *Guía Del Ocio*, available from newsstands all over town. *Activitats* is a monthly list of cultural events, published by the Ajuntament and available from its information office in Palau de la Virreina (Rambla 99).

The Arts

Concerts Catalans are great music lovers, and their main concert hall is the **Palau de la Música** (Sant Francesc de Paula 2, tel. 93/268–1000). The ticket office is open weekdays 11–1 and 5–8, Saturday 5–8 only. Sunday morning concerts (11 AM) are a popular tradition. Tickets range from 450 to 9,000 pesetas and are best purchased in advance. Concerts are held September–June. In September the city hosts an **International Music Festival** as part of its celebrations for the festival of the Mercè.

Dance **L'Espai de Dansa i Música de la Generalitat de Catalunya,** generally listed as **L'Espai** (The Space; Travessera de Gràcia 63, tel. 93/414–3133), was opened by the Catalonian government in February 1992 and is now Barcelona's prime venue for ballet, contemporary dance, and musical performances of varying kinds. **El Mercat de les Flors** (Lleida 59, tel. 93/426–1875) near Plaça de Espanya, is the more traditional setting for modern dance and theater.

Film Though some foreign films will be dubbed, there is always a good selection of films showing in their original language. Look in listing magazines for movies marked *v.o. subtitulada* (subtitled). The **Filmoteca** (Av. Sarrià 33, tel. 93/430–5007) shows three films daily in their original language, often English.

Flamenco Barcelona is not richly endowed with flamenco spots, as Catalans are only moderately fond of this very Andalucían spectacle. The best place is **El Patio Andaluz** (Aribau 242, tel. 93/209–3378), with *sevillanas* rather than flamenco and some audience participation, but it is quite expensive. **El Cordobés** (Rambla 35, tel. 93/317–6653) is the place most visited by tour groups, but it can be colorful and fun. Others are **El Tablao de Carmen** (Poble Espanyol, tel. 93/325–6895) and **Los Tarantos** (Plaça Reial 17, tel. 93/318–3067).

Opera Barcelona's opulent and beloved **Gran Teatre del Liceu** was gutted by flames in early 1994 and will in all probability not be restored until 1996. Originally constructed in 1848, the Liceu was destroyed by fire once before, in 1861. Considered one of Europe's finest opera houses, the Liceu was a Barcelona landmark. The box office, according to present plans, will remain open at San Pau 1 (tel. 93/318–9277); operas and musical events will be staged at the **Palau Sant Jordi** sports hall on Montjuïc, at the **Palacio Nacional** above Plaza España, or at the **Palau de la Música.** Some of the most spectacular halls and rooms of the Liceu were unharmed by the fire, and there may be some tours of these areas during the restoration.

Rock and Roll Keep an eye out for posters; in addition to some good Spanish bands (Radio Futura, El Ultimo de la Fila), many international bands pass through Barcelona. Major concerts are held in sports stadia or nightclubs such as Zeleste and K.G.B. For tickets, try any record shop; **Discos Castelló** (Tallers 79), just off Plaça Universitat, sells most concert tickets.

Theater Most theater performances are in Catalan, but Barcelona is also well known for its mime troupes (**Els Joglars** and **La Claca**). An international mime festival is held most years, as is the **Festival de Títeres** (Puppet Festival).

The best-known modern theaters are the **Teatre Lliure** (Montseny 47, in Gràcia, tel. 93/218–9251), **Mercat de les Flors** (Lleida 59, tel. 93/318–8599), **Teatre Romea** (Hospital 51, tel. 93/317–7189), **Teatre Tívoli** (Casp 10, tel. 93/412–2063), and **Teatre Poliorama** (Rambla

Estudios 115, tel. 93/317–7599) all of which offer a dynamic variety of classical, contemporary, and experimental theater.

Many of the older theaters specializing in big musicals are along the Paral.lel. They include **Apolo** (Paral.lel 56, tel. 93/241–9007) and **Victòria** (Paral.lel 67–69, tel. 93/441–3979). There is an open-air summer theater festival in July and August, when plays, music, song, and dance performances are held in the **Teatre Grec** (Greek Theater) on Montjuïc, as well as in other venues.

Nightlife

Cabaret Take in the venerable **Bodega Bohemia** (Lancaster 2, tel. 93/302–5061), where a variety of singers perform to an upright piano, or the minuscule **Bar Pastis** (Santa Mònica 4, tel. 93/318–7980), where the habitués form the cabaret and a phonograph plays the music of Edith Piaf.

Arnau (Paral.lel 60, tel. 93/242–2804) and **El Molino** (Vila i Vila 99, tel. 93/329–8854) are both traditional old-time music halls that have retained their popularity. **Belle Epoque** (Muntaner 246, tel. 93/209–7711), a richly decorated music hall, stages the most sophisticated shows.

Casinos The **Gran Casino de Barcelona** (tel. 93/893–3666), 42 km (26 mi) south in Sant Pere de Ribes, near Sitges, also has a dance hall and some excellent international shows in a 19th-century setting. The only others in Catalunya are in Lloret del Mar (tel. 972/36–65–12) and Perelada (tel. 972/53–81–25), both in Girona province up the coast north of Barcelona.

Jazz Clubs Try **La Cova del Drac** (Vallmajor 33, tel. 93/200–7032); **L'Auditori** (Balmes 245); or the Gothic Quarter's **Harlem Jazz Club** (Comtessa Sobradiel 8, tel. 93/310–0755), which is small but puts on atmospheric bands. The Palau de la Música stages an important **international jazz festival** in November, and the nearby city of Terrassa has its own jazz festival in March.

Nightclubs/ Barcelona is currently so hip that it is difficult to keep track of the
Discotheques trendiest places to go at night. Most clubs have a discretionary entrance charge that they like to inflict on foreigners, so dress up and be prepared to talk your way past the doorman.

Top ranked recently has been the prison decor–mimicking **Otto Zutz** (Lincoln 15, tel. 93/238–0722), just off Via Augusta. **K.G.B.** (Alegre de Dalt 55, tel. 93/210–5906) is another hot spot, while **Fibra Optica** (Beethoven 9, tel. 93/202–0069) and the city's nearly classic **Up and Down** (pronounced "Pendow") (Numancia 179, tel. 93/280–2922) are both anything but calm. **Oliver y Hardy** (Diagonal 593, tel. 93/419–3181) next to the Barcelona Hilton is a recent invention more popular with the older set (you won't stand out if you're over 35) while **La Tierra** (Aribau 230, tel. 93/200–7346) and **El Otro** (Valencia 166, tel. 93/323–6759) also accept post-graduates with open arms. **Zeleste** (Almogavers 122, tel. 93/309–1204) is one more standard hangout, especially popular with jazz and rock buffs.

For an old-fashioned *sala de baile* (dance hall) with a big band playing tangos, head to **La Paloma** (Tigre 27, tel. 93/301–6897); the kitsch 1950s decor creates a peculiar atmosphere that's great fun.

Late-night *Bar musical* is Spanish for any bar that plays modern music loud
Bars enough to drown out conversation. The pick of these are **Universal** (Marià Cubí 182–184, tel. 93/200–7470), **Mas i Mas** (Marià Cubí 199,

tel. 93/209–4502), and **Nick Havanna** (Rosselló 208, tel. 93/215–6591).

For a more laid-back locale, tall ceilings, billiards, tapas, and hundreds of students, visit the popular **Velodrom** (Muntaner 211–213, tel. 93/230–6022), just below Diagonal. Two blocks away is the intriguing *bar-museo* (bar-cum-museum) **La Fira** (Provença 171, tel. 93/323–7271). Downtown, deep in the Barrio Chino, try the **London Bar** (Nou de la Rambla 34, tel. 93/302–3102), an Art Nouveau old circus haunt with a trapeze suspended above the bar.

Barcelona Excursions

Numbers in the margin correspond to points of interest on the Barcelona Excursions map.

Montserrat

An almost obligatory side trip while you are in Barcelona is to the shrine of La Moreneta, the Black Virgin of **Montserrat,** 50 km (30 mi) west, high in the peaks of the Serra de Montserrat. These weird sawtoothed peaks have given rise to countless legends: Here, Parsifal found the Holy Grail, St. Peter left a statue of the Virgin Mary carved by St. Luke, and Wagner sought inspiration for his opera. A monastery has stood on the site since the early Middle Ages, though the present 19th-century building replaced the rubble left by Napoleon's troops in 1812. Montserrat is a world-famous shrine and one of Catalunya's spiritual sanctuaries. Honeymooning couples flock here by the thousands, seeking La Moreneta's blessing upon their marriage, and twice a year, on April 27 and September 8, the diminutive statue of Montserrat's Black Virgin becomes the object of one of Spain's greatest pilgrimages.

Follow the A2/A7 autopista on the new upper ring road (Ronda de Dalt) or from the western end of Diagonal as far as salida 25 to Martorell. Bypass this industrial center and follow signs to Montserrat. There is also train and bus service from Sants station to Montserrat, as well as guided tours (Pullmantur and Julià).

Only the Basilica and museum are readily open to the public. The **Basilica** (open daily 6–10:30 and noon–6:30) is dark and ornate, its blackness pierced by the glow of hundreds of votive lamps. Above the high altar stands the famous polychrome statue of the Virgin and Child to which the faithful can pay their respects by way of a separate door.

The monastery's **museum** has two sections: The Secció Antiga (open Tues.–Sat. 10:30–2) contains old masters, among them paintings by El Greco, Correggio, and Caravaggio, and the amassed gifts to the Virgin; the Secció Moderna (open Tues.–Sat. 3–6) concentrates on recent Catalan painters.

Time Out Amid a string of overpriced buffet establishments, the pick of lunching spots is the unremarkably named **Montserrat** (Plaça Apòstols, lunch only).

Montserrat is as memorable for its setting as for its religious treasures, so be sure to explore these strange pink hills. The vast monastic complex is dwarfed by the grandeur of the jagged peaks, and the crests are dotted with hermitages: Sant Joan hermitage can be reached by funicular. The views over the mountains away to the

Barcelona Excursions

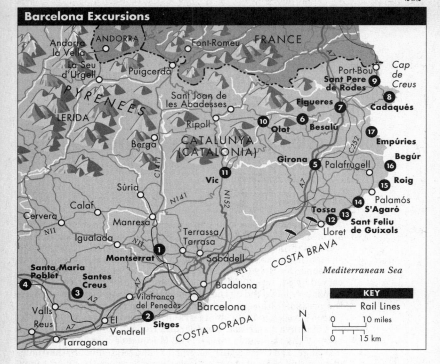

Mediterranean and, on a clear day, to the Pyrenees are breathtaking, and the rugged boulder-strewn setting makes for dramatic walking and hiking country.

Sitges, Santes Creus, and Poblet

These three attractions to the south and west of Barcelona can be seen comfortably in a day. Sitges is the prettiest and most popular resort in Barcelona's immediate environs and flaunts, apart from an excellent beach, a picturesque Old Quarter and some interesting Moderniste touches. The Cistercian monasteries west of here are characterized by restrained Romanesque architecture and beautiful cloisters.

Head southwest along Gran Via or Passeig de Colón to the freeway that passes the airport on its way to Castelldefels. From here, the new freeway and tunnels will get you to Sitges in 20 minutes. From Sitges, drive inland toward Vilafranca del Penedès and the A7 freeway. The A2 (Lleida) is the road for the monasteries.

Regular trains leave Sants and Passeig de Gràcia for Sitges; the ride takes a half hour. From Sitges, trains go to L'Espluga de Francolí, 4 km (2½ mi) from Poblet (Lleida line). For Poblet, stay with the train to Tarragona and catch a bus to the monastery (Autotransports Perelada, tel. 973/20–20–58).

2 In **Sitges,** head for the museums. Most interesting is the **Cau-Ferrat,** founded by the artist Russinyol, which contains some of his own paintings, together with two works by El Greco. Connoisseurs of wrought iron will be delighted to find here a beautiful collection of *cruces terminales,* crosses once erected to mark town boundaries. *Fonollar s/n, tel. 93/894–0364. Admission: 250 pesetas (free Sundays and holidays). Open Tues.–Sun. 9:30–2.*

Time Out You will find fine moderately priced seafood at **Vivero** (Passeig Balmins s/n, tel. 93/894–2149; closed Tues. from Dec. to May).

On leaving Sitges, make straight for the A2 autopista by way of Vilafranca del Penedès. If you are a wine buff, you may want to stop here to taste the excellent Penedès wine. You can visit and taste at the **Bodega Miguel Torres** (Comercio 22, tel. 93/890–0100), and there's an interesting **Museu del Vi** (Wine Museum; admission: 250 pesetas; open Tues.–Sun. 10–2 and 4–7; closed Mon.) in the Royal Palace, with descriptions of wine-making history.

❸ As it branches west to the province of Lleida, A2 passes two monasteries. The first you come to (salida 11) is **Santes Creus,** founded in 1157. Three austere aisles and an unusual 14th-century apse combine with the newly restored cloisters and the courtyard of the royal palace. *Admission: 350 pesetas. Open Oct.–Mar., daily 10–1 and 3–6; Apr.–Sept., daily 10–1 and 3–7.*

Another turning off the highway (salida 9) leads to the town of **Montblanc,** whose ancient gates are too narrow for cars. A walk through its tiny streets reveals Gothic churches with intricate stained-glass windows, a 16th-century hospital, and fine medieval mansions.

❹ Eight km (5 mi) farther on is the second and older monastery, **Santa Maria Poblet.** This splendid Cistercian foundation at the foot of the Prades Mountains is the most complete and representative masterpiece of Spanish monastic architecture. Founded in 1150 by Ramón Berenguer IV in gratitude for the Reconquest, it was initially inhabited by 12 Cistercians from Narbonne in France. The kings of Aragón used it for religious retreat and burial. It suffered extensive damage in the 1836 revolution, but since 1940 the monks of the reformed Cistercian order have successfully managed the difficult task of restoration. Today, monks and novices again pray before the splendid retable over the tombs of Aragonese rulers, restored to their former glory by sculptor Frederic Marés; sleep in the cold, barren dormitory; and eat their frugal meals in the stark refectory. The cloister is outstanding for its lightness and severity, two elements you rarely find blended so deftly as at Poblet. *Admission: 600 pesetas. Open for guided tours 10–12:30 and 3–6 (5:30 Oct.–Mar.).*

Girona and Northern Catalunya

The ancient city of Girona, often ignored by visitors who use its airport for the resorts of the Costa Brava, is full of interest and within easy day-tripping distance of Barcelona. The narrow medieval streets, with frequent stairways as required by the steep terrain, are what give Girona much of its charm. The historic buildings here include the cathedral, dominating the city from atop 90 steps; Arab baths; and an antique and charming Jewish Quarter.

Northern Catalunya boasts green rolling hills, the Aberes mountain range at the eastern tip of the Pyrenees, and the rugged Costa Brava. Meandering off into the countryside you see charming *masias* (farmhouses), whose austere grayish or pinkish stone, staggered rooftops, and ubiquitous square towers give them a look of fortresses. Churches confer dignity on the villages, and the tiniest of these contains its main arcaded square and *rambla* (promenade), where villagers stroll during the sacred evening paseo.

Arriving and Departing
By Car
Barcelona is now completely surrounded by a new network of *rondas*, or ring roads, with quick access from every corner of the city. Look for signs for these *rondas*, then follow signs to France (Francia); Girona; and the A7 autopista, which goes all the way. Leave the autopista at salida 7 for Girona. The 100 km (62 mi) to Girona takes 1½ hours.

By Train
Trains leave **Sants** and **Passeig de Gràcia** every 1½ hours for Girona, Figueres, and Port Bou. Some trains for northern Catalunya and France also leave from the França Station. Always double-check which station your train is leaving from. For Vic and Ripoll, catch a Puigcerdà train (every hour or two) from Sants or Plaça de Catalunya.

By Bus
Sarfa (Plaça Medinaceli 4, tel. 93/318–9434) has buses every 1½ hours to Girona, Figueres, and Cadaqués. For Vic try **Segalés** (at Fabra i Puig subway stop, tel. 93/231–2756) and for Ripoll call **Teisa** (Pau Claris 118, tel. 93/488–2837).

Guided Tours
Trenes Turísticos de RENFE (tel. 93/490–0202) operates guided tours to Girona by train May through September, leaving Sants at 10 AM and returning at 7:30 PM. It also has train tours to Vic and Ripoll, leaving Sants at 9 AM and returning at 8:40 PM. The cost for each is 1,500 pesetas for adults, 1,000 pesetas for children. Call RENFE to confirm these tours.

Exploring
5
In **Girona** you can park in the Plaça Independencia and find your way to the Tourist Information Office at Rambla Llibertat 1. Ask for their *oferta*, a card that will get you discount prices all over town. Then head to the Old Quarter across the River Onyar, past Girona's best-known view: the orange waterfront houses and their windows, draped with a colorful array of drying laundry, reflected in the waters of the Onyar. Use the cathedral's huge Baroque facade to guide you up through the labyrinth of streets.

At the base of 90 steps go left through the Sobreportes gate to the **Banys Arabs** (Arab Baths). Built by Morisco craftsmen in the late 12th century, long after Girona's Islamic occupation (795–1015) had ended, the baths are both Romanesque and Moorish in design. *Admission: 300 pesetas. Open May–Sept., Tues.–Sat., 10–2 and 4–7, Sun. 10–2; Oct.–Apr., Tues.–Sun. 10–1; closed Mon.*

Cross the River Galligants to visit the church of **Sant Pere** (Holy Father; finished 1131), notable for its octagonal Romanesque belfry and the finely detailed capitals atop the columns of the cloister. Next door is the **Museu Arquaeològic**, which documents the region's history since Paleolithic times. *Admission free. Church and museum open daily 10–1 and 4:30–7.*

Stroll back to and up the stepped Passeig Arquaeològic, which runs below the Old City walls. Climb to the highest **ramparts** through the Jardins de la Francesa. You get a good view from here of the 11th-century Romanesque Tower of Charlemagne, the oldest part of the cathedral.

Complete the loop around the **cathedral** to visit the interior. Designed by Guillem Bofill in 1416, it is famous for its immense, uncluttered Gothic nave—at 23 m (75½ ft), the widest in the world and the epitome of the goal of Catalan Gothic architects. The cathedral's museum contains the famous *Tapis de la Creació* (Tapestry of Creation) and a 10th-century copy of Beatus's manuscript *Commentary on the*

Apocalypse. Admission: 300 pesetas. Open Oct.–June, daily 9:30–1:15 and 3:30–7; July–Sept., daily 9:30–8.

The adjacent **Palau Episcopal** (Bishop's Palace) houses the **Museu d'Art**, a good mix of Romanesque, Catalan Gothic, and modern art. *Open Tues.–Sat. 10–1 and 4:30–7, Sun. 10–1; closed Mon. Same ticket as for Arab baths.*

Leave Plaça dels Apòstols along Carrer Claveria and turn right down Carrer Lluis Batlle i Prats. Plunge right down the tiny Carrer Sant Llorenç, formerly the cramped and squalid center of the 13th-century *Call*, or Jewish Quarter. Halfway down on the left is the small **Monastruc Çaporta**, a museum of Jewish history (open Tues.–Sat. 10–2 and 4–7, Sun. 10–2; closed Mon.), and the **Pati dels Rabís** (Rabbis' Courtyard).

❻ Three km (2 mi) north of Girona, turn left along C150. You pass through Banyoles by a large lake and countryside that grows steadily greener as you rise. The Pyrenees come into view on clear days, providing a spectacular backdrop to the ancient town of **Besalú**, capital of a feudal county from the 9th until the 12th century. Look for the carved, fortified bridge as you drive in, the porticoed **Plaça Llibertat**, the ruined **convent of Santa Maria** up on the hill, and the **church of Sant Pere**, whose window above the main portal is guarded by beautifully carved lions. The convent and churches can be visited by arrangement with the tourist office on Plaça Llibertat, with tours starting on the hour.

❼ Now follow C260, which runs through woods before descending to the ugly built-up plain and **Figueres**. Even if you aren't a great fan of Salvador Dalí's work, Figueres's **Museu Dalí** commands a halt. It's installed in a former theater, adjacent to the bizarre red Islamic-looking fortress where Dalí lived until his death in 1989. The remarkable collection includes a vintage Cadillac whose ivy-cloaked passengers you can water by putting 25 pesetas in a box at the side. Dalí is buried in a self-designed tomb beneath the museum. *Admission: 600 pesetas. Open Oct.–Mar., Tues.–Sun. 11:30–5:30; Apr.–Sept., Tues.–Sun. 9–8:30.*

❽ Our next destination is **Cadaqués**, 34 km (21 mi) away. Head past Roses and over the bleak heathland of the Sierra Alseda. Cadaqués's clustered, whitewashed houses set around a bay make it the most attractive of all Costa Brava resorts. The tiny beach is of a special kind of reddish-blue slate, used most decoratively in houses, walls, and streets, but uncomfortable to sit on and agony to walk over. The town has a strikingly situated 16th-century parish church and many steep, picturesque streets. It became an artists' haunt in the 1950s.

In summer, visit the **Museu Perrot-Moore** in the old town, which has an important collection of graphic arts dating from the 15th to the 20th century, including works by Dalí. *Admission: 400 pesetas. Open June 15–Oct. 15, daily 5–9.*

A few small, sandy beaches hug the side of the legendary **Cap** (Cape) **de Creus**. There remain only **Port de la Selva**, **Port de Llança**, and the frontier village of **Port-Bou** before you reach France. This road is unforgettably lovely as it winds its way around numerous bends, high above the turquoise sea, but the towns themselves are unremarkable.

❾ From Port de la Selva a rough track leads to a parking lot from which you can walk to the 10th-century monastery of **Sant Pere de Rodes**, a 610-m (2,000-ft) hilltop site with a perfect view of the coast. Built by Benedictine monks between 972 and 1022, the monastery was abandoned in 1789 and looted by the French. The bulk of the buildings have survived and are undergoing restoration. A paved road leads from the parking area onto C252. *Admission: 400 pesetas. Open daily 10–2 and 4–dusk.*

⑩ From Besalú, you can also go west to **Olot**, surrounded by basalt piles and largely destroyed by earthquakes in the 15th century. There is an interesting modern church here that flaunts a spring-board-shape steeple and a gigantic monk's head sculptured by Iloret on its facade. This is the **Church of Sant Pere the Martyr.** The **Museu Comarcal de la Garrotxa** contains an important assemblage of Moderniste art and design. *Carrer Hospici 8. Admission: 300 pesetas. Open Mon. and Wed.–Sat. 11–2 and 4–7, Sun. 11–2; closed Tues.*

⑪ From Olot follow C153 over a twisting, scenic road to **Vic.** The town rests on a 488-m (1,600-ft) plateau at the confluence of the Guri and Heder rivers, the business and industrial center of the region. It boasts a mostly neoclassical **cathedral** (open summer, Mon.–Sat. 10–1 and 4–7, Sun. 10–1 and 4–5; winter, Mon.–Sat. 10–1 and 4–6, Sun. 10–1 and 4–5), whose tremendous 11th-century Romanesque tower, El Cloquer, was built by Abbot Oliva. The cathedral is decorated with powerful modern murals by Josep Maria Sert. There is a good **museum** just opposite, containing very fine Romanesque and Gothic altarfronts, collected from local churches, as well as Gothic paintings. *Admission: 300 pesetas. Open Mon.–Sat. 10–1 and 4–7, Sun. 10–1:30.*

Before you go, be sure to see the vast **Plaça Mayor,** surrounded on all sides by Gothic arcades and well served by bars. A busy market takes place here on Tuesdays and Saturdays.

Dining
Cadaqués **Galiota** is the trendiest spot in town. Well-heeled arty types come here to eat fish and study the Dalí paintings on the walls. *Narcís Monturiol 9, tel. 972/25–81–87. Reservations required. Open only Sat., Sun., and holidays Oct.–May. $$*

Figueres **Ampurdán,** 1.5 km (1 mi) north on the NII, serves huge helpings of superb French/Catalan cooking; try one of the fish mousses. *Carretera NII, tel. 972/50–05–62. AE, DC, MC, V. $$$*
Mas Pau, 1.5 km (1 mi) west on the Olot road, is set in an old *masia* with a pretty garden; try one of the game specialties in season. *Carretera de Olot, tel. 972/54–61–54. DC, MC, V. $$$*

Girona **Alvereda** has excellent Ampurdan cuisine served in a bright and pleasant setting. Try the *galleta de calabacin con langostinos glaceada* (zucchini bisque with prawns). *Alvereda 7, tel. 972/22–60–02. Closed Sun. and many holidays. AE, DC, MC. $$*
El Po del Call is well situated near the center of Girona. The cuisine ranges from original creations like *bacalao a la miel* (cod in honey) to classical dishes. *La Força 14, tel. 972/22–37–74. Closed Sun. DC, MC, V. $$*

Lodging
Cadaqués **Hotel Playa Sol** has a pretty location—over a tiny beach, looking back at the town. *Platja Pianch 5, 17488, tel. 972/25–81–00, fax 927/25–80–54. 49 rooms. Facilities: coffee shop, garden, swimming pool, tennis. Closed Jan. 10–Feb. 15. MC, V. $$*

Girona **Ultònia's** attractive setting makes it Girona's best hotel. *Gran Via Jaume I 22, 08002, tel. 972/20–38–50, fax 972/20–33–34. 45 rooms. Facilities: coffee shop. AE, DC, MC, V. $$*

Vic **Parador de Vic** is 14 km (8½ mi) northeast of town on the road to Roda de Ter, with a stunning mountain setting and all the restrained good taste of the national chain. *Carretera Roda de Ter, 08500, tel. 93/888–3229 or 93/888–7211, fax 93/888–7311. 36 rooms. Facilities: coffee shop, garden, swimming pool, tennis. $$$*

The Costa Brava

The Costa Brava (rugged coast) is a jagged stretch of shoreline that begins at Lloret, northeast of Barcelona, and runs past 135 km (84 mi) of coves and beaches to the Franco-Spanish frontier town of Port-Bou. It is best to concentrate on selected pockets, just north of Tossa, around Cap de Begúr and around Cadaqués (*see above*), where the terrain is rocky and steep enough to have staved off the worst excesses of real-estate speculation. Here, on a good day, the luminous blue of the sea still contrasts with the red-brown headlands and cliffs; the distant lights of sardine boats reflect across wine-colored waters at dusk; and neat umbrella pines accompany you to the fringes of white, sandy beaches.

Arriving and Departing
By Car From Barcelona, go as if to Girona, leaving the autopista only when you are parallel with the bit you want to tackle, or you are in for a frustrating time competing with the coastal traffic.

By Train A slow train runs along the coast to Blanes, just south of Lloret, from Sants and Passeig de Gràcia.

By Bus Buses to Lloret, Tossa, Sant Feliu de Guíxols, Platja d'Aro, Palamós, Begúr, Roses, and Cadaqués are operated by **Sarfa** (Plaça Duc de Medinaceli 4, tel. 93/318–9434; metro: Drassanes).

Guided Tours Between May 1 and October 15, **Julià** and **Pullmantur** run coach and cruise tours, visiting the ports of Tossa, Lloret del Mar, and Fanals. A bus takes you from their Barcelona terminals (*see* Guided Tours, in Essential Information, above) up the coast to Tossa. From here, weather permitting, a boat will take you to the beach at Fanals, where you'll have time for swimming and lunch. Buses leave Barcelona at 9 AM, returning at 6 PM. The price per person is 9,000 pesetas, or 10,500 pesetas with lunch included.

Exploring
⑫ **Tossa** was the first place on the Costa Brava to attract foreigners, and one of the worst sufferers. It is only 23 km (15 mi) from here to Sant Feliu de Guíxols, but if you go by the beautiful coastal road, prepare for one sharp curve after another, as the road winds round innumerable deep-cut inlets. Parked cars indicate accessible coves, always involving a long walk down.

⑬ **Sant Feliu de Guíxols,** with its numerous *simpático* bars and restaurants, is much more agreeable than Tossa. Owing to the advent of plastics, the town has lost its cork industry and now lives from its port, fishing, and tourist trade. There is no beach, but a bus service runs to and from S'Agaró, 3 km (2 mi).

⑭ **S'Agaró,** one of the showpieces of the Costa Brava, is the creation of one man, José Ensesa, who bought the land to build his idea of a perfect seaside resort. Walk along the kilometer of hidden sea wall, beginning below the Hostal de la Gavina and ending at the magnificent Concha Beach.

Beyond S'Agaró, head for the rocky stretch opposite Palafrugell. Of the towns between the Cap de Sant Sebastià and Cap de Begúr, **Tamariu,** where umbrella pines fringe the silver-white strand, is the most beautiful.

⑮ Before stretching out on one of these idyllic beaches, visit **Roig,** reached by track from Calella, home to one of Spain's finest botanical gardens. *Admission: 350 pesetas. Open for guided visits, Mar.–Dec., daily 9–9; closed Jan. and Feb.*

Llafranc was an Iberian settlement in pre-Greek and pre-Roman times. From the 18th-century hermitage, with its Baroque sanctuary, set near the lighthouse that crowns the cape, you can see far along the loveliest stretch of the entire coast. From here to Aiguablava, the coast is precipitous and magnificent, but can be properly appreciated only from the sea. **Aiguablava** (Catalan for blue water) is a secluded little resort with a parador. Its beach at Fornells epitomizes what Mediterranean bathing should be—deep, clear blue water, sheltered by two headlands to form a natural yacht basin.

🔟 The neighboring town of **Begúr**, with a ruined medieval castle, contains a number of fine houses built during the last century by adventurers who went to Cuba to make their fortunes and returned to Spain rich enough to end their days in idle splendor.

If you are a devotee of the classics, don't miss visiting the Greek and Roman settlements at **Empúries**, 41 km (25 mi) north via Torroella. Emporion was founded by Greeks in 550 BC and used as an important trading station for three centuries until it was taken by the Romans, who built a larger city above the old Greek colony. *Admission: 350 pesetas. Open Apr.–Sept., Tues.–Sun. 9–7; Oct.–Mar., Tues.– Sun. 10–1 and 3–5; closed Mon.*

Dining
S'Agaró

La Gavina is a classy and elegant Relais and Chateaux hotel/restaurant. *Plaça de la Rosaleda, 08033, tel. 972/32–11–00. AE, MC, V.* $$$$

Sant Feliú

Eldorado Petit is the excellent (older) sister of its namesake in Barcelona. It serves diverse Catalan and international dishes. *Rambla Vidal 23, tel. 972/32–18–18. AE, MC, V.* $$$

Lodging
Aiguablava

Parador de la Costa Brava, stylish and modern, overlooks the bay. *Aiguablava, 08033, tel. 972/62–21–62, fax 972/62–21–66. AE, MC, V. Closed Nov.* $$$

Aiguablava has superb management and a delightful location above the beach. *Playa de Fornells, 08033, tel. 972/62–20–58, fax 972/62–21–12. AE, MC, V.* $$

9 Southern Catalunya and the Levante

Tarragona to Valencia

By Philip Eade

Updated by George Semler

This region straddles Catalunya (Catalonia) and Valencia, allowing you to compare the attributes of these two ancient kingdoms. The first thing that strikes visitors is the difference in language. Catalan prevails in Tarragona, a province of Catalunya, but Valenciano, a dialect of Catalan, is spoken and used in street signs in the Valencian provinces. The reason for this is that Jaime I (Jaume in Catalan), king of Catalunya, conquered Valencia in the 13th century, and the area became part of the Catalan empire until it was, in turn, incorporated into a united Spain in the 15th century.

The *huerta* (fertile, irrigated coastal plain) is largely devoted to citrus and vegetable farming, which lends color to the landscape and a fragrance to the air. Grayish, arid mountains provide a stark backdrop for the lush coast. These shores have seen Phoenician, Greek, Carthaginian, and Roman visitors. The Romans stayed several centuries, and there are archaeological reminders all the way down the coast, nowhere more so than in Tarragona, which was capital of Rome's Spanish empire by 218 BC. Rome's dominion did not go uncontested, the most serious challenge coming from the Carthaginians of North Africa. The three Punic Wars, fought over this territory between 264 BC and 146 BC, led to the immortalization of Hannibal, the most famous of the Carthaginian generals.

The coastal farmland and beaches that looked so attractive to the ancients have proved similarly popular for today's tourists, and a chain of ugly developments has marred much of the coast. Venturing inland, you discover a completely different world, where tourism is not the decisive fact of life and where local authenticity has survived intact. This rugged and often strikingly beautiful landscape is dotted with small fortified towns, several of which bear the name El Cid as proof of the battles he fought here against the Moors nine centuries ago. Each has its porticoed Plaza Mayor, whitewashed houses, and countless coats of arms as further reminders of the strategic importance of these towns in medieval times.

The city of Valencia, founded originally by the Greeks, was in Moorish hands from 712 to 1238, apart from a brief interlude from 1094 to 1102, when El Cid reconquered the city. The bright blue cupolas atop churches and the *azulejos* (glazed, patterned tiles) reflect Moorish traditions. Also striking are the products of Valencia's 15th-century Golden Age: the Gothic Lonja (silk exchange) and mansions and the Primitive paintings of Jacomart and Juan Reixach in the Fine Arts Museum. The flamboyant 18th-century Palacio de los Dos Aguas embodies the vitality of Churriguerismo, or early Spanish Baroque.

Essential Information

Important Addresses and Numbers

Tourist Information

Tourist offices that offer information covering the whole region are in **Castellón** (Plaza María Agustina 5, tel. 964/22–10–00), **Tarragona** (Ramon y Cajal 33, tel. 977/23–03–12), and **Valencia** (Paz 48, tel. 96/394–2222). Local tourist offices are as follows: **Benicàssim** (Médico Segarra 4, tel. 964/30–38–51), **Morella** (Torre San Miguel, tel. 964/17–30–32), **Peñíscola** (Paseo Marítimo, tel. 964/48–02–08), **Reus** (San Juan 27, tel. 977/32–03–49), **Sagunto** (Cronista Chabret, tel. 96/266–2213), **Tarragona** (Major 39, tel. 977/29–62–24), **Teruel** (Tomás Nogués 1, tel. 974/60–22–79), **Tortosa** (Plaza España, tel.

977/44–00–00), and **Valencia** (Paz 48, tel. 96/394–2222; and Estación RENFE, Játiva 24, tel. 96/352–8573).

There are information phone lines at Castellón (964/22–10–00) and Valencia (96/352–4000); in Valencia (Paz 46), a 24-hour machine dispenses information for 25-peseta coins.

Emergencies **Police:** tel. 091.

Ambulance: Castellón (Servicio Médico Urgencias, tel. 964/21–12–53), Gandesa (Servei d'Ambulancies, tel. 977/42–03–90), Morella (Cruz Roja, tel. 964/16–03–89), Tarragona (Creu Roja, tel. 977/23–65–11), and Valencia (Cruz Roja, tel. 96/380–2244).

General medical assistance: Castellón (Hospital Provincial, tel. 964/21–05–22), Morella (Ambulatorio, tel. 964/16–00–34), Tarragona (Hospital Joan XXIII, tel. 977/21–15–54), and Valencia (Hospital Clínico, tel. 96/368–2600).

Late-night Pharmacies Pharmacies (*farmacias de guardia*) operate on a rotating basis whereby one stays open 24 hours in every sizable town or city. To find the address of the one whose turn it is, look in the local press or on the door of any pharmacy.

Consulates **British:** Tarragona (Calle Real 33, 1º1ª, tel. 977/22–08–12). **U.S.** (agency only): Valencia (Ribera 3, tel. 96/351–6973).

Travel Agencies Tarragona: **Vibus SA** (Rambla Nova 125, tel. 977/21–91–56); Valencia: **Iberia** office (Paz 14, tel. 96/351–7237), and **Viajes Paz** (Paz 32, tel. 96/351–8080).

Arriving and Departing by Plane

The international airport nearest to the northern end of this tour is in **Barcelona** (*see* Chapter 8), 100 km (65 miles) from Tarragona. **Valencia** has an international airport (tel. 96/370–9500) with direct flights to London, Paris, Brussels, Frankfurt, and Milan. It is 8 km (5 mi) west of the center and best reached by taxi. For Iberia information, call 96/351–3739.

Arriving and Departing by Car, Train, Bus, and Boat

By Car The A7 *autopista* (motorway) provides excellent road access to the region at both ends. Having a car will be extremely valuable, even necessary, if you want to explore the inland areas of the Maestrazgo, where there is some excellent, uncrowded, and scenic motoring.

By Train Trains for Tarragona leave Barcelona's Passeig de Gràcia and Sants stations every half hour or so (*see* Chapter 8) or from Zaragoza. The RENFE office in Tarragona is at Rambla Nova 40 (tel. 977/23–25–34); the station is downhill from the Mediterranean balcony, south toward the port (tel. 977/24–02–02). Leaving the region at Valencia, you have a choice of train connections to Madrid, via Cuenca, or Alicante, via Játiva. The main station, Estación del Norte (tel. 96/352–0202), is on Calle Játiva, next to the bullring. It's very centrally located and involves only a short walk or cab ride to most hotels.

By Bus Again, the connection between Barcelona and Tarragona is easy; nine buses daily leave the Estación del Norte in Barcelona. **Bacoma, S.A.** (in Barcelona, tel. 93/231–3801) also dispatches buses from Tarragona (Plaça Imperial Tarraco s/n, tel. 977/22–20–72). From Valencia, buses continue down the coast and to Madrid. The bus depot is across the river (Av. Menendez Pidal 3, tel. 96/349–7222) and is reached by bus No. 8 from Plaza del Ayuntamiento.

By Boat **Trasmediterránea Ferries** (Av. Manuel Soto 15, tel. 96/367–6512, fax 96/367–3345) leave Valencia for Mallorca (Mon.–Sat.) and Ibiza (Tues. and Thurs. only).

Getting Around

By Car The roads are generally very good, but the main N340 becomes very clogged, and you're often much better off paying extra to use the autopista. For car rentals in Tarragona, **Avis** is at **Viajes Vibus** (Rambla Nova 125, tel. 977/21–91–56). In Valencia you have the choice of **Avis** (Isabel la Católica 17, tel. 96/351–0734), **Europcar** (Antiguo Reino de Valencia 7, tel. 96/374–1512, or airport, tel. 96/153–1369), or **Hertz** (Segorbe 7, tel. 96/341–5036, or airport, tel. 96/152–3791).

By Train Within the region, trains run more or less down the coast: Tarragona – Salou/Cambrils – Tortosa – Vinaròs – Peñíscola – Benicasim–Castellón–Sagunto–Valencia. A line also goes from Valencia to Zaragoza by way of Sagunto and Teruel, and local lines go around Valencia from the station on Cronista Rivelles (tel. 96/347–3750).

By Bus Again, connections up and down the coast between Tarragona and Valencia are frequent. Transport inland to Morella and Alcañiz can be arranged from Vinaròs, while Castellon or Sagunto have bus lines west to Teruel.

In Valencia buses provide the main method of public transport, and central services start from Plaza del Ayuntamiento. Services for the beaches and outlying suburbs leave from Plaza Puerta del Mar. The tourist office can supply details of bus routes.

Guided Tours

Orientation Tours For guided tours of Tarragona's sights, contact the municipal tourist office just below the cathedral (Carrer Major 39, tel. 977/23–22–08). The tour covers all the important archaeological sites, together with the cathedral. You can book guided tours of Valencia at the municipal tourist office (Plaza Ayuntamiento 1, tel. 96/351–0417). Leaving daily at 10 AM from the Ayuntamiento, a bilingual guide takes you around the Ayuntamiento itself, the Lonja, the cathedral, the Ceramics Museum, the bullring, the station, the Fine Arts Museum, and Viveros Park.

Special-Interest Tours RENFE (tel. 977/70–00–57) operates guided train tours of Amposta and the Ebro Delta, beginning and ending in Tarragona. In Amposta you'll visit the parish church of l'Assumpció, the Modernista Casa Fàbregues, and the bridge over the River Ebro before going on to a choice of a boat trip or bicycle ride around the delta proper.

In summer the municipal tourist office in Valencia (*see* Tourist Information, *above*) organizes tours of the Albufera, the marshlands to the south of Valencia, depending on demand. You tour the port area before continuing south to the Albufera lagoon, where you can visit a traditional *barraca* (thatched farmhouse). You'll end up in the Devesa Gardens, where you can hire boats to explore the canals through the paddy fields.

So, you're getting away from it all.

Just make sure you can get back.

AT&T Access Numbers
Dial the number of the country you're in to reach AT&T.

*AUSTRIA†††	022-903-011	*GREECE	00-800-1311	NORWAY	800-190-11
*BELGIUM	078-11-0010	*HUNGARY	00◇-800-01111	POLAND†♦2	0◇010-480-0111
BULGARIA	00-1800-0010	*ICELAND	999-001	PORTUGAL†	05017-1-288
CANADA	1-800-575-2222	IRELAND	1-800-550-000	ROMANIA	01-800-4288
CROATIA†♦	99-38-0011	ISRAEL	177-100-2727	*RUSSIA† (MOSCOW)	155-5042
*CYPRUS	080-90010	*ITALY	172-1011	SLOVAKIA	00-420-00101
*CZECH REPUBLIC	00-420-00101	KENYA†	0800-10	S. AFRICA	0-800-99-0123
*DENMARK	8001-0010	*LIECHTENSTEIN	155-00-11	SPAIN •	900-99-00-11
*EGYPT† (CAIRO)	510-0200	LITHUANIA♦	8◇196	*SWEDEN	020-795-611
*FINLAND	9800-100-10	LUXEMBOURG	0-800-0111	*SWITZERLAND	155-00-11
FRANCE	19◇-0011	F.Y.R. MACEDONIA	99-800-4288	*TURKEY	00-800-12277
*GAMBIA	00111	*MALTA	0800-890-110	UKRAINE†	8◇100-11
GERMANY	0130-0010	*NETHERLANDS	06-022-9111	UK	0500-89-0011

Countries in bold face permit country-to-country calling in addition to calls to the U.S. **World Connect**℠ prices consist of **USADirect**® rates plus an additional charge based on the country you are calling. Collect calling available to the U.S. only. *Public phones require deposit of coin or phone card. ◇Await second dial tone. †May not be available from every phone. †††Public phones require local coin payment through the call duration. ♦Not available from public phones. • Calling available to most European countries. 1Dial "02" first, outside Cairo. 2Dial 010-480-0111 from major Warsaw hotels. ©1994 AT&T.

Here's a travel tip that will make it easy to call back to the States. Dial the access number for the country you're visiting and connect right to AT&T. It's the quick way to get English-speaking AT&T operators and can minimize hotel telephone surcharges.

If all the countries you're visiting aren't listed above, call **1 800 241-5555** for a free wallet card with all AT&T access numbers. Easy international calling from AT&T. **TrueWorld Connections.**

AT&T

American Express offers Travelers Cheques built for two.

Cheques *for Two*℠ from American Express are the Travelers Cheques that allow either of you to use them because both of you have signed them. And only one of you needs to be present to purchase them.

Cheques *for Two* are accepted anywhere regular American Express Travelers Cheques are, which is just about everywhere. So stop by your bank, AAA* or any American Express Travel Service Office and ask for Cheques *for Two*.

Travelers Cheques

©1994 American Express Travel Related Services Company, Inc. *Available at participating clubs.

Bodegón Torre del Oro
Santander 15

Seville

Best Garlic chicken served
in individual Crock
pots. Delicious! Enjoy!

Exploring Southern Catalunya and the Levante

We begin our tour in Tarragona, which is distinguished by its extremely well-preserved Roman remains. Our second tour moves south to the Ebro Delta and the ancient town of Tortosa, where a splendid night can be spent in the hilltop parador. We make a rewarding loop inland here to explore the wild and remote Beceite and Maestrazgo mountains, the highlight being the ancient contoured town of Morella. Our third tour moves down the Costa del Azahar, characterized by orange groves against a backdrop of arid hills. Peñíscola, a cluster of white houses on a promontory, is very picturesque, although it is sadly becoming surrounded by tourist development. Farther south, the next stop of architectural note is the Roman town of Sagunto, with its hilltop fortress and amphitheater.

Our two final circuits explore Valencia, which offers a rich trove of art and architecture. Highlights include the Gothic Lonja (Silk Exchange), the outrageous Churrigueresque Palacio Marqués de Dos Aguas, and the superb Fine Arts Museum.

Highlights for First-time Visitors

Amphitheater, Sagunto (*see* Tour 3)
Amphitheater, Tarragona (*see* Tour 1)
Archaeological Museum, Tarragona (*see* Tour 1)
Cathedral, Tarragona (*see* Tour 1)
Fine Arts Museum, Valencia (*see* Tour 5)
Lonja, Valencia (*see* Tour 4)
Morella (*see* Tour 2)
Old town and castle, Peñíscola (*see* Tour 3)
Palacio Marqués de Dos Aguas, Valencia (*see* Tour 4)

Tour 1: Tarragona

Numbers in the margin correspond to points of interest on the Southern Catalunya and the Levante map.

❶ The name **Tarragona** promises rich classical remains, and the city does not disappoint. As capital of the Roman province of Tarraconensis (from 218 BC), Tarraco, as it was then called, formed the empire's principal stronghold in Spain. During the 1st century BC its population was double the present-day figure of 110,000, and the city was regarded as one of the empire's finest urban creations. Its wine was already famous, and the people were the first in Spain to become Roman citizens. St. Paul preached here in AD 58, and the city became the seat of the Christian Church in Spain until it was superseded by Toledo in the 11th century.

Coming from Barcelona, you pass by the **triumphal arch of Berà** (19 km/12 mi north of Tarragona), dating to the 3rd century BC, and from the Lleida road or autopista you can see the 1st century **Roman Aqueduct** that helped bring fresh water the 32 km (19 mi) from the River Gayo. Coming from the south, past the gasworks, you may think that modern Tarragona has forsaken her splendor, but, thankfully, some outstanding monuments remain and have received a valuable face-lift as part of city's preparations to host the 1993 World

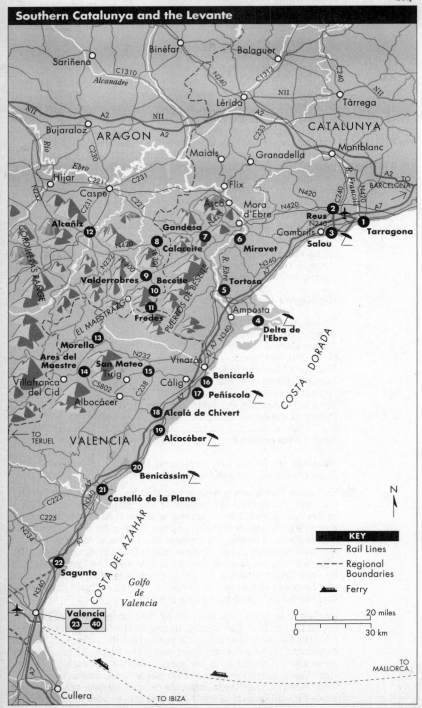

Southern Catalunya and the Levante

Sariñena

Binéfar

Balaguer

C1310

Alcanadre

N240

C1313

C240

Bujaraloz

Lérida

NII

Tàrrega

NII

ARAGON

A2

A2

NII

Maials

Granadella

Montblanc

Río

C230

Ebro

Flix

N420

C240

R. Francolí

A2

TO
BARCELONA

Híjar

C221

C231

Caspe

Ascó

Mora
d'Ebre

N420

A7

Reus

② ✈

①
Tarragona

N232

C231

C22

N420

Gandesa

⑦

⑥

Cambrils ○ **③**

N240

N420

A7

Alcañiz

⑫

⑧

Calaceite

Miravet

Salou

C400

N232

Valderrobres

⑨

Beceite

R. Ebre

Tortosa

N340

A7

⑩

⑤

N420

⑪

Fredes

PUERTOS DE BESEITE

Amposta

④

EL MAESTRAZGO

**Delta de
l'Ebre**

Morella

⑬

Vinaròs

COSTA DORADA

Ares del
Maestre

⑭

San Mateo
Tirig

N232

⑮

Cálig

Benicarló

⑯

Villafranca
del Cid

CS802

C238

⑰

Peñíscola

Albocácer

⑱

Alcalá de Chivert

TO
TERUEL

⑲

Alcocéber

VALENCIA

⑳

Benicàssim

N340

A7

㉑

Castelló de la Plana

C223

C225

N234

N340

A7

COSTA DEL AZAHAR

㉒

Sagunto

*Golfo
de
Valencia*

N

✈

Valencia

㉓ **㊵**

A7

TO
MALLORCA

Cullera

TO IBIZA

KEY

— Rail Lines

--- Regional
Boundaries

⛴ Ferry

0 ——— 20 miles

0 ——— 30 km

Archaeology Conference. Tarragona is clearly divided into old and new by the Rambla Vella: The old town and most of the Roman remains are to the north, while modern Tarragona spreads out to the south.

Start your tour at the acacia-lined Rambla Nova, at the end of which is a balcony overlooking the sea, the **Balcó del Mediterràni.** Walking leftward along the Passeig de les Palmeres, you arrive at a clear illustration of the dichotomy between ancient and modern. The remains of Tarragona's **amphitheater** are visible down toward the sea; above stands the modern semicircular Hotel Imperial Tarraco, artfully echoing the amphitheater's curve. If you descend the steps to the amphitheater, you will see just how well preserved it is. You are free to wander through the access tunnels and along the seating rows, and sitting with your back to the sea, you may understand why Augustus favored Tarragona as a winter resort. In the center of the amphitheater are the remains of two superimposed churches, the earlier of which was a Visigothic basilica built to mark the bloody martyrdom of Sant Fructuós and his deacons in AD 259. *Admission free. Open weekdays 10–7 (6 in winter), weekends 10–2.*

Cross the Rambla Vella to where students are excavating the vaults of the 1st-century AD Roman **Circus Maximus.** The plans just inside the gate show that the vaults you can see were only a small corner of a vast arena (320 m/350 yds long), where 23,000 spectators gathered to watch chariot racing. As medieval Tarragona grew, it gradually swamped the Circus. *Admission free. Open weekdays 10–1:45, weekends 10–1:45 and 4–7.*

Now head around the corner and up Passeig Sant Antoni to the tall former **Praetorium.** This was Augustus's town house and reputedly the birthplace of Pontius Pilate. It is Gothic-looking because of extensive alterations in the Middle Ages, when it served as the residence for the kings of Catalunya and Aragón during their visits to Tarragona. It now serves as the Museu d'Història (the city's History Museum), with plans showing the evolution of the city. The highlight is the Hippolytus sarcophagus, with a bas-relief depiction of the legend of Hippolytus and Fraeda, on the first floor. *Admission: 250 pesetas. Open Tues.–Sun. 10–1:30 and 4:30–8; closed Mon.*

Next door, a 1960s neoclassical building contains the **Museu Arqueològic** (Archaeological Museum), which has a collection of Roman statuary and domestic fittings. Look for the keys, bells, and belt buckles on the first floor. The beautiful mosaics displayed here include the Head of Medusa, famous for her piercing stare. *Admission: 250 pesetas. Open Apr.–Sept., Tues.–Sat. 10–1 and 4:30–8, Sun. 10–2; Oct.–Mar., Tues.–Sat. 10–1:30 and 4–7, Sun. 10–2; closed Mon.*

Follow Passeig Sant Antoni uphill, with the yellowish city walls to your left, and turn left up Passeig de Torroja to the gate through to the **Passeig Arqueològic.** This path skirts the formidable 3rd-century BC Ibero-Roman ramparts, built on pre-Iberian walls of giant rocks. You pass a curious oxidized bronze of what must be Romulus (founder of Rome) and Remus drinking from the udders of a she-wolf and, farther on, the glacis added by English engineers in 1707 to safeguard the city during the War of the Spanish Succession. *Admission: 250 pesetas. Open Apr.–Sept., Tues.–Sat. 10–8, Sun. 10–1; Oct.–Mar., Tues.–Sat. 10–1 and 3–6, Sun. 10–1; closed Mon.*

At the end, go through the arched Portada Roser (Rosary Gate) to Plaça Pallol, an old Roman **forum,** of which there is some evidence in a building on the left, Les Voltes, where the original Roman base has been surmounted by a Gothic upper story. Walking up Carrer Cavallers brings you to **Casa Castellarnau,** a Gothic mansion open as a museum, where you can see how a noble family of Tarragona once lived. Most impressive is the elaborate decor and furniture on the first floor, dating from the late 18th and the 19th century. The last member of the Castellarnau family vacated the house in 1954. *Admission: 250 pesetas. Open Mon.–Sat. 10–1 and 4–7, Sun. 10–1; closed Mon.*

This street leads into Carrer Major, full of rather pricey antiques stores. Turning right, downhill, brings you to the Plaça de la Font, home, at the far end, of the 19th-century neoclassical **Ajuntament** (Town Hall). Go left up to the cathedral.

Time Out At the foot of the cathedral steps on the left is the **Bar Vallmoll.** The decor is by no means sophisticated, but you can sit outside and drink a pitcher of the stiff local *priorato seco* (red wine), with a fine view of the cathedral.

Built in the 13th century on the site of the Roman Temple of Jupiter, mainly from blocks of Roman stone, the **cathedral** is a cross between the Romanesque and Gothic styles. The builders started with the former in the 12th century but switched when the latter came into vogue in the 13th century. You can see this in the main facade, where the central pointed Gothic portal is flanked by rounder Romanesque doors. The cathedral was never finished, leaving this main facade with a curious flat top. Entry is through the cloister (signposted), an idyllic, rose-garden enclosure that contrasts dramatically with the clustered columns of the stark interior. Look for the intricately decorated altarpiece of Santa Tecla in the main apse. Carved in 1470 by Pere Johan, it depicts the life of the city's patron, who was converted by the preaching of St. Paul on his visit to the city in AD 58. Harassed by unconverted townsfolk, Santa Tecla was saved each time by divine intervention. The showpiece of the museum is a rare Gothic tapestry. *Admission: 250 pesetas, including guide and museum. Open daily 10–1 and 4–7.*

Beside the cathedral, in Plaça de la Seu, you can catch a bus (No. 1) to the **Serallo** fishing quarter, where, at the quayside, boats create a hive of activity as they unload their catch. Sneak a look inside the market, where fish are swiftly auctioned off to impetuous fishmongers and restaurateurs. From here, go right, to the Passeig de la Independencia (also on the bus route), where just beyond the impressive tobacco factory is the **Necròpolis i Museu Paleocristià** (Paleochristian Tomb Museum). Both Christian and pagan tombs have been unearthed on this site. *Admission: 250 pesetas, free Tues. Open summer, Tues.–Sat. 10–1 and 4:30–8, Sun. 10–2; winter, Tues.–Sat. 10–1:30 and 4–7, Sun. 10–2; closed Mon.*

Tour 2: South Toward the Maestrazgo

2 **Reus** is an industrial town, 13 km (8 mi) inland from Tarragona along the N420 highway, with the distinction of having been the birthplace of Antoni Gaudí, as well as the longtime home of his fellow Moderniste architect, Lluís Domènech i Montaner. If Moderniste architecture interests you, Domènech's Casa Navàs is well worth the short detour. Following signs to the center, you arrive in the Plaça del Mercadal, where the Casa Navàs is beside the Ajuntament. The rich interior decoration includes mosaics, stained glass, tiles with characteristic Moderniste floral motifs, and weirdly shaped leather chairs. *Opening times are flexible; apply to the care-taker or the tourist office (San Juan 27, tel. 977/32–03–49).*

③ Turn onto the N240 and follow signs to **Salou,** a burgeoning beach resort with a long esplanade of young palms. If you can find the old port, it was from here that the conquerors of Mallorca set out in 1229. **Cambrils** is next, 7 km (4 mi) down the coast on N340, a target for gourmets who come to dine in the Gatell family restaurants (*see* Dining and Lodging, *below*). Less built-up than Salou, it also has a pretty marina.

The coast south of here doesn't have much to offer, and you may want to join the uncluttered autopista A7. The coastal N340 high-way tends to get very clogged, but the toll road will carry you rapid-ly to the **Delta de l'Ebre** (Ebro Delta). This flat piece of wetlands, resembling Holland, juts out into the Mediterranean; its Parc Natu-ral del Delta de L'Ebre is a major stopping and breeding place for huge numbers of birds. An impressive 60% of Europe's species are to be found here at some time during the year.

Take N230 south through orange groves. In Amposta, follow signs to Sant Jaume d'Enveja. You are now in the delta proper, weaving through rice fields. At Enveja you can get the ferry across to Deltebre. The Park Information Office (Plaça 20 de Maig, tel. 977/48–96–79) will tell you how to visit the reserve, which occupies the northeastern shore. West of here dramatic mountains soon rise, and farther on, the predominant agriculture switches from the vine to the orange tree.

⑤ Take C235 inland 10 km (6 mi) to the ancient town of **Tortosa,** which straddles the River Ebro. It was successively Roman, Visigothic, Moorish, and Christian. The parador, set in the ruined hilltop castle of La Zuda, is worth visiting even if you don't plan to stay here; keep to the left bank of the river and follow the signs. Originally a Tem-plar fortress, the citadel (and town) passed, around 713, into the hands of the Moors, who kept it until its reconquest by Ramón Berenguer IV, count of Barcelona, in 1153. For more than three cen-turies, Moors, Christians, and Jews lived peacefully together in the town. There are sweeping views from the castle walls across the fer-tile Ebro Valley to the Beceite Mountains.

Look for the cathedral from up here and then follow your nose to-ward it through the warren of streets. On the way, visit the Renais-sance Colegio Sant Lluís, which has a pretty arcaded patio, embellished with a frieze depicting the kings of Aragón. The **cathe-dral**'s main facade is Baroque, although if you enter through the cloister, you can see that behind the facade lies a pure Gothic design. It was common in Spain during the 18th century to tack these exu-berant stuccos onto the existing Gothic facade. The name given to the style is Churrigueresque, after its earliest practitioner, José Churriguera. *Cloister open daily; cathedral open for services only.*

Tortosa was the scene of one of the civil war's bloodiest battles. The Republicans, loyal to the democratically elected government and al-ready in control of Catalunya, crossed the Ebro here in July 1936 to attack the rebel Nationalists' rearguard. They got no farther than Tortosa, though, and were pinned down in trenches until they were forced to retreat with the loss of 150,000 lives. A conspicuously Na-tionalist monument rises from the Ebro to commemorate the victory of Franco's forces.

Leaving Tortosa to follow the Ebro upstream, you have a choice of routes: If you have time and a spirit of adventure, you can choose the east bank; a twisty and hilly drive through citrus groves and time-less stone villages keeps you within sight of the river. Allow an hour to cover the 40 km (25 mi) to Mora d'Ebre, and from there it is another 24 km (14 mi) to Gandesa along a faster road. You can try the ferry

6 across at **Miravet,** 9 km (5½ mi) before Mora, to cut the corner. Miravet has a large ruined Templar fortress-monastery in a dramatic rock setting, but don't count on the ferry, whose timetable cannot be described as regular.

The drive along the west bank is dramatic, too, and more direct, although it leaves the river after 10 km (6 mi). As the road climbs, the orange gives way to the olive and, farther on, to pine. West of the road are the craggy Beceite Mountains, which rise to 1,434 m (4,704 ft). In winter you can encounter a radical change in weather and temperature as you climb; you may easily find yourself in cloud or fog, having left Tortosa in sunshine. By this route it takes 45 minutes to reach Gandesa.

7 Renowned for its strong wine (up to 16% alcohol), **Gandesa** also contains two architectural landmarks. Out on the Mora road is the extraordinary Cooperativa Agrícola (Wine Cooperative; open working hours; closed Sun.), designed by the Moderniste architect Cèsar Martinell in 1919. Its white Islamic-looking facade does little to prepare you for the remarkable vaulting inside, constructed entirely of small bricks ingeniously arranged to allow for expansion and contraction. It is a working building, and you can buy some of the local wine here for a sleepy picnic on the way to Alcañiz or Beceite. Visit also the parish church (open daily) in the center of town, L'Assumpció, where the geometric patterns on the otherwise Romanesque doorway are attributed to Moorish influence.

Head west now along N420. The Beceite Mountains are again on your left, revealing their broader side. After 15 km (9 mi) you cross the border into the Aragonese province of Teruel. Turn right at

8 **Calaceite** to explore its ancient labyrinthine streets, which assemble at the arcaded Plaza Porticada. If a closer inspection of the Beceite massif interests you, go left at the Calaceite crossroads along TE301. Almost immediately on your right are some crumbling ocher walls marking the site of an ancient Iberian settlement. Turn right

9 after 18 km (11 mi) at a T-junction to reach **Valderrobres,** with a fortress palace and Renaissance town hall, thought to be so typical and elegant that it was reproduced in Barcelona's Poble Espanyol in 1929.

10 Continue to **Beceite,** and through here follow signs to a *panorama* for a bumpy drive along a track culminating in an impressive vista. Depending on the condition of these forest roads, you can drive all

11 the way to **Fredes,** due south of Beceite. Near here, on the Tossal dels Tres Reis (1,357 m/4,450 ft), the kings of Catalunya, Aragón, and Valencia are said to have met to iron out disputes. The best way to explore these hills is either by hiking or on horseback; a sign on the way into Beceite points you toward the tourist office, which provides maps of trails and arranges horseback riding. From Valderrobres, you can cut back to the Alcañiz road via TE300, which follows the River Matarraña.

12 **Alcañiz** lies on a plain and is encircled by the River Guadalope. It is surrounded by ugly modern apartment blocks, the result of a recent population explosion, stemming from the success of the surrounding olive and almond orchards. The highway (N420) enters the town along a modern street, busy with new construction. For the old town, turn left at the end of this street to Plaza Mayor. On the right is the Lonja (Exchange), with pointed arches defining its Gothic origin. Adjoining it on the corner is the Renaissance Ayuntamiento. The galleries and overhanging eaves on both these buildings mark them as Aragonese. The Collegiata Church, with its rhythmic Baroque facade, looms over the plaza. The ornate portal is very impressive, but the painted interior is disappointing. Next, climb to the hilltop castle, seat in the 14th century of the Calatrava knights and now a tiny parador.

Cut back from Alcañiz along the same N420 into the rugged hills known as El Maestrazgo (literally, "Domain of Knights"). Turn right after 15 km (9 mi) onto N232, toward Morella. This wild area offers the adventurous traveler some dramatic scenery, full of gorges, precipices, and rocky crags. Scattered throughout are villages that have changed little in the past 100 years.

El Cid charged through here nine centuries ago in his battle to wrest the Kingdom of Valencia from the Moors. This campaign, initially fought on behalf of King Alfonso VI of León and Castile but later as a private venture, began in 1088 and culminated in El Cid's capture of Valencia in 1094 (*see* Tour 4: Valencia Center, *below*). Many towns still bear his name.

13 You cross the border into Castellón, the northernmost Valencian province, 10 km (6 mi) farther on. The walled town of **Morella** stands on a towering crag, which is not immediately evident from the northern approach. To the south and east, the land drops away sharply, rendering it a natural fortress—one that was the scene of several bloody battles. Before you reach the town walls, you pass a well-preserved 14th-century aqueduct. The castle, the town's most prominent feature, can be reached through the gate on Plaza de San Francisco, on the uppermost of the town's contoured streets. Just inside the gate is the ruined cloister of an old Franciscan monastery. The walk up to the summit castle takes a good 15 minutes; the often high winds contribute to its air of impregnability. In 1088 El Cid scaled these walls and wrought havoc among the occupying Moors. During the Carlist Wars, the castle became a stronghold for General Cabrera, who captured Morella in 1838 for the pretender to the Spanish throne, Don Carlos. *Admission free. Open Oct.–Mar., daily 10–2 and 3–6; Apr.–Sept., daily 10–2 and 3–8.*

Walking left from the castle down Calle Hospital brings you to the beautiful church of **Santa María la Mayor.** Its blue-tile dome lends it an exoticism that complements the otherwise Gothic structure. The larger of the two doorways dates from the 14th century and depicts the Apostles. The raised flat-vaulted choir is reached by a spiral marble staircase. The sanctuary has received the full Baroque treatment, as has the high altar, which would glisten were it not for the gloom of the interior. The museum has a painting by Francisco Ribalta and some 15thcentury Gothic panels. *Admission free. Open daily 10–6.*

Descend the stepped Calle Cuesta de Prades to the arcaded Calle Don Blasco de Alagón, the town's main thoroughfare. There are numerous bars here, which are packed on the weekends. If you go right, you soon arrive at the old mansion of Cardinal Ram, now a hotel, and continuing uphill brings you into the pretty Plaza de los Estudios, whose white houses are distinguished by attractive wood balconies.

Leave Morella on N232. You can extend your Maestrazgo exploration by turning right 2 km (1 mi) out of Morella, just after the 57-km (35-mi) marker. This new road may not be signposted, but it does appear on some newer maps. If you get lost, ask for the new road to Villafranca del Cid. Ignore all the roads to the right, but after 16 km (9 mi) turn left at a T-junction and quickly left again toward

⑭ Albocácer (CS802). **Ares del Maestre** has the most dramatic site of any village in this area. Like Morella, it rests on a crag, but here the drop is more severe and the vistas are more rewarding. The village features a ruined castle (admission free; open daily). The ascent is a very windy climb in winter and a scorching one in the summer.

Time Out On the pass over which CS802 runs, just before you arrive at Ares del Maestre, is **Mesón el Coll** (tel. 964/44–16–85). This family-run restaurant serves a delicious set menu of local specialties. Try the *olla de Ares*, a thick stew typical of the Maestrazgo.

From Ares del Maestre, CS802 descends to Albocácer. Turn left **⑮** here to Tirig and continue to **San Mateo.** This small town proudly bears the title Capital del Maestrazgo because it was from here that King Jaime I set out on his decisive reconquering raids in the 13th century, freeing the region finally from Moorish control. The legacy of its regal past consists of sturdy Gothic mansions near the Plaza Mayor. Visit the Archpriest's Church on the corner of the plaza. Its nave is a fine example of the Catalan Gothic style; the vault covers a wide expanse, dispensing with the need for columns. The coast is now close again, and the nearest place to make for is Benicarló via Cervera del Maestre and Cálig.

Tour 3: The Costa del Azahar

⑯ **Benicarló** is the middle of the three northernmost towns of the Costa del Azahar, the stretch so called after the orange blossom whose fragrant aroma pervades the countryside inland. The entire central Mediterranean coastal area around Valencia is traditionally referred to as the Levante, or simply "east," where the sun rises (*se levanta*), and in ancient times was a favored place for Phoenician (Syrian) trading ships. Some of today's inhabitants still have a strongly Semitic countenance not found elsewhere in Spain. The Phoenicians never attempted the conquest of Spain, contenting themselves with trading posts. But it was these people, as they patrolled this stretch of coast and gazed uneasily at the menacing backdrop of mountains, who, according to one version, gave the country its present name—Spagna, or "hidden land."

Once an oasis, the area is now a busy haven for vacationers. Benicarló and Vinaròs, to the north, have suffered quite severely at the hands of the tourist building boom. Both have Baroque churches with characteristic blue-tile domes.

⑰ **Peñíscola,** 8 km (5 mi) down the coast, owes its foundation to the Phoenicians. It later became the bridgehead by which the Carthaginian Hamilcar (father of Hannibal) imported his elephants and munitions to wage the first of the three Punic Wars. Carthaginian influence in the peninsula rose to its zenith some 20 years later, in 230 BC, but was eroded by Rome's success in the subsequent campaigns.

The old town is a cluster of white-painted houses and tiny narrow streets leading up to the castle, whose promontory setting affords a perfect surveillance of the coast. You can drive up to the **castle,** but in summer it would be wiser to leave your car by the town walls and walk. Of chief interest now are the chapel and study of the Antipope Papa Luna, to whom the 14th-century castle passed in the 15th century. Hardly any of his effects remain, but while in his drafty quarters try to imagine this 90-year-old Frenchman, formerly Pope Benedict XIII, passing the last six years of his life attending Mass and composing schismatic bulls, while all the time surrounded by hostile Moorish townsfolk. *Admission: 250 pesetas. Open Apr.–Sept., daily 10–8:30; Oct.–Mar., daily 10–1 and 3:15–5:30.*

Leave Peñíscola on CS500, which angles away from the coast through carob and orange plantations. In summer the autopista is a far quicker way of heading south, but if you're in no mad rush, N340 shares the same scenery and allows access to places èn route. One

(18) town you pass on the right is **Alcalá de Chivert,** which boasts the tallest belfry in the Valencian provinces. The road here is cut off from the sea by the Sierra de Hirta, whose rugged outlines contain some ruined castles easily visible from the road. On the coast near here,

(19) **Alcocéber** is an expanding but still quiet holiday town with two good beaches.

(20) **Benicàssim** (salida 45 from the autopista) derives its appeal from the dramatic shapes in its mountainous background. Approach it by way of the coast road, which leaves N340 just before the town. Besides the setting, there is a long, sandy bathing beach and plenty of disco-type action at night.

(21) You are now very near the provincial capital, **Castelló de la Plana,** but there is nothing here to warrant the struggle through its suburbs unless you are an admirer of the Spanish Baroque painter Zurbarán, 10 of whose works are in the **Convento de las Religiosas Capuchinas** on Calle Nuñez de Arce (open for services).

(22) Again, the autopista is the best way of speeding you to **Sagunto,** 65 km (40 mi) from Benicàssim. If you were force-fed Caesar's history at school, the Roman name, Saguntum, will ring bells as the sparking point for the Second Punic War. When Hannibal laid seige to the town (at that time a port on the coast, from which the sea has since receded), the people heroically held out, faithfully expecting a Roman relief force, and burned the town rather than surrender to the Carthaginians.

Rambling Moorish hilltop fortifications dominate the town, and within this citadel earlier Roman remains are now being excavated. On the way up, visit the well-restored **amphitheater** (signposted from the town center), more complete than at Tarragona and a product of the Roman rebuilding five years after Hannibal's siege. Some of the finds from this era are housed in a fascinating and manageable museum just opposite the amphitheater. *Admission to amphitheater and museum: 300 pesetas. Open Tues.–Sat. 10–2 and 4–6, Sun. 10–2; closed Mon.*

Tour 4: Valencia Center

(23) It is only 23 km (14 mi) from Sagunto to **Valencia,** the third city of Spain, roughly equidistant from its two bigger sisters, Barcelona and Madrid, and the capital of the Levante.

Valencia's situation on a fertile *huerta* (or irrigated zone) has been fiercely contested ever since its foundation by the Greeks. El Cid captured the city from the Moors in 1094, and in 1099 won his strangest victory here: His corpse was strapped to his saddle and so frightened the waiting Moors as to cause a complete rout. In 1102, his widow, Jimena, was forced to return the city to Moorish rule; Jaume I finally drove them out in 1238.

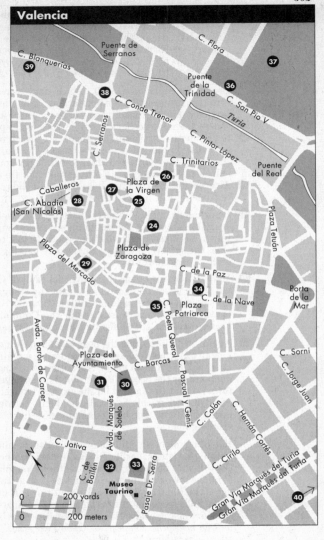

It is a somewhat confusing place, uneasily poised between old and new, with many of its finer monuments having suffered destruction or damage. The city walls were pulled down late in the 19th century in order to build a ring road and provide employment for the poor, and its river, the Turia, was later diverted to the south to prevent further flood damage, leaving the city's beautiful *puentes* (bridges) to span a municipal park.

Numbers in the margin correspond to points of interest on the Valencia map.

The city's historic buildings cluster around the 14th-century **catedral** (cathedral) in the Plaza de Zaragoza, a convenient place to begin your visit. The cathedral can be entered by three portals, respectively Romanesque, Gothic, and Rococo, the last leading off Plaza de Zaragoza. In the interior, Renaissance and Baroque marbles have been removed, as is now the trend in Spanish churches, in a successful restoration of the original pure Gothic.

In a side chapel is a purple agate chalice, said to be the Holy Grail (Christ's cup at the Last Supper), which, it is claimed, was brought to Spain in the 4th century. The most interesting feature of the museum (admission: 250 pesetas) is Goya's famous painting of St. Francis Borgia surrounded by devils eagerly awaiting his demise, on display in the treasury. *Open Mar.–Oct., daily 10–1 and 4–6; Nov.–Feb., daily 10–1.*

Dominating the cathedral at the near corner is the octagonal Miguelete Tower, which you can climb from inside the cathedral for good views over the city; 300 belfries are said to be visible. *Admission: 200 pesetas. Open daily 10:30–1 and 4:30–6:30.*

㉕ Leaving the cathedral by the Gothic Apostle Door brings you out into the trafficless **Plaza de la Virgen,** a lovely place for a drink in the late afternoon. Next to its portal, market gardeners of the huerta bring their irrigation disputes before the Water Tribunal, which has met every Thursday noon since 1350. Verdicts are given on the spot, and sentences range from fines to deprivation of water.

㉖ To the right of the plaza, down Calle Almudín, stands the old 14th-century granary, the **Almudín,** housing the **Museo de Paleontología,** which has an impressive collection of bones (including antediluvian skeletons from Argentina!) and shells. *Admission free. Open Oct.–May, Tues.–Fri. 10–1 and 4–6:30, weekends 10–1; June–Sept., Tues.–Sun. 10–1; closed Mon.*

㉗ On the left of the plaza, fronted by orange trees and box hedges, is the elegant east facade of the Gothic **Palau de la Generalitat,** home of the Valencia Cortes (Parliament) until its suppression by Philip V for supporting the wrong (losing) side during the War of the Spanish Succession. The two *salones* (reception rooms) in the elder of the two towers have superb woodwork on the ceilings. *Open weekdays 9–2. Permission required (tel. 96/332–0206).*

㉘ Next walk down Calle Caballeros (Horseman's Street), and look for the high door knockers, which could be reached without dismounting. Go left, down the tiny Calle Abadía San Nicolás (just after No. 41), to reach a small plaza containing Valencia's oldest church, **San Nicolás,** once the parish of the Borgia Pope Calixtus III. The first portal you come to, with a tacked-on rococo bas-relief of the Virgin Mary with cherubs, gives a good hint of what's inside, where every inch of the originally Gothic church has been covered with Churrigueresque embellishments.

㉙ Make your way from here to the **Lonja de la Seda** (Silk Exchange) by maintaining your direction downhill and turning left into Plaza del Mercado. The 15th-century Lonja is a product of the Golden Era here, when arts came under the patronage of Don Fernando de Antequerra, and it is generally held to be one of Spain's finest Gothic buildings. The perfect Gothic facade, dotted with ghoulish gargoyles, is complemented inside by high vaulting and twisted columns. *Admission free. Open Tues.–Fri. 10–2 and 4–8, weekends 10–1; closed Mon.*

㉚ Opposite stands the Iglesia de los Santos Juanes, whose interior was destroyed during the civil war, and, next to this, the Modernista Mercado Central (market), constructed entirely of iron and glass. Continue down Avenida María Cristina to the **Plaza del Ayun-**

tamiento. This is the hub of the city's life, a fact well conveyed by the massiveness of the Baroque facades.

Time Out On the right-hand side, at No. 2, is **Barrachina,** a venerable Valencian institution famous throughout Spain. It is a bar, café, restaurant, and delicatessen.

③① Just beyond Barrachina is the **Ayuntamiento** itself, which houses the municipal tourist office and a museum of the city's history. *Admission free. Open Sun.–Fri. 9–2; closed Sat.*

③② You can see the **Estación** (station) ahead of you, down Avenida Marqués de Sotelo. This is a splendid Modernista structure, designed by Demetrio Ribes Mano in 1917, replete with citrus motifs to let travelers know where it is they've arrived.

③③ Adjacent stands the **Plaza de Toros** (bullring); the best bullfighters are featured on July 25 and during the Fallas in March. The **Museo Taurino,** just beyond, down Pasaje Dr. Serra, is packed with bullfighting memorabilia, bulls' heads, and matadors' swords from this, one of Spain's oldest bullrings. *Admission free. Open weekdays 10–1:30; closed weekends.*

Head now along Calle Colón and take the first left up Calle Pascual y Genís, which runs into Calle Poeta Querol. Off to the right, down
③④ Calle Salva, is the Plaza Patriarca, where on the far side is the **Real Colegio del Patriarca.** Founded by San Juan de Ribera in the 16th century, it has a lovely Renaissance patio and an ornate church, and its museum contains works by Juan de Juanes, Francisco Ribalta, and El Greco. The entrance is off Calle de la Nave. *Admission: 200 pesetas. Open daily 11–1:30.*

Turning back to Calle Poeta Querol, you are soon face-to-face with
③⑤ the elaborate wedding-cake facade of the **Palacio del Marqués de Dos Aguas.** The famous Churrigueresque facade around the corner centers on the figures of the *Dos Aguas* (Two Waters) carved by Ignacio Vergara in the 18th century. The palace contains the **Ceramics Museum,** with a magnificent collection of mostly local ware, the highlight being the Valencian kitchen on the second floor. *Admission to palace and museum: 300 pesetas. Open Tues.–Sat. 10–2 and 4–6, Sun. 10–2; closed Mon.*

Tour 5: Outer Valencia

③⑥ Foremost among the more dispersed sights is the **Museo de Bellas Artes** (Fine Arts Museum), one of Spain's best art galleries. To get there, cross the riverbed by Puente de la Trinidad to No. 9, Calle San Pio V. On the first floor are the Valencian Primitives: In the 15th century Valencia was a thriving center of artistic talent, and many of the best works by Jacomart and Juan Reixach are here. Hieronymus Bosch, or El Bosco, as they call him here, is also represented. Still on the first floor are the murky 17th-century Tenebrist masterpieces of Francisco Ribalta and his pupil José Ribera, together with a Velázquez self-portrait and a room devoted to Goya. Upstairs, look for Joaquín Sorolla (gallery 66), the luminous Valencian painter of 19th-century Spanish everyday life. *Admission: 300 pesetas. Open Tues.–Sat. 10–2 and 4–6, Sun. 10–2; closed Mon.*

③⑦ Adjacent are the **Jardines del Real,** or Viveros, a pleasant park with fountains, rose gardens, tree-lined avenues, and a small zoo (open 9–dusk). On the way back you can cross Puente de Serranos to the
③⑧ **Torre Serranos,** a 14th-century fortified gate guarding the entrance

to the old city. Turning right, down Calle Blanquerías, at No. 23, is the **Casa Museo José Benlliure,** the elegant house of the modern Valencian painter/sculptor, which contains many of his works. *Admission free. Open Sept.–July, Tues.–Fri. 10–1:30 and 4–6, Sat. 10–1:30; Aug., Tues.–Fri. 10–1:30, Sat. 10–1:30; closed Sun. and Mon.*

After this, you could stroll south down the nascent riverbed park to the modern **Palau de la Música** (Concert Hall), whose location brings to mind the Sydney, Australia, opera house; for performance listings, look in the *Turia* guide.

What to See and Do with Children

The best **beach** for children is the southernmost one in Alcocéber, which is quiet and small. Or go for a few laps at one of the many *pistas de karts* (go-karting circuits); try the **Karting Benicàssim** (Av. Gimeno Tomás, Benicàssim, tel. 964/30–04–95). Check carefully that you are satisfied with the safety arrangements.

The **Grutas** (Caves) **de San José,** just west of Vall de Uxó, 25 km (15 mi) south of Castellón, are a spectacularly haunting setting in which to expand young imaginations. A guided tour, part by foot and part by boat, takes you through an incredible underground river. *Admission: 850 pesetas. Open daily 10:50–1 and 2:50–5 (dusk in summer).*

In Valencia, the **zoo** in the Jardines del Real (*see* Tour 5: Outer Valencia, *above*) is a safe bet to entertain youngsters.

Off the Beaten Track

The Maestrazgo and mountains farther south offer a wealth of unexplored territory. From Morella, follow the route of Tour 2 as far as Ares del Maestre before backtracking to **Villafranca del Cid** along the same CS802; then follow TE811, by way of Mosqueruela, to Teruel. Just before Linares de Mora, a right turn leads to the tiny ski station at **Valdelinares** where lodging can be found at the Meson de la Nieve (tel. 974/80–10–83) in the nearby village of La Virgen de la Vega. The ocher-red stone town of Valdelinares proclaims itself the third-highest village in Aragón; the other two are in the Pyrenees. **Linares de Mora** has a splendid site on a bend in the river, overlooked by tall cliffs. It's worth stopping to buy some of the delicious local ham produced here. Complete the trek across to Teruel via Mora de Rubielos.

Teruel is famous for Mudéjar architecture. Visit the Mudéjar Towers, built between the 12th and 16th centuries in a style more reminiscent of a Muslim minaret than a Christian belfry. The highlight in the cathedral is the coffered ceiling with 13th-century court and hunting scenes, visible from the upper gallery.

Shopping

Antiques/ Bric-a-brac You will have to be careful with the prices—haggle well—but Carrer Major in Tarragona has some exciting antiques stores, worth a thorough rummage, because the gems tend to be hidden away. Try also just in front of the cathedral and in the Plaza la Seu; **Antigüedades Ciria** (Plaza la Seu 2) has an interesting selection. In Valencia try **Salvador Ribes** (Vilaragut 7) for top-quality antiques with correspondingly daunting price tags. A local crafts market is held every day (10–8) in Plaza Alfonso Magnánimo at the bottom of Calle de la Paz. A flea market is held every Sunday morning in the streets around the cathedral.

Ceramics Just south of Cambrils, N340 is flanked by numerous tempting stores, with vast ranges of colorful Catalan pots and tiles at affordable prices. Farther south, the region inland from Castellón is a major ceramics-production area, and there are factories in Alcora, famed for its Rococo decoration, and Onda. In Valencia you can buy the famous Lladró porcelain or the slightly cheaper version, Nao porcelain; both of these are made locally. Check with the tourist office in the Ayuntamiento, which occasionally arranges visits to the factory. In Valencia itself, try **Cerámicas Lladró** (Poeta Querol 9) for purchases. Manises, 9 km (5½ mi) west of Valencia, is another center for Valencian ceramics, especially famous for its azulejos.

Textiles The Maestrazgo region produces brightly colored woven wool textiles. The best buys are the striped *mantas morellanas* (Morellan bedspreads). Morella's calles Blasco de Alagón and Hospital are good places to shop for them.

Sports

Golf The area is well provided with courses, all of them near to or on the coast. Call in advance to reserve tee times. Listed geographically north to south, they are: Club de Golf Costa Dorada (Apdo. 600, Tarragona, tel. 977/65–54–16), 9 holes; Club de Golf Costa de Azahar (Carretera Grao-Benicàssim, Grao de Castellón, tel. 964/28–09–79), 9 holes; Club de Campo del Mediterráneo (Urbanización La Coma, Borriol, Castellón, tel. 964/32–12–27), 18 holes; Club de Campo El Bosque (Chiva, 31 km/19 mi west of Valencia, tel. 96/326–3800), 18 holes; Club de Golf Escorpión (Apdo. 1, Betera, Valencia, tel. 96/160–1211), 18 holes; Campo de Golf de Manises (Apdo. 22029, Valencia, tel. 96/152–3804), 9 holes; Campo de Golf El Saler (Apdo. 9034, Valencia, tel. 96/161–1186), 18 holes.

Hunting/ Shooting For information and permits, contact the local wilderness management authorities in Tarragona (Av. Catalunya 50/51, tel. 977/21–79–28), Teruel (San Vicente 29), or Valencia (San Vicente 83, tel. 96/352–3369). You will need your passport, shooting license, and a temporary license issued by the relevant regional authority in Spain. The options include hunting the *cabra hispánica* (wild goat) in the **Beceite Mountains** (September–December), and outstanding waterfowl shooting on the **Ebro Delta** and the **Albufera lagoon** (October–February).

Sailing The safe waters off the coast make for good sailing conditions. Ask at local tourist offices or just chance upon places where you can rent boats. Some possibilities are Club Náutico Tarragona (port, tel. 977/24–03–60), Club Náutico Salou (Espigón del Muelle, no phone), Club Náutico Castellón (port, tel. 964/22–27–64), and Club Náutico Valencia (Camino del Canal 91, tel. 96/367–9011).

Beaches

If you've just come from the Costa Brava, you may well find the beaches in this area disappointing. There are, however, some good ones if you're careful with your choice. **Salou** has the best beaches at the northern end; there's a lively palm-lined promenade, and the sea is safe for youngsters. More tranquil are the beaches of the Ebro Delta: The best is the **Playa de los Eucalyptus**, reached by a pretty road from Amposta via Els Muntells. **Peñíscola**'s beach is seemingly never-ending; the sand is soft, and the old city rising up out of the sea at one end provides a scenic bonus. **Alcocéber** has a series of small, uncrowded, sandy crescents. Just to the north is the sophisticated new marina at Las Fuentes. **Benicàssim**'s long, crescent-shape beach has the most dramatic setting of all, with mountains rising steeply in the background. Valencia itself has a long beach that is great for sunning and for the numerous seaside restaurants, but not necessarily advisable for swimming. For cleaner water you need to head south as far as El Saler.

Dining and Lodging

Dining

Romesco (a spicy blend of hazelnuts, peppers, and olive oil) hails from Tarragona and is used as a sauce for fish and seafood, as well as a seasoning for salads. If you are here during the Festival of Santa Tecla, you can try the *espineta amb cargolins* (tuna fish with snails). You can accompany this with excellent wine from the nearby Penedés or Priorato vineyards. The Ebro Delta is renowned for its fresh fish—eels, in particular; *rossejat* (fried rice in a fish broth, dressed with garlic sauce) is another local specialty. *Jamones* (hams), *cecinas* (smoked meats) and *carnes a la brasa* (meats cooked over coals) all feature in Maestrazgan cooking, together with good *trucha* (trout) and *conejo* (rabbit). You should also try the *trufas* (truffles) that grow here. In Valencia and down the coast you are in the land of Spain's national dish, *paella valenciana* (based on rice flavored with saffron and embellished with tidbits of seafood, poultry, and/or meat). Prepared to order in a *caldero* (shallow pan), it takes a good 20 minutes to cook, so it is not for visitors in a hurry. Nor should it be chosen from a *menú del día*, when it is likely to be stodgy from having sat around. The alternative is *arroz a banda*, for which the fish and rice are cooked separately; the fish is fried in garlic, onion, and tomato, after which the rice is boiled in the resulting stock. Dress is casual but neat unless otherwise specified.

Highly recommended restaurants are indicated by a star ★.

Category	Cost*
$$$$	over 6,000 ptas
$$$	4,000–6,000 ptas
$$	2,000–4,000 ptas
$	under 2,000 ptas

per person, excluding drinks, service, and tax

Lodging

Tarragona's hotels are fairly uninspiring, but this is well compensated for by the time you reach the Ebro and the Maestrazgo, where antique one-of-a-kind places are in convenient abundance. Back on the coast, lodgings become more mundane, with modern high rises the predominant style. The selection of hotels elsewhere down the coast is provided more for the convenience of anyone who especially wishes to stop in these places than because the hotels themselves are particularly recommended. Just to the north and south of Valencia, in Puzol and El Saler, are some famous luxury hotels, while in the city itself there is a reasonable range, old and modern, to suit all pockets. If you plan to be in Valencia for its Falla celebrations, March 12–19, it is worthwhile to book your accommodations months ahead and to check whether prices are going to rise.

Highly recommended hotels are indicated by a star ★.

Category	Cost*
$$$$	over 16,500 ptas
$$$	9,500–16,500 ptas
$$	6,000–9,500 ptas
$	under 6,000 ptas

All prices are for a standard double room, excluding tax.

Alcañiz
Dining and Lodging
★

Parador de la Concordia. Installed in the sturdy castle of the Calatrava Knights, this hotel grandly surveys the surrounding fertile olive-growing plain and foothills of the Maestrazgo. Bedrooms have terra-cotta tile floors, patterned rugs, dark furniture, generous beds, and shutters. All have a good view. The restaurant serves *aragonés* specialties such as *cordero chilindrón* (lamb with a sauce of tomato, garlic, and peppers). *Castillo de Calatrara, Alcañiz, 44600 Teruel, tel. 974/83–04–00, fax 974/83–03–66. 12 rooms with bath. Facilities: restaurant, bar, parking. AE, DC, MC, V. Closed Dec. 15–Jan. 31. $$$*

Altafulla
Dining and Lodging
★

Faristol. The amiable Agustí Martí and his English wife, Lynne, administer this tiny hotel in the medieval village of Altafulla (11 km [7 mi] up the coast from Tarragona). The five bedrooms are decorated with period furniture from Agustí's family, and the dining room has a terra-cotta tile floor and murals. Specialties from the kitchen include meats *a la brasa* (cooked over coals) and *calçots* (a cross between spring onions and leeks) baked in roof tiles, dipped in romesco (Jan.–Apr.). *Carrer Sant Martí 5, Altafulla, 43893 Tarragona, tel. 977/65–00–77, fax 977/22–81–34. 5 rooms with bath. Reservations advised. MC, V. Restaurant closed weekdays except Fri. PM in winter and lunch every day in summer. $–$$*

Benicarló
Lodging

Parador de la Costa del Azahar. The main attraction of this modern parador, 6½ km (4 mi) north of Peñíscola, is its large semiformal garden, which runs down to the sea. It is a perfect place to rest up, in peace and quiet, away from the most crowded beaches. The decor doesn't match that of its more atmospheric cousins, but the public rooms are huge, bright, and tasteful, with white wicker furniture and white walls. The bedrooms have shiny tile floors, white walls, and functional furniture. Ask for a sea view. *Av. Papa Luna 3, Benicarló, 12580 Castellón, tel. 964/47–01–00, fax 964/47–09–34, 108 rooms with bath. Facilities: restaurant, bar, pool, tennis court, parking. AE, DC, MC, V. $$$*

Benicàssim
Dining

Villa del Mar. An old colonial-style house with a verdant terrace for dining, surrounded by palms and pines, forms an elegant and secluded setting. Inside, the decor is modern and the cuisine international as well as regional; try the *arroces Valencianos* (Valencian rice dishes). On summer evenings there is a barbecue in the garden. *Paseo Marítimo Pilar Coloma 24, tel. 964/30–28–52. Weekend reservations advised. AE, MC, V. Closed Oct.–Easter. $$*

Lodging

Orange. If facilities are what you're after, this huge, modern, chalet-style hotel possesses the widest range in town. It is centrally located, 150 yards from the beach, and surrounded by a garden and trees. Loud patterns of browns and oranges set the tone in the public rooms, and the plain bedrooms are no more than functional. Ask for a sea view; rooms over the pool may be noisy. *Gran Avenida s/n, Benicàssim, 12560 Castellón, tel. 964/39–44–00, fax 964/301–541. 415 rooms with bath. Facilities: restaurant, 2 bars, discothèque, hairdresser, 2 pools, tennis court, minigolf, parking. DC, MC, V. Closed Oct.–Mar. $$*

Voramar. At the north end of town, right on the beach, this small white hotel is encircled by classical balconies. It is the nearest thing to an old-fashioned resort hotel in town. The decor, though, is also rather plain and functional, with tile floors, white walls, and 1970s furniture. Ask for a bedroom overlooking the sea; each has a generous balcony. *Paseo Pilar Coloma 1, Benicàssim, 12560 Castellón, tel. 964/30–01–50. 55 rooms with bath. Facilities: restaurant, tennis court. AE, DC, MC, V. Closed mid-Oct.–Easter. $$*

Cambrils
Dining
★

Eugenia. Among the Gatell family restaurants (others are **Can Gatell,** tel. 977/36–01–06, and **Casa Gatell,** tel. 977/36–00–57), this has the edge because of its pretty terrace, pool, and marginally more adventurous cooking. The luxuriant plant life is continued inside, where the local cuisine is excellent. Try the *paella con bogavante* (paella with lobster) or *lubina con compota de cebolla* (sea bass with stewed onions). *Consolat de Mar 80, tel. 977/36–01–68. Summer and weekend reservations advised. AE, DC, MC, V. Closed Nov.–Dec. 15; Tues. evening and Wed. in winter; Wed. and Thurs. lunch in summer. $$$*

Gandesa
Dining and Lodging

Hostal Piqué. This modern roadhouse, although uninviting from the outside, has a large, smart dining room with a tile floor, pristine white tablecloths, and highly professional service. The menu ranges from everyday local options to more expensive rarities. Rooms are inexpensive and comfortable. *Via Catalunya 68, 43780, tel. 977/42–03–29, fax 977/42–00–68. No reservations for restaurant. 48 rooms with bath. MC, V. $*

Morella
Dining
★

Mesón del Pastor. A restored 14th-century stone mansion, down a side street off Calle Don Blasco de Alagón, houses this rustic mesón, which combines a family atmosphere with excellent cooking. Chef José Ferrer specializes in Maestrazgan dishes; try the *conejo relleno trufado* (rabbit and truffles enveloped in ham). Desserts, too, are homespun; try the *buñuelos con miel* (fried dumplings with honey). *Cuesta Jovaní 3 y 5, tel. 964/16–02–49. Weekend reservations advised. MC, V. Closed Wed. $*

Lodging
★

Cardenal Ram. Installed in one of Morella's handsomest mansions, originally Cardenal Ram's 14th-century ancestral home, this hotel oozes history from its bare stone walls and ubiquitous coats of arms. The tall lobby has a huge tapestry depicting the arrival of the Antipope Papa Luna in Morella in 1414. The bedrooms, all different, have pine floors, bare white walls, high beamed ceilings, and magnificent heavy furniture. The wide beds are covered with Morellan striped bedspreads. *Cuesta Suñer 1, Morella, 12300 Castellón, tel. 964/16–00–00. 19 rooms with bath. Facilities: restaurant. AE, DC, MC, V. $–$$*

★

Elías. If the Cardenal Ram is full, this friendly *residencia* (inn) in an old town house is an excellent alternative. There is a small, cozy sitting room with an open fire, and the L-shape bedrooms have terracotta tile floors, white walls, heavy wood furniture, and Morellan bedspreads. Ask for room No. 30, which has a good view of the Santa María Basilica. *Colomer 7, Morella, 12300 Castellón, tel. 964/16–00–92. 16 rooms with bath, 1 single without. MC, V. $*

Peñíscola **Hostería del Mar.** A semiparador, this modern white hotel next to
Lodging Peñíscola's long beach fits in with the paradors' high standards.
Most of the rooms have balconies overlooking the old town. The rustic, beamed public rooms surround a leafy pool terrace; the bedrooms have white walls, striped bedspreads, tile floors, and
Castellano-style dark wood and leather furniture. *Av. Papa Luna
18, Peñíscola, 12598 Castellón, tel. 964/48–06–00, fax 964/48–13–
63. 86 rooms with bath. Facilities: restaurant, bar, pool, tennis
court, parking. AE, DC, MC, V. $$–$$$*

Puzol **Monte Picayo.** If you enjoy the proximity of a casino and don't mind
Lodging looking at the sea from a distance, this is a hotel to consider. Set into
★ a hill, its greenery-draped modern, tiered structure overlooks the
huerta and offers a rare degree of luxury. Public areas and bedrooms are spacious and cheerful, each guest room has a balcony, and
the service is impeccable. *Urbanización Monte Picayo, 46530 Valencia, tel. 96/142–0100, fax 96/142–2168. 83 rooms with bath. Facilities: restaurant, 5 bars, 11 pools, tennis courts, minigolf, sauna,
discothèque, casino, parking. AE, DC, MC, V. $$$$*

El Saler **Sidi Saler.** On a stretch of coastline that suffers from being mid-development, Sidi Saler's contemporary khaki facade surrounds an oasis of luxury. The bedrooms are modern, bright, and unremarkable,
besides giving their inhabitants the impression that the beach belongs to them exclusively. *Playa del Saler, 46012 Valencia, tel. 96/
161–0411, fax 96/161–0838. 276 rooms with bath. Facilities: restaurant, 2 bars, 2 pools (indoor and out), sauna, massage, hairdresser,
shops, parking. AE, DC, MC, V. $$$$*
Parador Luis Vives. Definitely for golf enthusiasts, this modern
parador boasts a famous course with the first tee just outside the
front door. The hotel occupies an exposed position on the edge of a
pine forest, fronted by sand dunes. The bright reception rooms are
spacious, with cool marble floors, white walls, and baronial furniture. The bedrooms echo this style; insist on a sea view. *El Saler,
46012 Valencia, tel. 96/161–1186, fax 96/162–7016. 58 rooms with
bath. Facilities: restaurant, bar, pool, tennis court, 18-hole golf
course, parking. AE, DC, MC, V. $$$*

Tarragona **Sol Ric.** The flagship of the Tomas family restaurants remains the
Dining classiest in Tarragona. The menu changes constantly, as the chef experiments with variants of the regional cuisine. Try the *sepia
estofada con guisantes* (casseroled cuttlefish with peas) or the local
romesco. Located a kilometer out of town along the old Roman road,
it has a rustic interior and a leafy terrace. *Vía Augusta 227, tel. 977/
23–20–32. Weekend reservations required. AE, MC, V. Closed Sun.
evening, Mon., and Dec. 15–Jan. 15. $$$*
Les Coques. This up-and-coming hot spot in the old part of
Tarragona is decorated with wonderful antiques—a cash register,
sofas, clocks—and specializes in the *cucina de mercat* approach (cuisine based on the fresh ingredients available in the market that day)
with an emphasis on seafood. Try the house favorite: *rape al all
cremat* (monkfish in toasted garlic). *Bajada Nueva del Patriarca 2
bis, tel. 977/22–83–00. Reservations advised. AE, DC, MC, V.
Closed Sun. and July. $$*
La Puda. The quayside location, right opposite the fish auction
house, guarantees the freshness of seafood here. It is popular with
locals but obviously not unaccustomed to foreigners, as the menu
appears in several languages. The plain decor is marine oriented,
with a tile floor, blue walls, and white tablecloths. *Muelle Pescadores 25, tel. 977/21–15–11. No reservations. AE, DC, MC, V. $$*

Lodging **Imperial Tarraco.** This large, white half-moon hotel has a superb position overlooking the sea. The public rooms are large, with cool marble floors, black leather furniture, marble-top tables, and Oriental rugs. The bedrooms are plain but comfortable, each with a private balcony; insist on a sea view. *Rambla Vella 2, 43003 Tarragona, tel. 977/23–30–40, fax 977/21–65–66. 170 rooms with bath. Facilities: restaurant, bar, pool, tennis court, garden, parking, hairdresser. AE, DC, MC, V. $$$*

Lauria. A notch below the Imperial Tarraco in terms of space and comfort, this hotel is nevertheless well located, near the balcony on Rambla Nova. The public rooms have tile floors, black sofas, dark wood paneling, and patterned rugs, and they surround a pool in the courtyard. The bedrooms have wood-tile floors and white walls; the best either overlook the pool or have distant sea views. For most of the year this is a business hotel, with a smattering of tourists in the summer. *Rambla Nova 20, 43000 Tarragona, tel. 977/23–67–12, fax 977/23–67–00. 72 rooms, 62 with bath. Facilities: bar, pool, parking. AE, DC, MC, V. $$*

España. This modern town house offers comfort at a good value. The bedrooms have white walls, shiny tile floors, and functional 1970s furniture. Each of the exterior rooms has a balcony with a glimpse of the sea. *Rambla Nova 49, 43000 Tarragona, tel. 977/23–27–12. 40 rooms with bath. Facilities: breakfast room. AE, DC, MC, V. $*

Teruel **Parador de Teruel.** A modern, yellowish building in the Mudéjar
Dining and style, 2 km (1.2 mi) north on the Zaragoza road, houses the best
Lodging place to stay and eat in Teruel. The public rooms and bedrooms are spacious and rustic in tone. To the west are dramatic views of the Albarracín Sierra. The restaurant serves local fare. Try the *huevos con migas* (eggs with bread crumbs) and *jamón de Teruel* (Teruel ham). *Apartado 67, 44080 Teruel, tel. 974/60–18–00, fax 974/60–86–12. 58 rooms with bath. Facilities: restaurant, bar, tennis court, pool, parking. AE, DC, MC, V. $$–$$$*

Tortosa **San Carlos.** Joan Ros, chef-proprietor of this small restaurant on the
Dining northern edge of the old town, excels in seafood and freshwater fish from the Ebro Delta. Order *almejas* (marinated clams) or *rossejat* (fish broth with toasted rice). *Rambla Felip Pedrell 19, tel. 977/44–10–48. Summer weekend reservations advised. Jacket advised. DC, MC, V. $$*

Lodging **Parador Castillo de la Zuda.** Few sights near here equal the superb
★ view from this old Arab castle across the Ebro Valley to the Beceite Mountains. Dark shades of mahogany and numerous tapestries evoke a sense of the past. The bedrooms have wood furniture, terra-cotta floors, rugs, and plain walls. *Parador Castillo de la Zuda, Tortosa, 43500 Tarragona, tel. 977/44–44–50, fax 977/44–44–58. 82 rooms. Facilities: restaurant, bar, pool, parking. AE, DC, MC, V. $$–$$$*

Valencia **Civera.** Three blocks northwest of the Fine Arts Museum, this res-
Dining taurant, run by the Civera brothers, enjoys local renown for its fresh fish and seafood, cooked *a la plancha* (grilled), *hervidos* (boiled), or *a la sal* (baked in salt). The decor is marine oriented: white walls, beams, nautical motifs, and sumptuous displays of fish, fruit, and vegetables. *Lérida 11, tel. 96/347–5917. Dinner reservations advised. AE, DC, MC, V. Closed Sun. evening, Mon., and Aug. $$$$*

Eladio. Some way out of town, this welcoming restaurant has oak and marble in the decor. You can select from Galician fish dishes prepared with a mixture of tradition and invention by chef Eladio Rodríguez; try the *mero a la brasa* (charcoal-grilled grouper) and finish up with a mouth-watering Swiss pastry made by his wife,

Violette. *Chiva 40, tel. 96/384–2244. Dinner reservations advised. AE, DC, MC, V. Closed Sun. and Aug. $$$*

★ **La Hacienda.** Antiques, local lithographs, wood paneling, gilt mirrors, and salmon pink and bottle green combine to render this restaurant, two blocks east of the old center, the most elegant in Valencia. The cooking includes Valencian and international dishes; of the former, try the *filete de ganso con grosellas negras* (fillet of goose with black currants). To accompany this, there's an extensive list of Spanish and French wines. *Navarro Reverter 12, tel. 96/373–1859. Dinner reservations required. Jacket advised. AE, DC, MC, V. Closed midday Sat., Sun., and Holy Week. $$$*

El Timonel. Decorated to resemble the interior of a yacht, this central restaurant, two blocks east of the bullring, serves outstanding shellfish. The cooking is simple, yet benefits from the freshest ingredients. Try the *salmonetes* (whitebait) or *pescado de roca* (rockfish). The clientele ranges from business people at lunch to well-heeled, fashionable types at night. *Félix Pizcueta 13, tel. 96/352–6300. Dinner reservations advised. AE, DC, MC, V. Closed Mon., Holy Week, and Aug. $$$*

★ **Gargantua.** A series of apricot-colored rooms, crowded with pictures, sets the accent in this intimate and chic restaurant located in a 1910 town house. The excellent cooking is nouvelle and imaginative, the menu constantly changing. For a regional dish, try the *esgarrat* (grilled cod with green peppers). *Navarro Reverter 18, tel. 96/334–6849. Reservations advised. DC, MC, V. Closed Sun. evening and Mon. $$*

El Plat. The local press have dubbed this restaurant *el Rey del Arroz* (Rice, or *Paella*, King) because it offers a different variant of Valencia's most characteristic dish each day of the week. The simple decor consists of white, alcoved walls adorned with local ceramics, but the lighting is rather bright. The atmosphere is relaxed, the service attentive, and the location ideal should you feel like *marcha* (nightlife) after dinner. *Conde de Altea 41, tel. 96/395–1511. AE, MC, V. Closed Sun. evening, Mon., and Holy Week. $$*

Patos. Small and cozy, this restored 18th-century town house, just north of Calle Paz in the old quarter, is primarily for locals. Terra-cotta tiles, white tablecloths, wood-panelled walls, and overhead beams lend it an earthy look. In summer you can dine outside. The set menu (at 1,100 pesetas a real bargain) often includes duck (*pato*). It's very popular, so get here by 10 PM to be sure of a table. The service can be slow, and if you speak no Spanish, you risk trying the patience of the waiters. *Mar 28, tel. 96/392–1522. AE, DC, MC, V. $*

Lodging **Melia Valencia.** The average fate for a modern high rise nowadays is to be swallowed up by a large chain, and the former Rey Don Jaime has proved to be no exception. It is now slicker, with the emphasis implicitly on the business market. The decor is tasteful neo-Georgian, and it is a supremely comfortable choice if you don't mind the long walk into the town center. *Av. Baleares 2, 46023 Valencia, tel. 96/360–7300, fax 96/360–8921. 314 rooms with bath. Facilities: restaurant, 2 bars, pool, hairdresser, parking (tennis club next door). AE, DC, MC, V. $$$$*

★ **Reina Victoria.** The grand old lady of Valencia's hotels has recently received a much-needed face-lift, making her an excellent choice for comfort, as well as time-worn charm and centrality. The spacious reception rooms have cool marble floors with rugs to take the chill off; the bedrooms are clothed in green chintz and deep-pile carpets with a subdued pattern. *Barcas 4, 46002, tel. 96/352–0487, fax 96/352–0487. 97 rooms with bath. Facilities: restaurant, bar. AE, DC, MC, V. $$$*

Bristol. Central, but hidden away in a narrow street by the church of San Martín, just behind the Inglés hotel, this is an unpretentious but well-maintained hotel. It has little in the way of public rooms, but the bedrooms are perfectly comfortable, with their plain decor and functional furniture. *Abadía San Martín 3, 46002, tel. 96/352–1176, fax 96/352–8502. 40 rooms with bath. AE, DC, MC, V. Closed Dec.–mid-Jan. $$*

★ **Excelsior.** In a central 1930s building, this hotel provides the best value in this price category. From the Art Deco restaurant-cum-bar, a spiral marble staircase leads to a dark, wood-paneled salón, with a terrace for the summer. The bedrooms have olive-green carpets, the beds have brass headboards, and old prints hang on the white walls. The atmosphere is very friendly. *Barcelonina 5, 46002, tel. 96/351–4612, fax 96/352–3478. 67 rooms with bath. Facilities: restaurant, bar. AE, DC, MC, V. $$*

Inglés. Once the palace of the dukes of Cardona, this hotel stands next door to the Palacio del Marqués de Dos Aguas (*see* Tour 4: Valencia Center, *above*). There is nothing very grand about it, but it's extremely central for the old part of town. The polished wood floors and striped Regency chairs in the public rooms look rather more Spartan than they must have been in the duke's day. The bedrooms have a jaded appearance, born of the passé modern decor, but are perfectly comfortable. All are exterior; ask for one overlooking Hipolito Roviro's alabaster doorway into the next-door palacio. *Marqués de Dos Aguas 6, 46002, tel. 96/351–6426, fax 96/394–0251. 62 rooms with bath. Facilities: restaurant, bar. AE, DC, MC, V. $$*

Continental. This friendly establishment taking up two floors of a town house, just off the central Plaza del Ayuntamiento, offers excellent value for the money if all you need is a clean and comfortable room. It has a small salón and a restaurant that serves breakfast only. *Correos 8, 46002, tel. 96/351–0926, fax 96/351–0926. 46 rooms with bath. Facilities: breakfast room. AE, DC, MC, V. $*

Vinaròs
Dining

Casa Pocho. This is named after the chef Paco Puchal, known as "El Pocho," or "The Tubby One." Wood paneling and maritime motifs set the scene for the famously good seafood prepared here. The *langostinos* make the best choice. *San Gregorio 49, tel. 964/45–10–95. Weekend reservations advised. AE, DC, MC, V. Closed Sun. eve., Mon., and Dec. $$–$$$*

The Arts and Nightlife

The Arts

Many of the towns along this route have arts festivals. Tourist offices can supply details of programs and make ticket reservations. Most ayuntamientos (city/town halls) produce a cultural timetable, weekly or monthly, and local newspapers provide current listings. For Castellón and Valencia, *Que y Donde* is the major listings magazine; for Valencia only, there is *Turia*, with events, prices, and reviews.

Morella The reconquest of the town from the Moors is commemorated annually on January 7 with processions and mock battles.

Sagunto The festival of classical Mediterranean drama, *Sagunto a Escena*, takes place during the first two weeks of August, when Spanish and overseas theater groups perform a variety of ancient plays in the authentic setting of Sagunto's Roman amphitheater. For information, contact the tourist office there or in Valencia (Barcas 15, tel. 96/351–0051).

Tarragona Tarragona's most important fiestas are those of *Sant Magi* (August 19) and *Santa Tecla* (September 23), both characterized by colorful processions.

Valencia The *Fallas* are held for a week in March and reach their climax on March 19, San José, or St. Joseph's, Day, when families throughout Spain celebrate Father's Day. The fact that St. Joseph is also the patron saint of carpenters is what gave rise to this bizarre and time-honored fiesta. Back in medieval days the guilds of carpenters burnt their wood shavings in huge bonfires on St. Joseph's Day. Today Valencia explodes into a week-long celebration of fireworks, flower-strewn floats, carnival processions, top bullfights, and uncontrolled merrymaking to which tourists and Spaniards alike flock. On March 19, the huge and monstrous satirical effigies of popular and not-so-popular figures are ceremoniously burnt on massive bonfires. If you are allergic to firecrackers, stay away from this one.

Throughout July, Valencia hosts a festival of theater; classical, jazz, and pop music; film; and dance. Contact the Ayuntamiento (tel. 96/352–0694). If you're homesick, there is the Instituto Shakespeare (Av. Blasco Ibañez 28, tel. 96/360–1950), which holds performances in English and Spanish.

Nightlife

Nightlife along the coast is largely confined to music bars and discotheques. The liveliest of these are in Salou, Peñíscola (**Disco Fleca,** Plaza Ayuntamiento, old town), and Benicàssim (**K'asim,** Av. Gimeno Tomas). They really get going only during the summer months and Holy Week; at other times the atmosphere is decidedly tame. In Tarragona there are some rustic older bars; try **Poetes** (Sant Llorenç 15), near the cathedral, a music bar set in a bodega-like cellar.

Valencia is altogether different; here sleep seems to be anathema. The best time to experience this is anytime but summer, when everybody has disappeared on holiday. Plaza Canovas del Castillo and the surrounding streets are the liveliest zone, closely followed by Plaza Xuques, near the university. For a rougher breed, head to the beach. Calle de Eugenio Vines is lined with numerous loud discotheques and bars. One of these, **A'C T'V** (No. 152), opens on Sunday afternoon.

For more sophisticated clubs, try **Belle Epoque** (Cuba 8) or **Xuquer Palace** (Plaza Xuquer 8), and for Sevillanas, **Albahaca** (Almirante Cadarso 30, tel. 96/334–1484) or **Triana** (Crabador Esteve 11, tel. 96/374–3001).

To gamble, you'll have to head out to the Monte Picayo Hotel in Puzol (*see* Dining and Lodging, *above*).

10 The Southeast

Valencia to Almería

By Philip Eade

Updated by George Semler

The southeastern corner of Spain is a land of geographic contrasts. In the north, the flat, fertile *huerta* (coastal plain) produces an orange harvest spread over five months, from late November until the end of April; in spring, you can see fragrant flowers and fruit growing on the same tree. The rice paddies stretching from the Albufera (lagoon) south of Valencia to Gandía are what gave rise to the Valencian specialty, paella. The farther south you go, the drier and more mountainous the country becomes, until you reach the strange desert/lunar landscape of Almería, made famous by the advent of spaghetti western film crews in the 1960s. The inland province of Albacete, historically part of Murcia, is of interest chiefly for having been the scene of Don Quixote's exploits in the upland district of La Mancha.

The striking white architecture that you encounter in most towns attests to the long Moorish occupation. Alicante was in Moorish hands from 718 to 1249; Murcia, from 825 to 1243; and Almería, the longest of all, from 712 to 1489, when it was reconquered by Ferdinand and Isabella.

Most visitors come for the beaches, of which there is an endless variety, from the crowded Costa Blanca to near-deserted stretches around Cabo de Gata in Almería, renowned for its scuba diving. Mild temperatures in spring and fall permit vacationing before or after the worst of the crowds.

Essential Information

Important Addresses and Numbers

Tourist Information
Tourist offices offering information on the whole region are in **Valencia** (*see* Chapter 9); **Alicante** (Explanada de España 2, tel. 96/521–2285, information phone line 96/520–0000); **Almería** (Hermanos Machado 4, tel. 951/23–08–58); and **Murcia** (Alejandro Seiquer 4, tel. 968/21–37–16). Local tourist information offices are at **Albacete** (Virrey Morcillo 1, tel. 967/21–56–11); **Benidorm** (Avenida Martínez Alejos 166, tel. 965/585–3224); **Calpe** (Avenida Ejércitos Españoles s/n, tel. 96/583–1350); **Cartagena** (Plaza Castellini 5, tel. 968/50–75–49, and Ayuntamiento, tel. 968/50–64–63); **Cullera** (Calle del Riu 56, tel. 96/152–0974); **Denia** (Plaza Oculista Builges 9, tel. 96/578–0724); **Elche** (Parque Municipal, tel. 96/545–3831); **Gandía** (La Marqués de Campo s/n, tel. 96/287–7788); **Játiva** (Moncada, tel. 96/288–2561); **Jávea** (Plaza Almirante Basterreche 24, tel. 96/579–0736); **Lorca** (López Gisbert, tel. 968/46–61–57); **Orihuela** (Francisco Díez 25, tel. 96/560–2747); **Santa Pola** (Plaza Diputación, tel. 96/541–1100); and **Torrevieja** (Costera del Mar s/n, tel. 96/685–1371).

Emergencies
Police: 091. *Ambulance:* **Alicante** (tel. 96/510–0822); **Murcia** (tel. 968/25–69–00). *General medical assistance:* **Alicante,** Hospital del SVS (tel. 96/525–0060); **Almería,** Torrecárdenas (tel. 951/25–22–11), Emergencies (tel. 951/23–56–93).

Consulate
British: Alicante (Plaza Calvo Sotelo, tel. 96/521–6022). **U.S.:** Valencia (Ribera 3, tel. 96/351–6973).

Late-night Pharmacies
Pharmacies in each town take turns staying open 24 hours. All pharmacies display the address of the *farmacia de guardia,* the one on duty that night.

Travel Agencies
Alicante: Viajes Barceló (San Telmo 9, tel. 96/521–0011). Benidorm: Viajes Barceló (Gerona, Edif. Pinos, tel. 96/585–4733). La Manga del Mar Menor: Viajes Hispania (Urbanización Las Sirenas 3, tel.

968/56–41–61). Murcia: Viajes Internacional Expreso 9 (Jaime I El Conquistador, tel. 968/23–16–62).

Arriving and Departing by Plane

The Southeast has four major airports: Valencia (*see* Chapter 9), Alicante (El Altet, 12 km/7.2 mi south, tel. 96/528–5011), San Javier (for Mar Menor and Murcia, tel. 968/57–00–73), and Almería (6 km/ 3.6 mi east, tel. 951/22–06–46). Iberia has the most flights (tel. 96/ 520–6000, 968/24–00–50, or 951/23–09–33).

Arriving and Departing by Car, Train, Bus, and Boat

By Car   The autopista A7 from Barcelona now runs through Valencia and Alicante as far as Murcia. Tolls, though quite high, are often worth it for the time saved. The other main links with the region are the NIII from Madrid to Valencia and the N301 from Madrid to Murcia via Albacete.

By Train   For RENFE information, contact its offices in Valencia (tel. 96/352– 9362), Alicante (tel. 96/522–3642), Murcia (tel. 968/25–21–54), or Almería (tel. 951/25–11–22).

By Bus   Private companies run buses down the coast, and from Madrid to Valencia/Benidorm/Alicante/Murcia/MarMenor/Almería (*see* Getting Around, *below*).

By Boat   From Alicante, Trasmediterránea (tel. 96/512–3187) boats sail to Ibiza in summer. Contact Agencia Romeu (Jorge Juan 6, tel. 96/520– 8333) for boats to Oran in Algeria. From Denia, Flebasa Lines (Puerto de Denia, tel. 96/578–4200) sails to Ibiza. From Almería, Trasmediterránea (tel. 951/23–61–55) sails to Melilla, a Spanish outpost on the Moroccan coast.

Getting Around

By Car   Except for short distances, coastal roads are best avoided in summer, apart from the stunning road that hugs the Almerian coast, although in places this requires a good head for heights. Cars can be rented in the provincial capitals and all major resorts, though it is less expensive to rent ahead of time from the United States.

By Train   Frequent and comfortable RENFE trains connect the chief cities of the region. In addition there's an independent FGV line running along the Costa Blanca from Denia to Alicante.

Alicante has a RENFE station (Avenida Salamanca, tel. 96/522– 6840) and a RENFE office (Explanada de España 1, tel. 96/521– 1303); the FGV station is at the far end of Playa Postiguet (Avenida Villajoyosa, tel. 96/526–2731), reached by buses C1 and C2 from downtown. Murcia's RENFE station is some way out (Industria, tel. 968/25–21–54), but there is an office in town (Barrionuevo, tel. 968/21–28–42). Almería's station is off Carretera de Ronda (tel. 951/ 25–11–35).

By Bus   Regular bus service connects the towns and cities of the region. Main bus depots are as follows: Alicante (Avenida Portugal, tel. 96/ 522–0700); Murcia, west of town (Plaza San Andres, tel. 968/29–22– 11); and Almería (Plaza Barcelona, tel. 951/22–10–11).

By Boat   In summer there are crossings from both Alicante (tel. 96/521–6396) and Santa Pola (tel. 96/541–1113) to the island of Tabarca. From

Benidorm, there are hourly crossings to the island of Plumbaria
(10–8; 750 pesetas round-trip).

Guided Tours

Orientation Tours The *ayuntamiento*, or town hall (Plaza del Ayuntamiento), and travel agencies in Alicante organize guided tours of the city and bus and
train tours to Guadalest, the Algar waterfalls, Benidorm, the Peñón
de Ifach (Calpe), and Elche. From Benidorm, similar excursions are
arranged by large hotels. The ayuntamiento in Elche (Plaça de Baix,
tel. 96/545–1240) organizes tours of the city and *environs*. From
Mojácar, **Horizon** (Pueblo Indalo, tel. 950/47–83–76) tours the local
countryside. In Murcia, contact **Alquibla** tour guides (Gonzalez
Adalid 13, tel. 968/22–12–19) for tours of the city and region, and in
Almería, **Viajes Cemo** (Avenida Las Gaviotas, Urbanización
Roquetas de Mar, tel. 950/33–35–02).

Special-Interest Tours The ayuntamiento in Alicante also runs tours to Jijona, where you
can visit one of the famous *turrón* (nougat) factories before going on
to the Cuevas de Canalobre (Canalobre Caves) to see the amazing
stalactites and stalagmites. This sometimes includes a concert in the
cave, but check beforehand.

Exploring the Southeast

Orientation

Our first tour moves south from Valencia (*see* Chapter 9), between
the sea and Albufera lagoon, before following the coast around the
Cabo de la Nao to the Costa Blanca. Our second tour branches inland
just south of Cullera and passes through the historic towns of Játiva
and Alcoy on the way to Alicante, where it meets with the end of
Tour 1. Our third tour begins in Alicante, an exotic and bustling
Mediterranean port, before moving inland toward Murcia, past the
palm forest at Elche and the ancient town of Orihuela. Tour 4 covers
the vast inland areas that fall within the bounds of the Southeast. It
is designed primarily for travelers approaching Murcia from Madrid
or readers of Cervantes keen to explore the setting for *Don Quixote*.
Our final tour takes you from Murcia, with its superb cathedral, to
the African-looking Almería, by way of Lorca and the stunning, uncrowded coast around the Cabo de Gata.

Highlights for First-time Visitors

Old Quarter, Jativa (*see* Tour 2)
Bridges of Alcoy (*see* Tour 2)
View from the Castillo de Santa Bárbara, Alicante (*see* Tour 3)
Alcazaba fortress, Almería (*see* Tour 5)
Cabo de Gata Nature Reserve (*see* Tour 5)
Peñón de Ifach, Calpe (*see* Tour 1)
Huerto del Cura, Elche (*see* Tour 3)
Ducal Palace, Gandía (*see* Tour 1)
Old town, Lorca (*see* Tour 5)
Murcia's cathedral (*see* Tour 5)
El Salvador Cathedral, Orihuela (*see* Tour 3)

Tour 1: From Valencia to the Costa Blanca

Numbers in the margin correspond to points of interest on the Southeast map.

❶ Going south from **Valencia** (*see* Chapter 9), the coastal road runs along a thin strip of land (La Dehesa) that barely separates the sea from the Albufera lagoon, rimmed with rice fields and shady pine woods. There are large-scale duck shoots here in the fall. For a closer

❷ whiff of the Albufera's unique aura, turn right to **El Palmar**. A single-track road hugs the edge of the lagoon, passing thatched *barracas* (fishing shacks). In El Palmar, you can hire boats to explore the lagoon.

Time Out Lining the main street of El Palmar are numerous bars where you should venture to try the local delicacy, *all-i-pebre* (eel fried in garlic and served with a hot-pepper sauce).

Back on the main highway, N332, continue south, with sand dunes

❸ on your left, to the lighthouse at **Cullera**. Around the rocky point is modern Cullera, a rapidly mushrooming resort, marked by futuristic, curved high rises. The climb up to the hermitage of **Nuestra Señora del Castillo** and castle ruins culminates in views of the sea, the huerta, and the mountains.

Some 10 km (6 mi) south of Cullera, the N332 passes the turning to Játiva (*see* Tour 2, *below*). For the coastal route, continue toward

❹ **Gandía,** whose old town lies 4 km (2½ mi) inland from the modern beach development. This became the Borgia (Borja, in Spanish) fief after Ferdinand the Catholic granted the duchy to the family in 1485. The canny Borgia Pope Alexander VI (*see* Játiva in Tour 2, *below*) was one of the most notorious of all Renaissance prelates. The family's reputation was later redeemed, however, by the Jesuit St. Francis Borgia (1510–72), born in Gandía and canonized in 1671.

In Gandía, you can visit the **Palacio de los Duques** (Ducal Palace), signposted from the center. It was founded by St. Francis in 1546 and still serves as a Jesuit college. Elaborate ceilings and brightly colored *azulejos* (tiles) adorn the 17th-century state rooms. One room contains the crucifix said to have announced the imminent death of Francis's wife, after which he devoted his life to God. *Admission: 300 pesetas. Guided tours, summer, Mon.–Sat. 10, 11, noon, 5, 6, and 7; winter, Mon.–Sat. 11, noon, 4:30, and 5:30; Sun. and fiestas, 10 and 11.*

As you head south, parchment-colored hills mark the beginning of the province of Alicante. Once past Ondara, which has an unusual

❺ stone bullring, you can detour to the **Cueva de las Calaveras** (Skull Cave), near Benidoleig, inhabited by prehistoric humans some 40,000 years ago. *Admission: 300 pesetas. Open daily 9–6.*

Gata de Gorgos, the next town, specializes in basketwork. A road

❻ branches off from here to the coastal resorts of **Denia** and pictur-

❼ esque **Jávea.**

❽ **Cabo de la Nao** (Cape Nao) is a great spur of land that juts out into the Mediterranean toward Ibiza, barely 100 km (62 mi) away. As you round the point, you turn from a coast that looks toward Italy to one that mirrors Africa. In the course of a few kilometers, you pass from an agriculture of oranges and rice to one of olives and palms, from a benign, if variable, climate to tawny aridity.

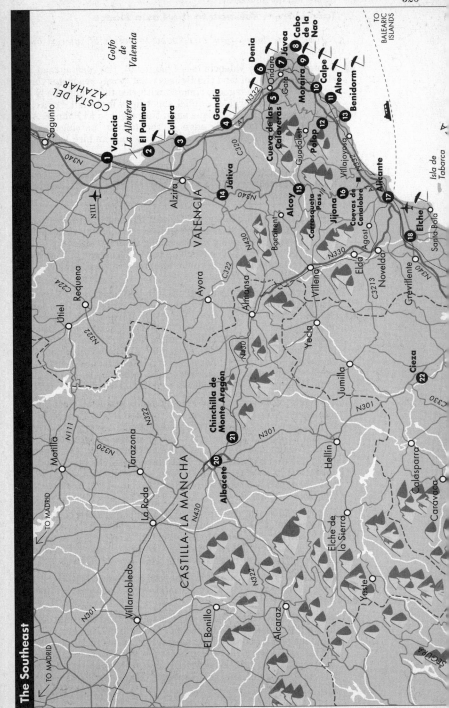

The Southeast

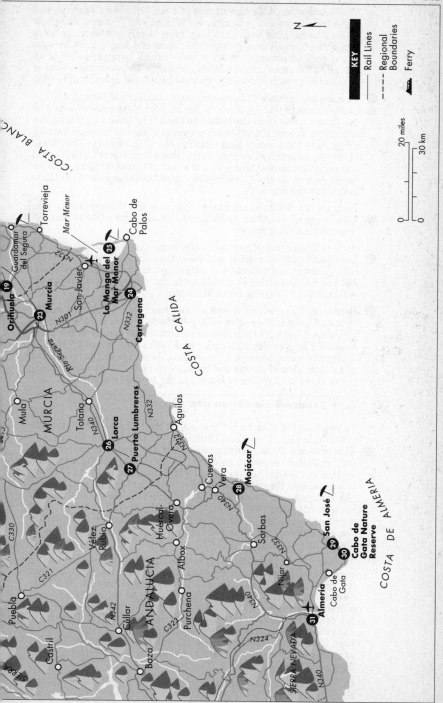

KEY

Rail Lines

Regional Boundaries

Ferry

N

0   20 miles
0   30 km

COSTA BLANCA

Torrevieja

Guardamar del Segura

Mar Menor

Cabo de Palos

La Manga del Mar Menor **25**

San Javier

Orihuela **19**

Murcia

23

N332

N301

Cartagena **24**

COSTA CALIDA

Río Segura

N340

MURCIA

Mula

Totana

Lorca **26**

Puerto Lumbreras **27**

N332

Aguilas

N332

Cuevas

Vera

Mojácar **28**

COSTA DE ALMERIA

Vélez Rubio

Huércal-Overa

Albox

Purchena

Sorbas

San José **29**

30 Cabo de Gata Nature Reserve

C330

C321

Puebla

Castril

SIERRA

N342

Cúllar

Baza

ANDALUCIA

C323

Níjar

Cabo de Gata

Almería **31**

N332

N340

N324

SIERRA NEVADA

The popular name for the stretch of coast between Cape Nao and Cape Palos is the Costa Blanca, or "White Coast." Carnations grow in such abundance here that they even faintly perfume the local wine. The Costa Blanca includes the towns of Alicante and Cartagena, as well as numerous beach resorts, which have expanded at an uncontrolled rate since the 1960s and early '70s, creating a kind of sub-Miami growth of endless concrete hotels and apartment blocks.

⑨
⑩ **Moraira** has managed to preserve an atmosphere of seclusion in the narrow streets leading down to the harbor. Next comes **Calpe** and the dramatic outcrop, the **Peñón de Ifach.** The town was utterly deserted for nearly 100 years after Barbary pirates killed or carried off as slaves the entire population in the 17th century. The 305-m (1,000-ft) monolith of the Peñón rises sheer from the sea into the sky; the summit is accessible by way of a tunnel. Goatlike spirits are reputed to hurl to their deaths those unwise enough to scale these heights at full moon.

⑪ Back on the N332, which plunges periodically through rocky tunnels, you arrive at **Altea,** an old fishing village with white houses and blue ceramic-tiled domes.

⑫ You can branch inland here along the route that leads to the C3318, a beautiful mountain road on which lies the village of **Polop.** In its center is a surprising collection of water taps, each donated by a different town or province, that still serve the villagers with mountain water. Follow C3318 south to Benidorm.

⑬ **Benidorm** is a hideously overdeveloped resort whose current capacity is said to be in the region of 300,000 beds! Praise is quite justifiably heaped upon its twin white crescent-shape beaches, which are enhanced by a continual topping-up of sand from Morocco. Hidden among the concrete blocks, the original old village still survives. For a fantastic view of all this and more, climb up to the **Rincón de Loix;** follow signs to Club Sierra Dorada at the far east end of town.

Tour 2: Inland via Játiva and Alcoy

⑭ To reach Játiva (Xàtiva in Catalan), on the inland N340, follow the N332 10 km (6 mi) south of Cullera, and turn right on the road to Tabernes and Simat. **Játiva** rests on the dry vine- and cypress-covered slopes of the Sierra de Alcoy, 43 km (26 mi) from Cullera, and retains a pink Old Quarter dotted with fountains. Under the Moors, it was famous for paper production, and centuries later it became the birthplace of two of the Borgia popes—Calixtus III and his nephew Alexander VI. The latter issued the famous 1493 Papal Bull granting the Indies to Ferdinand and Isabella, though he's more often remembered for his scandalous private life and as the father of Caesar and Lucrezia.

The picturesque **Castillo** is set on the slopes of Mount Bernisa. To reach it, follow signs up a steep path to the Castillo from the Plaza del Espanoleto. Halfway up, the 13th-century **Ermita de San Feliú** (Hermitage of St. Felix) has a beautiful group of Valencian Primitive paintings (open daily 10–1 and 4–8). Felipe V did a fairly thorough job of destroying the fortress as part of his fierce retribution for Játiva's opposition during the War of the Spanish Succession, but a partial restoration of the castle and a panoramic view over the town and huerta reward your efforts. (Apply to the caretaker; closed Mon.)

On the Plaza del Seo stands the monumental **Collegiata** Church, chiefly remarkable for its size, but also housing some Borgia Renais-

sance marbles. Opposite is the ornate 16th-century Plateresque facade of the **hospital.** Down Calle Corretgeria, the **Museo Municipal**
(Municipal Museum, open Tues.–Sat. 10–2; closed Sun. and Mon.)
has a small collection of archaeological finds, as well as paintings by
Játiva's other famous son, José de Ribera.

The N340 south climbs steeply behind the castle walls toward Alcoy.
This is a rugged and twisty drive with sweeping vistas on clear days.
⓯ Sixty-five km (105 mi) from Játiva, **Alcoy** has a dramatic site at the
confluence of three rivers and is famous for its bridges spanning
their deep gorges. It owes its size (population, 67,000) to textile, pa-
per, and fruit-canning industries. The annual Moros y Cristianos
(Moors and Christians) festival around Sant Jordi (St. George's
Day), April 23, is the most spectacular fiesta of its kind in Spain.
Colorful processions and mock battles commemorate the battle of
Alcoy in 1275, when St. George's intervention helped liberate the
city from the besieging forces of Al-Azraq, ensuring victory for the
Christians.

If you miss this week, go down Calle Sant Miquel, which leads off
Plaza de España, to **Casal de Sant Jordi,** which houses paraphernalia
from the event, including costumes worn by the combatants. *Sant
Miquel 62. Admission: 300 pesetas. Open Tues.–Fri. 11–1 and
5:30–8; closed Sat.–Mon.*

Time Out Through arches from the Plaza de España is the enclosed **Plaza de
Dins,** whose sidewalk cafés are an ideal place for a drink and some
local stuffed olives.

The N340 south passes La Sarga, 6 km (3½ mi) east of the road, with
some ancient cave paintings, before climbing over the dramatic
Carrasqueta Pass (990 m/3,300 ft). As the road begins its rapid descent, Alicante and the Costa Blanca can usually be seen clearly
across terraced vineyards, in dramatic contrast to the surrounding
⓰ parched and jagged peaks. You pass through **Jijona,** famous for
turrón production (*see* Guided Tours, *above*).

Tour 3: Alicante, Elche, and Orihuela

⓱ **Alicante,** at the convergence of inland and coastal roads, has always
been known for its luminous skies. The Greeks called it Akra Leuka
(White Summit) and the Romans Lucentum (City of Light). The city
is dominated by the castle of Santa Bárbara, set on a rocky peak.
From the palm-lined harbor, ships sail regularly to the island of Ibiza and to Algeria. The pride of the city is its date-palm-lined avenue,
the Explanada.

Begin your tour in the arcaded Plaza de Ayuntamiento at the tourist
office. Look inside the Baroque ayuntamiento; ask gate officials for
permission to explore the ornate state rooms and Rococo chapel on
the first floor (open daily 9–3). Walk through to Plaza Santísima Faz
behind the ayuntamiento, a trafficless square crowded with sidewalk cafés and restaurants.

Continue down the busy, pedestrianized Calle Mayor and turn right
to the **cathedral of San Nicolás de Bari** (open for services), set on the
site of a former mosque. It has both an austere 17th-century Renaissance facade in the style of Herrera (architect of the Escorial) and a
lavish Baroque side chapel.

Retrace your steps to the **Museo de Arte Siglo XX** (Museum of 20th-
Century Art), at the other end of Calle Mayor. The surprisingly

good collection of abstract art includes works by Picasso, Miró, Braque, Tàpies, Hockney, and Rauschenberg, all donated by the painter Eusebio Sempere. *Admission free. Open Oct.–Apr., Tues.– Sat. 10–1 and 5–8; May–Sept., Tues.–Sat. 10:30–1:30 and 6–9; closed Sun. and Mon.*

Across the small plaza stands the **Church of Santa María,** which boasts a lavish Baroque facade with finely carved twisted columns. From here, it's a short walk down some steps, and then left along the back of Playa Postiguet to the foot of Mt. Benacantil (210 m/700 ft) and the elevator up to the castle.

Originally built as a Carthaginian fortress around 3 BC, the **Castillo de Santa Bárbara** was extensively modified for numerous wars. From it you have a spectacular bird's-eye view of the city. Within the castle walls, a small museum displays objects associated with the San Juan bonfires, burned on midsummer night's eve each year. *Castle admission: 250 pesetas. Castle and elevator open Sun.–Fri. 9–9; closed Sat. eve. Museum admission: 100 pesetas. Open Sun.– Fri. 10–1 and 5–8, Sat. 10–1. Closed Mon., winter.*

Time Out The cafés along the Explanada offer a picturesque, if noisy, place for a drink. The bar below the **Delfín** restaurant has a wide selection of tapas, and tables are set out on the pavement.

⑱ If Alicante is torridly hot in summer, **Elche,** 23 km (14 mi) along the inland N340, is even hotter. Escape from the worst of the heat is fortunately made possible in the largest palm forest in Europe, which surrounds the city. The Moors first planted the palms for dates, and the palms still produce Europe's most reliable crop, as well as providing the whole of Spain with yellow Palm Sunday fronds, which, once blessed, are hung on balconies to ward off evil during the coming year. This town, colonized by ancient Rome, was later ruled by the Moors for 500 years. The remarkable stone bust known as *La Dama de Elche,* discovered here in 1897 (now in Madrid's Archaeological Museum), is one of the earliest examples of Iberian sculpture. The *Misteri* (Mystery Play), performed in the Basilica de Santa María on the Feast of the Assumption, draws many visitors. The performances on August 14 and 15 are spectacular, involving the winching of a platform bearing the Virgin Mary and a band of guitar-playing angels 47 meters (150 feet) up into the dome of the church.

Be sure to visit the Palm Grove, with more than 200,000 trees, and the beautiful **Huerto del Cura,** where flowers of vibrant colors grow beneath magnificent palms. *Admission: 300 pesetas. Open Apr.– Sept., daily 9–8; Oct.–Mar., daily 9–6.*

⑲ Palm and orange groves are scattered through market gardens as far as **Orihuela,** on the banks of the Segura—another excuse to linger on the N340 south. The town's air of fading grandeur stems from its former status as capital of Murcia until the Reconquest. Stroll through Orihuela's winding streets and visit the Gothic **El Salvador Cathedral** (whose handsomest portal happens to be Renaissance) to see the rare spiral vaulting. The adjoining museum has paintings by Velázquez and Ribera (open Mon.–Sat. 10:30–12:30).

Tour 4: Approaching Murcia via Albacete and La Mancha

From Madrid to Albacete, along the N301, it is 250 km (155 mi). **⑳** **Albacete** is an agricultural town famous for wines and saffron. Lying

900 m (3,000 ft) above sea level, it has a 15th- and 16th-century quarter on the crest of a hill, known as **Alto de la Villa,** and the **Ermita de San Antonio** (Hermitage of St. Anthony) is a good example of 17th-century Castellano architecture.

Visit the **Museo Arqueológico** (Archaeological Museum) in the Parque Abelardo Sánchez, with Roman mosaics, ivory dolls, and objects dating from the Paleolithic era. *Admission: 300 pesetas. Open Tues.–Sat. 10–2 and 4–7, Sun. 10–2; closed Mon.*

㉑ If you detour slightly along the N430, you'll soon see the imposing 15th-century fortress-prison-castle of **Chinchilla de Monte Aragón** away on your left, and, if the day is clear, the distant Sierra de Alcaraz rising to nearly 1,830 m (6,000 ft) to the south. Chinchilla is a fine old pottery town.

㉒ Back on the N301, most of the 146 km (91 mi) to Murcia run adjacent to the bleak uplands of La Mancha, where Don Quixote went adventuring in Cervantes's famous novel. Across the border into Murcia and through the Roman town of **Cieza,** dominated by its feudal castle, the road drops some 800 m (2,700 ft) to green farmland before reaching the provincial capital.

Tour 5: Murcia and Almería

Soon after Orihuela, you enter the province of Murcia, where the N340 follows the course of the Segura, though the foothills of the Sierra de Carrascoy often intervene between road and river. This is the driest part of Spain, and the least visited. The tawny hills are punctuated by stretches of fertile huerta, moistened by life-giving rivers whose waters irrigate three crops in succession a year. Rich metal deposits supply a busy mining industry. As you cross into Murcia, the Valenciano language gives way to the Castilian dialect, which is now the standard form of the language spoken throughout Spain.

㉓ **Murcia,** the capital of the province, was first settled by Romans. The conquering Moors later used Roman bricks to build the 8th-century Murcia. The city was liberated and annexed to the crown of Castile only in 1243; the Murcian dialect contains many Arabic words, and in appearance many of its inhabitants clearly reveal their Moorish ancestry. Modern Murcia is a bustling university city with a population of more than 300,000.

The **cathedral** is a masterpiece of eclectic architecture. Begun in the 14th century, it received its magnificent facade—described by the 19th-century English traveler Richard Ford as "rising in compartments, like a drawn out telescope"—as late as 1737. This facade is considered the fullest expression of the Churrigueresque style. From the 15th century are the Gothic Door of the Apostles and the splendid Isabelline Vélez Chapel, with beautiful star vaulting and carvings by the 18th-century Murcian sculptor Francisco Salzillo. Look in the museum, off the north transept, to see Salzillo's polychrome wood sculpture of the penitent St. Jerome. Ask the keeper for the keys to climb the monumental bell tower, built between 1521 and 1792, 95 m (312 ft) high. *Museum and bell tower admission: 250 pesetas. Open daily 10–noon and 5–7:30.*

On leaving the belfry, go down Calle Trapería, the pedestrianized main shopping street. You will soon reach the 19th-century **Casino,** well worth a peep for its style and aura of a British gentleman's club. The intricate Mudéjar decor was modeled on the Alhambra in Granada. Gambling hasn't taken place here for years; Murcians (men only!) come here instead to read newspapers and play billiards.

Time Out At the end of Trapería is a cluster of sidewalk cafés serving a wide variety of Murcian tapas.

The **Salzillo Museum,** some way out by the bus station, has the main collection of Francisco Salzillo's disturbingly realistic polychrome *pasos* (carvings), carried every Easter in the processions. *Admission: 250 pesetas (free Sun.). Open Mon.–Sat. 9:30–1 and 4–7 (winter, 3–6), Sun. 11–1.*

Leaving Murcia, if you are a naval devotee, you might want to go 24 south along the N301 to **Cartagena,** founded in the 3rd century BC by the Carthaginians, and Spain's principal naval base ever since. From 25 here there is easy access to the resort of **La Manga del Mar Menor** (*see* Beaches, *below*) and a twisty, if scenically attractive, 100 km (62 mi) along the N332 to the start of the Costa de Almería.

If you stay on the N340, after 32 km (20 mi) the market gardens suddenly give way to the dramatically stark hillscape for which this corner of Spain is known. To the north, the Sierra de Espuña does a near faultless job of imitating Arizona, fun for an exploratory drive if you have time for a picnic away from the traffic.

26 Leave the main highway for a glimpse of **Lorca,** a picturesque old market town and the scene of some of Spain's most colorful Holy Week celebrations. Your first stop should be the tourist office on Lope Gisbert, housed in the beautiful, dilapidated Casa de los Guevara; note the doorway and lovely tiled patio. Head down Alamo to the elegant Plaza de España, ringed by a string of unexpectedly rich Baroque buildings, particularly the ayuntamiento, law courts, and Colegiata Church. You can follow signs from this plaza up to the **castle.**

27 **Puerto Lumbreras** lies 17 km (11 mi) farther south, home to a parador, but nothing more than a glorified truck stop. If you are heading for Granada, this is where to turn off. On the way to Granada is **Guadix,** famous for its cave dwellings in the Barrio Santiago. Before expressing shock at the existence of such dwellings in this modern, industrialized nation, have a look inside one or two of the caves: They are warm in winter, cool in summer, and have electricity to power all the modern conveniences.

As the N340 enters Almería province, it straightens out and continues for mile upon mile, seemingly toward the end of the earth. You can either go direct to Almería along the N340—by way of the dramatically positioned **Sorbas,** whose houses rest on a high cliff above a river, and the various film locations (*see* Mini Hollywood, *below*)— or reach it from the coast.

The most attractive part of the Almerían coast lies to the south of Mojácar, so stay on the N340 until Vera. Turn left here, and after 10 28 km (6 mi), turn right to **Mojácar.** Nestling a couple of miles inland on a hillside overlooking the sea, Mojácar's clustered white Cubist houses attest to the town's Moorish past.

As you drive south, numerous hairpins wind around deep coves; it's not a road for squeamish motorists. Don't stop in Carboneras, but continue by the AL101 and N332 to the junction with the road to Níjar, and turn left to San José. The road passes through field upon field of tomatoes, growing under oceans of plastic sheeting. This *plástico* agriculture has revolutionized the fortunes of this previously impoverished corner of Spain. Leaving the plain, the road enters the wild and beautiful Sierra del Cabo de Gata, a range of green hills that belies the area's arid reputation and produces a stunning coastline.

㉙ **San José** is a small, relaxed village, as yet out of developers' clutches, and well placed to take advantage of the near-deserted beaches nearby. It has one tiny hotel, a handful of *hostales* (hostels), and a
㉚ campsite. Just to the south is the **Cabo de Gata Nature Reserve,** meaning that for 16 km (10 mi) there are no buildings whatsoever to spoil the countryside. Follow signs south to the beaches of **Genovese** and **Monsul;** a dirt track follows the coast around the spectacular cape, eventually linking up with the N332 to Almería.

㉛ **Almería** has tree-lined boulevards and gardened squares. Its dazzling white houses give it a Moroccan flavor. A mild climate makes this capital of the grape industry pleasant in spring and autumn. Its core still consists of distinctly Mudéjar flat-roofed houses in a maze of narrow, winding alleys, though now framed by modern apartment blocks.

Dominating the city is its main sight, the **Alcazaba fortress,** built by the Caliph Abdu'r Rahman, entered by the Gothic gate of the Reyes Católicos, and provided with a bell tower by Carlos III. The fortifications command sweeping views of the port and city. Among the ruins of the fortress, damaged by earthquakes in 1522 and 1560, are landscaped gardens of rock flowers and cacti. *Admission: 300 pesetas. Open Apr.–Oct., daily 10–2 and 5–8; Nov.–Mar., daily 9–1 and 3–6.*

Below stands the **cathedral,** whose buttressed towers give it the look of a castle. The reason for these defenses was the frequency of raids by Barbary pirates in the 16th century. The overall design is Gothic, with some classical touches around the doors. *Open 10:30–noon and for services.*

Time Out The liveliest cafés line the main Paseo de Almería and nearby smaller streets. Head down the narrow Calle Tenor Iribarne, near the top on the left, for numerous seafood bars. Left from here, down Calle Fructuoso Perez, is **Las Botas Bodega,** a tavern with hams hanging from the ceiling.

If you are a film devotee intent on seeing where spaghetti westerns were—and to a lesser extent, still are—shot, head to **Mini Hollywood,** 24 km (15 mi) north on the N340, a curious film set open to the public when there's no filming taking place. *Tel. 950/36–52–36. Admission: 650 pesetas adults, 350 pesetas children. Open daily 10–6 (and later in summer).*

What to See and Do with Children

Beaches provide the best entertainment for children in this area (*see* Beaches, *below*). Or take them to one of the caves. The **Cueva de las Calaveras,** near Denia (*see* Tour 1, *above*), and the **Cuevas de Canalobre** (admission: 400 pesetas; open summer, daily 10:30–8:30; winter, daily 11–6:30), off the main road between Alicante and Jijona, should both interest children.

Safari parks are at Vergel (tel. 96/575–0285; admission: 1,350 pesetas adults, 900 pesetas children; open daily 10–6:45) and between Elche and Santa Pola (Rio Safari, tel. 96/545–2288; admission: 1,350 pesetas adults, 900 pesetas children; open daily 10:30–8:30).

Fort West, El Campello (between Alicante and Villajoyosa), is a cowboy-oriented amusement park. *Admission: 1,350 pesetas adults, 900 pesetas children. Open year-round; shows start 1:30 and 5:30.*

Off the Beaten Track

In **Villena,** 40 km (25 mi) west of Alcoy, a remarkable collection of priceless Bronze Age rings, bracelets, coronets, and bowls, all of solid gold, was discovered on a dry riverbed in 1963. It is displayed in the Archaeology section of the ayuntamiento. On the way back to the N340, find time to stop in **Bocairent,** where the Museo Parroqial displays paintings by Juan de Juanes, who died here in 1579, along with works by Francisco Ribalta and Joaquín Sorolla.

Detouring east from Alcoy, along the C3313 toward Guadalest, pass through some of the most tempting, mountainous scenery behind the Costa Blanca. **Guadalest** is an old town within the walls of a ruined castle, perched formidably atop a crag, with tiny stepped streets to overcome the steep terrain. Continue as far as Callosa, turn left to Tarbena, and brave a dip at the foot of the **El Algar falls,** icy whatever the time of year. **Tarbena,** a mountain village famed for its sausages, introduces you to the most spectacular scenery here.

Shopping

Local **crafts** include basketwork, embroidery, leatherwork, and weaving, each peculiar to a single town or village in the Southeast. You will find all these crafts for sale in major tourist resorts, although the prices may be inflated. Often the most satisfying places to shop are local markets, so be sure to check whether it is market day while you are in town.

Among the best buys in **antiques,** if you can find them at a reasonable price—800–1,000 pesetas each—are antique azulejos. Look, too, for copper and brass, especially old Art Deco oil lamps. For top quality and equally pricey antiques, visit **Domínguez Cazorla** in Almería (Miguel Segura 3).

For **ceramics,** go to Agost, 20 km (12 mi) inland from Alicante, where they make good jugs and pitchers from the local white clay, whose porosity is ideal for keeping liquids cool. Biar, Chinchilla, and Níjar (north of Almería) are also well known for their ceramics.

Sports

Golf
: Be sure to reserve tee times in advance, and expect to pay around 8,000 pesetas for 18 holes, 4,000 pesetas for nine. The region's golf courses are as follows (listed north to south): **El Saler** (*see* Chapter 9, Valencia); **Club de Golf Jávea** (tel. 96/579–2584), 9 holes; **Club de Golf Don Cayo** (Conde de Altea 49, Altea, tel. 96/584–0716), 9 holes; **Campo de Golf Villa Martín** (Apartado 35, Torrevieja, tel. 96/676–5154), 18 holes; **La Manga Club de Golf** (Los Belones, tel. 968/56–45–11), two 18-hole courses; and **Golf Almerimar** (tel. 950/48–09–50), 18 holes.

Horseback Riding
: You can go horseback riding at the **La Manga Club** (Los Belones, tel. 968/56–45–11).

Tennis
: Most of the coastal hotels have tennis courts, although few will let you use them if you're not a guest. Some exceptions are **Hotel Eurotennis** (Villajoyosa, tel. 96/589–1250), **La Manga Club** (Los

Belones, tel. 968/56–45–11, ext. 1666), and **Club de Tenis V. Alegre** (Paraje El Olive, Huercal de Almería, tel. 950/30–03–90).

Water Sports Swimming, waterskiing, jet skiing, and windsurfing are popular all along the coast, and you can rent the necessary equipment (on leaving a substantial deposit) in every resort. Try the **Dos Mares** watersports center (La Manga del Mar Menor, tel. 968/14–12–83) and the **Pueblo Indalo** (Mojácar, tel. 950/47–83–76). For scuba diving, contact the **Federación Andaluza de Actividades Subacuáticas** (Club Náutico Almería, Almadrabillas 10, tel. 950/27–06–12).

Beaches

The Southeast coastline offers abundant variety: from the long stretches of sand dunes north of Denia and south of Alicante to the rocky coves and sweeping crescents of the Costa Blanca. The benign climate means you can be on the beach for most of the year. Major beaches have Red Cross (Cruz Roja) stations with helicopters and flags to warn swimmers of conditions: green for safe, red for danger.

Altea, popular with families, is somewhat busy and rather pebbly, but the old town provides a pretty setting. **Benidorm's** two white crescent-shape beaches extend for more than 5 km (3 mi) and are widely considered the best in Spain. For backup entertainment, Benidorm takes all the prizes; however, you are unlikely to be the only one on the beach, and in summer you will be sunbathing head to toe. **Calblanque** is on the road between Los Belones and Cape Palos, which takes you down a longish rough track to a succession of near-deserted beaches frequented by young Murcians. **Calpe's** beaches have the scenic advantage of the sheer Peñon de Ifach, which stands guard over stretches of sand to either side. **Denia** and **Jávea** both have ideal family beaches where children build sand castles and paddle in the relatively safe waters. **Gandía's** sandy beach is well kept, with bars and restaurants lining the promenade. Although the narrow **La Manga del Mar Menor** (Manga refers to a thin "sleeve" of land), which encloses a huge lagoon, offers some stunning views, it has been ruined by a tasteless sprawl of hotels and holiday apartments. **Mojácar** has a shingly beach backed by bars and good sports facilities, but if you are mobile, try some of the deserted beaches to the south (*see* Tour 5, *above*). Needless to say, there aren't any facilities, bar the odd water tap for campers. Nudity seems quite accepted here, as it does just north of **Cullera** and at **Calblanque.** In **Moraira,** the best is Castillo beach, just outside the center. Santa Pola and **Guardamar del Segura** are good options, with fine, clean sand and pine trees behind the dunes, though they are unexciting scenically, and facilities for sports and eating are rather limited.

Dining and Lodging

Dining

In the Valencian provinces, rice grows better than anywhere else in Spain—which explains why the now ubiquitous paella originated here. Another rice dish to try is *arroz a banda* (meat or fish and vegetables cooked over a wood fire). Remember that paella should be eaten directly after cooking, so don't order it from a *menú del día* (menu of the day) before checking its freshness. Alicante and Jijona are famous for their turrón, a kind of nougat made with almonds and flavored with honey. In Elche you can eat fresh dates. Murcian cooking uses products of the huerta and the sea, with a marked Arab influence in the preparation. The *caldero de Mar Menor* deserves special mention: Traditionally a fisherman's rice dish, it is cooked in huge iron pots and has a distinctly oily consistency, flavored by fish cooked in its own juices. Delicious as tapas or a first course are *muchirones* (broad beans in a spicy sauce), similar to the Catalan *habas a la catalana*, as well as *cocas* (meat pies similar to *empanadas*). In Almería, *gazpacho andaluz* (often described as a spicy, liquid salad—and here characterized by the addition of croutons) appears on the menu. It is also the place for *pescaditos fritos* (small fried fish), as well as grapes.

Highly recommended restaurants are indicated by a star ★.

Category	Cost*
$$$$	over 6,500 ptas
$$$	4,500–6,500 ptas
$$	2,000–4,500 ptas
$	under 2,000 ptas

*per person, for a three-course meal excluding drinks, service, and tax

Lodging

Many of the hotels on the coast are modern high rises. When trying to avoid this grouping, one is often faced with a choice between character and comfort. Paradors have traditionally solved this conundrum, and there are four in the region: Jávea, Puerto Lumbreras (Lorca), Mojácar, and Albacete. The last of these, likely to be off most people's itineraries, is the most representative of the rustic, parador style. The others are tasteful, albeit modern. There are older, one-of-a-kind hotels in Calpe, Alicante, San José, and Almería. It is safest always to make reservations in advance; you never know when a local trade fair is going to snag your plans. Be aware that some coastal hotels close for the winter.

Highly recommended hotels are indicated by a star ★.

Category	Cost*
$$$$	over 18,000 ptas
$$$	11,500–18,000 ptas
$$	7,000–11,500 ptas
$	under 7,000 ptas

*All prices are for a standard double room, excluding tax.

Albacete
Dining and Lodging
★

Parador de la Mancha. Set back from the highway, this low-rise white-washed, *manchego*-style parador has a rustic wood-beamed interior and comfortable, cozy bedrooms. The restaurant serves local cuisine; try the *chuletas de cordero* (lamb chops grilled with garlic). *Apdo. 384, Carretera N-301, 02000 Albacete, tel. 967/22–94–50, fax 967/22–60–92. 70 rooms with bath. Facilities: restaurant, bar, tennis courts, pool, parking. AE, DC, MC, V. $$*

Alcoy
Dining
★

Venta del Pilar. Two and a half km (1½ mi) out on the Valencia road, this 18th-century inn serves superb food. When reserving, ask to be downstairs, where the decor is more in keeping with the building. The cooking includes both local and international dishes; try the *salmón al vinagre de cava* (fresh baked salmon with champagne sauce). *Carretera Valencia 118, tel. 96/559–2325. Reservations advised. Dress: casual. AE, DC, MC, V. Closed Sun., Holy Week, and Aug. $$–$$$*

Lodging

Reconquista. There is nothing at all memorable about the modern high-rise Reconquista, but it is the most comfortable option for miles around. You can compensate for the plain, dated decor in the bedrooms by requesting a view over the river gorge to old Alcoy. The public rooms have an institutional air, with their spotty gray-tiled floors and functional plastic furniture. *Puente San Jorge 1, 03803 Alicante, tel. 96/533–0900, fax 96/533–0955. 77 rooms with bath. Facilities: restaurant, bar, discothèque, parking. AE, DC, MC, V. $$*

Alicante
Dining

Delfin. Don't let the fantastic view over the palm-lined Explanada and Alicante's yacht culture distract you from the imaginative food offered here. Opened in 1961, Delfin remains in the gastronomic front line and wholly modern in its bright first-floor decor and breezy terrace. The cooking is divided equally between seafood and meat dishes. Try the *tosta de salmon* (toasted salmon). *Explanada de España 14, tel. 96/521–4911. Reservations strongly advised. Jacket advised. AE, DC, MC, V. $$$*

★

Quo Vadis. Clocks, chains, and shields hang from the walls in the medieval interior of this most "Spanish" of Alicante's restaurants, just behind the ayuntamiento. Friendly and fast service brings to you, indoors or out, dishes ranging from local seafood like *dorada a la sal* (dorada baked in salt) to Castilian favorites like the various *carnes flambés* (barbecued meats). Come here at any time of day to pick at the tapas that line the bar. *Plaza Santísima Faz 3, tel. 96/521–6660. No reservations. Dress: casual. AE, DC, MC, V. Closed Sun. evening and Mon. in winter. $$*

Lodging

Meliá Alicante. For proximity to the sea and good comfort, you needn't look farther than the Meliá. This huge hotel stands on a reclaimed peninsula jutting out into the Mediterranean, close to the city center. The bedrooms have bright, modern decor and furniture and command sweeping views eastward to the beaches and west to the marina. Downstairs is a shrine to postmodernism, with cool marble floors and low black tables. *Playa del Postiguet, 03001 Alicante, tel. 96/520–5000, fax 96/520–5746. 545 rooms with bath. Facilities: 2 restaurants, piano bar, discothèque, 2 pools, gymnasium, parking. AE, DC, MC, V. $$$–$$$$*

★

Palas. This is Alicante's oldest hotel, and from the ornate lobby up it's also the most stylish. Upstairs, the bedrooms, with Regency furniture, lack carpets, but these shouldn't be necessary in any but the coldest months. Ask for a front room if you value a sea view more than tranquillity. The restaurant, with its summer terrace, is popular for its rice dishes. *Plaza del Mar 5, 03002 Alicante, tel. 96/520–9310, fax 96/514–0120. 49 rooms with bath. Facilities: restaurant, bar, parking. AE, DC, MC, V. $$*

★

Residencia Palas. The Palas's sister hotel has the same prices, less extensive and elegant public rooms, but more comfortable bedrooms, with carpets and restrained rustic decor. The other advantage is the quieter and more picturesque setting on Alicante's arcaded Plaza del Ayuntamiento. *Plaza Ayuntamiento 6, 03002 Ali-*

cante, tel. 96/520–6690, fax 96/514–0120. 53 rooms with bath. Facilities: bar, breakfast room, parking. AE, DC, MC, V. $$

Almería
Dining

Anfora. Fresh food and outstanding fish dishes make Anfora the best restaurant in town. Almerían specialties are cooked with care and accompanied by wines from a huge *bodega* (wine cellar). A good choice is the *ensalada del mar* (seafood salad). The only drawback is the rather gloomy interior. *Teniente Acosta Laynez 3, tel. 950/23–13–74. Reservations advised. Dress: neat but casual. AE, DC, MC, V. Closed Sun. and July 15–31. $$*

Rincón de Juan Pedro. A traditional family-run mesón waits behind the door of Juan Pedro's. Seafood is the specialty; try the *lenguado a la naranja* (sole in orange sauce). The game is also worthwhile in season. The friendly atmosphere is enhanced by a vaulted-cellar dining room. *Plaza del Carmen 5, tel. 950/23–58–19. Reservations advised. Dress: casual. AE, DC, MC, V. Closed Sun. $$*

Imperial. White walls and orange tablecloths set the Andalusian scene for the local seafood and meat recipes cooked here. Outstanding dishes include the *zarzuela de marisco* (mixed seafood), *solomillo a la pimienta verde* (filet mignon with green peppers), and gazpacho andaluz. It is popular with Spanish families at lunchtime and has old-fashioned semiformal service. You can also dine outside on the canopied terrace. *Puerta Purchena 13, tel. 950/23–17–40. Reservations advised. Dress: casual. MC, V. Closed Wed. in winter. $*

Lodging

Gran Hotel Almería. The Gran Hotel has recently undergone redecoration, allegedly at the prompting of King Juan Carlos, who stayed here in 1988. The bedrooms now contain brightly painted walls and chintz coverings to complement their fine views over Almería's harbor. The huge marbled reception rooms evoke the hotel's golden era, when it played host to the film directors who came to make spaghetti westerns in the desert interior. *Avenida Reina Regente 8, 04001 Almería, tel. 950/23–80–11, fax 950/27–06–91. 117 rooms with bath. Facilities: bar, breakfast room, pool, parking. AE, DC, MC, V. $$$*

Torreluz II. Value for money is the overriding attraction of this comfortable, elegant, and modern hotel. The bedrooms are slick and bright, with the kind of installations you'd expect to have to pay more for. *Plaza Flores 1, 04001 Almería, tel. 950/23–47–99. 73 rooms with bath. Facilities: bar, parking. AE, DC, MC, V. $–$$*

Hostal Andalucía. If you stay in only one *hostal* during your time in Spain, make it this one. A scruffy white facade leads through to a large, ornate lobby, off which open an azulejo-tiled restaurant and the bedrooms. Ask for a room with a view and then bask in the old-fashioned atmosphere and fantastic value of it all. The non–air-conditioned sea air can make beds slightly damp, so air them on arrival. *Granada 9, 04003 Almería, tel. 950/23–77–33. 76 rooms, 37 with bath. No credit cards. $*

Altea
Dining

La Costera. This restaurant offers bizarre decor as well as a nightly show. The excellent cooking, with Swiss specialties, includes the delicious *rostit con carne troceada y champiñon* (chopped meat with mushrooms and potatoes). It is extremely popular and often booked long ahead. *Costera del Mestre la Música 8, tel. 96/584–0230. Reservations strongly advised. Dress: neat but casual. DC, MC, V. Closed Wed. and Aug. $$$*

Los Belones
Lodging

La Manga Club-Hotel. Golf pervades this superbly situated luxury clubhouse/hotel, just above Mar Menor. Most of its patrons come here to wallow in the golfy ambience of what has become Sevy Ballesteros's home course. It includes a cricket pitch, which probably accounts for the surfeit of British-registered Range Rovers in the parking lot. You can also rent apartments or villas. *La Manga Club, Los Belones, 30385 Murcia, tel. 968/56–45–11, fax 968/56–47–50. 47 rooms with bath. Facilities: restaurant, bar, sauna, Jacuzzi, 2 squash courts, 17 tennis courts, 2 pools, 2 golf courses, parking. Reservations required. AE, DC, MC, V. $$$$*

Benidorm
Dining

Tiffany's. The red and white tones of Tiffany's are where Benidorm's jet set come for intimacy and fine international cuisine. Delicacies like *salmón con langostinos* and *entrecote al roquefort* (steak in roquefort sauce) are brought to you to the accompaniment of piano music. *Avenida Mediterráneo, Edificio Coblanca 3, tel. 96/585–4468. Reservations strongly advised. Dress: casual chic. AE, DC, MC, V. Closed for lunch and Jan. 6–Feb. 6. $$$*

I Fratelli. Like its name and owners, the cooking here is Italian, with nouvelle French and international touches. Neapolitan music complements the stylish *modernista* decor: sleek black chairs, white tablecloths, and exotic potted plants. Try the *pescados a la sal* (fish baked in salt) or a pasta dish. *Dr. Orts Llorca, tel. 96/585–3979. Reservations strongly advised. Dress: neat but casual. AE, DC, MC, V. Closed Nov. $$*

Lodging

Gran Delfín. Of the umpteen-thousands of hotel beds in Benidorm, those in the Gran Delfín are the most quietly situated. This does not preclude taking optimum advantage of Benidorm's attractions. The *salón* downstairs is filled with a motley collection of furniture. The bedrooms are furnished Castellano- (Castilian-) style with a smattering of bric-a-brac on the walls. Ask for a room at the front overlooking the beach. *Playa de Poniente, Benidorm, 03500 Alicante, tel. 96/585–3400, fax 96/585–2100. 87 rooms with bath. Facilities: restaurant, bar, pool, tennis courts, parking. AE, DC, MC, V. Closed Oct.–Apr. 5. $$$*

More economical options in Benidorm include: **Don Pancho** (Avenida Mediterráneo 39, tel. 96/585–2950; $–$$), well furnished with Spanish colonial and Aztec motifs in its decor, and **Las Garzas** (Avenida Marina Española s/n, tel. 96/585–4850; $$), in a quiet location by Poniente Beach.

Calpe
Lodging
★

Venta la Chata. This pretty hotel represents good value. The downstairs is rustic, as are the dark wood furnishings and azulejo-tiled floors in the bedrooms. The premises include terraced gardens with views down to the sea and a good restaurant serving fresh fish and vegetables. You won't find a happier roadside halt. *Carretera de Valencia (N332, Km 150), 03710 Alicante, tel. 96/583–0308. Facilities: restaurant, bar, ping-pong, tennis courts, parking. AE, DC, MC, V. $*

Cullera
Dining
★

Les Mouettes. On the road up to the castle, this tiny restaurant with only a dozen tables has a lovely terrace with stunning sea views. The French owner/chef Jacqueline Lagarce prepares secret recipes from home; try the *mousse de salmón con coulis de tomate fresco* (salmon mousse with slices of tomato). *Carretera subida al Castillo, tel. 96/172–0010. Reservations strongly advised. Dress: neat but casual. AE, DC, MC, V. Closed Dec. 15–Feb. 15, Sun. evening, and Mon. in winter; open daily July–Sept. $$$*

Elche
Dining and Lodging
★

Huerto del Cura. A subtropical location and a large private garden in Elche's palm grove render this a perfect place for rest and relaxation. The main building of the modern low-rise semiparador houses the excellent Els Capellans restaurant, which serves regional rice and fish dishes. Bungalow huts contain the bedrooms, somewhat gloomy due to the shady location, but with tasteful decor in keeping with the surroundings. The palm-ringed swimming pool resembles something you might hope for on a trip to the Seychelles. *Porta de la Morera, Elche, 03200 Alicante, tel. 96/545–8040, fax 96/542–1910. 70 rooms with bath. Facilities: restaurant, bar, cafeteria, 2 pools, sauna, tennis courts, parking. AE, DC, MC, V. $$$*

Gandía **Meson Gallego.** This restaurant serving northern cuisine (from Gali-
Dining cia) in the heart of paella country is a lucky discovery in the port area. The rough and simple decor is a good setting for putting away hearty Gallegan dishes such as *pulpo* (octopus), or fish and meat specialties cooked over coals. Ask for the typically Gallegan shallow ceramic bowls for drinking the young *ribeira* wines. *Levante 37, Grao de Gandía, tel. 96/284–1892. Reservations advised. Dress: casual. AE, DC, MC, V. $$*

Jávea **Parador Costa Blanca.** Enjoying an unbeatable location on a head-
Dining and land between Jávea's two beaches, this modern parador has a large
Lodging garden with pines, palms, and an attractive swimming pool. Although the restrained pale tones are a lot better than you'll find in its nearby competitors, the interior doesn't quite meet the near-universal parador standard. *Parador de la Costa Blanca, Jávea, 03730 Alicante, tel. 96/579–0200, fax 96/579–0308. 65 rooms with bath. Facilities: restaurant, bar, pool, parking. AE, DC, MC, V. $$–$$$*

Lorca **Cándido.** On the road into town, this is a rustic, old-fashioned res-
Dining taurant that has been going strong on its home cooking for more
★ than half a century. The ambience is relaxed, and the clientele a happy mix of Lorcans and travelers. The inspiration in the kitchen comes from the region; try the *trigo con arroz y caracoles* (wheat with rice and snails), a typical Lorca offering. *Santo Domingo 13, tel. 968/46–69–07. No reservations. Dress: casual. No credit cards. Closed Sun. in summer. $–$$*

Lodging *See* Puerto Lumbreras, *below.*

La Manga del *See* Los Belones, *above.*
Mar Menor

Mojácar **El Palacio de Mojácar.** Installed in an old white Mojácar house with
Dining exposed beams and fireplace, this restaurant specializes in good food. The friendly owner-chef doesn't have a large menu, but what there is tends to be highly original and inventive. Ask for local specialties such as *ajo colorao* (red garlic) or *Caldo de pescado* (fish broth). *Plaza del Cano, tel. 950/47–82–79. Reservations advised in summer. Dress: casual. AE, MC, V. Closed Thurs. and Nov.–Feb. $$*

Lodging **Parador Reyes Católicos.** If you agree that it is preferable to be by
★ the sea than up in the old town, this rambling white modern parador is the best option in Mojácar. The public rooms are some of the most spacious and tasteful you'll find anywhere. Large open-plan fireplaces contribute the rustic ingredient. Bedrooms are similarly bright, with parador-style Castellano furniture. *Carretera de Carboneras, 04638 Almería, tel. 951/47–82–50, fax 951/478–183. 98 rooms with bath. Facilities: restaurant, bar, tennis courts, pool, parking. AE, DC, MC, V. $$$*
El Moresco. Up in the village itself, this hotel has a stunning position and tasteful country decor, but it tends to be descended upon by large tour groups. *Avda. Horizón s/n, 04638 Almería, tel. 951/47–8025. 147 rooms with bath. Facilities: pool. AE, DC, MC, V. $$*

Moraira **El Girasol.** An elegant, ivy-cloaked villa on the Calpe road houses
Dining one of the finest restaurants in this region. Owners Joachim and Vic-
★ toria Koerper preside over a small dining room and terrace. Their cooking is outstanding and imaginative, with the emphasis on

French dishes. Highlights on the menu include *ensalada de salmonetes a la vinagretta de naranja* (red mullet salad with orange vinegar). *Carretera Moraira a Calpe, tel. 96/574–4373. Reservations strongly advised. AE, DC, MC, V. Closed Mon. (except July–Aug.), lunch July–Aug. (except Sun.), and Jan. 15–Mar. 1. $$$*

Lodging **Hotel Swiss Moraira.** With a secluded location in a pine forest above Moraira (off the road to Calpe) and well-decorated rooms around an artistically conceived swimming pool, this low-rise luxury hotel is ideal for peace and comfort. During the day, guests leave for the beach and marina, 3.2 km (2 mi) away. *Club Moraira, 03724 Alicante, tel. 96/574–7104, fax 96/574–7074. 26 rooms with bath. Facilities: restaurant, bar, tennis, pool, parking. AE, DC, MC, V. Closed mid-Jan.–Feb. 5. $$$*

Murcia **Rincón de Pepe.** A rambling series of casually decorated dining
Dining rooms greets locals and visitors. Chef Raimundo Frutos doubles as
★ an organic farmer and sticks closely to these ingredients, with only the freshest supplements, such as the fish from Mar Menor. Highlights on the extensive menu include *ensalada de mariscos y trufas* (shellfish and truffle salad). *Apóstoles 34, tel. 968/21–22–39. Reservations advised. Jacket advised. AE, DC, MC, V. Closed Sun. in summer, Sun. evening in winter. $$$*

Hispano. For a typically Spanish brand of rusticity, including walls crowded with heavy oil paintings, look no farther than the Hispano. A well-known Murcian family of restaurateurs-hoteliers created this restaurant some 20 years ago, and it is still extremely popular for Murcian, traditional, and nouvelle cuisine. *Lucas 7, tel. 968/21–61–52. Reservations advised. Dress: neat but casual. AE, DC, MC, V. Closed Sat. in summer. $$*

Lodging **Rincón de Pepe.** The name of this modern hotel is more famous for the restaurant next door. The location could not be better, in the center of the old town, 45 m (50 yds) from the cathedral's apse. It offers good comfort and hospitality. The bedrooms all have modern, bright, and restrained decor. The lobby and reception rooms have cool marble floors. *Apóstoles 34, 30001 Murcia, tel. 968/21–22–39, fax 968/22–17–44. 115 rooms with bath. Facilities: bar, parking. AE, DC, MC, V. $$$*

Hispano 1. The functional decor of this budget hotel has been well chosen. The bedrooms are bright and airy; ask for an exterior one. The first-floor sitting room is large, with tasteful furnishings. The location is very central, and the street outside is pedestrianized. *Trapería 8 y 10, 30001 Murcia, tel. 968/21–61–52, fax 968/21–68–59. 46 rooms with bath. Facilities: breakfast room, parking. AE, DC, MC, V. $*

Puerto **Parador de Puerto Lumbreras.** South of Lorca, where the road di-
Lumbreras vides to Granada or Almería, stands this modern parador with a gar-
Lodging den and swimming pool. The tranquil setting and smart modern decor provide a good base where you can pause before deciding which route south to take. *Carretera N340, 30890 Murcia, tel. 968/40–20–25, fax 968/40–28–36. 60 rooms with bath. Facilities: restaurant, bar, pool, parking. AE, DC, MC, V. $$*

San José **San José.** For access to the beautifully rugged coast toward Cape
Lodging Gata, you couldn't choose a happier spot than this tiny hotel in the
★ laid-back village of San José. The medium-size villa, superbly positioned above San José's bay, has just eight very large bedrooms, all tastefully decorated and with great sea views, around a central large sitting room with an open fire. Its size means that it is crucial to book well ahead of your visit. *Carretera a Monsul y Genoveses,*

04118 Almería, tel. 950/38–01–16, fax 951/38–00–02. 8 rooms with bath. Facilities: restaurant, parking. MC, V. Closed mid-Jan.–mid-Mar. $$

The Arts and Nightlife

The Arts

Local festivals all provide excellent entertainment. Tourist offices will point you toward the best of the action, while local papers are useful for cinemas and the like.

Alcoy's spectacular *Moros y Cristianos* (Moors and Christians) festival takes place April 21–24 (*see* Tour 2, *above*). Altea (third Sunday in May), Lorca (Nov.), Murcia (Sept.), and Villajoyosa (July 21–24) all hold similar events. **Alicante's** main festival is the *Hogueras de San Juan* (St. John's Day Bonfires), June 21–24. **Almería's** *Festival Internacional de Títeres* (Puppet Theater Festival) is held in January. **Denia** holds a mini *Fallas*, March 16–19. In **Elche** *El Misteri* (The Mystery Play) is performed in two parts, August 14–15, and preceded by a public dress rehearsal (Aug. 13). The *Semana Santa* (Holy Week) processions in **Murcia** and **Lorca** are among the most impressive and famous in Spain.

Nightlife

There is no shortage of discothèques and flamenco *tablaos* (floor shows) along the Costa Blanca, and most towns are lively after dark if you find the right places.

Discotheques In **Alicante** roughish but lively bars are found all through the small streets behind the ayuntamiento. Among the slicker pubs and discotheques are **O Chic** (Serrano 11) and the **Discoteca Bugatti** (San Fernando 37). In summer, the liveliest nighttime place is the beach at San Juan; **O'Ku** (Avenida Costa Blanca), a discothèque, and **Caligula** (Playa de San Juan), a pub, are both popular.

In **Benidorm,** countless bars and discos, with names like Jockey's and Harrods, line Avenida de Europa and the Ensanche de la Playa de Levante.

Flamenco In **Almería** go to the ayuntamiento for names and locations of tablaos. You won't have any difficulty finding a flamenco tablao in **Benidorm.** They do vary a lot in quality, so consult the Tourist Office first.

Cabaret For cabaret, try the **Benidorm Palace** (Diputación, tel. 965/85–1661). Alternatively, visit the **Nuevo Gran Castillo Conde de Alfaz** (Camino Viejo del Albir, tel. 96/588–8592), don a crown, and dine in front of jousting medieval knights. If it sounds touristy, that's because it is. Price per person is 3,500 pesetas (children: 2,500 pesetas), including dinner, drinks, and the show.

Casinos There are two casinos in the area, in **Villajoyosa** (tel. 96/589–0700; open 8 AM–4 AM) and **La Manga del Mar Menor** (tel. 968/56–38–50). Remember to bring your passport to play at the tables.

11 The Balearic Islands

By Sean
Hignett

Updated by
George Semler

The Balearic Islands of Mallorca, Menorca, Ibiza, and Formentera
lie between 80 and 242 km (50 and 150 mi) from Spain's Mediterranean
an coast, halfway between France and Africa. Their strategic position made the islands an important maritime staging post, and they
became, in turn, dominions of the Phoenician, the Roman, and the
Byzantine empires before being occupied by the Moors in 902.

The Moors remained until they were ousted by Jaume I of the House
of Aragón in the 13th century. For a brief but much-celebrated period, the islands were an independent kingdom; then, in 1343, they
were subsumed once more under Pedro IV, and on the marriage of
Isabella of Castile to Ferdinand of Aragón in 1469, the Balearics became part of a united Spain. During the War of the Spanish Succession, however, Britain occupied Menorca in 1704 to secure the
superb natural harbor of Mahón as a naval base. The British remained in Menorca for almost a century, interrupted only by a surprise invasion in 1756 that gave the French control for 12 years and a
shorter reoccupation by the Spanish 20 years later. Under the Treaty of Amiens, Great Britain finally returned Menorca to Spain in
1802.

Menorca diverged once more during the Spanish civil war, declaring
staunchly for the Republican cause while Mallorca and Ibiza supported the Fascists. To this day, the topic is still one to be broached
delicately within the islands, which, in many ways, remain fiercely
independent of one another.

The tourist boom, which started during the regime of General
Franco, turned great stretches of the coastlines of Mallorca and Ibiza into unplanned strips of high-rise hotels, fast-food restaurants,
and discos. Recently, ecology-minded inhabitants have made some
headway in lobbying for laws to restrict shoreline development.

In 1983 the Balearics became an autonomous province, and one
effect has been the gradual replacement of Castilian Spanish by
the Catalan language (banned for official use by Franco) in its
Mallorquín, Menorquín, and Ibizencan dialects. The only occasions
on which this is likely to confuse the visitor is with regard to place
names, particularly because outside the islands, and especially in
the travel industry, the Spanish names are still used. Within the islands the problem is compounded by the fact that where road signs
have not been officially altered, they are sometimes obliterated by
aerosol spray paints. In the sections that follow, Catalan or Spanish
is used according to whichever seems to be used locally. *Carrer*
(street) and *Plaça* (square) are Catalan; *Calle* and *Plaza* are Spanish.

Place names that may cause confusion are (Spanish version first):

Mallorca: La Puebla—Sa Pobla; Santa Margarita—Santa Margalida; Colonia San Pedro—Colonia Sant Per; San Juan—Sant Joan.
Road signs are sometimes sprayed with the word "Ciutat," meaning
"the city"—i.e., Palma.

Menorca: Mahón—Maó; Ciudadela—Ciutadella.

Ibiza: Santa Inés—Santa Agnes; San Miguel—Sant Miquel; San
Jorge—Sant Jordi; San Antonio Abad—Sant Antoni de Portmany;
San José—Sant Josep; San Juan—Sant Joan; Ibiza—Eivissa (Ibiza
town is also "Ciutat").

Formentera: San Francisco—Sant Francesc; San Fernando—Sant
Ferran.

Essential Information

Important Addresses and Numbers

Tourist Information The regional tourist office for the Balearic Islands is the **Consellaria de Turismo de Balear** (Av. Jaume III 10, Palma, tel. 971/71–22–16).

The **Mallorcan Tourist Board** (Palma Airport, tel. 971/26–08–03) is supplemented in **Mallorca** by municipal tourist offices in **Alcúdia** (Carretera Port d'Alcúdia–Arta s/n, tel. 971/54–86–15), **Palma** (Carrer Sant Domingo 11, tel. 971/72–40–90; kiosk on northeast side of Plaça d'Espanya, facing railway station, tel. 971/71–15–27; open weekdays 9–2:30, Sat. 9–1:30, closed Sun.), **Pollença** (Carrer Miquel Capllonch, Port de Pollença, tel. 971/53–46–66), **Sóller** (Plaça de Sa Constitució 1, tel. 971/63–02–00; Carrer Canónigo Oliver, Port de Sóller, tel. 971/63–01–01), and **Valldemossa** (at ticket office adjacent to monastery, Cartuja de Valldemossa, tel. 971/61–21–06).

Local tourist information for **Menorca** can be obtained in **Mahón** (Oficina de Información Turística de Menorca, Plaça Explanada 40, tel. 971/36–37–90) and in **Ciutadella** (mobile office, open irregularly Apr.–Sept., and at the police station in the Ajuntament, Plaça d'Es Born, open 24 hours); the best map for all purposes is the *Mapa Arqueológico de Menorca*, available in bookshops and some hotels.

Local tourist offices in **Ibiza** and **Formentera** are in **Eivissa** (Oficina de Información Turistica de Ibiza, Passeig Vara de Rey 13, tel. 971/30–19–00; open weekdays 9:30–1:30 and 5:00–7, Sat. 10–1), **Santa Eulalia** (Carrer Mariano Riquer Wallis s/n, tel. 971/33–07–28), **Sant Antoni** (Passeig de Ses Fonts s/n, tel. 971/34–33–63), and **Port de la Sabina** (Formentera, tel. 971/32–08–01).

Emergencies **Police,** tel. 091 or 092 (except Ciutadella, tel. 971/38–10–95; and Formentera, tel. 971/32–02–10). **Medical emergencies,** Clinica Juaneda (Son Espanyolet, tel. 971/72–22–22).

Consulates: United States: Avinguda Jaume III 26, Palma, Mallorca, tel. 971/72–26–60; **United Kingdom:** Plaça Major 3D, Palma, Mallorca, tel. 971/71–24–47, and Torret 28, Sant Lluis, Mahón, Menorca, tel. 971/36–64–39.

Pharmacies Pharmacies are open late by rotation. Schedules are posted on the door of each pharmacy and in local newspapers.

Travel Agencies **Viajes Barcelos** (*Palma, Mallorca:* Av. Jaume III 2, tel. 971/559–0874; *Mahón, Menorca:* Av. Josep María Cuadrado 1, tel. 971/36–02–50; *Ciutadella, Menorca:* Cami de Maó 5, tel. 971/38–04–87; *Eivissa, Ibiza:* Av. d'Espanya s/n, tel. 971/30–32–50); **Viajes Wagons-Lits Cook** (*Mahón, Menorca:* Plaça Constitució 9, tel. 971/36–41–62; *Eivissa, Ibiza:* Passeig Vara de Rey 3, tel. 971/30–15–03).

Car Rental Cars are available through **Avis** and **Betacar** (Palma, Mahón, and Ibiza airports), **Hertz** (Palma and Ibiza airports), **Hiper Rent-a-Car** (Mallorca, Son Garcias, Apartado de Correos 50, Ca'n Pastilla, tel. 971/26–99–11 or 971/26–22–23, fax 971/49–20–00), and **Pitiusas** (Ibiza Airport); local firms rent motorbikes, scooters, mopeds, and bicycles as well (ask for a crash helmet).

Arriving and Departing by Plane

Serving **Mallorca,** Iberia and Aviaco have several direct flights daily between Palma (tel. 971/26–46–24) and Barcelona, Madrid, Alicante, Valencia, Menorca, and Ibiza, as well as direct flights two or three times a week to Bilbao and Vitoria. The interisland flights (Ibiza and Menorca) are very full in the summer months and should be booked well in advance. Iberia and a large number of charter operators also have flights between Palma and major European cities. Bus No. 17 runs between Palma Airport and the out-of-town bus station on Plaça d' Espanya, next to the Inca railway terminus. On both outward and inward journeys, it travels first to Terminal B, then to Terminal A, every 30 minutes until 9 PM, then about once an hour. The last bus from town is at 11 PM; the last bus from the airport is at midnight. (Fare: 350 pesetas; evenings and holidays, 400 pesetas. Journey time: 30 minutes.) Taxi fare from Palma Airport to downtown starts at 2,500 pesetas.

Aviaco flies direct to Mahón, **Menorca,** from Barcelona and from Palma three or four times daily. A large number of direct charter flights go to Menorca from many European cities in the summer. A metered taxi to Mahón costs about 1,100 pesetas.

Aviaco (tel. 971/30–25–77 or 971/30–67–72) has several direct scheduled flights daily to **Ibiza** from Barcelona, Madrid, Valencia, and Palma. These are supplemented in season by numerous charter flights from many European cities. For airport information, call 971/30–03–00. An hourly bus service runs between Ibiza Airport and Eivissa (Ibiza Town) from 7 AM to 10:30 PM (on the hour from town, on the half-hour from the airport; fare: 350 pesetas; journey time: 15 minutes). A taxi costs about 2,500 pesetas.

Arriving and Departing by Ferry

Serving **Mallorca, Trasmediterránea** (Est. Marítima 2, Muelle de Peraires 07012, tel. 971/40–50–14, fax 971/40–59–64) sails at least once a day between Palma and Barcelona and Valencia; once a week (Sunday) between Palma and Mahón (Menorca) and Palma and Ibiza. Fares are, oddly enough, higher than the airline fares. From May to October there is also a daily hydrofoil (**Hidrojet**) service between Palma and Ibiza: **Naviera Mallorquina** (tel. 971/71–01–53). From France a service operates between Sète and Palma twice a week, June to September. The short sea crossing between **Ciutadella,** at the western tip of Menorca, and **Alcúdia,** in the north of Mallorca, has been reopened; details are available at the ticket offices in Ciutadella and Alcúdia harbors.

Serving **Menorca, Trasmediterránea** (tel. 971/36–60–50) sails from Mahón three times a week to Barcelona Easter and summer (June 15–Sept. 15), daily except Fridays, once a week to Palma and Valencia. Journey times: Barcelona, 9 hours; Valencia, via Palma, 16 hours overall.

Serving **Ibiza, Trasmediterránea** (tel. 971/31–50–11) sails at least twice a week to and from Barcelona, Palma, and Valencia. From May until October there is also daily hydrofoil (**Hidrojet**) service from Palma, Alicante, and Denia, as well as less frequent services from Valencia and Barcelona. A service operates between Sète (France) and Ibiza twice a week, June to September, calling at Palma on the way.

Between San Antonio in the west of Ibiza and Denia on the mainland, **Flebasa** (Estació Marítim, Eivissa, tel. 971/31–09–27; Edificio Faro, San Antonio, tel. 971/34–28–71; Madrid, tel. 91/473–20–55; Denia, tel. 96/78–40–11) operates both a car ferry and a fast hydrofoil with coach connections to Madrid, Alicante, and Valencia.

Flebasa can also ferry you and your car from Alcudia, Mallorca to Ciutadella, Menorca in 2½ hours. Finally, a Hovercraft covers the journey between San Antonio and Benidorm on the mainland in 2½ hours, daily in the summer months; for information and reservations, contact **Coral Travel** (Carrer Mar 11, Sant Antoni, tel. 971/34–37–11 or 971/34–37–52, fax 971/34–42–66; Carrer Isadora Macabich 14, Santa Eulàlia, tel. 971/33–05–12 or 971/33–05–61).

Frequent services to **Formentera** from Ibiza by car ferry, catamaran, and hydrofoil are operated by **Transmapi** (tel. 971/31–45–13, 971/31–07–11; Formentera, tel. 971/32–07–03), **Marítima de Formentera** (tel. 971/32–01–57), and **Flebasa** (tel. 971/31–09–27).

Getting Around

By Car In **Mallorca** main highways are well surfaced, and traveling times can be reasonably fast on the flat plain that comprises most of the island. Driving in the mountains that run the length of the northwest coast and descend to a cliffside corniche is a different matter. Not only will the winding roads slow you down; so will the tremendous views and the cars of other tourists.

If you want to go beach hopping in **Menorca,** a car is essential because few of the island's beaches and *calas* (coves) are served by public transport. However, most of the sights are in Mahón or Ciutadella, both of which have a reasonable bus service from other parts of the island, and once you are in town, everything is within walking distance. The island's archaeological remains can easily be seen in a day's drive, so, where cost matters, a reasonable compromise might be to rent a car for just a part of your visit. The main roads are good; others may be narrow.

A car or motor scooter is the best means of exploring **Ibiza,** because many of the beaches lie at the end of rough, unpaved roads. The main highways are well surfaced and relatively straight, making for fast driving. Several new roads, crossing the island in the north, have recently been constructed, replacing twisting country lanes.

By Train **Mallorca** has two separate railway systems. The Palma–Inca line travels to Inca, with stops at Santa María and Consell, from the Palma terminus (Ferrocarriles de Mallorca, Plaça d'Espanya, tel. 971/75–22–24). A journey on the privately owned Palma–Sóller railway is a must. Built by the rich citrus-fruit farmers of Sóller at the beginning of the century, it still uses the carriages of that era. The line trundles across the plain to Bunyola, then winds through tremendous mountain scenery to emerge high above Sóller, to whose station it circles slowly down. An ancient tram connects the Sóller terminus to Port de Sóller, leaving every hour on the hour, 9–7. The Palma terminal (tel. 971/75–20–28) is in the corner of Plaça d' Espanya, on Calle Eusebi Estada, just north of the Inca railway station.

By Bus A good network of bus services fans out from Palma to towns and villages throughout **Mallorca.** Most of these leave from the out-of-town bus station (Estació Central, tel. 971/75–22–24) adjacent to the Inca railway terminus on Plaça d'Espanya, but a few terminate at other points within the city. Full details and timetables are available from the Tourist Office.

Several buses a day run the length of **Menorca,** between Mahón and Ciutadella, calling at the island's other principal towns—Alayor, Mercadal, and Ferreries—en route. From the smaller villages there are buses each day to Mahón and, to a lesser extent, to Ciutadella. A regular bus service from the west end of the Plaça Explanada in Ciutadella ferries visitors between the town and the tourist resorts to the south and west.

In **Ibiza** buses run every half hour from Eivissa (bus terminal, Avinguda Isadora Macabich) to Sant Antoni and to Playa d'En Bossa and about once an hour to Santa Eulàlia. Buses from Eivissa to other parts of the island are much less frequent, as is the cross-island bus between Sant Antoni and Santa Eulàlia. The timetable is published in the daily newspapers.

A very limited bus service operates between the villages of **Formentera,** shrinking to one bus each way between San Francisco and Pilar on Saturdays and disappearing altogether on Sundays and holidays. Details are in Ibizan newspapers.

By Boat Boats from Palma, **Mallorca,** to neighboring beach resorts leave from the jetty opposite the Auditorium on the Passeig Marítim. The Tourist Office has a detailed timetable.

Despite the fact that many of **Menorca's** beaches are difficult to reach by road, the only bays to which boat trips are organized are Macarella, Cala Mitjana, and Cala Trebaluger, all reached from Cala Galdana.

By Carriage In **Mallorca** horse-drawn carriages, accommodating four to five passengers, can be found in Palma at the bottom of the Born, on Avinguda Antonio Maura, in the Cathedral Square nearby, and on Plaça d'Espanya—the side farthest from the railway station. A city tour costs about 4,000 pesetas.

By Taxi Taxis in Palma, **Mallorca,** have meters. For trips beyond the city, there are standard charges, displayed at the taxi ranks. In **Menorca** taxis can be found at the airport and in Mahón (Explanada; radio taxi, tel. 971/36–71–11) and Ciutadella (Carrer Josep Antoni; radio taxi, tel. 971/38–18–96). In **Ibiza**, taxis are available at the airport (tel. 971/30–52–30) and in Eivissa (Passeig Vara de Rey, tel. 971/30–17–94; radio taxi, tel. 971/30–70–00 or 971/30–66–02), Figueretas (tel. 971/30–16–76), Santa Eulalia (tel. 971/33–30–33), and San Antonio (tel. 971/34–00–74 or 971/34–17–21). In **Formentera** taxis are in La Sabina (tel. 971/32–20–02 or 971/32–30–16) and Es Pujols (tel. 971/32–80–16).

Guided Tours

Most hotels in **Mallorca** offer a variety of guided tours—ask the hotel porter for information. Typical itineraries are to the Caves of Artà or Drac on the east coast, taking in the Auto-Safari Park nearby and stopping off at an artificial pearl factory in Manacor on the way; to the Chopin museum in the former monastery at Valldemossa, returning through the writers' and artists' village of Deya; the port of Sóller and the Arab gardens at Alfabia; the Thursday market and leather factories at Inca; Port de Pollença; Cape Formentor; and northern beaches.

Boat Tours Around **Mallorca,** almost every resort has excursions to neighboring beaches and coves, many of them inaccessible by road, and to the offshore islands of Cabrera and Dragonera. There are also morning shopping trips by boat from Magaluf and Palma Nova to Palma. A detailed timetable is available from the Tourist Office.

In **Menorca** there are various types of sightseeing trips around Mahón harbor, all originating at quayside near the Xoriguer gin factory. Tickets for the day trips on the *Don Pancho,* which run between 10 AM and 5 PM, can be bought at the Aquarium (tel. 971/35–05–37). The cost is around 4,000 pesetas, with lunch; special prices for groups can be negotiated. Tickets for one-hour trips are available at the Xoriguer ginnery and cost about 900 pesetas. Outings can be organized directly with the captain of the *Menorquin*, Olegario Preto (tel. 971/35–31–52). Excursions from Es Grau to the Illa d'en Colom can be reserved at the Bar Can Bernat (Es Grau, tel. 971/36–99–36).

Trips from **Ibiza** to Formentera include an escorted coach tour, and every resort offers trips to neighboring beaches and to islands off the coast. At San Antonio, which has little to offer in the way of a beach itself, a whole flotilla advertises trips.

Mallorca

Mallorca, more than five times the size of either Menorca or Ibiza, is roughly saddle shaped. A tough mountain range, the Sierra de Tramuntana, soaring to nearly 1,550 meters (5,000 feet), runs the length of the northwest coast; a ridge of hills borders the southeast shores; and between lies a great flat plain that in early spring is a sea of almond blossoms, the "snow of Mallorca." Though the island, with more than 5 million visitors per year, has the reputation of a cheap getaway, especially among British holidaymakers, the package-tour industry is confined to a narrow coastal strip. Elsewhere, Mallorca has a great deal of relatively undiscovered character and charm, particularly in the mountains of the northwest. Architecturally, it is closest to mainland Spain. It offers a wealth of natural and historic sightseeing opportunities in caves, bird sanctuaries, abandoned monasteries, tiny museums, and village markets.

Our tours are confined to the rugged west of the island. The east is made up of flat farmland dotted with iron-and-timber windmills that used to pump water for irrigation. The beach resorts are easy of access but predictably developed. Exceptions to this blanket avoidance advice include Artà and surrounding hills (*see* Off the Beaten Track, *below*) and the amazing Caves of Drac (*see* What to See and Do With Children, *below*).

Numbers in the margin correspond to points of interest on the Mallorca map.

Tour 1: Palma

❶ If you look at a map of the city of **Palma,** you will see, north of the cathedral—or La Seu, as it is known to Mallorcans—the jumble of tiny streets around the Plaça de Cort that made up the very early town. A little farther out, a circle of wide boulevards, known as "the Avenues," zigzags around. These follow the path of the walls built by the Moors to defend the larger city that had grown up by the 12th century. The zigzags mark the position of bastions that jutted out at regular intervals. By the end of the last century the walls had largely been torn down, and the only place where the massive defenses can still be seen is along the seafront.

Through the middle of the old city ran a stream bed (*torrent*), dry for most of the year but, in the rainy season, often a raging flood that annually caused destruction and drowning. In the 17th century this was diverted to the east, along the moat that ran outside the city walls. What was its natural course is now La Rambla and the Passeig d'Es Born, two of the principal shopping streets of Palma. The Born is also the place for the traditional evening *paseo* (promenade).

Mallorca

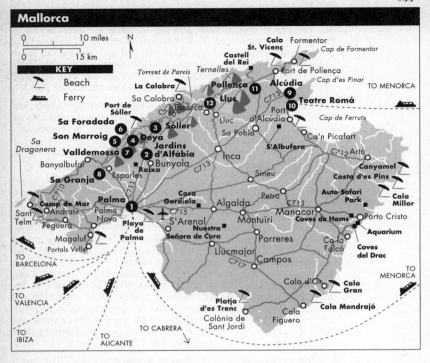

0	10 miles
0	15 km

KEY

Beach

Ferry

Torrent de Pareis · Ternelles · Cala St. Vicenç · Formentor · Cap de Formentor

Castell del Rei · Port de Pollença · Cap d'es Pinar · TO MENORCA

La Calobra · Pollença **11** · Alcúdia

Sa Calobra · Lluc **12** · **9** Teatre Romà

Port de Sóller · Escorca · Port d'Alcúdia **10** · Cap de Ferrutx

Sa Foradada · **6** · **3** Sóller · Lluc · Ca'n Picafort

Son Marroig · **5** · **4** Deià · Sa Pobla · S'Albufera · C712 · Artà

Sa Dragonera · Valldemossa · **7** · **2** Jardins d'Alfàbia · Inca · Sineu · Canyamel · Costa d'es Pins

Banyalbufar · Raixa · Bunyola · C713

Sa Granja · **8** · Esporles · Petra · Auto-Safari Park · Cala Millor

Camp de Mar · Palma · **1** · Casa Gordiola · Algaida · C715 · Manacor · Coves de Hams · Porto Cristo

Sant Telm · Andratx · Palma Nova · C715 · S'Arenal · Montuïri · Aquarium

Peguera · Playa de Palma · Nuestra Señora de Cura · Porreres · Ca-la Falcó · Coves del Drac

Magaluf · Llucmajor · Campos · C717

Portals Vells · TO BARCELONA · TO MENORCA

TO VALENCIA · Cala d'Or · Cala Gran

Platja d'es Trenc · Cala Figuero · Cala Mondrajó

TO IBIZA · TO ALICANTE · TO CABRERA · Colònia de Sant Jordi

If you are traveling by car, use the underground garage beneath the **Parc de la Mar.** On exiting, take a short stroll along the park. Beside it run the huge bastions guarding the Almudaina Palace and the cathedral, golden and pinnacled. In the park itself are examples of modern sculpture, as well as ceramic murals by the late Catalan artist and Mallorca resident Joan Miró.

From the park, follow Avinguda Antoni Maura past the steps that climb to the palace. At Plaça de la Reina, the Born begins—a wide avenue with a tree-covered pedestrian promenade running down its center and fashionable shops.

At the top of the Born, turn right on Carrer de la Unió, a little way along Plaça Santa Catalina Tomás. On the far side of the square the ornate facade of the building on the corner of Carrer Santacilia, now a bank, was designed by Antoni Gaudí.

Continue past the Palace of Justice, and on the right, tucked in just before the steps leading up alongside the Teatro Principal, is the **Forn Teatro** (Theater Bakery). You'll see pictures of it as a "typical Mallorcan shop" in all the tourist literature, but in fact it's the only shop like this, with a facade that looks as though it came from a fairground organ. Forn Teatro is famous for its *ensaimadas* (pastries) and its *cocas* (sugary breads). At the top of the steps is Plaça Marqués Palmer. On the left an archway leads to the greater expanse of the **Plaça Major.** A good craft market is held here on Monday, Friday, and Saturday mornings (10–2).

Make your way down Carrer Colon to Plaça Cort, where, on the south side of the square, is the 17th-century **Ajuntament** (Town Hall). The olive tree in the center of the square is reputed to be 500 years old. To the west of the Ajuntament, the Caja de Baleares Sa Nostra, on the corner of Carrer Jaume II and Plaça Cort, occupies a superb building designed in the style of Gaudí.

East of the Ajuntament, follow Carrer Cadena across Plaça Santa Eulàlia to Carrer Arquitecto Reynes and Plaça Sant Francesc. On the north of the plaza is the beautiful 13th-century monastery church of **Sant Francesc** (admission: 350 pesetas; open Mon.–Sat. 9:30–1 and 3:30–7, closed Sun.), founded by Jaume II when his eldest son took monastic orders and gave up all rights to the throne. Later, Fray Junípero Serra, the missionary who founded San Francisco and other California towns, was educated here. The entrance to the church and the finely arched cloisters is through the adjoining collegiate buildings on the east side.

Return to Plaça Santa Eulàlia. Ramón Llull, the 13th-century scholar much celebrated in Mallorca, is said to have ridden his horse into the church of **Santa Eulàlia** in pursuit of a married lady of whom he was enamored in his wild young days before he turned to scholarship and religion. It was in this church also that in 1435, 200 Jews were converted to Christianity when their rabbis were threatened with being burned at the stake.

| **Time Out** | For a light lunch on the plaza, **Café Moderno** has tables outside and good *bocadillos* (sandwiches), while **Bar Santa Eulàlia** has a selection of *tapas* (hors d'oeuvres) indoors at the bar. |

Just south of the plaza, off Carrer Morey, is Carrer Almudaina. The **archway** crossing the narrow street was one of the gates to the early Moorish citadel and, with the Arab Baths, is one of the few relics of Moorish occupation remaining on the island.

To reach the baths, continue down Carrer Morey and take the left fork down Carrer Portella. On the left at No. 5 is the **Museu de Mallorca** (Museum of Mallorca; open Tues.–Sat. 10–2 and 4–7, Sun. 10–2; closed Mon.), with paintings and pottery ranging back to Moorish times. At the bottom of Carrer Portella, turn left onto Carrer Formiguera, a short street that tunnels through the adjoining buildings, then turn left again—it's the only way you can go. A few yards up Carrer de la Serra, in a small garden, are the 10th-century **Banys Arabs** (Arab Baths; admission: 250 pesetas; open daily 10–1:30 and 4–6). The 12 columns supporting the domed roof are all different and are recycled from Roman sites.

At the top of Carrer de la Serra, go left and follow the meandering streets west, until you reach Plaça Almoina, with its antiques shops and restorers, to the north of the **cathedral.** The visitor's entrance to the cathedral is here, through the museum (admission: 300 pesetas; open weekdays 10–12:30 and 4–6:30, Sat. 10–1:30; closed Sun.), which displays ancient manuscripts, religious paintings, and precious jeweled crucifixes and reliquaries. The cathedral proper is an architectural wonder. It took more than 300 years to build, from 1230 to 1601, and the great open expanse of the nave is supported on 14 extraordinarily slender 22-meter (70-ft) columns, which fan out like palm trees at the top. Look up the nave and you will see suspended above the Chapel Royal the curious asymmetrical canopy constructed by Gaudí, who remodeled much of the interior at the beginning of this century. The lights, shining from within the canopy and illuminating the nave, come on at regular intervals, permitting photographs.

Be sure to take note of the bell tower above the cathedral's Plaça Almoina door. It holds nine bells, the largest of which is known as "N'Eloi." N'Eloi was cast in 1389, weighs 4 tons, needs 12 men to ring it, and has been known to shatter the stained-glass windows with its sound. Continuing around the cathedral, you will come to the impressive west facade. The blocked windows are the result of alterations following earthquake damage in 1851.

Opposite is the **Palau de l'Almudaina** (Almudaina Palace), originally an Arab citadel, which was the residence of the royal house of Mallorca in the Middle Ages. It is now a military headquarters and can be visited only on guided tours (every half hour). If you go on Wednesdays and have an EC passport, you will get in free. *Admission: 400 pesetas. Open weekdays 9:30–1:30 and 4–6:30, Sat. 9:30–1:30; closed Sun.*

Steps lead back from the palace to the Parc de Mar.

Other highlights of Palma can also be visited. The **Llotja** (Exchange; open Tues.–Sat. 11–2 and 5–9, Sun. 11–2, during exhibits only, closed Mon.), on the seafront, a little way west of the Born, was built in the 15th century as a commodities exchange. Its slim columns look even more like delicate stone palm trees than do those in the cathedral. The **Poble Espanyol** (Spanish Village; Carrer Capitán Mesquida Veny 39; admission: 300 pesetas; open daily 9–8, crafts shops 10–6), in the western suburbs of the city, is a kind of Disneyland of reproductions of Spanish buildings and styles, intermingled with shops and crafts studios. A little farther, overlooking the city and the bay from a hillside above the Terreno nightlife area, is **Castell de Bellver** (Bellver Castle; admission: 300 pesetas; open Oct.–Mar., Mon.–Sat. 8–6; Apr.–Sept., Mon.–Sat. 8–8; closed Sun.), built on a circular design in the 14th century. There is a terrific view of Palma and the bay from its ramparts.

Tour 2: The Northwest Corniche, Valldemossa, and La Granja

Leave Palma via the Avenues and turn into Carrer 31 de Desembre, C711, just north of Plaça d'Espanya, toward Sóller. Look on the left after about 13 km (8 mi) to see **Raixa**, a beautiful 18th-century palace in landscaped gardens, at the top of a great flight of steps in the Italian style, with statues and fountains on each side. The gates to ❷ **Jardins d'Alfàbia** (Alfàbia Gardens) are 4 km (2½ mi) farther on the right. At the top of the steps is a huge vaulted cistern, built by a Moorish overlord to irrigate the gardens. A path leads around to a café and then winds through a small, thick woods. The chief attraction of the gardens is that they are there at all in a climate where water is not abundant. The house itself is furnished with antiques and lined with painted paneling. *Admission: 400 pesetas. Open Nov.–Mar., Mon.–Sat. 9:30–5; Apr.–Oct., Mon.–Sat. 9:30–6:30; closed Sun. and holidays.*

Continuing from Alfàbia, the road climbs rapidly in a series of hairpins to a *mirador* (vantage point) with excellent views to the south and then reaches a second mirador from which you will see Sóller lying below in a great amphitheater brooded over by Mallorca's highest peaks.

❸ **Sóller** is an attractive gray stone town with a hardy, outdoorsy feel. Find your way to the main Plaça Constitució, dominated by the cathedral; arm yourself with a map from the Tourist Office in the

Ajuntament; then hop on a tram down to the harbor (*see* Getting Around by Train, *above*).

Time Out Opposite the town hall on the Plaça Constitució, with white walls and azulejos, is the earthy **Sa Cova d'En Jordi** (tel. 971/63–32–22), a great restaurant for typical Mallorcan fare—try the *caracoles* (snails).

Leaving Sóller, look for a left turn to C710 to Deya (Deià), just where the urban area of Sóller ends. The road winds uphill and takes you high above the sea, with magnificent views all the way, to **Deya**, about 9 km (5 mi) away. On the way you'll pass the hamlet of Llucalcari, where Picasso once stayed. Deya was made famous by the writer Robert Graves, who lived for some time in the village. The local bar—up some steps on the left as you enter the village—is still the haunt of writers and artists. On warm afternoons, you'll find them congregated in the beach bar in the rocky cove, a 2-km (1-mi) walk down from the village. You can park here and walk up the narrow street, which is lined with titled Stations of the Cross, to the village church. From the small cemetery behind it, there are marvelous views of the mountains inland, terraced with gnarled and ancient olive trees, and of the coves below.

A little way beyond Deya is **Son Marroig**, one of the estates of Austrian archduke Luis Salvador (1847–1915), who arrived in Mallorca as a young man and fell in love with the island. The archduke, who spoke 14 languages and wrote innumerable books on every aspect of Mallorca, its history, its wildlife, and its folklore, acquired estates and built great houses, mostly along the northwest coast, which he adorned with miradors at each spectacular viewpoint. Son Marroig, now a museum but much as it was in the time of the archduke, contains his collection of Mediterranean pottery and ceramics, old Mallorcan furniture, and paintings. *Admission: 350 pesetas. Open Apr.–Oct., Mon.–Sat. 9:30–2:30 and 4:30–8; Nov.–Mar., Mon.–Sat. 9:30–2:30 and 4:30–6; closed Sun.*

From the mirador you can see, nearly 310 meters (1,000 ft) below, **Sa Foradada** ("perforated"), a spectacular rock peninsula, pierced by a huge archway under which the archduke moored his yacht. A pathway, adjacent to the café in the parking area, leads down to Sa Foradada (1 hour down, 1½ hours up). Four km (2½ mi) farther, behind a restaurant on the right, is another of the archduke's miradors, **Ses Pites.**

Now the road moves slightly inland and, in 2 km (1 mi), a left turn will take you into **Valldemossa.** The Tourist Office, in the plaza next to the church, sells a ticket that gives admission to the monastery's various attractions. The **Reial Cartuja** (Royal Carthusian Monastery) was founded in 1339 but, on the expulsion of the monks in 1835, was privatized, and the cells became lodgings for travelers. Later they were leased as summer apartments, which they largely remain today. The most famous lodgers were Frederic Chopin and his mistress, the French novelist George Sand, who spent three tempestuous months here in the winter of 1839.

The guided tour of the monastery begins in the **church.** Note the frescoes above the nave—the monk who painted them was Goya's brother-in-law. The next stop, in the cloisters, is perhaps the most interesting: a **pharmacy,** equipped by the monks in 1723 and still almost exactly as it was. Up a long, wide corridor are the apartments occupied by Chopin and George Sand, furnished in period style. Only the piano is original—the effort required to transport it here from France and up the mountains was monumental. Nearby, another set of apartments houses the local **museum,** with mementos of archduke Luis Salvador and a collection of old printing blocks. From here, you return to view the ornately furnished rooms of what was originally **King Sancho's Palace,** where you may find a performance of local folk dancing. *Admission: 850 pesetas. Open Nov.–Mar., Mon.–Sat. 9:30–1 and 3–5:30; Apr.–Oct., Mon.–Sat. 9:30–1 and 3–6:30; closed Sun.*

Leave Valldemossa the way you entered and, at the junction for Deya, drive straight on toward Banyalbufar. After 8 km (5 mi), turn **⑧** left toward Esporles. Look for a sign to La Granja on the right. **Sa Granja** (the Farm) was built by a noble family in the 17th century on what had been a farm belonging to monks in Palma. The family created pools and landscaped gardens. The house itself is now a historical museum of the Mallorcan countryside, including an olive mill and free samples of country produce and pies made on the premises. If you are there at the right time, you may be able to see an exhibition of folk dancing. *Tel. 971/61–00–32. Admission: 850 pesetas includes sampling of local wines and pastries. Open daily 10–6 (until 7 in June). Folk dancing Wed. and Fri. 3:30–5 (400 pesetas extra).*

From Sa Granja continue to Esporles, from which it is an easy 17-km (10-mi) run to Palma.

Tour 3: Alcúdia, Lluc, and the Torrent de Pareis

Drive east along the Passeig Marítim from Palma and take the bypass north. Follow it for about 3 km (2 mi) to the Inca turnoff, a fast autopista for the first 8 km (5 mi) until it rejoins the old Inca road, C713. **Inca** is known for its leather factories and Thursday market.

⑨ Drive on to **Alcúdia,** circling around the much-restored remains of the Moorish city walls outside which, on Sundays and Tuesdays, you'll find a market. Inside, in the maze of narrow streets, are some fine 17th-century houses and the excellent **Museu Argueològic Municipal** with Roman and prehistoric items. *Carrer Sant Jaume 2. Open Tues.–Sat. 10:30–1:30 and 3:30–6:30, Sun. 10:30–1:30; closed Mon.*

Just past Alcúdia on the right, a signposted road leads to the small **⑩** **Teatre Romá** (Roman Amphitheater), which is carved directly from the rock. This was excavated in the 1950s and is permanently open. Return toward town and, at the Inca junction, keep right for Port de Pollença.

Time Out **Port de Pollença** is less hectic than many of Mallorca's coastal resorts, and there are a number of cafés and bars along the seafront where you can relax and watch the windsurfers and sailors on the bay.

⑪ Follow signs to the town of **Pollença** itself, 5 km (3 mi) inland. The road to Lluc bypasses the town, but you may wish to drive in and climb the **Calvari,** a tree-lined stone staircase of 365 steps. From the top there is a good view of the two bays, Alcúdia and Pollença, and capes Formentor and Pinar jutting out to sea. Almost opposite the turnoff to Ternelles is Pollença's **Roman Bridge,** the only one on the island.

The road now climbs through a dramatic landscape of weirdly eroded rock formations for 20 km (12 mi) until a side road to the Monastir de **⑫** **Lluc** goes off to the right. The monastery has a 17th-century church and a **museum** (admission: 500 pesetas; open Nov.–Mar., daily 10–5:30; Apr.–Oct., daily 10–6:30), with an eclectic collection of ceramics, paintings, clothing, folk costumes, and religious items. A boys' choir performs in the chapel at 11:15 AM and 8 PM (except June–mid Sept.).

Return to C710; turn right; and, at a junction just a short way farther, remain on C710, signposted right to Escorca and Sóller. For the next 10 km (6 mi), jagged canyons cut between sheer 155-meter (500-ft) rock faces down to the sea, distracting you from the careful driving needed on this mountain road. From Sant Pere Church in Escorca you can hike down the **Torrent de Pareis,** a ravine that drops dramatically to the sea. (Use proper footwear and don't go alone.)

The turn to Sa Calobra is worth taking if you want to see the bottom of the Torrent without climbing down. The road descends in a series of sharp loops to the Mediterranean, but the touristy town and beach at its end is an unwarranted letdown.

Beyond the Sa Calobra junction, C710 passes through tunnels and beside reservoirs, with terrific views of Sóller, the mountains above, and the bay below. If you have time, a short detour left through **Fornalutz** and **Biniaraix** is worthwhile before you reach Sóller. Both have been spruced up in recent years by tourist money, but their honey-colored cobbled plazas and stepped streets are still undeniably charming. Each has its resident artist colony. Follow the signposts marked Palma through Sóller to C711, the main Sóller–Palma road.

Alternatively, wiggle your way around the deeply indented southwest coast, densely populated by hotels but scenically spectacular. The C710 south passes neat terraces planted with vines and tomatoes before reaching the village of **Banyalbufar,** perched high on a cliff overlooking its tiny harbor. Continue through Estellencs, where apricot and almonds grow on the terraces, to Andratx. This twisty road virtually runs along the cliff edge. **Andratx** is a pleasantly laid-back town overlooked by the 1,023-meter (3,300-ft) Mt. Galatzo. There is an enjoyable route, on foot or by car, from here through S'Arracó to the **Castell Sant Telmo,** and on to the rocky shore opposite the Isla Dragonera. Past sandy but rather built-up coves at Camp de Mar, Paguera, and Cala Fornells, you arrive at the fishing and gin palace town of **Santa Ponsa.** Return by way of C719 and the autopista to Palma.

What to See and Do with Children

Water Parks   **Aqua City** (Km 15 on the motorway between Palma and S'Arenal, tel. 971/49–07–04); **Aquapark** (Carretera Cala Figuera, Magaluf, tel. 971/68–08–11; open mid-Apr.–Oct., daily 10–8); **Hidropark** (Av. Tucán s/n, Pt Alcúdia, tel. 971/54–70–72); **Aqualandia** (Foro de Mallorca, Carretera Palma–Inca Km 25, Binissalem, tel. 971/51–12–28; Aqualandia also boasts a Wax Museum, open daily 9–7; until 8 in summer); and **Marineland** (Costa d'en Blanes, tel. 971/67–51–25), which has sea lions, dolphins, sharks, amusement rides, a minitrain, an aquarium, and a beach. The **Aquarium** (Porto Cristo, tel. 971/82–09–71, open daily 9–7) is the east coast water park.

Caves   The **Coves del Drac** (Caves of Drac; tel. 971/82–07–53; admission: 850 pesetas) and the **Coves de Hams** (Caves of Hams; tel. 971/82–09–88; admission: 950 pesetas) in Porto Cristo are both exciting places for children to visit. Each has a labyrinth of fancifully named caverns crammed with strange limestone formations and underground lakes on which musicians appear by boat to give a concert. **Artà Caves** are farther north on the east coast near Canyamel (tel. 971/56–32–93; admission: 500 pesetas; open Apr.–Oct., daily 9:30–7, Nov.–Mar., daily 9:30–5).

Other Attractions **Auto-Safari Park** (Sa Coma s/n, Son Servera, Km 5, tel. 971/58–54–25; admission: 850 pesetas adults, 500 pesetas children; open Nov.–Mar., daily 9–5; Apr.–Oct., daily 9–7) has exotic animals, and **Poble Espanyol** (Palma, tel. 971/23–70–75) has authentic reproductions of castles, palaces, and houses from all over Spain (*see* Tour 1, *above*).

Off the Beaten Track

Even at the height of summer, you can find relatively uncrowded areas in Mallorca, particularly if you're willing to walk a little. The hills of the northeast, beyond Artà, are almost without roads, and **Artà** itself is less frequented by tourists. The north side of the town is dominated by its castle and the church of San Salvador. Just below the church, a sign points (somewhat ambiguously—confirm the direction locally) to the **Ermita de Betlem,** some 9 km (5 mi) farther on. The road soon degenerates into a rocky track that twists hairraisingly up between dwarf palms and sea holly and then circles down to the isolated hermitage, the home of a small number of hermit monks. Behind it, a path leads up the hillside to a mirador with fine views of the jagged capes beyond Alcúdia.

For another jaunt, closer to Palma, take C715 east from the city to PM501, turn right, and follow signs to Llucmajor until, after about 3 km (2 mi), a left turn leads to Randa. At the center of this tiny village, turn right and follow a twisting road up the Puig de Randa, on which are three separate hermitages. From the terrace of the Franciscan monastery of **Nuestra Señora de Cura** (admission: 300 pesetas; open Tues.–Thurs. 10–1 and 4–6, Fri. 10–1; closed Sat.–Mon.) on the summit you will find the best views, north over the plain to the mountains of the northwest coast and south to the sea and the island of Cabrera. The monastery was founded in the 13th century by philosopher Ramón Llull (*see* Tour 1, *above*), and its library contains many valuable books that, during quiet times, you may be able to see. Adjacent to the terrace are a bar and restaurant, and the monastery has rooms and apartments to rent.

Finally, if you enjoy twisty, scenic roads to nowhere, pack a picnic and drive to **Cap de Formentor,** north of Puerto de Pollença. The road threads its way among huge teeth of rock before reaching a lighthouse at the extreme tip, where there is a spectacular view.

Shopping

Specialties of Mallorca are leather shoes and clothing, porcelain, souvenirs carved from olive wood, and artificial pearls.

In Palma big-name fashion stores line the Avinguda Jaume III; less expensive shopping areas are Carrer Sindicat and Carrer Sant Miquel, both pedestrian streets running north from Plaça Major, and the jumble of small streets south of Plaça Major. The square itself has an excellent crafts market (*see* Tour 1, *above*).

Here's a selection, all central in Palma: **leather:** Loewe (Borne 2), Pink (Plaça Pio XII), Piza (Carrer Sant Nicolau 20); **pearls:** Perlas Majorica (Avinguda Jaume III 11); **antiques:** Persepolis (Avinguda Jaume III 22), Casa Belmonte (La Rambla 8), and shops on Plaça Almoina; **pottery:** Las Columnas (opposite Tourist Office, Carrer

Sant Domingo 24); **gift-wrapped ensaimadas** (fluffy, sweet Mallorcan pastry) of all sizes: Forn Teatro (Plaça de Weyler, at the foot of the steps leading up to Plaça Major).

Along the Inca road you'll find **siurells** (brightly colored ceramic whistles) at Cabaneta, **pottery** at Marratxi, and **ilengos** (a traditional peasant fabric) at Santa María, where the amusingly named Mas Vieja que mi Abuela ("older than my grandmother") sells **antiques.** Inca has, in addition to **leather** factories, **galletas** (traditional local biscuits). **Suspiros** (sighs), a local delicacy, are on sale at C'an Roca in Manacor, **basketry** and **woven palms** in Artà. Manacor is also the home of the **Majorica Pearl Factory,** where you can see how Mallorca's famous artificial pearls are made (open weekdays 9–12:30 and 3–7, weekends 10–1).

Sports and Fitness

Bicycling The flatlands around Port de Pollença, Alcúdia, and C'an Picafort on the north coast are ideal for cycling. The roads have special bike lanes, and there are rental outlets on every block.

Golf **Canyamel** (Carretera de las Cuevas, tel. 971/65–44–57; 18 holes). **Palma,** 18 holes: **Son Vida** (adjacent to Sheraton Son Vida Hotel, 5 km/3 mi from Palma, tel. 971/23–76–20), **Poniente** (Carretera Cala Figuera, Calvia, tel. 971/68–01–48), and **Santa Ponsa** (Calvia, tel. 971/69–02–11); 9 holes: **Real Golf de Bendinat** (Carrer Formentera, Calvia, tel. 971/40–52–00). **Pollença** (Carretera Palma–Pollença Km 49.3, tel. 971/53–32–16; 9 holes). **Vall d'Or** (Carretera Porto Colom–Cala d'Or Km 7.7, s'Horta, tel. 971/57–60–99; 9 holes). **Son Servera** (Costa de Los Piños, tel. 971/56–78–02; 9 holes).

Horseback Riding stables can be found in a number of tourist resorts. The Riding **Riding** School of Mallorca is at Km 12 on the Palma–Sóller road (tel. 971/61–31–57).

Walking Mallorca is a walker's paradise, particularly in the mountains of the northwest, the Serra de Tramuntana. It's worth asking the Tourist Office for the excellent free booklet *20 Hiking Excursions on the Island of Mallorca,* with detailed maps and itineraries, although, sadly, it's now out of print. *12 Classic Hikes Through Majorca,* by the German author Herbert Heinrich, has excellent drawings and maps.

Water Sports Windsurfers and dinghies are available for rental at most beach resorts. Yacht-berthing facilities are available all around the island. The Club de Mar in Palma (tel. 971/40–36–11), with its own hotel, bar, disco, and restaurant, is famous with yacht sailors and can provide details of other clubs on the island.

Beaches

The closer it is to Palma, the more crowded a beach is likely to be. Going west from the city, **Palma Nova/Magaluf,** with a good narrow beach, is backed by one of the most crowded and noisy package resorts on the Mediterranean; **Paguera,** with several small sandy beaches, is the only sizable resort in this area not overshadowed by high-rise developments. **Camp de Mar,** a little farther along, with a good beach of fine white sand, is small and relatively undeveloped but, by the same token, can be overrun with day-trippers arriving by bus and boat from other resorts. At the end of this coast, **Sant Telm** has a very pretty little bay, with a tree-shaded parking lot.

East of Palma, a 5-km (3-mi) stretch of sand runs beside the main coast road from C'an Pastilla to Arenals, the overbuilt package-tour mecca also known collectively as **Playa de Palma.** There's nothing wrong with the beach, but it's crowded.

The only real beach on the northwest coast is at **Port de Sóller,** an attractive bay almost totally enclosed by its headlands. **Cala St. Vicenç,** at the top end of this coast, has fine, soft sand in an attractive narrow bay and is not overdeveloped. A little farther, on the north coast at **Port de Pollença,** sand has been imported, but it's an attractive resort, with good water sports and free of high-rise development. From Port de Pollença, there is a frequent water-taxi service to **Formentor,** one of the most attractive beaches on the island.

The north coast has the longest sand beach on the island. Shelving gently and backed in part by pines, it stretches 8 km (5 mi) east from **Port de Alcúdia** to **C'an Picafort** and beyond.

On the map, the east coast may seem to be peppered with beaches and coves, but few are large. **Canyamel,** close to the Caves of Artà, is not overcommercialized.

A little farther south, **Costa d'es Pins** is an extensive, expensive urbanization, but it has a good sandy stretch of public beach, backed by a thin line of pines. Tourist buses, disguised and decorated to look like train engines, run from here to **Cala Millor,** which has a long, narrow, sloping beach of soft sand. Much of the resort has pedestrian access only to the beach, so Cala Millor is ideal for children.

Moving south, **Cala d'Or** is a pleasant resort, and **Cala Gran,** a short walk away, is even more attractive. **Cala Mondrajó,** a tiny sandy bay with little development and most easily reached by boat from Portopetre or Cala Figuera, is also a good bet.

On the south coast, the sand-dune-backed beach at **Es Trenc,** near Colònia de Sant Jordi, is one of the few good beaches on Mallorca without development pressing upon it and is very popular with Mallorcans.

Dining and Lodging

Dining Seafood forms the basis of many local specialties, such as *espinigada* (a pie topped with tiny eels and spinach) and *panades de peix* (fish pies). Pork and its derivatives are also traditional. *Sobrasada* (the bright red Mallorcan sausage) is basically pork and red pepper. Even the light and fluffy *ensaimada* (the spiral pastry that ranges in size from a breakfast snack to a gift-boxed party special a foot or more across) has *saim* (pork fat) as its essential ingredient. Other specialties are *butifarra* and *llonganissa* sausages and *cocas* (pastries filled with meat or a mixture of vegetables). *Frits* (fried sheep's intestines) may be offered as tapas or included in a main course, along with *seisos* (brains), and accompanied by *tumbet* (a ratatouille with potatoes). *Sopa Mallorquina* is fried vegetables in meat stock, usually served over pieces of thinly sliced bread; *escaldum* is a chicken broth thickened with potatoes and ground almonds.

Dress is casual but neat unless otherwise stated.

Highly recommended restaurants are indicated by a star ★.

Category	Cost*
$$$$	over 7,500 ptas
$$$	5,500–7,500 ptas
$$	2,000–5,500 ptas
$	under 2,000 ptas

per person, excluding drinks, service, and tax

Lodging
Mallorca has more than 1,200 hotels, mostly serving the package-tour industry in the newer coastal resorts. Because they are often fully booked by tour operators and because attempting to obtain a reservation privately may be fruitless, hotels in these resorts are not included in the selection below.

Highly recommended hotels are indicated by a star ★.

Category	Cost*
$$$$	over 20,000 ptas
$$$	10,000–20,000 ptas
$$	4,000–10,000 ptas
$	under 4,000 ptas

All prices are for a standard double room, including tax.

Alaró
Dining and Lodging
★

Castell d'Alaró. The dormitory-style rooms are simply furnished, and because water is collected in the stone cisterns during the rainy season, showers are limited. Nevertheless, the location and views are incomparable, and the restaurant serves hearty country cooking. To reach here, turn left a mile out of Alaró on the road to Orient—the sign says *Castillo Es Pouet*. A nerve-shattering drive up a mountain track leads to a parking area half a mile below the castle. The rest of the journey is on foot up a rocky but not difficult path. Older guests or those with a considerable amount of luggage should phone two to three days ahead for a donkey to meet them. *Alaró, tel. 971/51–04–80. 17 rooms (68 beds). Facilities: restaurant, bar. MC, V. $*

Artà
Dining and Lodging
★

El Sureda. This is possibly the best French restaurant on the island. Jean St-Jours, one of the two partners, worked for the French Line and at Maxim's in Paris. The building itself is unprepossessing, at the edge of an unfinished *urbanización* (development) on the north coast, between Alcúdia and Artà, and very out of the way. Nevertheless, senior French politicians, the Liechtenstein royal family, and European ambassadors make their way here to dine. Accommodations are available in six adjoining apartments. *Colonia San Pedro, 07570, tel. 971/58–91–24. Reservations advised. MC, V. Closed lunch, Thurs., Jan. and Feb. $$$*

Banyalbufar
Dining and Lodging
★

Mar y Vent. The small, modern, family-run hotel is at the north end of this very quiet village where the land was terraced by the Romans. Paths lead down to two small rocky coves for sea bathing. All the rooms, furnished in traditional style, have good sea views. *Carrer Major 49, 07191, tel. 971/61–00–25. 19 rooms with bath. Facilities: restaurant, bar, pool, tennis courts. No credit cards. Closed Dec. and Jan. $$*

Deya
Dining and Lodging
★

La Residencia. A former 16th-century manor house, set in olive and citrus groves above the village, the hotel is superbly furnished with antiques, modern canvases, and four-poster beds. The arched dining room was formed from an old olive mill. *Son Moragues, 07179, tel. 971/63–90–11, fax 971/63–93–70. 65 rooms with bath. Facilities: restaurant, bar, pool, tennis courts. AE, DC, MC, V (extra charge). $$$$*

Costa d'Or. This attractive villa, a little way north of Deya, is set on the terraced cliffside with a footpath down to the cove. *Llucalcari, 07179, tel. 971/63–90–25. 42 rooms with bath. Facilities: restaurant, pool. Closed Nov.–Apr. $*

Lodging

Hostal Miramar. Follow signs uphill from the main street and park on the left of the track under a eucalyptus tree. Set in an old villa, this is a charming family-run inn. The hall is crowded with a mish-mash of antiques and old junk. The bedrooms are homey, and most have great views over terraces of gnarled olive trees to the sea. *Deya, 07179, tel. 971/73–90–84. 9 rooms (shared bath). No credit cards. Closed Jan.–Mar. $*

Lluc
Lodging
★

Santuari de Lluc. This is one of several monasteries on Mallorca that offer accommodations. Some of the simply furnished monastic cells have kitchens; not all have baths. All have tiled floors and rather meager beds. The setting is terrific, high in the mountains between Sóller and Pollença. *Santuari de Lluc, 07315, tel. 971/51–70–25. 108 rooms (50 with bath). Facilities: refectory, 3 restaurants. MC, V. $*

Orient
Lodging

L'Hermitage. In a hidden valley close to the rustic village of Orient, this hotel was converted in 1982 from a private 17th-century hunting lodge where Farouk of Egypt, the former king of Bulgaria, and Juan Carlos, then prince of Spain, had stayed as family guests. Most of the rooms are in a new annex overlooking farmland, but those in the lodge itself, each with its own fireplace and supply of logs, have much more character, though they lack the spacious balconies of the former. *Orient, 07000, tel. 971/61–33–00, fax 971/61–33–00. 20 rooms with bath. Facilities: restaurant, bar, sauna, 2 tennis courts, outdoor pool, bicycles. DC, MC, V. Closed Nov.–Dec. 15. $$$$*

Palma
Dining
★

Koldo Royo. The eponymous owner, formerly the prize-winning chef at Porto Pi (*see below*), conjures up Basque specialties, such as lamprey, salt cod, baked hake, tripe, and stuffed quail. The chic yellow dining room, crowded with modern art, overlooks the marina. Try the *pechuquitas de codorniz rellenas de pétalos de rosas* (quail breasts stuffed with rose petals). *Passeig Marítim 3, tel. 971/45–70–21. Reservations advised. AE, MC, V. Closed Sat. lunch and Sun. $$$*

Porto Pi. Dining in this old Mallorcan villa in the Terreno area, 1 km (.6 mi) west of Plaza Gomila, is not unlike eating in a private home. Several high-ceilinged dining rooms, with round tables and oil paintings, lead off the elegant central hall-cum-drawing room, and there's a terrace for the summer. The fine cooking is international—try the *escalopines de foie gras a la parrilla* (barbecued escallops of foie gras). Disappointingly, the once-excellent views over the bay have been almost totally obliterated by ugly modern apartment blocks. *Av. Joan Miró 174, tel. 971/40–00–87. Reservations advised. Jackets and tie not strictly required. AE, MC, V. Closed Sat. lunch and Sun. $$$*

El Pilón. In an old vaulted building tucked between the top of the Born and Avinguda Jaume III, El Pilón has the widest range of tapas in town, from cheaper clams to more expensive eels. More substantial fish dishes can be chosen fresh from the tank. *Carrer Cifre 1, tel. 971/72–60–34. AE, DC, MC, V. Closed Sun. and Feb. $$*

Bon Lloc. Just off the Born, decorated with New Age advertisements for massage and meditation, modern square tables, and a tiled floor, this is the place for vegetarian food. There's a very good menú del día at lunch. *Carrer Sant Feliu 7, tel. 971/71–86–17. No credit cards. Lunch only, except Fri. Closed Sun. and Mon.* $

Dining and Lodging **Son Vida.** One of less than a dozen hotels in Spain in the Grand Luxe category, this Sheraton envelops a 13th-century castle on a hillside outside Palma. Antique furniture contrasts with the futuristic bronze-mirror interior of the El Jardín restaurant. Most rooms have panoramic views of Palma Bay to the south; a few standard rooms overlook the service area and hillside but are double size to compensate. *Castillo Son Vida, 07015, tel. 971/79–00–00, fax 971/79–00–17. 166 rooms with bath. Facilities: 2 restaurants, 2 bars, boutiques, library, hairdresser, indoor heated pool, 2 outdoor pools, health club, 4 tennis courts, children's playground, golf course adjacent, free bus service to Palma. AE, DC, MC, V.* $$$$

★ **Valparaiso Palace.** This hotel stands in landscaped gardens with spectacular illuminated fountains and a small lake in a quiet district west of the Poble Espanyol and Bellver Castle. The rooms are richly furnished in the Spanish style, with carved woodwork and fabric-covered walls. *Carrer Fr. Vidal s/n, La Bonanova, 07015, tel. 971/40–04–11, fax 971/40–59–04. 138 rooms with bath. Facilities: restaurant (jacket and tie required after 8 PM), grill room, nightclub, 4 bars (jacket and tie required in Conde Duque bar after 8 PM), heated outdoor and indoor pools, health center, art gallery, boutiques, beauty salon, 2 tennis courts, minigolf. AE, DC, MC, V.* $$$$

Lodging **Hotel Borne.** Right in the middle of Palma in a pedestrian street, the ★ building is a former noble's mansion. The bedrooms are totally refurbished, but prices remain very reasonable. Romanesque arches surround the central courtyard and reception area. *Carrer Sant Jaume 3, 07012, tel. 971/71–29–42, fax 971/71–86–18. 29 rooms with bath. AE, DC, MC, V.* $$

Port de Pollença **Dining and Lodging** **Formentor.** This famous hotel, founded in 1929, is beautifully situated at the northern tip of the island, with terraced gardens descending to an attractive private beach where there is a barbecue at lunchtime. The building is long and white, the bedrooms comfortable but no more than par for hotels of this price; despite the remote site, it lacks intimacy. Former guests include the Duke of Windsor, Winston Churchill, Charlie Chaplin, Aristotle Onassis, and the Spanish royal family. *07470, tel. 971/53–13–00, fax 971/53–11–55. 127 rooms with bath. Facilities: restaurant (jacket and tie required at dinner), grill room, 3 bars, boutiques, hairdresser, children's playground, 2 pools, minigolf, 5 tennis courts, riding (instruction available for both tennis and riding), waterskiing, windsurfing, sailing, limousine service from Palma airport. AE, DC, MC, V. Closed Nov.–Easter.* $$$$

Sóller **Dining and Lodging** **Es Port.** The 15th-century manor house, built around a central courtyard, is the ancestral home of the Montis family, who have added a modern extension and now run it as a hotel. The heavily beamed restaurant is in an old mill, where the huge olive press makes a striking centerpiece. Rooms in the old part have much more character—heavy, dark wood furniture and four-posters. The hotel's only drawback is its size, which attracts tour groups. *Carrer Antoni Montis s/n, Port de Sóller 07108, tel. 971/63–16–50, fax 971/63–16–62. 156 rooms with bath (plus 10 cottage accommodations). Facilities: restaurant, bar, pool, 3 tennis courts, children's playground. AE, MC, V.* $–$$

★ **El Guía.** An elegant old house typical of those built by the merchants of this town on the rich rewards of the citrus trade, El Guía is furnished in keeping with its fin de siècle style. The excellent restaurant serves Mallorcan specialties. The bedrooms have rather small beds and Spartan decor, but they are clean. *Carrer Castanyer 3, 07100, tel. 971/63–02–27. 20 rooms with bath. Facilities: restaurant. AE, MC, V. Restaurant closed Mon. dinner; hotel closed Nov.– Mar. $*

Valldemossa
Dining and
Lodging
Vistamar. An old *finca* set in 100 hectares (250 acres) of olive groves overlooking the sea provides the setting for this charming small hotel. The building has been faithfully restored; the sitting rooms and bedrooms have exposed beams, heavy furniture, and modern art. The Vistamar first won popularity for its excellent Mediterranean cooking, and it is still a fantastic place to stay for gourmets looking to get away from it all. *Ctra. Valldemossa–Andratx, Km 2, 07170, tel. 971/61–23–00, fax 971/61–25–83. 16 rooms with bath. Facilities: restaurant, bar, pool (tennis 1 km away). Closed Nov.–Feb. 15. AE, MC, V. Restaurant: $$$. Inn: $$$$*

The Arts and Nightlife

The Arts
The City of Palma Symphony Orchestra performs about twice a month throughout the winter at the **Auditorium** (Passeig Marítim 18, tel. 971/23–47–35), which also has ballet and theatrical performances throughout the year, as does the **Teatre Principal** (adjacent to the Plaça Major, tel. 971/78–47–35).

Given the Chopin connection, it is not surprising that there is an International Chopin Piano Competition during the first week of November at the Teatre Principal, which, with the Auditorium, also hosts an International Segovia Guitar Competition at the end of that month. There is a week of organ music in Santa Eulàlia Church, in Palma, at the beginning of March and a Historic Organs of Mallorca celebration at churches throughout the island during the first week in October.

Pollença has a music festival in August and September every year, with performances each Saturday by international artists in the cloisters of **Sant Domingo Church** (tel. 971/53–10–08).

A 30-page leaflet, *Festivals, Fairs, and Festivities in the Balearics*, published by the Tourist Office in Palma, has a wealth of information on these and other events.

Nightlife
With some 200 discos and music bars scattered throughout the city and all over the island, Mallorca's nightlife is never difficult to find. In Palma itself, the **Plaça de la Lonja** is the place to go for "copas" (drinks, tapas-sampling, and general carousing).

The most incandescent hot spots, however, are concentrated six km west of Palma at **Punta Portals** in Portals Nous, where King Juan Carlos I moors his yacht along with those of many of Europe's most beautiful people. **D.P.P.** is the disco of choice, and **Tristan, Flannigan's,** and **Diablito** are other places to dine.

In the center of Palma, on the west side of the Born, **Carrer Apuntadores** is always lively at night, and many of the bars are still genuinely local.

Mallorca's **Casino** (tel. 971/45–40–12; open Sun.–Thurs. 7 PM–4 AM, Fri. and Sat. 7 PM–5 AM) is at Calvia, west of the city, and has a beach and tennis club as well as gaming—take your passport with you.

Menorca

Menorca, northernmost island of the archipelago, is a cliff-bound, rather knobbly plateau with a single central hill, Monte Toro, from whose 336-m (1,100-ft) summit the whole island can be seen. Prehistoric monuments—*taulas* (huge stone T shapes), *talayots* (spiral cones made of stone), and *navetes* (stone structures shaped like upturned boats)—left by the first Neolithic settlers are thickly scattered over the countryside. Menorca shows the influence of its century of British rule in its Georgian-style architecture (especially in Mahón); its landscape of small and tidy fields bounded by hedgerows and dry-stone walls and grazed by Holsteins; and in its language, which is sprinkled with English words. Tourism came late to Menorca, partly because it was traditionally more prosperous and, thus, less eager than its neighbors to encourage visitors, but also because Franco deliberately punished the Republican island by restricting tourist development there. Starting late, Menorca has managed to avoid many of the teething troubles of the other islands. There are no high-rise hotels, and its herringbone road system, with a single central highway, has meant that each resort is small and separate.

Numbers in the margin correspond to points of interest on the Menorca map.

Tour 1: Mahón

❶ In **Mahón,** start from the northwest corner of the Plaça de S'Esplanada and turn right onto Carrer Comte de Cifuentes. At No. 25 is the **Ateneo,** a cultural and literary society where visitors are welcome to view the collection of wildlife, seashells, seaweed, minerals, and stuffed birds. On the staircase are ceramics and old tiles and, in side rooms, paintings, prints, maps, and mementos of Menorcan writers, poets, and musicians. *Admission free. Open daily 10–2 and 3–10.*

At the end of Carrer Comte de Cifuentes, turn left onto Carrer Dr. Orfila, one of the principal shopping streets; then take the second right onto Carrer Bastió (Costa d'en Ga). Where the street curves left is the **Teatre Principal,** built in 1824 as an opera house and now a cinema and theater. You can usually manage to peep inside at the semicircular auditorium, whose columns support tier after tier of boxes and a gilded ceiling. Continue down Costa d'en Ga into Plaça Reial.

Time Out The **American Bar** on Plaça Reial is the place to watch the passing parade, although service is incredibly slow. If you run out of patience, try the **Andalucía** next door.

S'Arravaleta, a pedestrian street with more smart shops, leads from Plaça Reial to Plaça del Carme. Up to the right is the **Verge del Carme Church,** which houses a fine painted and gilded retablo. Adjoining the church, you'll find the cloisters, now surprisingly a public **market.** As you pick your way between the colorful piles of fruit and vegetables, notice the carvings on the west and north walls.

Return up S'Arravaleta and turn right onto Carrer Nou. At the end is Plaça de la Constitució, dominated by the **Church of Santa María,** originally 13th-century but largely rebuilt in the 18th century during the British occupation. It was restored once more after being

Menorca

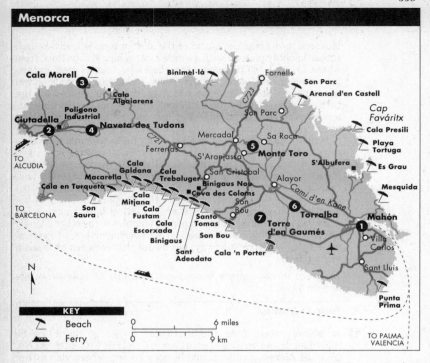

KEY

☞ Beach

⛴ Ferry

0 ——— 6 miles
0 ——— 9 km

N

TO ALCUDIA

TO BARCELONA

TO PALMA, VALENCIA

sacked during the Spanish civil war. The pride of the church is the 3,200-pipe Baroque organ, imported from Austria in 1810.

Behind the church is Plaça de la Conquesta, with a statue of Alfons III of Aragón. At the end of the tiny Carrer Alfons III that leads off the square, you'll be rewarded with the best view of Mahón harbor.

Returning to the Plaça de la Constitució, you will find the **Ajuntament** on the right. Stroll up Carrer Isabel II, a pleasant street of fine houses. Notice the statue of the Virgin up on the wall on the corner of Carrer de Rosari and the **Governor's Palace** and courtyard on the right.

Return to the Ajuntament, and follow Carrer Port de Sant Roc immediately opposite. Ahead you'll see the 16th-century **San Roque Gate,** the only remnant of the city walls, which were built to protect Mahón from the pirate Barbarossa (Redbeard).

Tour 2: Ciutadella

② Before the British came and set up their capital in Mahón, **Ciutadella** was capital of Menorca, and its history and architecture are much richer than Mahón's. As you arrive from Mahón by way of the main road across the island, turn left at the traffic lights and circle the old part of the city to the north end of the coniferous Plaça de s'Explanada. Turn left here, down Camí de Sant Nicolau. At the end, near an old watchtower and two rather rusty cannons, is a monument to David Glasgow Farragut, the first admiral of the U.S. Navy, whose father emigrated from Ciutadella to the United

States. From here you also get a good view of the distant jagged peaks of Mallorca.

Return up Sant Nicolau and park as near the Plaça d'es Born as possible. Next to the Ajuntament, on the west side of the Born, steps lead up to the **Mirador d'Es Port,** from which you can survey the whole length of Ciutadella Creek. The **Ajuntament** houses the local museum (open daily 10–1 and 4–6), a repository of anything and everything to do with the city—old street signs, keys, shoes, even a record of land grants made by Alfons III after defeating the Moors.

Circle the Born to the north, with more views of the narrow harbor. The monument in the center of the plaza commemorates the resistance of the citizens to an invasion by the Moors in 1588. Continue south along the east side of the Born. The whole of this first block is the palace of the Torresaura family. It's worth going into one of the tiny shops here to take a closer look at the complex pattern of archways and stairwells.

Turn left into Carrer Major to enter the old city, where you'll find many interesting brass and bronze door fixtures. On the left, at No. 8 (even palaces have street numbers!), over the doorway of the **Palau Torresaura,** is a strange carving of a veiled female face. On the right is the **Palau Salort,** its door knockers carved to resemble entwined serpents. The latter is the only noble's house regularly open to the public (open Mon.–Sat. 10–2). The coats of arms on the ceiling are those of the families Salort (a salt pit and a garden: *sal* and *ort*, or *huerta*) and Martorell (a marten).

Continue up Carrer Major to Plaça de la Catedral (Plaça Píus XII). Inside the Gothic **cathedral** you'll find beautifully carved woodwork and choir stalls. The side chapel has round Moorish arches with intricate carving, remnants of the mosque that was originally on this site.

Turn south from the Plaça de la Catedral onto Carrer Roser. Turn left onto Carrer Santíssims, where, on the right, there is another noble home, one of the Saura palaces. Its ground floor is occupied by one of the best antiques shops in the Balearic Islands. Don't miss the coat of arms dated 1718, some primitive naval paintings at the end of the entrance hall, and the carved, domed ceiling.

Turn left onto Carrer del Seminari (Carrer Obispo Vila). Immediately on the right is the **Seminari,** whose cloisters are the setting for Ciutadella's annual music festival (*see* The Arts and Nightlife, *below*).

Return, keeping north of the cathedral, along Carrer Sant Sebastià. Twisting left and right, you'll reach the steps leading down into the port. The waterfront here is lined with seafood restaurants, some of which burrow into caverns far under the Born. Between the restaurants, Carrer Costa del Moll leads left up to the Born again.

Many of the archaeological curiosities for which Menorca is famous are close to Ciutadella. Returning around the Avenues, continue straight at the traffic lights, take the next right (Carrer de Pere ❸ Martorell), and follow the signs for **Cala Morell.** Soon you'll be in open countryside, where numerous talayots of stone dot the fields.

Returning, take a shortcut through the Polígono Industrial on the left to the Ciutadella–Mahón road. Turn left toward Mahón, and in a mile or so on the right are a parking lot and a path leading to the ❹ **Naveta des Tudons,** one of the best preserved of Menorca's mysterious prehistoric remains. The name derives from its shape, that of an upturned boat.

Menorca Excursions En route between Mahón and Ciutadella, or on the way to the beach, three other pieces of the Menorcan countryside may be fitted in at your leisure.

⑤ Monte Toro. Follow the signs in Mercadal to the peak of Monte Toro, Menorca's highest point. From the monastery on top, you can see the whole island and, on a clear day, across the sea to Mallorca.

⑥ Torralba. Coming from Mahón, turn south immediately upon entering Alayor toward Cala 'n Porter. Torralba, a megalithic site with a number of stone constructions, is 2 km (1.2 mi) ahead at a bend in the road, marked by an information kiosk on the left that, as is so often the case in Menorca, you will be lucky to find open. The massive T-shape taula is through an opening to the right. Behind it, from the top of a stone wall, you can see, in a nearby field, the monolith Fus de Sa Geganta.

⑦ Torre d'en Gaumés. Turn south toward Son Bou on the west side of Alayor. In about a mile, the first fork left will lead you to Torre d'en Gaumés, a much more complex set of prehistoric ruins, with fortifications, monuments and deep pits of ruined dwellings, huge vertical slabs, and taulas. How much longer it will last is difficult to say. Motorists already drive right through on a tiny path, and sightseers clamber all over it, pulling stones from top to bottom. See it while you can.

What to See and Do with Children

Cala Galdana and Urbanización San Jaime at Son Bou both have **water parks** and, inland, **go-carting** is available at the Hippodrom on the Mahón–San Luis road. **Equestrian Spectacular** offers displays of horsemanship a few yards down the road from Ferreries to Cala Galdana.

Off the Beaten Track

Cova des Coloms. The Cave of Pigeons is the most spectacular cave on the island. To reach it, take the Ferreries road at San Cristobal and turn up to the primary school. Beyond the school the paved road continues for about 3 km (2 mi) toward Binigaus Nou. At an easily recognized parking place—you'll see wheel marks and possibly cars as well—leave the car. Climb a stile and take a path that follows the right-hand side of the barranca (ravine) toward the sea. You'll come to a well-trodden path bearing down into the bottom of the barranca and up the other side. The entrance to the cave is around an elbow, well camouflaged by a tree. Remember to bring a flashlight.

Shopping

Menorca is known for shoemaking and **gin,** both introduced by the British. The Xoriguer distillery on Mahón quayside, close to the ferry terminal, offers a guided tour, free samples, and bottles for sale. **Fashionable footwear** can be found along Carrer Dr. Orfila in Mahón and under the arches of Ses Voltes in Ciutadella. The industrial estate (*polígono*) on the right as you enter Ciutadella has a number of shoe factories, each with shops. Prices may be no lower, but the range on view is likely to be greater. The Rubrica shoe factory in Ferreries is where locals head.

In Mahón, there's **leatherwear** at Marks (S'Arravaleta 18 and Hanover 38), Patricia (31/33 Carrer Dr. Orfila), and Musupta (S'Arravaleta 26) and **costume jewelry,** also a local specialty, at Bali (corner of Carrer de Lluna). Up on the Esplanade, there's an open-air market with cheap clothing and souvenirs.

In Ciutadella, Carrer del Seminari 36 has designer leatherwear. Sa Celeria (33 Carrer de Santa Clara), a saddler and harness maker, stocks elegant riding boots and, opposite, No. 48 has interesting pottery. One of the few antiques shops on the island is on the ground floor of the Saura Palace (Carrer de Santíssim).

Sports and Fitness

Bird-watching S'Albufera, a wetland nature reserve north of Mahón, attracts many species of migratory birds.

Diving Equipment and lessons are available at Cala En Bosc, Son Parc, and Cala Tirant. Compressed air is available at Club Marítimo, Mahón, and Club Náutico, Ciutadella. The only decompression chamber on the island is at S'Algar.

Golf **Urbanización Son Parc** (tel. 971/36–88–06; 9 holes, with 9 more under construction) has the only course.

Horseback Riding There are stables on the left of the main road between Alayor and Mercadal, just after the turn to the new *urbanización* of Torre Son Bou, as well as between Sant Climent and Cala 'n Porter. Elsewhere on the island, look for the sign *picadero* (riding school). **Es Fornás** (Box 842, tel. 971/36–44–22) in Mahón organizes equestrian tours of the island by day or night for beginner and advanced riders, and tours by carriage.

Walking In the south, each cove has a barranca (ravine or gully) leading down to it, often from several miles inland, which makes a pleasant, untaxing excursion. The head of **Barranca Algendar** is down a small, unmarked road immediately on the right of the Ferreries–Cala Galdana road. The barranca, which by Menorcan standards is a lush oasis, ends in the beach resort of Cala Galdana.

Windsurfing and Sailing Knowledgeable windsurfers and dinghy sailors head for Fornells Bay. Several miles long and a mile wide, but with a narrow entrance to the sea, it gives the beginner a feeling of security and the expert plenty of excitement. **Windsurfing Fornells** (tel. 971/37–66–36) rents boards and offers excellent lessons in English and Spanish.

A little south of Fornells, at Ses Salines on the same bay, **Minorca Sailing Holidays** offers a package that includes airfare and accommodations with opportunities to enjoy the rest of the island. *No local reservations. 256 Green La., London N13 4XE, tel. 81/886–7193.*

Beaches

North of Mahón, **Mesquida** is popular with the Mahonese, and you'll see few tourists. Beyond a watchtower on a headland is a second beach, free of development.

Continuing west, **Es Grau,** a sandy stretch with dunes behind it, is sometimes a bit littered. Behind Es Grau is the nature reserve of S'Albufera. Before the lighthouse at the end of Cap Favàritx are **Cala Presili** and **Playa Tortuga,** both nudist beaches. **Arenal d'en Castell,** a circular bay, sheltered and almost completely enclosed, and Arenal de Son Saura, now known as **Son Parc,** are the biggest sandy beaches in the north of the island.

At the junction of the Mahón-Fornells and the Mercadal-Fornells roads, take the small lane leading west and follow signs to **Binimel-lá,** an excellent sandy beach. It's often deserted, and the tiny coves to the west have small caves that give welcome shade in the summer months.

The only reasonable and generally accessible beach to the north of Ciutadella is **Cala Morell.** Menorcans claim that the coves of **Cala Algaiarens** are the nicest on the island, but unless you have a Menorcan friend, forget about them. A permanent guard with a radio telephone will allow only Menorcans onto the beach.

Son Saura, Cala en Turqueta, and **Macarella,** the beaches at the west end of the south coast, are all reached by driving southeast from Ciutadella toward Son Saura. You'll be halted by a gate and a sign prohibiting entry, but no one will bother you, provided you close the gate behind you. All are classical Menorcan beaches with trees to the water's edge, a horseshoe bay, and white sand. To the east, **Cala Mitjana, Cala Trebaluger, Cala Fustam,** and **Cala Escorxada** are accessible by land only on foot, but boats with outboard engines can be rented to reach them, as well as the Son Saura calas to the west. The long, straight sandy stretches of **Binigaus, Sant Adeodato,** and **Santo Tomas** are reached from Mercadal, and **Son Bou** is reached from Alayor.

Cala 'n Porter is a British enclave. The rectangular cove has a sandy beach that stretches back a long way inland, is sheltered by cliffs, and is itself not too overrun.

Dining and Lodging

Dining   Until recently Menorcan restaurant cuisine consisted entirely of seafood, offered by establishments lining the harbors in Mahón, Ciutadella, and the fishing village of Fornells. The last is famous for its very expensive *llagosta* (lobster), sold by weight and grilled or served as *caldereta* (soup). Lately, a country cuisine has developed, based on the slow-baked dishes traditionally served in the home.

Mayonnaise, which was invented in Menorca during the French occupation and named after Mahón, is usually freshly prepared. Local tapas include *tornellas* (sheep's intestines stuffed with bread crumbs, garlic, and meat, and braided and cooked). (*See* price chart for Mallorca, *above*.)

Lodging   Apart from a few hotels and hostels in Mahón and Ciutadella, almost all the tourist accommodations are in newly developed beach resorts. As with the other Balearic islands, many of the hotels are fully reserved by travel operators in the high season, and it is more economical to book a package, including airfare and accommodations. (*See* price chart for Mallorca, *above*.)

Ciutadella   **Casa Manolo.** This well-established paella and seafood restaurant is
Dining   at the seaward end of the many eating places that rub shoulders along the east side of the narrow harbor. The maritime dining rooms with white walls and exposed beams extend back into the rock face. *Marina 117, tel. 971/38–00–03. Reservations advised. AE, DC, MC, V. Closed Dec.–Mar. $$*

Lodging   **Patricia.** Opened in 1988 in a quiet boulevard just south of the main plaza, it is close to Ciutadella creek. The hall is marble, light, and modern. Bedrooms have pale carpets, pastel wallpaper, and watercolors. *Camí Sant Nicolau 90–92, 07760, tel. 971/38–55–11, fax 971/*

48–11–20. 44 rooms with bath. Facilities: restaurant, bar. AE, DC, MC, V. $$$

Hostal Ciutadella. In the center of town, a block southwest of Plaça Alfonso III, is a pleasant modern bar with bedrooms upstairs. The latter have white walls, shutters, shiny tiled floors, and comfortable beds. *Carrer Sant Eloi 10, 07760, tel. 971/38–34–62. 17 rooms with bath. Facilities: bar/cafeteria. MC, V. $*

Cala Galdana
Lodging

Hotel Audax. Remaining reasonably secluded in this busy beach resort, the modern high rise is situated below a pine-covered slope on the west of the bay. A footbridge over a small creek leads to the main beach. *Cala Galdana, Ferreries, 07760, tel. 971/37–31–25, fax 971/37–31–25. 244 rooms with bath. Facilities: restaurant, bar, movie theater, pool, children's pool, tennis courts, beach. AE, MC, V. Closed Nov.–Mar. $$$*

Ferreries
Dining
★

Vimpi. Legend has it that the owner once worked in England in a fast-food Wimpy bar. When he returned home, he opened a restaurant of the same name. One day a Wimpy executive on holiday in Menorca complained. The owner immediately removed half the "W"— hence, Vimpi. But don't let the name put you off; Vimpi serves excellent tapas, and its newly extended restaurant has a good local menu. *Plaça Principe Juan Carlos 5, tel. 971/37–31–99. AE, MC, V. $$*

Fornells
Dining

Es Pla. Right on the harbor in a village famous for its seafood restaurants and lobster dishes, Es Pla is a little more famous than the others because when King Juan Carlos moors the royal yacht in the bay each summer, he dines here. The floor has black and white tiles, the ceiling is stained pine, and the tables have coral-color cloths. *Port s/n, 07748, tel. 971/37–66–55. AE, MC, V. $$–$$$*

Dining and Lodging

Passeig Maritim. This newly built snack bar and pizzeria facing the bay also has a few rooms to rent. Diners are welcome to use the swimming pool in the patio. *Port s/n, 07760. No credit cards. Closed Nov.–Apr. $*

Mahón
Dining

Jágaro. Here you find an open-air feel with lots of greenery in the recently enlarged garden and huge windows overlooking the harbor. The conservatory is understandably very popular in summer. The seafood dishes are more inventive than elsewhere—try the carpaccio *de mero* (halibut). *Moll de Llevant 334, tel. 971/36–23–90. AE, MC, V. Closed Mon. dinner and Sun. dinner, Oct.–Apr. $$$*

Rocamar. At the extreme end of the twisting quayside road in the direction of Villa Carlos, this restaurant is an established favorite that serves simply prepared fresh seafood. You dine four floors up overlooking the creek, surrounded by dark wood paneling and maritime lights. The *pimientos rellenos de langostinos* (peppers stuffed with prawns) are superb. *Cala Fonduco 32, Port, tel. 971/36–56–01. Reservations advised. AE, DC, MC, V. Closed Sun. evening in winter, Mon. $$$*

★ **Bar Europa.** An ordinary town bar just behind the Esplanade, Europa serves the best tapas in Menorca. The long list includes *pescado escabeche* (pickled fish), *caracoles* (snails), *cranca* (crab), *lomo con col* (meat in cabbage leaves), *marejas* (lamb tripe), *frito* (chitterling), *pulpo* (octopus), and *callos* (tripe). Red *Damm* beer crates and Formica tables make up the decor. *Carrer Cifuentes 68, tel. 971/36–13–79. No credit cards. Closed Wed. $*

Lodging

Port Mahón. The only high-quality hotel actually in Mahón is magnificently situated overlooking the estuary in extensive terraced gardens in a quiet residential district. Steps lead directly down to the fashionable bars and restaurants that line the harbor. *Av. Fort de L'Eau s/n, 07700, tel. 971/36–26–00, fax 971/36–45–95. 74 rooms* *with bath. Facilities: restaurant, bar, piano bar, boutique, hair-dresser, pool. AE, DC, MC, V. $$–$$$*

Almirante (Collingwood House). The 18th-century residence of Admiral Lord Collingwood is located between Mahón and Villa Carlos, with spectacular views over the creek. The Georgian house became a hotel in 1964 but retains its original character. Cottage accommodations around a swimming pool were added later. *Carretera Villacarlos s/n, 07720, tel. 971/36–27–00. MC, V. 38 rooms with bath. Facilities: restaurant, bar, game room, 1 tennis court, pool. Closed Nov.–Apr. $$*

Mercadal **Ca'n Olga.** Difficult to find but worth it, off the Camino de
Dining Tramuntana, Olga's is under an archway to the left (or ask for direc-
★ tions). Make for the small patio and try the excellent and inventive country cuisine, such as local snails or quail in sherry. Inside are a terra-cotta floor, white walls, bottle-green woodwork, and a very friendly owner. *Pont Na Macarrana s/n, tel. 971/37–54–59. AE, MC, V. Closed Mon. and Tues. Jan.–Feb. $$*

Bar Sa Plaça. This local bar serves substantial helpings of good local food. Try *pan amb oli con jamón serrano* (bread and oil with cured ham) for starters and *guisantes con cerdo* (pork with peas) to follow. *Sa Plaça 2. No credit cards. $*

The Arts and Nightlife

The Arts Ciutadella holds a **Classical Music Festival** during July and August in the cloisters of the 17th-century Seminary (for information, tel. 971/ 38–41–23; for tickets, Foto Born, Carrer Seminari (Calle Obispo Vila) 14, tel. 971/38–17–54). Mahón hosts an **Opera Week** in April and an **International Music Festival** in July and August. An **organ festival,** using the famous organ in Santa María, takes place in Mahón in July with recitals each Tuesday and Thursday (tel. 971/36–51–61).

Fiestas Menorca's traditional fiestas are still essentially celebrations for the townsfolk and villagers and have changed not at all in deference to tourism. The summer round begins with the Feast of Sant Joan, in Ciutadella, on June 23, when *caixeres* (townspeople representing all classes) take part in a *jaleo,* dancing their horses to the sound of a band while the youths of the town attempt to make the animals rear up on their hind legs and to prove their virility by standing beneath. From July onward, fiestas follow one after another, ending with Mahón's Senyora de Gràcia (Nostra) in early September.

Nightlife The bars opposite the ferry terminal in Mahón harbor are the late-night spots for locals. In Ciutadella nighthawks descend on the creek, unfortunately also the island's drug scene.

Discos **Lui** is in a cave at the edge of Mahón, just past the traffic circle on the Villa Carlos road (Sá Sinia de's Muret, tel. 971/36–63–68). **Pachá,** a branch of Ibiza's famous night spot, is on the left at the entrance to San Luis. **Cova d'en Xoroi** is set in a pirate's cave in the cliff high above the sea at Cala 'n Porter.

Ibiza and Formentera

Settled by the Carthaginians in the 5th century BC, Ibiza (Eivissa in Mallorquín and Catalan) in the 20th century was transformed by tourism. From a peasant economy, it became a wild, anything-goes gathering place for the international jet set and for the hippies of the 1960s, only to enter the 1990s with its principal resort, Sant Antoni,

Ibiza and Formentera

Ibiza

Cala Xarraca
Caló d'Es Porcs
Puerto San Miguel
Portinaitx
Cala San Vicente
San Vicente
Sant Joan
Sant Miquel
San Mateo
Santa Agnes
Sant Llorenç
Balafi
San Carlos
TO BARCELONA
Santa Gertrudis
Bahía de San Antonio
Santa Agnes
Sant Antoni
Santa Eulàlia del Riu
Santa Eulàlia
San Rafael
Sant Josep
Eivissa
TO PALMA
TO VALENCIA
Es Vedra
Sant Jordi
Playa d'En Bossa
Mitjorn
Cavallet
Formentera
Es Palmador
Puerto de La Sabina
Trucadors
Estany Prudent
Es Pujols
Sant Francesc Xavier
Sant Ferran
Cala Sahona
Playa de Mitjorn
El Pilar
Cabo de Barbiera

N

KEY
Beach
Ferry

0   10 miles
0   15 km

regarded as one of the most boorish, noisy, and brash on the Mediterranean. And yet, of the islands, only on Ibiza and on tiny Formentera, just off Ibiza's southern tip, will you still see women in the fields dressed in the simple country costume of long black skirt and wide-brimmed straw hat, gathering almonds in their aprons or herding errant goats.

Tour 1: Eivissa and the d'Alt Vila

Running along the quayside in the town of **Eivissa** is the area known as **Sa Penya** (the crag or cliff). Once a quiet fisherman's quarter, since the 1960s it has been a tourist mecca, springing into life each evening with lively bars and restaurants and flea markets.

Enter Sa Penya via Carrer Rimbau, which you'll find at the end of Passeig Vara de Rey, opposite Hotel Montesol, whose fashionable pavement café is a favorite place for people-watching. Carrer Rimbau has some of the more exotic fashion boutiques for which Ibiza is renowned, and off it are alleys crammed with stalls, boutiques, and restaurants.

Continue on Carrer Major, just east of San Telmo Church. In this part of Sa Penya none of the streets is quite straight, and the miniature houses appear to have been randomly dumped along tiny passageways whose staircases are narrow enough to scrape the padded shoulders of fashionable promenaders.

Return to Plaça de la Constitució, just north of San Telmo, where a pretty little building that looks something like a miniature Parthenon houses the local market. Beyond it a ramp leads up to Las

Tablas, the main gate of **d'Alt Vila,** the walled upper town. On each side stands a statue, Roman in origin, both now headless, Juno on the right, an armless male on the left.

Inside, the ramp continues to the right between the outer and inner walls and opens into a long, narrow plaza lined with stalls and pavement cafés. Don't worry about losing your way in the d'Alt Vila. Aim uphill and you will arrive at the cathedral. Aim downhill and you will return to the gate. A little way up Sa Carroza, a sign on the left points back toward the **Museu d'Art Contemporani** (Museum of Contemporary Art; Ronda Pintor Narcis Putget s/n, tel. 971/30–27–23; admission: 350 pesetas; open daily 10:30–1 and 6–8:30) housed in the gateway arch. Farther uphill is a sculpture of a priest sitting on one of the stone seats in the gardens. On the left the wide **Bastion of Santa Lucia** offers a panoramic view over Sa Penya.

Wind your way up past the 16th-century church of **Sant Domingo,** its roof an irregular landscape of tiled domes, and turn right in front of the **Ajuntament,** housed in the church's former monastery, then follow any of the streets or steps leading uphill to Carrer Obispo Torres (Carrer Major).

Time Out   Take a break at **Café Torre Canónigo** on the ground floor of an ancient mansion, halfway up the street. Immediately opposite is a small art gallery.

At the top of Carrer Major is the **cathedral** (open Sun.–Fri. 10–1 and 4–6:30, Sat. 10–1), on the site of religious structures from each of the cultures that have ruled Eivissa since the Phoenicians. Built in the 13th and 14th centuries and renovated in the 18th century, the cathedral has a Gothic tower and a Baroque nave. The painted panels above the small vault adjoining the sacristy depict souls in purgatory being consumed by flames and tortured by devils while angels ascend to heaven. A visit to its museum (admission: 250 pesetas), reached through the nave, is well worthwhile. Inside the sacristy is a collection of religious art, relics, and ecclesiastical treasures.

Across the plaza, the **Museu d'Alt Vila** (Museum of Archaeology) has a collection of Phoenician, Punic, and Roman finds. *Plaça Catedral 3, tel. 971/30–12–31. Admission: 450 pesetas. Open Mon.–Sat. 10–1; closed Sun.*

A passageway leads between the cathedral and the castle, which has recently been restored, to the **Bastion of Sant Bernardo.** From here there is a panoramic view of the wide bay from Playa d'En Bossa to Figueretas, and of the chain of islands that stretches across the sea to Formentera. Steps lead down to a small gate in the bastion from which it is not too difficult to pick your way along the clifftop to Figueretas, where you can also continue along the top of the wall, the Route of St. John the Baptist, by way of the bastions of Sant Joan and Santiago, until you reach the steps to the **Portal Nou** (New Gate).

Go down the dark curving tunnel of Portal Nou and up the Vía Romana to reach, on the left, the **Puig des Molins,** so called because it was once covered in windmills. A major Punic necropolis, with more than 3,000 tombs, has been excavated here, and many of the finds can be seen in the new **Museu Puig d'Es Molins** (Punic Archaeological Museum) adjacent to it. *Vía Romana 31, tel. 971/30–17–71. Admission: 450 pesetas (same ticket as for museum above). Open Mon.–Sat. 10–1; closed Sun.*

From here you can return downhill to the Passeig Vara de Rey.

Tour 2: By Boat to Formentera

You can begin this tour from Eivissa, Sant Antoni, or Santa Eulàlia, all of which have ferries to Formentera. Because **Formentera** is essentially an island of beach and countryside, you may wish to organize a picnic lunch, for which you should buy supplies in Ibiza. During the short passage it's well worth standing on deck. You'll have excellent views of the d'Alt Vila and of the smaller islands en route—look for Trucadors, the long stretch of sand almost linking Formentera to Es Palmador.

From the port of La Sabina it's only 3 km (2 mi) to the island's tiny capital, **Sant Francesc Xavier,** which is a few yards off the main road. In the small plaza before the church, there's an active hippie market. The interior of the whitewashed church is quite simple, its rough, old wooden door encased in iron and studded with nails. Down a short street directly opposite the church, there's a good antiques and junk shop on the left, with a small art gallery displaying paintings and olive-wood carvings.

Time Out At **Estrella Dorada,** a few yards down Carrer Jaume I, you can sit outside and enjoy good coffee and a selection of tapas. In an alleyway to the right of Estrella Dorada is a chocolate house, **Café Matinal,** white and tiled and very stylish.

Returning to the main road, turn right toward Sant Ferran, 2 km (1 mi) away. Beyond Sant Ferran the road travels for 7 km (4 mi) along a narrow isthmus, keeping slightly closer to the rougher northern side where, if a wind is blowing, the waves come crashing over the rocks. Just beyond El Pilar you'll see, on the right, a **windmill,** still in good order, with all its sails flying.

The plateau that forms the east end of the island ends at the lighthouse, **Faro de la Mola.** Nearby is a monument to Jules Verne, who used Formentera as a setting in his novel *Journey Through the Solar System*. Around the lighthouse, in autumn and spring, the bare rock, despite the feet of thousands of tourists, is carpeted with flowers and covered with purple thyme and sea holly, while below hundreds of swallows soar. At the edge of the cliff you may see luminous turquoise-viridian lizards.

Back on the main road, turn right at Sant Ferran toward Es Pujols. Its few hotels are the nearest Formentera comes to having a beach resort, although the beach is not the best. Beyond Es Pujols the road skirts **Estany Pudent,** one of two lagoons that almost enclose La Sabina. Salt is extracted from Pudent—hence its name, which means "stinking." The other lagoon, **Estany de Peix** (Fish Pond), is a fish farm.

At the northern tip of Pudent, a road to the right leads to a footpath that runs the length of **Trucadors,** the narrow sand spit that reaches out to the island of Es Palmador. For a swim before leaving Formentera, the beaches here are excellent.

What to See and Do with Children

Aqualandia (Urbanización Punta Martine, Playa Talamanca, tel. 971/31-40-60) is a leisure complex just north of Eivissa, with a children's park, children's pool, minigolf, river rapids, a "spirotube," and water slides. Portinaitx also has an **Aquapark.**

Go-Carting is available on the right of the Eivissa–Santa Eulàlia road, just before the junction left to Portinaitx and also south of San Antonio Bay. Playa d'En Bossa has a **fairground** with dodge-'em cars and similar attractions.

Off the Beaten Track

A visit to the church at **Santa Eulàlia del Riu** is a must. At the edge of the town, to the right just below the road, a Roman bridge crosses what is claimed to be the only permanent river in the Balearics (hence, "del Río"), although nowadays it is usually no more than damp. Ahead, on the hilltop, are the cubes and domes of the church. Look for a narrow lane to the left, signed Puig de Missa, and follow it to the church. A stoutly arched, cryptlike covered area, clearly of Moorish influence, guards the entrance. Inside are a fine gold reredos and blue-tiled Stations of the Cross.

To reach the fortified village of **Balafi,** take the Sant Joan road from Eivissa and, passing the left turn to Sant Llorenç, look for a bar on the right next to a ceramics workshop, and turn right onto Sant Carles. Almost opposite on the left, a rough, narrow track leads to Balafi. In the distance you will be able to make out some towers. These have no entrance on the ground floor and, in times of peril, the local inhabitants climbed a ladder to the first floor and pulled the ladder up after them.

Shopping

During the late 1960s and '70s, Ibiza built a reputation for extremes of fashion, of which not much survives, though the softer designs of Smilja Mihailovich, under the **Ad Lib** label, still prosper. While Sa Penya still has a few designer boutiques, much of that famous area is now a so-called hippie market of overpriced tourist ephemera. You'll still find designer leather clothing at **Azara 5** (tel. 971/31–06–71) in front of the Teatro Pereira. **Pink Fly** (Rimbau 4, tel. 971/31–06–55) and **The End** (Carrer de la Creu 26) are well-known boutiques.

In the newer part of town, **Krystal** (corner of Carrers Canarius and Aragón) specializes in designer glassware. **Casa del Café** (corner of Carrers Bisbe Carrasco and Médico Rapuchin) has an amazing range of coffees, teas, and preserves. **Front Line** (Bartolomé Rosello 1) stocks fashions for adults and children.

In Santa Eulàlia, **Broch** on Plaça de Espanya has leatherwear.

Sports and Fitness

Bicycling On Formentera, cycling is very popular, with numerous rental outlets in La Sabina, the port of arrival.

Horseback Riding In Sant Antoni **Club Hípico** (Carretera de Circunvalación) has horses and equipment.

Sports and Fitness Complex **Ahmara,** on the road to Sant Josep, has tennis courts (lessons available), four squash courts, badminton, indoor football, a gymnasium, an exotic Turkish bath, massage, sauna, Jacuzzi, a pool, a grill-restaurant, and a bar. *Centro Deportivo, Carretera Sant Josep Km 2.7, tel. 971/30–77–62 or 971/30–79–50.*

Tennis **Ibiza Club de Campo** (Carretera Sant Josep Km 2, tel. 971/30–00–88); **Aqualandia** (Urbanización Punta Martinet, Playa Talamanca, tel. 971/31–40–60); **Port Sant Miquel** (tel. 971/33–30–19; 5 public courts); **Formentera:** municipal tennis courts (Av. Port Saler, Sant Francesc).

Walking   *Landscapes of Ibiza* (Sunflower Press) is about walking in Ibiza, with itineraries for 22 different walks, none very strenuous, and six bicycle tours of Formentera.

Beaches

Proceeding clockwise from Eivissa, immediately southwest is one of Ibiza's longest stretches of sandy beach at **Playa d'En Bossa,** now almost entirely developed. Farther on, a left turn at Sant Jordi on the way to the airport leads across the salt pans to the beaches of **Cavallet** and **Mitjorn,** two of the best on the island, with no development other than a couple of beach bars. All beaches on Ibiza are topless, but Es Cavallet is the official nudist beach. The remaining beaches in this part of the island are all reached from the Eivissa–Sant Josep–Sant Antoni highway, down side roads that often end in rough tracks.

From Sant Antoni north, there are no easily accessible beaches until you reach **Puerto San Miguel,** an almost rectangular cove with a relatively restrained development of two identical hotels up on the cliffs and a few bars and restaurants at beach level. Next along the north coast, reached via San Juan, is **Portinaitx,** a series of small coves with sandy beaches, of which the first and last, Cala Xarraca and Caló d'Es Porcs, are the best.

The beaches on the east coast have been developed, but **Santa Eulàlia** remains attractive. The resort has a narrow sloping beach in front of a pedestrian promenade that, despite being entirely lined by hotels and apartment blocks, is not frenetic, like Sant Antoni.

Best of all for beaches is **Formentera. Playa de Mitjorn** is completely undeveloped and stretches for 7 km (4 mi) of soft sand and dunes along the south of the island. **Trucadors,** a long, thin spit at the north, has a mile of sand on each side, and it's sometimes possible to wade to Es Palmador, where there are more sandy beaches. On Formentera, nudity is practically the norm.

Dining and Lodging

Dining   Because most produce comes to Ibiza and Formentera from the mainland via Palma, the cost of dining is often high. Sa Penya, the old fisherman's quarter that became famous as a hippie haven in the 1960s, is lined with restaurants of all styles, outside which you can sit and watch the passing parade each evening. Dress is generally casual at restaurants on these islands. (*See* price chart for Mallorca, *above*.)

Lodging   The greatest concentration of hotels is in the coastal resorts of Sant Antoni and Playa d'En Bossa. Many of them are excellent, but unless you are anxious to be part of a mob, Sant Antoni has little to recommend it. Playa d'En Bossa, newer and close to Eivissa, is less brash, but because it lies under the flight path of the airport, it can hardly be recommended to light sleepers. (*See* price chart for Mallorca, *above*.)

Eivissa   **S'Oficina.** The entrance from Avinguda d'Espanya is uninviting but
Dining   leads to an attractive restaurant with a small patio and some of the best Basque cuisine on the island. Marine prints hang on white walls, and ships' lanterns from the ceiling. *Lomo de merluza con almejas* (hake with clams) and *kokotxas* (cod cheeks) are house spe-

cialties. *Av. d'Espanya 6, tel. 971/30–00–16. AE, MC, V. Closed Sun. $$–$$$*

El Porralón. Just inside and left of the main gate into d'Alt Vila, a front terrace announces this intimate French restaurant, the most stylish in town. One dining room is medieval—exposed heavy beams, antiques, oils, coats of armor—another modern, blending dark orange walls with sleek modern furniture. *Pato con salsa de frambuesa* (duck with raspberry sauce) is worth trying if you can't decide. *Plaza Desamparados 1–2, tel. 971/30–39–01 or 971/30–08–52. AE, DC, MC, V. $$–$$$*

Comidas San Juan. This small café at the beginning of Sa Penya has marble-top tables, reminiscent of a Paris bistro. The gloss-painted decor is sterile, but the owners are cheerful and the fish dishes usually good—try the grilled sole. *Carrer Montgri 8, tel. 971/31–07–66. No credit cards. Closed Sun. and holidays. $*

Lodging **Los Molinos.** Technically in Figueretas but only a five-minute walk
★ from the center of Eivissa, Los Molinos is the best hotel in town, at the end of a relatively quiet street. The bedrooms are standard modern; the more expensive ones have balconies that look out over attractive gardens to the bay. *Carrer Ramón Muntaner 60, Apdo 504, 07800 Figueretas, tel. 971/30–22–50/54, fax 971/30–25–04. 147 rooms with bath. Facilities: restaurant, bar, hairdresser, pool, waterskiing from hotel jetty, beach. AE, DC, MC, V. $$–$$$*

La Torre Canónigo. These modern apartments, built into a 16th-century tower at the top of the d'Alt Vila, 50 m (55 yd) from the cathedral, have open fireplaces and the flavor of their ancient surroundings. *Carrer Major 8 Calle Obispo Torres 8, d'Alt Vila, 07800, tel. 971/30–38–84. 7 apartments with bath. Facilities: parking, snack bar, TV room. No credit cards. Closed Nov.–Mar. $–$$*

La Peña. This small, very simple guest house is in an ancient fisherman's cottage right at the end of Sa Penya and close to the lively nighttime scene. *Carrer Verge 76, Sa Penya, 07800. 13 rooms, 2 with shower, 2 with WC. No credit cards. Closed Nov.–Mar. $*

Sant Antoni **Rias Baixas.** One of the best fish restaurants on the island, serving
Dining Galician cuisine, provides possibly the only reason for visiting Sant Antoni. Leave your car on the seafront—the one-way street system is impossible to divine. *Carrer Ignacio Riquer 4, tel. 971/34–04–80. AE, DC, MC, V. Closed Dec. 15–Feb. 15. $$*

Santa Eulàlia **Doña Margarita.** This elegant restaurant on the waterfront has won
Dining several awards for its Ibizan seafood cuisine. You eat at pine tables, overlooked by Ibizan landscapes that hang on the white walls. The outside terrace, next to the crescent beach, is especially pleasant in the evenings. *Passeig Marítim s/n, tel. 971/33–06–55. Reservations advised. Closed Mon. and Dec. AE, DC, MC, V. $$–$$$*

★ **C'as Pagès.** This old farmhouse with bare stone walls, wood beams, and columns made of olive-press "screws" is for meat eaters only. The staff is slow to bring the menu, quick to serve the food. Try the leg of lamb with baked potato or roast peppers or *sofrit pagès* (lamb and chicken stew), followed by *graixonera* (a mixture of sugar, milk, eggs, and cinnamon). *Carretera de San Carlos Km 10 (Pont de S'Argentara), no phone. No credit cards. Closed Tues. and Feb.–Mar. $$*

Lodging **Sol Los Loros.** Striking architecture in extensive gardens and well-designed interiors are the appeal here, but it is a bit isolated at the end of a half-finished development and nearly a half mile from the town center. *Urbanizacion S'Argamassa, 07840, tel. 971/33–07–61, fax 971/33–95–42. 262 rooms with bath. Facilities: restaurant, bar, discothèque, hairdresser, boutique, outdoor and indoor pools, ten-*

nis courts, children's playground. AE, DC, MC, V. Closed Nov.–Mar. $$

Sant Josep
Dining
★

Ca Na Joana (formerly Can Pujolet). A small 200-year-old country house on a hillside combines homey decor and personal attention to give the feeling of dining in a private home. Joana Biarnés, in a former life a well-known journalist, has put together one of the finest restaurants in the Balearics, complete with famous clients and one of the few acclimatized wine cellars in the islands. The *estafado de buey* (ragout of beef) is excellent. *Carretera Eivissa–Sant Josep Km 10, tel. 971/80–01–58. Reservations advised. AE, MC, V. Closed Sun. evening, Mon. Dec. 30–May 31. Open daily June–Oct. $$$*

Sant Miquel
Dining and Lodging
★

Hacienda Na Xamena. Ibiza's most exclusive hotel is also the most isolated, on a rocky headland in the north of the island. Access to the sea is difficult and involves a long hike down steep steps, but the rooms are elegant, around a pretty little central patio with a fountain and trees. Reserve well in advance. *Apdo 423, Sant Miquel, 07815, tel. 971/33–30–46, fax 971/33–31–75. 63 rooms with bath, 33 with Jacuzzis. Facilities: restaurant, bar, 3 pools (including children's pool), boutiques, health club, 1 tennis court. AE, DC, MC, V. Closed Nov.–Mar. $$$–$$$$*

The Arts and Nightlife

The Arts
Sant Josep is known for its **folk dancing**—the Tourist Office in Eivissa will advise on dates and times. You can also see folk dancing at Sant Joan each Thursday evening and on June 24, the Feast of St. John the Baptist. July 15 and 16 are celebrated in honor of the Virgen del Carmen, the patron saint of sailors, with boat processions in the bay at Sant Antoni. Sant Francesc, on Formentera, has a **fiesta** with dancing on July 25, the Feast of St. James, the patron saint of Spain.

Nightlife
If the arts are relatively neglected, nightlife certainly is not, and the discos of Ibiza are famous throughout Europe. In Eivissa, the trendy place to begin the evening is **Keeper** (Passeig Marítim), where you can sip your drink perched atop a carousel horse. There is also a lively, very young scene at **Divino,** another of the music bars on the Passeig Marítim. The in place for older nighthawks is the foyer of the former **Teatre Pereira** (Carrer Comte Roselló; expensive).

Long-established favorites are **Pachá** (Passeig Marítim s/n), **Amnesia** in San Rafael (Sant Antoni road, opposite the Km 5 marker), and **Ku** (a little farther along the same road). Hardened discomanes end the night at **Space** (at the far end of Playa d'En Bossa), which doesn't even open until 5 AM.

Ibiza's **casino** is in a Cubist building whose architectural style resembles that of an Ibizan church, with a pizzeria and piano bar in the side chapels. *Passeig Marítim s/n, tel. 971/31–33–12. Open weekdays 10 PM–4 AM, weekends 10 PM–5 AM.*

12 The Costa del Sol

By Hilary
Bunce

Updated
by Mark
Potok

The stretch of Andalusian shore known as the Costa del Sol runs officially from Cabo de Gata, beyond Almería in the east, all the way to the tip of Tarifa, past Gibraltar in the west. For most of the vast hordes of European vacationers who have flocked here during the 35 years of its popularity, though, the Sun Coast has been largely restricted to 70 km (43 mi) of concrete playground between Torremolinos, just west of Málaga, and Estepona, 50 km (31 mi) short of Gibraltar. Since the late 1950s this area has mushroomed from a string of impoverished fishing villages afflicted with malaria and near starvation into a hugely overdeveloped package-tour mecca of the sunseekers of northern Europe and a retirement haven for Britons and Americans.

In the '60s and early '70s, hundreds of concrete high rises shot up to scar the skylines of Torremolinos and Fuengirola, and luxury hotels and leafy villas erupted on the shoreline of Marbella, pushing this former fishing village to the forefront of Europe's upscale resorts. The late 1980s witnessed a second boom, generating new golf courses, luxury marinas, villa developments, and yet more world-class hotels.

The Costa averages some 320 days of sunshine a year, and balmy days are not unknown even in January or February. It's also a good place to unwind. You can bask or stroll on mile upon mile of beaches and enjoy a full range of land and water sports.

Sunseekers from bleaker climes seem crammed into every corner of the Costa. If you're planning to spend some time here, it's particularly important to choose your resort carefully. Málaga and Ronda, though not strictly resorts, are the most authentically Spanish cities—especially Ronda. Torremolinos caters almost exclusively to the mass market; it's a budget destination that appeals very much to singles and to those who come to soak up the sun and disco the night away. Fuengirola is quieter and much more geared to family vacations, whereas farther west, the Marbella–San Pedro de Alcántara area is more exclusive and, of course, more expensive.

In places, mountains roll down to the sea; in others, unfolding hillsides of olive groves, cork oaks, and terraced vineyards provide vistas of the Mediterranean glinting in the distance. The developed coastal strip contrasts vividly with its hinterland. Just a few miles up in the mountains, you'll find remote villages where black-shawled women go about their daily routine much as they did a quarter century or so ago, and donkeys and mules are still used for farm work. Steeped in medieval lore and the scene of many turbulent battles of the Reconquest, the perched white villages (*pueblos blancos*) belong to a world light-years away from the hedonistic carnival of the coast. Gibraltar, of course, provides yet another atmosphere, with its British policemen, pubs, and regal guardsmen.

Essential Information

Important Addresses and Numbers

Tourist
Information

The Costa del Sol's main information office is in **Málaga** (Pasaje de Chinitas 4, tel. 95/221–3445 or 95/222–8948; open weekdays 9–2:30, Sat. 9–1). Local tourist offices can be found in **Algeciras** (Juan de la Cierva, tel. 956/57–26–36), **Antequera** (Palacio de Najera, Coso Viejo, tel. 95/284–1827), **Benalmádena Costa** (Av. Antonio Machado 14, tel. 95/244–2494), **Estepona** (Paseo Marítimo, tel. 95/280–0913), **Fuengirola** (Av. Jesús Santos Rein 6, tel. 95/246–7457), **Gibraltar**

(Cathedral Sq., tel. 9567/74950), **La Linea** (Av. 20 de Abril, tel. 956/76–99–50), **Málaga Airport** (tel. 95/224–0000), **Marbella** (Glorieta de la Fontanilla, tel. 95/277–1442 or 95/277–4693), **Nerja** (Puerta del Mar 2, tel. 95/252–1531), **Ronda** (Plaza de España 1, tel. 95/287–1272), **Torremolinos** (Plaza Pablo Ruíz Picasso, tel. 95/237–1159 or 95/237–1125).

Consulates **British** (Duquesa de Parcent 3, Málaga, tel. 95/221–7571; Av. Fuerzas Armadas 11, Algeciras, tel. 956/66–16–00). **Canadian** (Plaza de la Malagueta 3, Málaga, tel. 95/222–3346). **U.S.** (Ramón y Cajal, Edificio El Ancla, Fuengirola, tel. 95/247–4891).

Travel The chief international agencies are **American Express** (Av. Arias
Agencies Maldonado 2, Marbella, tel. 95/282–1494 or 95/282–2820; Viajes Alhambra, Especerías 10, Málaga, tel. 95/221–3774 or 95/221–4636) and **Wagons Lits Viajes** (Strachan 20, Málaga, tel. 95/221–7695).

Arriving and Departing by Plane

Airports and **Gibraltar Airport** (tel. 9567/73026) is worth considering if you're ar-
Airlines riving from Great Britain, especially if you're visiting the coast west of Marbella. It is next to the frontier, and once you've crossed into Spain, you can make bus connections at La Linea for all coastal resorts.

Málaga Airport (95/224–0000, switchboard, or 95/213–6166/67 for Iberia information) lies 10 km (16 mi) west of Málaga. If you're flying from the United States, you'll have to make connections in Madrid. Iberia and British Airways operate several scheduled flights a day from London; Dan Air operates from London Gatwick, as do numerous other charter flights. Most major European cities have direct flights to Málaga on either Iberia or their own national airlines. Iberia and its subsidiary, Aviaco, have up to eight flights a day from Madrid (journey time: 1 hour), three flights a day from Barcelona (1½ hours), and regular flights from other Spanish cities.

Iberia has offices in Málaga (Molina Lario 13, tel. 95/213–6146/47/48) and at the airport (tel. 95/213–6166 for arrival and departure information).

From the From Málaga Airport, a train service runs regularly to nearby cities
Airport to (*see* Getting Around, *below*), and an Iberia bus leaves every 20 min-
Downtown utes for downtown Málaga (6:20 AM–10:40 PM; fare: 100 pesetas). Taxis are plentiful at both terminals, and official fares to Málaga, Torremolinos, and other resorts are posted inside the terminal buildings. The trip from the airport to Torremolinos will cost about 1,500 pesetas. When you return to the airport, make sure to get off the bus at the right stop: *Vuelos Nacionales* for domestic flights, *Vuelos Internacionales* for international flights. The two terminals are a long way apart, and there's no connecting bus.

Arriving and Departing by Car, Train, and Bus

By Car Málaga is 580 km (360 mi) from Madrid by way of N IV to Córdoba, then N331 to Antequera and N321; 182 km (114 mi) from Córdoba via Antequera; 214 km (134 mi) from Seville; and 129 km (81 mi) from Granada by the shortest route of N342 to Loja, then N321 to Málaga. Numerous highway projects completed in connection with the 1992 International Exposition in Seville improved highways and traveling time between Seville and Granada and the Costa del Sol.

By Train Málaga is the main rail terminus, with five through trains a day from Madrid and one from Barcelona and Valencia. Most Málaga trains leave from Madrid Chamartín, though most of those also stop at Atocha. Travel time varies between 7 and 10 hours; the best trains are the daytime Pendular (7 hours) and the overnight Talgo (9½ hours), both from Chamartín. All Madrid–Málaga trains stop at Córdoba; there are also local trains direct from Córdoba to Málaga. From both Seville (4 hours) and Granada (3–3½ hours), you will have to change at Bobadilla for Málaga, making buses a better bet for those traveling from these cities. In fact other than the direct Madrid–Córdoba–Málaga line, trains in Andalucía can be slow because of the terrain, and you may find buses quicker and more convenient.

Málaga Station (Explanada de la Estación, tel. 95/236–0202) is 15 minutes' walk from the center, across the river. For tickets and information, the central RENFE office (Strachan 2, just off Larios, tel. 95/221–4127; open weekdays 9–1:30 and 4:30–7:30; closed weekends) is much more convenient.

By Bus   Long-distance buses serve Málaga from Madrid, Cartagena, Almería, Granada, Úbeda, Córdoba, Seville, and Badajoz. Málaga's main bus station is on Paseo de los Tilos (tel. 95/235–0061). Marbella and Algeciras can be reached direct from Madrid or Seville; other services are between Fuengirola and Seville, and Cádiz and Algeciras. Marbella's bus station is at Avenida Ricardo Soriano 21 (tel. 95/277–2192).

Getting Around

By Car   A car will enable you to explore some of the picturesque mountain villages for which Andalucía is famous. Mountain driving can be an adventure because hair-raising curves, precipices, and mediocre road services are often the norm. But this is changing rapidly as highways throughout the region are resurfaced and widened; in some cases completely new roadbeds have been built. Though the busy coastal N340 is good by Spanish standards and is currently being widened in parts, it is a notorious death trap known locally as the Carretera de la Muerte (the Highway of Death). A useful tip: When you want to turn left from N340, you do so in most cases by exiting right and looping in a circle, often controlled by traffic lights. To take a car into Gibraltar, drivers, in theory, need an international driver's permit, an insurance certificate, and a logbook; in practice, all you need show is your passport. Be prepared for parking problems on the Rock—space is scarce—but beware of phony offers of help from "parking/insurance agents" on the frontier approach.

By Train   A useful suburban train service runs between Málaga, Torremolinos, and Fuengirola, calling at the airport and all resorts along the way. It leaves Málaga every half hour between 6 AM and 10:30 PM and from Fuengirola every half hour from 6:35 AM to 11:35 PM. Its terminus in Málaga is the **Guadalmedina** Station, more or less opposite the Corte Inglés; it also calls at Málaga RENFE Station. Its Fuengirola terminus is just across from the bus station, where you can make connections for Mijas, Marbella, Estepona, and Algeciras.

Two trains a day run between Málaga and Ronda through dramatic El Chorro gorge. Journey time is around three hours, and you have to change at Bobadilla. Between Ronda and Algeciras three direct trains a day (two hours) travel a spectacular mountain track built in the 19th century by the British.

By Bus   Buses are the best way of getting around the Costa del Sol (as well as reaching it from Seville or Granada). Málaga's bus station is on the Paseo de los Tilos (tel. 95/235–0061). The **Portillo** bus company, with offices at the Málaga Station (tel. 95/236–0191), serves most of the Costa del Sol. Another company with offices at the station, **Alsina Gräells** (tel. 95/231–8295), has service to Granada, Córdoba, Seville, and Nerja. Málaga Tourist Office has details on other bus lines serving outlying villages.

Guided Tours

Excursions Numerous one- and two-day excursions from Costa del Sol resorts are run by **Julia Tours** (Emilio Esteban 1, Torremolinos, tel. 95/238–7222), **Pullmantur** (Pontevedra 3, Torremolinos, tel. 95/238–4400), and various smaller companies. Leaflets are available in most hotels, and tours can be booked through your hotel desk or any travel agent. Excursions operate from Málaga, Torremolinos, Fuengirola, Marbella, and Estepona; prices vary slightly, according to your departure point; in most cases, you can be picked up from your hotel.

Local Tours Most of the following local tours are half-day: Málaga, Cuevas de Nerja, Mijas, Marbella, and Puerto Banús; Burro safari in Coín; countryside tour to villages of Alhaurín de la Torre, Alhaurín el Grande, Coín, Ojén, and Ronda. Night tours include a barbecue evening, a bullfighting evening with dinner, and a night at the Casino Torrequebrada.

Exploring the Costa del Sol

Orientation

Our tour of the Costa del Sol moves from east to west along the coastal highway N340. It starts in the province of Granada, then heads west along the entire coastline of Málaga province, to enter Cádiz province briefly at Sotogrande and San Roque, before terminating at the Rock of Gibraltar. The main centers along this route are Nerja, Málaga (the region's capital and only major city), Torremolinos, Fuengirola, Marbella, and Estepona. You'll also find some suggestions for short detours inland to mountain villages and the dramatic scenery of El Chorro gorge. A major detour from the coastal highway, and one not to be missed, is to Ronda, high in the mountains, 54 km (34 mi) inland.

Highlights for First-time Visitors

Views from Nerja's Balcón de Europa (*see* Tour 1)
Garganta del Chorro (*see* Tour 2)
View from Málaga's Gibralfaro (*see* Tour 2)
View from terrace of Mijas church (*see* Tour 3)
Nerja Caves (*see* Tour 1)
Cable-car ride up the Rock of Gibraltar (*see* Tour 5)
El Tajo gorge seen from the Puente Nuevo, Ronda (*see* Tour 4)

Tour 1: The Costa del Sol Oriental

Numbers in the margin correspond to points of interest on the Costa del Sol map.

To the east of Málaga, the so-called Costa del Sol Oriental has escaped the worst excesses of the property developers. Housing developments inspired by Andalusian village architecture, rather than faceless concrete tower blocks, are the norm and the tourist onslaught has been much milder. That's not to say you won't find packed beaches and traffic-choked roads at the height of the season, but for most of the year, it's relatively free from tourists, if not from foreign expatriate residents.

❶ Dropping down through the mountains from Granada or continuing west from Almería, you pick up the N340 coast road near **Salobreña.** A short detour to the left from the highway brings you to this unspoiled village whose near-perpendicular streets and old white houses perch on a steep hill beneath a Moorish fortress. Salobreña is picturesque in a totally natural way, providing a sample of the Andalusian pueblo atmosphere.

❷ The road from Motril to Málaga passes through the former heart of the empire of sugar barons who brought prosperity to Málaga province in the 19th century. Today, the traditional cane fields are giving way to litchis, limes, mangoes, papaws, and olive groves. Dark green avocado groves line your route on the descent into **Almuñécar,** a fishing village since Phoenician times, 3,000 years ago, when it was called Sexi. The Moors built a castle here, where the kings of Granada once kept their treasures. Today Almuñécar is a small-time resort with a shingle beach, popular with Spanish and Belgian vacationers.

❸ Between Almuñécar and Nerja, giant cliffs and dramatic seascapes provide the best scenery on this eastern stretch of the Costa. Above the village of Maro, 4 km (2 mi) before Nerja, signs point to the entrance to the **Cuevas de Nerja.** These huge Paleolithic caves, thought to be between 12,000 and 20,000 years old, were discovered in 1959 by children playing on the hillside. Over the past 30 years, thousands of tourists have tramped through the floodlit caverns furnished with spires and turrets created by centuries of dripping water. One suspended pinnacle, 62 meters (200 feet) long, claims the title of world's largest stalactite. In summer these awesome subterranean chambers provide an impressive setting for concert and ballet performances. *Tel. 95/252–0076. Admission: 300 pesetas. Open Sept.–June, daily 10:30–2 and 3:30–6; July–Aug., daily 10:30–6.*

❹ **Nerja**—its name comes from the Moorish word *narixa,* meaning "abundant springs"—is a rapidly developing resort. Happily, the high rises have been kept at bay, and much of Nerja's growth has been confined to *urbanizaciones* ("village" developments). The old village of Nerja is clustered on top of a headland above several small beaches and rocky coves that offer reasonable bathing despite the gray grit sand. In high season Nerja's beaches are packed with sun-worshiping north Europeans, but at other times wandering the narrow whitewashed streets and courtyards of the old town is enjoyable. Nerja's highlight is the **Balcón de Europa,** a lookout high above the sea on a promontory just off the central square.

Time Out **Cala Bella** (Puerta del Mar 10, tel. 95/252–0700) and **Portofino** (Puerta del Mar 4, tel. 95/252–0150) are medium-priced restaurants in neighboring Andalusian houses close to the main square. Their dining rooms, with outdoor balconies offering dramatic cliff-top sea views, are an ideal setting for lunch, or dinner on a summer evening.

❺ Six km (3.7 mi) inland, the village of **Frigiliana** perches on a mountain ridge overlooking the ocean. In 1567, one of the last battles between the Moors and Christians was fought here. Spectacular views of the Mediterranean and an old quarter with twisting cobbled streets and ancient houses reward this short drive off the main road. Frigiliana can also be reached by bus from Nerja.

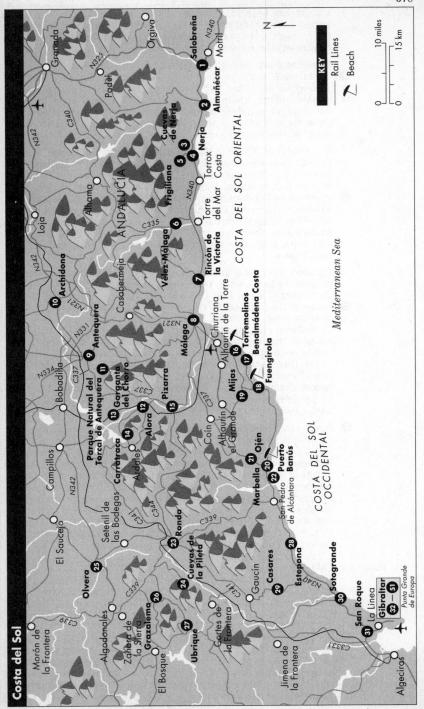

Costa del Sol

KEY
Rail Lines
Beach

0 ___ 10 miles
0 ___ 15 km

N

Granada

N323

Padul

Órgiva

Salobreña

Motril

①

Almuñécar

②

Cuevas de Nerja

③

Nerja

⑤ ④

Torrox Costa

N340

ANDALUCÍA

C340

N342

Alhama

Loja

Casabermeja

C335

⑥

Torre del Mar

Frigiliana

Vélez-Málaga

⑦

Rincón de la Victoria

COSTA DEL SOL ORIENTAL

Archidona

⑩

N321

N331

Antequera

⑨

Churriana

Alhaurín de la Torre

⑧

Málaga

N321

Torremolinos

⑯

Benalmádena Costa

⑰

Bobadilla

N334

C337

Parque Natural del Torcal de Antequera

⑪

Garganta del Chorro

Pizarra

⑮

C337

Fuengirola

⑱

⑲ Mijias

C337

Coín

Campillos

N342

⑬ ⑫

Álora

⑭

Ardales

Carratraca

Alhaurín el Grande

Ojén

㉑ ⑳ Puerto Banús

Mediterranean Sea

Setenil de las Bodegas

C341

C344

Ronda

Marbella

㉒

San Pedro de Alcántara

COSTA DEL SOL OCCIDENTAL

El Saucejo

Morón de la Frontera

C339

Olvera

㉕

Cuevas de la Pileta

㉓

C339

㉘

Estepona

Sotogrande

㉚

Algodonales

㉖

Zahara de la Sierra

Grazalema

㉔

Gaucín

Casares

㉙

C341

N340

San Roque

㉛

La Línea

Gibraltar

㉜ ⟶ 51

Punta Grande de Europa

Cortes de la Frontera

㉗

Ubrique

El Bosque

Jimena de la Frontera

C3331

Algeciras

The remaining road to Málaga leaves little to explore. Ruins near the lighthouse at Torrox Costa bear witness to the town's Roman past. If you have time, turn inland at Torre del Mar and drive up to

❻ **Vélez-Málaga,** the capital of the Ajarquía region. A pleasant agricultural town of white houses, Vélez-Málaga is a center for strawberry growing and vineyards producing the sweet muscatel grapes for which Málaga is famous. A Thursday market, ruins of a Moorish castle, and the church of Santa María la Mayor, built in Mudéjar (Spanish Muslim) style on the site of a mosque destroyed when the town fell to the Christians in 1487, all merit a quick visit.

❼ One km (⅔ mi) outside **Rincón de la Victoria** you can visit the Cueva del Tesoro (Treasure Cave), where Moorish kings reputedly hid their treasure as they fled Christian attackers. The caves were inhabited in prehistoric times, and early domestic utensils are on display. *Open Apr.–Sept., daily 10–2 and 4–7; Oct.–Mar., Tues.–Sun. 10–2 and 4–7, closed Mon.*

Tour 2: Málaga and Inland

❽ The city of **Málaga,** with about 575,000 inhabitants, claims the title of Capital of the Costa del Sol, though in reality most tourists simply use its airport and bypass the city itself. Approaching the city from the airport, you'll be greeted by urban sprawl, where the huge high rises flung up in the 1970s march determinedly toward Torremolinos. But don't despair, for in its center and eastern suburbs, Málaga is a pleasant port city, with ancient streets and lovely villas set amid exotic foliage. It enjoys a subtropical climate, is blessed with lush vegetation, and averages some 324 days of sunshine a year.

Arriving from Nerja, you'll come into Málaga through the suburbs of El Palo and Pedregalejos, once traditional fishing villages in their own right. Here you can eat wonderfully fresh fish in the numerous rough-and-ready *chiringuitos* (fishermen's restaurants) on the beach and enjoy a stroll on Pedregalejos's seafront promenade or on the tree-lined streets of El Limonar. At sunset take a walk along the **Paseo Marítimo,** and watch the lighthouse start its nightly vigil.

Once you reach the center, the **Plaza de la Marina,** with its bustling outdoor cafés and illuminated fountain overlooking the port, is a pleasant place for a drink. From here you can stroll through the shady palm-lined gardens of the **Paseo del Parque,** scene of Málaga's August fair, or browse the stores on Calle Marqués de Larios, the main shopping street.

The narrow streets and alleyways on each side of Calle Marqués de Larios have a charm of their own. Wander the warren of passageways around Pasaje Chinitas, off Plaza de la Constitución; peep into the dark, vaulted bodegas where old men down glasses of *seco añejo* or *Málaga Virgen*, local wines made from Málaga's muscatel grapes. Silversmiths and vendors of religious books and statues ply their trade in shops that have changed little since the turn of the century. Across Larios, in the streets leading through to Calle Nueva, you'll find shoe-shine boys, lottery ticket vendors, carnation-sporting Gypsies, beggars, and a wealth of tapas bars dispensing wine from huge barrels.

A word of warning: Málaga has one of the highest unemployment rates in Spain; poverty and crime are rife (although drug peddling, once fairly common in the streets, has declined). There have been numerous reports of muggings, and you're better off not carrying purses or valuables in the streets or on the way up to Gibralfaro (*see below*).

Time Out   **El Boquerón de la Plata** (Alarcón Luján 6) is one of Málaga's most famous tapas bars. The counter is piled high with fresh seafood, and the floor is ankle deep in discarded shells.

After exploring the alleyways of the old town, visit the **cathedral,** built between 1528 and 1782 on the site of the former mosque. Mainly Renaissance in style, Málaga Cathedral is not one of the great cathedrals of Spain and is unfinished, the funds having run out before a second tower could be built to match the single existing one. One story has it that the allocated money was donated instead to the American War of Independence. The lovely enclosed choir, which miraculously survived the burnings of the civil war, is the work of the great 17th-century artist Pedro de Mena, who in places has carved the wood wafer-thin to express the fold of a robe or shape of a finger. *Calle de Molina Lario, tel. 95/221–5916. Admission: cathedral free; choir, 100 pesetas. Open daily 10–12:30 and 4–5:30.*

Nearby, the **Museo de Bellas Artes** (Fine Arts Museum) is set in the old Palace of the Counts of Buenavista, reached across a courtyard off Calle San Agustín. Inside, you'll find Roman mosaics and minor canvases by Luis de Morales, Alonso Cano, Murillo, Zurbarán, and Ribera, as well as 19th- and 20th-century paintings. Its most interesting treasure is a gallery of early childhood drawings by Málaga's most famous native son, Pablo Picasso, who was born only a few hundred yards away in a house on Plaza de la Merced (No. 15). *San Agustín 6, tel. 95/221–8387. Admission: 250 pesetas. Open Apr.–Oct., Tues.–Sat. 10–1:30 and 5–8, Sun. 10–1:30; Nov.–Mar., Tues.–Fri. 10–1:30 and 4–7, Sat. and Sun. 10–1:30; closed Mon.*

The **Alcazaba,** undoubtedly the city's best sight, is a fortress begun in the 8th century, when Málaga was the principal port of the Moorish kingdom. The ruins of the Roman amphitheater at its entrance were uncovered when the fort was restored. The inner palace was built between 1057 and 1063, when the Moorish emirs took up residence here. Ferdinand and Isabella lived here, too, for a while, after their conquest of Málaga in 1487. Orange trees and bougainvillea have been planted among the ruins, whose heights offer great views of the park and port. Inside the enclosure you'll find the **Museo Arqueológico** (Archeological Museum), with displays from Málaga's Roman and Moorish periods. *Entrance on Alcazabilla. Tel. 95/222–0043. Admission: 20 pesetas. Open Apr.–Sept., Mon.–Sat. 11–2 and 5–8, Sun. 10–2; Oct.–Mar., Mon.–Sat. 10–1 and 4–7, Sun. 10–2.*

Magnificent views will reward a climb up through the Alcazaba gardens to the summit of **Gibralfaro.** (There have been reports of thieves here, so don't go alone, and don't carry valuables.) Alternatively, you can drive to Gibralfaro by way of Calle Victoria or take a minibus that leaves roughly every 1½ hours from near the cathedral on Calle Molina Larios for the parador at the top of Gibralfaro. The Gibralfaro fortifications were built for Yusuf I in the 14th century. The Moors called them Jebelfaro, meaning "rock of the lighthouse," after a beacon that stood here to guide ships into the harbor and warn of invasions by pirates. Today the beacon is gone, succeeded by the small parador, a delightful place for a meal or a drink.

On the far side of the city center, beside the river, you'll find the **Museo de Artes Populares** (Arts and Crafts Museum), housed in the old Mesón de la Victoria, a 17th-century inn. On display are horse carriages and carts, old agricultural implements, folk costumes, a forge, a bakery, an ancient grape press, and Málaga ceramics and sculptures. *Pasillo de Santa Isabel 10, tel. 95/221–7137. Admission free. Open Apr.–Oct., Tues.–Sat. 10–1:30 and 5–8, Sun. 10–1:30; Nov.–Mar., Tues.–Sat. 10–1:30 and 4–7, Sun. 10–1:30; closed Mon.*

From Málaga you can either continue westward along the coast to Torremolinos or, if time permits, make a detour inland to visit the old Moorish town of Antequera, returning to the coast road by way of El Chorro gorge and Alora. If you opt for the detour, head north on N321, then N331, to Antequera, 64 km (40 mi) from Málaga. On the way there, look for the village of **Casabermeja,** where tall cypresses shelter one of the prettiest cemeteries in Andalucía. As you approach Antequera, stop near Los Dólmenes gas station to visit the Menga and Viera Dolmens, mysterious funeral chambers constructed from giant monoliths. A third chamber, Romeral, lies 5 km (3 mi) away, near the sugar factory (ask here for the key).

❾ Antequera became one of the great strongholds of the Moors following their defeat at Córdoba and Seville in the 13th century. Its fall to the Christians in 1410 opened the gateway to Granada. The Moors retreated, leaving behind a fortress on the town heights in whose midst the parador now stands. Of the town's many churches, the collegiate church of **Santa María la Mayor,** a 16th-century sandstone building with a fine ribbed vault, used today as a concert hall and crafts training center, is one of the best. Another landmark is the church of **San Sebastián,** with a brick Baroque-Mudéjar tower.

Antequera's pride and joy is **Efebo,** a beautiful bronze statue of a boy that stands almost 5 feet high and dates back to Roman times. It's on display in the **Museo Municipal** (Municipal Museum). *Palacio de Nájera, Coso Viejo. Open Tues.–Sat. 10–1:30, Sun. 11–1; closed Mon.*

From Antequera several options are open to you. To the east of town along N342 the dramatic silhouette of the **Peña de los Enamorados** (Lovers' Rock) is an Andalusian landmark. Legend recounts how a Moorish princess and a Christian shepherd boy eloped here one night and next morning cast themselves to their deaths from its famous peak. Its outline is often likened to the profile of the Cordoban bullfighter Manolete. Eight km (5 mi) beyond the Peña, the village of **❿ Archidona** winds its way up a steep mountain slope beneath the ruins of a Moorish castle. This picturesque white cluster is worth a detour for the sake of its contrasting **Plaza Ochavada,** a magnificent 17th-century square resplendent in red and ocher stone.

⓫ Ten km (6 mi) to the south of Antequera on C3310, the **Parque Natural del Torcal de Antequera** has well-marked walking trails (you'll need strong shoes) that guide you among eerie pillars of pink sandstone sculpted by millennia of wind and rain.

C337 to the southwest of Antequera will bring you to the turnoff for **⓬ Alora.** From Alora follow a small road north to the awe-inspiring **⓭ Garganta** (gorge) **del Chorro.** Here, in a deep chasm in the limestone cliff, the Guadalhorce River churns and snakes its way some 186 meters (600 ft) below the road. The railroad track that worms in and out of tunnels in the cleft is, amazingly, the main line out of Málaga heading north for Bobadilla junction and, eventually, Madrid.

⓮ The road continues in a circle to Ardales, then on to the old spa town of **Carratraca,** with its Moorish-style Ayuntamiento (City Hall) and unusual polygonal bullring. It was formerly a favorite watering hole of the Spanish and foreign aristocracy. Its hotel, the Hostal del Príncipe, once sheltered Empress Eugénie, wife of Napoleon III. Lord Byron, too, came to partake of the cure. Today you can still relax in the sulfur baths of Carratraca's splendid marble and tile bathhouse.

From Carratraca return to Alora, from which C337 takes you back to the coast through groves of citrus and olives. At **Pizarra,** you may be able to visit the **Hollander Museum.** Gino and Barbara Hollander, originally from the United States, founded the museum in their converted 18th-century farmhouse home, with an exceptional collection of paintings and objets d'art. But the Hollanders have left, and you'll have to ask for information at the local ayuntamiento (Town Hall, tel. 95/248–3015).

Tour 3: The Costa del Sol Occidental

Rejoin N340, the coastal highway, and 12 km (7 mi) to the west of Málaga, the sprawling outskirts of **Torremolinos** mark the beginning of the "real Costa del Sol."

Fun in the sun is what Torremolinos is all about. Swarms of northern European vacationers, the young and not so young, throng its streets in season. Scantily attired and pink fleshed, they shop for bargains on the Calle San Miguel, down sangría in the bars of La Nogalera, and dance the night away in discothèques. By day the sunseekers flock to the El Bajondillo and La Carihuela beaches, whose sand is the usual fine gray grit, and in high summer it's hard to find a patch to call your own.

Torremolinos has two distinct sections. The first, Central T-town, is built around the Plaza Costa del Sol; Calle San Miguel, the main shopping street; and the brash Nogalera Plaza, full of overpriced bars and "foreign" restaurants. The Pueblo Blanco area off Calle Casablanca is pleasant, and the Cuesta del Tajo, at the far end of San Miguel, winds down a steep slope to the Bajondillo Beach. Here, crumbling walls, bougainvillea-clad patios, and old cottages give a hint of the fishing village this once was.

The second section of Torremolinos is the much nicer district of **La Carihuela,** easily missed if you don't know where it is. To reach it, head west out of town on Avenida Carlota Alessandri, and turn left by the Hotel La Paloma. Far more authentically Spanish, the Carihuela retains many of its old fishermen's cottages and several excellent fish restaurants. Its traffic-free esplanade makes for an enjoyable stroll, especially on a summer evening or at Sunday lunchtime, when it's packed with Spanish families.

Time Out   **La Casita** (Calle Bulto 42) is a small bar in an old fisherman's cottage. Look in here any night after dinner (10 PM onward) to see if there's flamenco; performances are often fun, spontaneous, and fairly authentic.

If you want something "to do," you'll find the **Atlantis Mundo Aquatico** just off the bypass, near the Palacio de Congresos Convention Center, complete with water chutes, artificial waves, water mountains, and pools. *Tel. 95/238–8888. Admission: 1,595 pesetas adults, 975 pesetas children 3–12. Open May–Oct., daily 10–7.*

West of Torremolinos come the similar but more staid resorts of Benalmádena Costa and Fuengirola. **Benalmádena Costa** is run almost exclusively by package-tour operators and offers little to draw the independent traveler, though there's a pleasant-enough marina.

Two km (1 mi) inland, at Arroyo de la Miel, you can visit **Tivoli World,** the Costa del Sol's leading amusement park. Don't expect the sleek perfection of Disneyland, but there's a 4,000-seat open-air auditorium that often features international stars alongside the cancan, flamenco, or Spanish ballet. You'll also find roller coasters, a Ferris wheel, illuminated fountains, a Chinese pagoda, Wild West shows, and some 40 or so restaurants. *Tel. 95/244-2848. Admission: 600 pesetas includes access to more than 30 rides and attractions. Open year-round, afternoon and evening only.*

❶⑧ Fuengirola is the poor stepsister of Torremolinos. It is duller and generally cheaper; many of the concrete pyramids along its 6-km (4-mi) promenade are holiday apartments catering to budget-minded vacationers from northern Europe. Fuengirola is above all a British and American retirement haven.

Every half hour buses leave Fuengirola bus station for the 8-km (5-mi) drive through pine-clad hills to the picturesque village of **❶⑨ Mijas** in the foothills of the sierra. If you have a car and don't mind a mildly hair-raising drive, there's a far prettier approach from Benalmádena Pueblo by way of a winding mountain road (currently being widened and straightened) that affords some great views. Though Mijas was discovered long ago by the foreign-retiree community (foreign residents here now outnumber locals), and the large touristy square where you arrive may well seem like an extension of the Costa, beyond this are hillside streets of whitewashed houses and a somewhat authentic village atmosphere.

Park in the Plaza Virgen de la Peña, where you can hire a "burro taxi" to explore the village, take a quick look at the Chapel of Mijas's patroness, the Virgen de la Peña, or, if such things appeal, visit the **Carromato de Max** (admission: 400 pesetas; open weekdays 11–8, weekends 10–8) with its collection of miniature curiosities from all over the world.

Wander over to the Plaza Constitución, the real village square, then walk up the slope beside the Mirlo Blanco restaurant to Mijas's tiny bullring. It's one of the few square bullrings in Spain. *Tel. 95/248-5248. Admission to the ring and its bullfighting museum: 400 pesetas.*

Next, visit the delightful **church** just up the hill. It is immaculately decorated, especially at Easter, and its terrace and surrounding gardens afford a splendid panorama down the hillside to Fuengirola and the coast.

Wander at will through any of the white streets of Mijas; be sure to head up the hill behind the village; the higher you go, the more authentic the atmosphere. Take a peep inside the tiny church at the bottom of Calle San Sebastián; it's filled with flowers, and Rococo decorations on gleaming white walls.

Time Out Next door, at No. 4, the **Bar Menguine** (or **Casa de los Jamones**) has row after row of hams strung from its ceiling and a couple of tables set aside for inexpensive meals.

❷⓪ Return to the coast and head west to **Marbella,** playground of the rich and home of movie stars, rock musicians, and dispossessed royal families of Europe, which has attained the top rung on the ladder of social chic. Dip into any Spanish gossip magazine, and the glittering parties that fill its pages are doubtless taking place in Marbella.

Much of the action takes place on the fringes, for grand hotels and luxury restaurants line the waterfront for 20 km (12 mi) on each side of the center. In the town itself, you may well wonder just why Marbella became so famous. The main thoroughfare, Avenida Ricardo Soriano, is singularly lacking in charm, and the Paseo Marítimo, though pleasant enough, with its array of seafood restaurants and pizza houses overlooking an ordinary beach, is far from spectacular.

The real charm of Marbella is to be found in the heart of the old village, which remains miraculously intact, a block or two back from the main highway. Here, narrow alleyways of whitewashed houses cluster round the central Plaza de los Naranjos, where colorful restaurants vie for space under the orange trees. Climb up on what remains of the old fortifications and stroll along the quaint Calle Virgen de los Dolores to the Plaza de Santo Cristo. Wander the maze of lanes and enjoy the geranium-bedecked windows and splashing fountains.

Time Out Virgen de Dolores is lined with inviting restaurants whose prices are rather more manageable than those of the nearby Plaza de los Naranjos. Here, **Casa Eladio** (No. 6, tel. 95/277–0083) has a charming indoor patio.

㉑ For a complete contrast to the glamour of the coast, drive up to **Ojén,** in the hills above Marbella. When you reach this ancient village, it's like entering another world. Don't miss the pretty pottery sold here or the typical Andalusian cemetery, with its rows of chambers for burial urns.

The road to Puerto Banús has been dubbed the Golden Mile. Here, a mosque, Arab banks, and the onetime residence of King Fahd of Saudi Arabia proclaim the influence of petrodollars in this enclave of the rich. Seven km (4 mi) west of central Marbella (between Km 175 ㉒ and Km 174), a sign indicates the turnoff that leads down to **Puerto Banús.** Marbella's plush marina, with its 915 berths, is a gem of ostentatious wealth, a kind of Spanish answer to Saint-Tropez. Huge flashy yachts, beautiful people, and countless expensive shops and restaurants make up the glittering parade that continues long into the night. The set is an Andalusian pueblo of the 1980s built to emulate the typical fishing villages that once lined this coast.

Tour 4: Ronda and the Pueblos Blancos

From San Pedro de Alcántara a well-maintained road, C339, leads up through the mountains of the Serranía de Ronda to the town of ㉓ **Ronda,** 54 km (34 mi) inland. One of the oldest towns in Spain, Ronda was a stronghold of the legendary Andalusian bandits. Secure in its mountain fastness, perched atop a rock high above the River Guadalevín, Ronda is famed for its spectacular position and views. Its most dramatic feature is its ravine, 360 feet deep and 210 feet across, known as **El Tajo,** which divides La Ciudad, the old Moorish town, from El Mercadillo, the "new town," which grew up after the Christian Reconquest of 1485. Tour buses roll in daily with sightseers from the coast, and on weekends affluent Sevillanos flock to their second homes here; stay overnight midweek and you'll see this noble town revert to its true identity.

Begin in El Mercadillo, in the **Plaza de España,** where it's a good idea to drop into the Tourist Office for a map and to double-check opening times of sights. Immediately to the south is the most famous of Ronda's bridges, the **Puente Nuevo,** an amazing architectural feat built between 1755 and 1793, whose lantern-lit parapet offers dizzying views of the river far below. Just how many people have met their deaths in this gorge nobody knows, but the architect of the Puente Nuevo fell to his death here while inspecting work on the bridge. During the civil war hundreds of victims of both sides were hurled from it.

Cross the bridge into **La Ciudad,** the old Moorish town, where you can wander through twisting streets of white houses with bird-cage balconies, punctuated every now and again by a stately Renaissance mansion. Turn left down Santo Domingo until you come to the **Casa del Rey Moro.** This so-called House of the Moorish King was, in fact, built in 1709 on the site of an earlier Moorish residence. Despite its name and the *azulejo* (tile) plaque of a Moor on its facade, it's unlikely that Moorish rulers ever lived here. Its garden offers a great view of the gorge, and from here a stairway of some 365 steps, known as La Mina, descends to the river.

Just down the street you'll come to the **Palacio del Marqués de Salvatierra,** a Renaissance mansion with wrought-iron balconies and an impressive portal. Note the strange figures carved on its facade. Though the house is still occupied by descendants of the original family, you can visit the interior with a guide. *Tel. 95/287–1206. Admission: free. Open Mon.–Wed., Fri., and Sat. 11–2 and 4–6; Sun. 11–2. Closed Aug. 1–Sept. 15.*

Below the Salvatierra palace, a road leads down into the ravine, where two more bridges span the river: the **Puente Viejo** (Old Bridge), built in 1616 on Roman foundations, and the **Puente Arabe,** a much-restored Moorish bridge. Beside the river are the excavated remains of the **Baños Arabes** (Arab Baths), from Ronda's time as capital of a Moorish *taifa* (kingdom). (Gangs of youths have been known to threaten tourists for money here, so it's wise to be careful.) The star-shaped vents in the roof are a somewhat inferior version of the ceiling of the beautiful bathhouse in Granada's Alhambra. *Admission free. Open Tues.–Sun. 9–2 and 4–6; Mon. 4–6.*

Climb back up the hill and make your way to the Plaza de la Ciudad. At the end of Marqués de Salvatierra you'll pass the restored **Minarete Árabe** (Minaret of San Sebastián). The minaret is all that remains of a mosque destroyed after the Reconquest of 1485. The collegiate church of **Santa María la Mayor,** which serves as Ronda's cathedral, also has roots in Moorish times. Originally the Great Mosque of Moorish Ronda, it was rebuilt as a Christian church and dedicated to the Virgen de la Encarnación following the Reconquest. Today, its flamboyant mixture of styles reflects Ronda's heterogeneous past. While the naves are late Gothic and the main altar is heavy with Baroque gold leaf, the Renaissance belfry incorporates part of the original minaret.

Below the cathedral stands the ruined **Alcazaba,** blown up by the French in 1809, and beyond it, the Moorish **Puerta de Almocobar,** through which a triumphant Ferdinand led his troops in 1485.

From the west front of Santa María, the Ronda de Gameros leads to a stone palace with twin Mudéjar towers, known as the **Casa de Mondragón** (Plaza de Mondragón). Appropriated by Ferdinand and Isabella following their victory in 1485, it was probably the residence of Ronda's Moorish kings. Today it is used as an exhibition center where you can wander around the patios, with their brick arches and delicate Mudéjar stucco tracery, and admire the mosaics and *artesonado* (coffered) ceiling. *Tel. 95/287–3265. Admission: 200 pesetas. Open daily 9–6.*

The nearby Plaza Campillo offers good views of the gorge and terraced hillsides. From here, Calle Tenorio leads back up to the Puente Nuevo and into **El Mercadillo,** the commercial heart of town, where you'll find the hotels, restaurants, bars, banks, and stores. Most of the activity takes place around the Plaza del Socorro and along the Carrera de Espinel, the main shopping street.

Time Out   The **Mesón Santiago** (Marina 3, tel. 95/287–1559), a colorful Andalucían tavern with a pretty vine-covered patio, is a good place to break for a moderately priced lunch.

The main sight here is the **Plaza de Toros,** one of the oldest—it was completed in 1784—and most picturesque bullrings in Spain. Here, Pedro Romero (1754–1839), father of modern bullfighting and Ronda's most famous native son, is said to have killed 5,600 bulls during his long career, and in the **Museo Taurino** (Bullfighting Museum) beneath the plaza, you can see posters for the very first fights, held in the ring in 1785. The plaza, rarely used for fights now except during Ronda's May and September fairs, is owned by the famous now-retired bullfighter Antonio Ordóñez, on whose nearby ranch Orson Welles had his ashes scattered. The ring has become a firm favorite with moviemakers. Each year, in September, the bullring is the scene of Ronda's *corridas goyescas*, named after the artist Goya, whose bullfight sketches, known as the *tauromaquías*, were inspired by the skill and art of Pedro Romero. Seats for these fights cost a small fortune and are booked long in advance; both the participants and the dignitaries in the audience don the costumes of Goya's day for the event. *Tel. 95/287–6967. Admission to ring and museum: 200 pesetas. Open daily 10–6:30.*

Beyond the bullring you can relax in the shady **Alameda del Tajo** gardens, one of the loveliest spots in Ronda. Stroll on along the clifftop walk to the Old World **Reina Victoria** hotel, (*see* Dining and Lodging, *below*), built by the British from Gibraltar at the turn of the century as a fashionable resting place on their Algeciras–Bobadilla railroad line.

㉔ About 30 km (18 mi) west of Ronda are the prehistoric **Cuevas de la Pileta** (Pileta Caves). Head out along C339 toward Algodonales and turn left after a few miles where you see the sign to the caves. The road winds up through the villages of **Montejaque** (worth a stop) and **Benaoján** to peter out at the entrance to the caves. A guardian from the farm in the valley below will show you around, but you will probably have to ask a local where to find him. Armed with lamps, you'll set off on a visit of about 1½ hours that will reveal prehistoric wall paintings of bison, deer, and horses outlined in black, red, and ocher. One of the highlights is the *Cámara del Pescado (Chamber of the Fish)*, where the drawing of a huge fish, thought to be 15,000 years old, is outlined on the chamber wall.

Clinging to the mountainsides of the vast, impressive landscape that surrounds Ronda are villages of white houses with honey-colored tile roofs. These are the remote **pueblos blancos** of Cádiz province, on the onetime frontier between Moors and Christians, all within a day's drive of Ronda. Below is a selection of villages you might visit; if you've time for only one, then make it Grazalema.

㉕ North of Ronda is **Olvera.** The easiest way to get there is by continuing on the C339 to Algodonales and then turning right on the N342.

Two imposing silhouettes dominate the crest of the hill on which the town stands: the 11th-century castle of Vallehermoso, legacy of the Moors, and the neoclassical church of La Encarnación, reconstructed in the 19th century on foundations of the old Arab mosque.

Setenil de las Bodegas lies south of the N342 just east of Olvera, on a small mountain road. The village nestles in a cleft in the rock cut by the River Guadalporcín. Its houses seem to be sculpted from the rock itself; streets resemble long, narrow caves; and on many houses the roof is formed by a projecting ledge of heavy rock, a kind of weighty overhanging thatch that all but shuts out the sunlight from the narrow streets.

To the west of Setenil is **El Gastor,** south of which lie the twin ravines of Alagarines. Nearby are the remains of an ancient dolmen known as La Sepultura del Gigante (Giant's Tomb). **Ronda la Vieja,** site of the Roman settlement of Acinipo, is found down a track off the Setenil–El Gastor road (another track off C339 also leads to it). A reconstructed theater is the only vestige of the Roman town.

West of the C339, a little south of Algodonales, a solitary watchtower dominates a crag above the village of **Zahara de la Sierra,** its outline visible for miles around. The tower is all that remains of a Moorish castle where Alfonso X once fought the emir of Morocco. It remained an important Moorish stronghold until its fall to the Christians in 1470. Along the streets of Zahara you can see door knockers fashioned like the hand of Fatima. The fingers represent the five laws of the Koran and serve to ward off evil.

The winding mountain road between Zahara and Grazalema, via the Puerto de las Palomas (1,312 m/4,300 ft), is for only the most adventurous driver. The views from its heights are breathtaking, but unless you have nerves of steel and a head for heights, take a more conventional approach.

㉖ The safest access to **Grazalema** is heading south on the C339, then right (west) on C344. Nestled in the Sierra del Endrinal, 28 km (17 mi) from Ronda, the town is the prettiest of the pueblos blancos. Because it's on a west-facing slope where rain clouds roll in from the Atlantic, Grazalema is also the wettest spot in Spain. Cobbled streets of houses with pink-ocher roofs wind up the hillside, red geraniums splash white walls, and black wrought-iron lanterns and grilles cling to the house fronts.

㉗ **Ubrique,** spread on the slopes of the Saltadero Mountains southwest of Ronda and Grazalema on C3331, is known for its leather tanning and embossing industry. Worth looking for are the Convento de los Capuchinos and the churches of San Pedro and Nuestra Señora de la O.

From Ronda you have a choice of routes. You can drop down to the coast near Gibraltar on C341 through rugged scenery dotted with ruined medieval castles by way of **Gaucín** and **Jimena de la Frontera.** The train from Ronda to Algeciras also follows this route and offers spectacular views as the line twists and turns its way through the ravine of the churning Guadiaro. Steeped in history that ranges from Moorish intrigue in the Middle Ages to the adventures of genteel English travelers of the late 19th century, both the road and the rail track are exciting routes for the adventurous. The alternative, and more straightforward option for drivers, is to return to the coast at San Pedro de Alcántara by way of C339.

Tour 5: Estepona to Gibraltar

28 Until recently, **Estepona** marked the end of the urban sprawl of the Costa del Sol, but today, thanks largely to the increasingly important role of Gibraltar Airport, it's fast becoming the biggest boomtown on the coast. Nevertheless the old fishing village can still be detected. Its beach, over 1 km (⅔ mi) long, is lined with fishing boats, and along the promenade are well-kept gardens with aromatic flowers. Back from the main Avenida de España, the old Moorish village is surprisingly unspoiled.

29 Twenty km (12 mi) northwest of Estepona the mountain village of **Casares** lies high in the Sierra Bermeja. Streets of ancient white houses, piled one on top of the other, perch on the slopes beneath a ruined but impressive Moorish castle. Its heights afford stunning views over orchards, olive groves, and cork woods to the Mediterranean sparkling in the distance.

From Estepona to Gibraltar the highway is flanked by urbanizaciones, which have mushroomed since the border between Spain and Gibraltar was reopened in 1985. Today's architects appear to have learned from the mistakes of earlier developers, and the architecture is more in keeping with the traditional spirit of Andalucía. Sparkling white marinas and rolling green golf courses have blossomed on what, prior to 1985, was a largely unexploited terrain of silted-up riverbanks and infertile scrubland. For a glimpse of the Costa's latest showpieces, drive down to the Puerto de la Duquesa,
30 near Manilva, or the Puerto de **Sotogrande.**

31 **San Roque** is the point at which you leave the coastal highway and drive the final 8 km (5 mi) to La Linea and Gibraltar along the peninsula that forms the east side of Algeciras Bay. The town of San Roque was founded within sight of Gibraltar by Spaniards who fled the Rock when the British captured it in 1704. Almost 300 years have done little to diminish the chauvinism of San Roque's inhabitants, who have protested their displeasure at the prominence Gibraltar is now assuming at this end of the Costa del Sol by declaring a ban on the use of English on all billboards and other advertising.

Gibraltar The tiny British colony of **Gibraltar,** fondly nicknamed Gib, whose
32 impressive silhouette dominates the straits between Spain and Morocco, is a rock just 5.8 km (3 mi) long, .8 km (½ mi) wide, and 424 meters (1,369 ft) high. In ancient times Gibraltar was one of the two Pillars of Hercules, which marked the western limits of the known world. Its position commanding the narrow entrance to the Mediterranean led to its seizure by the Moors in 711 as a preliminary to the conquest of Spain. They held it longer than either the Spaniards or the British ever have—a fact to which tribute is paid unconsciously whenever anyone pronounces its name, for Gibraltar is a corruption of Jebel Tariq (Tariq's Rock), Tariq being the Moorish commander who built the first fort of Gibraltar.

After 750 years of Moorish rule, the Spaniards recaptured Tariq's Rock in 1462, on the feast day of St. Bernard, now co-patron of the colony along with Our Lady of Europe, whose shrine you will see at the Rock's southernmost tip. The English, heading an Anglo-Dutch fleet in the War of the Spanish Succession, seized the Rock in 1704, after three days of fighting. Following several years of skirmishing in the vicinity, Gibraltar was finally ceded to Great Britain by the Treaty of Utrecht, in 1713. With the exception of the Great Siege, when a Franco-Spanish force battled at its ramparts for three years (1779–82), Gibraltar has lived a relatively peaceful existence ever since. During the two World Wars, it served the Allies well as an important naval and air base.

Today, much of Gibraltar creates the impression of a somewhat faded garrison town of 20 or 30 years ago. The number of British troops stationed here is being cut back, and millions of dollars are currently being invested in developing the Rock's tourist potential. A further big boost has been given to the economy of this tiny colony by the 100,000-plus expatriate Britons living on the Costa del Sol, many of whom zoom in daily to take advantage of Gibraltar's reasonable pound-sterling prices, free-port status, and British consumer goods.

There can be few places in the world that one enters by walking or driving across an airport runway. But that's what you'll have to do in Gibraltar. First show your passport, then make your way out onto the narrow strip of land linking Spain's La Linea with the Rock. Here, you have a choice: Either plunge straight into exploring Gibraltar town or opt first for a tour of the Rock's circumference. If you don't have your own transport, several minibus tours of the latter route are readily available at the point of entry.

Numbers in the margin correspond to points of interest on the Gibraltar map.

The circumference tour is best begun on the Rock's eastern side, so turn left down Devil's Tower Road as you enter Gibraltar. Here, on
㉝ the eastern shores, you'll find **Catalan Bay,** a small fishing village founded by Genoese settlers and now a picturesque resort; massive
㉞ water catchments that supply the colony's drinking water; **Sandy Bay,** another resort; and the Dudley Ward tunnel, which brings you
㉟ out at the Rock's southern tip, **Punta Grande de Europa** (Europa Point). Stop here for the view across the straits to the coast of Morocco, 23 km (14 mi) away. You are standing on one of the two Pillars of Hercules; across the water, in Morocco, a mountain between the cities of Ceuta and Tangiers formed the second pillar. In front of you, the **Europa Point lighthouse** has dominated the meeting place of the Atlantic and the Mediterranean since 1841. Sailors can see its light from a distance of 27 km (17 mi). Nearby, on Europa Flats, you
㊱ can see an ancient Moorish cistern, known as the **Nun's Well,** and the
㊲ **Shrine of Our Lady of Europe,** venerated by seafarers since 1462.

Now follow Europa Road along the western slopes of the Rock, high
㊳ above **Rosia Bay,** to which Nelson's flagship, HMS *Victory,* was towed after the Battle of Trafalgar in 1805. Aboard were the dead of the battle, who were buried in Trafalgar Cemetery on the southern edge of town—except, that is, for Admiral Nelson, whose body went home to England preserved in a barrel of rum.

㊴ Continue on Europa Road as far as the **Casino,** above the Alameda
㊵ Gardens. Make a sharp right here up Engineer Road to **Jews Gate,** an unbeatable lookout point over the docks and Bay of Gibraltar to Algeciras, in Spain. Here you can gain access to the **Upper Nature Preserve,** which includes St. Michael's Cave, the Apes' Den, the Great Siege Tunnel, and the Moorish Castle (*see below*). *Admission, including all attractions: £4.50 adults, £2.25 children under 6, plus £1.50 per vehicle. Open daily 10–6. Alternatively, you can take the cable car from Gibraltar town. Admission: £4 (includes cable-car ride, St. Michael's Cave, and Apes' Den).*

㊶ Queens Road leads to **St. Michael's Cave,** a series of underground chambers adorned with stalactites and stalagmites, which provides an admirable setting for concerts, ballet, and drama. Sound-and-

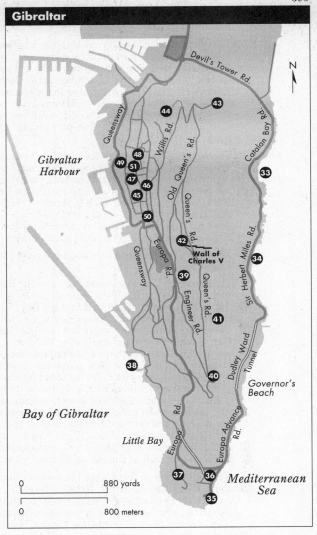

Gibraltar

light shows are held here most days (at 11 and 4). The skull of a Neanderthal woman (now in the British Museum in London) was found nearby at Forbes Quarry some eight years *before* the world-famous discovery in Germany's Neander Valley in 1856.

42 Drive down Old Queens Road to the **Apes' Den,** near the **Wall of Charles V.** The famous Barbary Apes are a breed of cinnamon-colored, tailless monkey, native of the Atlas Mountains in Morocco. Legend holds that as long as the apes remain, the British will keep the Rock. Winston Churchill himself issued orders for their preservation when the ape colony's numbers began to dwindle during World War II. Today, they are the responsibility of the British Army, and a special officer in charge of apes is assigned to feed them twice daily, at 8 and 4. The apes are mischievous, as well as expert purse and camera snatchers.

43 At the northern end of the Rock, the **Great Siege Tunnel,** formerly known as the Upper Galleries, was carved out during the Great Siege of 1779–82. Here, in 1878, Governor Lord Napier of Magdala entertained ex–United States President Ulysses S. Grant at a banquet in St. George's Hall. The Holyland Tunnel leads to a vantage point on the east side of the Rock high above Catalan Bay.

44 The **Moorish Castle** on Willis Road, restored and reopened in 1993 after being closed for many years, was built originally by the descendants of Tariq, who conquered the Rock in 711. The present Tower of Homage dates from 1333, and its walls bear the scars of countless sieges when first stones from medieval catapults, and later cannonballs, were hurled against it. Admiral Rooke hoisted the British flag from its summit when he captured the Rock in 1704, and it has flown here ever since.

Willis Road leads steeply down to the colorful, congested town of Gibraltar, where the dignified Regency architecture of Great Britain blends well with the shutters, balconies, and patios of southern Spain. Call in at the tourist office on Cathedral Square. Apart from the shops, restaurants, and pubs that beckon on busy Main Street, **45** you'll want to see the **Governor's Residence,** where the ceremonial **Changing of the Guard** and **Ceremony of the Keys** take place irregu- **46** larly, usually about five times a year; the **Law Courts,** where the famous case of the *Mary Celeste* sailing ship was heard in 1872; the **47 48** Anglican **Cathedral of the Holy Trinity;** and the Catholic **Cathedral of St. Mary the Crowned.**

49 Don't miss the recently reorganized and refurbished **Gibraltar Museum,** whose exhibits recall the history of the Rock throughout the ages. Its well-presented displays include a beautiful 14th-century Moorish bathhouse, evocations of the Great Siege and of the Battle of Trafalgar, and an 1865 model of the Rock. *Bomb House La., tel. 9567/74289. Admission: £1.50 adults, £1 children. Open Mon.–Fri. 10–6, Sat. 10–2, closed Sun.*

50 The **Nefusot Yehudada Synagogue** on Line Wall Road is worth a look for its inspired architecture, and, if you're interested in guns, the **51** **Koehler Gun** in **Casemates Square** at the northern end of Main Street is an impressive example of the type of gun developed during the Great Siege. Finally, take a ride on the **cable car** to the top of the Rock. The cable car, which resembles a ski gondola, isn't especially high off the ground, but the views of Spain and Africa from the rock's pinnacle are superb. It runs every day except Sunday from the cable-car station on Grand Parade at the southern end of Main Street. Admission: £4 (includes cable car, St. Michael's Cave, and Apes' Den).

What to See and Do with Children

Parque Aquatico Mijas, a water theme park in Fuengirola, offers some wild slides. *Marbella–Fuengirola highway, Km 209, tel. 95/246-0404. Admission: 1,450 pesetas adults, 1,100 pesetas children under 12. Open May–Oct., daily 10–6; July–Aug. daily 10–8.*

Fuengirola also has a **zoo** (admission free for children under 12; open year-round) with more than 300 kinds of animals and reptiles. Gibraltar offers many diversions for children. On the east side of the Rock energetic types can walk down the **Mediterranean Steps.** The **Changing of the Guard** a few times a year at the Governor's Residence, the **laser show** in the tunnels of the Rock, and a **Dolphin Safari** in Gibraltar Bay (details from the Gibraltar tourist office) are also likely to captivate young visitors.

Shopping

Most of the stores in the Costa del Sol resorts cater almost exclusively to the tourist trade or to the Costa's foreign-resident community. You'll find endless mass-produced souvenirs in places like Torremolinos and outlets for a vast array of Scandinavian furniture and imported household goods in Fuengirola. The most genuine stores—those catering to Spaniards—are in Málaga. Marbella and Puerto Banús have plenty of highfashion boutiques if you're willing to pay the prices. Málaga, Marbella, Torremolinos, and Mijas are the main shopping centers. Don't expect to find any bargains. The one exception is Gibraltar, which because of its tax-free status (no VAT is levied on goods) has become a mecca for bargain-hunters.

Crafts Handicrafts to look out for include **pottery** and **ceramics** (Málaga, Mijas, Ronda, Vélez-Málaga); **leather goods** (Málaga, Mijas, Campillos, Ronda); **guitars** (Málaga, Ronda); **wood carvings** (Málaga, Ronda); embossed **copper** plates (Málaga); **esparto-grass wares** (Antequera, Grazalema, Mijas, Ronda); **basketry** (Vélez-Málaga, Benamocarra); **palm-leaf** articles (Cártama); and **castanets** (Alora).

Department Store In Málaga, the **Corte Inglés** department store (Av. de Andalucía 4–6, tel. 95/230–0000; open daily 10 AM–9 PM), the only store open during siesta, provides English interpreters, mailing, tax-refund, and money changing facilities.

Sports

Golf Certain hotels cater almost exclusively to golfers, offering guests reduced greens fees: **Parador de Golf** (tel. 95/238–1255), halfway between Málaga and Torremolinos; the **Golf Hotel Guadalmina** (tel. 95/288–2211), near San Pedro de Alcántara; the **Hotel Atalaya Park** in Estepona (*see* Dining and Lodging, *below*); and the **El Paraíso** (tel. 95/288–3000), between San Pedro and Estepona. Other hotels, such as **Los Monteros** (tel. 95/277–1700) near Marbella (*see* Dining and Lodging, *below*), also have their own golf courses.

Indispensable for anyone trying to make his or her own golfing arrangements is a copy of *Costa Golf*, a monthly magazine available from all newsstands. The *Andalucía Golf Guide*, published by the tourist department of the Regional Government of Andalucía, lists details of all courses on the Costa del Sol; it is available free from the Tourist Office of Spain.

Horseback Riding Horseback riding is becoming increasingly popular; you'll find stables advertised in your hotel or local tourist office. One of the leading riding agencies is **Alora Riding Holidays,** Alora (Málaga), where you should contact Ann Warnock.

Sailing Sailing can be enjoyed all along the coast, and there are notable marinas at (from east to west) **Marina del Este,** between Almuñécar and La Herradura; **Benalmádena Costa; Puerto Cabo Pino** near Marbella; **Puerto Banús; Puerto La Duquesa,** near Manilva; and **Puerto de Sotogrande.**

Water Sports Windsurfing and waterskiing are available in every resort. Boats of all kinds can be rented at the main beaches.

Beaches

The beaches of the Costa del Sol run from shingle and pebbles at worst (Almuñécar, Nerja, Málaga) to a fine gray gritlike sand (Torremolinos westward). Swimming in the sea is not always pleasant because of pebbles underfoot and pollution. Look for a beach flying the blue EC flag, which indicates that the water conforms to European Community standards.

All the beaches are very crowded in July and August, when Spanish families take their annual vacation, and on Sundays from May to October, when they become picnic sites.

All Spanish beaches are free; changing facilities are usually not available, though you'll find free, cold showers on the major beaches. It's quite acceptable (not officially) for women to go topless on beaches. If you want to take it all off, you'll have to drive to the more deserted beaches, and beware the odd awkward civil guard who can, and often does, make arrests for total nudity. **Costa Natura,** 3 km (2 mi) west of Estepona, is the coast's official nudist colony.

The best, though inevitably the most crowded, beaches are **El Bajondillo** and **La Carihuela** in Torremolinos; the long stretch between Carvajal, Los Boliches, and Fuengirola; and those on both sides of Marbella. You may just be able to find the odd secluded beach to the west of Estepona.

Dining and Lodging

Dining

The Costa del Sol has thousands of places to eat. Málaga is best for traditional Spanish cooking, with a wealth of bars and seafood restaurants serving *fritura malagueña* (Málaga's famous fried fish). Torremolinos's Carihuela district is also a paradise for lovers of Spanish seafood. In the resorts you'll find every kind of foreign repast, from Scandinavian *smörgåsbord* to the delicacies of Thailand. Marbella has internationally renowned restaurants like Paul Schiff's La Hacienda. At the other end of the scale, but just as enjoyable, are the Costa's traditional *chiringuitos* or *merenderos*. Strung out along the beaches, and open in summer only, these rough-and-ready restaurants serve seafood fresh off the boats.

Casual dress is acceptable in most Costa del Sol restaurants.

Reservations are advisable for all Marbella restaurants listed as $$$–$$$$ and for the Café de París and parador dining room in Málaga. Elsewhere, reservations are rarely essential unless specified. Expect beach restaurants, such as Málaga's Casa Pedro and all those on Torremolinos's Carihuela seafront, to be packed on Sundays after 3 PM.

Highly recommended restaurants are indicated by a star ★.

Category	Cost*
$$$$	over 6,500 ptas
$$$	4,000–6,500 ptas

$$	2,500–4,000 ptas
$	under 2,500 ptas

per person for a three-course meal, including house wine and coffee, and excluding tax

Lodging

The most highly developed stretch of the Costa del Sol lies between Torremolinos and Fuengirola, where the concrete high rises of the '60s and early '70s are now showing their age; poorly built in the first place, they're often in need of total refurbishment and improvement in standards of service. They do offer large, functional rooms close to the sea at competitive rates. The never-waning popularity of this area as a low-budget vacation destination means that most such hotels are booked in high season by foreign package-tour operators. Finding a room at Easter, in July and August, or around the October 12 holiday weekend can be difficult if you haven't prebooked.

Málaga is poorly endowed with hotels for a city of its size. It has an excellent but small parador that can be hard to book, and few other hotels of note. Marbella, conversely, boasts more than its fair share of grand hotels, with five five-star hotels, three of which are classed as "grand deluxe" and rank among Spain's most expensive lodgings.

Highly recommended hotels are indicated by a star ★.

Category	Cost*
$$$$	over 23,000 ptas
$$$	11,000–23,000 ptas
$$	7,000–11,000 ptas
$	under 7,000 ptas

All prices are for a standard double room and do not include breakfast, tax, or service charge.

In Gibraltar, $$$: £65–£75 ($104–$120); $$: £40–£46 ($64–$74) (not including tax).

Antequera
Dining

Las Pedrizas. This best bet for regional Andalusian cooking is actually owned by a local fraternal organization, La Sociedad de las Pedrizas–Las Fuentes, but is open to the public. Local favorites include *choto* (roast kid) and *jamon ibérico* (Iberian ham). *Carretera Malaga–Madrid at Km 527, tel. 95/275–1250. MC, V. $–$$*

Lodging

Parador de Antequera. This white parador is set among the ruins of a Moorish fortress on the heights overlooking Antequera. The public rooms are sparsely decorated in Andalusian Moorish style, with Alpujarran rugs on tile floors and paintings on the walls. Potted plants freshen the hallways, and the comfortable rooms have twin beds, covered with woven rugs, and spacious tile bathrooms. *García de Olmo, 29200, tel. 95/284–0261, fax 95/284–1312. 55 rooms. Facilities: restaurant, pool, garden, covered parking. AE, DC, MC, V. $$*

Benalmádena
Dining

Casa Fidel. Rustic touches like heavy beams and a large fireplace adorn this restaurant in Benalmádena Pueblo. The menu is based on expertly cooked international dishes. For appetizers, you could try *entremeses Casa Fidel* (a tasty selection of hors d'oeuvres); main courses include old favorites such as grilled sole, or you could go for something more exotic, like *perdiz en salsa de vino de Málaga* (partridge in Málaga wine). *Maestra Ayala 1, tel. 95/244–8221. Reservations advised in summer. AE, DC, MC, V. Closed Tues. and Nov.* $$

Ventorillo de la Perra. If you've been searching the coast for somewhere typical, then this old inn, which dates to 1785, could well be the place. Outside there's a leafy patio, and inside a cozy, rustic atmosphere prevails in the dining room and in the bar, with its hamhung ceiling. You can choose between local Malagueño cooking, regular Spanish fare, or established international favorites. The *ajo blanco* (a cold garlic soup) makes a particularly good appetizer. *Av. Constitución, in Arroyo de la Miel, tel. 95/244–1966. Dinner reservations advised. AE, DC, MC, V. Closed Mon. and 2 weeks in Nov.* $$

Campamento
Dining

Los Remos. The dining room inside this gracious Colonial villa has peach-colored walls adorned with gilt rococo mirrors, swirling cherubs, friezes of grapes, and crystal lamps. It overlooks a formal, leafy garden full of palms, cedars, and trailing ivy. Among the main courses offered is *urta del estrecho en salsa de erizos marinos* (perch from the Straits of Gibraltar in sea urchin sauce). All the fish and seafood are from the Bay of Algeciras area, and the wine cellar boasts some 20,000 bottles. *Villa Victoria, Campo de Gibraltar, between San Roque and Campamento, tel. 956/10–68–12. Reservations advised. Dress: Jacket and tie advised. AE, DC, MC, V. Closed Sun. (except Aug.).* $$$$

Estepona
Dining

El Molino. Situated in an old windmill, 12 km (8 mi) out on the road to Málaga, this restaurant has provided professional service and classic French cuisine for the past three decades. Try the *lubina al hinojo* (sea bass in fennel), *perdiz al champán* (partridge in champagne), or the delicious Chateaubriand steak. *Carretera N340 at Km 166, tel. 95/288–2135. Reservations advised. AE, DC, MC, V. No lunch. Closed Tues., Sun., and Jan.* $$$

Alcaría de Ramos. José Ramos, winner of the National Gastronomy Prize, opened this restaurant in a restored building outside town in 1990, and it has quickly garnered a large and enthusiastic following. Try the *ensalada de lentejas con salmón ahumado* (lentil salad with smoked salmon), followed by *cordero asado* (roast lamb) and the chef's justly famous fried ice cream. *Carretera N340 at Km 167, tel. 95/288–6178. Reservations advised. V. No lunch. Closed Sun. and June 15–July 15.* $$–$$$

Costa del Sol. This friendly French bistro offers French and Spanish dishes in an informal setting. It's located on a side street beside the Portillo bus station. French favorites include *bouillabaisse* and duck in orange sauce. *San Roque s/n, tel. 95/280–1101. Reservations advised in high season. AE, MC, V. Closed Mon. lunch and Sun. AE, DC, MC, V.* $

Lodging

Atalaya Park. Closer to San Pedro de Alcántara than to Estepona itself, this very comfortable resort hotel is set in subtropical gardens beside the sea and offers extensive sporting facilities. Rooms overlooking the sea are more expensive than those at the back facing the mountains. *Carretera N340 at Km 169, 29680, tel. 95/288–4801, fax 95/288–5735. 246 rooms. Facilities: restaurant, 2 bars, golf course, putting green, 9 tennis courts, table tennis, 4 outdoor pools, 1 indoor pool, hairdresser, sauna, massage. AE, DC, MC, V.* $$$

Santa Marta. This is a small, quiet hotel with rooms in chalet bungalows arranged in a large, peaceful tropical garden. Some of the rooms are a little faded after 30-odd years, but the tranquil setting is a definite plus. In summer, good lunches are served by the pool.

Carretera N340 at Km 173 between Estepona and San Pedro, 29680, tel. 95/288–8180. 37 rooms. AE, DC, MC, V. Closed Oct.–Mar. $$

Fuengirola
Dining

La Cazuela. An old fisherman's cottage, with low ceilings and white walls decorated with ceramic plates, houses this small Andalusian restaurant. The menu offers inexpensive daily specials as well as regular à la carte selections. Old favorites include chicken Kiev, pork chop and applesauce, and pepper steak. *Miguel Márquez 8, tel. 95/247–4634. Reservations advised Easter–Sept. AE, MC, V. $$*

Lodging

Florida. A simple hotel offering fairly basic accommodations, the Florida, almost opposite the water chute, is set back from the seafront behind a shady semitropical garden where you can sunbathe and enjoy a drink in the poolside bar. One of Fuengirola's original hotels, it dates back to the years before the land boom and is actually run by its owners. *Paseo Marítimo, 29640, tel. 95/247–6104. 116 rooms. Facilities: restaurant, bar, pool, garden. AE, DC, MC, V. $$*

Sedeño. This small, family-run hostel, renovated in 1992, makes an ideal base for anyone seeking simple budget accommodations. It's in the center of town, one block back from the harbor, just off Jacinto Benavente, the café-lined street running down to the seafront. The rooms have balconies overlooking a tree-filled garden, and breakfast is served in a glass-enclosed dining room. *Don Jacinto 5, 29640, tel. 95/247–4788. 30 rooms. AE, DC, MC, V. $*

Gibraltar
Dining

La Bayuca. One of the Rock's oldest restaurants, La Bayuca is renowned for its onion soup and Mediterranean dishes. Prince Charles and Prince Andrew both dined here while on naval service. *21 Turnbull's La., tel. 9567/75119. Reservations advised. AE, DC, MC, V. Closed Sun. lunch and Tues. $$$*

Country Cottage. Set back from Main St., this is the place to go for a taste of Old England. You can dine by candlelight on white linen tablecloths with pink napkins and enjoy old favorites such as steak and kidney pie, roast beef and Yorkshire pudding, and Angus steak. *13 Giro's Passage, tel. 9567/70084. Reservations advised. AE, MC, V. Closed Sun. $$–$$$*

Strings. This small, popular bistro is one of the few places open in Gibraltar on Sunday nights. Prints, nautical paraphernalia, ensigns, and badges cover every inch of the walls, and there are just six dark wooden booths clustered around a small bar. Red and orange lamps complete the cozy cavelike decor. The menu is English bistro-style and daily specials are chalked up on a blackboard. *44 Cornwall La., tel. 9567/78800. AE, DC, MC, V. Reservations advised. Closed Sun. and Mon. lunch. $$*

Lodging
★

The Rock. The Rock has undergone a massive refurbishment program, with the aim of bolstering its reputation as Gibraltar's supreme luxury hotel. The predominance of muted pink, peach, and beige in the decor of the rooms and restaurant, the deep fitted carpets, glowing table lamps, and cane furniture evoke the atmosphere of good "international" hotels everywhere, yet the establishment manages to preserve something of the old English Colonial style with ceiling fans and a fine bar-terrace. Located on Gibraltar's western slopes, the hotel overlooks the town and harbor. *3 Europa Rd., tel. 9567/73000. 143 rooms, 10 suites. Facilities: restaurant, bar, pool, garden, beauty salon. AE, DC, MC, V. $$$*

Bristol. This Colonial-style hotel lies right in the heart of town, overlooking the cathedral. The rooms are spacious, with pink carpets and bedspreads and comfortable dark-blue floral settees and armchairs. The tropical garden is a real haven. The wood-paneled lounge has two pool tables. *10 Cathedral Sq., tel. 9567/76800. 60* *rooms. Facilities: breakfast room, bar, outdoor pool, garage. AE, DC, MC, V. $$*

Málaga
Dining
★

Café de París. The owner of this elegantly intimate restaurant with warm pink decor, in the Paseo Marítimo area, is a former chef of Horcher, in Madrid, and La Hacienda, in Marbella. Sophisticated Spanish diners come from far afield for such specialties as *rodaballo sobre espinacas* (turbot on a bed of spinach) and *hojaldre de langostinos* (giant shrimp en croûte). The *menú degustación* allows you to try a little of everything. *Vélez-Málaga 10, tel. 95/222-5043. Reservations required. AE, DC, MC, V. Closed Sun. $$$*

Antonio Martín. Established in 1886, this Málaga standby, at the beginning of the Paseo Marítimo, has several dining rooms furnished in various Spanish rustic styles and a splendid terrace overlooking the ocean. It's long been famous for its fresh seafood and paella. Try the local fritura malagueña. *Paseo Marítimo 4, tel. 95/222-2113. Reservations advised; required Sun. lunch. AE, DC, MC, V. Closed Sun. evening. $$*

Casa Pedro. It's crowded and noisy, but Malagueños have been flocking to this no-frills fish restaurant for more than 50 years. Out in El Palo, the restaurant has a huge, bare dining room that overlooks the ocean. If you know a little Spanish, are adventurous and above all patient, and like local color, try joining the hordes of families who come here for lunch on Sundays. It's quieter at other times. *Quitapenas 121, El Palo beach (bus No. 11), tel. 95/229-0003. Reservations advised Sun. AE, DC, MC, V. Closed Mon. evening. $$*

La Cancela. Located in an alley off Calle Granada at the top of Molina Lario, this pretty bistro serving standard Spanish fare is ideal for lunch after a morning's shopping in the town center. The two dining rooms—one upstairs, one down—are crowded with knickknacks: iron grilles, bird cages, potted plants, and plastic flowers. In summer, tables are placed on the sidewalk for outdoor lunching on what amounts to a sheltered patio. *Denís Belgrano 3, tel. 95/222-3125. AE, DC, MC, V. $*

Lodging

Los Naranjos. This compact hotel owned by the Luz chain is situated on a pleasant but busy avenue in a residential district a little to the east of the city center. There's a small garden with *naranjos* (orange trees) in front, but rooms overlooking the street can be noisy. *Paseo de Sancha 35, 29016, tel. 95/222-4317 or 95/222-4319. 41 rooms. Facilities: breakfast room, bar, garage. AE, DC, MC, V. $$$*

★ **Parador de Gibralfaro.** Surrounded by pine trees on top of Gibralfaro mountain 3½ km (2 mi) above the city, this tiny modern two-story parador built of gray stone and smothered in ivy offers spectacular views of the city and bay. Its typical parador accommodations (twin beds, matching curtains and bedspreads, and woven rugs on a bare floor) are the best in Málaga. The parador was closed for renovations in 1993 and was not expected to reopen until spring 1995; check with the tourist office. *Gibralfaro, 29016, tel. 95/222-1902, fax 95/222-1904. 12 rooms. Facilities: restaurant, garden, bar, parking. Reservations required long in advance. AE, DC, MC, V. $$-$$$*

★ **Las Vegas.** In a pleasant, though noisy, part of town, just east of the center, this late-1950s-style concrete-and-glass hotel backs onto the Paseo Marítimo and is the best choice if you can't get into the parador. Parts of the hotel were renovated in 1991, and you now have a choice between older, less expensive rooms, and 33 new doubles with king-size beds, marble floors, TV, and air conditioning. Older rooms are functional, but a bit sterile and fading. The rooms at the back enjoy a good view of the ocean, as does the spacious, panoramic dining room. There's an outdoor pool in the large, leafy garden. *Paseo de Sancha 22, 29016, tel. 95/221–7712. 107 rooms. Facilities: restaurant, bar, outdoor pool, garden. AE, DC, MC, V. $$*

Victoria. This small, recently renovated hostel offers excellent budget accommodations in a very central location. Situated in a 19th-century stone row house whose facade has been painted gleaming white, it is on a side street just off Calle Larios. *Sancha Lara 3, 29015, tel. 95/222–4223. 13 rooms. AE, DC, MC, V. $*

Marbella
Dining
★

La Hacienda. La Hacienda is one of the highest-rated restaurants in Spain. The menu reflects the influence of both chef-proprietor Paul Schiff's native Belgium and his adopted Andalucía. The menú degustación (about 6,500 pesetas) will enable you to sample creations such as *tortilla fría de trufas y foie-gras* (cold truffle and foie gras omelette) and *solomillo de pato relleno de aceitunas* (duck stuffed with olives). The setting is an elegant villa on a hillside overlooking the ocean. *Urbanización Las Chapas, at Km 193 on N340, 12 km (7½ mi) east of Marbella, tel. 95/283–1116. Reservations required in summer. Dress: Jacket and tie advised. AE, DC, MC, V. Closed Mon., Tues., and mid-Nov.–mid-Dec. $$$$*

La Meridiana. Another of Marbella's outstanding restaurants, and a favorite with the local jet set, La Meridiana is located west of town, behind the mosque. Moorish influence is apparent in its striking modern architecture, and an enclosed terrace makes "outdoor" dining possible year-round. The cuisine is famous for its quality and the freshness of the ingredients, and here, too, there's a menú degustación. This is a good place to sample *ajo blanco* (a garlicky local version of gazpacho). *Camino de la Cruz, tel. 95/277–6190. Reservations strongly advised, especially for dinner. Dress: Jacket and tie advised. AE, DC, MC, V. Closed Nov.–Dec., and Mon. and Tues. lunch, Sept.–May; open dinner only June–Aug. $$$$*

Cenicienta. A friendly welcome, superb cuisine and good professional service await you at "Cinderella's." The modern white stucco villa surrounded by a leafy garden and pine grove is on the ring road about a mile from the center of town. *Cánovas del Castillo, tel. 95/277–4318. Reservations advised but not essential. AE, DC, V. $$$*

La Dorada. Fresh fish and shellfish top the menu in this two-story building with an outdoor dining area on each floor. Specialties of the house include fritura malagueña served sizzling from the pan, and excellent *mariscos* (shellfish), such as *coquinas* (small cockles), *cigalos* (small crayfish), and *bogavantes* (similar to crayfish). *Carretera Cádiz-Málaga (N340) at Km 176, tel. 95/282–1034. AE, DC, V. Closed Aug. $$$*

★ **La Fonda.** This is an 18th-century house filled with antique furniture in one of the loveliest squares in Marbella's old town. La Fonda is owned by Horcher, one of Madrid's leading restaurateurs, and its cuisine combines the best of Spanish, French, and Austrian influences. A garden-patio filled with potted plants allows summer dining alfresco. *Plaza del Santo Cristo 9, tel. 95/277–2512. Reservations advised. Dress: Jacket and tie advised. AE, DC, MC, V. Open for dinner only. Closed Sun. $$$*

La Tricycleta. Located in an old house on a narrow alley in the center of town, English-owned La Tricycleta has become something of an institution among Marbella restaurants. You can have a predinner drink in the downstairs bar, which is furnished like a private sitting room, and then dine upstairs beside a log fire in winter or outside on the covered rooftop patio. A long-standing favorite is the *brochette Tricycleta* (a kebab of fillet steak and shrimp flambéed in brandy). *Buitrago 14, tel. 95/277–7800. Reservations advised in summer. AE, MC, V. Closed Sun. $$*

Mesón del Pasaje. A warren of small dining rooms and bars awaits you in this old house just off the Plaza Naranjos. The decor is pure Victoriana, with several Spanish touches. The menu features a wide variety of pastas and such international favorites as chicken curry or pepper steak. *Pasaje 5, tel. 95/277–1261. Reservations advised in summer. V: Closed for lunch in summer and mid-Nov.–mid-Dec.* $

Mesón del Pollo. A small, charming, and delicious "house of chicken" that illustrates how Marbella, despite its tourism, can remain truly Spanish. Porcelain lampshades, azulejo tiles, and the scents of roasting chicken fill this popular lunch spot. Try the *pollo a la sevillana* dinner (roast chicken with squid, fried potatoes, salad, and cider), fritura malagueña, or tapas of octopus or meatballs. *Antonio Martín, across from the El Fuerte Hotel, no phone. No credit cards.* $

Dining and Lodging **Los Monteros.** Situated 5 km (3 mi) east of Marbella, on the road to Málaga, this exclusive hotel stands surrounded by pine woods and luxurious gardens on the sea side of the highway. It offers a wide range of facilities, including gourmet dining in its famous El Corzo Grill restaurant. The rooms are formally decorated, and the service is impeccable. British visitors make up some 80% of the guests. *Urbanización Los Monteros, Carretera N340 at Km 187, 29600, tel. 95/277–1700, fax 95/282–5846. 161 rooms. Facilities: 2 restaurants, 18-hole golf course, 10 tennis courts, 5 squash courts, 1 indoor and 2 outdoor pools, horseback riding, gymnasium, sauna, hairdresser, shops, nightclub. AE, DC, MC, V.* $$$$

Lodging **Marbella Club.** This grande dame of Marbella hotels was the creation of Prince Alfonso von Hohenlohe, the man who "founded" Marbella. The club attracts a long-established clientele as well as local patricians who descend from their villas for drinks and dinner. The bungalow-style rooms range from cramped to spacious, and the decor varies from regional to modern. The grounds are exquisite, and breakfast is served on a patio where songbirds flit through the lush, subtropical vegetation. *Carretera N340 at Km 178, 3 km (1¾ mi) west of Marbella, 29600, tel. 95/277–1300. 76 rooms. Facilities: restaurant, pool, gymnasium, sauna, nightclub, hairdresser. AE, DC, MC, V.* $$$$

★ **Puente Romano.** The spectacular, super deluxe modern hotel and apartment complex of low, white stucco buildings is located west of Marbella between the Marbella Club and Puerto Banús. The "village" has a genuine Roman bridge in its beautifully landscaped grounds, which run right down to the beach. A disco (Olivia Valere) and two outstanding restaurants, El Puente and Tai Pan, complete the picture. *Carretera N340 at Km 184, 29600, tel. 95/277–0100. 220 rooms. Facilities: 2 restaurants, indoor pool, outdoor pool, tennis courts, nightclub, shopping galleries. AE, DC, MC, V.* $$$$

El Fuerte. The hotel was built in the 1950s, and the decor, featuring dark wood paneling and green velour chairs, is very much in keeping with that era. The rooms are simply but adequately furnished and have balconies overlooking the sea. A five-minute walk from the town center, El Fuerte stands at the end of the Paseo Marítimo, separated from the beach by a pleasant palm-filled garden with an outdoor pool. *Av. El Fuerte, 29600, tel. 95/286–1500. 262 rooms. Facilities: outdoor and indoor pools, parking, tennis courts, gardens. AE, DC, MC, V.* $$$

Las Chapas. Located about 12 km (19 mi) out on the road to Málaga, this modest (by Marbella standards) hotel stands in pleasant grounds surrounded by a pine wood. It features a private bullring for teaching bullfighting with hornless calves. *Carretera N340 at Km 198, 29600, tel. 95/283–1375. 117 rooms. Facilities: indoor and*

outdoor pools, bar, tennis courts, minigolf. V. Closed Oct.–Mar.
$$–$$$

Finlandia. If you're looking for clean, inexpensive accommodations in the heart of town, try this simple, recently renovated white hostel on a quiet residential street. The atmosphere is friendly and informal, with a small bar and TV lounge in the lobby. The large rooms have white walls and bright blue paintwork; those at the front have balconies. The hot water is not totally reliable. *Calle Finlandia, 29600, tel. 95/277–0700. 11 rooms. MC, V. $*

Pilar. This may be the best find in Marbella: a cheerful and charming hotel in a central location—and very fairly priced to boot. It was taken over in 1992 by Scotsman Michael Wright, a former butler and master of guest houses in Edinburgh. It's clean and intimate and includes such delightful surprises as a log fire in winter. *Mesoncillo 4, tel. 95/282–9936. 17 rooms. Facilities: bar serving breakfast. No credit cards. $*

Mijas
Dining

Valparaíso. The setting is the attraction of this restaurant on the road leading up from Fuengirola to Mijas. The villa stands in its own garden with a swimming pool; you can dine on the outdoor terrace in summer, and afterward dance the night away to live music. In winter logs burn in a cozy fireplace. Try the *pato a la naranja* (duck in orange sauce). *Carretera de Mijas, Km 4, tel. 95/248–5996. AE, MC, V. No lunch. Closed Sun. except June–Oct. $$$*

Mirlo Blanco. Here you can sample Basque specialties such as *txangurro* (crab) and *merluza a las vasca* (hake with asparagus, eggs, and clam sauce). *Plaza de la Constitución 13, tel. 95/248–5700. Reservations accepted. AE, MC, V. $$*

El Padrasto. Perched on a clifftop above the Plaza Virgen de la Peña, this restaurant is reached via an elevator from the square or by steps if you're energetic. The views over Fuengirola and the coast are its main drawing card. The menu features international and Spanish dishes, and there's a pool and outdoor terrace. *Paseo del Compás, tel. 95/248–5000 or 95/248–5197. AE, DC, MC, V. $$*

Dining and
Lodging
★

Byblos Andaluz. In this luxury hotel (the coast's most expensive) set in a huge garden of palms, cypresses, and fountains, you'll find every comfort for a pampered vacation. It is first and foremost a spa hotel, French owned, and famed for its thalassotherapy, a treatment that uses seawater and seaweed and is applied in a Roman temple of cool white marble and blue tiles. There are two outstanding restaurants: El Andaluz, which offers lunchtime buffets and low-calorie menus, and the superb Le Nailhac, with elegant decor and the cuisine of top French chef Patrick Bausier, formerly of Bocuse in Paris. *Urbanización Mijas-Golf, 29640, tel. 95/247–3050, fax 95/247–6783. 144 rooms. Facilities: indoor and outdoor pools, 18-hole golf course, tennis courts, nearby riding school, shops, hairdresser, gymnasium, sauna, beauty treatments. AE, DC, MC, V. $$$$*

Mijas. This beautifully situated hotel at the entrance to Mijas village offers a poolside restaurant and bar, gardens with views of the hillsides stretching down to Fuengirola and the Mediterranean, marble floors, wrought-iron window grilles, and Moorish shutters. The reception area is large and airy, and there's a delightful glass-roofed terrace where afternoon tea is served every day from 4 to 6 PM. *Urbanización Tamisa, 29650, tel. 95/248–5800, fax 95/248–5825. 97 rooms with bath. Facilities: indoor and outdoor pools, health center, Jacuzzi, solarium, sauna, gymnasium, massage, beauty treatments. AE, DC, MC, V. $$$*

Nerja
Dining
★

Casa Luque. One of the most authentically Spanish of Nerja's restaurants, Casa Luque is located in a charming old Andalusian house behind the Balcón de Europa Church. The menu features dishes from northern Spain, often of Basque or Navarese origin, with an emphasis on meat and game, though good fresh fish is available, too. A lovely patio makes a perfect setting for summer dining. *Plaza Cavana 2, tel. 95/252–1004. AE, V. Closed Mon. and Feb.* $$

Udo Heimer. Your host is a genial German who will give you a warm welcome at his Art Deco villa in a new development to the east of town. The menu is a combination of traditional German dishes and local products. Ham-stuffed pumpkin, giant prawns wrapped in bacon and served in a curried banana sauce, and pork knuckle and sauerkraut are just some of the concoctions you might try. *Pueblo Andaluz 27, tel. 95/252–0032. AE, DC, MC, V. Reservations advised. No lunch. Closed Wed. and Jan.–Feb.* $$

Dining and
Lodging

Parador de Nerja. This modern (as opposed to a castle) parador is located east of Nerja's center and stands in a pleasant, leafy garden on the cliff edge. Rooms in the original, two-story building have balconies overlooking the garden and, obliquely, the sea, and those in the newer, single-story wing, open onto their own patios. An elevator will take you down to the rocky beach. As with all paradors, the restaurant concentrates on local cuisine and is especially well known for its fish dishes; try the *pez espada a la naranja* (swordfish in orange sauce) or the giant langostino shrimp. *Almuñecas 8, 29780, tel. 95/252–0050, fax 95/252–1997. 73 rooms. Facilities: restaurant, outdoor pool. AE, DC, MC, V.* $$$

Lodging

Mónica. Opened in 1986, the Mónica is spacious and luxurious, with cool, Moorish-style architecture and lots of marble. Popular with package tours, it's also within easy walking distance of the center of town. *Playa Torrecilla, 29780, tel. 95/252–1100. 234 rooms. Facilities: restaurant, bar, tennis, pool, nightclub, discothèque. AE, DC, MC, V.* $$$

Ronda
Dining

Don Miguel. The restaurant stands at the end of the bridge over the Tajo gorge, and its two terraces offer breathtaking views of the ravine (though river pollution can sometimes be a problem here). Baby lamb, reared on the owner's farm, is the house specialty; it's called *pierna de cordero lechal*. The bar, set inside the bridge in what was once Ronda's prison, is a good place for a drink and tapas. *Villanueva 4, tel. 95/287–1090. Reservations advised on holiday weekends. AE, DC, MC, V. Closed Sun., Wed. in summer; mid-Jan.–mid-Feb.* $$–$$$

Pedro Romero. You'll find this restaurant right opposite the bullring and inevitably (it's named after the father of modern bullfighting), it's packed with colorful taurine decor. Melancholy-eyed bulls peer down at you from the walls as you tuck into *sopa del mesón* (the house soup) or enjoy a *tocino del cielo al coco* (a sweet caramel custard flavored with coconut). *Virgen de la Paz 18, tel. 95/287–1110 and 95/287–1618. AE, DC, MC, V.* $$

Lodging
★

Reina Victoria. This grande dame of Spanish hotels was built in 1906 by the British in Gibraltar as a weekend retreat for passengers traveling the newly constructed rail line between Algeciras and Bobadilla. In 1912 it became famous when the ailing German poet Rainer Maria Rilke came here to convalesce. His room has been preserved as a museum. Today, the Reina Victoria maintains its air of faded English gentility. Its spacious rooms and suites are furnished with comfortable sofas and armchairs, and most have balconies. Perched on a clifftop, amid luxuriant gardens, this hotel commands one of the most striking locations in Andalucía. It is popular with tour groups.

Jerez 25, 29400, tel. 95/287–1240, fax 95/287–1075. 89 rooms. Facilities: restaurant, pool, garden. AE, DC, MC, V. $$–$$$

Polo. A cozy, old-fashioned, homey hotel in the center of town, the Polo offers comfortably furnished rooms and a good, reasonably priced restaurant. *Mariano Soubirón 8, 29400, tel. 95/287–2447. 33 rooms. Facilities: restaurant. AE, DC, MC, V. $$*

Torremolinos
Dining:
Torremolinos
Center

El Atrio. There's a definite French feel—white walls, pink table-cloths, dark wood tables and chairs in the small dining room—to this restaurant. Snails, onion soup, and quiche lorraine are often on the menu; the entrées are predominantly meat (a welcome change in this mecca of seafood), and for dessert, you'll find it hard to resist the mouth-watering profiteroles. On summer evenings you can dine outside in the square. *Casablanca 9, Plaza Pueblo Blanco, tel. 95/238–8850. Reservations advised. AE, MC, V. No lunch. Closed Sun. and Dec. $$*

Dining:
La Carihuela
★

Casa Guaquin. On a seaside patio at what is widely known as the best seafood restaurant in the region, changing daily catches are served alongside such menu stalwarts as *coquillas al ajillo* (sea cockles in garlic sauce). *Paseo Marítimo 63, tel. 95/238–4530. AE, MC, V. Closed Thurs. and mid-Dec.–mid-Jan. $$*

Europa. A short walk from the Carihuela, this villa in a large garden is a very Spanish institution (rare for Torremolinos). You can dine in leafy surroundings, and it's best on Sundays when local families come here for a leisurely lunch. *Via Imperial 32, tel. 95/238–8022. Reservations advised for Sun. lunch. AE, MC, V. Closed Mon. and mid-Jan.–mid-Feb. $$*

Juan. This is a good place for seafood in summer, with a sunny outdoor patio facing the sea. The specialties include the great Costa del Sol standbys—*sopa de mariscos* (shellfish soup), *dorada al horno* (oven-roasted giltheads), and fritura malagueña. *Paseo Marítimo 29, La Carihuela, tel. 95/238–5656. AE, DC, MC, V. $$*

Marrakech. If you haven't time for a trip to Tangiers, then at least sample some of the magic of Morocco in this splendid stucco-and-tile palace with delicately molded lacelike decorations on the walls. Couscous and tajine are served in big earthenware dishes; tasty *pastilla* (pigeon pie) comes glazed with sugar; lamb is stewed with prunes, raisins, or almonds; and delicious honey-coated pastries round off a sumptuous repast. It's worth a visit for the decor alone. *Av. Joan Míro 7, tel. 95/238–2169. No reservations. No credit cards. Closed Sun. and Mon. lunch. $$*

Lodging

Cervantes. This busy cosmopolitan hotel—one of Torremolinos's consistently good places to stay—in the heart of town is ideal for those who want to be in the center of things. It's not by the beach, but there's a pool, and the rooms are well furnished and comfortable. The service is good, and the panoramic dining room on the top floor is a favorite with locals. *Las Mercedes, 29620, tel. 95/238–4033, fax 95/238–4857. 393 rooms. AE, DC, MC, V. $$–$$$*

Tropicana. Located on the beach at the far end of the Carihuela in one of the most pleasant and leafy parts of Torremolinos, this is a relaxing resort hotel with its own beach club. A whole range of good restaurants are within five minutes' walk. *Trópico 6, 29620, tel. 95/238–6600, fax 95/238–0568. 86 rooms. Facilities: beach club, subtropical garden, pool. AE, DC, MC, V. $$–$$$*

Lago Rojo. In the heart of the old Carihuela district, this three-story modern white apartment building stands just two blocks back from the seafront. The well-maintained rooms all have balconies that overlook the small tree-filled garden and pool. There's no great view, but advantages are the modest prices and location close to the best bars and restaurants in town. *Miami 1, 29620, tel. 95/238–7666, fax 95/238–0891. 144 rooms. AE, DC, MC, V. $$*

Miami. Set in an old Andalusian villa in a shady garden west of the Carihuela, this is something of a find amid the ocean of concrete high rises. Staying here is like visiting a private Spanish home; the rooms are individually furnished, and there's a sitting room with a cozy fireplace. It's very popular, so book ahead. *Aladiño 14 (on the corner of Miami), 29620, tel. 95/238–5255. 26 rooms. Facilities: pool, patio, garden. No credit cards. $*

The Arts and Nightlife

The Arts

The best place to look for news of what's on along the coast is in *Lookout*, an English-language glossy monthly available on newsstands. Its "Costa del Sol Events" section lists art exhibitions, concerts, theater, local fiestas, and films in English. Try also Málaga's daily newspaper, *El Sur*, or its weekly English-language version, *Sur in English*.

Art Exhibitions are held in private galleries in Málaga and Marbella (see *Lookout* for details) and in several of Marbella's leading hotels, especially the Puente Romano. The Hotel Mijas in Mijas Pueblo often has small exhibitions in its lobby.

Film English and American films are shown at the **Cine Puerto Banús** in Puerto Banús (tel. 95/281–5750). There are also two cinemas in Gibraltar.

Music The Málaga Symphony Orchestra gives a winter season of orchestral concerts and chamber music, and most performances are held at the **Teatro Cervantes** in Málaga (Ramos Marín 2, tel. 95/222–4100 or 95/222–4109). Evening concerts (chamber music, organ, and choral recitals) are held in the beautiful setting of the **Hotel la Bobadilla** (tel. 958/32–18–61), in the heart of the countryside about 60 km (37 mi) north of Málaga on the Málaga–Granada provincial border, near the village of Las Salinas.

Theater The region's main theater is the **Teatro Cervantes** (Ramos Marín 2, Málaga, tel. 95/222–4100). It puts on plays (in Spanish), concerts, dance, and flamenco performances. For plays in English, try the **Salón de Variétés Theater** in Fuengirola (Emancipación 30, tel. 95/247–4542).

Nightlife

Casinos There are two casinos on the Costa del Sol: **Casino Torrequebrada** (Km 226 on N340 between Benalmádena Costa and Carvajal, tel. 95/244–2545 or 95/244–2354) and **Casino Nueva Andalucía** (west of Marbella, on the N340 next to the Andalucía Plaza hotel, tel. 95/281–4000). Both are open 8 PM–4 AM and require passport and jacket and tie for the gaming salons. In Gibraltar the **Casino** (Europa Rd., tel. 9567/76666) is open 9 PM–4 AM, and jacket and tie are advised but not required for the gaming rooms.

Flamenco and Cabaret Don't expect to see any pure, serious flamenco in the coastal resorts. Go instead for the fun and the colorful spectacle.

Arroyo de la Miel The theater of the amusement park **Tivoli World** (tel. 95/244–2848; *see* Tour 3, *above*) often puts on cabarets with international stars and plenty of flamenco dancing.

Benalmádena Costa   The **Fortuna Nightclub** of the **Casino Torrequebrada** (tel. 95/244–2545) has flamenco and an international show with dancing to an orchestra, beginning at 9:30 PM.

Málaga   Famous flamenco stars perform at the **Teatro Cervantes** (*see* The Arts, *above*).

Marbella   The **Bar Ana María** (Plaza Santo Cristo 4–5; closed Mon. and Nov.) is a crowded, colorful tapas bar packed with noisy locals who come here to enjoy the spontaneous singing and dancing of the owner and her cronies. **Casino Nueva Andalucía** (8 km [5 mi] west of Marbella, tel. 95/281–4000 for reservations) has *sevillanas* and flamenco dancing in **La Caseta del Casino** from midnight onward in summer.

Nerja   **El Colono** (Granada 6, tel. 95/252–1826) is a flamenco club set in a typical Andalusian house in the town center, and dinner shows begin at 9 PM Wednesday through Saturday. There's a choice of three set-price menus.

Torremolinos   **El Jaleo** (or **Taberna Flamenca Pepe López;** Plaza de la Gamba Alegre, tel. 95/238–1284) is the best bet here. **Molino de la Bóveda** (Cuesta del Tajo 8, tel. 95/238–1185) has South American guitar music and flamenco singing and dancing.

Discos
Málaga   The main nightlife districts are along the Paseo Marítimo and out in the eastern suburbs on Avenida Juan Sebastián Elcano and the beachfront at Pedregalejos, where **Krystal** is one of the best-known discos.

Marbella   **Olivia Valere** (tel. 95/277–0100; closed Mon.) at the Puente Romano hotel is the Costa del Sol's most exclusive disco; call ahead and take your passport. Not far away, at Km 186 on N340, is **Willy Salsa** (tel. 95/277–0279); M–25, another favorite, about 5 km (3 mi) out on the road to Cádiz.

Torremolinos   **New Pipers,** right in the center just off Plaza Costa del Sol, is the longest-established disco.

13 Andalucía

Granada to Córdoba

By Hilary Bunce

Updated by Mark Potok

From the dark mountains of the Sierra Morena in the north to the mighty snowcapped peaks of the Sierra Nevada in the south, Andalucía (Andalusia) rings with echoes of the Moors. These Muslim invaders from North Africa dwelled here for almost 800 years, from their first conquest of Spanish soil (Gibraltar) in 711 to their expulsion from Granada in 1492. The name Andalucía itself comes from the Moors' name Al-Andalus for the land they conquered from the Vandals (although a competing theory has it deriving from Vandalusia). Two of Spain's most famous monuments, the great mosque of Córdoba and the magical palace of the Alhambra in Granada, were the inspired creations of Moorish architects and craftsmen working for the Arab emirs. The brilliant white villages with narrow, shady streets; the sturdy-walled houses clustered around cool inner patios; and the whitewashed facades with modestly grilled windows all stem from centuries of Moorish occupation. The Guadalquivir, the "great river" of the Arabs, traverses the whole region; town names like Úbeda and Jaén are derivations of old Arabic names; ruined *alcázares* (fortresses) dot the landscape; and *azahar* (orange blossom) perfumes its patios. It's hard to find a church in Andalucía that wasn't built on the site of an Arab mosque, and high on the southern slopes of the Sierra Nevada, the villages of the Alpujarras, with their cube-shape houses, flat roofs, and chimney stacks, could be North African.

In the 13th century King Ferdinand III (Fernando el Santo, canonized in 1671), one of the Reconquest's greatest soldiers, captured Baeza, Úbeda, Córdoba, and Jaén from the Moors. From their defeats, the Moors fled south to Granada, where they tarried for another 250 years. The next two centuries (14th and 15th) were punctuated by constant battles and skirmishes between Moors and Christians, until Ferdinand of Aragón and Isabella of Castile, known jointly as the Catholic Monarchs, scored the ultimate victory of the Reconquest in 1492. They entered Granada and accepted the Moors' final surrender. In honor of this victory, the Catholic Monarchs chose to be buried in Granada.

The Moors left a legacy, but so did the Christian conquerors and their descendants. There are Gothic chapels, Renaissance cathedrals, and fanciful Baroque monasteries and churches. The sturdy golden-stone mansions of Úbeda and Baeza contrast intriguingly with the humble whitewashed villages of much of Andalucía.

The landscape is varied and powerful, too. To the south, the fertile plain of Granada, known as *la vega*, with its tobacco and poplar groves and lush orchards, stretches to meet the mountains of the majestic Sierra Nevada. In this range, snowclad for most of the year, you'll find Spain's highest peaks—the 11,407-foot (3,536-meter) Mulhacén and the 11,125-foot (3,449-meter) Veleta. The Guadalquivir River rises in the east in the heights of the Sierra de Cazorla. Flowing westward toward Córdoba, it is bounded on the north by the rugged shrub-covered Sierra Morena, and in the south by the rolling olive groves of Jaén. Next come the orchards of Córdoba, where cherry, peach, apricot, pear, apple, and almond trees line the river's banks. Vineyards cover the Cordoban *campiña* (fertile plain south of the Guadalquivir), and white villages cling to hillsides below ruined castles perched on crags.

Essential Information

Important Addresses and Numbers

Tourist
Information

The main tourist office for the region is in **Granada** (Plaza Mariana Pineda 10, tel. 958/22–66–88), with information on both the province and the city. A much smaller regional office is found in **Córdoba** (Plaza de Judá Leví, tel. 957/47–20–00).

Local tourist offices in major towns covered in this chapter are **Baeza** (Plaza del Pópulo, tel. 953/74–04–44), **Córdoba** (Palacio de Congresos y Exposiciones, Torrijos 10, tel. 957/47–12–35), **Granada** (Corral del Carbón, Mariana Pineda, tel. 958/22–59–90 or 958/22–10–22), **Jaén** (Arquitecto Bergés 1, tel. 953/22–27–37), and **Úbeda** (Plaza del Ayuntamiento, tel. 953/75–08–97).

Travel Agency

American Express, Viajes Bonal, Avenida de la Constitución 19, Granada, tel. 958/27–63–12 or 958/27–63–16.

Emergencies

Police, emergency telephones: Policía Nacional, 091; Policía Municipal, 092.

Arriving and Departing by Plane

Granada Airport (tel. 958/44–64–11 or 958/44–70–81) is 18 km (11 mi) west of Granada. **Aviaco** has daily flights to and from Madrid and Barcelona and three flights weekly to Valencia.

*Between the
Airport and
Downtown*

J. Gonzalez buses (tel. 958/13–13–09) run between the airport and city center, leaving Plaza Isabel la Católica approximately 1¼ hours before flight departures. Times are listed at the bus stop.

Arriving and Departing by Car, Train, and Bus

By Car

From Madrid take N IV, 401 km (250 mi) direct to Córdoba, or if you're heading for Granada first, take N IV as far as Bailén, then turn left, heading south on the N323 via Jaén. Scores of millions of dollars were spent to improve the N IV and most of the smaller highways in the region in connection with the International Exposition hosted by Seville in 1992, and the result is greatly reduced traveling times throughout Andalucía—as well as some very pleasant driving in a place once infamous for its poor infrastructure. The construction is now complete, and the N IV is a fairly major highway, although some of the more mountainous roads in the region, particularly the eastern area, can still be somewhat slow going.

By Train

Córdoba is on both the main Madrid (Chamartín)–Seville–Cádiz and Madrid (Chamartín)–Málaga lines, so there are several trains daily in each direction, including a daytime and a nighttime Talgo. There are also daily services between Barcelona (Sants), Valencia, and Córdoba. Córdoba Station is on the Glorieta de Guadalorce. Call for RENFE information (tel. 957/49–02–02). For information and tickets in advance, go to the **RENFE office** (Ronda de los Tejares 10, tel. 957/47–58–84).

Granada has two trains a day from Madrid (Chamartín). One train a day connects Barcelona, Valencia, and Granada. Granada can also be reached from Seville, Córdoba, Málaga, Ronda, and Algeciras, though most of these routes involve changing trains at Bobadilla junction. Granada Station is at the end of Avenida Andaluces and can be reached by Bus 11 from the Puerta Real or Gran Vía Colón. Call for RENFE information (tel. 958/27–12–72). For information or advance ticket purchase, go to the **RENFE office** (Reyes Católicos 63, corner of Sillería, tel. 958/22–31–19).

By Bus   Buses connect several Spanish cities and **Córdoba.** For bus information, go either to the main tourist office (Torrijos 10) or to the following bus companies: **Alsina Gräells** (Av. Medina Azahara 29, tel. 957/23–64–74) for services to Badajoz, Cádiz, Granada, Seville, and Málaga; **Ureña** (Av. Cervantes 22, tel. 957/47–23–52) for Seville and Jaén; **Priego** (Paseo de la Victoria 29, tel. 957/29–01–58 or 957/29–07–69) for Madrid (via N IV), Barcelona, and Valencia; **López** (Paseo de la Victoria 5, tel. 957/47–75–51 or 957/47–45–92) for Ciudad Real and Madrid (via Ciudad Real). **Ramírez** (Avda. de la República Argentina, tel. 957/41–01–00 or 957/41–09–01) serves small towns in Córdoba province.

Granada's main bus station is **Alsina Gräells** (Camino de Ronda 97, tel. 958/25–13–58), with services to and from Madrid, Algeciras, Málaga, Córdoba, Seville, Jaén, Motril, and Almería. The other main bus company is **Bacoma** (Av. Andaluces 10, tel. 958/28–42–51), which runs services from Granada to Murcia, Alicante, Valencia, and Barcelona. Both can be reached on the circular Bus 11 from Puerta Real or Gran Vía Colón.

Getting Around

By Car   In the cities of Granada and Córdoba, be prepared for parking problems and, particularly in Granada, the ever-present threat of break-ins. Most of Córdoba's hotels are located in a labyrinth of narrow streets that can be a nightmare to negotiate, even with a small car; with anything bigger, you'll probably find them impassable. In Córdoba, all sights are within easy walking distance of one another; in Granada, it's simpler to take a taxi up to the Alhambra or the Albaicín Quarter than to negotiate the extremely complicated one-way system and narrow Moorish streets in a rented car.

If you do decide to go by car, the route from Granada to Jaén, Baeza, Úbeda, and Cazorla is not one of Andalucía's most tourist-packed, though between Granada and Jaén you'll no doubt encounter the odd tour bus. Still, the roads have been smoothed and straightened, and driving through the region is one of the more pleasant ways to see the countryside.

By Train   Services from Córdoba to Granada are poor. There is no train service between Granada and Jaén or between Jaén and Córdoba. Both Córdoba and Jaén have trains to Linares–Baeza Station, but from there you must take a bus into Baeza or Úbeda.

By Bus   If you're not driving, buses are the best method of transportation in this region. They run to most of the outlying towns and villages, and bus connections between major cities are generally faster and more frequent than by train (*see* Arriving and Departing, *above*). If you're using public transportation to reach the villages of the Alpujarras, check details of bus schedules and accommodations carefully with the Granada Tourist Office and the Alsina Gräells bus company before you set off.

Guided Tours

Orientation   **Pullmantur** and **Julia Tours** (*see* Getting Around by Bus in Chapter 1) run numerous tours to this region, which can be booked through most travel agents, many hotels, or with their Madrid (*see* Chapter 3) or Costa del Sol (*see* Chapter 12) offices.

Special-Interest *The Andalusian Express* is a luxury vintage train with cars from the '20s that makes a weekly trip in season from Madrid to Aranjuez, Úbeda, Córdoba, Seville, Jerez, Málaga, and Granada. For reservations and information contact **Abercrombie & Kent** (*see* Getting Around by Train in Chapter 1).

Horseback riding tours—some with English guides—are offered in the villages of the Alpujarras and the Sierra Nevada and sometimes elsewhere. Contact tourist offices for information; one agency in the Alpujarras is **Cabalgar** (Bubeon, Granada, tel. 958/76–31–35, fax 958/76–32–36).

In the **Cazorla Nature Park,** four-wheel-drive or horseback excursions and more specific nature tours, such as bird-watching, can be arranged through the Torre de Vinaigre Visitor Center (tel. 953/72–01–02).

Walking Tours In **Córdoba,** English-speaking guides for the Mezquita and Synagogue can be contacted through the **Asociación Profesional de Informadores Turísticos** (Torrijos 2, Córdoba, tel. 957/48–69–97). In **Granada,** multilingual guides can be contacted through the **Asociación Provincial de Guías** (Puerta del Vino, La Alhambra, Granada, tel. 958/22–99–36). In **Jaén** and **Úbeda,** ask at the Tourist Office.

Exploring Andalucía: Granada to Córdoba

Our tours move westward through three of Andalucía's eight provinces, Granada, Jaén, and Córdoba. First we concentrate on the city of Granada, where you can explore the Alhambra, the Generalife, the Albaicín, and the Capilla Real (Royal Chapel), with excursions to the Sierra Nevada, Santa Fe, Fuente Vaqueros, and the Alpujarras. The second tour takes you to the province of Jaén, where dramatic scenery is combined with the delights of the small, quiet, historic towns of Úbeda, Baeza, and Cazorla and the pure, fresh air of the Cazorla Nature Park. Finally, you tour Córdoba, where you can visit the Mezquita (mosque) and see Andalucía's Moorish heritage in thick white walls, hidden squares, winding alleys, and picturesque patios.

Highlights for First-time Visitors

The gardens of the Alcázar, Córdoba (*see* Tour 3)
The Alhambra, Granada (*see* Tour 1)
View of the Alhambra from San Nicolás balcony in the Albaicín, Granada (*see* Tour 1)
Baeza's palaces and fountains (*see* Tour 2)
Scenery in the Cazorla Nature Park (*see* Tour 2)
View from Jaén's castle-parador (*see* Tour 2)
Mezquita, Córdoba (*see* Tour 3)
Úbeda's Plaza Vásquez de Molina (*see* Tour 2)
Capilla Real, Granada (*see* Tour 1)
View of the Sierra Nevada from the Veleta summit (*see* Tour 1)

Tour 1: Granada, the Sierra Nevada, and the Alpujarras

Numbers in the margin correspond to points of interest on the Andalucía: Granada to Córdoba and Granada maps.

❶ The city of **Granada** rises majestically from a fertile plain onto three hills, dwarfed—on a clear day—by the mighty snowcapped peaks of the Sierra Nevada. Atop one of these hills perches the pink-gold palace of the Alhambra, at once splendidly imposing and infinitely delicate. From it can be seen the roofs of the old Moorish quarter, the Albaicín; the caves of the Sacromonte; and, in the distance, the fertile *vega* (plain), rich in orchards, tobacco fields, and poplar groves.

Granada's Moorish Nasrid dynasty, split by internal squabbles, presented Ferdinand of Aragón with the chance he needed in 1491. Spurred by Isabella's religious fanaticism, he laid siege to the city for seven months. On January 2, 1492, the Rey Chico (Boy King), Boabdil, was forced to surrender the keys of the city to the triumphant Catholic Monarchs. As Boabdil fled the Alhambra by the Puerta de los Siete Suelos (Gate of the Seven Sighs), he asked that this gate be sealed forever.

We begin our tour at the Plaza Nueva, from which the Cuesta de Gomérez leads up a steep grade to the cool vale of the Alhambra precincts. Pass beneath the Puerta de las Granadas, a Renaissance gateway built by Charles V (note that it is topped by three pomegranates—a symbol of Granada) and climb the slopes of green elms, planted by the duke of Wellington, until you come to the main en-
❷ trance of the Alhambra, the **Puerta de la Justicia.** Yusuf I built this Gate of Justice in 1348. On its two arches are carved a hand and a key, the five fingers representing the five laws of the Koran.

❸ The **Alhambra** was founded in the 1240s by Ibn el-Ahmar, or Alhamar, the first king of the Nasrids. The great citadel once comprised an entire complex of houses, schools, baths, barracks, and gardens surrounded by defense towers and seemingly impregnable walls. Today, only the Alcazaba fortress and the Royal Palace, built chiefly by Yusuf I (1334–54) and his son Mohammed V (1354–91), remain. The palace is an intricate fantasy of endless patios, arches, and cupolas fashioned from wood, plaster, and tiles; lavishly colored and adorned by geometric patterns of marquetry and ceramics; and surmounted by delicate, frothy profusions of lacelike stucco and *mocárabes* (ornamental stalactites). Built of perishable materials, it was never intended to last but to be forever replaced and replenished by succeeding generations.

By the early 17th century, ruin and decay had set in, and it was abandoned by all but vagabonds and Gypsies, tramps and stray dogs. Napoleon's troops commandeered it in 1812, but their attempts to blow it up were happily foiled. In 1814 the Alhambra's fortunes took a turn for the better with the arrival of the duke of Wellington, who came to it to escape the pressures of the Peninsular War. Soon afterward (1829), Washington Irving came to live in it and did much to promote a revival of interest in the fortunes of the crumbling palace. His 1832 book, *Tales of the Alhambra*, played an important role in this. In 1862 Granada finally embarked upon a complete restoration program that has been carried on ever since.

Purchase your entrance ticket and wander over to your left, to the original fortress of the **Alcazaba.** Its ruins are dominated by a tower, the **Torre de la Vela,** whose summit offers superlative views of the city; to the north, the Albaicín; to the northeast, the Sacromonte;

and to the west, the cathedral. The tower's great bell was used as an alarm signal by the Moors, and later by the Christians, to control the opening and closing of the gates of the Granada vega's irrigation system.

The Renaissance **Palacio de Carlos V** (Palace of Charles V), with a perfectly square exterior but a circular interior courtyard, stands imposing but totally incongruous on the site where the sultans' private apartments once stood. Begun in 1526, and designed by Pedro Machuca, a pupil of Michelangelo, the palace was once used for bullfights and mock tournaments. Today, its perfect acoustics make it a fine setting for symphony concerts during Granada's International Festival of Music and Dance, held annually in June and July.

Next, a wisteria-covered walkway leads into the heart of the Alhambra, the **Casa Real** (Royal Palace). Delicate apartments, lazy fountains, and tranquil pools form a vivid contrast to the sturdy surrounding defense walls. The Royal Palace is divided into three sections. The first is the *mexuar*, where the business, government, and administration of the Alhambra were conducted. Here are the Oratory and the Cuarto Dorado (Golden Room); make sure you don't miss the views of the Albaicín and Sacromonte from their windows.

Next comes the *serrallo*, a series of state rooms where the sultans held court and entertained their ambassadors. In the heart of the serrallo, you'll find the **Patio de los Arrayanes** (Court of the Myrtles), with a long goldfish pool surrounded by fragrant shrubs. At its northern end, in the **Salón de Embajadores** (Hall of the Ambassadors)—which has a magnificent cedar dome and fine tile and stucco decoration—Boabdil signed the terms of surrender and Isabella received Christopher Columbus.

The final section, the *harem*, was entered only by the sultan, his family, and their most trusted servants, most of them eunuchs. To reach it, you pass through the Sala de los Mozárabes—note its splendid but damaged ceiling. The **Patio de los Leones** (Court of the Lions) is the heart of the harem. From the fountain in the center of the patio, 12 lions, which may represent the months or signs of the zodiac, leer out at the hordes of tourists. Four streams flow symbolically to the four corners of the Earth, and more literally to the surrounding state apartments. On the south side is the **Sala de los Abencerrajes,** perhaps the most beautiful gallery in the Alhambra, with a stalactite ceiling and a star-shaped cupola reflected in the pool below. Here Boabdil's father is alleged to have massacred 16 members of the Abencerrajes family, whose chief was the lover of his own favorite, Zoraya, and piled their blood-stained heads in this now-serene font.

On the patio's east side lies the **Sala de los Reyes** (Kings' Gallery), decorated with ceiling frescoes that may have been painted by Christians in the last days of the Moors' tenure. To the north, the **Sala de las Dos Hermanas** (Hall of the Two Sisters) was the abode of the king's favorite. Its name comes from the two white marble slabs in its floor, and its ceiling is resplendent with some of the Alhambra's most superb stucco work, an intricate pattern of honeycomb cells.

From here, signs lead you to the **Baños Arabes,** the Alhambra's semisubterranean bathhouse, where the sultan's favorites luxuriated in baths of brightly tiled mosaic and performed their ablutions lit by star-shaped pinpoints of light in the ceiling above. You'll notice a balcony that looks out over one of the rooms; from here, the sultan

Andalucía: Granada to Córdoba

TO MADRID

NIV

E. del Jándula

La Carolina

E. del Rumblar

Bailén

N322

Linares

Arquillos

C3210

N322

Villacarrillo

E. de Guadalmena

Puente de Génave

Embalse del Tranco

Baeza (20)

(21) **Úbeda**

Río Guadalquivir

Torre de Vinaigre (23)

Cazorla (22)

PARQUE NATURAL DE CAZORLA

N323

N321

C328

C328

C325

Jódar

C328

C328

Jaén (19)

N323

N324

Huéscar

Pozo Alcón

Cúllar Baza

N342

Baza

C323

Fuente Vaqueros (16)

Viznar

Granada (1)—(14)

Guadix

N324

(15) **Santa Fe**

C340

Solynieve

N323

Pico Veleta

Sierra Nevada (17)

Mulhacen

N340

Dúrcal

Trevélez

Alpujarras (18)

Capileira

Lanjarón

C333

Orgiva

N331

Almería

Motril

Salobreña

N340

Adra

N340

N

0 ____ 40 miles
0 ____ 60 km

KEY
— Rail Lines
- - - Regional Boundaries

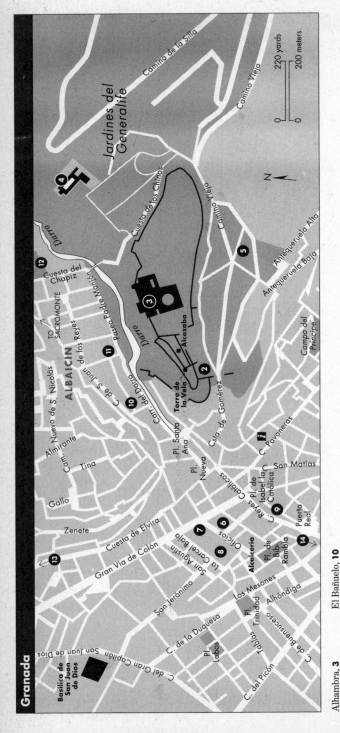

Granada

Basílica de San Juan de Dios

Alhambra, **3**
Capilla Real, **7**
Casa de Castril, **11**
Casa del Chapiz, **12**
Casa de Manuel de
Falla, **5**
Catedral, **8**
Corral del Carbón, **9**

El Bañuelo, **10**
Generalife, **4**
La Cartuja, **13**
La Huerta de San
Vicente, **14**
Palacio Madraza, **6**
Puerta de la Justicia, **2**

Alhambra

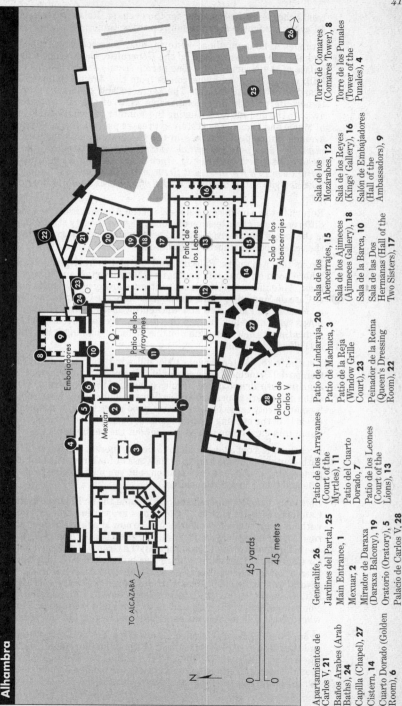

TO ALCAZABA

N

0 — 45 yards
0 — 45 meters

Embajadores

Mexuar

Patio de los Arrayanes

Patio de los Leones

Patio de Lindaraja

Sala de los Abencerrajes

Palacio de Carlos V

Apartamientos de Carlos V, **21**
Baños Arabes (Arab Baths), **24**
Capilla (Chapel), **27**
Cistern, **14**
Cuarto Dorado (Golden Room), **6**

Generalife, **26**
Jardines del Partal, **25**
Main Entrance, **1**
Mexuar, **2**
Mirador de Daraxa (Daraxa Balcony), **19**
Oratorio (Oratory), **5**
Palacio de Carlos V, **28**

Patio de los Arrayanes (Court of the Myrtles), **11**
Patio del Cuarto Dorado, **7**
Patio de los Leones (Court of the Lions), **13**

Patio de Lindaraja, **20**
Patio de Machuca, **3**
Patio de la Reja (Window Grille Court), **23**
Peinador de la Reina (Queen's Dressing Room), **22**

Sala de los Abencerrajes, **15**
Sala de los Ajimeces (Ajimeces Gallery), **18**
Sala de la Barca, **10**
Sala de las Dos Hermanas (Hall of the Two Sisters), **17**

Sala de los Mozárabes, **12**
Sala de los Reyes (Kings' Gallery), **16**
Salón de Embajadores (Hall of the Ambassadors), **9**

Torre de Comares (Comares Tower), **8**
Torre de los Punales (Tower of the Punales), **4**

would choose his bed partner for the evening. Relax or stroll in the adjacent gardens before climbing up to the Generalife.

❹ Avenues of bougainvillea, wisteria, neat boxwood hedges, cedars, and soaring cypresses lead to the **Generalife,** the ancient summer palace of the Nasrid kings. The palace stands on the Cerro del Sol (Hill of the Sun); its name comes from the Arabic Gennat Alarif (Garden of the Architect). The terraces and promenades of the Generalife provide an incomparable view of the city, stretching away to the distant vega. During the summer International Festival of Music and Dance, the stately cypresses provide the backdrop for evening ballet performances in the Generalife amphitheater. *Admission: 600 pesetas, which includes the Alhambra and the Generalife (free Sun. after 3). Open Mar.–Oct., daily 9–8, floodlit visits Tues., Thurs., and Sat. 10 PM–midnight; Nov.–Feb., daily 9–6, floodlit visits Sat. 8 PM–10 PM. Ticket office closes 1 hour before closing time.*

Return to town on the opposite side of the Alhambra hill for a totally different, though no less spectacular, view of the city stretching out at the foot of the Sierra Nevada. Pass through the elm groves toward the ocher-red Alhambra Palace hotel.

❺ From the Alhambra Palace, head up along Antequeruela Baja, where soon on your left another rather deserted and dilapidated road, Antequeruela Alta, leads past some lovely old Granada houses to **Casa de Manuel de Falla,** the house where the Cádiz-born composer Manuel de Falla lived and worked for many years. His house is now a small museum. In 1986 Granada finally paid tribute to him by dedicating its new concert hall in his memory, naming it the Manuel de Falla Auditorium.

Return to the Antequeruela Baja and wind your way down to the **Campo del Príncipe.** In the center of this square is a much-venerated crucifix with Cristo de los Faroles (Christ of the Lanterns). Women often come here to pray and offer flowers. The square is surrounded by many lively tapas bars, and it's a good place to come at lunchtime or early in the evening to sample plates of seafood or *jamón serrano* (mountain-cured ham prized throughout the peninsula).

From here it's not a long walk to Calle Pavaneras, where you'll find a 16th-century mansion known as the **Casa de los Tiros.** The building is undergoing a long-term restoration, but you may be able to step inside and take a look at the patios.

Continue down Pavaneras and you'll come to the **Plaza de Isabel la Católica,** with its statue of Columbus presenting Queen Isabella with his maps of the New World. You're now at one of the main crossroads of the city, and you may well feel like a break. Ahead of you lies one of Granada's main thoroughfares, the Gran Vía de Colón, named for Columbus. This thoroughfare was built in the late 19th century in an effort to modernize cross-town transportation; unfortunately, several wonderful old palaces were destroyed in the process. To your left, Calle de los Reyes Católicos leads down to Puerta Real, the commercial hub of the city; and up to your right is the Plaza Nueva, where townsfolk meet in outdoor cafés and restaurant terraces.

From Plaza Isabel la Católica, follow Gran Vía de Colón to Oficios and turn left to explore the alleys of the adjoining **Alcaicería,** once the Arabs' silk market. This was the hub of the Moorish city, and though the Alcaicería is not authentic—the old one burned down in the 1840s and was rebuilt as arcades of souvenir shops—it is particularly beautiful at night, when its arches and courtyards are lit by rows of white lanterns.

Back on Oficios, at the Gran Vía de Colón, the Baroque facade of the ➏ **Palacio Madraza** conceals the old Moorish university, built in 1349 by Yusuf I. Inside you'll find an octagonal room crowned by a dome of Moorish inspiration. The building is now a university exhibition and cultural center. *Admission free but only open during exhibitions.*

➐ Opposite, you'll find the entrance to the **Capilla Real** (Royal Chapel), a shrine of Granada history second only to the Alhambra. This is the burial place of the Catholic Monarchs, Isabella of Castile and Ferdinand of Aragón. They had originally planned to be buried in San Juan de los Reyes, in Toledo, but following their conquest of Granada in 1492, Isabella decreed that their final resting place would be here. When Isabella died in 1504, her body was at first laid to rest in the Convent of San Francisco (now the parador) on the Alhambra hill. In 1506 the architect Enrique Egas began work on the Royal Chapel and completed it 15 years later. It is a masterpiece of the ornate Gothic style known in Spain as Isabelline. In 1521 Isabella's body was brought to a simple lead coffin in the Royal Chapel crypt, where it was joined by that of her husband, Ferdinand, and later her unfortunate daughter, Juana la Loca, and son-in-law, Felipe el Hermoso. Felipe died young and Juana la Loca—Joan the Mad in English—had his casket borne about the peninsula with her for years, opening the lid each night to kiss her embalmed spouse good night. The elaborate marble tombs in which Ferdinand and Isabella now lie side by side were commissioned by their grandson, Charles V, and fashioned by the sculptor Domenico Fancelli. The intricate wrought-iron *reja* (grille) is by Master Bartolomé of Baeza. The altarpiece by Felipe Vigarini (1522) shows Boabdil surrendering the keys of the city to its conquerors. In the sacristy you'll find Ferdinand's sword, Isabella's crown and scepter, and a fine collection of Flemish paintings once owned by Isabella. *Oficios. Admission: 200 pesetas. Open Mar.–Sept., daily 10:30–1 and 4–7; Oct.–Feb., daily 11–1 and 3:30–6.*

➑ Adjoining the Royal Chapel, you'll find the huge **catedral** (cathedral), commissioned in 1521 by Charles V, who considered the Royal Chapel "too small for so much glory" and determined to house his illustrious grandparents somewhere more worthy. Charles undoubtedly had great designs; Granada cathedral is the creation of some of the greatest architects of its time: Enrique Egas, Diego de Siloé, Alonso Cano, and sculptor Juan de Mena. But his ambitions came to little, for the cathedral is a grandiose and gloomy monument, not completed until 1714, and never used as the crypt of his parents and grandparents. *Admission: 200 pesetas. Open Mar.–Sept., Mon.–Sat. 10:30–1 and 4–7, Sun. 4–7; Oct.–Feb., Mon.–Sat. 11–1 and 3:30–6, Sun. 3:30–6.*

➒ From the cathedral, cross Reyes Católicos to the **Corral del Carbón.** Its name means Coal House or Coal Store, and this is what it was used for in the 19th century, but its origins are much earlier. One of the oldest Moorish buildings in the city, it dates back to the 14th century, when Moorish merchants used it as a lodging house and stored their goods on the upper floor. This old Arab inn, the only one of its kind in Spain, was later used by Christians as a theater. It's been expertly restored and now displays Spanish furniture and handicrafts. *Mariana Pineda, 1 block from Reyes Católicos, tel. 958/22–45–50. Admission free. Open weekdays 10–8, Sat. 10–2; closed Sun.*

Head next for the **Albaicín,** a very special part of Granada. Standing on a hill of its own, across the ravine of the Darro from the Alhambra, this old Moorish quarter is a fascinating mix of dilapidated white houses and immaculate *carmenes* (private villas in gardens enclosed by high walls). Its steep, twisting streets, cobbled alleyways, and secret corners capture perfectly the peculiar charm of Granada. This hillside quarter was founded in 1228 by Moors who were expelled from Baeza after its capture by the Saint King Ferdinand. The Albaicín guards its old Moorish atmosphere jealously, though its 30 mosques have long been converted into Baroque churches. A stretch of the original Moorish city wall runs beside the Cuesta de la Alhacaba.

If you're on foot, you can enter the Albaicín from either Cuesta de Elvira or Plaza Nueva. On foot or by car—take a taxi rather than your own car; parking is impossible—begin in Plaza Santa Ana and follow the Carrera del Darro, Paseo Padre Manjón, and the Cuesta del Chapiz.

The first place you'll come to is the 11th-century Arab steam baths, known locally as **El Bañuelo** (Little Bath). The bathhouse may be a little dark and dank now, but try to imagine how it would have been some 900 years ago when it was filled with Moorish beauties, and bright ceramic tiles and hangings adorned the dull brick walls. From the ceiling, light comes in through star-shaped vents, just as it does in the Alhambra bathhouse. *Carrera del Darro 31, tel. 958/22–23–39. Admission: 100 pesetas. Open Tues.–Sat. 10–2; closed Sun. and Mon.*

Just up the street, you'll find the **Casa de Castril,** a richly decorated 16th-century palace that once belonged to Bernardo Zafra, secretary to Queen Isabella. Before you go inside, notice the exquisite portal and the facade carved with a phoenix and scallop shells. The house is the home of the **Museo Archeológico** (Museum of Archaeology); here you'll find a beautiful Moorish room, Egyptian burial urns from near Almuñécar, and artifacts from the caves of Granada province. *Carrera del Darro 41, tel. 958/22–56–40. Admission: 250 pesetas. Open Tues.–Sat. 10–2; closed Sun. and Mon.*

On the Paseo Padre Manjón, look for the **Palacio de los Córdoba,** a noble house of the 17th century. It's used today as a center for art exhibitions and municipal functions. Around the corner, on the Cuesta del Chapiz, at its junction with Camino del Sacromonte, is the **Casa del Chapiz,** a fine 16th-century Morisco house with a delightful garden. It's the home of the School of Arabic Studies, which researches the history of Moorish culture in Spain, and, as such, is not generally open to the public. But if you knock, the caretaker may well show you around.

Once you've reached the top of the Albaicín, wander on through it. Don't miss the **balcony** in front of **San Nicolás Church,** which gives one of the finest views in all Granada. Before you, on the hill opposite, the turrets and towers of the ocher-colored Alhambra are dramatically silhouetted against the snowcapped peaks of the Sierra Nevada. This view is at its most magical at dawn, dusk, and when the Alhambra is floodlit.

Rising behind the Albaicín, the third of Granada's three hills, the **Sacromonte,** is dotted with prickly-pear cacti and riddled with caverns. From *garnathah* (mountain cave) comes the name of Granada. These caves may possibly have sheltered early Christians, for 15th-century treasure hunters found instead a collection of bones there. Some of these they assumed belonged to San Cecilio, the city's patron saint, and so the hill was sanctified (*sacro monte,* or holy mountain), and a monastery built on its summit.

The Sacromonte is the domain of Granada's Gypsies. Though fewer and fewer of them actually live in the district today, a good number still earn a healthy living there fleecing the city's tourists. The flamenco shows they stage are generally abysmal, the drinks watered down, and the prices vastly inflated for performances that are not so very *auténtico.* But on another level, these shows can be fun, they're certainly colorful, and they do provide a chance to go inside the famous *cuevas* (caves). Richly colored rugs and gleaming copper utensils adorn their caves—as do such modern conveniences as refrigerators and dishwashers. So, too, does grandfather's photo, a crude image of the Virgin Mary, and an assortment of banderillas retrieved from bullfights. On summer evenings enterprising Granadinos run minibus tours to the Gypsy caves—your hotel can often put you in touch. The price of the trip usually includes a drink in the Albaicín first, and though not cheap, it may well be the safest way to visit the Sacromonte. Only the most adventurous should attempt the trip on their own. Don't bring valuables up here or more cash than you can afford to lose.

In the north of the city, about 2 km (1 mi) from the center, lies a Carthusian monastery known as **La Cartuja.** It was begun in 1506 and moved to its present site in 1516, and its construction continued for the next 300 years. It became one of the most outstanding examples of lavish Baroque style in Andalucía. When you enter the church and gaze at its twisted, multicolored marble columns; the profusion of gold and silver, tortoiseshell, and ivory; the intricate stucco; and the extravagant Churrigueresque sacristy, you'll see why the Cartuja has often been called the Christian answer to the Moors' Alhambra. *Camino de Alfacar, tel. 958/20-19-32. Admission: 200 pesetas. Open May-Sept., daily 10-1 and 4-7; Oct.-Apr., daily 10-1 and 3:30-6.*

If you're interested in Granada's most famous native son, the poet Federico García Lorca, you may want to see his family's summer home on the western fringes of the city. From Puerta Real, head down Recogidas, cross Camino de Ronda, and head straight along Neptuno. Turn right onto Arabial, and where Arabial crosses Virgen Blanca, you'll find **La Huerta de San Vicente.** Lorca's family first spent the summer here in 1909, and the house is being restored as part of its conversion to a museum; the museum was expected to open in early 1994, but check with the tourist office to save a fruitless trip.

Numbers in the margin correspond to points of interest on the Andalucía: Granada to Córdoba map.

Excursions from Granada Eight km (5 mi) west of Granada, just south off N342, you'll come to the village of **Santa Fe,** founded in the winter of 1491 as a campground for the 150,000 troops of Ferdinand and Isabella as they prepared for the Siege of Granada. It was in Santa Fe, in April 1492, that Isabella and Columbus signed the agreements that were to finance his historic voyage. Often known as the "Cradle of America," Santa Fe is full of historic monuments.

Just beyond Santa Fe, a side road turns to the right, heading north to the village of **Fuente Vaqueros,** where, on June 5, 1898, Federico García Lorca was born. His birthplace was opened as a museum in 1986, when Spain was commemorating the 50th anniversary of Lorca's assassination and celebrating his reinstatement as a national figure after 40 years of nonrecognition during the Franco dictatorship. *Poeta García Lorca 4, tel. 958/51–64–53. Admission: 150 pesetas. Open July–Sept., Tues.–Sun. 10–1 and 6–8; Oct.–Mar., Tues.–Sun. 10–1 and 4–6; Apr.–June, 10–1 and 5–7; closed Mon. Tours (in Spanish only) at 10, 11, noon, and 1 year-round; also, Oct.–Mar. at 4, 5, and 6 PM; Apr.–June at 5, 6, 7 PM; July–Sept. at 6, 7, 8 PM.*

The nearby village of **Valderrubio** inspired Lorca's *Libro de Poemas* and one of his best-loved plays, *La Casa de Bernarda Alba*. If you're a devotee of Lorca, you may also want to make the short trip to **Viznar,** 9 km (6 mi) northeast of Granada (the easiest route is to head northeast on the N342, then turn left, and left again, when you see signs for Viznar). The Federico García Lorca Memorial Park, between the villages of Viznar and Alfacar, marks the spot where Lorca was shot without trial by Nationalists at the beginning of the civil war in August 1936 and where he is probably buried. Lorca, who today is positively venerated by most Spaniards, was hated by Fascists both for his liberal ideas and for his homosexuality.

17 A popular and easy excursion, even if you do not have a car, is to the mountains of the nearby **Sierra Nevada.** From December to May, the **Solynieve** ski resort at Pradollano draws crowds of winter-sports enthusiasts, but it is quiet in the summer. The drive from Granada to Pradollano along C420 by way of Cenes de la Vega takes around 45 minutes, and you'd be wise to carry snow chains even as late as April or May. Buses leave Granada daily at 9, returning at 5 (Autobuses Bonal, tel. 958/27–31–00). Buses depart year-round from the Bar El Ventorillo (where you also buy tickets, 590 pesetas), next to the Palacio de Congresos. In July and August you can drive right up to the summit of the Veleta on one of Europe's highest roads. It's cold up here, so be sure to bring a warm jacket, scarf, and sunglasses, even when the weather in Granada is sizzling hot. The **Veleta,** Spain's third-highest mountain, stands at 11,125 feet, and the view from its summit across the Alpujarra range to the sea at distant Motril is stunning. On a very clear day you can even see the coast of North Africa. Away to your left, the mighty Mulhacén, continental Spain's highest peak, soars to 11,407 feet.

18 A trip to the villages of the **Alpujarras** region, on the southern slopes of the Sierra Nevada, will take you to one of the highest, most remote, and most picturesque regions of Andalucía. If you're driving, the road as far as Lanjarón and Orgiva is plain sailing; after that you should be prepared for twisting, steeply ascending mountain roads and few gas stations.

A few kilometers east of Granada on N323, the road reaches a spot known as the **Suspiro del Moro** (Moor's Sigh). Pause here a moment and look back at the city, just as the boy king Boabdil, last ruler of the Moors of Granada, did 500 years ago. As he wept over the city he'd surrendered to the Catholic Monarchs, his scornful mother bestowed upon him the now famous rebuke: "You weep like a boy for the city you could not defend as a man."

When you come to the Venta de las Angustias, take the indicated left turn to Lanjarón on C333. **Lanjarón,** 46 km (29 mi) from Granada, is a faded spa town. Its famous mineral water, gathered from the melting snows of the Sierra Nevada, is drunk throughout Spain. The road continues on to **Orgiva,** the main town of the western Alpujarra, where you leave C333 and follow the signs for Pampaneira and Capileira in the Alpujarra Alta (High Alpujarra).

The remote Alpujarras region—known for its poverty—was populated originally by Moors fleeing the Reconquest, first from Seville after its fall in 1248 and later, after 1492, from Granada. It was also the last fiefdom of the unfortunate Boabdil, conceded to him by the Catholic Monarchs after his surrender of Granada. From the Alpujarras in 1568, the Moors made their final stand against Spain's Christians. Their revolt was ruthlessly suppressed by Philip II and followed by the forced conversion of all Moors to Christianity.

The villages of the Alpujarras were then repopulated with Christians from Galicia in northern Spain. The Galicians and their descendants have continued to this day the Moorish custom of weaving rugs and blankets in traditional Alpujarran colors of red, green, black, and white, and you'll find such craft items on sale in many of the villages. The houses of the Alpujarran villages are squat and square, built of slate and compacted mud, with low, flat roofs punctuated by smoking chimneys. One on top of another, they spill down the mountainside, bearing a strong resemblance to the Berber homes in the Rif Mountains across the sea in Morocco. Herds of goats with tinkling bells roam the lanes and hillsides.

The villages of the Poqueira Ravine—Pampaneira, Bubión, and Capileira—are the best known. The looms of **Pampaneira's** workshops produce many of the woven goods you'll see on sale in the surrounding villages. **Capileira,** at the end of the road, is one of the prettiest villages; in the Plaza Mayor, the **Museo Alpujarreno** has a colorful display of local crafts. From Capileira, a winding track leads over the mountain peaks to join the road to the Veleta summit. It's passable only in July or August, and then only in a four-wheel-drive vehicle.

If you make it as far as **Trevélez,** which lies on the slopes of the Mulhacén at 4,840 feet above sea level, you will have driven on one of the highest roads in Europe. Reward yourself with a plate of the locally produced jamón serrano.

Tour 2: Jaén, Baeza, Úbeda, and Cazorla

19 The city of **Jaén** nestles in the foothills of the Sierra de Jabalcuz, surrounded by towering peaks and rolling olive-clad hillsides. The Arabs called it Geen, meaning Route of the Caravans, because it formed a crossroad between Castile and Andalucía. Captured from the Moors by the Saint King Ferdinand in 1246, Jaén became a frontier province and, for the next 200 years, witnessed many battles and skirmishes between the Moors of Granada and Christians from the north and west. Today, the province of Jaén has lead and silver mines and endless olive groves.

In the city of Jaén drive up to the **Castillo de Santa Catalina,** perched on a rocky crag 5 km (3 mi) from the center. The origins of the castle may have been a tower erected by Hannibal, and the site was fortified continuously over the centuries. The Nasrid king, Alhamar, builder of Granada's Alhambra, constructed an alcázar, but King Ferdinand III captured it from him in 1246 on the feast day of Santa Catalina. Santa Catalina consequently became Jaén's patron saint, and when the Christians built a new castle and a chapel on this site, they dedicated them to her. The castle ruins make a dramatic setting for the parador that has been built in their midst.

The imposing hulk of Jaén **Cathedral** looms above the modest buildings around it. It was begun in 1500 on the site of a former mosque and not finished until the end of the 18th century. Its chief architect was the brilliant Andrés de Vandelvira (1509–75), many more of whose buildings can be seen in Ubeda and Baeza. The ornate facade was sculpted by Pedro Roldán, and if you look up at the figures on top of the columns, you can see San Fernando (King Ferdinand III) surrounded by the four evangelists. Inside the cathedral, the altarpiece of the Chapterhouse is by Pedro Machuca, who designed the Palace of Charles V in the Alhambra. In the Cathedral Museum (open weekends only, 11–1; admission: 100 pesetas), look for the *Immaculate Conception* by Alonso Cano, *San Lorenzo* by Martínez Montañés, and a Calvary scene by Jácobo Florentino. There are also some fine pieces of wrought iron by Maestro Bartolomé—you may recall his *reja* in Granada's Royal Chapel. *Plaza Santa María. Admission free. Open daily 8:30–1 and 4:30–7.*

You can explore the narrow alleyways of the old part of town as you walk from the cathedral to the **Baños Arabes** (Arab Baths), which once belonged to Ali, a Moorish king of Jaén, and probably date back to the 11th century. Four hundred years later, a viceroy of Peru chose to build himself a mansion, the Palacio de Villardompardo, right over them, and it has taken years of painstaking excavation to restore the baths to their original form. *Palacio de Villardompardo, Plaza Luisa de Marillac, tel. 953/22–33–92. Admission free. Open Tues.–Sat. 10–2 and 5–8, Sun. 10:30–2; closed Mon.*

Finally, the **Museo Provincial** is a delightful small museum housed in a 1547 mansion. In its patio stands the facade of the Church of San Miguel, another work of Andrés de Vandelvira. Roman mosaics, Greek vases, sculptures from the 5th century BC, and the *toro ibérico*, an Iberian bull found at Porcuna, halfway between Jaén and Córdoba, feature in its archaeological display. One of the highlights of the fine arts section is a room of Goya lithographs. *Paseo de la Estación 29, tel. 953/25–03–20. Admission free. Open Tues.–Fri. 10–2 and 4–7:30, weekends 10–2; closed Mon.*

❷⓿ Forty-eight km (30 mi) northeast of Jaén on the N321, the small town of **Baeza**, set among rolling hills and olive groves, dates back to the Romans, who called it Beatia, after Betis, their name for the Guadalquivir. The Visigoths lived here, too, and under the Moors Baeza became the head of a *taifa* (Moorish kingdom). Saint King Ferdinand captured it in 1227, and for the next two centuries, Baeza stood on the frontier with the Moorish kingdom of Granada. In the 16th and 17th centuries Baeza's noble families endowed the city with a wealth of splendid Renaissance palaces.

Begin in the central paseo, where the Plaza del Pópulo (or Plaza de los Leones) and Plaza del Mercado Viejo merge to form a delightful cobbled square. Here, you'll find the **Casa del Pópulo,** a beautiful Plateresque structure built around 1530, which now houses the Tourist Office. On its curved balcony the first Mass of the Reconquest is reputed to have been celebrated.

In the center of the square is an ancient Iberian-Roman statue, thought to be of Imilce, wife of Hannibal. The hapless figure is now headless, having been decapitated by an anticlerical crowd who apparently mistook her for the Virgin in the 1930s. At the foot of her column is the **Fuente de los Leones** (Fountain of the Lions).

Steps on the south side of the plaza lead you to the old **university,** which, when it opened in 1542, was one of 32 universities in Spain. It closed in 1824 and later became a high school where, from 1912 to 1919, the poet Antonio Machado *(Tierras de Castilla)* taught French.

The next building on the Cuesta de San Felipe is the golden-stoned **Palacio de Jabalquinto,** built by Juan Alonso Benavides, second cousin of Ferdinand of Aragón. Its facade is a true gem of late-15th-century Isabelline Gothic. The main portal is the work of sculptor Juan Guas.

Opposite the cathedral, at the end of Cuesta San Felipe, the **Seminary of San Felipe Neri** dates from 1660. The ancient student custom of inscribing names and graduation dates in bull's blood is still evident on the walls.

Baeza **Cathedral** was begun originally by Ferdinand III on the site of a former mosque, but it has undergone many transformations since his day. It was largely rebuilt by Vandelvira, architect of Jaén's cathedral, between 1570 and 1593, though if you go around to the west front, you'll see architectural traits of an earlier period. A fine 14th-century rose window crowns the 13th-century Puerta de la Luna (Door of the Moon). Inside, the beautifully painted wrought-iron choir screen is yet another example of the skill of local craftsman Maestro Bartolomé. Don't miss the decorative Baroque silver monstrance, which is carried in Baeza's Corpus Christi processions. It's kept in a concealed niche behind a painting, and if you want to see it in all its flamboyant splendor, you'll have to put a coin in a slot to reveal its hiding place and light it up—it's money well spent. In the cathedral's Gothic cloisters, you can see the remains of the original mosque. *Open daily 10:30–1 and 4–6.*

Wander around the Old Quarter between the cathedral and the Paseo de las Murallas to see noble old mansions with emblazoned facades. From the balcony of Paseo de las Murallas, there's a view over the wheat fields and olive groves.

The **Ayuntamiento** (City Hall) on Plaza Cardenal Benavides, just north of Plaza del Pópulo, features an ornate Plateresque facade, making it one of Baeza's most beautiful monuments. Its architect was Vandelvira. Look up at its facade between the balconies and you'll see the coats of arms of Felipe II, the city of Baeza, and the Magistrate Juan de Borja.

㉑ Nine km (6 mi) to the northeast on the N321, **Úbeda** stands in the heart of the olive groves of Jaén. Olive oil production is its main concern, and the modern town of 30,000 is fairly dull and uninteresting, but seek out the **Casco Antiguo** (Old Town), a superb example of a pure Renaissance town, and one of the most outstanding enclaves of 16th-century architecture in Spain. Follow the signs to the **Zona Monumental,** where you're bound to pass countless Renaissance palaces and stately mansions, each with its own distinctive features—an unusual balcony or a fine sculptured facade. Though many of Úbeda's churches are open to visitors, most of its palaces can be viewed from the outside only.

Begin at the **Hospital de Santiago,** on Avenida Cristo Rey, in the modern section, only a short walk from the bus depot and the main street, Ramón y Cajal. This huge quadrangular building, often jokingly known as the Escorial de Andalucía, is the masterpiece of Andrés de Vandelvira, who was responsible for most of Úbeda's monuments. It was begun in 1568 for Diego de los Cobos, bishop of Jaén, and completed in 1575. Its generally plain facade is decorated with ceramic medallions and a relief of St. James as a warrior on horseback over the main entrance. Inside are a fine arcaded patio and a grand staircase.

Head into the Old Town now, to the **Plaza del Ayuntamiento,** where in the northeast corner you'll pass the **Palacio de Vela de los Cobos,** built in the mid-16th century by Vandelvira for the magistrate of

Úbeda, Francisco de Vela de los Cobos. Its special feature is the corner balcony, with its central column of white marble, which you can see echoed in the gallery above.

Cross the square to the Ayuntamiento, housed in the **Palacio de las Cadenas** (House of Chains), so called because iron chains were once fixed to the columns of its main doorway. It was built by Vandelvira in 1562 for Vásquez de Molina, secretary to Felipe II. From here you can go around to **Plaza Vásquez de Molina,** the heart of the Old Town.

At the eastern end of the plaza is the **Sacra Capilla del Salvador,** the most elaborate and ornate of Úbeda's churches, which is photographed so often that it has become the city's unofficial symbol. It was built by Vandelvira, though he based his design on some 1536 plans by Diego de Siloé, architect of Granada cathedral. It was sacked in the frenzy of church burning at the outbreak of the civil war, but retains its ornate west front and a lavish altarpiece with a rare Berruguete sculpture. In the crypt you'll find the tomb of Francisco de los Cobos, secretary to Carlos V and chief benefactor of Úbeda.

Calle Horno Cantador leads you to the **Plaza del Mercado.** In the southwest corner is the **Ayuntamiento Antiguo** (Old City Hall), begun in the early 16th century but restored as a beautiful arcaded Baroque palace in 1680. From its upper balcony the Town Council watched celebrations and *autos da fe* ("acts of faith"—executions of heretics sentenced by the Inquisition) in the square below. On the north side is the 13th-century church of **San Pablo,** with its Isabelline south portal.

㉒ Some 48 km (35 mi) from Úbeda, C328 brings you to the remote, unspoiled Andalusian village of **Cazorla,** in the far east of Jaén province. The pine-clad slopes and towering peaks of the Sierras of Cazorla and Segura rise above the village, and below it stretch endless miles of olive groves. Steep streets of low white houses wind their way up mountainsides, and in spring, purple Judas trees blossom in picturesque squares.

Cazorla is the gateway to the **Parque Natural de Cazorla** (Cazorla Nature Park), an area of remote mountain scenery, 80 km (50 mi) long and 30 km (19 mi) wide, where deer, wild boar, and mountain goats roam the slopes and forests, and hawks, eagles, and vultures soar over 2,000-m (6,000-ft) peaks. This carefully protected wilderness is the source, at Cañada de las Fuentes, of Andalucía's great river, the Guadalquivir. The road through the park follows the course of the river to the shores of the **Tranco de Beas** lake. The park's alpine meadows, pine forests, springs, and waterfalls make it a perfect place for hiking.

㉓ At the Visitor Center at **Torre de Vinaigre** (tel. 953/72–01–02), a short film will introduce you to the park's main sights, and you can get information on camping, fishing, and hiking trails. There are also a small **hunting museum** and displays on the park's flowers, plants, trees, and geology. Nearby is a **botanical garden** and a **game reserve.** The park has four well-equipped campsites (open June–October).

Tour 3: Córdoba

㉔ On the right bank of the Guadalquivir stands one of Spain's oldest cities. **Córdoba** is a chilly, small, and lonely place—despite its popularity as a tourist destination—that hugs the banks of the graceful Guadalquivir River and contains some of the most interesting cul-

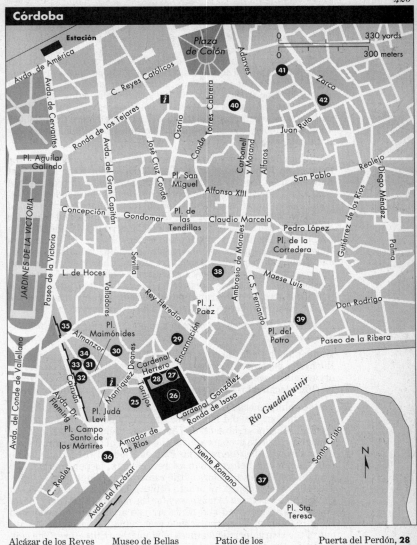

Córdoba

Estación

Plaza de Colón

Avda. de América

Avda. de Cervantes

C. Reyes Católicos

Adarves

Zarco

Juan Rufo

41

42

Ronda de los Tejares

Avda. del Gran Capitán

José Cruz Conde

Osario

Conde Torres Cabrera

40

Carbonell y Morand

Alfaros

San Pablo

Realejo

Diego Méndez

Pl. Aguilar Galindo

Concepción

Gondomar

Pl. San Miguel

Alfonso XIII

Pl. de las Tendillas

Claudio Marcelo

Pedro López

Gutiérrez de los Ríos

Palma

JARDINES DE LA VICTORIA

Paseo de la Victoria

L. de Hoces

Sevilla

Valladares

Rey Heredía

Pl. J. Paez

38

Ambrosio de Morales

C. S. Fernando

Pl. de la Corredera

Maese Luis

Don Rodrigo

35

Pl. Maimónides

Almanzor

30

34

33 31

32

Cardenal Herrero

28 27

29

Encarnación

39

Pl. del Potro

Paseo de la Ribera

Avda. del Conde de Vallellano

Carrión

Avda. Dr. Fleming

Manríquez Deanes

Torrijos

25

26

Cardenal González

Ronda de Isasa

Río Guadalquivir

Santo Cristo

N

Pl. Judá Levi

Pl. Campo Santo de los Mártires

36

Amador de los Ríos

C. Reales

Avda. del Alcázar

Puente Romano

37

Pl. Sta. Teresa

330 yards

300 meters

0 | 0

Alcázar de los Reyes Cristianos, **36**

Callejón de las Flores, **29**

Judería, **30**

Mezquita, **26**

Museo Arqueológico, **38**

Museo de Bellas Artes, **39**

Museo Taurino, **31**

Palacio de Congresos y Exposiciones, **25**

Palacio de los Marqueses de Viana, **42**

Patio de los Naranjos, **27**

Plaza de los Dolores, **40**

Plaza Santa Marina de las Aguas, **41**

Puerta de Almodóvar, **35**

Puerta del Perdón, **28**

Statue of Maimónides, **32**

Synagogue, **33**

Torre de la Calahorra, **37**

Zoco, **34**

tural monuments on the peninsula. The city was both the Roman and the Moorish capital of Spain, and its Old Quarter, clustered around its famous mosque (Mezquita), remains one of the best examples of Moorish heritage in Andalucía. From the 8th to the 11th century, the Moorish emirs and caliphs of the West held court here. During these 300 years, Córdoba's magnificence and opulence were legendary. Its population grew to around a million, making it the largest city in Europe (today, just 285,000 residents remain). Under the Moors it became one of the Western world's greatest centers of art, culture, and learning; one of its libraries boasted more than 400,000 volumes. Moors, Christians, and Jews lived together in harmony within its walls.

Córdoba remained in Moorish hands until it was conquered by the Saint King Ferdinand in 1236. The Catholic Monarchs held court here and used the city as a base from which to plan the conquest of Granada. Under the Catholic Monarchs, Gonzalo Fernández de Córdoba, better known as El Gran Capitán, reaped glory for himself and his native city by capturing the Kingdom of Naples and Sicily for Spain. It was in Córdoba that Queen Isabella granted Columbus the commission for his first voyage to the New World. In Columbus's time the Guadalquivir was navigable as far upstream as Córdoba, and great galleons sailed its waters. Today, the muddy water and unkempt banks of Andalucía's great river evoke little of the city's glorious past, but the impressive bridge of Roman origin—though much restored by the Arabs and successive generations—and the old Arab waterwheel are vestiges of a far grander era.

Numbers in the margin correspond to points of interest on the Córdoba map.

Wander along Calle Torrijos, on the west side of the mosque, where the heady perfume of orange blossom and music from an old barrel organ set the scene of this very Andalusian city. Drop into the Tourist Office located in the **Palacio de Congresos y Exposiciones.**

㉖ The **Mezquita** (mosque), built between the 8th and 10th centuries, is one of the earliest and most breathtakingly beautiful examples of Spanish Muslim architecture. The shabby crenellated walls of the outside do little to prepare you for the beauty of the interior. As you enter through the **Puerta de las Palmas** (Door of the Palms), some 850 columns rise before you in a forest of onyx, jasper, marble, and granite, reflecting all colors of the rainbow in oblique rays of light. The pillars are topped by ornate capitals taken from the Visigoth church that was razed to make way for the mosque. Crowning these, an endless array of red-and-white striped arches curves away into the dim interior. These horseshoe arches in alternating colors are one of the characteristic features of Moorish architecture. The ceiling is of carved and delicately tinted cedar.

The Mezquita has served as a Christian cathedral since 1236, but its origins as a mosque are only too clear. Built in four stages, by four emirs, it was founded in 785 by Abd ar-Rahman I (756–788) on a site he bought from the Visigoth Christians. He pulled down their church and replaced it with a mosque, one-third the size of the present one, into which he incorporated marble pillars from earlier Roman and Visigothic shrines—the white marble columns came from the Roman theater in Mérida. Under Abd ar-Rahman II (822–852) the Mezquita, which boasted possession of an original copy of the Koran and a bone from the arm of the prophet Mohammed, became a place of Muslim pilgrimage second only to Mecca.

Al Hakam II (961–976) built the beautiful **Mihrab,** the Mezquita's greatest jewel. Make your way over to the **Qiblah,** the south-facing wall in which this sacred prayer niche was hollowed out. (Muslim law decrees that the Mihrab face east, toward Mecca, as it is the point in the mosque toward which worshippers turn to pray. Here, in Córdoba, because of an error in calculation, the Mihrab faces more south than east. Al Hakam II spent hours agonizing over a means of correcting such a serious mistake but was persuaded by wise architects to let it be.) Before the Mihrab, you'll find the **Maksoureh,** a kind of anteroom reserved for the caliph and his court. Its delicate mosaic and plasterwork make it a masterpiece of Oriental art. The final stage of the mosque was completed around 987 by Al Mansur (976–1002), who more than doubled its size.

After the Reconquest, the Christians, for the most part, left the Mezquita undisturbed. They simply dedicated it to the Virgin Mary and set about using it as a place of Christian worship. The Christian clerics did erect a wall closing off the mosque from its courtyard, dimming the interior. In the 13th century Christians had the **Villaviciosa Chapel** built by Moorish craftsmen, its Mudéjar architecture blending harmoniously with the lines of the mosque. Not so the heavy, incongruous Baroque structure of the **cathedral** sanctioned in the very heart of the mosque by Charles V in the 1520s. To the emperor's credit—though it didn't stop him from tampering with the Alhambra (the Palacio Carlos V) and with Seville's Alcázar—it must be said that he later regretted this action and accused the clergy of having destroyed something unique to build something commonplace. *Torrijos and Cardenal Herrero, tel. 957/47–05–12. Admission: 600 pesetas. Open May–Sept., daily 10:30–1:30 and 4–7; Oct.–Apr., daily 10:30–1:30 and 3:30–5:30.*

Head out now into the **Patio de los Naranjos,** perfumed in springtime by orange blossoms. Cross to the **Puerta del Perdón** (Gate of Forgiveness) in the north wall, and climb the **campanario** (bell tower). A Baroque belfry now adorns the minaret from which the faithful were summoned to prayer. It's well worth climbing the uneven steps to the top for the view of the Guadalquivir and tiled rooftops of the old city. *Open same times as the mosque.*

A little farther along the mosque's north wall, on Cardenal Herrero, you'll find a niche where the **Virgen de los Faroles** (Virgin of the Lanterns) stands demurely behind a lantern-hung grille, rather like a lovely lady awaiting a serenade. The painting of the Virgin is by Julio Romero de Torres, an early 20th-century Cordoban artist. Velázquez Bosco, a narrow alleyway to your left, will bring you to the **Callejón de las Flores** (Alley of the Flowers), its houses decked with hanging flower baskets. You'd be hard put to find prettier patios than these, with their abundant foliage, ceramics, and wrought-iron grilles. Patios are very much the key to Córdoba's architecture, at least in the old town, where life is lived behind sturdy outer walls—a legacy of the Moors, who believed in the sanctity of the home just as much as they did in shutting out the fierce summer sun. In early May Córdoba celebrates its Patio Festival, when private patios are filled with flowers and opened to the public.

Return to Cardenal Herrero and make your way westward, through the labyrinth of narrow streets lined with ancient white houses and souvenir stores selling filigree silver and embossed leather, to the **Judería,** the old Jewish Quarter.

Here, on the Plaza Maimónides (or Plaza de las Bulas), you'll find the **Museo Taurino** (Museum of Bullfighting), housed in two adjoining

Cordoban mansions. Whatever your thoughts on bullfighting, this museum is worth visiting, as much for the chance to see inside a restored mansion as for the welldisplayed collection of posters, Art Nouveau paintings, and memorabilia of famous bullfighters who were native sons of Córdoba. *Plaza Maimónides, tel. 957/47–20–00, ext. 211. Admission: 200 pesetas. Open May–Sept., Tues.–Sat. 9:30–1:30 and 5–8; Oct.–Apr., Tues.–Sat. 9:30–1:30 and 4–7; closed Sun. and Mon.*

㉜ Next to the museum, in the Plaza Tiberiades, you'll pass a **statue of Maimónides,** the famous Jewish philosopher who was born nearby in the Judería in 1135. A few paces along Judíos, the main street of the
㉝ Jewish Quarter, lies the entrance to the only **synagogue** in Andalucía to survive the expulsion of the Jews in 1492 (though it is no longer in use as a place of worship). It is one of only three remaining ancient synagogues in Spain—the other two are in Toledo. The outside is plain, but inside you'll find some exquisite Mudéjar stucco tracery—look for the fine plant motifs and the Hebrew inscription stating that the synagogue was built in 1315. The women's gallery still stands, and in the east wall you can see the arch where the sacred scrolls of the law were kept. *Calle Judíos, tel. 957/29–81–33. Admission: 75 pesetas. Open Tues.–Sat. 10–2 and 3:30–5:30, Sun. 10–1:30; closed Mon.*

Across the way, through an arch, you enter an inner courtyard
㉞ called the **Zoco,** a former Arab souk, where now, on summer evenings, you can see flamenco performances, and stalls display local handicrafts for sale.

㉟ The **Puerta de Almodóvar** marks the western limit of the Judería. Outside this old Moorish gate is a **statue of Seneca,** the Cordoban-born philosopher who rose to prominence in Nero's court in Rome and who, on his emperor's command, committed suicide.

A walk south down Cairuán will bring you to the Plaza Campo Santo
㊱ de los Mártires and the entrance to the **Alcázar de los Reyes Cristianos,** a Mudéjar-style palace with splendid gardens. The original Moorish Alcázar stood beside the Mezquita on the site of the present Bishop's Palace. This one was built by Alfonso XI in 1328. In the 14th century the Catholic Monarchs often held court here, using it as a base from which to launch their conquest of Granada. Boabdil was imprisoned here for a time in 1483, and for nearly 300 years the Alcázar served as a base for the Inquisition. *Plaza Campo Santo de los Mártires. Admission: 250 pesetas (Tues. free). Open May–Sept., Tues.–Sat. 9:30–1:30 and 5–8, Sun. 9:30–1:30; Oct.–Apr., Tues.–Sat. 9:30–1:30 and 4–7, Sun. 9:30–1:30; closed Mon.*

From Plaza Campo Santo, three choices are possible: Hire a *coche caballo* (horse and buggy) for a tour of the city—but haggle over the price first (around 3,500 pesetas an hour is enough); wander back to the shops on Deanes and Cardenal Herrero by way of Manríquez and Plaza Judá Levi; or walk back along Amador de los Ríos to the bottom of Torrijos, turn down past the Puerta del Puente (Gate of the Bridge), and cross the **Puente Romano** (Roman Bridge), whose 16 arches span the Guadalquivir. From the bridge you'll get a good view of **La Albolafia,** the huge wheel used by the Arabs to carry water to the gardens of the Alcázar.

㊲ The **Torre de la Calahorra,** on the far side of the bridge, was built in 1369 to guard the entrance to Córdoba. It now houses the **Museo Histórico** (Córdoba City Museum), where multiscreen shows and audiovisual guides in English will help you learn more of Córdoba's history. The museum focuses on Cordoba's tricultural past. *Tel. 957/*

29–39–29. Admission: 350 pesetas. Open May–Sept., Mon.–Sat. 10–2 and 4:30–8:30, Sun. 10–2; Oct.–Apr., Mon.–Sat. 10–6, Sun. 10–2.

Next, visit the old town to the north and east of the mosque. Warning: It's best to avoid exploring this area in the deserted siesta hours; the narrow streets are a prime spot for muggers. A good **38** place to begin exploring is the **Museo Arqueológico** on the Plaza Jerónimo Paez, which houses finds from Córdoba's Iberian, Visigoth, Roman, and Muslim past, as well as later Mudéjar and Renaissance displays. *Plaza Jerónimo Paez, tel. 957/47–10–76. Admission: 250 pesetas. Open June 15–Sept. 15, Tues.–Sat. 10–2 and 6–8, Sun. 10–1:30; Sept. 16–June 14, Tues.–Sat. 10–2 and 5–7, Sun. 10–1:30; closed Mon.*

Now wind your way southeast to the **Plaza del Potro** (Colt Square) through the maze of narrow alleys. The plaza, named after the Fountain of the Colt in its center, was mentioned by Cervantes in *Don Quixote*. Cervantes himself reputedly stayed at the nearby inn, the beautifully restored **Posada del Potro**, now used for shows of local craftwork and painting.

39 In a courtyard off to your right is the **Museo de Bellas Artes** (Fine Arts Museum). Its deep pink facade belongs to a former Hospital de la Caridad (Charity Hospice) founded by Ferdinand and Isabella, who twice received Columbus here. Its art collection includes paintings by Murillo, Valdés Leal, Zurbarán, Goya, and Sorolla. *Off Plaza del Potro, tel. 957/47–33–45. Admission: 250 pesetas. Open June 15–Sept. 15, Tues.–Sat. 10–2 and 6–8, Sun. 10–1:30; Sept. 16–June 14, Tues.–Sat. 10–2 and 5–7, Sun. 10–1:30; closed Mon.*

Head north to the **Plaza de la Corredera** (some maps call it Plaza Constitución), an intriguing, if sadly dilapidated, arcaded square that dates from around 1690. A market is held here most mornings.

Time Out Head now for the Plaza de Las Tendillas, the central square of modern Córdoba. Here, the outdoor terraces of the **Café Boston** or **Café Siena** are good places to relax over a coffee and pastry.

On the north side of the Plaza, Calle Diego León will lead you to the small **Plaza San Miguel,** whose 13th-century Gothic-Mudéjar church dates back to the time of Córdoba's conquest by Saint King Ferdi- **40** nand. More twisting streets will eventually bring you to the **Plaza de los Dolores** (Square of Sorrows). This small square, surrounded by the 17th-century Convento de Capuchinos, is a secret place, one where you can sense most deeply the city's languid pace. In its center a statue of **Cristo de los Faroles** stands amid eight lanterns that hang from twisted wrought-iron brackets. If you can, come back here at night to see the lanterns shed their light on this moving Calvary scene. Around the corner you'll come upon the Plateresque facade of the **Casa de los Fernández de Córdoba,** home of El Gran Capitán.

41 At the **Plaza Santa Marina de las Aguas,** a statue of the legendary bullfighter Manolete stands on the edge of the Barrio de los Toreros, the quarter where many of Córdoba's famous bullfighters were born and lived. Not far away, on the **Plaza de la Lagunilla,** you'll find a bust of Manolete by Juan Avalos.

42 Our final stop is the 17th-century **Palacio de los Marqueses de Viana,** one of Córdoba's most splendid aristocratic palaces. It is known as the Museum of Patios for its 14 patios, each of them different. Inside are a carriage museum, a library, many embossed leather wall hangings, fine filigree silver, and grand galleries and staircases. The patios and gardens are planted with cypresses, orange trees, and myrtles. *Plaza Don Gomé, tel. 957/48-22-75. Admission: 200 pesetas. Open June-Sept., Thurs.-Tues. 9-2, closed Wed.; Oct.-May, Mon., Tues., and Thurs.-Sat. 10-1 and 4-6, Sun. 10-2, closed Wed.*

Numbers in the margin correspond to points of interest on the Andalucía: Granada to Córdoba map.

Excursion to Medina Azahara

43 Eight km (5 mi) to the west of Córdoba lie the ruins and partial reconstruction of a fabulous Muslim palace. Begun in 936, **Medina Azahara** was built by Abd ar-Rahman III for his favorite, az-Zahra ("The Flower"). According to contemporary chroniclers, it took 10,000 men, 2,600 mules, and 400 camels 25 years to erect this fantasy of 4,300 columns in dazzling pink, green, and white marble and jasper brought from Carthage. Here, on three terraces, stood a palace, a mosque, luxurious baths, fragrant gardens, fish ponds, and even an aviary and a zoo. In 1013 this Moorish paradise was sacked and destroyed by Berber mercenaries. In 1944 the Royal Apartments were rediscovered and there followed a careful reconstruction of the Throne Room. The outline of the mosque has also been excavated. *Off C431, follow signs on the way toward Almodóvar del Río, tel. 957/23-40-25. Admission: 250 pesetas. Open May-Sept., Tues.-Sat. 10-2 and 6-8:30, Sun. 10-2; Oct.-Apr., Tues.-Sat. 10-2 and 4-6:30, Sun. 10-2; closed Mon.*

44 If you're driving, continue to **Almodóvar del Río**, a further 18 km (11 mi) along C431, where just beyond the town a restored castle towers dramatically over the surrounding countryside.

What to See and Do with Children

In **Cazorla, La Iruela castle** is a dramatic ruin likely to inspire young imaginations. The **Cazorla Nature Park** has horseback riding and canoeing (*see* Sports, *below*).

In **Córdoba**, a ride in a coche caballo outside the Alcázar gardens can offer a peaceful interlude. The **bell tower** of the Mezquita challenges climbers, and the **zoo** in the Cruz Conde Park has a rare black lion called Chico.

In **Granada**, the Alhambra provides exciting climbs and views from the **Torre de la Vela** and spooky explorations in the underground cisterns of the **Patio de los Aljibes**. Splashing at an **aqua park** (Aquaola, 4 km/2½ mi from Granada in Cenes de la Vega on the road to the Sierra Nevada) will refresh parched sightseers. In winter, the Solynieve ski resort in Pradollano in the Sierra Nevada has a **children's ski school** (*see* Sports, *below*). A late **flamenco** evening (Jardines Neptuno) may be a new and memorable experience for children.

In **Jaén**, the **castle** is another time machine for young imaginations. In **Úbeda, potters** at work (Calle Valencia) may fascinate children.

Off the Beaten Track

In the southeastern corner of Córdoba province lies a cluster of villages and small towns unknown to most tourists. You'll need a car to explore them, and in places you'll find the roads bumpy and rather rough going.

Just inside the southern tip of Córdoba province, southeast of Lucena, C334 crosses the **Embalse de Iznájar** (reservoir of Iznájar) amid spectacular scenery. Midway between Lucena and the reservoir on the C334, in **Rute,** you can sample the potent *anís* liqueur for which this small white town is famous. In **Lucena** you can see the Torre del Moral, where Boabdil was imprisoned in 1483 after he launched an unsuccessful attack on the Christians. Today, the town makes furniture and brass and copper pots.

The jewel of this area is **Priego de Córdoba,** a town of 14,000 people lying at the foot of Mt. Tinosa (from Lucena, head north 9 km/6 mi on the C327 to Cabra, where you'll turn right, or east, on the C336; after 32 km/20 mi, you'll reach Priego). Wander down Calle del Río opposite the Ayuntamiento to see the fine mansions with which the silk merchants embellished their town in the 18th century. At the end of the street is the Fuente del Rey, with some 130 jets of water, built in 1803. Don't miss the lavish Baroque churches of La Asunción and La Aurora or the Barrio de la Villa, an old Moorish quarter.

Baena, surrounded by chalk fields producing top-quality olive oil, is an old town of narrow white streets, ancient mansions, and churches clustered beneath Moorish battlements. **Castro del Río** has an old Roman bridge; here in 1592 the unfortunate Cervantes was jailed in the City Hall. At **Espejo,** a majestic castle towers over the countryside. You're now in the Montilla-Morilés vineyards of the Cordoban campiña. Each autumn 47,000 acres' worth of Pedro Ximénez grapes are crushed here to produce the rich Montillas of the region, a fortified wine not unlike sherry. You can visit the bodegas.

Shopping

Córdoba Córdoba's typical handicrafts are fine embossed **leather** (a legacy of the Moors) and filigree **silver** (from the mines of the Sierra Morena) **jewelry. Artesanía Andaluza** (Tomás Conde 3), near the Museum of Bullfighting, sells a wide range of Córdoban handicrafts. The **Association of Córdoban Artisans** (Calle Judíos, opposite the synagogue) sells craft wares in the Zoco (many stalls open May–Sept. only). **Meryan** (Callejón de las Flores 2) and **Hijos de Rafael Bernier** (Encarnación 8) are leather workshops. The main shopping district is around Avenida Gran Capitán, Ronda de los Tejares, and Plaza de Colón.

Granada Granada's handicrafts are very much a legacy of the Moors and include **brass** and **copperware, ceramics, marquetry** (objects made of inlaid wood), and **woven goods.** The main shopping streets, centering on the Puerta Real, are Reyes Católicos, Zacatín, Ángel Ganivet, and the Gran Vía de Colón. Most of the antiques stores are on Cuesta de Elvira. In the villages of the Alpujarras you can find handwoven carpets, blankets, and tapestries and handmade basketware, leather goods, pottery, glass, ceramics, and mirrors.

Jaén Province Jaén province is well known for its **pottery** and **ceramics.** Wares woven from **esparto grass**—baskets, mats, and ornaments—are also a specialty.

Úbeda Calle Valencia is Úbeda's crafts center. **Antonio Almazara** (Valencia 34, tel. 953/75–12–00), **Juan Martínez** (Valencia 32, tel. 953/75–13–02), and **Paco Martínez** (Valencia 44, tel. 953/75–14–96) specialize in Úbeda's green-glazed pottery. **Millan,** also on Valencia, will make coats of arms on tiles to order. Other ceramics specialists are **Hermanos Alameda** (Carretera de Linares) and **Alfarería Góngora** (Merced 32, tel. 953/75–46–05). For esparto wares try **Ana Ubalde Plaza** (Calle Real, 47, tel. 953/75–04–56). **Garrido Plaza** (Jurado Gómez,

tel. 953/75–12–81) sells wrought-iron items. Finally, Úbeda has its
own brand of olive oil, Oro de la Loma; ask for Extra Virgin.

Sports

Cazorla **Cazorla Nature Park** is administered by the Agencia de Medio
Ambiente (AMA—the Environmental Agency of the Andalucían
Regional Government). For information on hiking, camping, canoeing, jeep excursions with park guides, or horseback-riding tours,
contact its offices at Cazorla village, Jaén, or the Park Visitor Center: AMA, Cazorla (Tejares Altos, Cazorla [Jaén], tel. 953/72–01–
25), AMA, Jaén (Av. de Andalucía 79, tel. 953/21–50–00), or AMA,
Sierra (Centro de Visitantes, Torre del Vinaigre, Parque Natural de
Cazorla [Jaén], tel. 953/72–01–02). For fishing and hunting permits,
apply well in advance to IARA (Jefatura de Jaén, Avenida de Madrid 25, Jaén, tel. 953/22–11–50).

Córdoba **Horseback riding:** The **Club Hípico** (Riding Club) is at Km 3 on the
Carretera de Trassierra.

Granada **Bicycling:** Bicycles can be rented from **Taller Manolo** (Manuel de
Falla 12, one block off Recogidas).

Horseback riding: In the Alpujarras, contact **Cabalgar** in Bubeon,
tel. 958/76–31–35, fax 958/76–32–36.

Skiing: The **Solynieve** ski resort, at Pradollano in the Sierra Nevada,
has 21 lifts, 29 runs, and around 50 km (31 mi) of marked trails. Contact the Sierra Nevada Information Center (Plaza de Pradollano,
Edificio Telecabina, Pradollano [Granada], tel. 958/24–91–00). You
can also call for snow, weather, and road conditions (tel. 958/48–01–
53). To reserve hotels or apartments around the area, call 958/24–
91–11.

Dining and Lodging

Dining

Córdoba's restaurants are a gourmet's paradise, whereas Granada's
are undistinguished. Córdoba's specialties are *salmorejo* (a thick,
very garlicky version of gazpacho) and *rabo de toro* (bull's tail or ox-
tail stew). Many of the city's restaurants are now coming up with
creative dishes based on old Arab recipes from Córdoba's Moorish
past. Here, *finos* or *Montillas*, from the province's Montilla-Morilés
district, make good aperitifs or bar drinks. Granada's typical dishes
are *tortilla al Sacromonte* (omelet made of calf's brains, sweet-
breads, diced ham, potatoes, and peas), *habas con jamón* (ham
stewed with broad beans), and *sopa sevillana* (tasty fish and seafood
soup made with mayonnaise). Trout are also good in the Riofrío-
Loja area.

Lunch, not dinner, is the main meal here. Restaurants start serving
lunch around 2 PM, but most tables don't fill up until at least 3. Most
people are still at the table at 5 or later. After such a long, late lunch,
few locals dine out in the evening. Instead, they do the rounds of the
bars (*see* Nightlife, *below*), dipping into tapas and plates of ham or
cheese. Ham from the Alpujarran village of Trevélez is famous
throughout Spain; ask for it in Granada.

Generally speaking, neat casual dress is acceptable in all restaurants in this region, unless we have specified otherwise. Shorts and

cut-off jeans are best avoided in all but inexpensive restaurants. In the restaurants listed in our two more expensive categories ($$$ and $$$$), jackets are advisable, but not essential, for men, and ties are rarely needed. Spanish diners are more casually dressed in summer than in winter. Reservations are rarely needed (except where specified) if you go for lunch around 2 PM; wait until 3 PM and you may have trouble finding a table. In the evening, if you dine early, say 9–10 PM, you shouldn't have problems.

Highly recommended restaurants are indicated by a star ★.

Category	Cost*
$$$$	over 12,000 ptas
$$$	8,500–12,000 ptas
$$	5,000–8,500 ptas
$	under 5,000 ptas

*per person for a three-course meal, including house wine and coffee, and excluding tax and service

Lodging

Córdoba has seen a recent spate of building and is now blessed with some very pleasant hotels set in typical old houses in the old town close to the mosque. It's rarely difficult to find accommodations in Córdoba if you haven't booked, though watch out for Holy Week and the May Patio Festival. Granada, on the other hand, can be very difficult—it contains the Alhambra, which is Spain's most-visited monument. Hotels on the Alhambra hill need to be booked long in advance; those in the city center around the Puerto Real and Acera del Darro are unbelievably noisy; ask for rooms at the back. Avoid chain hotels like the **Luz** and the **Meliá;** we've received complaints from readers on them. Granada has plenty of hotels, but the busy season runs from Easter until late October. Beware Holy Week, the International Festival of Music and Dance (mid-June–mid-July), and the weekend around October 12, when rooms are particularly hard to find.

Highly recommended hotels are indicated by a star ★.

Category	Cost*
$$$$	over 15,000 ptas
$$$	11,000–15,000 ptas
$$	8,000–11,000 ptas
$	under 8,000 ptas

*Prices are for a double room, excluding tax.

Baeza
Dining and Lodging

Juanito. Located on the edge of town on the way to Úbeda, this small, unpretentious hotel provides simple accommodations—the best you'll find in Baeza. Its rooms are clean and comfortable. Juanito's real drawing card is its well-known restaurant. The menu is based on fresh local produce cooked in top-quality olive oil; the chef has done much to revive the art of cooking regional specialties of Jaén province, such as *ensalada de perdiz* (partridge salad), and *cordero con habas* (lamb and broad beans). Desserts are based on old

Moorish recipes. *Paseo Arca de Agua, 23440, tel. 953/74–00–40, fax 953/74–23–24. 36 rooms, 1 suite. Facilities: restaurant (closed Sun. evening and Mon. evening, Nov. 1–15; $$). $*

Bubió
Lodging
★
Villa Turística del Poqueira. This recently built apartment-hotel offers individual whitewashed houses, each with its own sitting room, kitchen, bathroom, and bedrooms that sleep two, four, or six people. The traditional architectural style of the Poqueira ravine is carried through in curtains and headboards and in open fireplaces and woven rugs. The hotel nestles beneath the Veleta and overlooks Bubión village and splendid mountain scenery. *Barrio Alto, 18412, tel. 958/ 76–31–11, fax 958/76–31–36. 43 rooms. Facilities: restaurant, bar, TV room. AE, DC, MC, V. $$*

Cazorla
Lodging
Parador El Adelantado. This modern, whitewashed parador with a red-tile roof stands isolated on a pine-covered mountain slope on the edge of Cazorla Nature Park, 26 km (16 mi) above Cazorla village. Popular with hunters and fishermen, it is perfect for anyone seeking tranquillity and splendid scenery. The restaurant specializes in regional cooking, such as *ajo blanco* (almond soup with garlic), fresh trout from the nearby lakes, and game dishes in season. *23470, tel. 953/72–10–75. 33 rooms. Facilities: restaurant, pool, garden. AE, DC, MC, V. $$*

Sierra de Cazorla II. A low, white two-story hotel nestles in a bend of the road leading up into the mountains 2 km (1¼ mi) above Cazorla village at La Iruela. Rooms in the modern section, opened in 1987, are functional but comfortable. *Carretera Sierra de Cazorla, Km 2, 23476, La Iruela (Jaén), tel. 953/72–00–15, fax 953/72–00–17. 58 rooms. Facilities: restaurant, pool. AE, DC, MC, V. $*

Córdoba
Dining
El Blasón. Owned by El Caballo Rojo (*see below*), this restaurant opened in 1987 and has fast gained a name for fine food and unbeatable ambience. It's tucked away in an old inn one block west of Avenida Gran Capitán. A Moorish-style entrance bar leads onto a patio enclosed by a glass roof and ivy-covered walls. Upstairs are two elegant dining rooms. Blue walls, aquamarine silk curtains, candelabras, and scrolled mirrors create the atmosphere of early 19th-century luxury. The innovative menu includes *salmón con naranjas de la mezquita* (salmon in oranges from the mosque) and *musclo de oca al vino afrutado* (leg of goose in fruited wine). And for dessert there are delicious pastries from the cart. *José Zorrilla 11, tel. 957/ 48–06–25. Reservations advised. Jacket advised Nov.–Mar. AE, DC, MC, V. $$$*

★
El Caballo Rojo. The Red Horse, on the north side of the mosque, is Córdoba's best restaurant, winner of the National Gastronomy Prize. The decor resembles a cool, leafy Andalusian patio, and the menu features traditional specialties such as rabo de toro and salmorejo, as well as exotic creations inspired by Córdoba's Moorish and Jewish heritage. *Cardenal Herrero 28, tel. 957/47–53–75. Reservations advised. Jacket advised Nov.–Mar. AE, DC, MC, V. $$$*

La Almudaina. This attractive restaurant is located in a 15th-century house across the square from the Alcázar gardens, at the entrance to the Judería. There's an Andalusian patio and a mesón bodega in the cellar. The menu concentrates on fresh market produce and local recipes. You might try *pudding de calabacines* (pumpkin mousse), or *lubina al hinojo* (sea bass in fennel). For dessert, there's *espuma de higos a la crema de fresas* (figs in strawberry cream sauce). *Campo Santo de los Mártires 1, tel. 957/47–43–42. AE, DC, MC, V. Closed Sun. evening. $$*

El Cardenal. Opposite the bell tower of the mosque, this restaurant, in the heart of Córdoba's tourist center, offers a stylish setting for lunch or dinner. Flamenco shows are performed downstairs in the evening, and a carpeted marble staircase leads to a spacious dining room upstairs decorated with paintings, plants, and ceramic plates. Good Spanish food and professional service complement the cool, agreeable atmosphere. *Cardenal Herrero 14, tel. 957/48–03–46. AE, DC, MC, V. Closed Sun. evening, Mon. in winter. $$*

★ **El Churrasco.** A long-standing Córdoba institution that ranks second only to El Caballo Rojo, El Churrasco is located in the heart of the Judería, just two minutes' walk from the mosque. Its colorful mesón entrance bar is an ideal place for prelunch tapas. There's a wine museum and bodega specializing in the restaurant's own Montilla-Morilés wine, and a pictureseque patio beneath a glass roof in winter, open in summer. It is known for its succulent grilled meats, such as *churrasco* (pork in pepper sauce), and an excellent salmorejo. *Romero 16, tel. 957/29–08–17. AE, DC, MC, V. Closed Aug. $$*

Federación de Peñas Cordobesa. You'll find this popular budget restaurant on one of the main thoroughfares of the old town halfway between the mosque and the Plaza Tendillas. You can eat at one of several outdoor tables around the fountain in the spacious courtyard surrounded by horseshoe arches or inside in a pretty restaurant with dark green cloths and white linen. The food is traditional Spanish fare. *Conde y Luque 8, tel. 957/47–66–98. MC, V. Closed Wed. $*

Mesón El Burladero. This one's located off a small patio at the end of an alley off Deanes, near the back entrance to El Caballo Rojo. There are a few tables outside on the patio, and indoors the decor is that of a typical mesón, with bullfight posters and red, white, and coffee-colored cloths. An eclectic array adorns the whitewashed walls: stags' heads, stuffed birds, and a boar's head, among other things. The *menú Manolete* offers *revuelto de la casa* (scrambled eggs) and *solomillo de cerdo* (pork steak), with bread, wine, and dessert included. *Calleja la Hoguera 5, off Deanes, tel. 957/47–27–19. AE, DC, MC, V. $*

Lodging **Conquistador.** On the east side of the mosque, this contemporary hotel is built in Andalusian Moorish style, making good use of ceramic tiles and inlaid marquetry in the bar and public rooms. The reception area overlooks a colonnaded patio, fountain, and small enclosed garden. The rooms are comfortably and elegantly furnished. Those at the front have small balconies overlooking the walls of the mosque, floodlit at night. *Magistral González Francés 17, 14003, tel. 957/48–11–02 or 957/48–14–11, fax 957/47–50–79. 100 rooms, 3 suites. Facilities: bar, garage, sauna. AE, DC, MC, V. $$$$*

Parador La Arruzafa. Five km (3 mi) north of town, this modern parador is set in a peaceful, leafy garden on the slopes of the Sierra de Córdoba. Rooms are traditional parador-style, with somber dark wood fittings, and many have balconies overlooking the garden or with good views toward Córdoba. Rates are determined by the view. *Av. de la Arruzafa, 14012, tel. 957/27–59–00, fax 957/28–04–09. 94 rooms. Facilities: outdoor pool, tennis courts. AE, DC, MC, V. $$$*

El Califa. This recently renovated modern hotel in the old town is convenient to both the mosque and the shopping area around Plaza Tendillas. The rooms are fairly spacious, with tile floors and matching russet brown, beige, or gold headboards, curtains, and chairs. The patio has red and white flagstones and Moorish-style arches. In summer snacks are served outdoors among the potted palms and geraniums. *Lope de Hoces 14, 14003, tel. 957/29–94–00. 66 rooms. Facilities: cafeteria, bar, garage. AE, MC, V. $$–$$$*

Albucasis. Tucked away in the heart of the old town is a friendly family-run hotel, opened in 1989. Its air-conditioned rooms are spotlessly clean, with marble-tile floors, white and green decor, and green-tile bathrooms. Doubles overlook the pretty ivy-covered patio and have a limited view of the mosque tower. Breakfast and drinks are served in the attractive reception-bar area. *Buen Pastor 11, 14003, tel. 957/47–86–25. 15 rooms. Facilities: bar. MC, V. $$*

González. The hotel opened in 1989 in a restored 16th-century palace in the heart of the Judería, near the mosque. The entrance hall, with a white marble floor, a massive 18th-century brass lamp, and huge gold scrolled mirrors, opens off the Plaza Judá Levi. The rooms are simply but comfortably furnished: tile floors, white walls, twin beds, and air-conditioning. The quietest rooms have black wrought-iron balconies heaped with flowerpots and overlook the fountain in the central patio. Some readers have noted security problems; think twice about leaving valuables in the hotel safe. *Manríquez 3, 14003, tel. 957/47–98–19. 17 rooms. Facilities: restaurant (open Mar.–Oct. 15), bar. MC, V. $$*

Marisa. The Marisa's facade is an old Andalusian house that overlooks the north side of the mosque and the Patio de los Naranjos. Inside, the hotel has been modernized, and the rooms are simple and sparsely furnished. Those on the front face the mosque walls, magnificent when floodlit. If you dislike noise and bright lights in the small hours, ask for an inside room. Breakfast and drinks are served in the bar area. The staff is friendly and helpful. *Cardenal Herrero 6, 14003, tel. 957/47–31–42. 28 rooms. Facilities: parking. AE, DC, MC, V. $–$$*

Durcal
Dining and Lodging
★

El Molino. The setting is an 18th-century mill house on a wooded hillside. Besides a restaurant, you'll find a gastronomy museum with a working mill and old cooking implements, a wine museum-cum-bodega, a center for research into the ancient cuisine of Andalucía, and a cooking and restaurant-management school. The center, partly sponsored by the Andalusian Regional Government and the European Union, is staffed by 60 students. Its owner-director, Manuel Carrillo, runs regular open cooking courses on such themes as Sephardic Jewish cuisine, tapa cookery, and Moorish breads and pastries. Instruction is available in English by arrangement. The elegant but rustic dining room overlooks leafy hillsides and an aromatic herb garden. The seasonal menu makes good use of local almonds and olive oil and offers only ancient Andalusian, Jewish, and Moorish dishes. Your best bet is to try the *menú degustación*—seven dainty courses that won't leave you feeling overfed and sleepy. Hors d'oeuvres may include *remojón* (a salad of oranges and codfish); a main course might be *pastel de pichón* (a flaky pigeon pie dusted with cinnamon). Desserts are of Arab origin: you might try the figs in caramel-almond sauce. Country breads and Moorish pastries are baked in a traditional Arab wood-burning oven. For details and enrollment in cookery courses, write to the Center for Andalusian Culinary Research at the address below. *Camino de las Fuentes, Paraje de la Isla, 18650 Durcal (Granada), tel. 958/78–02–47. Reservations advised. AE, DC, MC, V. Closed Mon. $$$*

Granada
Dining
★

Baroca. Locals consider this restaurant, located one block above the Camino de Ronda, Granada's best. The menu favors international cuisine; desserts are especially good. Service is professional and the ambience agreeable. *Pedro Antonio de Alarcón 34, tel. 958/26–50–61. Reservations advised. AE, DC, MC, V. Closed Sun. and Aug. $$$*

Carmen de San Miguel. Superbly set on the Alhambra hill in a villa with a glass-enclosed dining room, an Andalusian patio and fountain, and a terrace, this restaurant offers magnificent views over Granada. The food is a little less spectacular. Entrées may include *paletilla de cordero con piñones* (shoulder of lamb with pine nuts). *Paseo Torres Bermejas 3, tel. 958/22–67–23. Reservations advised June–Aug. AE, DC, MC, V. Closed Sun. evening. $$$*

Cunini. Just below the cathedral, Cunini is Granada's best fish restaurant. Fresh seafood is heaped on the long tapas bar, and the menu offers fish dishes from all over Spain, including some Basque specialties. Both the fried (*pescaditos fritos*) and the grilled (*parrillada*) fish are good choices, or you may prefer *zarzuela* (fish stew). *Pescadería 9 or Capuchinas 14, tel. 958/25–07–77. AE, DC, MC, V. Closed Mon. $$$*

★ **Ruta del Veleta.** Just over 5 km (3 mi) out in Cenes de la Vega, this typically decorated restaurant offers some of Granada's best cuisine. Its specialties are *carnes a la brasa* (succulent grilled meats), and fish dishes from Cantabria and the Levante cooked in rock salt. Dessert might be *puding de manzanas en salsa de moras* (apple pudding in blackberry sauce). *Carretera Sierra Nevada, Km 5.4, tel. 958/48–61–34. AE, DC, MC, V. Closed Sun. evening. $$$*

Alacena de las Monjas. In the heart of town, by the Casa de los Tiros, this restaurant, whose name means "Nuns' Closet," specializes in the regional dishes and wines of Granada province. The menu is short and based on what's available in the market. In winter it features wholesome meaty stews; *chuletas de cordero* (lamb chops) are another favorite, or you might try *lomos de salmón en salsa de naranja y estragón* (salmon in orange and tarragon sauce). *Plaza Padre Suárez, tel. 958/22–40–28. AE, V. Closed Sun. and Mon. $$*

★ **Sevilla.** García Lorca and Manuel de Falla used to dine in this colorful restaurant, which has been going strong since 1930 and got a facelift in 1993. There's a superb tapas bar and four picturesque dining rooms, or you can eat on the outdoor terrace overlooking the Royal Chapel. The menu features such Granadino favorites as *sopa sevillana* (white soup made with mayonnaise, white fish, clams, eggs, and peas) and *tortilla Sacromonte* (omelet with kid's brains, ham, and vegetables). *Oficios 12, tel. 958/22–12–23. Reservations advised. AE, DC, MC, V. Closed Sun. $$*

Los Manueles. The food frankly isn't that special, but the decor, atmosphere, and friendly old-fashioned waiters at this traditional inn off Reyes Católicos make it popular with Granadinos and visitors alike. Alpujarran rugs, copper plates, and other knickknacks cover the walls, and gigantic hams adorn the bar; this ancient mesón is usually packed and fun. *Zaragoza 2, tel. 958/22–34–13. AE, DC, MC, V. $*

Lodging **Alhambra Palace.** This flamboyant ocher-red Moorish palace was
★ built in 1910 and commands a superb position, in leafy grounds on the back of the Alhambra hill. The interior is exotic and Oriental, with green-and-blue tile walls, ornate wooden ceilings, gleaming brass lamps, and Moorish arches and pillars. Even the bar is incongruously decorated as a mosque. The rooms overlooking the town have the most magnificent views; so, too, does the terrace, a perfect place to watch the sun set on the Sierra Nevada. *Peña Partida 2, 18009, tel. 958/22–14–68, fax 958/22–64–04. 123 rooms, 9 suites. Facilities: restaurant, 2 bars, garden, barbecue. AE, DC, MC, V. $$$$*

Parador de San Francisco. Magnificently located within the Alhambra precincts, Spain's most popular parador stands in an old Franciscan convent built by the Catholic Monarchs after their capture of Granada. The rooms in the old section are furnished with antiques, woven curtains, and bedspreads; those in the new wing are simpler and less expensive. The public rooms are decorated with antiques and local handicrafts. *Alhambra, 18009, tel. 958/22–14–43, fax 958/ 22–22–64. 38 rooms. Facilities: restaurant, bar. AE, DC, MC, V. Reservations required, 4–6 months in advance. $$$$*

Triunfo. Opened in 1988, this comfortable hotel is at the far end of Gran Vía de Colón. The public rooms have gleaming marble floors, deep antique-style sofas and armchairs, and a generous number of paintings on the walls. The rooms are furnished in traditional style, with dark wood fittings and apricot curtains and bedspreads. *Plaza Triunfo 19, 18010, tel. 958/20–74–44, fax 958/27–90–17. 37 rooms. Facilities: restaurant, cafeteria, piano bar, garage. AE, DC, MC, V. $$$*

América. This simple but charming hotel, located within the Alhambra precincts, is very popular; you should book months ahead. It feels like a private home, with simple bedrooms, a sitting room decorated with local handicrafts, and a shady patio where home-cooked meals are served in the summer months. *Real de la Alhambra 53, 18009, tel. 958/22–74–71. 14 rooms. Facilities: restaurant. No credit cards. Closed Nov.–Feb. $$*

★ **Victoria.** An absolute gem of an Old World hotel, it overlooks the bustling Puerta Real—from which the noise may be a disadvantage. The tone is set by an impressive entrance lobby with a glittering chandelier and coral-colored marble decor. Upstairs, hallways with half-tiled walls lead to fully carpeted bedrooms furnished with old-fashioned headboards, dark polished furniture, and individual color schemes of dark green, burnt orange, or deep pink. *Puerta Real 3, 18005, tel. 958/25–77–00. 66 rooms, 3 suites. Facilities: 2 restaurants, 2 bars. AE, DC, MC, V. $$*

Reina Cristina. Located in an old house near the lively Plaza Triunfo in the heart of the city, this hotel has been thoroughly modernized inside. Plants trail from the windowsills of the patio-reception area, where a small marble fountain splashes beneath a Moorish lamp. A marble stairway leads to the bedrooms, which are simply but cheerfully furnished with red curtains and red-and-white checked bedspreads. *Tablas 4, 18002, tel. 958/25–32–11, fax 958/25–57–28. 43 rooms. Facilities: restaurant, bar-cafeteria, parking. AE, DC, MC, V. $–$$*

Britz. In a clean, pleasant building, the hotel is conveniently located at the base of the Alhambra hill and close to downtown attractions. Rooms are small but comfortable, with modern characterless decor. *Plaza Nueva y Gomerez 1, 18009, tel. 958/22–36–52. 22 rooms. MC, V. $*

Inglaterra. Set in a period house just two blocks above the Gran Vía de Colón in the heart of town, this is a hotel that will appeal to those who prefer Old World charm to creature comforts, though the accommodations are perfectly adequate for the reasonable rates. *Cetti Meriem 6, tel. 958/22–15–59, fax 958/22–15–86. 36 rooms. AE, DC, MC, V. $*

Montecarlo. This friendly, old-fashioned hotel overlooks the Fuente de las Batallas in the city center. The entrance lobby and stairways have some nice old touches—ornate tables, mirrors, and Moorish lamps. Most rooms have been refurbished, but avoid front rooms, which are horrendously noisy. *Acera del Darro 44, 18005, tel. 958/ 25–79–00, fax 958/25–64–62. 73 rooms. Facilities: cafeteria, bar. AE, MC, V. $*

Jaén
Dining

Mesón Vicente. Hidden away on a narrow pedestrian street near the cathedral square, this popular restaurant is usually packed with locals. Enter through a colorful mesón-bar, where you can have prelunch drinks and tapas, then move on to a cozy dining room with wood paneling and tile decorations. Traditional Jaén dishes, such as game casseroles, are especially good. *Arco del Maestra 8, no phone. AE, MC, V. Closed Sun. $$*

Dining and Lodging
★
Parador de Santa Catalina. Built on a rocky crag amid the towers of a medieval Moorish castle, Jaén's parador is one of the showpieces of the parador chain, and one of the main reasons for visiting Jaén. Lofty ceilings, tapestry-hung walls, baronial shields, and suits of armor add to the medieval-castle atmosphere. The comfortable bedrooms with canopied beds all have balconies overlooking the mountains. Reserve ahead in the summer. *Castillo de Santa Catalina, 23001, tel. 953/23–00–00, fax 953/23–09–30. 45 rooms. Facilities: restaurant, pool. AE, DC, MC, V. $$$*

Loja
Dining and Lodging
★
La Bobadilla. Opened in 1986 in the heart of the Andalusian countryside, halfway between Granada and Málaga, this luxurious hotel is the brainchild of German businessman Rudolph Staab. The complex, with its white walls, tile roofs, patios, fountains, and artificial lake, resembles a Moorish village or a rambling Andalusian *cortijo* (ranch). The buildings cluster around a 16th-century-style chapel whose 1,595-pipe organ is used for weekend concerts. Each bedroom is individually designed and decorated, with its own terrace, patio, or garden. The elegant haute-cuisine restaurant, La Finca, features fresh organically grown produce from the hotel garden and meat reared on the hotel farm. The two *menús de degustación* (tasting menus) offer up to seven light courses that enable you to sample a little of everything. *Finca La Bobadilla, north of the Granada–Seville highway between Salinas and Rute, 18300, tel. 958/32–18–61, fax 958/32–18–10. Restaurant: reservations advised. 60 rooms. Facilities: 2 restaurants, pools, gymnasium, Jacuzzi, 4 saunas, tennis courts, horseback riding, hunting, clay-pigeon shooting, convention facilities. AE, DC, MC, V. $$$$*

Úbeda
Dining and Lodging
★
Parador Condestable Dávalos. Really the *only* place to stay or dine in Úbeda is at this splendid parador, located in a 16th-century ducal palace. Recently refurbished, the palace retains its original wooden beams and old fireplaces. A grand stairway leads up to the bedrooms, which have tile floors, lofty wood ceilings, antique furnishings, and deliciously big baths. In the dining room the condestable's portrait hangs above the fireplace, the menu features regional dishes, and the waitresses wear local costumes. You might try one of the *perdiz* (partridge) specialties. Desserts have intriguing names like *suspiros de monja* (nun's sighs). *Plaza Vázquez de Molina 1, 23400, tel. 953/75–03–45, fax 953/75–12–59. 31 rooms. Reservations advised in summer. AE, DC, MC, V. Hotel: $$$; restaurant: $$$*

La Paz. This modern, homey hostel offers simply furnished rooms, all with private bathroom and telephone. Breakfast is served, but not dinner. *Andalucía 1, 23400, tel. 953/75–08–48 or 953/75–21–40. 53 rooms. DC, MC, V. $*

The Arts and Nightlife

The Arts

Córdoba
Fiestas
Carnival celebrations before Lent; **Holy Week** processions at Easter; **Las Cruces de Mayo, Fiesta de los Patios,** and **Feria de Nuestra Señora de la Salud** in May; and **Nuestra Señora de Fuensanta** in September.

Music and Flamenco
Córdoba City **Orchestra concerts** are given in the Alcázar garden, Sundays in summer; **flamenco performances** take place in the Zoco, off Calle Judíos, summer evenings or at flamenco clubs like **Mesón la Bulería** (Pedro López 3, tel. 957/48–38–39). The most reliable way to

see flamenco is to attend a performance at **El Cardenal** restaurant (*see* Dining and Lodging, *above*).

Granada The **Granada International Theater Festival,** organized by the Gra-
Festivals nada Ayuntamiento (City Hall, tel. 958/27–40–00), is held for 10 days annually in May. The **Granada International Festival of Music and Dance** is held annually from mid-June to mid-July; tickets and information are available at Paseo de los Martires 64, tel. 958/22–96–81. For information about the **November Jazz Festival,** contact Granada City Hall or the tourist office.

Fiestas Celebration of **Granada's 1492 surrender** to the Catholic Monarchs, January 2; **Día de los Reyes,** procession of the three Wise Men, January 6; **pilgrimage to the Monastery of San Cecilio** on Sacromonte, February 1; **Carnival,** February 28; **Holy Week,** Apr. 9–15; **Day of the Cross,** May 3; **San Isidro,** May 15; **Mariana Pineda,** May 26; **Corpus Christi,** June 15; **San Pedro,** June 29; **Nuestra Señora de las Angustias,** last Sunday in September; **Romería de San Miguel,** September 29. Check with local tourist offices for details of fiestas in the Alpujarras.

Flamenco The show at **Jardines Neptuno** (Calle Neptuno, tel. 958/52–25–33 or 958/25–11–12), though tourist oriented, can be colorful and often includes a mixture of ballet and folk music. There's a similar nightly show in a somewhat smaller venue at **Reina Mora** (Mirador de San Cristobal, tel. 958/27–82–28). Tickets are available from many hotels. Flamenco is performed at **El Corral del Príncipe** (Campo del Príncipe, tel. 958/22–80–88). Never go before 11 PM; the best time is around 1 AM. For *zambra* (singing and dancing) performances by Gypsies in the Sacromonte caves, join one of the tours organized for tourists through a travel agent or your hotel. If you want to go on your own (call ahead for times of performances and be prepared to part with lots of money), these are some of the caves: **Cueva la Zíngara** (Camino del Sacromonte 71, tel. 958/28–00–28), **Cueva los Tarantos** (Camino del Sacromonte 9, tel. 958/22–24–92), **Cueva El Rocío** (tel. 958/22–71–29), and **Zambra María la Canastera** (tel. 958/12–11–83).

Nightlife

Córdoba Most sidewalk cafés are on or near the Plaza Tendillas. For atmos-
Bars and Cafés phere and color, hunt out the old Andalusian bodegas and mesónes tucked away in the narrow streets of the old town, such as **Bodegas Campos** (in an alleyway just off Plaza del Potro), **Casa Rubio** (Puerta de Almodóvar 5), Casa Salinas (Puerta de Almodóvar 2), **Mesón de la Luna** (Calleja de la Luna), **Los Pilares** (Ángel Saavedra 2), **Sociedad de Plateros** (Plaza de Seneca 4), **Taberna de Pepe** (Romero 1), and **Taberna San Miguel** (Plaza San Miguel).

Granada For the most colorful bars, look around the Albaicín, Campo del
Tapas Bars Príncipe, Plaza del Carmen–Calle Navas, and Pedro de Alarcón–Martínez de la Rosa. Among them are **Aben Humeya** (Carril de las Tomasas 12, Albaicín), **Bar El Ladrillo** (Plaza de Fatima, Albaicín), **Bar La Trastienda** (Plaza Cuchilleros 11), **Bodegas Castañeda** (Elvira 6), **Casa Enrique** (Acera del Darro 8, on Puerta Real), **Casa Yanguas** (San Buenaventura, off Plaza Aliatar, Albaicín), **Chikito** (Plaza del Campillo 9), and **La Puerta del Vino** (Paseo Padre Manjón 5).

14 Western Andalucía

Seville and the Guadalquivir Delta

By Hilary
Bunce

Updated
by Mark
Potok

Through a triangle formed by the cities of Huelva, Seville, and Cádiz flows the estuary of Andalucía's great river, the Guadalquivir. This flat landscape of fertile pastures, muddy marshlands, chalky vineyards, and sandy beaches contrasts vividly with the mountainous provinces of eastern Andalucía. Here, the banks of the Guadalquivir are lined with fields of cotton and rice, orange groves, stud farms, and bull ranches.

This is a land with a proud seafaring history. The career of Christopher Columbus can be traced here, from the monastery at La Rábida, whose friars pleaded his cause with Queen Isabella, to Palos, where he set sail on his epic voyage of 1492; to Cádiz and Sanlúcar, departure points of his second and third voyages; and to Seville. Its shores and rivers echo with the names of other maritime adventurers: Ferdinand Magellan, Juan Sebastián de Elcano, Sir Francis Drake, and Pierre de Villeneuve, to name just a few. For more than two centuries Spain's trade with the New World centered on Seville. Treasures from the Americas flowed into her coffers. Later, when this maritime and trading role passed to Cádiz, its lucrativeness funded the notable buildings of that city.

Many towns of this region are called "de la frontera," such as Arcos, Jerez, or Palos, because for 250 years they stood on the battlefront between Christian Spain and Infidel Granada.

Flamenco, wildlife, horses, and sherry are some of the region's keynotes. Seville and Jerez are widely acknowledged as the home of flamenco, and Jerez now has an institute dedicated to the history and performance of this very Andalusian art form. The Doñana National Park, on the estuary of the Guadalquivir, is one of Europe's most valuable nature reserves, sheltering rare birds and endangered wildlife. Here, you may just sight a lynx or an imperial eagle. In Jerez, you can see highly trained horses at the Royal School of Equestrian Art.

This western corner of Andalucía is well known in Spain as a gourmet's paradise. Many Spaniards drive for miles to sample the giant shrimp and succulent seafood of Puerto de Santa María or Sanlúcar and to enjoy the finos and manzanillas from the vineyards of Jerez. Others come to enjoy the tapas of Seville, legendary across the land.

Finally, the fame of the region's fiestas has spread far beyond the borders of Spain. Cádiz's carnival is the best in the land. Visitors come from far and wide, from within Spain and beyond, to witness the pageant of Seville's Holy Week processions and to join in the fun of its April Fair. On top of the charms that have drawn visitors for centuries, the city offers the panoply of new attractions that are the legacy of the International Exposition it hosted in 1992. Crowds flock to the revelries of Jerez's May Horse Fair and September Vintage Festival. The Whitsuntide pilgrimage to the shrine of the Virgen del Rocío, through the marshlands of the Doñana National Park, has reached television screens around the world.

Essential Information

Important Addresses and Numbers

Tourist
Information
Local tourist offices in major towns covered in this chapter are **Arcos de la Frontera** (Cuesta de Belén, tel. 956/70–22–64), **Cádiz** (Calderón de la Barca 1, tel. 956/21–13–13), **Jerez de la Frontera** (Alameda Cristina 7, tel. 956/33–11–50), **Puerto de Santa María** (Guadalete 1,

tel. 956/54–24–75), **Sanlúcar de Barrameda** (Calzada del Ejército, tel. 956/36–61–10), and **Seville** (Av. de la Constitución 21B, tel. 95/422–1404 or 95/421–8157, fax 95/422–9753; and the less useful offices at Costurero de la Reina, Paseo de las Delicias 9, tel. 95/423–4465; and at the airport, tel. 95/425–5046).

Consulates   **Canada** (Av. Constitución 30-2°-4, Seville, tel. 95/422–9413). **United Kingdom** (Plaza Nueva 8, Seville, tel. 95/422–8875 or 95/422–8874). **United States** (Paseo de las Delicias 7, Seville, tel. 92/423–1833/84/85).

Travel Agency   **American Express** (Viajes Alhambra, Teniente Coronel Seguí 6, Seville, tel. 95/421–2923 or 95/421–8321).

Emergencies   Tel. 091. **Police:** *Cádiz* (Av. de Andalucía 28, tel. 956/28–61–11), *Jerez de la Frontera* (Plaza de Silos, tel. 091), *Seville* (Plaza de la Concordia 1, tel. 95/422–8840). **Ambulance:** *Seville* (tel. 061).

Crime

WARNING: With chronic high unemployment, Seville has developed a bad reputation for petty crime such as purse snatching and thefts from parked cars, even the occasional robbery. Drive with your car doors locked, lock all your luggage out of sight in the trunk, never leave *anything* in a parked car, and keep a wary eye on scooter riders, who have been known to snatch purses or even smash the windows of moving cars. Take only a small amount of cash and just one credit card out with you. Leave your passport, traveler's checks, and other credit cards in the hotel safe, and avoid carrying purses and expensive cameras or wearing valuable jewelry.

Arriving and Departing by Plane

The region's main airport is Seville's **San Pablo Airport** (tel. 95/451–0677), 12 km (7½ mi) east of the city on N IV to Córdoba. It has international flights from Amsterdam, Brussels, Frankfurt, London, and Paris; and domestic flights from Madrid, Barcelona, Valencia, and other major cities. Seville's **Iberia** office is on Almirante Lobo 3 (toll-free reservations, tel. 901/33–31–11). There is no bus or train service to the airport; you'll have to take a taxi.

The region's other airport is Jerez de la Frontera's **Aeropuerto de la Parra** (tel. 956/15–00–00), 7 km (4½ mi) from Jerez on the road to Seville. It has domestic flights only, on **Aviaco,** which is owned by Iberia Airlines (Plaza Arenal 2, tel. 956/15–00–10). Aviaco has flights to Madrid, Barcelona, Valencia–Palma de Mallorca, and Zaragoza.

Arriving and Departing by Car, Train, and Bus

In general, Seville is most easily reached from Córdoba by train, while buses are a better choice between Seville and Granada, as trains on that route are slow and involve a change. Buses are also a better choice for trips from the Costa del Sol.

By Car   The main road into the region from Madrid is the N IV highway through Córdoba. It has recently been made into a four-lane *autovía*, but it's one of Spain's busiest roads, and trucks can cause delays. From Granada or Málaga, head for Antequera, then take N334 by way of Osuna to Seville. Several highways in and around Seville were improved and rebuilt in connection with 1992's International Exposition; road trips from Córdoba, Granada, and the Costa del Sol by way of Ronda have all become far quicker and more pleasant as a result. From the Costa del Sol, the coastal N340 highway is well paved and rarely very busy beyond Algeciras.

By Train Seville, Jerez, and Cádiz all lie on the main rail line between Madrid and the southwest corner of Spain. From Madrid there are approximately six trains a day, via Córdoba, to Seville; three of these continue on to Jerez and Cádiz. RENFE also operates the high-speed AVE train between Madrid and Seville; it makes the journey in less than three hours, but at a considerably higher cost than the regular train. From Granada, Málaga, Ronda, and Algeciras, trains run to Seville by way of Bobadilla junction, where, more often than not, you have to change.

By Bus Long-distance bus services connect Seville with Madrid and with Cáceres, Mérida, and Badajoz in Extremadura and Córdoba, Granada, Málaga, Ronda, and Huelva in Andalucía. Through buses take the coastal route from Granada, Málaga, and Marbella to Cádiz. Buses from Ronda run to Arcos, Jerez, and Cádiz. Bus services throughout Andalucía, and between Extremadura and Seville, tend to be more frequent and convenient than trains.

Getting Around

By Car Driving in the region is easy—the terrain is mostly flat or gently rolling hills, and the roads are straight. From Seville to Jerez de la Frontera and Cádiz, you can choose between N IV and the slightly faster A4 toll road. The only access by road to the Coto Doñana is to take the A49 Seville–Huelva highway, exit for Almonte/Bollullos del Condado, and then follow the signs for El Rocío and Matalascañas. Getting into and out of Seville, long a nightmarishly confusing ordeal, has become far easier as a result of a new ring road and several altered accesses, although getting around the city by car is still trying. Try to avoid the 7:15–8:30 PM rush hour in Seville and Cádiz; the lunchtime rush hour around 2–3 PM can be another problem. Don't try taking a car to Cádiz at Carnival time (pre-Lent) or to Seville during Holy Week or the April Fair—processions close most of the streets to traffic. *See* Crime, *above*, for a safety warning about driving and parking in Seville.

By Train A dozen or more local trains each day connect Cádiz with Puerto de Santa María, Jerez de la Frontera, and Seville. Journey time from Cádiz to Seville is 1½ to 2 hours. There are no trains to the Coto Doñana, Sanlúcar de Barrameda, or Arcos de la Frontera or between Cádiz and the Costa del Sol.

Cádiz station is on Plaza de Sevilla (tel. 956/25–43–01 or 956/26–21–04) near the docks. **Jerez** station is on Plaza de la Estación, off Diego Fernández Herrera, in the east of town (tel. 956/34–23–19 or 956/33–48–13). The sprawling new Santa Justa station (Jose Laguillo and Av. Kansas City) is some distance from the city center; you'll have to take a cab or a long hike into town. The downtown RENFE Office is on Zaragoza 29 (information and reservations, tel. 95/454–0202).

By Bus There are services connecting all the towns and villages in the region. **Cádiz** has two bus depots: **Comes** (Plaza Hispanidad, tel. 956/21–17–63 or 956/22–42–71) runs buses to most destinations in Spain; **Los Amarillos** (Av. Ramón de Carranza 31, tel. 956/28–58–52) runs services to Jerez, Seville, and Córdoba and to Puerto de Santa María, Sanlúcar de Barrameda, and Chipiona. **Jerez** bus station is on the Plaza Madre de Dios (tel. 956/34–52–07). In **Seville**, there are now two bus stations. The older one is the **Estación de San Sebastian** (Prado de San Sebastian, tel. 95/441–7111), just off the Plaza de San Sebastian between Manuel Vázquez Sagastizabal and José María Osborne; buses from here serve points to the west and northwest. The second, a glittering modern terminal on the banks of the Guadalquivir River downtown, is the **Estación Plaza de Armas** (on Arjona, next to the east end of the Cachorro Bridge, tel. 95/490–8040). This station serves central and eastern Spain. Check with the tourist office to make sure which station you need.

By Boat   A popular way to reach Puerto de Santa María from Cádiz is to take the boat known as *El Vapor* across the Bay of Cádiz. The crossing takes 40 to 45 minutes and costs around 200 pesetas each way. In Cádiz *El Vapor* leaves from the back of Plaza Sevilla at 10 AM, noon, 2 PM, and 6:30 PM (and 8:30 PM, June–Aug. only). Departures from Puerto de Santa María are at 9 AM, 11 AM, 1 PM, and 3:30 PM (and 7:30 PM, June–Aug. only).

Guided Tours

Orientation   In Seville, any of the following organizations can put you in touch with qualified English-speaking guides: **Asociación Provincial de Informadores Turísticos** (Glorieta de Palacio de Congresos, Sevilla, tel. 95/425–5957), **Guidetour** (Lopez de Rueda 13, tel. 95/422–2374–2375; office open 9–1:30 and 5–8), **ITA** (Sta. Teresa 1, tel. 95/422–4641). For English-speaking local guides in Cádiz or Jerez, contact the tourist office.

Special-Interest   From **Seville** Pullmantur (Paseo de Colón 11, tel. 95/421–6100) offers
Jerez Horse   day trips to Jerez to see **Como Bailan los Caballos Andaluces** (the
Show   Dancing Horses of Andalucía) at the Royal Andalusian School of Equestrian Art. Tours include visits to sherry bodegas as well. The **Cádiz** tourist office can direct you to travel agencies that arrange similar tours from that city.

Sherry Bodegas   Tours can be arranged from Seville and Cádiz (*see above*). In **Jerez,** bodegas are open (weekdays 10:30–1:30; closed Aug. and some of Sept. for harvest) to visitors; tours, which include a tasting of brandy and sherry, should be booked in advance; English-speaking guides are usually available. Call the bodega and ask for Public Relations: Domecq (tel. 956/33–19–00; admission free) and González Byass (tel. 956/34–00–00; admission free) *must* be prebooked; Harvey (tel. 956/15–10–30; admission free) has one visit at noon; Williams (tel. 956/34–65–39; admission: 300 pesetas) and Wisdom (tel. 956/18–43–06; admission free) have differing schedules; check by telephone or with the Jerez tourist office.

To visit bodegas in **Puerto de Santa María,** contact Osborne (Fernán Caballero 3, tel. 956/85–52–11) or Terry (Cielo 1, tel. 956/48–30–00). Ask locally for other bodegas in **Sanlúcar de Barrameda** and **Lebrija.**

Doñana   Jeep tours of the reserve depart twice daily (Tues.–Sun., 8:30 AM
National Park   and 3 PM) from the park's reception center, 2 km (1 mi) from Matalascañas. Tours (maximum 125 people) should be booked well in advance. Passengers can often be collected from hotels in Matalascañas. Write or call Parque Nacional de Doñana (Cooperativa Marisma del Rocío, Centro de Recepción, 21760 Matalascañas, Huelva, tel. 955/43–04–32).

Exploring
Western Andalucía

Orientation

This region covers the provinces of Seville and Cádiz and part of Huelva, in western Andalucía. For touring purposes it can be divided into three parts, starting with Seville. From there you can go on to visit the Doñana National Park, Matalascañas or Mazagón, and the villages of the Columbus story. Next, you can visit Jerez de la Frontera, Arcos de la Frontera, and Cádiz.

Highlights for First-time Visitors

Arcos de la Frontera (*see* Tour 3)
Old Cádiz (*see* Tour 3)
Doñana National Park (*see* Tour 2)
A Jerez bodega (*see* Tour 3)
Jerez's Royal Andalusian School of Equestrian Art (*see* Tour 3)
Puerto de Santa María's Ribera del Marisco (*see* Tour 3)
Seville's Alcázar and Barrio de Santa Cruz (*see* Tour 1)
Seville's catedral and Giralda (*see* Tour 1)

Tour 1: Seville

Numbers in the margin correspond to points of interest on the Western Andalucía: Seville and the Guadalquivir Delta map and the Seville map.

❶ Lying on the banks of the Guadalquivir, **Seville** is Spain's fourth-largest city and the capital of Andalucía. Its whitewashed houses bright with bougainvillea, its ocher-colored palaces, and its Baroque facades have long enchanted visitors to the region. Today Seville benefits from much-needed improvements made for Expo '92, including a new train station and new bus station; an enlarged and modernized airport; new highways in and around the city; an opera house; seven new bridges; a new riverfront esplanade; a completely renovated Fine Arts Museum and several dozen other buildings; and high-speed rail and four-lane highway links with Madrid.

Of course, this bustling city of almost 700,000 people also has a negative side: traffic-choked streets; high unemployment; a notorious petty crime rate (*see* warning under Crime in Essential Information, *above*); and, at times, the kind of impersonal treatment you won't find in smaller cities like Granada or Córdoba. But Seville's artistic heritage and its citizens' zest for life more than compensate for the city's disadvantages. Be warned, however, that schedules for the city's monuments and other institutions have a habit of changing almost monthly.

Seville has a long and noble history. Conquered by the Romans in 205 BC, it gave the world two great emperors, Trajan and Hadrian (you can see the latter's birthplace at nearby Itálica). The Moors held Seville for more than 500 years and bequeathed to it one of the greatest examples of their art in the form of the well-loved Giralda tower. Saint King Ferdinand (Ferdinand III) lies enshrined in glory in the cathedral, one of Seville's greatest monuments. His rather less saintly descendant, Pedro the Cruel, builder of the splendid Alcázar, is buried here, too.

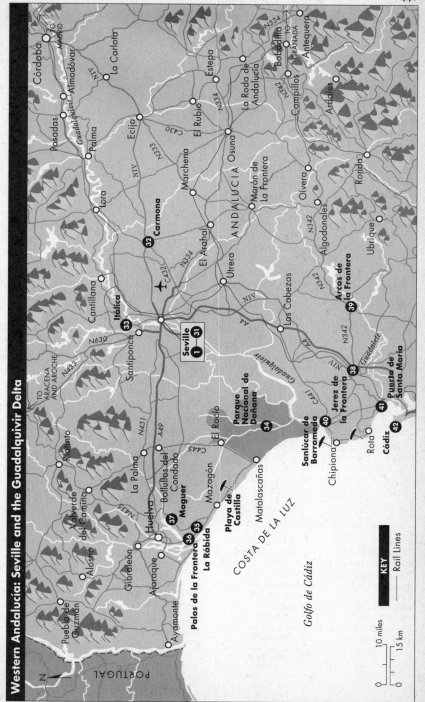

Western Andalucía: Seville and the Guadalquivir Delta

PORTUGAL

Córdoba
TO MADRID
Posadas
Palma
Lora
Cantillana
Almodóvar
La Carlota
Guadalquivir
Écija
El Rubio
Estepa
La Roda de Andalucía
Osuna
Marchena
Morón de la Frontera
Olvera
Ronda
Algodonales
Ubrique
Bobadilla
TO GRANADA
Campillos
Antequera
Ardales
N334
N334
N342
N342
N342
N342
N330

Itálica
Santiponce
Carmona 32
Itálica 33
Seville 1 — 31
El Arahal
Utrera
Las Cabezas
Arcos de la Frontera 39

Puebla de Guzmán
Alosno
Valverde del Camino
Riotinto
La Palma
Bollullos del Condado
El Rocío
Parque Nacional de Doñana 34
Sanlúcar de Barrameda
Chipiona
Rota
Jerez de la Frontera 40
Puerto de Santa María 41
Cádiz 42
Arcos de la Frontera

Gibraleón
Ajaraque
Huelva
Moguer 37
Palos de la Frontera 36
La Rábida 35
Mazagón
Playa de Castilla
Matalascañas
COSTA DE LA LUZ
Golfo de Cádiz

Ayamonte

N630
N431
N433
A49
C445
CA441
N340
N342

ANDALUCÍA

N

KEY
— Rail Lines

10 miles
15 km
0
0

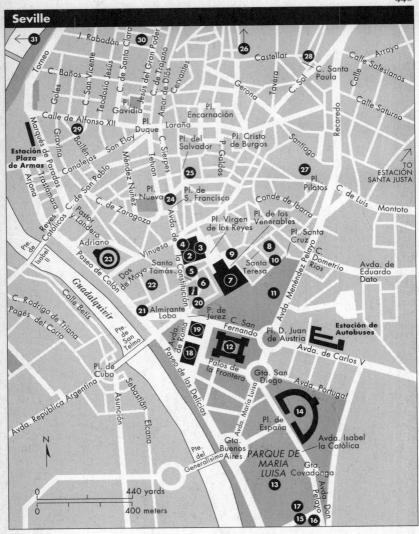

Seville

Alcázar, **7**

Alfonso XIII, **19**

Archivo de Indias, **5**

Ayuntamiento, **24**

Barrio de Santa
Cruz, **8**

Basílica de la
Macarena, **26**

Casa de Murillo, **10**

Casa Pilatos, **27**

Catedral, **2**

Convento de Santa
Paula, **28**

Expo site, **31**

Fábrica de Tabacos, **12**

Giralda, **3**

Hospital de la
Caridad, **22**

Hospital de los
Venerables, **9**

Iglesia del
Salvador, **25**

Jardines de Murillo, **11**

La Maestranza, **23**

Museo
Arqueológico, **16**

Museo de Arte
Contemporáneo, **6**

Museo de Artes y
Costumbres
Populares, **17**

Museo de Bellas
Artes, **29**

Palacio de San
Telmo, **18**

Palacio de Yanduri, **20**

Parque de María
Luisa, **13**

Patio de los
Naranjos, **4**

Plaza de América, **15**

Plaza de España, **14**

San Lorenzo y Jesús
del Gran Poder, **30**

Torre de Oro, **21**

Seville is justly proud of its literary and artistic associations. The painters Diego Rodríguez de Silva Velázquez (1599–1660) and Bartolomé Esteban Murillo (1617–82) were natives of Seville, as were the poets Gustavo Adolfo Becquer (1836–70), Antonio Machado (1875–1939), and Nobel Prize-winner Vicente Aleixandre (1898–1984). The tale of that ingenious knight of La Mancha was begun in a Seville jail, for Don Quixote's creator, Miguel de Cervantes, twice languished in a debtors' prison here. Tirso de Molina's character Don Juan carried on his amorous pursuits in the mansions of Seville, later scheming as Don Giovanni in the Barrio de Santa Cruz. The barrio also provided the setting for the nuptials of Rossini's barber, Figaro. Nearby, at the old tobacco factory, Bizet's sultry Carmen first met Don José.

The vivacity and color of Seville can be seen at their most intense during Holy Week, when the lacerated Christs and bejeweled weeping Virgins of the city's 24 parishes are paraded through the streets on floats borne by barefoot penitents.

Two weeks later, the *sevillanos*, this time clad in flamenco costume, take to the streets to celebrate the Feria de Abril, the greatest parade of the year. Begun as a horse-trading fair in 1847, today it recalls its equine origins in the midday horse parades, with men in broad-brimmed hats and Andalusian riding gear astride prancing steeds, their women in long flounced dresses riding side-saddle behind them. Bullfights, fireworks displays, and the all-night singing and dancing of sevillanas in the *casetas* (tents) of the fairground complete the spectacle.

The best place to start your exploration of Seville is in the **Plaza Virgen de los Reyes.** From next to the central fountain you can gaze up at the magnificent Giralda, symbol of Seville, and at the east facade of the great Gothic cathedral.

2 Begin at the **catedral** (cathedral), Seville's leading monument. After Ferdinand III captured Seville from the Moors in 1248, the great mosque begun by Yusuf II in 1171 was at first simply reconsecrated to the Virgin Mary and used as a Christian cathedral, in much the same way the mosque at Córdoba was. But in 1401 the citizens of Seville saw fit to erect a new and glorious cathedral, one more worthy of the status of their great city. They promptly pulled down the old mosque—all, that is, but its minaret and outer court—and set about their task with a zeal and enthusiasm unparalleled elsewhere. This mighty building was completed in just over a century—a remarkable record for the time. The clergy renounced their incomes for the cause, and a member of the chapter is said to have proclaimed: "Let us build a church so big that we shall be held to be insane." And this they proceeded to do, for today Seville's cathedral can be described only in superlatives: It is the biggest and highest cathedral in Spain, the largest Gothic building in the world, and the world's third-largest church (the world's *largest*, if you aren't counting patios and gardens, Sevillanos say) after St. Peter's in Rome and St. Paul's in London.

The exterior of the cathedral, with its rose windows and magnificent flying buttresses, is a monument to pure Gothic beauty. But the badly lit interior can be disappointing, its seven naves and numerous side chapels shrouded in gloom. Gothic purity has been submerged in ornate Baroque decoration lit only by flickering candles. Just inside the main entrance, on the south side off Calle Fray González, is the flamboyant **monument to Christopher Columbus.** The great explorer knew triumph and disgrace and found no repose.

He died at Valladolid, bitterly disillusioned. His body was buried at Santo Domingo although this monument was built at his tomb. Columbus's coffin is borne aloft by the four medieval kingdoms of Spain: Castile, León, Aragón, and Navarra.

Between the great west door, the Puerta Mayor, and the central choir, you'll find the tombstone of Columbus's son Hernando Colón (1488–1539), inscribed with the words *A Castilla y a León, mundo nuevo dió Colón* (To Castile and León, Columbus gave a New World).

Spend awhile in the **Capilla Mayor,** in the central nave, and study the intricately carved altarpiece begun by a Flemish carver in 1482. This magnificent retablo, the largest in Christendom (65 feet high by 43 feet wide), depicts some 36 scenes from the life of Christ; its pillars are carved with more than 200 figures; and the whole work is lavishly adorned with immeasurable quantities of gold leaf.

Move on to the **Capilla Real,** where, above the grille, you can see Ferdinand III, on horseback, receiving the keys of Seville. At the sides of this chapel stand the tombs of Ferdinand's wife, Beatrix of Swabia, and his son, Alfonso X, called the Wise (died 1284). In a silver urn before the high altar rest the precious relics of Ferdinand III, Seville's liberator (canonized in 1671), who was said to have died from excessive fasting. In the vault below (rarely open) lie the tombs of Ferdinand's descendant, Pedro the Cruel, and his mistress, María de Padilla.

Between the Capilla Real and Columbus's tomb, you'll find the main treasure houses of the cathedral, displaying a wealth of gold and silver (much of it brought from the New World), historic relics, and many rather neglected works of art. In the dome of the **Sala Capitular,** in the cathedral's southeast corner, you'll see one of Murillo's finest *Immaculate Conceptions*, painted in 1668. Next, in the **Sacristía Mayor,** are two Virgins by Francisco de Zurbarán (1598–1664) and the keys of the city, which the Moors and Jews of Seville presented to its conqueror, Ferdinand. Finally, in the **Sacristía de los Cálices,** look for Martínez Montañés's crucifixion, *Cristo de la Clemencia;* Valdés Leal's *St. Peter Freed by an Angel;* Zurbarán's *Virgin and Child;* and Goya's *St. Justa* and *St. Rufina*.

❸ The **Giralda,** undisputed symbol of Seville, dominates the skyline and can be glimpsed from almost every corner of the city. Built originally as the minaret of Seville's great mosque, from which the faithful were summoned to prayer, it was constructed between 1184 and 1196 under the Almohad dynasty, just 50 years before the Reconquest of Seville. When the Christians tore down the mosque, they could not bring themselves to destroy this tower and so incorporated it into their new cathedral as the bell tower. In 1565–68 they added a lantern and belfry to the old minaret, installing 24 bells, one for each of Seville's 24 parishes and the 24 Christian knights who fought with Ferdinand III in the Reconquest. They also added the bronze statue of Faith, which turns as a weather vane (*el giraldillo*—something that turns), providing the name Giralda.

With its Baroque additions, the slender Giralda now rises 322 feet. In its center, in place of steps, a gently sloping ramp, wide enough for two horsemen to pass abreast, climbs to a viewing platform 230 feet up. It is said that Ferdinand III rode his horse to the top to admire the view of the city he had conquered. If you follow in his footsteps, your efforts will be rewarded by a glorious view of pan-tile roofs and the Guadalquivir shimmering beneath palm-lined banks. *Plaza Virgen de los Reyes. Tel. 95/421–4971. Admission to cathe-*

*dral and Giralda: 500 pesetas. Open Mon.–Sat. 10–5, Sun. 10–4;
cathedral also open for Mass.*

➍ Before you leave the cathedral precincts, take a look inside the **Patio de los Naranjos** (Courtyard of Orange Trees). The old fountain in the center was used for ritual ablutions before entering the mosque. See if you can find the alligator by the Puerta del Largata in the corner near the Giralda—thought to have been a gift from the emir of Egypt in 1260 as he sought the hand of Alfonso the Wise's daughter—and the ivory elephant tusk found in the ruins of Itálica. Across the patio, the **Sacristy** houses the Columbus Library, a collection of 3,000 volumes bequeathed by his son Hernando.

➎ The **Archivo de Indias** (Archives of the Indies) opened in 1785 in the former Lonja, the Merchants' Exchange, designed by the architect of the Escorial, Juan de Herrera, in 1572. This dignified Renaissance building houses an impressive collection of documents relating to the discovery of the New World. Its collection of maps includes Juan de la Cosa's *Mappamundi*, and among the logbooks you'll find one kept by Columbus. There are drawings, trade documents, plans of South American towns, and even the autographs of Columbus, Magellan, and Cortés. Many of the 38,000 documents have yet to be sorted and properly catalogued, and the exhibits on display are constantly being shifted. *Avenida de la Constitución, tel. 95/421–1234. Admission free. Open Mon.–Fri. 10–1 (8–3 for researchers); closed weekends.*

➏ Beside the Archives of the Indies, you'll find the **Museo de Arte Contemporáneo** (Museum of Contemporary Art), housed in a fine old mansion. Its collection of 20th-century Spanish paintings and sculpture includes works by Romero de Torres, Carlos Saura, Antoni Tàpies, Fernando Zobel, and the sculptor Eduardo Chillida. Temporary exhibitions by contemporary Andalusian artists are also held here. *Santo Tomás 5, tel. 95/421–5830. Admission: 250 pesetas. Open Mon.–Fri. 10–7, weekends 10–2.*

➐ On the Plaza Triunfo you'll find the entrance to the **Alcázar** (Reales Alcázares), the Mudéjar palace built by Pedro I (1350–69), on the site of the former Moorish alcázar (fortress). Don't mistake the Alcázar for a genuine Moorish palace, like the Alhambra in Granada. It may look like one, and was indeed designed and built by Moorish workers brought in from Granada, but it was commissioned and paid for by a Christian king, more than 100 years after the Reconquest of Seville. Into its construction, Pedro the Cruel incorporated stones and capitals he pillaged from elsewhere—from Valencia, from Córdoba's Medina Azahara, and from Seville itself. The Alcázar is the finest example of Mudéjar architecture in Spain today, though its purity of style has been much diluted by the alterations and additions of successive Spanish rulers. The Catholic Monarchs, whose only son, Don Juan, was born here in 1478, added a new wing to serve as an administration center for their New World Empire. Today, the Alcázar is the official residence in Seville of the king and queen of Spain.

You enter the Alcázar through high, fortified walls of genuine Moorish origin that belie the exquisite delicacy of its interior. Cross the **Patio de la Montería** to Pedro's Mudéjar palace, arranged around the beautiful **Patio de las Doncellas** (Court of the Damsels). Its name most likely pays tribute to the annual gift of 100 virgins to the Moorish sultans. Resplendent with the most delicate of lacelike stucco and gleaming *azulejo* (tile) decorations, its Granada craftsmanship is instantly reminiscent of the Alhambra, though the upper galleries were added by Carlos V. Opening off this patio, the **Salón de Embajadores** (Hall of the Ambassadors), with its cedarwood cupola of green, red, and gold, is the most sumptuous hall in the palace. It was here in 1526 that Carlos V married Isabel of Portugal—for which occasion he added the wooden balconies.

Next, you'll find Felipe II's dining hall and the three apartments of Pedro's wily and beautiful mistress, María de Padilla. María's hold over her royal lover, and seemingly over his courtiers, too, was so great that they apparently lined up to drink her bathwater. The **Patio de las Muñecas** (Court of the Dolls) takes its name from two tiny faces carved on the inside of one of its arches, no doubt as a joke on the part of its Moorish creators. Here, in 1358, Pedro reputedly had his half-brother Don Fadrique, master of the Order of Santiago, slain. And here, too, he murdered his guest Abu Said of Granada for the sake of his jewels. One of these, a huge uncut ruby, Pedro presented to the Black Prince (Edward Prince of Wales [1330–76], eldest son of England's Edward III) in 1367. It now sits among other priceless gems in the Crown of England.

Next, you'll come to the **Apartments of Carlos V,** built by the emperor at the time of his marriage. The walls carry a rich collection of Flemish tapestries depicting Carlos's victories at Tunis. Look at the tapestry of the map of Spain—it shows the Iberian Peninsula upside down, as was the custom in Arab mapmaking.

The end of your visit will bring you out into the **Alcázar Gardens,** where you can enjoy the fragrance of jasmine and myrtle, the beautiful terraces and ornamental baths, the palm trees, and the well-stocked goldfish pond covered in water lilies. In the midst of this oasis of green is an orange tree said to have been planted in the time of Pedro the Cruel. From the gardens, a passageway leads to the **Patio de las Banderas,** which offers a classic view of the Giralda. *Plaza del Triunfo, tel. 95/422–7163. Admission: 600 pesetas. Open Tues.–Sat. 10:30–5, Sun. 10–1.*

8 The twisting alleyways, cobbled squares, and whitewashed houses of the **Barrio de Santa Cruz,** the old Jewish Quarter, were much favored by Seville's nobles in the 17th century. Today its houses are beautifully preserved, and the barrio boasts some of Seville's most expensive properties. Wrought-iron lanterns cast shadows on whitewashed walls, ocher-framed windows hide behind potbellied grilles, petunias and geraniums splash color on balconies and patios. In places bars nestle side by side with antiques shops and souvenir stores, but most of the quarter is made up of quiet residential streets. The Callejón del Agua, beside the wall of the Alcázar Gardens, boasts some of the quarter's finest mansions and patios.

Pause awhile to enjoy the antiques shops and the outdoor café in the **Plaza Alianza.** A starkly simple crucifix hangs on the dazzling white wall shrouded in bougainvillea, and blue-and-white tiles bear the square's name. In the **Plaza de Doña Elvira,** with its fountain and azulejo benches, the youth of Seville gather to play guitars. The heart of the barrio is the colorful **Plaza de los Venerables.**

Time Out   Enjoy a drink or a plate of ham here in the fine old bar known as **Casa Román,** or stop for lunch in either of the two outdoor restaurants (**Hostería del Laurel** or **Restaurante Santa Cruz**).

9 The **Hospital de los Venerables,** once a retirement home for priests, has opened after extensive renovation; don't miss its splendid azulejo patio and small museum of floats from the Cruces de Mayo processions (tel. 95/456–2696; admission: 500 pesetas; open daily 10–2 and 4–8). Follow Justino de Nieve and Agua to the **Plaza Alfaro,** where Rossini's Figaro serenaded Rosina on her famous balcony. In the **Plaza Santa Cruz** a 17th-century filigree iron cross marks the site of the Santa Cruz church destroyed by Napoleon's General Soult. Here, the painter Murillo was buried in 1682. A few paces away, up Calle Santa Teresa, you can visit **Casa de Murillo** (Santa Teresa 8, tel. 95/421–7535; admission free; open Mon.–Fri. 10–2). The street is named for Santa Teresa de Ávila (1515–82), who stayed here once on a visit to Seville and was so enchanted by the city that she decreed that anyone who stayed free from sin in Seville was indeed on the path to God.

⓫ From the Plaza Santa Cruz, make your way down to the **Jardines de Murillo** (Murillo Gardens), where you'll find a statue of Christopher Columbus. At the far end you'll come out on the Plaza Don Juan de Austria. The handsome square building opposite you, across Calle San Fernando, is the **Fábrica de Tabacos** (old tobacco factory), built between 1750 and 1766 (the new factory is across the river). Less than a century later, some 10,000 *cigarreras* were employed here, including, of course, the heroine of Bizet's opera *Carmen,* who rolled her cigars on her thigh. These tobacco women constituted the 19th century's largest female work force. This splendid building was once the second-largest monument in Spain, after the Escorial. Since the 1950s it has been the home of Seville University.

Continue down to the Glorieta San Diego, with its statue of El Cid (Rodrigo Díaz de Vivar, 1043–99, who fought for and against the Muslim rulers during the Reconquest), and in front of you, the old Casino building of the 1929 Exhibition, now the Teatro Lope de Vega, stands at the entrance to the **Parque de María Luisa** (María Luisa Park). This park, one of the loveliest in Spain, was formerly the garden of the Palacio de San Telmo. It's a blend of formal design and wild vegetation, shady walkways, and sequestered nooks. In the burst of development and expansion that gripped Seville in the 1920s, it was redesigned to form the site of the 1929 Hispanic-American Exhibition, and the impressive villas you'll see here today are the fair's remaining pavilions, many of them now used as consulates or schools.

Turn left on Avenida Isabel la Católica and you'll come to the monumental **Plaza de España.** This grandiose structure, designed by architect Aníbal González, was Spain's pavilion at the fair, and formed the centerpiece of the whole exhibition. The brightly colored azulejo pictures in its arches represent the 50 provinces of Spain, and the four bridges over the ornamental lake, the medieval kingdoms of the Iberian Peninsula.

Opposite the plaza you'll come upon a monument to the 19th-century Romantic poet Gustavo Adolfo Bécquer. Stroll across the park, past the Isla de los Patos (Island of Ducks), until you reach the **Plaza de América.** This plaza, also designed by Aníbal González, is a blaze of color, with deep orange sand; flowers; shrubs; ornamental stairways; and fountains of yellow, blue, and ocher tiles. It's also home to hundreds of greedy white pigeons who are used to being indulged by Seville's children and busloads of tourists. The three impressive buildings in neo-Mudéjar, Gothic, and Renaissance style that surround the square were built by González for the 1929 fair. Today, two of them serve as museums.

⓰ The **Museo Arqueológico** (Archaeology Museum), in the Renaissance building, houses finds from Phoenician, Greek, Carthaginian,

Iberian, Roman, and medieval times. Its best exhibits include marble statues and mosaics from the Roman excavations at Itálica and the fabulous Carambolo treasure found on a hillside outside Seville in 1958. It consists of 21 pieces of jewelry, all of 24-karat gold, that date from the 7th and 6th centuries BC. *Plaza de América, tel. 95/ 423–2401. Admission: 250 pesetas. Open daily 9–2.*

⑰ The Mudéjar pavilion opposite is the home of the **Museo de Artes y Costumbres Populares** (Museum of Folklore). Here, on the first floor, you'll find re-creations of a forge, a bakery, a winepress, a tanner's shop, and a pottery. Upstairs, the exhibits include 18th- and 19th-century court dress, regional folk costumes, carriages, musical instruments, farm implements, votive offerings, weaving, and lace. *Plaza de América, tel. 95/423–2576. Admission: 250 pesetas. Open Tues.–Sat. 9–2:30; closed Sun. and Mon.*

⑱ Wander through the park to the **Palacio de San Telmo,** on Avenida de Roma. This splendid Baroque palace, built between 1682 and 1796, was chiefly the work of architect Leonardo de Figueroa. Look for the exotic main portal. It dates from 1734 and is a superb example of the fanciful Churrigueresque style, but now is the seat of the Presidencia de Junta de Andalucía, the regional government's executive. The grand Mudéjar-style building behind San Telmo is
⑲ Seville's leading hotel, the **Alfonso XIII,** built—and named—for the king's visit to the 1929 fair. You can explore its inner courtyard or take a drink in the bar and enjoy its ornate Moorish decor. On the
⑳ north side of Puerta de Jerez is the **Palacio de Yanduri,** where the Nobel Prize–winning poet Vicente Aleixandre was born.

From the Puerta de Jerez walk down Almirante Lobo to the riverside, where you'll find another of Seville's great landmarks, the
㉑ **Torre de Oro** (Tower of Gold), a 12-sided tower built by the Moors in 1220 to complete the city's ramparts. The Moors used to close off the harbor by attaching a chain across the river from the base of the Tower of Gold to another tower on the opposite bank. In 1248 Admiral Ramón de Bonifaz succeeded in breaking through this barrier, thus enabling Ferdinand III to capture the city. Today, the tower houses a small but well-displayed Naval Museum. *Tel. 95/422–2419. Admission: 100 pesetas. Open Tues.–Fri. 10–2, weekends 10–1; closed Mon.*

You can now cross the San Telmo Bridge and take a scenic walk along the Calle Betis—a street famed for night life, terraced restaurants facing the river, and tapas bars—on the far side of the river to the
㉒ Isabel II Bridge, or you can head for the **Hospital de la Caridad.** (Opposite it is Seville's new opera house, Paseo de Colón, which opened in 1991; the Maestranza, as it is known, has become one of Europe's leading houses and offers opera, classical music, zarzuela, or comic opera, and even jazz; Nuñez de Balboa 5, tel. 95/422–6573.) Today, this Baroque charity hospital is an almshouse for the sick and elderly, run by a religious institution. It was founded in 1674 by Seville's original Don Juan. The story goes that Miguel de Mañara (1626–79), a nobleman of licentious character, who loved drunken brawls and carnal pleasures, was returning one night from a riotous orgy when he had a vision of a funeral procession in which the partly decomposed corpse in the coffin was his own. Accepting the apparition as a sign from God, Miguel de Mañara renounced his worldly goods and joined the Brotherhood of Charity, whose unsavory task it was to collect the bodies of executed criminals and bury them. He devoted his fortune to building this hospital and is buried before the high altar in the chapel. La Caridad's chief attractions are its six paintings by Murillo—the artist was a personal friend of Mañara's—and two

gruesome works by Valdés Leal (1622–90) showing the Triumph of Death. *Calle Temprado 3, tel. 95/422–3232. Admission: 200 pesetas. Open Mon.–Sat. 10–1 and 3:30–6, Sun. in summer 10:30–12:30.*

㉓ Nearby, on the Paseo de Colón, stands **La Maestranza.** Built between 1760 and 1763, this deep ocher-painted bullring is the oldest and most beautiful *plaza de toros* in Spain (tel. 95/422–4576; admission to plaza and bullfighting museum: 250 pesetas; open Mon.–Sat. 10–1:30). From there, walk up to the Plaza Nueva in the heart of Seville's commercial center. In the middle of this square stands the ㉔ **Ayuntamiento** (City Hall), designed by Diego de Riaño and built between 1527 and 1564. The facade, which overlooks the Plaza Nueva, dates from the 19th century, but walk around to the opposite side on the Plaza de San Francisco, and you'll find Riaño's original building, exquisitely decorated in Plateresque style.

At the beginning of Calle Sierpes, a plaque and a small bronze bust of Cervantes mark the spot where the Carcel Real (Royal Prison) once stood. In one of its cells Cervantes began work on *Don Quixote*. ㉕ Around the corner, on the Plaza del Salvador, the **Iglesia del Salvador** (Church of El Salvador, 1671–1712) stands on the site of Seville's first great mosque. In this exuberantly Baroque church you'll find ornate side chapels and some fine carvings. Look especially for the image of *Jesús de la Pasión,* carved by Martínez Montañés in 1619. This statue is borne through the streets on Holy Thursday in one of Semana Santa's most moving processions. *Plaza San Salvador, tel. 95/421–4777. Admission free. Open Mon.–Sat. 6:30–9 PM; Sun. 10–1 and 6:30–9.*

Calle Gallegos will lead you back to Sierpes. A small alleyway on your right is named Monardes, after the apothecary who opened the first herbalist store in Seville with samples of American flora brought back from the New World. Sierpes is Seville's main shopping artery, a lively pedestrian street.

Time Out | At the far end of Sierpes you can relax over a coffee at one of the sidewalk tables of the old-fashioned **Café Campaña** or enjoy a beer or pastry at its long polished wooden counter.

If you've time to spare, Seville has several other interesting sights located somewhat away from the center, though, with the possible exception of the Macarena, they are all still within walking distance of it.

㉖ At the **Basilica de la Macarena** you'll find Seville's most revered image, the Virgin of Hope, more familiarly known as the Macarena, because her church adjoins the Puerta de la Macarena (Macarena Gate), a remnant of the old Roman wall. Bedecked with candles and carnations, her cheeks streaming with glass tears, La Macarena is the focus of the procession on Holy Thursday that is the highlight of Seville's Holy Week pageant. She is the patroness of Gypsies and the matador's protector. Few matadors would dream of entering the ring without addressing a prayer to her. So great are her charms that the Sevillian bullfighter Joselito spent half his personal fortune buying her four emeralds. When, in 1920, he was killed in the ring at the tender age of 25, the Macarena was dressed in widow's weeds for a full month. *Puerta de la Macarena, tel. 95/437–0195. Admission to basilica: free; admission to treasury: 250 pesetas. Basilica open daily 9–9. Treasury open daily 9:30–12:30 and 5:30–7:30.*

㉗ The **Casa Pilatos** was built at the turn of the 16th century by the dukes of Tarifa, ancestors of the present owner, the duke of

Medinaceli. It's known as Pilate's House because of a popular belief that Don Fadrique, first marquis of Tarifa, modeled it on Pilate's house in Jerusalem, where he went on a pilgrimage in 1519. This palace, with its fine patio and superb azulejo decorations, is, in fact, a beautiful blend of Spanish Mudéjar and Renaissance architecture. *Plaza Pilatos, tel. 95/422–5298. Admission: 500 pesetas to lower floor; 500 pesetas to upper floor. Open daily 9–6.*

28 The 15th-century Gothic **Convento de Santa Paula** boasts a fine facade and portico with ceramic decoration by Nicolaso Pisano. The chapel has some beautiful azulejos and sculptures by Martínez Montañés. *Calle Santa Paula, tel. 95/442–1307. Admission free, but voluntary donations accepted. Open daily 10:30–1 and 4:30–6:30.*

29 The **Museo de Bellas Artes** (Fine Arts Museum), which recently underwent extensive renovations, contains a fine collection of Murillo, Zurbarán, Velázquez, Valdés Leal, and El Greco, said by locals to be second only to the Prado's. *Plaza del Museo, tel. 95/422–0790. Admission: 250 pesetas. Open Tues.–Sun. 9–2 and 4–7; June–Sept. mornings only; closed Mon.*

30 The church of **San Lorenzo y Jesús del Gran Poder** has many fine works by such artists as Montañés and Pacheco, but its most outstanding piece is Juan de Mesa's *Jesús del Gran Poder* (Christ Omnipotent). The *paso* (float) for the famous procession of El Gran Poder that takes place early on Good Friday morning is the work of Ruíz Gijón (1690). *Calle Jesús del Gran Poder, tel. 95/438–5454. Admission free. Open daily 8–1:30 and 6–9.*

31 The year 1992 brought the universal exhibition, Expo '92, to Seville's island of La Cartuja, on the Guadalquivir. Seven new bridges across the river were constructed, as well as numerous pavilions and other facilities. Although some pavilions were dismantled in late 1992, most of the **Expo site** remains as a permanent public area. Concerts, audiovisual shows, and other events are regularly held here; inquire at the tourist office. Part of the site is going to be converted into a scientific theme park similar to Florida's Epcot Center (the consultant to the project had long experience with Disney); other areas are to be used for a technological business center and a campus extension to the University of Seville. Planners expected the theme park to be open by 1995, but check with the tourist office.

Numbers in the margin correspond to points of interest on the Western Andalucía: Seville and the Guadalquivir Delta map.

Excursions from Seville **32** Some 32 km (20 mi) east of Seville off N IV, **Carmona** claims to be one of the oldest inhabited places in Spain. The Phoenicians and the Carthaginians had settlements here, and it became an important town under both the Romans and the Moors. Today, Carmona is a quiet, unspoiled Andalusian town occupying a dramatic position on a steep fortified hill. Its chief attraction is in what in Moorish times was the **Alcázar de Arriba** (Upper Fortress), built by the Moors on Roman foundations, and later, in the 14th century, converted by King Pedro the Cruel into a fine Mudéjar palace. Pedro's summer residence was destroyed in 1504 by an earthquake, but the parador (*see* Dining and Lodging, *below*) that now stands amid its ruins commands a breathtaking view.

As you wander Carmona's ancient, narrow streets, you'll come upon a wealth of Mudéjar and Renaissance churches, medieval gateways, and simple whitewashed houses of clear Moorish influence, punctuated here and there by an occasional Baroque palace. Pick up a street plan in the parador and stroll down to the **Puerta de Córdoba** (Córdoba Gate) on the eastern edge of town. This old gateway was first built by the Romans around AD 175, then altered by Moorish and Renaissance additions.

Climb back up into town and make your way to the Gothic church of **Santa María,** built between 1424 and 1518 on the site of the former Great Mosque. Santa María is a contemporary of Seville cathedral, and it, too, retains its Moorish courtyard, once used for ritual ablutions. The heart of the old town is the Plaza San Fernando, whose 17th-century houses show clear Moorish inspiration.

From the square, Calle Prim leads down to the **Puerta de Sevilla** (Seville Gate), where the imposing **Alcázar de Abajo** (Lower Fortress), another Moorish fortification built on Roman foundations, marks the limits of the old town.

Across the road, on the edge of the "new town," stands the church of **San Pedro,** which was begun in 1466. Its extraordinary interior is an unbroken mass of sculptures and gilded surfaces, and the church's Baroque tower, erected in 1704, is an unabashed imitation of Seville's famous Giralda.

At the far end of town lies Carmona's most outstanding monument, its splendid **Roman Necropolis.** Here, in huge underground chambers, some 900 family tombs dating from the 2nd century BC to the 4th century AD have been chiseled out of the rock. The necropolis's walls, decorated with leaf and bird motifs, are punctuated with niches for burial urns. The most spectacular tombs are the Elephant Vault and the Servilia Tomb, with colonnaded arches and vaulted side galleries. A museum houses the chambers' archaeological finds. *Calle Enmedio, tel. 95/414–0811. Admission: 250 pesetas. Open Tues.–Fri. 10–2 and 4–6, Sat. and Sun. 10–2; closed Mon.*

③③ The ruins of the Roman colony of **Itálica** lie about 1 km (⅔ mi) beyond Santiponce on N630 toward Extremadura, about 12 km (7 mi) from the center of Seville. Itálica was founded by Scipio Africanus in 206 BC as a home for veteran soldiers. By the 2nd century AD, it had grown into one of Roman Iberia's most important cities and had given the Roman world two great emperors, Trajan (52–117) and Hadrian (76–138). Itálica once had 10,000 inhabitants who lived in 1,000 dwellings. About 25% of the site has been excavated, and work is still in progress. The most important monument is the huge elliptical amphitheater that once held 40,000 spectators. You'll find traces of city streets, cisterns, and the floor plans of several villas, some with mosaic floors, though all the best mosaics and statues have been removed to Seville's Archaeological Museum. A small museum contains relics found on the site of a fully excavated Roman theater in Santiponce. Itálica was abandoned and plundered as a quarry by the Visigoths, who preferred Seville. It fell into decay around AD 700. For information about the excavation, call 95/599–6583. *Admission: 250 pesetas. Open Tues.–Sat. 9–5, Sun. 10–4; closed Mon.*

Tour 2: Doñana National Park to Moguer

③④ **Parque Nacional de Doñana** (Doñana National Park) lies beside the Guadalquivir estuary in the southeast corner of Huelva province. These wetlands, one of Europe's last corners of wilderness, constitute Spain's largest national park. They cover an area of 188,000 acres, 64 km (40 mi) by 14½ km (9 mi), and are a paradise for nature lovers, especially bird-watchers. The park lies on the migratory route from Africa to Europe and is the winter home and breeding ground for as many as 150 species of rare birds. Their habitats range from beaches and shifting sand dunes to marshes, dense brushwood, and sandy hillsides of pine and cork oak. Two of Europe's most endangered species, the imperial eagle and the lynx, make their homes here. Sightings of lynx are fairly rare, but you may be lucky enough to spot a wild boar, a fox, or even a mongoose. Kestrels, kites and buzzards, egrets, storks, and spoonbills breed among the cork oaks. The marshlands are home to some 40,000 geese and to one of Europe's last remaining colonies of flamingos. More than 14,000 come here to nest each February.

The Doñana park reception center is just under 100 km (66 mi) from Seville. Turn off the Seville–Huelva highway, drive through Almonte and El Rocío, scene of the famous Whitsuntide pilgrimage to the Virgin of the Dew, and you'll come to the **Information Center** of La Rocina (tel. 955/44–23–40; open daily 8–7). A short distance away, an exhibition at the **Acebron Palace** (open daily 8–7, last entrance 1 hour before closing) explains the park's ecosystems. Two km (1 mi) before Matalascañas, you'll find the park's main **Reception and Interpretation Center** at Acebuche (tel. 955/44–87–11; open daily 8–7). Jeep tours of the park, which must be reserved in advance, start from here. Tours last four hours, cost 2,400 pesetas, and take you on a 70-km (43-mi) route across beaches, sand dunes, marshes, and scrubland. Off-season (November–February), you can usually book a tour with just a day's notice; at other times, book as long in advance as possible (*see* Guided Tours, in Essential Information, *above*).

35 You may want to extend your Doñana tour to include the monastery of **La Rábida**, "birthplace of America," just 30 km (19 mi) along the coast to the west (this place was inundated with tourists in 1992, the 500th anniversary of Columbus's first trip to the New World). In 1485 Columbus came from Portugal with his son Diego to stay in this Gothic Mudéjar monastery. Here, he discussed his theories with friars Antonio de Marchena and Juan Pérez, who interceded on his behalf with Queen Isabella. In its church, which dates from the early 1400s, you'll find a much-venerated 14th-century statue of the Virgen de los Milagros (Virgin of Miracles). The frescoes in the gatehouse were painted by Daniel Vázquez Díaz in 1930. *Open Tues.–Sun. 10–1 and 4–7, with visits every 30 min.; closed Mon.*

36 Four km (2½ mi) away you'll come to **Palos de la Frontera,** from which, on August 2, 1492, Columbus's three caravels, the *Pinta*, the *Niña*, and the *Santa María*, set sail. Most of his crew were men of Palos and neighboring Moguer. Here, you can see the church of San Jorge (1473), at whose door the royal letter ordering the levy of the crew and equipment of the caravels was read aloud; and the Fontanilla, the well from which the caravels took their water supplies.

37 In **Moguer,** 12 km (7 mi) to the north, you can visit the **Monastery of Santa Clara** (admission: 200 pesetas; open Tues.–Sat. 11–12:30 and 2–5:30), which dates from 1337, and the home of Nobel Prize–winning poet Juan Ramón Jiménez, author of the much-loved *Platero y Yo* (Calle Nueva; admission: 100 pesetas; open Mon.–Sat. 10–2 and 4–8). Moguer's inhabitants now spend more of their time growing strawberries than they do in seafaring, as you'll see from the surrounding fields.

Tour 3: Jerez de la Frontera to Cádiz

㊳ Jerez de la Frontera, the home of sherry, is surrounded by immense vineyards of chalky soil, whose famous Palomino grapes have funded a host of churches and noble mansions. An hour's stroll around the center is all you'll need to get a feel for this small, unprepossessing town. The 12th-century **Alcázar** was once the residence of the caliph of Seville; its terrace provides views down on the **cathedral,** with its octagonal cupola and separate bell tower. Nearby, on the **Plaza San Dionisio,** one of Jerez's most intimate squares, you'll find the Mudéjar church of San Dionisio and the ornate Cabildo Municipal (City Hall), with a lovely Plateresque facade (1575). Jerez also has two interesting and unusual museums: the **Museo de los Relojes** (Clock Museum, tel. 956/18–21–00), in the Palacio de la Atalaya on Calle Leales, and the **Centro Andaluz de Flamenco** (Flamenco Center), in the Palacio Pemartín, on Plaza San Juan (tel. 956/34–92–65; admission free; open weekdays 9:30–1:30, with frequent showings of Spanish-language movies on flamenco).

Names such as González Byass, Domecq, Harvey, Sandeman, and Williams are inextricably linked with Jerez, and the word *sherry,* first used in Great Britain in 1608, is an English corruption of the town's old Moorish name of Xeres. Both sherry and horses are very much the domain of Jerez's Anglo-Spanish aristocracy, whose Catholic ancestors came here from England two or three centuries ago.

At any one time there are more than a million barrels of sherry maturing in Jerez's vast aboveground wine cellars. If you visit a bodega, the guide will explain the *solera* method of blending old wine with new and the importance of *flor* (a sort of yeast) in determining the kind of sherry. Afterward you'll be able to sample generous amounts of pale, dry fino; nutty amontillado; or rich, deep oloroso. Domecq is Jerez's oldest bodega, founded in 1730.

The **Real Escuela Andaluza del Arte Ecuestre** (Royal Andalusian School of Equestrian Art) stands on the grounds of the Recreo de las Cadenas, a splendid 19th-century palace. The establishment of this prestigious school was masterminded by Alvaro Domecq in the 1970s. From 11 to 1 on Monday–Wednesday and Friday, you can visit the stables and tack room and watch the horses being schooled, and see the rehearsals for the Thursday show, *Como Bailan los Caballos Andaluces,* in which horses (a breed created from a cross between the native Andalusian workhorse and the Arabian) and skilled riders in 18th-century riding costume demonstrate intricate dressage techniques and jumping. *Av. Duque de Abrantes, tel. 956/31–11–11. Admission: 1,750 pesetas for numbered seats; 1,425 pesetas for unnumbered seats. Show every Thurs. 12–1:30. Box office opens at 11—go early.*

May and September are the most exciting times to visit Jerez, when spectacular fiestas transform this otherwise modest town into an exuberant, colorful pageant. In early May Jerez's Feria del Caballo (Horse Fair) fills the streets with carriages and riders, and purebreds from the School of Equestrian Art are entered in races and dressage displays. September sees the celebration of the Vintage Festival, when the grapes are blessed on the steps of cathedral.

㊴ Thirty km (18 mi) east of Jerez, the white village of **Arcos de la Frontera** is perched dramatically on a wild crag crowned by a castle, overlooking the gorge of the Guadalete River. On the main square, the Plaza de España, the **Church of Santa María** is a fascinating blend of architectural styles: Romanesque, Gothic, and Mudéjar, with a Plateresque doorway, a Renaissance retablo, and a 17th-century Baroque choir.

Twenty-four km (15 mi) west of Jerez, through seemingly endless **40** manzanilla vineyards, you reach **Sanlúcar de Barrameda** at the mouth of the Guadalquivir. In 1498, Columbus sailed from here on his third voyage to the Americas. Twenty years later, Magellan steered his ships out of the same harbor on the start of his world-circling exploit. Today this unspoiled fishing town is primarily known for its *langostinos* (giant shrimp) and manzanilla (a light, dry sherry with a tangy taste of salt). From its *puerto pesquero* (fishing port), 4 km (2½ mi) north of the town center, there's a fine view of fishing boats and the pine trees of the Doñana on the opposite bank of the Guadalquivir.

Sandy beaches extend along Sanlúcar's southern promontory to Chipiona, where the Roman general Scipio Africanus built a beacon tower.

41 On the northern shores of the Bay of Cádiz, **Puerto de Santa María** is an attractive, if somewhat dilapidated, small fishing port whose white houses have fading, peeling facades and floor-length green grilles covering their doors and windows. The town is dominated by the sherry and brandy bodegas of Terry and Osborne. Columbus once lived in a house on the square that bears his name (Cristobal Colón), and at Calle Palacios 57, Washington Irving spent the autumn of 1828.

Time Out The *marisco* bars along the Ribera del Marisco (Seafood Way) constitute Puerto Santa María's current claim to fame. **Casa Paco** and neighboring **Bar Salva** are two of the most popular.

To the south of Puerto de Santa María, a bridge across the bay **42** brings us to the ancient city of **Cádiz,** surrounded on three sides by the Atlantic Ocean. Spaniards flock here in February to revel in its famous Carnival celebrations, but as yet, few foreigners have discovered its very real charms. Founded as Gadir by Phoenician traders in 1100 BC, Cádiz claims to be the oldest continuously inhabited city in the Western world. The Romans called it Gades, and here Hannibal lived and Julius Caesar first held public office.

After centuries of decline during the Middle Ages and under Moorish rule, Cádiz regained its commercial importance following the discovery of America. Columbus set out from here on his second voyage, and Cádiz later became the home base of the Spanish fleet. Its merchants competed fiercely with those of Seville. In the 18th century, when the river to Seville silted up, Cádiz took over the monopoly of New World trade and became the wealthiest port in Western Europe. Most of its buildings date from this period, and the cathedral was begun then, built with gold and silver brought from the New World.

The old city is African in appearance and immensely intriguing—a cluster of narrow streets opening onto charming small squares. The golden cupola of the cathedral looms above low white houses, and the whole place has a slightly dilapidated air. In an hour's walk around the headlands, you'll encompass the entire old town and pass through some enchanting parks with fine views of the bay.

You might begin your explorations in the **Plaza de Mina,** a large, leafy square with palm trees and plenty of benches for relaxation. On the square's western flank, the ornamental pink facade of the College of Architects is especially beautiful. Look, too, for the house on the south side, in which the composer Manuel de Falla was born in 1876. On the west side, you'll find the **Museo de Bellas Artes y Arqueología** (Fine Arts and Archaeology Museum), well worth visiting for its works by Murillo and Alonso Cano and the *Four Evangelists* and set of saints by Zurbarán, which have much in common with his masterpieces at Guadalupe in Extremadura. *Plaza de Mina, tel. 956/21–22–81. Admission: 250 pesetas. Open Tues.–Sun. 9:30–2.*

Calle San José brings you out on another impressive square, the Plaza de San Antonio, and to Calle Ancha, the main street of the old city. Don't forget to look up here—the facades are quite splendid. Farther down San José you'll come to the **Oratorio de San Felipe Neri.** This impressive church was the scene of the declaration of Spain's first liberal constitution in 1812, and here the Cortes of Cádiz met when the rest of Spain was subjected to the rule of Napoleon's brother, Joseph Bonaparte—more popularly known as "Pepe Botella" for his love of the bottle. On the main altar is an *Immaculate Conception* by Murillo, the great Sevillian artist who in 1682 fell to his death from a scaffolding while working on his *Mystic Marriage of St. Catherine* in the Chapel of Santa Catalina in Cádiz. You'll need to call in advance to arrange a visit. *Santa Inés, tel. 956/21–16–12. Admission free. Open daily 8:30–10 and 7:30–10.*

Next door, the small but pleasant **Museo Histórico Municipal** (Municipal Museum) has a 19th-century mural depicting the establishment of the Constitution of 1812. Its real showpiece is a fascinating ivory and mahogany model of the city made in 1779, which depicts in minute detail all the streets and buildings much as they are now. *Santa Inés, tel. 956/22–17–88. Admission free. Open Tues.–Fri. 9–1 and 5–8, weekends 9–1; closed Mon.*

Four blocks to the west is the Plaza Manuel de Falla, overlooked by an amazing neo-Mudéjar redbrick building, the **Gran Teatro Manuel de Falla.** There's a model of this unusual theater in the nearby parador, the Atlántico (*see* Dining and Lodging, *below*).

On the other side of town, the **cathedral,** with its gold dome and Baroque facade, was begun in 1722, when Cádiz was at the height of its power. The Cádiz-born composer Manuel de Falla, who died in 1946 at the age of 70, is buried in the crypt. The cathedral museum overflows with gold, silver, and precious jewels brought from the New World. One of its most priceless possessions is Enrique de Arfe's processional cross, which is carried in the Corpus Christi parades. *Cathedral, Plaza Catedral; admission free; open evenings for services, 6:30–7:30. Cathedral museum, entrance on Calle Acero, tel. 956/28–61–54. Admission: 250 pesetas. Open Mon. 10–12, Tues.–Sat. 10–1; closed Sun.*

Walk across to the Plaza San Juan de Diós, one of the city's liveliest hubs. It's overlooked by the impressive **Ayuntamiento** (City Hall), built in two parts, in 1799 and 1861, and attractively illuminated at night. Walk up Calle San Francisco to the **Oratorio de la Santa Cueva,** an oval 18th-century chapel that contains three frescoes by Goya. *Calle Rosario. Admission: 50 pesetas. Open Mon.–Fri. 10–1; closed weekends.*

Just up the hill, the Plaza San Francisco, surrounded by old houses painted white, cream, and yellow, is a pretty square filled with orange trees and beautiful street lamps. It's especially lively at paseo time.

What to See and Do with Children

Cádiz offers **steamer rides** across the bay on *El Vapor* (*see* Getting Around, in Essential Information, *above*). **Chipiona, Rota,** and **Sanlúcar** have good, sandy **beaches.** In **Jerez,** the Thursday **Horse Show** at the Royal Andalusian School of Equestrian Art (*see* Tour 3, *above*) is likely to enthrall young horse lovers. On N IV, just north of **Puerto de Santa María,** an **aquapark** (AquaSherry) provides opportunities for splashers.

One of **Seville's** attractions for children is climbing the **Giralda** for a spectacular view. **Horse and buggy** (*coche caballos*) **rides** can be fun either in the Plaza Virgen de los Reyes, on Adolfo Rodríguez Jurado, or in the María Luisa Park at the Plaza de España. (Rates are set by the city and posted; an hour's ride will cost at least 3,500 pesetas, but prices can double during Holy Week and the April Fair.) The Plaza de España also offers **donkey carts, rowboats,** and **pedaloes,** as well as ducks to feed on the Isla de los Patos. Seville's children enjoy feeding the white pigeons of the Plaza de América. The Guadalquivir has a variety of choices for boating enthusiasts: pedaloes or canoes (ask at the tourist office or on the riverbank near the Torre del Oro); or **Cruceros Guadalquivir** (Paseo Marqués de Contadero, beside the Torre del Oro; **Cruceros del Sur,** tel. 95/421–1396). The excitement and color of a late-evening **flamenco** performance may be a memorable experience for older children and teenagers (*see* Nightlife, *below*).

Off the Beaten Track

If you've a day to spare in Seville and want to go somewhere that not too many tourists know about, then drive out to **Aracena,** 90 km (56 mi) northwest of Seville along N630, then N433, in the Sierra Morena mountains in the north of Huelva province. The main attraction in this town of 5,100 people is the spectacular cave known as the **Gruta de las Maravillas** (Cave of Marvels). There are 12 natural caverns with stalactites and stalagmites arranged in wonderful patterns, long corridors, and beautiful natural-colored lakes. *Plaza Pozo de Nieves, Pozo de Nieves, tel. 955/11–03–55. Admission: 750 pesetas adults, 550 pesetas children. Guided tours daily at 10:30, 11:30, 12:30, 1:30, 3, 4, 5, and 6.*

Aracena has many fine old mansions that were once the summer homes of wealthy Sevillian families. Be sure to sample a plate of the local serrano ham from nearby Jabugo, famous for its acorn-fed gray pigs.

For something really off the beaten track, you could continue 40 km (25 mi) west of Aracena on N433 to **Aroche,** a village of 4,000 people with a 12th-century Arab castle and ancient Gothic and Baroque houses. Here you'll find the **Museo del Santo Rosario** (Rosary Museum), with a collection of more than 1,100 rosaries donated by famous Catholics. *Alferez Lobo 7. Admission: 100 pesetas. Open daily 10–1.*

Shopping

Cádiz   In Cádiz, you'll find all the usual Andalusian handicrafts, especially ceramics and wicker, but no specialized local crafts. Antiques stores: **Antiquaria** (Cánovas del Castillo 7), **Belle Epoque** (Antonio López 2), **Casa Rodríguez** (Enrique de las Marinas 1).

Jerez   In Jerez, look for wicker and ceramics. This town of famous horses naturally has specialized saddle shops: **Duarte** (Larga 15), **Arcab** (Av. Duque de Abrantes), **Guarnicionería Jerezana** (Calle Zaragoza).

Seville   Seville is the region's main shopping center, and here you'll find all the souvenirs associated with Andalucía. You'll find most of these souvenirs in the Barrio de Santa Cruz and on the streets around the cathedral and Giralda, especially Calle Alemanes.

The main shopping area—for sevillanos, as opposed to tourists—is the Calle Sierpes, and its neighboring streets of Tetuan, Velázquez, Plaza Magdalena, and Plaza Duque. The **Corte Inglés** department store on the Plaza Duque stays open during siesta hours. **Galerías Preciados** is on Plaza Magdalena.

Antiques   Look along Mateos Gago opposite the Giralda; on Jamerdana in the Barrio de Santa Cruz; and Rodrigo Caro, between Plazas Alianza and Doña Elvira in the Barrio Santa Cruz.

Books   In English: **Libros Vértice** (Mateos Gago 24), **Pascual Lázaro** (Sierpes 2), **Tarsis** (Méndez Núñez 17).

Castanets   **Filigrana** (Cereza 3), out beyond the Macarena Gate, is a good source.

Ceramics   **Martian Ceramics** (Sierpes 76) has a good range of high-quality plates and dishes. Try also along Mateos Gago; Romero Murube, between Plaza Triunfo and Plaza Alianza, on the edge of the barrio; and between Plaza Doña Elvira and Plaza de los Venerables Sacerdotes, also in the barrio.

Embroidery   **Juan Foronda** (Argote de Molina 18).

Fans   **Casa Rubio** (Sierpes 56), **Zadi** (Sierpes 48).

Flamenco Dresses   Beware, these are prohibitively expensive. You'll find the cheapest ones in the **Corte Inglés**, or surprisingly, in the souvenir shops on Calle Alemanes. For serious costumes, go to **Pardales** (Cuna 23) or **Lina** (Lineros 7).

Leather and Suede   **Artesanía Textil** (García de Vinuesa 33), **Juan Foronda** (Plaza Virgen de los Reyes), **Feliciano Foronda** (Alvarez Quintero 52).

Porcelain   **Las Cadenas** (Calle Vida in Barrio Santa Cruz), **Zadi** (Sierpes 48), **El Corte Inglés** (Plaza Duque).

Street Markets   Plaza del Duque, daily crafts and jewelry stalls; El Jueves flea market, Calle Feria on Thursday mornings; Alameda de Hercules, crafts market on Sunday mornings; Plaza del Cabildo, coin and stamp market on Sunday mornings.

Sports

Water Sports   There are yacht clubs and marinas in most towns on and around the
Sailing   Bay of Cádiz. About 50 regattas are held each year for all kinds of boats. For information on sailing, inquire at the local tourist office.

The region's newest marina is **Puerto Sherry** (tel. 956/85–53–00 and 956/85–25–27), on the Bay of Cádiz, near Puerto de Santa María.

Windsurfing Windsurfing is available at Matalascañas in Huelva province. Tarifa, 90 km (56 mi) southeast of Cádiz, has some of the best windsurfing in Europe, but winds and currents are strong and suitable for experienced windsurfers only.

Spectator Sports
Racing

Formula One Grand Prix car and motorcycle races are held at the race circuit at Jerez de la Frontera. Late September and early October see the Formula One Tío Pepe Grand Prix. For information, call the Circuit Office (tel. 956/30–80–16).

Bullfights The season runs from Easter until late October. Most corridas are held on Sundays, with the exception of special fiestas. In **Seville,** bullfights take place at the Maestranza bullring, on the Paseo de Colón (tel. 95/422–4576). This is one of Spain's leading bullrings—few toreros gain nationwide recognition until they have fought here. The best season is during the April Fair, when fights take place each day with Spain's leading toreros. Tickets for these fights are expensive, and you should buy them in advance from the official *despacho de entradas* (ticket office) on Calle Adriano, beside the Maestranza ring. Other genuine, but unofficial, *despachos* on Calle Sierpes sell tickets, too, but they charge a 20% commission.

Jerez's bullring is situated on Calle Circo, northeast of the city center. Tickets are sold at the official ticket office on Calle Porvera (tel. 956/34–61–48), although there are now only about four bullfights held each year.

Beaches The Atlantic beaches of the Costa de la Luz generally offer better bathing than those on the Costa del Sol. The sea here is rougher and more exciting than the Mediterranean, and the sand is mostly golden rather than fine gray grit. You'll find some of the best beaches on the shoreline between **Rota, Chipiona,** and **Sanlúcar de Barrameda** in Cádiz province and around **Mazagón** and **Matalascañas** in Huelva province. In the city of **Cádiz** there are some stretches of sandy beach along the **Paseo Marítimo** in the new town on the isthmus.

Dining and Lodging

Dining

Seafood and sherry wines are the specialty of this region. Puerto de Santa María and Sanlúcar de Barrameda are famed as the best places to eat fried fish and shellfish in Andalucía. Most locals drink finos or manzanillas with their meals rather than table wine.

The restaurants listed for Seville are those within easy walking distance of the center of town. Two well-known restaurants farther out are **La Dorada** and **Rincón de Curro Maitres.** Unless specifically mentioned, neat casual dress will suffice in all of our listings. Restaurants in the $$$ category tend to be more formal in winter than in summer. In these places jacket and tie are advisable but rarely essential, especially in hot weather. Formal dress is usually required only in restaurants of five-star hotels. Reservations are rarely essential, and we have mentioned those places where they are advisable. Many restaurants are closed on Sunday evenings, and several in Seville close for a month's vacation in August.

Highly recommended restaurants are indicated by a star ★.

Category	Cost*
$$$$	over 12,000 ptas
$$$	8,000–12,000 ptas
$$	4,500–8,000 ptas
$	under 4,500 ptas

per person for a three-course à la carte meal, excluding tax and service

Lodging

This region has several fine hotels. You'll find four paradors; those at Carmona and Arcos de la Frontera are ancient palaces with great views, and both are worth a special visit. Those at Mazagón (Huelva) and the Atlántico in Cádiz are modern, comfortable hotels. In addition, you can stay at converted monasteries in Puerto de Santa María and Sanlúcar de Barrameda or on a private luxury ranch near Arcos de la Frontera. Seville has grand old hotels like the famous Alfonso XIII and the Colón, both newly renovated. Thanks to Expo '92, it also has a total of 22 new hotels—nine of them four-star establishments.

If you plan to visit during famous festivals, such as Seville's Holy Week or April Fair or Jerez's May Horse Fair or September Vintage Festival, it is essential to book early—four to eight months in advance in Seville, though that's not to say you won't find a room somewhere if you simply turn up. If you intend to visit Cádiz during its February Carnival celebrations, it would be wise to book at least a month or so in advance.

Seville's hotel prices skyrocketed to absurd levels during Expo '92, but a post-party reality check convinced officials to lower rates to fill the city's many hotels. As a result, prices have fallen sharply, in some cases as much as 30%. It's also still possible to find genuinely inexpensive lodging, but the rooms will be tiny, and you'll have to scour areas far from the city center. Prices fluctuate dramatically with the seasons—much more so than in most other parts of Spain—so you'd be wise to check ahead for prices.

During Holy Week and the April Fair, all hotel rates in Seville rise steeply and legitimately by at least half as much again.

Highly recommended hotels are indicated by a star ★ .

Category	Cost*
$$$$	over 20,000 ptas
$$$	11,500–20,000 ptas
$$	8,000–11,500 ptas
$	under 8,000 ptas

Prices are for a standard double room for two, excluding tax.

Arcos de la Frontera
Lodging
★

Cortijo Faín. This exclusive resort hotel is set in a 17th-century farmhouse on a ranch 3 km (1.8 mi) southeast of Arcos. The old *cortijo* is surrounded by olive groves and enclosed in high white walls covered in bougainvillea. The atmosphere is personal and intimate, with just 10 suites, all with their own fireplaces. The ranch has an outstanding 10,000-volume library. Advance reservations are essential. *Carretera de Algar, Km 3, 11630, tel. 956/70–11–67; for reservations in U.S., call 818/907–0642, fax 818/981–7910. 10 suites. Facilities: restaurant, pool, gardens, conference rooms, horseback riding, hunting. AE, MC, V. $$$*

★ **Parador Casa del Corregidor.** From the semicircular terrace of this parador on Arco's main square, you can see both Arcos castle and the rolling valley of the Guadalete River. Charles de Gaulle wrote part of his memoirs while staying here. Among the public rooms are a bar decorated with ceramic tiles and bullfight pictures, a panoramic restaurant that opens onto the terrace, and an enclosed patio filled with leafy potted plants. Rooms are furnished in traditional parador style. Book well in advance. Local dishes in the restaurant include *berenjenas arcenses* (spicy eggplant with ham and chorizo) and *chocos con judías* (squid with beans). *Plaza de España, 11630, tel. 956/70–05–00, fax 956/70–11–16. 24 rooms. Facilities: restaurant (reservations advisable), bar. AE, DC, MC, V. $$$*

El Convento. This tiny hotel, in part of an old convent, is a real find. Perched on top of the cliff right behind the parador, it shares the same splendid view of the rolling farmlands of the Guadalete Valley. It consists of just eight rooms, a bar, and a four-table restaurant with a large sunny patio. The owners, Sr. and Sra. Roldán, who obviously love their work, will make you very welcome. Dishes in the restaurant are lovingly prepared and often include local game specialties, such as *perdiz estofado* (partridge stew). Desserts are pastries and cookies made from old convent recipes. *Maldonado 2, 11630, tel. 956/70–23–33. 8 rooms. Facilities: restaurant, bar. AE, MC, V. $*

Cádiz **El Faro.** Gonzalo Córdoba's restaurant, located in a fishing quarter,
Dining justly deserves its fame as the best restaurant in the province. On
★ the outside it's one of many low white houses decorated with bright blue flowerpots. Inside the decor is warm and inviting, with half-tile walls, glass lanterns, oil paintings, and photos of old Cádiz. Hams hang from the ceiling of the bar, and the counter is piled high with oranges. Fish and seafood dominate the menu, but there are plenty of alternatives, such as *cebón al queso de cabrales* (venison in blue cheese sauce). *San Felix 15, tel. 956/21–10–68. Reservations advisable. AE, DC, MC, V. $$$*

El Anteojo. Located in a glass-front modern building on the headland, El Anteojo has good views over the bay toward Rota. Its walls are hung with photos of Cádiz dignitaries and famous diners. The menu offers specialties from different regions of Spain. You could try *merluza con kokotxas y almejas* (hake with crab and clams) from the Basque country or the local *frito gaditano* (Cádiz fried fish). *Alameda Apodaca 22, tel. 956/22–13–20. AE, V. $$*

Lodging **Atlántico.** This parador stands in a privileged position on the headland overlooking the bay. Its spacious public rooms have gleaming marble floors, and in a small outdoor patio chairs and tables are set around a fountain. The cheerful bright-green bar, decorated with ceramic tiles and bullfight posters, is a popular meeting place for Cádiz society. The rooms have white walls, polished wood floors, elegant black furniture, and small balconies facing the sea. *Parque Genovés 9, 11002, tel. 956/22–69–05, fax 956/21–45–82. 152 rooms. Facilities: restaurant, bar, pool, garden. AE, DC, MC, V. $$–$$$*

Francia y París. The advantage of this hotel is its central location on a pretty pedestrian square in the heart of the old town. The house has a rather boring, modern interior that includes a vast lobby, a big sitting room, and a small bar and breakfast room (no other meals). The rooms are simple, but comfortable. Room Nos. 108–114 have small balconies facing the square, where you can watch the lively paseo and savor the perfume of orange blossoms. *Plaza San Francisco 2, 11004, tel. 956/22–23–48. 57 rooms. Facilities: bar. AE, DC, MC, V. $*

Carmona
Dining and Lodging
★

Parador Alcázar del Rey Don Pedro. This delightful parador commands superb views from its hilltop position among the ruins of Pedro the Cruel's summer palace. The public rooms open off a central Moorish-style patio built of brick and ceramic tiles with slender columns, capitals, and horseshoe arches. The vaulted dining hall and adjacent bar open onto an outdoor terrace that overlooks the sloping garden—where even the pool is tiled in Moorish patterns—and rolling landscapes. The rooms are spacious, with polished tile floors, dark wood furniture, and green and blue woven rugs and bedspreads. All the rooms have south-facing balconies with spectacular country views. Advance reservations are advisable. *41410, tel. 95/414–1010, fax 95/414–1712, telex 72992. 59 rooms. Facilities: restaurant, bar, pool, garden. AE, DC, MC, V. $$$*

Jerez de la Frontera
Dining

Gaitán. This restaurant, within walking distance of the riding school, has white walls and brick arches decorated with colorful ceramic plates and photos of famous diners. It's very popular and crowded with business people at lunchtime. The menu is basically Andalusian with a few Basque dishes. When in season, *setas* (wild mushrooms) make a delicious starter. An entrée might be *perdiz al chocolate* (partridge in chocolate sauce). *Gaitán 3, tel. 956/34–95–49. AE, DC, MC, V. Closed Sun. evening and Aug. $$–$$$*

Tendido 6. This restaurant is near the bullring, opposite Gate 6—hence its name. The tables, which are set in an enclosed patio decorated with bullfight posters and potted plants, are draped with bright red tablecloths. The menu lists all the Spanish standbys: *jamón serrano* (cured ham), *gambas al ajillo* (garlic shrimp), and *tarta de almendra* (almond tart). *Circo 10, tel. 956/34–48–35. AE, MC, V. Closed Sun. $$*

Venta Antonio. Crowds come from far and wide to dine in this humble inn on the outskirts of Jerez. The decor is functional, but what counts is the superb fresh seafood cooked in top-quality olive oil. Here you can try the specialties of the Bay of Cádiz, such as *sopa de mariscos* (shellfish soup) for starters and *bogavantes de Sanlúcar*, a succulent local lobster, for your entrée. *Carretera de Sanlúcar, Km 5, tel. 956/14–05–35. Closed Mon. Oct.–Apr. AE, DC, MC, V. $$*

La Posada. The tiny white-walled dining room, decorated with iron grillwork, has only half a dozen tables. It is tucked away behind a bar in the side streets of central Jerez, just a three-minute walk from the Hotel Ávila. The menu is small, but both the meat and the fish dishes are well prepared. Let the chef advise you on the daily specials. *Arboledilla 2, tel. 956/33–74–74. V. Closed Sat. evening, Sun. $–$$*

Lodging

Jerez. This luxury hotel, recently upgraded to four-star classification, is set in a low, white three-story building in the residential neighborhood north of town. The bar and elegant El Cartujano restaurant overlook the sun terrace, the large outdoor pool, and a big leafy garden. There's an atmosphere of peace and quiet, and the public rooms are light and airy. The best rooms overlook the pool and garden; back rooms face the tennis courts and parking lot. *Av. Alvaro Domecq 35, 11405, tel. 956/30–06–00. 121 rooms, 4 suites. Facilities: restaurant, bar, pool, garden, tennis. AE, DC, MC, V. $$$*

★ **Royal Sherry Park.** Opened in 1988, this gleaming modern hotel is set back from the road in an unusually large, tree-filled garden. It is designed around several patios filled with ceramic plant pots and exotic green foliage, and modern paintings decorate its light, sunny hallways. The rooms are bright and airy, with dark blue bedspreads and pale gray carpets; most have balconies overlooking the garden. The elegant restaurant serves buffets on the terrace on Thursdays and Sundays. *Av. Alvaro Domecq 11, 11405, tel. 956/30–30–11, fax 956/31–13–00. 173 rooms. Facilities: restaurants, coffee shop, bar, pool, garden, conference rooms, shops. AE, DC, MC, V. $$$*

Avenida Jerez. Opposite the Royal Sherry Park, this modern, functional hotel opened in 1987. The light, airy, and sunny rooms are decorated in white and pale gray. Ask for a room at the back; those at the front are close to the road and can be noisy despite double glazing. *Av. Alvaro Domecq 10, 11405, tel. 956/34–74–11, fax 956/33–72–96. 95 rooms. Facilities: coffee shop, bar, garden. AE, DC, MC, V. $$*

Ávila. This simple, friendly hotel in a side street off Calle Arcos offers good-value accommodations in the center of town. A television lounge and a small bar and breakfast room open off the lobby. The rooms are modern with basic furnishings and tile floors. *Ávila 3, 11401, tel. 956/33–48–08. 32 rooms. Facilities: breakfast room. AE, DC, MC, V. $*

Matalascañas
Lodging

El Cortijo. Located near the Doñana National Park, this hotel provides overnight accommodations for visitors to the park. *Sector E, Parcelas 15 y 46, tel. 955/43–02–59. 24 rooms. Facilities: café, garden, pool, tennis. AE, MC, V. $$*

Tierra Mar. If you want to stay longer to explore the Doñana park, you can find lodging nearby at the Tierra Mar. *Matalascañas Parc. 120 Sector M, tel. 955/44–03–00. 253 rooms. Facilities: café, discothèque, garden, pool, tennis, sauna. AE, DC, MC, V. Closed Nov.–Mar. $$*

Mazagón
Dining and Lodging

Parador Cristobal Colón. This peaceful, modern parador, 3 km (2 mi) southeast of Mazagón, stands on a cliff surrounded by pine groves and overlooks a sandy beach. It was refurbished in 1989, and the rooms are all well equipped; most have balconies overlooking the garden, which is a blaze of color and flowering shrubs. Traditional Andalusian dishes and local seafood specialties are served in the restaurant. Typical entrées include *choquitos rellenos* (stuffed baby squid with peppers). *Carretera Matalascañas, 21130, tel. 955/53–63–00. 43 rooms. Facilities: restaurant, bar, pool, garden, beach, tennis. AE, DC, MC, V. $$$*

Puerto de Santa María
Dining

Eating at any of the outdoor bars along the Ribera del Marisco can often be more fun than dining formally in a restaurant. If you enjoyed **El Faro** in Cádiz, there's another branch, run by Gonzalo's son, in Puerto (Carretera de Rota, Km 0.5, tel. 956/85–80–03 or 956/85–09–52; closed Sun. evening).

Don Peppone. Jose Luis Gomez Heredia has made his restaurant a seafood lover's destination of choice. In winter, a fireplace warms the dining room; in summer, you can eat on an outdoor terrace. Some of the tempting offerings are the *caracoles al horno* (oven-baked snails), *rodaballo al grill* (grilled turbot), and *ensalada de pimientos rojos con ajo* (sweet red-pepper salad with garlic). There's also an excellent wine cellar. *Caceres (Playa de Valdelagrana), tel. 956/56–10–99. AE, DC, V. Closed Wed. $$$*

El Patio. Tucked away in a corner, one block behind the Ribera del Marisco, this pretty restaurant is built around an 18th-century patio. Colorful ceramic plates and potted plants decorate the dining room. The menu combines local seafood from the Bay of Cádiz with Andalusian dishes like *rabo de toro* (oxtail). The homemade desserts are especially good. *Plaza de la Herrería, tel. 956/54–05–06. AE, DC, MC, V. $$*

Lodging **Monasterio de San Miguel.** In the summer of 1989 this monastery,
★ which dates to 1733, opened as a luxury hotel. It's in the heart of town, a few blocks from the harbor. There's nothing Spartan about the former cells, now air-conditioned rooms with all the modern conveniences. The Baroque church is a concert auditorium, and the cloister gardens provide a peaceful refuge for visitors. Beamed ceilings, polished marble floors, and huge brass lamps help retain the 18th-century atmosphere. *Monasterio de San Miguel, 11500, tel. 956/54–04–40. 177 rooms. Facilities: restaurant, bar, garden, pool, squash courts. AE, DC, MC, V. $$$*

Sanlúcar de **Bigote.** On the Bajo de Guía beach, this fish restaurant is colorful
Barrameda and informal. *Tel. 956/36–26–96 or 956/36–32–42. Reservations es-*
Dining *sential during Spanish vacation time. AE, DC, MC, V. Closed Sun. $$*

Seville **La Albahaca.** One of Seville's prettiest restaurants is located in the
Dining heart of the Barrio de Santa Cruz. This typical Andalusian house was built by the celebrated architect Juan Talavera as a home for his own family. Inside, three dining rooms are colorfully decorated with ceramic tiles and leafy potted plants. The service is friendly and professional, and the menu combines traditional Spanish and French dishes with innovative *nouvelle* creations. The entrées include *suprema de lubina al hinojo fresco* (sea bass supreme with fresh fennel). *Plaza Santa Cruz 12, tel. 95/422–0714. Reservations advisable. AE, DC, MC, V. Closed Sun. $$$*

★ **Egaña-Oriza.** One of Seville's newest and most acclaimed restaurants, the Egaña-Oriza is on the edge of the Murillo Gardens. The decor is modern, with walls painted in deep peach and air-force blue. Large windows create an atmosphere of sunshine and light. José Mari Egaña, the owner, is Basque, and the menu reflects the influence of his homeland's cuisine. For an entrée you could try *estofado de jabalí con ciruelas y pasas* (casserole of wild boar with cherries and raisins). *San Fernando 41, tel. 95/422–7271. Reservations advised. AE, DC, MC, V. Closed Sat. lunch, Sun., and Aug. $$$*

La Isla. At this restaurant in the Arenal district, fresh fish is brought in daily from the Cádiz and Huelva coasts. Some of the dishes are based on traditional Galician fish cuisine. The downstairs dining room has cream stucco walls and high-backed black chairs; the upstairs dining room, with blue-and-white tile decor, is a little less formal. *Parrillada de mariscos y pescados*, a fish and seafood grill for two people, is one of the best bets. Simply cooked meat dishes are also available. *Arfe 25, tel. 95/421–5376. AE, DC, MC, V. Closed Mon. and Aug. $$$*

San Marco. Ask a sevillano to recommend a really good restaurant, and he will probably send you to San Marco. This is an Italian restaurant in an old neoclassical-style house in Seville's shopping district. It has a leafy patio and is furnished with antiques. The owner and the chef are of Italian origin, and the menu is a happy combination of Italian, French, and Andalusian cuisines. You'll find good pasta dishes, such as ravioli stuffed with sea bass in clam sauce. *Cuna 6, tel. 95/421–2440. Reservations essential. AE, DC, MC, V. Closed Sun. and Aug. $$$*

Enrique Becerra. This small, cozy restaurant, a short walk from the cathedral, is in a whitewashed house with wrought-iron window grilles. Inside, a lively crowded bar, decorated with Sevillian ceramic tiles, is a meeting place for locals who enjoy its excellent selection of tapas. The menu concentrates on traditional Andalusian home-cooked dishes, such as *jarrete de ternera a la cazuela* (veal stew). *Gamazo 2, tel. 95/421– 3049. Reservations advisable. AE, DC, MC, V. Closed Sun. $$–$$$*

El Bacalao. Its specialty is, of course, *bacalao*, or salt cod, which you'll find prepared in 101 different ways. The decor is modern mesón: rough white walls, wooden tables and chairs, and just a touch of Sevillian ceramics. The bar is popular for tapas and sherry or white wine. *Plaza Ponce de León 15, tel. 95/421–6670. AE, DC, MC, V. Closed Sun. and Aug. $$*

Hostería del Laurel. This restaurant is geared to tourists, but its big advantage is its location in the Barrio de Santa Cruz. In summer you can dine on the outdoor terrace in the square, surrounded by beautiful white-and-ocher painted houses and balconies bright with geraniums or petunias. It has two indoor dining rooms decorated in traditional Castilian style: wood paneling, white walls, heavy wooden tables, and leather-backed chairs. There's a menu in English offering a wide choice of traditional Spanish fare, and the service is friendly. *Plaza de los Venerables 5, tel. 95/422-0295. AE, DC, MC, V. $$*

★ **La Judería.** This bright, modern restaurant near the Hotel Fernando III is fast gaining recognition for the quality of its Andalusian and international cuisine and reasonable prices. Fish dishes from the north of Spain and meat from Avila are specialties. Try *cordero lechal* (roast baby lamb) or *urta a la roteña* (a fish dish unique to Rota). *Cano y Cueto 13, tel. 95/441–2052. Reservations required. AE, DC, MC, V. Closed Tues. and first 2 weeks in Aug. $$*

Modesto. This restaurant, on the edge of the Barrio de Santa Cruz, is popular among Sevillanos, who come here for its excellent value and efficient service. Downstairs is a lively crowded tapas bar, and upstairs is a restaurant with white stucco walls above blue and white tiles. Try the *menú del día* or the Tío Diego (Uncle Jim's) specialty of ham, mushrooms, and shrimp. *Cano y Cueto 5, tel. 95/441–1816. AE, DC, MC, V. Closed Wed. $$*

La Cueva del Pez de Espada. The Swordfish's Cave is a colorful, tourist-oriented mesón just off Plaza Doña Elvira. The tables have bright red cloths, and the white walls are hung with cheerful oil paintings, ceramic tiles, trailing plants, and other typical Sevillian paraphernalia. The service is friendly and helpful, and an English menu offers a good choice of traditional Spanish meat and fish dishes. *Rodrigo Caro 18, tel. 95/421–3143. AE, DC, MC, V. $–$$*

Girarda. You'll find this kitschy but charming tourist restaurant (which doubles as a small hostel) in the heart of the Barrio de Santa Cruz. Half a dozen tables with bright blue, red, green, and pink plastic coverings are set in the patio of a private house. Antonia Miranda, who, with black hair scraped back and huge gold earrings, looks like a retired flamenco dancer, runs the place in the absence of her bullfighter husband. A canary sings in its cage on the stairs, and colorful tiles, trailing plants, and horse brasses abound. The fare is traditional Spanish. *Justin de Neve 8, tel. 95/421–5113. No credit cards. $*

Mesón Castellano. This recently refurbished old house opposite the church of San José is an ideal place for lunch after a morning's shopping on Calle Sierpes. Specialties are Castilian meat dishes. *Jovellanos 6, tel. 95/421–4028. Lunch only. AE, DC, MC, V. Closed Sun. $*

Mesón Don Raimundo. This small restaurant is in an alleyway off Calle Sierpes. It's prettily decorated with blue-and-white tile walls, pink linen tablecloths, stained-glass windows, fans, and a picture of the American bullfighter John Fulton. The house specialties are meat dishes from the north, such as *solomillo a la castellana* (steak

Castilian style), though you'll find fish dishes, too. *Argote de Molina 26, tel. 95/422–3355. AE, DC, MC, V. Closed Sun. evening.* $

Lodging ★ **Alfonso XIII.** Inaugurated by King Alfonso XIII on April 28, 1929, this splendid Mudéjar Revival palace is in many ways one of the great hotels of Europe. Its public rooms are resplendent with marble floors, wood-paneled ceilings, heavy Moorish lamps, stained glass, and ceramic tile decor in the typical blue, green, and yellow of Seville. The hotel is built around a huge central patio surrounded by ornate brick arches and filled with potted plants and a central fountain. The restaurant, with its painted wood-paneled ceiling, heavy drapes, huge central table, and ornate wrought-iron gate, is imposing. Much of the hotel, both inside and out, was renovated for Expo '92. *San Fernando 2, 41004, tel. 95/422–2850, fax 95/421–6033. 149 rooms and suites. Facilities: 2 restaurants, bar, pool, garden, shops, conference facilities. AE, DC, MC, V.* $$$$

★ **Colón.** Seville's other grand old hotel, the Colón, was also built for the 1929 Exhibition and was completely restored in 1988. A white marble staircase leads up to the central lobby, which is surmounted by a magnificent stained-glass dome and crystal candelabra. The reception area, La Fuente restaurant, and the Bar Majestic open off this circular lobby. Downstairs is the renowned El Burladero restaurant, with bullfight ambience, and La Tasca tavern. The stylish old-fashioned rooms are elegantly furnished in pink and green, with silk drapes and bedspreads and dark wooden fittings. *Canalejas 1, 41001, tel. 95/422–2900, fax 95/422–0938. 204 rooms, 14 suites. Facilities: 2 restaurants, 2 bars, rooftop garden, hairdressers, garage, convention rooms. AE, DC, MC, V.* $$$$

Meliá Sevilla. This vast, modern, airy hotel behind the Plaza de España opened in 1987. In its spaciousness, facilities, and careful attention to detail, it resembles the best American business hotels. Ask for a room at the front facing the pool and Plaza de España, which is illuminated Friday to Sunday; those at the back have poor views. The best rooms and suites, on the ninth floor, have striking deep blue-and-pink decor and balconies overlooking the pool. *Dr. Pedro de Castro 1, 41004, tel. 95/442–2611, fax 95/442–1608. 366 rooms, 5 suites. Facilities: restaurant, coffee shop, bar, pool, sun terrace, garage, convention facilities, shopping gallery. AE, DC, MC, V.* $$$$

Dona Maria. Close to the cathedral, this is one of Seville's most charming hotels. Some rooms are small and plain; others are tastefully furnished with antiques. Room 310 has a four-poster double bed, and 305 two single four-posters; both have spacious bathrooms. There's no restaurant, but there's a rooftop pool with a good view of the Giralda. *Don Remondo 19, tel. 95/422–4990, fax 95/421–9546. 60 rooms. AE, DC, MC, V.* $$$

★ **Inglaterra.** This modern hotel overlooking the central Plaza Nueva has long had a reputation for individual attention and excellent service. No tour groups stay here, and the staff make an effort to call their guests by name. The best rooms are on the fifth floor; they are furnished with comfortable settees, armchairs, and flowered curtains, and have big balconies. The wood-paneled first-floor dining room overlooks orange trees and the Plaza Nueva. On the ground floor, the bar and sitting rooms serve as meeting places for Seville society. *Plaza Nueva 7, 41001, tel. 95/422–4970, fax 95/456–1336. 114 rooms, 3 suites. Facilities: restaurant, bar, garage, gift shop. AE, DC, MC, V.* $$$

Pasarela. Close to the Meliá, behind the Plaza de España, the Pasarela is smaller and cozier than its giant neighbor. On the ground floor you'll find several small sitting rooms furnished with comfortable armchairs and settees. Oil paintings and table lamps give it a homey atmosphere. The rooms are large and fully carpeted, with predominantly brown-and-beige modern decor and white bedspreads. *Av. de la Borbolla 11, 41004, tel. 95/441–5511, fax 95/442–0727. 82 rooms. Facilities: bar, breakfast room, Finnish sauna, gym, garage. AE, DC, MC, V. $$$*

Bécquer. This well-maintained modern hotel dates from the late 1960s and has marble floors, dark wood and leather furniture, and huge mirrors in the public areas. A small sitting room with a wood-paneled ceiling is dedicated to the poet Gustavo Adolfo Bécquer. The rooms are traditionally Spanish, with white walls, carved wood headboards, and woven bedspreads. *Reyes Católicos 4, 41001, tel. 95/422–8900, fax 95/421–4400. 120 rooms. Facilities: bar, breakfast room, garage. AE, DC, MC, V. $$*

Giralda. This modern hotel, in a cul-de-sac off Recaredo, caters largely to tour-bus groups, but the service is friendly and professional. Paintings of Spanish scenes, an enormous cage, and Moorish grilles decorate the lobby. The adjoining restaurant has glazed half-tile walls ornamented with ceramic plates and urns. The spacious, light rooms are furnished in typical Castilian style. *Sierra Nevada 3, 41003, tel. 95/441–6661, fax 95/441–9352. 65 rooms, 5 suites. Facilities: restaurant, bar, garage, convention facilities. AE, DC, MC, V. $$*

Murillo. In the very heart of the Barrio de Santa Cruz, the Murillo can be reached only on foot; take a taxi to the Plaza de Santa Cruz and a porter will collect your luggage. The rooms are simple, with bare floors, white walls, and bright red bedspreads. But the location, friendly atmosphere, and wonderfully ornate public rooms with heavy wood-paneled ceilings are splendid. *Lope de Rueda 7, 41004, tel. 95/421–6095, fax 95/421–9616. 61 rooms. Facilities: bar, breakfast room. AE, DC, MC, V. $–$$*

Girarda. One of several very basic family-run hotels in the Barrio Santa Cruz, the Girarda is in an old, Moorish-style building with a colorful interior patio that also serves as a restaurant. Antonia Miranda runs the place in the absence of her bullfighter husband, Pedro Sanchez Martínez. *Justin de Neve 8, tel. 95/421–5113. 5 rooms. No credit cards. $*

Internacional. If you value charm and Spanish atmosphere above creature comforts, this pretty old Andalusian house near Casa Pilatos is unbeatable. The friendly, family-run hotel has a heavy wrought-iron gate that opens into the central patio-reception area. Ivy cascades from the balconies of the first-floor gallery; the patio's glass roof lets in plenty of sunlight. A white marble staircase leads to the upstairs bedrooms, which are very simply furnished with twin beds. *Aguilas 17, 41003, tel. 95/421–3207. 26 rooms. Facilities: parking. MC, V. $*

★ **La Rábida.** A charming old Andalusian house in the Arenal district has been converted into a comfortable, modestly priced hotel that retains all its Old World Sevillian atmosphere. The spacious modernized bedrooms are fully carpeted; many overlook a leafy patio with oblique views of the Giralda. The hotel is popular with both tour groups and individual travelers. *Castelar 24, 41001, tel. 95/422–0960, telex 73062. 87 rooms. Facilities: restaurant, bar. AE, MC, V. $*

The Arts and Nightlife

The Arts

To find out what's on in **Seville,** look in the local press, in the *ABC*, *Correo de Andalucía, Sudoeste,* or *Nueva Andalucía,* or pick up a copy of the free monthly leaflet *El Giraldillo.* It lists classical music and jazz venues, movies, theater performances, art exhibitions, and dance events in Seville and all major Andalusian cities, including Cádiz. You can also call a city information line (tel. 010) for up-to-the-minute information on art shows and cultural events; most operators speak English. The major venue for all cultural events in **Cádiz** is the **Gran Teatro Manuel de Falla** (Plaza de Falla, tel. 956/22–08–28).

Music A city that has long figured prominently in the opera world, Seville opened its new opera house in late 1991 (Paseo de Colón, at the corner of Nuñez de Balboa, tel. 95/422–6573). Classical concerts are held at the **Teatro Lope de Vega** (Av. María Luisa, tel. 95/423–1835), the **Conservatorio Superior de Música** (Jesús del Gran Poder), and in the **cathedral** and the church of **San Salvador.** Ballet performances are sometimes staged in the Teatro Lope de Vega.

Movies For films in English, look in the press or *El Giraldillo* for films marked *V.O. Subtitulada* (V.O. = Original Version).

Theater Seville has two theaters, the **Teatro Lope de Vega** and the **Teatro Alameda** (Calle Calatrava 13, tel. 95/438–8312). Tickets are sold at the theaters' box offices. A quarterly leaflet of events at both theaters (*Programación Teatros Municipales*) is published by Seville City Hall and is available from the tourist office. Be sure to check out what's at the opera house (*see* Music, *above*), which is formally known as the Teatro de la Maestranza—it's usually the best show in town.

Major Festivals and Fiestas Many of Spain's best-known fiestas take place in this region. Remember to book accommodations long in advance for any of these spectacles.

Feb. Week-long **Carnival** celebrations in Cádiz.
Mar. or Apr. Seville's **Holy Week** processions are the most famous in Spain. Jerez and Cádiz also have Semana Santa processions.
Apr. The **Feria de Abril,** Seville's annual Horse Fair, is celebrated with top bullfights; horse parades; flamenco costumes; and singing, dancing, and fireworks nightly in the fairground across the river.
May. The Andalusian horses of Jerez de la Frontera are the showpiece of this city's **Feria del Caballo** (May Horse Fair).
May or June. Famous Whitsuntide pilgrimage to the shrine of the **Virgen del Rocío** (Virgin of the Dew) in the village of El Rocío (Huelva). **Corpus Christi** (second Thursday after Whitsun) is celebrated with processions in Cádiz, Jerez, and Seville.
Aug. International **flamenco courses** are held in Jerez de la Frontera. The **Assumption** of the Virgin Mary is celebrated everywhere on the 15th, but especially in Seville, where it's the day of the city's patroness, the Virgen de los Reyes.
Sept. The **Fiesta de la Vendimia** (Grape Harvest Festival) is celebrated in all the wine-producing towns of Cádiz province. Jerez's Harvest Festival is particularly spectacular.
Oct. Celebrations for Cádiz's patroness, the **Virgen del Rosario.**
Dec. National **Contest of Flamenco Guitar** at the Fundación Andaluza de Flamenco in Jerez de la Frontera.

Nightlife

Casinos   The **Casino Bahía de Cádiz**, on the road between Jerez and Puerto de Santa María, is the only casino in this part of Andalucía. You can play roulette, baccarat, or blackjack, and there's a restaurant, a disco-thèque, and slots. *N IV, Km 650, tel. 956/87–10–42. Admission: 250 pesetas. Open daily 5 PM–5 AM. Passport required. Jacket required.*

Flamenco   Seville and Jerez are the capitals of flamenco. In Jerez, ask at the Tourist Office for details of flamenco events. Seville has three regular flamenco clubs, patronized more by tourists than by locals. Tickets are sold in most hotels; otherwise, make your own reservations (essential for groups, advisable for everyone in high season) by calling the club during the evening.

El Arenal (Rodo 7, tel. 95/421–6492; admission: 3,500 pesetas, not including dinner; performances nightly 9:30 and 11:30) is in the back room of the picturesque Mesón Dos de Mayo. Here, you have your own table rather than sit in rows.

Los Gallos (Plaza Santa Cruz 11, tel. 95/421–6981 or 95/422–8522; admission: 3,500 pesetas) is a small, intimate club in the heart of the Barrio de Santa Cruz that has good, fairly pure flamenco.

El Patio Sevillano (Paseo de Colón, tel. 95/421–4120 or 95/422–2068; admission: 3,500 pesetas; performances nightly 9:30, 11:15, sometimes 7:30 and 10) caters mainly to tour groups; the show is a mixture of regional Spanish dances (often performed to taped music) and pure flamenco by some outstanding guitarists, singers, and dancers.

Bars and   Because most of the locals eat their main meal at lunchtime, Seville's
Cafés   bars are packed in the evenings with people making a supper of tapas. Among the best are **Alhucema** (Carlos Canal 20A), **La Alicantina** (Plaza del Salvador 2), **Bodega El Arenal** (Pavia 11), **Casa Morales** (García de Vinuesa 11), **Casa Román** (Plaza de los Venerables), **Cervecería Giralda** (Mateos Gago 1), **Patio San Eloy** (top of San Eloy near Campana), **Rincón San Eloy** (San Eloy 24), and **El Rinconcillo** (Gerona 42).

15 Extremadura

By Michael
Jacobs

Updated by
Deborah
Luhrman

The very name Extremadura—the "land beyond the Douro"—suggests the wild, remote, and isolated character of this haunting region. The area, which has poor soil and is scarcely industrialized, has experienced extreme poverty. The film director Luis Buñuel established his reputation in the 1930s with a powerful documentary about the mountainous district of Las Hurdes, in northern Extremadura, then desperately poor, virtually unchanged since the Middle Ages, and still accessible only on foot or donkey. The Nobel Prize–winning novelist Camilo José Cela made his own debut with *The Family of Pascual Duarte*, a bleakly realistic study of a murderer brought up in the southern half of Extremadura, in a village "crouched over a road as long and as flat as a day without bread."

In 1601, at Fuente de Cantos, only a few miles from the village of Pascual Duarte, one of the greatest of Spain's artists, Francisco de Zurbarán, was born. A visit to the town, which lies on the main road between Andalucía and Extremadura, is essential for an understanding of Zurbarán's art. The simplified forms, flat, unmodulated colors, and powerful austerity of his works are mirrored in the treeless, undulating ocher expanses that surround his birthplace; it is one of the most abstract landscapes imaginable. In the 19th century, after a long period of neglect, Zurbarán's art was hailed as representing all that was most profound in the Spanish temperament. Similarly, today the region of Extremadura has been recognized as the pure, unsullied essence of Spain. It is a region that has resisted more than any other the onslaught of the 20th century, a place where raising pigs continues to be the major activity, where lizards are eaten, and where travel remains an adventure.

Though a strong backward character pervades the whole of Extremadura, the diverse lands that surround it have had their influence also. Officially, Extremadura comprises two provinces: Badajoz to the south, and Cáceres to the north. The dazzlingly white villages and sunbaked landscape of the former have much in common with neighboring Andalucía; Cáceres, meanwhile, with its wooded mountain valleys and half-timbered gray stone houses, is reminiscent of both Castile and northern Spain. Yet another influence is that of Portugal, which borders on both Badajoz and Cáceres.

Extremadura has not always been such an isolated and impoverished region. No other place in Spain has so many Roman monuments as the Extremaduran town of Mérida, which, in fact, was the capital of the vast Roman province of Lusitania. Economic and artistic decline set in after the Romans, but in the 16th century the region revived as the survivors among the famous and ruthless men who conquered and explored the New World—from Francisco Pizarro and Hernán Cortés to Nuñez de Balboa and Francisco de Orellana, first navigator of the Amazon—returned to their birthplace. They were responsible for the magnificent palaces that today constitute the glory of towns such as Cáceres and Trujillo. They, too, turned the remote monastery of Guadalupe—the miraculous Virgin of which had inspired their exploits overseas—into one of the great artistic repositories of Spain.

Essential Information

Important Addresses and Numbers

Tourist Information The most helpful and well equipped of Extremadura's tourist offices is at the entrance to **Mérida**'s Roman Theater (Pedro María Plano s/n, tel. 924/31–53–53). The other tourist offices in the region are in **Alcántara** (Avenida de Mérida 21, tel. 927/39–08–63), **Badajoz** (Pasaje de San Juan s/n, tel. 924/22–27–63), **Cáceres** (Plaza Mayor 36, tel. 927/24–63–47), **Plasencia** (Calle Trujillo 17, tel. 927/41–27–66), and **Trujillo** (Plaza Mayor 8, tel. 927/32–06–53). In places without tourist offices, information and maps can generally be found at the town hall *(ayuntamiento)*.

Emergencies **Police:** tel. 091.

Guided Tours

City Tours The main tourist centers of Extremadura offer city tours, but not on a regular basis; for information on these, contact the local tourist offices.

Bus Tours For specialized art tours, accompanied by an expert, contact the English-based firm **Prospect Art Tours Ltd.** (10 Barley Mow Passage, London W4 4PH, tel. 081/995–2163).

Arriving and Departing by Plane

The international airports nearest to Extremadura are at Madrid and Seville; Iberia runs daily flights from both cities to Badajoz, the Extremaduran capital.

Arriving and Departing by Car, Train, and Bus

It is best to rent a car outside the region, either in Madrid or Seville, or before leaving for Spain.

By Car The main highway from Madrid to Extremadura, the NV, was upgraded to four lanes in 1993, greatly reducing travel time from the capital. The N630, or Via de la Plata, which crosses Extremadura from north to south, is currently being improved as well, with construction expected to finish in 1996. The fastest approach from Portugal is along N4 from Lisbon to Badajoz.

By Train The principal train link with Extremadura is the line running from Madrid to Seville, passing through Plasencia, Cáceres, Mérida, and Zafra. The journey from Madrid to Plasencia takes three hours; from Seville to Zafra, 3½ hours. There is also a direct train from Lisbon, in Portugal, to Badajoz (five hours).

By Bus The bus links between Extremadura and the other Spanish provinces are far more frequent, extensive, and reliable than are the links by plane or train; the journeys also tend to be shorter. There are regular bus services to the main centers of the province from Madrid, Seville, Lisbon, Valladolid, Salamanca, and Barcelona. All the buses from Madrid go past Trujillo. The main company serving the province is **Auto Res** (Plaza Conde de Casal 6, tel. 91/551–7200).

Getting Around

By Car This is the most feasible way of exploring Extremadura if you are in a hurry. Off the autoroute, the main roads through the province are well surfaced and not too congested; the side roads, particularly those that traverse the wilder mountainous districts, such as the Sierra de Guadalupe, can be poorly paved and badly marked.

By Train Only the main towns in the province can be reached by train, and the services are very infrequent: For instance, the line connecting Plasencia, Cáceres, Mérida, and Zafra has just two trains a day, one of which runs at night. The stations also tend to be some distance from the town centers.

By Bus As with most of the traditionally poor parts of Europe, nearly every village in Extremadura is accessible by bus. However, on the lesser routes, buses tend to set off at a depressingly early hour in the morning and to leave you stranded at your destination for many hours, if not overnight.

Exploring Extremadura

A round-trip by car, covering the tours described below, can feasibly be done in three days: An excellent three-day tour from Madrid would be to take the slow, winding, but very beautiful C501 to Plasencia (via the monastery of Yuste), then go south to Cáceres and Mérida, and finally return to Madrid by way of Trujillo and Guadalupe. Alternatively, you could get a lightning impression of the region in the course of the day's drive between Madrid and Seville (take N V to Mérida, and then N630), stopping off for sightseeing and an excellent lunch at Trujillo; this is unquestionably the most enjoyable way of getting to the south of Spain, and infinitely preferable to the more usual route through La Mancha. If you are seeking outdoor activities and beautiful landscapes, you should take the tour to Plasencia, which will also appeal to anyone interested in the life of the emperor Carlos V. If Roman ruins attract you, go to Mérida, while Cáceres and Trujillo are a must if you love good food and are fascinated with the Spain of the conquistadors. The single outstanding attraction of the region is Guadalupe, which is worth a special journey: It combines a spectacular setting, an appealing village, two hotels situated in beautiful old buildings, and one of the most richly endowed and historically important monasteries in Spain.

Highlights for First-time Visitors

The old town of Cáceres (*see* Tour 2)
The monastery of Guadalupe (*see* Tour 3)
The Roman theater of Mérida (*see* Tour 4)
Trujillo (*see* Tour 2)
The monastery of Yuste (*see* Tour 1)

Tour 1: Plasencia

Numbers in the margin correspond to points of interest on the Extremadura map.

The most important town in the far north of Extremadura, ❶ **Plasencia** is situated on the banks of the narrow Jerte River, with good views of the Sierra de Gredos. It was founded by Alfonso VIII in 1180, just after he had captured the whole area from the Moors. The town's motto of *placeat Deo et hominibus* ("it pleases both God and men") might well have been a ploy on Alfonso's part to attract settlers to this wild and isolated place on the southern borders of the former kingdom of León. In 1196 the town was briefly recaptured, and many of its inhabitants were packed off to Morocco to work on the Great Mosque at Rabat. Badly damaged during the Peninsular War of 1808, Plasencia has today preserved far less of its medieval quarter than have other Extremaduran towns. Nonetheless, it still retains extensive fragments of its medieval walls and boasts a scattering of fine old buildings.

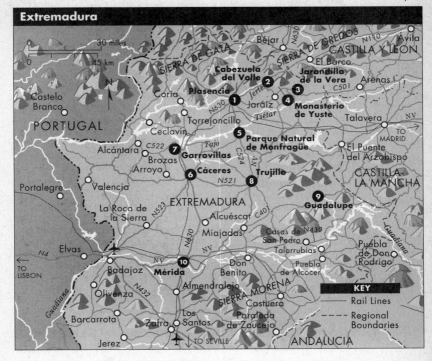

Extremadura

The **cathedral,** rising above the town's western fortifications, was founded in 1189 and rebuilt after 1320 in an austere Gothic style. Then, in 1498, the great Enrique de Egas, famous for his work in the Toledo cathedral and in the Royal Chapel at Granada, designed a new structure, which was to be only partially completed. The entrance to this curious and not wholly satisfactory complex is through the portal on the new cathedral's ornate but somber north facade (overlooking the Plaza de la Catedral). The dark, truncated interior of the new cathedral is notable for its delicate Renaissance ornamentation and, above all, for the beauty of its pilasters, the unbroken shafts of which sprout treelike into the ribs of the vaulting. The furnishings are mainly from the Baroque and neoclassical periods—for instance, the high altar by Gregorio Fernández, a leading 17th-century sculptor known for his realistic works in polychromed wood. You enter the old cathedral through the Gothic cloister, off which also stands the oldest surviving part of the building, the 13th-century chapter house (now the chapel of San Pablo)—a late Romanesque structure with an idiosyncratic Moorish-inspired dome. The museum installed within the truncated nave of the old cathedral contains a miscellaneous collection of ecclesiastical bric-a-brac, including vestments; a small archaeological display; and paintings by the 16th-century artist Morales. *Tel. 927/41–48–52. Admission to old cathedral: 150 pesetas. Open daily 9–1 and 4–6.*

Surrounding the old and new cathedrals are several austerely elegant structures of the Renaissance, all built in the gray stone of the area, most notably the **Palacio Episcopal** (Bishop's Palace, closed to the public), the **Hospital de Santa María** (now a cultural center), and the **Casa del Deán** (Dean's House; now a rather run-down police station). From the Plaza de la Catedral, head north along the Calle Blanca to the Plaza de San Nicolás, beyond which is the narrow Plaza de San Vicente. This carefully preserved square, lined with orange trees, is dominated on its northern side by the Renaissance **Palacio de Mirabel** (Palace of the Marquis of Mirabel); go through the arch in its middle and you will come to an alley affording a back view of the palace and its intricately carved coat of arms (admission: tip to caretaker, ask for Señor Felipe; usually open 10–2 and 4–6). East from the Plaza de San Vicente, at the other end of the Rua Zapatería, is the Plaza Mayor, a cheerful, arcaded square, animated by a market that has been held here every Tuesday morning since the 12th century. Farther east, you come to a large section of the town's medieval wall, on the other side of which, leading directly into the surrounding landscape, is a heavily restored Roman aqueduct.

Two of the finest excursions from Plasencia are along the valleys of the rivers Jerte and Tiétar, which run, respectively, to the north and south of the Sierra de Gredos. The N110 from Plasencia north to Ávila (150 km/90 mi) follows the narrow, fast-flowing Jerte almost to its source, then climbs above it to leave Extremadura and enter the bleak plateau of Castile. To the Greeks, the Jerte Valley was supposedly "the Valley of Pleasure." Its lower slopes are covered with a dense mantle of ash, chestnut, and cherry trees, their richness contrasting with the granite cliffs of the Sierra de Gredos above; try to come here either in the spring, when the colors are at their most varied, or in the fall, when the trees turn into a rippling carpet of browns, ochers, and reds. One of the best preserved of its many attractive villages is **Cabezuela del Valle,** 34 km (21 mi) from Plasencia on the N110, full of half-timbered stone houses. Like other settlements in this area, it once had a significant Jewish population.

Twelve and a half km (20 mi) farther north, at **Tornavacas,** a rough track (passable only on foot or in a strong car) leads over the Sierra de Gredos and down toward the village of Jarandilla de la Vera, in the valley of the Tiétar. (You'll have to turn right off the N110, following signs into the village, to pick up the track.) The track, with extensive views in its upper stages, descends into a narrow gorge with the dramatic name of La Garganta de los Infiernos (the Gorge of Hell). The excitement of the route is heightened by the knowledge that you are following in the footsteps of the Holy Roman Emperor Carlos V, who took this very path in 1556. Ill with gout, and weary after a lifetime of constant travel around Europe, Carlos had abdicated and decided to end his days in the monastery of Yuste, 12 km (7.2 mi) west of Jarandilla.

An easier approach to Jarandilla and Yuste is along winding C501, which runs from Plasencia in a northeasterly direction almost to Madrid. The village of **Jarandilla de la Vera,** 55 km (33 mi) from Plasencia, has a fortified palace of the 15th and 16th centuries (this is now the Parador Nacional Carlos V; *see* Dining and Lodging, *below*); Carlos V stayed here for a year while waiting for his quarters to be ready at Yuste.

The **Monasterio de Yuste** (Monastery of Yuste), in a wooded setting 2 km (1 mi) north of C501 (turn left, or northwest, at Cuacos, 45 km/27 mi from Plasencia, the way is well-marked with signs for the monastery), was founded by Hieronymite monks in the early 15th century. It was badly damaged in the Peninsular War and left to decay after the suppression of Spain's monasteries in 1835, but has recently been restored and taken over again by the Hieronymites. You can visit the Royal Chambers where Carlos stayed from February 1557 until his death on September 21 the following year. The bedroom where he died has a view into the church, which enabled Carlos to hear Mass from his bed (Felipe II was later to appropriate this idea at El Escorial). A ramp, originally intended to be climbed on horseback, leads up to a terrace overlooking an enchanting fish pond and the verdant valley of the Tiétar. *Tel. 927/17–21–30. Admission: 100 pesetas. Open Oct.–May, daily 9:30–12:30 and 3–6; June–Sept., daily 9:30–12:30 and 3:30–6:30.*

⑤ Parque Natural de Monfragüe (Monfragüe Nature Park) is 20 km (12 mi) south of Plasencia, at the confluence of the rivers Tiétar and Tajo; C524, which connects Plasencia with Trujillo, runs through the middle of it. Turned into a national park in 1979, this beautiful wild area is known for its wide range of plant and animal life, including imperial eagles and the world's largest colony of black vultures.

Tour 2: Cáceres and Trujillo

⑥ Originally a Roman colony and later heavily disputed between the Moors and Christians, **Cáceres** is today a provincial capital and prosperous agricultural town. The bus and railway stations are next to each other, a good half-hour walk from the old center, along the characterless Avenida de España. Once you are on the Calle San Anton, the look of the town improves considerably, particularly as you reach the intimate Plaza de San Juan, where you will find one of Extremadura's greatest restaurants, El Figón de Eustaquio (*see* Dining and Lodging, *below*). Beyond this square is the long, inclined, and stony-looking **Plaza Mayor,** arcaded on its western side and bustling with the life of this surprisingly animated town; in the middle of the arcade is the entrance to the lively Calle General Ezponda, lined with tapas bars and busy as a hive in the evening.

On high ground on the eastern side of the Plaza Mayor are the town's fortifications—intact though heavily restored—which contain one of the best-preserved old quarters in Spain. The old town of Cáceres is small but without a single distracting modern building—a cold, stony, and dream-like place that is one of the high points of a visit to Extremadura. Almost empty of shops, restaurants, and even bars, virtually deserted outside the tourist season, and crammed with medieval and Renaissance palaces somberly constructed out of heavy gray blocks of stone, it looks like the stage set for a tragedy—and in fact has served as a background in numerous movies. Try to come here at night, when the buildings and narrow streets take on an especially haunting quality. Enter the old town by the gate next to the Torre de la Hierba from the Plaza Mayor. Immediately inside, turn right along the Adarves de San Juan, and you will soon pass the **upper Palace of the Golfines,** which is dominated by a soaring tower dating from 1515. Continue to skirt the town walls until you reach, on the southern side of the old town, the Mérida Gate. Leading from here to the old town center is the Calle Ancha, at the beginning of which is the **Casa de Sanchez de Paredes,** a 16th-century palace that has been converted into a parador (*see* Dining and Lodging, *below*).

Time Out Adjoining the parador, at No. 4 Calle Ancha, is **El Palacio de los Vinos,** a stylish but intimate snack bar and liquor store installed around the patio of an old palace. Among the offerings is a creation of the bar's Mexican owner, Leonardo Rodríguez, called *El Beso Extremeño* (The Extremaduran Kiss), a liqueur made of acorns.

On the Plaza San Mateo, at the northern end of the Calle Ancha, stands one of the town's most important churches, **San Mateo.** Built mainly in the 14th century, but with a 16th-century choir, it has an impressively austere interior, the main decorative notes being the Baroque high altar and the heraldic crests surmounting the tombs of noblemen. On the square facing the southern side of the building is the battlemented tower of **Las Cigueñas** (Palace of the Storks), so called because of the stork's nest attached to it.

Farther down the square, with vistas over the rolling landscape to the east of the town, is the **Casa de las Veletas** (House of the Weathervanes). This now contains a small provincial museum, the **Museo Arqueológico,** devoted to archaeology and folklore. Its basement comprises the Moorish cistern over which the palace was constructed; horseshoe arches rise in the gloom above murky waters fed by pipes leading from both the roof and the sloping square outside. *Tel. 924/24-73-34. Admission: 200 pesetas. Open Tues.-Sun. 10:30-2:30; closed Mon. and holidays.*

The narrow street that descends from the eastern end of San Mateo to the town's other main church, Santa María, passes first the Jesuit church of **San Francisco Xavier** and then the lower **Palacio de los Golfines.** The latter has the finest exterior of any Cáceres palace, the austerity of the stone relieved by Mudéjar (Spanish Muslim) and Renaissance decorative motifs. The Gothic church of **Santa María** (can be visited during Mass), now serving as the town's cathedral, was built mainly in the 16th century and has an elegantly carved high altar of 1551, just about visible in the surrounding gloom. Nearby is the **Palacio de Caruajal** (Plaza de Santa María), the only old palace apart from the Casa de las Veletas that can be toured. Ask at the tourist office to arrange a visit.

A 100-m (110-yd) walk from here down Calle Tiendas will take you to the northern walls of the town. Turn left and you will come, in the northwestern corner of the old town, to the 16th-century **Casa de los Toledo-Moctezumas** (now a bank), which was built by Juan Cano de Saavedra with the dowry provided by his wife—none other than the princess daughter of the Aztec ruler Montezuma. Follow the town walls south until you reach the Estrella Gate, which will lead you back down a long stone stairway to the main square.

The chief building of interest outside the town walls is the church of **Santiago** (instead of turning left at the Calle Tiendas, go through the Socorro Gate, and continue north along the Calle de Villalobos). It was rebuilt in the 16th century by Rodrigo Gil de Hontañon, the last great Gothic architect of Spain. The interior has a dynamic high altar (1561) by Berruguete, a sculptor much influenced by Michelangelo and one of the outstanding figures of the Spanish Renaissance.

❼ A possible excursion from Cáceres is to **Garrovillas,** 10 km (6 mi) off the main road between Cáceres and Plasencia (turn left, or northwest, onto C522, 25 km/15 mi north of Cáceres). Now partially deserted, it is a perfectly preserved village of the late 15th century, built on the banks of the peaceful Alcántara reservoir to replace the abandoned ancient settlement of Alconétar.

❽ Anyone who comes to Cáceres province should not fail to visit **Trujillo,** 48 km (30 mi) east of Cáceres, at the junction of N521 and N V. It is an extreme version of the Extremaduran look—a lonely, nearly deserted place built of cold and imposing stone that is nonetheless thrilling to both eye and soul. The stork nests that top several towers in and around the center of the old town—and that have become something of a symbol of the town—only add to this strange effect. Unlike Cáceres, Trujillo has none of the hustle and bustle of the new Spain; Indeed, it seems almost stuck in the time when Extremadura was a symbol of Spanish poverty. Dating to at least Roman times, when its castle was first constructed, Trujillo was captured from the Moors in 1232 and colonized by a number of leading military families; Ferdinand and Isabella stayed here in 1478 during their war against the king of Portugal. Only after the discovery of America in 1492 did the fame of the town begin to spread far and wide. Known today as "The Cradle of the Conquistadors," Trujillo gave birth to some of the leading explorers and conquerors of the New World, men who were later to bring great wealth to their native town and build here, in the course of the 16th and 17th centuries, a splendid series of palaces—radically changing what had been a poverty-stricken provincial town into a showcase of 16th-century and 17th-century conspicuous consumption. The most famous of these conquistadors was Francisco Pizarro, conqueror of Peru, born in Trujillo in 1475. Pizarro, though illegitimate and illiterate, was the son of one of the most illustrious noblemen in town. A particularly brutal conquistador, he was killed in Peru in 1541 by jealous compatriots. His educated half-brother Hernando, also an adventurer in Peru, was luckier in this respect, ending his days in Spain and building perhaps the most magnificent palace in Trujillo. Others from Trujillo who made their mark in the New World include Alonso de Monroy, Francisco de Orellana, and Hernando de Alarcón, famous, respectively, for their exploits in Chile, the Amazon jungle, and California.

Trujillo's economic boom during the Golden Age of Spain led the town to expand well beyond its medieval walls. Then, from the mid-17th century onward, building ceased almost completely, and the town went into a long decline. Today, it is possible to wander endlessly and at random around its maze of streets and still uncover at every turn poignant memorials of its glorious past. A word of warning, however: It is only practical to see Trujillo on foot, as the streets are mainly cobbled or crudely paved with stone and rarely flat. The two main roads through Trujillo leave you at the singularly unattractive and unspectacular bottom of the town, where there is a small bus station (with regular connections to Cáceres and Madrid). Most of the streets leading up the hill converge on the Plaza Mayor. The town becomes progressively older the farther you climb, but even on the lower slopes—where most of the shops are concentrated—you need walk only a few yards to step into what seems like the Middle Ages.

The large **Plaza Mayor,** one of the finest in Spain, is a superb 16th- and early 17th-century creation, one of the few features that mar it being, ironically, the modern tourist office in its center. The spirit of the conquistadors dominates the town. Appropriately, at the foot of the stepped platform that rises on the north side of the Plaza Mayor, stands a large bronze equestrian statue of the great conqueror of Peru, Francisco Pizarro, by two American artists of the early years of this century, Charles Runse and Mary Harriman (an exact replica is found in Lima, Peru). The church behind the Pizarro statue, **San Martín,** is a Gothic structure of the early 16th century, with some fine Renaissance tombs and an old organ.

Facing the church, in the northeastern corner of the square, is the **Palacio de los Duques de San Carlos** (Palace of the Dukes of San Carlos), which has a majestically decorated facade of around 1600; the building is now a convent of Hieronymite nuns, one of whom will show you around the austere, arcaded inner courtyard, where fragments of the Visigothic castle that once stood here are kept. *Tel. 927/ 32–00–58. Admission: offering to nuns. Open daily 9–1 and 4–6.*

Time Out The Clarisse nuns now live in a modern building between the palace and the Trujillo parador. They make some of the best sweets and pastries in town. If you stop by during normal shopping hours, you can buy a delectable range of cakes, meringues, sponge biscuits, and doughnuts from them.

The most interesting part of Trujillo extends to the west of the Plaza Mayor. Your tour proper of the town could begin near the southwestern corner of the square, outside the **Palacio de la Conquista** (Palace of the Conquest), the most dramatic building on the plaza. This was built by Francisco Pizarro's brother Hernando and is immediately recognizable by its rich covering of exquisite Renaissance ornamentation. Flanking its corner balcony, around which most of this ornamentation is concentrated, are lively, imaginative busts of the Pizarro family. On the left-hand side are Francisco Pizarro and his Inca princess wife, Yupanqui Huaynas, while on the right is Yupanqui's daughter, Francisca Pizarro Yupanqui, together with her uncle and husband, Hernando. Prominent in the coat of arms above, and an interesting reflection of the spirit of brutal subjugation in which the conquest of the New World was carried out, are representations of chained Indians. The magnificent interior of the palace has now been partially opened to the public and features a grandiose staircase, a courtyard, and some 16th-century stables. You can walk out onto the corner balcony and see its sculptural decoration from close quarters. Restoration on this building has continued at a snail's pace for years, although one glance serves to tell you how richly it is deserved. *Admission: tip to caretaker. Open daily 10:30–2 and 4:30–6; if you don't find caretaker, ask at tourist office.*

Adjacent to the palace is the arcaded former town hall (now a law court), which has much Renaissance painted and stuccoed ornamentation inside. The alley that runs through this building's central arch will take you to the **Palacio de Pizarro de Orellana** *(now a school), where you will find the most elegant Renaissance courtyard in town. Admission free. Open daily 10–2 and 4–6.*

The oldest part of Trujillo, known as **La Villa,** is entirely surrounded by its original, if much restored, walls. The Calle Almenas, which runs west from the Palace of Pizarro de Orellana, skirts these walls up to the **Puerta de San Andrés,** one of the four surviving gates of the Villa (there were originally seven). Once inside, you enter a world inhabited by storks, who, in the spring and early summer months, adorn the many crumbling chimneys and towers of old palaces and churches. Through the Gate of San Andrés and past the church of that name, you come to a stagnant pond, which was once a public bath established by the Arabs. Head north up the Calle Palomas, passing on your left the birthplace of the Amazon explorer Francisco de Orellana.

The cobbled climbing street leads you into the Plaza de Santa María, on which stands the town's major monument of artistic interest, the church of **Santa María.** This Gothic structure attached to a Romanesque bell tower is occasionally used for services; to go inside, you usually have to apply to the surly old woman who lives in the first of a small group of houses directly in front of the west facade. The interior has been virtually untouched since the 16th century and has wonderful network vaulting as well as an upper choir with an exquisitely carved balustrade. The coats of arms at each end of this balustrade indicate the seats that were used by Ferdinand and Isabella when they attended Mass here. The chief attraction in the church is the high altar of c.1480, adorned with one of the greatest Spanish paintings of the 15th century (to see this properly illuminated, you must place a 100-peseta coin in the box adjacent to the church entrance). Executed by the Salamanca artist Fernando Gallego, it combines delightful Flemish detail and naturalism with Spanish harshness and power. *Admission: 50 pesetas plus tip. Open daily, usually 10–2 and 4–6. (Ask for Señora Tomasa.)*

Climbing north from the church, you will come almost immediately to the Pizarro family home. The small house has been restored and turned into a museum dedicated to the links between Spain and Latin America. There is a colorful mural in the entry depicting the agricultural products, such as corn, tomatoes, and tobacco, that were brought from the New World. There are also rooms decorated in the style of the period. The upper floor displays drawings, maps, and objects related to the conquistadors. *Admission: 250 pesetas. Open June–Oct., Tues.–Sun. 11–2 and 6–8; Nov.–May, Tues.–Sun. 11–2 and 4:30–6:30.*

Standing in isolation beyond this are the perimeter walls of the large **castle,** built by the Moors on Roman foundations. *Admission free. Open daily 10–6:30.*

Head down toward the Plaza Mayor by way of the Calle Santiago, which will deposit you in a square named after the founder of Trujillo in Venezuela, Diego García de Paredes (a plaque on the square records the site of his birthplace). Leave the Villa by the Santiago Gate and approach the Plaza Mayor, on the Calle de Ballesteros. You will find yourself at the upper end of the square, next to the two best restaurants in town—Hostal Pizarro and Mesón La Troya (*see* Dining and Lodging, *below*).

Tour 3: Guadalupe

If you could visit only a single site in Extremadura, the choice would have to be the monastery of **Guadalupe.** The journey here is in itself worthwhile. Whether you are coming from Madrid, Trujillo, or Cáceres, the last stage of your trip will take you through wild, breathtakingly beautiful mountain scenery. Finally, you catch your first glimpse of the monastery clinging to the slopes above you and forming with its towers, pinnacles, and spires a magical profile echoing that of the gaunt wall of mountains behind. Hawks wheel in the piercing azure skies that seem to endlessly dominate this town, which despite its high perch has a warm and welcoming feel to it. Pilgrims have been coming here since the 14th century, but only in relatively recent years have they been joined by a growing number of tourists. Even so, the monastery's very isolation—it is a good two- to three-hour drive to the nearest town—has saved it from the worst excesses of tourism and ensured that a visit here is still an adventure.

The story of Guadalupe goes back to around 1300, when a shepherd uncovered a miraculous statue of the Virgin, this one supposedly carved by St. Luke. Its fame might have been only local had it not come to the attention of King Alfonso XI, who frequently hunted here. Alfonso had a church built to house the statue and later vowed to found a monastery, should he defeat the Moors at the battle of Salado of 1340. After his victory, he kept his promise. The greatest period in the monastery's history was between the 15th and 18th centuries, when, under the rule of the Hieronymites, it was rebuilt, enlarged, and endowed and turned into a pilgrimage center rivaling even Santiago de Compostela in importance. Situated as it was in the heart of Conquistador Spain, the place emerged in the Golden

Age as a symbol of Spain's territorial expansion: Documents authorizing Columbus's first voyage to America were signed here, a West Indian island and numerous other locations in the New World were named after this monastery, and the first American Indians to be converted to Christianity were also brought here to be baptized. Thus the Virgin of Guadelupe became the patroness of Latin America, testimony to which is found in the thousands of churches and towns dedicated to her in the New World. The decline of the monastery coincided with Spain's loss of overseas territories in the 19th century. Abandoned for 70 years and left to decay, it was taken over after the civil war of 1936–39 by Franciscan brothers, who slowly restored it.

The bus station lies just below the village of Guadalupe, leaving you with a steep climb up to the monastery. The village is filled with wood arcades and russet brown–tiled roofs; on sale everywhere is the copperware that has been made here since the 16th century. In the middle of the tiny, irregularly shaped main square (transformed during festivals into a bullring) is a 15th-century **fountain** where Columbus's two Indian servants were baptized in 1496. Looming in the background is the late-Gothic south facade of the **monastery church,** covered in swirling decorative motifs and flanked by battlemented towers.

To visit the monastery itself, you are obliged to follow a guided tour that lasts about an hour (the entrance to the building is to the left of the church). From the large Mudéjar cloister you progress to the chapter house, with its collection of choir books, illustrated manuscripts, and paintings, including a series of small panels by Zurbarán that originally covered the predella of the sacristy altarpiece. Next you are led through the raised choir of the church, an excellent vantage point from which to view the building's Gothic nave and chancel, with its exquisite Renaissance grille and high altar carved partially by one of El Greco's sons. The ornate 17th-century sacristy contains the monastery's most important works of art—a series of eight paintings of 1638–47 by Zurbarán. These powerfully austere works representing monks of the Hieronymite order and scenes from the life of St. Jerome are the only important paintings by this artist still in the setting for which they were originally intended. The tour concludes with the garish late-Baroque Camarín—the chapel where the miraculous Virgin is housed. It is a riot of color and rich materials and is given further distinction by its superb canvases by the Italian Baroque artist Luca Giordano. Outside, the monastery's gardens have been renovated in the geometric Arab style in which they were originally laid out. However, the focal point is the Virgin of Guadalupe, a dark and shriveled wood object hiding under a great veil and mantle. *Tel. 927/36–70–00. Admission: 300 pesetas. Open daily 9:30–1 and 3:30–6:30.*

Tour 4: Mérida

Founded by the Romans in 25 BC on the banks of the River Guadiana and strategically situated at the junction of major Roman roads between Salamanca and Seville and Lisbon and Toledo, **Mérida** today is a rather unattractive, lifeless town—with the exception of the dramatic Roman complex which has made it a major Spanish tourist attraction. After its founding, the city soon became capital of the vast Roman province of Lusitania. A bishopric in Visigothic times, Mérida never regained the importance that it had had under the Romans. Today, it is an ugly town of mainly modern appearance, yet it boasts a series of Roman monuments finer than those in any other town in Spain.

The new glass-and-steel bus station stands in a modern district on the other side of the River Guadiana from the center of Mérida. It commands a good view of the exceptionally long **Roman Bridge,** which spans two forks of this sluggish river and comprises 64 arches formed of heavy blocks of granite.

As you cross the bridge, you see in front of you the impressively sturdy square **alcazaba** (fortress), built originally by the Romans and later strengthened by the Visigoths and Moors. To go inside, follow the fortress walls around to the side farthest from the river. The dusty precinct is worth a visit for the Moorish cistern that lies at its center, to which you descend by way of a dimly lit flight of steps; you should also climb up to the battlements for the sweeping views of the river. *Tel. 924/31–25–30. Admission (including entrance to the Roman theater and amphitheater; see below): 200 pesetas. Open Mon.–Sat. 9–1:45 and 5–6:45, Sun. 9–1:45.*

The main square, the Plaza de España, adjoins the northwestern corner of the fortress and is extremely animated both by day and by night. Its oldest building is the 16th-century palace that served for many years as the Hotel Emperatriz. Between this hotel and the town's stylish parador (*see* Dining and Lodging, *below*) stretches the most charming and best-preserved area of Mérida, comprising Andalucían-style white houses shaded by palms.

Off the tiny Plaza de Santa Clara, at the heart of this area, is an abandoned 18th-century church that has been turned into a dusty, old-fashioned **Museo Visigótico** (Visigothic Museum), filled with fragments of Visigothic stonework. *Tel. 924/31–16–90. Admission: free. Open June–Sept., Tues.–Sat. 10–2 and 5–7, Sun. 10–2; Oct.–May, Tues.–Sat. 10–2 and 4–6, Sun. 10–2, closed Mon.*

Time Out The Plaza de España and nearby Plaza de Santa Clara are the best places in town to linger at bars and have good snacks. **Bar Lusi** (Plaza de Santa Clara s/n) serves regional delicacies and has a number of quiet, shaded tables outside.

From the Plaza de España, head north along the Calle Santa Eulalia, a lively pedestrian shopping street. Continue north along the Rambla **Mártir Santa Eulalia** until you reach the church of that name, which was originally a Visigoth structure marking both the site of a Roman temple and the supposed place where the child martyr Eulalia was roasted alive in AD 304 for spitting in the face of a Roman magistrate. From here you have views of the long Roman aqueduct.

Alternatively, you could head east up the Calle José Ramon Mélida to Mérida's superb, modern **Museo Nacional de Arte Romano** (Museum of Roman Art), housed in an adventurous and monumentally large brick building and containing outstanding mosaics, jewelry, statues, and other Roman works. *José Ramón Mélida 2, tel. 924/31–16–90. Admission: 200 pesetas. Open June–Sept., Tues.–Sat. 10–2 and 5–7, Sun. 10–2; Oct.–May, Tues.–Sat. 10–2 and 4–6, Sun. 10–2; closed Mon.*

Just past the museum are the town's best-preserved Roman monuments, the **teatro** (theater) and **anfiteatro** (amphitheater) **Romano,** arranged in a verdant park. The former, dating from 24 BC, is notable for the elegant colonnade on its stage (plays are put on in front of this during the summer months). *Admission (includes entrance to the alcazaba;* see above*): 200 pesetas. Open 8 AM to dusk daily.*

What to See and Do with Children

Extremadura is traditional Spain, and you will not find here the zoos, entertainment parks, and other children's attractions that characterize sophisticated tourist resorts. The main entertainment for both adults and children alike is provided by the local festivals, usually held during the summer months in honor of a town's or village's saint. Fun fairs always accompany these occasions, and children tend to stay up most of the night, enjoying the music, dancing, and general animation as much as their parents do. (Information on local festivals can be obtained from the regional tourist offices.)

Off the Beaten Track

Almost everywhere in Extremadura is "off the beaten track," although in recent years such wild and forlorn areas as Las Hurdes (of Buñuel fame) are becoming increasingly popular with travelers from Madrid. If you want a taste of a still virtually unchanged Spain, visit the "Extremaduran Siberia," which lies between Mérida and the La Mancha town of Ciudad Real (leave N430, which links the two towns, by following signs for Casas de Don Pedro, and continue south toward Talarrubias). This poor area of wild, rolling scrubland owes its exotic name to the 12th duke of Osuna, who came here after 10 years as Spanish ambassador in Russia and was reminded of the Siberian steppes; the rickety old bus that until a few years ago served this area was even known as "the Trans-Siberian." Of the handful of villages here, the oldest is **Puebla de Alcocer,** which has an arcaded square. More unusual is the nearby village of **Peloche,** to the north of Talarrubias, where you can still see women embroidering in the streets; this same place also continues to have its ferryman, "Tío Vito," an old man in traditional costume who, for many years, has ferried people and cattle over the River Guadiana.

Shopping

Extremadura is a region rich in traditional folk crafts, though you have to go farther and farther afield to find the genuine article at a reasonable price. Crafts shops in the main tourist centers tend to sell increasingly commercialized and garish products. The town of Trujillo has a wider range of crafts products on sale than almost any other place in the region.

Copper For copper and tinware, the place to go is **Guadalupe,** where the industry has been established for more than four centuries.

Pottery The best-known pottery comes from the south of the region and is reddish brown, with delicate designs incised into the wet clay with a stone. It can be bought in **Mérida,** for instance, at two shops along the Calle José Ramon Mélida, the street that leads to the Roman theater and amphitheater—**Balbinas Esteban** (at No. 18) and **Antonio Zambrano** (at No. 40).

Weaving and Needlework Among the most attractive of Extremadura's crafts products are its multicolored rugs, blankets, and embroideries—good examples of which are to be found in the **Cáceres** shop **Acebo** (Plaza San Jorge 4). But for the very best embroidered and woven products, you should go to **Maribel Vallar** in **Trujillo** (at the junction of the Calles Domingo de Ramas and Juana Bazaga), where a centuries-old loom is still in use.

Woodworking Products Among Trujillo's other specialties are wood carvings, basketwork, and furniture, all of which are on sale at **Domingo Pablos Barquilla** (Plazuela de San Judas).

Sports

Boating All sorts of water sports are practiced in Extremadura, thanks to the presence of numerous artificial lakes, most notably Borbollón and Gabriel y Galán in northern Cáceres and Cíjara and García Sola in northwestern Badajoz.

Fishing Trout fishing is popular in the Vera and Jerte districts, while tench, carp, royal carp, barbel, and pike abound in the dams and basins of the Tajo and Guadiana rivers. A fishing permit can be obtained from **Agencia de Media Ambiente** offices (Enrique X Canedo, Mérida, tel. 924/38–14–15; and **ICONA** offices at Avenida General Primo de Rivera 2–7, Cáceres, tel. 927/22–76–01).

Dining and Lodging

Dining

The food of Extremadura reflects the austerity of the landscape. It is true peasant cuisine, conditioned by poverty, but with a strong character and a reliance on fresh produce. Its basis is the pig, of which no part is spared, including the *criadillas* (testicles), although these are not to be confused with the *criadillas de la tierra* (earth testicles), which are truffles. The charcuterie products are outstanding, most notably the sweetish cured hams from Montánchez, the *chorizo* (spiced sausage), and *morcilla* (blood pudding), which is often made here with potatoes, a legacy of the days of the conquistadors. Game is also common, a famous specialty being *perdiz al modo de Alcántara* (partridge cooked with truffles). Certain Extremaduran dishes appall many foreigners, as well as many other Spaniards—in particular, those involving *ranas* (frogs) and *lagartos* (lizards), the latter usually eaten with an almond sauce. In the south, numerous Andalusian specialties are to be found, such as *gazpacho* and *ajo blanco* (cold almond and garlic soup). A common accompaniment throughout the region is *migas* (bread crumbs soaked in water and fried in olive oil with garlic and specks of bacon). The excellent local cheeses generally have a crumbly texture and strong flavor; the most famous is the *torta de Casar* from Casar, near Cáceres. The little-known wines of the area are equally full of character: Try Lar de Lares. Almendralejo is the wine-growing center.

There is little tradition in Extremadura for going to restaurants, and some of the best food is to be found in modest bars. The two best restaurants in Extremadura serving regional food are the El Figón de Eustaquio in Cáceres and the Hostal Pizarro in Trujillo. Dress is generally casual throughout the region unless otherwise specified. Reservations are usually unnecessary.

Highly recommended restaurants are indicated by a star ★.

Category	Cost*
$$$$	over 6,500 ptas
$$$	4,000–6,500 ptas
$$	2,300–4,000 ptas
$	under 2,300 ptas

per person for a three-course meal, excluding tax

Lodging

No other region of Spain can boast such a remarkable group of state-run paradors as can Extremadura. They cover all the main tourist areas of the region, and all are in buildings of great historical and architectural interest; early reservations are usually needed on weekends. The other luxury hotels of the region are generally in modern buildings of little character. If you prefer character to luxury, you might try your luck with the region's modest *fondas* (inns). The best place to stay is Cáceres, and from here easy day trips can be made to Trujillo, Mérida, and Plasencia.

Highly recommended hotels are indicated by a star ★ .

Category	Cost*
$$$$	over 13,000 ptas
$$$	11,000–13,000 ptas
$$	7,000–11,000 ptas
$	under 7,000 ptas

All prices are for a standard double room, excluding tax and service.

Badajoz
Dining

La Toja. This smart yet intimate family-run restaurant specializes in Galician food, and its decor immediately makes you aware of this fact. At the entrance is one of the more familiar sights of the Galician countryside: a *horreo*, or small barn raised on stilts. The walls of the restaurant's three small dining rooms are covered with oars, fishing tackle, and other reminders of northern shores. The emphasis is on fish, including such delicacies as *merluza a la Gallega* (hake stewed in onions, potatoes, parsley, and paprika). *Sanchez de la Rocha 22, tel. 924/27–34–77. AE, MC. Closed Sun. evening and Aug. $$$*

Lodging

Gran Hotel Zurbarán. This large modern block dating back to the 1970s has a beautiful position near the River Guadiana and overlooking the Castelar park. The look of the place is brash and slightly dated, with an abundance of chrome in the entrance lobby. The service is nonetheless impeccable, and there are few hotels in Extremadura that offer such a range of luxury features. *Paseo Castelar s/n, 06001, tel. 924/22–37–41, fax 924/22–01–42. 215 rooms. Facilities: parking, garden, pool, tennis, discothèque, conference room (with translation facilities), shopping arcade, and bookshop. AE, MC, V. $$$$*

Cáceres
Dining

Atrio. Slickly elegant in an unprepossessing modern setting, this restaurant offers adventurous and ultrarefined modern cooking. Truffles feature in many of the dishes—for instance, in the tastefully presented version of *perdiz al modo de Alcántara* (partridge), a traditional Extremaduran delicacy. *Avenida España 30, Bloque 4, 10003, tel. 927/24–29–28. AE, MC, V. $$$*

★ **El Figón de Eustaquio.** Situated on the quiet and pleasant Plaza San Juan, this is a justly famed Extremaduran gastronomic institution. Comprising a jumble of small, old-fashioned, intimate dining rooms, it is always busy, especially at lunchtime. Its traditional local cuisine is presented without fanciful embellishment. Excellent cured ham from Montánchez, *angulas en ensalada* (eel salad), and *truchas del Jerte a la Extremeña* (trout from the Jerte Valley) are among its specialties. *Plaza San Juan 12, 10003, tel. 927/24–81–94. Reservations required at lunchtime. AE, MC, V. $$$, but set menu is reasonable.*

Lodging **Meliá Cáceres.** Equally historic and somewhat more comfortable
★ than the parador (*see below*), the Meliá Cáceres occupies a renovated 16th-century palace just outside the walls of the old town. It gracefully blends exposed stone, indirect spot lighting, and designer furnishings. Rooms feature huge double beds, wall-to-wall carpeting, and ample baths. The street-level bar, with charming wine-bottle lighting, is the town's most popular meeting spot. *Plaza San Juan 11, 10003, tel. 927/21–58–00, fax 927/21–40–70. 86 rooms. Facilities: restaurant, bar. AE, DC, MC, V. $$$*

Parador Nacional de Cáceres. Transformed in 1989 from a restaurant into the latest of the state-run paradors, this one is installed in a 16th-century palace. The peace and location could not be better, but the gray stone architecture is plain and undecorated, and the white corridors have a cold, unwelcoming character. *Ancha 6, 10003, tel. 927/21–17–59, fax 927/21–17–29. 27 rooms. Facilities: restaurant, parking. AE, DC, MC, V. $$$*

Quinto Centenario. Opened in 1992 just outside Cáceres on the road to Plasencia, the Quinto Centenario offers remarkable warmth and comfort for a modern high-rise hotel. Rooms are large and carpeted, with oversize beds and luxurious baths. The swimming pool and outdoor terrace dining make it a good choice for hot summer days. *Manuel Pacheco s/n, 10003, tel. 927/23–22–00, fax 23–22–02. 138 rooms. Facilities: restaurant, bar, shops, pool, tennis court, parking. AE, DC, MC, V. $$$*

Guadalupe **Hospedería del Real Monasterio.** An excellent alternative if the
Dining and parador is full, this inn is situated around the 16th-century Gothic
Lodging cloister of Guadalupe's monastery. The simple, traditionally furnished rooms with dark wood-beamed ceilings were once taken up by a pharmacy, medical school, and infirmary. It is exceptionally quiet. Despite its grand, unforgettable setting in the cloister, the restaurant is a place of unpretentious charm, specializing in modest local dishes such as *sopa de tomate* (tomato soup) and *migas Extremeñas* (fried bread crumbs with ham and garlic). *Plaza Juan Carlos I s/n, 10140, tel. 927/36–70–00, fax 927/36–71–77. 46 rooms. Facilities: restaurant, parking, garden. MC, V. Closed Jan. 15–Feb. 15. $*

Lodging **Parador Nacional Zurbarán.** Occupying a former hospital and pil-
★ grim's hostel dating to the 15th century, this parador has a particularly sensual and luxuriant character, owing to its Mudéjar architecture, Moorish-style rooms with blue tile bathrooms, and the exotic vegetation of its garden and whitewashed cloister. *Marqués de la Romana 10, 10140, tel. 927/36–70–75, fax 927/36–70–76. 40 rooms. Facilities: restaurant, garage, garden, pool, tennis. AE, DC, MC, V. $$$*

Jarandilla **Parador Nacional Carlos V.** Historically this is one of the most im-
Lodging portant buildings in the parador chain: the emperor Carlos V having

stayed here for a year prior to moving to the nearby monastery of Yuste. Built in the early 16th century as a fortified palace, it has an arcaded patio with flattened arches. Thoroughly overhauled in 1986, this stylish hotel, filled with pseudomedieval furnishings and suits of armor, has only one drawback: the food, which is quite unworthy of the setting. *Carretera Plasencia s/n, 10450, tel. 927/56–01–17, fax 927/56–00–88. 53 rooms. Facilities: restaurant, parking, pool, tennis. AE, DC, MC, V. $$$*

Mérida
Lodging
★

Parador Nacional Via de la Plata. Though originally a Baroque convent, and for a while even a prison, this spacious whitewashed building exudes an Andalusian cheerfulness. The rooms are bright, with traditional dark wood furniture. The brilliant white interior of the former church has been turned into a particularly restful lounge. *Plaza Constitución 3, 06800, tel. 924/31–38–00, fax 924/31–92–08. 82 rooms. Facilities: restaurant, parking, garden. AE, DC, MC, V. $$$$*

Plasencia
Dining and Lodging

Alfonso VIII. The sturdy gray exterior of this centrally located hotel shields an interior attempting a French rococo elegance with gilt plaster and red upholstery. Grand, but past its prime, and evocative more of the 1950s than of the 18th century, it is a curious survival of the Franco era. The hotel restaurant has long been renowned for its food, which has a strong Extremaduran accent despite the general atmosphere of international refinement. Certainly, the Parisian-style dining room seems the least likely setting for *lagarto en salsa* (lizard in a green sauce)—this is one of the few restaurants in the region that provide this traditional Extremaduran dish. The menu changes seasonally; the lizards are available only in the spring. *Alfonso VIII 32, 34, 10600, tel. 927/41–02–50, fax 927/41–80–42. 57 rooms. Facilities: restaurant, garage. AE, DC, MC, V. $$*

Trujillo
Dining
★

Hostal Pizarro. Occupying a small but quietly elegant upstairs room, this is a celebrated establishment with a warm and friendly atmosphere. It is run by two sisters, one of whom does the cooking and the other the serving; the place was founded by their father more than 60 years ago, and they have lovingly maintained traditional Extremaduran home cooking. A specialty of the house is *gallina truffada* (an elaborately prepared chicken pâté with truffles), which was once a common Christmas dish in Extremadura but which few today know how to make. Main courses include such exotica as *cordero con criadillas de tierra al queso de Ibores* (fried lamb served with truffles and cheese sauce). You could end your meal with the succulent *torta de almendras* (almond pie) from Badajoz. *Plaza Mayor 13, tel. 927/32–02–55. AE, V. $$*

Mesón La Troya. The food here, though good and simple, is not up to the standard of the neighboring Hostal Pizarro, but there can be few more entertaining places to spend a lunch or evening. Occupying the vaulted ground-floor room of a beautiful old building, this lively and raucous restaurant is often filled with carousing soldiers. The elderly woman who runs the place is a known eccentric, who scolds you if you are unable to finish the remarkably copious helpings. At the beginning of the meal you are served a *tortilla de patatas* (potato omelet), whether you want it or not. *Plaza Mayor 10, tel. 927/32–13–64. No credit cards. $*

Lodging
★

Parador Nacional de Trujillo. This unusually friendly parador is entered through a cheerful, whitewashed courtyard reminiscent of that of a farm. The building was originally the convent of St. Clare, and its bedrooms surround a harmonious Renaissance courtyard. The decoration aims for the mock-medieval chic common to most of the paradors, but the atmosphere, for a change, is endearingly homey. *Santa Clara s/n, 10200, tel. 927/32–13–50, fax 927/32–13–66. 46 rooms. Facilities: restaurant, garage, pool, conference room. AE, DC, MC, V. $$$*

★ **Mesón La Cadena.** Situated in a rambling 16th-century palace on the Plaza Mayor, this bar and restaurant has some simple but very comfortable upstairs rooms, with wonderful views of both the square and the fortifications of the Villa. *Plaza Mayor 8, 10200, tel. 927/32–14–63. 7 rooms with shower. Facilities: restaurant, bar. AE, MC, V. $*

Zafra
Lodging
★
Parador Nacional Hernán Cortés. The parador, which is the dominant building in this attractive and lively town, occupies the 15th-century castle where Cortés stayed before going to Mexico. The building's military exterior conceals an elegant 16th-century courtyard attributed to Juan de Herrera. The rooms are white and cheerful, some with wood-beam ceilings, others with windows overlooking the marble courtyard. There is a suite with a superbly elaborate *artesonado* (coffered) ceiling. Other such ceilings adorn the bar and dining room, as well as the magnificent chapel, which now serves as the conference room. The hotel was restored and remodeled in 1991. *Plaza Corazón de María 7, 06300, tel. 924/55–45–40, fax 924/55–10–18. 45 rooms. Facilities: pool. AE, DC, MC, V. $$$*

The Arts and Nightlife

The Arts

Cultural life is provincial in Extremadura. The exceptional event on the region's artistic calendar is the **Theater Festival** at Mérida, which is held in the town's Roman theater every summer from late June to early August; for tickets and information, contact the Festival Office (Reyes Huerta 3, Mérida 06800, tel. 924/31–28–11).

Nightlife

The region is not renowned for its nightlife, although bars in Cáceres are lively until the wee hours. The southern half of the region is by far the livelier at night, and Mérida's Calle John Lennon has a number of bars and discos; the center of Badajoz nightlife is Avenida República Argentina; should you want to go to a discothèque in Cáceres, the street to find is Dr. Fleming.

16 The Canary Islands

By Deborah Luhrman

The Canary Islands are Europe's winter place in the sun. The volcanic archipelago lies 1,280 km (800 mi) southwest of mainland Spain, 112 km (70 mi) off the coast of southern Morocco, at about the same latitude as central Florida. There are seven major islands in the chain, each with its own personality. Some are fertile and overgrown with exotic tropical vegetation; others are as dry as a bone, with lava caves and desert sand dunes. Spain's highest peak, Mt. Teide, which is snowcapped for much of the year, juts up among these islands as well.

The best thing about the islands is their climate, warmed by the sun in winter and tempered by cool Atlantic breezes in summer. Swimming is possible year-round. The first modern-day tourists arrived around the turn of the century from England to spend the winter months at Puerto de la Cruz in Tenerife. The steamer trip took eight days down and eight days back. Today huge charter flights from Düsseldorf, Stockholm, Zürich, Manchester, and dozens of other northern European cities unload 6 million pasty-faced visitors a year, flying them back two weeks later tanned and relaxed.

The Canary Islands fell one at a time to the Spanish conquistadors during Spain's Golden Age, at the end of the 1400s. They were known then as the Fortunate Isles, because of the climate, and for centuries they lay on the edge of navigators' maps. Columbus resupplied his ships in the Canaries in 1492 before heading west to the New World. Columbus is sometimes called the islands' first tour operator, because he stopped at the Canaries on all his subsequent voyages to America, bringing settlers and establishing the archipelago as an important trading port between the New and the Old World.

Before the arrival of the Spanish, the islands were populated by cave-dwelling people called Guanches. Their ranks were decimated by slave traders by the end of the 16th century, and the Guanche civilization died out, leaving behind only a few Stone Age implements (now in island museums), some geometrical cave scratchings, and the Cenobio de Valerón ruins on Gran Canaria.

To really get to know the Canaries, try to combine a visit to one of the more touristy islands—Tenerife, Gran Canaria, or Lanzarote—with trips to one or more of the less-developed islands, such as Fuerteventura, La Palma, La Gomera, or El Hierro. Each has something distinct to offer.

Tenerife has suffered most at the hands of developers, but it also has the largest number of attractions to tempt visitors, who can ride a cable car up the slopes of Mt. Teide, swim in a huge man-made lake, explore botanical gardens, or dance at glittering discos. The beaches are small, with black sand. The verdant north coast retains unspoiled villages, while the southern Playa de las Americas is built chockablock with hotels.

Gran Canaria was the hot spot of the '60s and has an image of being passé, but its Maspalomas beach is one of the most beautiful in all the islands, and an area of sand dunes behind the beach is being turned into a nature reserve. The island capital, Las Palmas, is a vibrant Spanish city with good cultural offerings and a sparkling sandy beach right downtown.

Lanzarote is a desert isle made beautiful through thoughtful development. It has golden-sand beaches, carefully preserved white villages, caves to explore, and a volcanic national park where heat from an eruption in 1730 is still rising through vents in the earth. Vegetation is scarce, but grapes grown by farmers in volcanic ash produce a distinctive Canarian wine.

Fuerteventura was ignored until recently, but construction is now racing to keep up with the demands of tourists who come to windsurf and enjoy its endless white-sand beaches. The barren interior of the island is largely the domain of goatherds.

La Palma, called the garden isle, has only recently been discovered by tourists. It has luxuriant foliage, tropical storms, rainbows, and black crescents of beach. The capital city is a beautifully preserved example of Spanish colonial architecture.

La Gomera is a paradise for the backpacking crowd. Ruggedly mountainous, it offers good hiking, and UNESCO protects its primeval forests. The black-sand beaches are usually fringed by banana plantations.

El Hierro is the smallest and least-visited island. For tourists who really want to be alone, it offers a few beaches of black sand and a cool, highland pine forest for walking and picnicking.

Many places in the Canary Islands share the same names. Be careful not to confuse the island of La Palma with the city of Las Palmas, which is the capital of Gran Canaria. Equally confusing, the capital of the island of La Palma is called Santa Cruz and the capital of the island of Tenerife is also called Santa Cruz. When writing to an address on one of the islands, note that there are two provinces: The province of Santa Cruz de Tenerife includes the islands of Tenerife, La Palma, La Gomera, and El Hierro, while the province of Las Palmas includes the islands of Gran Canaria, Lanzarote, and Fuerteventura.

Essential Information

Important Addresses and Numbers

Tourist Offices Each of the Canary Islands has its own tourist offices. They are generally open 9 to 2 and are located in **Tenerife** (Plaza de España 1, Santa Cruz, tel. 922/60–55–92; Plaza de la Iglesia, Puerto de la Cruz, tel. 922/38–60–00), **Gran Canaria** (Parque Santa Catalina, Las Palmas, tel. 928/26–46–23), **Lanzarote** (Parque Municipal, Arrecife, tel. 928/81–18–60), **Fuerteventura** (1 de Mayo 33, Puerto de Rosario, tel. 928/85–10–24), **La Palma** (Palacio Salazar, Calle O'Daly 22, Santa Cruz de la Palma, tel. 922/41–21–06), **La Gomera** (Calle del Medio 20, San Sebastian, tel. 922/87–01–03), and **El Hierro** (Dr. Quintero 11, Valverde, tel. 922/55–00–78).

Arriving and Departing

By Plane **Iberia** and its sister carrier **Aviaco** offer several direct flights a day to Tenerife, Gran Canaria, and Lanzarote from most cities in mainland Spain (2½ hours from Madrid). **Air Europa** and **Spanair** have fewer flights but slightly lower prices. The other four main islands are reached by connecting flights.

From the United States, **Air Europa** (136 E. 57th St., Suite 1602, New York, NY 10022, tel. 212/888–7010) flies once a week directly from New York to Tenerife (6 hours). Package information is available from **Spanish Heritage Tours** (116–47 Queens Blvd., Forest Hills, NY 11375, tel. 718/544–2752 or 800/221–2580). Seats can sometimes be purchased without the hotel package if space is available.

By Boat **Trasmediterranea** (Pedro Muñoz Seca 2, Madrid, tel. 91/431–0700) operates a slow, comfortable ferry service between Cádiz and the Canary Islands (Tenerife, 42 hours; Gran Canaria, 54 hours; Lanzarote, 66 hours). The boat is equipped with cabins, a tiny swimming pool, restaurants, a game room, and a discothèque, but it is not a luxury cruise.

Getting Around

By Plane All the Canary Islands are served by air except La Gomera. **Tenerife** has two airports. **Reina Sofia** (TFS) is near Playa de las Américas in the south, and **Los Rodeos** (TFN) is in the north near Puerto de la Cruz. As a general rule, long-distance flights arrive at the southern terminal and interisland flights use the northern one, but there are exceptions. Try to book a flight that gets you to the part of the island where you are staying, and be sure to allow plenty of time to travel between airports for connecting flights. Driving time from one airport to the other is about 1½ hours; taxis charge up to 7,500 pesetas, or you can rent a car for about 4,000 pesetas.

Airport information can be obtained in Tenerife (Reina Sofia, tel. 922/77–00–50; Los Rodeos, tel. 922/25–23–50), Gran Canaria (tel. 928/25–41–40), Lanzarote (tel. 928/81–14–50), Fuerteventura (tel. 928/85–08–52), La Palma (tel. 922/44–04–27), and El Hierro (tel. 922/55–02–78).

Interisland flights are handled by **Iberia** and its regional subsidiary, **Binter Airlines,** using small turbo-prop planes that allow great low-altitude views of the islands. Reservations can be made in Tenerife (Av. de Anaga 23, Santa Cruz, tel. 922/28–80–00), Gran Canaria (Alcalde Ramirez de Bethancourt 8, Las Palmas, tel. 928/36–01–11), Lanzarote (Av. Rafael Gonzalez 2, Arrecife, tel. 928/81–03–58), Fuerteventura (23 de Mayo 11, Puerto de Rosario, tel. 928/85–05–16), La Palma (Apurón 1, tel. 922/41–13–45), and El Hierro (Dr. Quintero 6, tel. 922/55–02–78).

By Boat **Trasmediterranea** (*see* Arriving and Departing by Boat, *above*) operates interisland **car ferries.** Trips often take all night, and the ferries are equipped with sleeping cabins. Schedules and reservations are available in Tenerife (Marina 59, Santa Cruz, tel. 922/27–75–00), Gran Canaria (Muelle Rivera Oeste s/n, Las Palmas, tel. 928/26–00–70), Lanzarote (Jose Antonio 90, Arrecife, tel. 928/81–10–19), La Palma (Av. Perez de Brito 2, Santa Cruz de la Palma, tel. 922/41–24–15), La Gomera (Calle del Medio 41, San Sebastian, tel. 922/87–08–02), Fuerteventura (Leon y Castillo 46, 928/85–00–95), and El Hierro (Puerto de la Estaca, tel. 922/55–01–29).

Passenger-only **hydrofoil** service is also available through Trasmediterranea three times a day between Las Palmas and Tenerife (80 minutes). One hydrofoil a day links Morro Jable in southern Fuerteventura with Las Palmas (90 minutes) and Tenerife (3½ hours). La Gomera can be reached by hydrofoil (30 minutes) from Los Cristianos in southern Tenerife.

The **Ferry Gomera** takes cars and people between Tenerife (Muelle Los Cristianos, tel. 922/21–90–33) and La Gomera (Av. Fred Olsen, San Sebastian, tel. 922/87–10–07) three times a day. **Trasmediterranea** also operates a 35-minute hydrofoil.

A T L A N T I C

La Palma

Caldera de
Taburiente

San Andres y Sauces

El Paso

Santa Cruz
de la Palma

Tazacorte

Breña Alta

Puerto Naos

Fuencaliente

Punta de
Fuencaliente

Tenerife

San
Andrés

La Laguna

Puerto de
la Cruz

Garachico

La
Orotava

Santa Cruz
de Tenerife

Punta de Teno

Icod de los Vinos

La Gomera

Los Gigantes

Mt. Teide

Alojera

Las Rosas

Valle
Gran Rey

Playa de las Américas

San Sebastián

Playa de Santiago

Parque Nacional
de Garajonay

El Abrigo

El
Golfo

Valverde

El Hierro

La Restinga

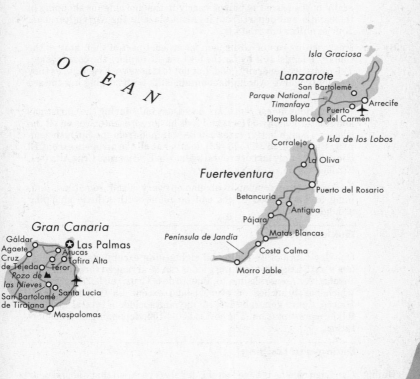

Isla Graciosa

Lanzarote

San Bartolomé

Parque National Timanfaya

Playa Blanca Puerto del Carmen Arrecife

Corralejo *Isla de los Lobos*

La Oliva

Fuerteventura

Puerto del Rosario

Betancuria

Antigua

Pájara

Península de Jandía Matas Blancas

Costa Calma

Morro Jable

Gran Canaria

Gáldar

Agaete Las Palmas

Cruz Arucas

de Tejeda Tafira Alta

Pozo de Teror

las Nieves

San Bartolomé Santa Lucia

de Tirajana

Maspalomas

O C E A N

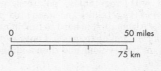

N

0   50 miles
0   75 km

AFRICA

Southern Lanzarote and northern Fuerteventura are linked by two ferry companies. **Linea Fred Olson** (Av. de Llegada s/n, Playa Blanca, tel. 928/51–73–01) makes five round-trips a day, and so does **Ferry Betancuria** (Dr. Ruperto Gonzalez Negrin s/n, Arrecife, tel. 928/81–21–86). The voyage takes about one hour, and the ferries take cars.

By Bus In Tenerife, buses meet all arriving Iberia flights at Reina Sofia Airport and transfer passengers to the bus terminal on the outskirts of Santa Cruz de Tenerife. From there you can get a taxi or another bus to the northern side of the island. Buses also meet the Gomera hydrofoil and ferry to take passengers on to Santa Cruz.

Each island has its own bus service geared for local residents. Generally buses leave the villages early in the morning for shopping in the capital and depart from its main plaza in the early afternoon. Tourist offices have details.

By Car Most visitors rent a car or jeep for at least part of their stay in the Canary Islands. It is by far the best way to explore the countryside. The roads are generally good, but not for those with vertigo, as they frequently curve over high mountain cliffs with nothing but the sea below.

Reservations for car rental are necessary only during the Christmas and Easter holidays. **Hertz** and **Avis** have representatives on all the islands, though better rates can be obtained from the Spanish company **Cicar** (tel. 928/27–73–08), located at all the airports except El Hierro. The only airport rental agency in El Hierro is **Cruz Alta** (tel. 922/55–00–04).

Local car-rental companies abound on every island, sometimes doubling as bars. Good prices can be found with a little shopping around.

Guided Tours

One-day tours of Tenerife and sightseeing excursions to other islands with English-speaking guides can be arranged through **Viajes Insular** (Av. Generalisimo 15, Puerto de la Cruz, tel. 922/38–02–62), which has branches on every island except La Gomera and El Hierro. Tours generally last all day and include a typical lunch or folklore presentation. The cost is $50–$100, depending on transportation.

Dining and Lodging

Dining Canarian cuisine is based on the delicious rockfish that abound near the coast and features some distinctive specialties that are worth searching out.

A typical meal begins with a hearty stew, such as *potaje canario* (a soup with vegetables, potatoes, and garbanzo beans), *rancho canario* (vegetables and meat), or *potaje de berros* (a watercress soup). Although it is hard to find in restaurants, Canarian residents eat *gofio* (similar to mashed potatoes, but made by toasting wheat, corn, or barley flour and then adding milk or broth) with their first course.

The next course is fresh native fish, the best of which are *vieja*, *cherne*, and *sama*, all firm-fleshed white rockfish. Accompanying the fish are *papas arrugadas* (literally, wrinkled potatoes), tiny new potatoes boiled in seawater so that salt crystals form on them as they dry. They are served with two delicious *mojo* sauces: a red one, made from sweet red peppers, olive oil, and vinegar, and a green one, made with fresh coriander, garlic, oil, vinegar, and sometimes avocado. Other specialties include *cabrito* (roast baby goat) and *conejo* (rabbit), both served in *salmorejo*, a slightly spicy paprika sauce.

Dessert is tropical fruit, often papaya, or sometimes various custards drenched in a syrup made from palm trees. Bananas flambé is strictly a tourist innovation.

Another island specialty is goat's-milk cheese; the best variety comes from La Palma. Canarian malmsey wines from Lanzarote, a favorite with Falstaff in Shakespeare's *Henry IV*, are still produced today. Wines from El Hierro and Tenerife are also delicious.

Meals are generally informal on the islands, although dressy clothing is appropriate when you dine in luxury hotels. Prices are lower than in mainland Spain.

Restaurants are listed in individual island sections. Highly recommended restaurants are indicated by a star ★.

Category	Cost*
$$$$	over 4,000 ptas
$$$	3,000–4,000 ptas
$$	1,500–3,000 ptas
$	under 1,500 ptas

per person, including tax but excluding drinks and service

Lodging There are hundreds of hotels in the Canary Islands, but they tend to fray rapidly with the masses of tourists who use them. With a few exceptions noted in the hotel descriptions, it is best to stay in the newest facilities.

Through package tours, most visitors pay reasonable prices for hotel rooms, but rates for independent travelers are exorbitant and out of line with the quality offered. This is especially true in the middle price range, where tourists are offered dingy lobbies, broken beds, and rusty swimming pools for prices up to $175 a night. This category has not been included in the book.

For economy-minded individual travelers, the solution is to stay in newly constructed apartment complexes. Although simply furnished, they have reception desks and swimming pools, and many have restaurants. There is also the added advantage of a kitchenette in each unit.

Accommodations are listed in individual island sections. Highly recommended properties are indicated by a star ★.

Category	Cost*
$$$$	over 19,000 ptas
$$$	12,000–19,000 ptas
$$	6,500–12,000 ptas
$	under 6,500 ptas

All prices are for a double room, including tax.

Highlights for First-time Visitors

Banana plantations (every island except Lanzarote and Fuerteventura)
Cuevas Verdes and Jameos del Agua (*see* Lanzarote, Tour 1)
Maspalomas beach and dunes (*see* Gran Canaria, Beaches)
Mt. Teide (*see* Tenerife, Tour 3)
Parque National Timanfaya (*see* Lanzarote, Tour 2)
Santa Cruz de la Palma (*see* La Palma, Tour 1)

Tenerife

Tenerife is the largest of the Canary Islands and roughly triangular in shape. It is towered over by the volcanic peak of Mt. Teide, which at 12,198 feet is Spain's highest mountain. The slopes leading up to it are forested with pines in the north, or barren lava fields in the south.

Tenerife's capital, Santa Cruz de Tenerife, is an important shipping port and the site of Spain's wildest fiesta, the pre-Lenten Carnival. Puerto de la Cruz, on the green north coast, has been welcoming tourists for decades (hotels hand out awards to regular visitors, some of whom have spent 30 consecutive winters here) but retains a charming small-town atmosphere. In the north, mixed in among the tourist attractions, are banana plantations and vineyards.

In the dry south, the resort of Playa de las Américas has sprung up at the edge of the desert over the past 15 years. It is especially popular with young couples and singles, who appreciate the world-class hotels and swinging nightlife.

Numbers in the margin correspond to points of interest on the Tenerife map.

Tour 1: Santa Cruz

❶ The port city of **Santa Cruz** is the capital of Tenerife and home to about 210,000 people. Begin with a visit to the city's heart, the **Plaza de España.** The cross is a monument to those who died in the Spanish Civil War, actually launched from Tenerife by General Franco, who had been exiled to the island. For two weeks before Lent each year, during Carnival, Santa Cruz throbs to a Latin beat emanating from the plaza. Be sure to make hotel reservations if you plan to visit during this period.

The **tourist office** is on the plaza, and just around the corner in the same building is the **Museo Arqueológico Provincial** (Archaeology Museum; Bravo Murillo 5, 3rd floor, tel. 922/24–20–90), which displays primitive ceramics and mummies. The ancient Guanches mummified their dead by rubbing the bodies with pine resin and salt and leaving them in the sun to dry for two weeks before placing them in caves. *Admission: 200 pesetas. Open weekdays 9–1 and 4–6; closed weekends.*

Follow Calle Bravo Murillo south along the opposite side of the building, and you will arrive at the quaint Plaza de la Iglesia. The **Iglesia de la Concepción** (Church of the Conception), noted for its six-story Moorish bell tower, is expected to remain closed for restoration until the year 2000, as part of a massive urban-renewal project that has already razed blocks of slums in this area.

Tenerife

Cross the bridge and turn right up Avenida de San Sebastián to get to the colorful **Mercado de Nuestra Señora de Africa** (Market of Our Lady of Africa). It is part bazaar and part food market. Stalls outside sell household goods; inside, stands selling everything from flowers and tropical fruits to canaries and parrots are arranged around a sunny patio. Downstairs a stall sells homemade cheesecakes and pineapples from El Hierro, while a stroll through the seafood section will acquaint you with the local fish. The market opens at 5 AM and is busy from about 6 AM to noon, Monday–Saturday.

Back toward the center of town is the Plaza del Príncipe de Asturias, location of the **Museo de Bellas Artes** (Museum of Fine Arts). Two floors of paintings, both Old Masters and modern works, include canvases by Breughel and Rivera. Many works depict local events. *José Murphy 4, tel. 922/24–43–58. Admission free. Open Tues.–Fri. 10–3.*

Time Out   The **Bar Avenida,** an old-style sidewalk café in front of the taxi stand on the Plaza de España, is a favorite meeting place for Santa Cruz residents.

Continue north on Calle de la Rosa. It dead-ends into the **Museo Militar** (Military Museum; C. de San Isidro 2, tel. 922/27–16–62; admission free; open Tues.–Sat. 10–2), with its exhibits of Tenerife's military past. On the northern outskirts of town, a plaza preserves 18th-century cannons on the site of what was once the **Paso Alto** fortress. In 1794 these weapons held off an attack led by Britain's Admiral Nelson; the cannon on the right, called Tiger, fired the shot that cost Nelson his right arm.

Santa Cruz's beach, **Las Teresitas,** is about 6½ km (4 mi) farther east.

If time permits, drive north to the university town of **La Laguna,** which was the first capital of the island and still retains many colonial buildings. Most are along Calle San Agustin. One of these, Casa Lercaro, the 400-year-old home of a former slave trader, has been carefully restored and was reopened in 1994 as the **Tenerife History Museum.** Here you can see antique navigational maps and learn about the evolution of the island's economy as it shifted from dependence on wine to sugarcane to bananas. *Calle San Agustin 22. Admission: 400 pesetas. Open Tues.–Sat. 10–5, Sun. 10–2.*

Tour 2: Puerto de la Cruz and the North Coast

❷ Puerto de la Cruz is the oldest resort in the Canary Islands. Despite high-rise hotels and mass tourism, it remains a town with character. Start your visit at the seafront **Lago Martianez,** an immense public swimming pool with landscaped islands and bridges, and fountains that spray sky-high. Because Puerto de la Cruz has uninviting black-sand beaches, the town in 1965 commissioned Lanzarote artist Cesar Manrique to build this forerunner of today's water parks. The complex also includes a restaurant-nightclub and several smaller pools.

Stroll from Lago Martianez along the coastal walkway until you reach the central **Plaza de la Iglesia,** which is beautifully landscaped with seasonal flowering plants. Here you can sit and listen to the street musicians, or stop at the **tourist office** for a copy of a walking tour in English that details all the architecturally important buildings.

Time Out The **Hannen Tab**—a beer bar of burlap and rough-hewn wood, between the Plaza de Charco and the fishing port—is a great place to stop for dark German beer on tap or a light meal of shish kebabs, bratwurst, hamburgers, or Scandinavian-style open-face sandwiches.

Heading uphill and out of town by car, pay a visit to the **Jardín Botanico** (Botanical Gardens). Now filled with thousands of varieties of exotic tropical plants, the gardens were founded on the orders of King Carlos III in 1788 to propagate warm-climate species brought back to Spain from the Americas. *Tel. 922/38–35–72. Admission: 150 pesetas. Open Oct.–Mar., daily 9–6; Apr.–Sept., daily 9–7.*

❸ Take the coastal highway, C820, west 29 km (18 mi) through the banana plantations to **Icod de los Vinos,** where a 3,000-year-old **dragon tree** towers 18 meters (57 ft) above the highway. These trees were worshiped as a symbol of fertility and knowledge by the Guanches; the sap, which turns red on contact with air, was used in healing rituals and later exported to Europe, where it became an ingredient in hair dye and a stain for violins.

Adjacent to the dragon tree are attractive plazas of unspoiled Colonial architecture and Canarian pine balconies. At Plaza de la Pila 4 is the **Casa Museo del Vino,** a tasting room where you can sample the sweet local malmsey and other Canary Island wines and cheeses.

❹ Backtrack through town and take the turnoff for **Garachico,** 5 km (3 mi) toward the sea. One of the most idyllic and best-preserved towns in the islands, it was the main port of Tenerife until May 5, 1706, when Mt. Teide blew its top, sending twin rivers of lava downhill. One filled in Garachico's harbor, and the other destroyed most of the town. Legend has it that the eruption was unleashed by an evil monk who put a curse on the town in anger over being banished.

One of the buildings that withstood the eruption was the **Castillo San Miguel,** the tiny 16th-century fortress on the waterfront. Island crafts such as embroidery and basketmaking are demonstrated inside. From the roof you can see the two rivers of lava, which are now solidified on the mountainside. The **Convento de San Francisco,** also untouched, can be visited, as can the 18th-century parish church of **Santa Ana.**

From here you can return or continue along the coast on a newly paved road to the lighthouse on the volcanic **Punta de Teno.** A paved road winding along high cliffs to the south coast is only for the adventurous.

Tour 3: Orotava to Mt. Teide

Four roads lead to Mt. Teide from various parts of the island, but the most beautiful approach is the road from **Orotava,** which takes you through four distinct types of vegetation.

Begin with a visit or drive through the town to see the stately mansions built by traders and ranchers of the fertile Orotava valley on **Calle San Francisco,** just north of the Baroque church **Nuestra Señora de la Concepción.** At the **Casa de los Balcones** (Calle San Francisco 3) and just across the street at the **Casa del Turista** (Calle San Francisco 2) you can see a variety of island craftspeople at work: women stitching intricate Canarian embroidery, basketmakers, cigar rollers, and potters. You may also come upon a remarkable demonstration of painting with sand, which is done on the street during Orotava's fiestas. *Admission free. Open daily 8:30–6:30.*

As you head out of town to the higher altitudes, the banana plantations give way to fruit and almond orchards that bloom in January. Then you enter a fragrant pine forest that allows views of the snow-capped peak towering over the evergreens.

At **El Portillo** you enter the **Parque Nacional del Teide,** which is made up of the volcano itself and a 6-km- (4-mi-) long sunken crater at the foot of the mountain called the Cañadas del Teide. The cañadas area is a violent jumble of swirling rocks and minerals created by millions of years of volcanic activity. At the visitor's center in El Portillo you can see a video and exhibits explaining the region's natural history. The center also offers trail maps, guided hikes, and bus tours. *Tel. 922/29–01–29. Open every day 9–4.*

From El Portillo the road descends into **Las Cañadas del Teide,** a stark landscape that looks as if it belongs to another planet. About 10 km (6 mi) farther on, in the middle of the sunken crater, a cable car (admission: 1,000 pesetas, children 500 pesetas; open daily 9–5, last trip up at 4) carries you to 3,616 meters (11,664 ft) in eight minutes, leaving the final 166-meter (534-ft) climb to your own feet and lungs. Allow at least an hour for the round-trip to the crater rim. On the way you will notice sulfur steam vents, and from the top there is a glorious view of most of the archipelago.

The trail to the rim is closed to cable-car riders when it is snowy, usually about four months a year. In that case you can still get a good view of southern Tenerife and Gran Canaria from the top of the cable-car line, but you will be confined to the tiny terrace of the bar by whistle-blowing guards posted on the roof to make sure no one strays.

After descending in the cable car, continue another 3 km (2 mi) to the **Roques de Garcia**, across from the Parador Nacional Cañadas del Teide (*see* Dining and Lodging, *below*). The rocks have eroded into fantastic shapes and provide a good foreground for a photo of Mt. Teide.

From here you can head south for about 30 km (18 mi) on a slow, twisting road that meets the coastal highway near Reina Sofia Airport, or you can backtrack to the park entrance at El Portillo and return to Orotava. The road to the right at El Portillo runs along the ridge of Tenerife through pine forests and eucalyptus groves to La Esperanza, ending near Los Rodeos Airport.

What to See and Do with Children

In addition to swimming and mountain climbing, Tenerife offers numerous attractions geared for young visitors.

Loro Parque is a subtropical garden that is home to 1,300 parrots, many of which are trained to ride bicycles and perform other tricks. The recently renovated park also includes a dolphin show, an amusing film that shows the world through a parrot's eyes, and a replica of a village in Thailand. *Puerto de la Cruz, tel. 922/37–38–41. Admission: 1,500 pesetas. Open daily 8:30–5.*

The **Yellow Submarine** cruises beneath the coastal waters, allowing glimpses of the rich undersea life of Tenerife's south coast. *Las Galletas, tel. 922/73–00–13. Admission: 4,000 pesetas adults, 2,000 pesetas children. Operates in good weather daily 10–5.*

Octopus Aguapark, a huge water park, has tall slides, meandering streams for innertubes, and swimming pools and lounge chairs. *San Eugenio, Playa de las Americas, tel. 922/79–22–66. Admission: 1,000 pesetas. Open daily 10–6.*

Shopping

Tenerife, like all the Canary Islands, is a free port, meaning no value-added tax is charged on luxury goods such as jewelry, electronics, alcohol, and cigarettes. The streets are packed with shops selling these items to Europeans, but the prices do not represent a significant saving for Americans.

The islands are also famous for lacy, hand-embroidered tablecloths and place mats. The largest selection is available in Puerto de la Cruz at **Casa Iriarte** (San Juan 17), located in the patio of a ramshackle Canarian house.

Contemporary island crafts and traditional musical instruments can be found at the government-sponsored shop **Casa Torrehermosa** (Tomás Zerolo 27) in Orotava.

Beaches

Along the north coast, rock ledges are used for beaches, but swimming is safe only during the summer months, when the sea is calm. **Las Teresitas** beach, 7 km (4 mi) east of Santa Cruz, was constructed using white sand imported from the Sahara Desert. It is planted with palms and especially popular with local families. **Playa del Médano** on the southern coast, a large bay surrounded by yellow sand, is considered the best beach on Tenerife. It is often windy and consequently a favorite with windsurfers, who hold international windsurfing competitions here. **Los Cristianos** is a small crescent of gray sand surrounded by apartment houses. **Playa de las Américas** is a man-made yellow-sand beach protected by an artificial reef. **Los Gigantes** is a smallish gray-sand cove surrounded by rocks and cliffs of great natural beauty.

Sports

Diving Information on diving and underwater fishing can be obtained from the **Club Nautico** (tel. 922/27–37–00) in Santa Cruz or the school in Playa de las Américas at **Las Palmeras Hotel** (Av. Maritima, tel. 922/79–09–91). The rugged and isolated west coast of the island boasts marine habitats unspoiled by development, but diving is safe only in the calm summer months.

Fishing Fishing trips can be arranged at the harbor in Los Cristianos.

Golf There are four 18-hole golf courses on the island. In the north, **Club de Golf de Tenerife** (tel. 922/25–02–40) in El Peñon can be used by nonmembers on weekdays only. In the south, **Campo Golf de Sur** (tel. 922/73–10–70) has 27 holes near Reina Sofia Airport, and not far away there are two 18-hole links at the **Amarilla Golf Club** (tel. 922/79–24–61 or 922/79–35–59) in San Miguel.

Horseback Riding The **Club Hipica La Atalaya** (Camino de San Lazaro s/n, tel. 922/25–57–39) on the outskirts of Santa Cruz can help arrange excursions on horseback.

Windsurfing Windsurfing rentals and lessons can be arranged at the **SunWind Windsurf School** (tel. 922/17–61–74) in Playa del Médano.

Dining and Lodging

El Médano
Lodging
Hotel Windsurf. The lobby of this beach hotel on the southeast coast is arranged around a fountain made from a windsurfing board in full sail. The rooms have separate sleeping and sitting areas, with modern black furniture, white tile floors, and terraces. A breakfast buffet is included, and children under 12 stay free. *38612 El Médano, tel. 922/17–54–60. 155 rooms with bath. Facilities: restaurant, piano bar, outdoor pool, Jacuzzi, sauna, playground, bike rental, squash, gym, windsurfing school. AE, MC, V. $$*

La Orotava
Dining and Lodging
Parador Nacional Cañadas del Teide. Built of stucco in the style of a ski chalet, with green shutters and balconies, the parador offers basic accommodations amid fantastic rock formations in the center of the Las Cañadas plateau at the foot of Mt. Teide. The large rooms have heavy, dark furniture and tile floors. The parador restaurant serves local specialties including roast goat and rabbit in *salmorejo* sauce. *38300 La Orotava, tel. 922/38–64–15. 23 rooms with bath. Facilities: restaurant, bar, outdoor pool (summer only), tennis court. AE, DC, MC, V. $$*

Playa de las Américas
Dining
El Patio. Located on the grounds of the Jardín Tropical hotel, this restaurant is spectacularly located by the sea in the midst of flowering gardens. This famous patio ranks as the south coast's top gourmet dining spot, serving up such dishes as cold mussel soup with saffron and duck breast in mandarin orange sauce. A pianist provides soft background music that, with the candlelight and splashing fountain, enhances the romantic atmosphere. *Hotel Jardín Tropical, tel. 922/79–41–11. Reservations recommended. Jacket and tie advised. Closed Mon. and June. AE, DC, MC, V. $$$*

★ **Masia del Mar.** There's no menu here; you simply point to what you want from the vast display of fresh fish and shellfish in a big refrigerator case. Add a salad and a bottle of white wine to the order and then find a seat on a wide terrace for a simple feast of the best food the Canary Islands has to offer. Overlooking Las Caletas cove, the Masia del Mar is about 5 km (3 mi) west of Playa de las Americas. *Caleta de Adeje, tel. 922/71–02–41. Reservations not required. Dress: casual. MC, V. $$*

Lodging **Jardín Tropical.** Spread on many levels over several hills, the Jardín Tropical has white turrets and archways, Moorish tile floors, and bright flowering plants cascading everywhere. The rooms are decorated with carved-pine and wicker furniture and pastel paisley prints; all have balconies. The baths are decorated with colorful Spanish tile. One swimming pool has islands and bridges. *38660 San Eugenio, Adeje, tel. 922/79–41–11, fax 922/79–44–51. 376 rooms with bath. Facilities: restaurant, bar, 2 outdoor pools, gym, sauna, beauty shop. AE, MC, V. $$$$*

Mediterranean Palace. Replicas of Greek statues line the entrance and the vast swimming pool, while the six-story lobby is a high-tech synthesis of marble, neon, and chrome. Glass elevators glide up to the rooms, which are decorated with black leather and brass furniture. The beds are extra large, the baths are black marble, and each room has a terrace. *Av. del Litoral s/n, 38660 Arona, tel. 922/79–44–00, fax 922/79–36–22. 532 rooms with bath. Facilities: restaurant, piano bar, outdoor pool, children's pool, tennis, squash, aerobics, gym, sauna, nude-sunbathing terrace, beauty parlor, TV room. AE, DC, MC, V. $$$$*

★ **Gran Hotel Bahia del Duque.** A cross between a Canarian village and an Italian hill town, this sprawling hotel is a striking jumble of pastel-colored houses and palaces, with Renaissance windows, loggias, and quiet courtyards all presided over by a clock tower copied from the Torre de la Concepción in Santa Cruz. The five-story lobby is a marvel in itself, with tropical birds, palm-filled bars, and two glass elevators. All employees are dressed in traditional Canarian costumes. Guest rooms feature oversize beds, summery wicker and pine furnishings, and distinctive architectural details such as scalloped plasterwork and hand-painted ceramics. There are four swimming pools with natural lava rock walls, which spill one into the other. The hotel provides opportunities for sailing and diving and runs boat trips to see a colony of whales that cavort just off the coast. *Adeje 38660, tel. 922/75–00–00, fax 922/75–16–16. 362 rooms. Facilities: 5 restaurants, bars, 4 outdoor pools, gymnasium, squash, sauna, beauty shop, tennis, sailing, diving. AE, MC, V. $$$*

Compostela Beach. This new five-story apartment complex near the Mediterranean Palace offers one- and two-bedroom units furnished in earth tones with pine furniture and terraces. The landscaping is sparse, but the complex has a large pool and sunbathing area. *Av. del Litoral s/n, 38660 Arona, tel. 922/79–30–07, fax 922/79–60–57. 110 apartments with kitchen and bath. Facilities: restaurant, bar, outdoor pool, playground, discothèque. AE, V. $*

Puerto de la Cruz *Dining* **La Magnolia.** Perched in the upscale neighborhood near the botanical gardens, La Magnolia offers dining in the garden or in the main dining room, where the decor stalled in the '60s with a purple ceiling, gold tablecloths, and autographed photos of all the celebrities who have enjoyed the Catalan cuisine served here. The open kitchen serves huge platters of seafood in garlicky sauces. *Carretera Botanico 5, tel. 922/38–56–14. Reservations advised. Dress: Jacket and tie advised. AE, MC, V. $$$*

El Pescador. This restaurant claims to be located in the oldest house in town, and you'll believe it when you feel the wood floor shake as the waiters walk by. Slatted green shutters, high ceilings, and rhythmic salsa music give the dining room the atmosphere of a tropical fiesta. A guitarist entertains at night. Specialties include avocado stuffed with shrimp and local fish. Ask for papas arrugadas or you'll get french fries. *Puerto Viejo 8, tel. 922/38–40–88. AE, DC, MC, V. $$*

Lodging **Melia San Felipe.** This 19-story hotel has the best location in Puerto de la Cruz, with million-dollar views of the coast and Mt. Teide. It has been a landmark for decades, but the large, carpeted rooms are well cared for. They feature pastel bargello drapes and bedspreads, balconies, and large baths. An elegant champagne breakfast buffet is included in the room rate. *Av. de Colón 22, 38400, tel. 922/38–33–11, fax 922/37–37–18. 260 rooms with bath. Facilities: restaurant, bar, Olympic-size outdoor pool, tennis, sauna, satellite TV. AE, MC, V. $$$*

Hotel Monopol. One of the town's first inns, the Monopol has been lodging tourists for 102 years. Before that it was a private home, built in 1742. The rooms are arranged on four stories of wooden balconies around a central courtyard shaded by tropical plants. The small, carpeted rooms have chenille spreads and tile baths. The balconies of most overlook the sea or the town's main plaza. *Quintana 15, 38400, tel. 922/38–46–11, fax 922/37–03–10. 100 rooms with bath. Facilities: restaurant, 2 bars, outdoor pool, TV room. AE, MC, V. $$*

Santa Cruz **Mesón El Drago.** Located in the village of El Socorro, 6 km (3 mi)
Dining from Los Rodeos Airport, this green-and-white 18th-century farmhouse with brick floors and flower-filled patio has been converted into a showcase of typical Canarian cookery. Among the best dishes on the menu are fish casserole, rabbit in spicy salmorejo sauce, and *puchero canario,* a tangy stew of vegetables and meats. *Urbanizacion San Gonzalo, tel. 922/54–30–01. Reservations recommended on weekends. Dress: casual. Open Tues.–Sun. for lunch and Fri. and Sat. for dinner. AE, MC, V. $$$*

Los Troncos. In a middle-class neighborhood near the bullring is one of the few restaurants in Santa Cruz serving Canarian cuisine. A white Andalusian entryway greets diners, who enjoy *rancho canario* stew, *potaje de berros,* and local fish. Steak and spare ribs are grilled to perfection. *Calle de General Goded 15, tel. 922/28–41–52. AE, V. $$*

Lodging **Hotel Mencey.** "Mencey" was the name for the ancient Guanche kings, and you'll probably feel like one if you stay at this grandiose beige stucco-and-marble hotel. Crystal chandeliers and gold-leaf columns ornament the lobby. The rooms feature French Louis XIV–style furnishings. *José Naveiras 38, 38001, tel. 922/27–67–00. 298 rooms with bath. Facilities: restaurant, bar, outdoor pool, tennis, satellite TV, shopping, beauty parlor. AE, DC, V. $$$$*

Hotel Taburiente. Right across the street from the city park, this hotel is favored by businesspeople and visitors who need to catch early morning flights at Los Rodeos Airport. The white marble lobby is downright luxurious, and the rooms are large and comfortable, despite the linoleum floors. Try to get one with a balcony facing the park. *Dr. José Naveiras, 24A, 38001, tel. 922/27–60–00, fax 922/27–05–62. 116 rooms. Facilities: restaurant, outdoor pool. AE, MC, V. $$*

The Arts and Nightlife

Casinos For gambling, Tenerife has the **Casino Taoro** (Carretera del Taoro s/n, tel. 922/38–57–19), in a stately former hotel in Puerto de la Cruz, and the **Casino Playa de las Américas** (Av. Marítima s/n, tel. 922/79–37–12), in the hotel Gran Tenerife in Playa de las Américas.

Dancing Almost all hotels have live music at night. For dancing in Puerto de la Cruz try **Victoria** at the Hotel Tenerife Playa (Av. de Colón s/n), a favorite with all age groups, or **El Coto** (Av. Litoral 24, next door to the Melia San Felipe hotel), which is usually jammed with a young, fast crowd.

Bar In Santa Cruz, the wood and brass-laden **Andén** (General Goded 41) attracts a hip young crowd with loud rock music.

In Playa de las Américas most bars are within a three-building complex called **Veronica's.** There you'll find places like the **Kangaroo Pub, Busby's,** and **Sgt. Pepper's,** all with young rowdy crowds. **The Banana Garden** (tel. 928/79–03–65) attracts an older but no less sedate crowd with live salsa music, and the disco **Prismas** (in the Hotel Tenerife Sol) remains on top after nearly a decade.

Gran Canaria

The circular island of Gran Canaria has three distinct identities. Its capital, Las Palmas, with 370,000 people, is a thriving business center and shipping port, while the white-sand beaches of the south coast are a tourist mecca and the towns of the interior continue a simple agricultural existence.

Las Palmas, the largest city in the Canary Islands, is very Spanish, with traffic jams, diesel-spewing buses, and hordes of shoppers. One side of the city is lined with docks for huge container ships, while the other harbors the 7-km- (4-mi-) long Canteras Beach. In the evening Spanish families, with children on bikes and in strollers, join sailors and tourists for a *paseo* up and down the beachfront.

The south coast, developed in the '60s in a boxy, low-rise style along wide avenues, is a family resort. At the southern tip of the island the popular Playa del Ingles, with its strip of fast-food restaurants, gives way to the empty dunes of Maspalomas and miles of beach.

The interior of Gran Canaria is steep highlands that reach an elevation of 1,995 meters (6,435 ft) at Pozo de las Nieves. Although it is green in winter, Gran Canaria does not have the luxurious tropical foliage of the western islands of the archipelago.

Numbers in the margin correspond to points of interest on the Gran Canaria map.

Tour 1: Las Palmas

❶ Las Palmas is strung out for 10 km (6 mi) along the waterfront. Begin in the old quarter, called La Vegueta, at the **Plaza Santa Ana,** with its bronze dog statues. You may be surprised to learn that the Canary Islands were not named after the yellow songbirds, but for a breed of dog (*canum* in Latin) found here by ancient explorers. The birds were named after the island.

The smog-stained **Catedral Santa Ana** faces the plaza. The cathedral took four centuries to complete, so the 19th-century exterior with its neoclassical Roman columns contrasts sharply with the Gothic

Gran Canaria

0 — 10 miles
0 — 15 km

N

Gáldar
Bañaderos
Playa de las Canteras
⓫ C810
Cenobio de Valerón
Moya
Arucas ❾
Las Palmas ❶
TO TENERIFE, FUERTEVENTURA
⓭ ⓬ **Puerto de las Nieves**
Agaete
Firgas
Teror ❿
Tafira Alta ❽
Punta de la Aldea
Santa Brígida
Atalaya ❼
C810
San Mateo
❻
Telde
Parador Cruz de Tejeda ❹
Valsequillo
San Nicolás de Tolentino
Mirador Los Pechos ❺
Pozo de las Nieves
Punta de Cruz Grande
GC1
San Bartolomé de Tirajana
❷
Ingenio
Gran Canaria Airport
Mogán
❸
Santa Lucía
Agüimes
Fataga
Playa Mogán
GC520
Arinaga
Puerto de Mogán
C810
GC1
Puerto Rico
Playa de Puerto Rico
Playa de Tarajalillo
Playa de San Agustín
Maspalomas
Playa de las Burras
Playa de la Mujer
Playa del Inglés
Playa de Maspalomas

ceiling vaulting of the interior, which was begun in the 15th century.

Baroque statues carved in the Andalucían style are on display in the cathedral's **Museo de Arte Sacro** (Museum of Religious Art), which is arranged around a peaceful cloister with Canarian carved-wood balconies. Ask the curator to open the *sala capitular* so you can see the 16th-century Valencian tile floor. The flower pattern, part of the cathedral's shield, is repeated in several of the windows of the nave. The treasury is closed to the public. *Admission: 150 pesetas. Open weekdays 9–1:30 and 4–6:30, Sat. 9–2; closed Sun.*

Behind the cathedral, the **Casa Museo Colón** (Columbus Museum) is housed in a palace where Christopher Columbus may have stayed when he stopped to repair the rudder on the *Pinta* before leaving to discover America. Models of Columbus's three ships, nautical instruments, and copies of early navigational maps are on display. Two rooms showcase pre-Columbian artifacts brought back from Colombia and Mexico. *Calle Colón 1. Admission free. Open weekdays 9:30–5:30, Sat. 9–1; closed Sun. and Aug.*

It's worth stopping in next door to see what temporary exhibits are showing at the **Centro Atlántico de Arte Moderno** (Atlantic Center for Modern Art). Although it has only been open since 1991, the center has already earned a reputation for putting together some of the best avant-garde shows in Spain. *Los Balcones 11. Admission free. Open Tues.–Sat. 10:30–1:30 and 4:30–8:30.*

Wander the narrow, cobbled streets, then hop on bus No. 1 at the Teatro Perez Galdos. Line 1 runs the length of Las Palmas and brings you back again. A stop at the **Parque Doramas** will let you peek at the elegant Santa Catalina hotel and casino. Inside the park you will also find the **Pueblo Canario,** a model village designed with typical Canarian architecture by artist Nestor de la Torre, as well as a museum devoted to his work. Regional folk dancing takes place in the village on Thursdays (5:30–7) and Sundays (11:30–1).

Back on bus No. 1, you can continue as far as the **Castillo de la Luz,** a fortress in the port district that dates to 1494 and is currently closed to the public. You can also get off near the sparkling, white sands of **Las Canteras Beach** for a swim or a stroll along the paseo.

Tour 2: Central Highlands

From Maspalomas on the southern coast, take Rte. GC520 toward Fataga. This is sagebrush country, with interesting rock formations and cactus as well as tiny valleys of palm trees and goats grazing on stubby grass. A **mirador** about 7 km (4 mi) uphill offers good views of the coast and mountains. Fruit trees begin to replace the cactus as you climb higher on the winding road. **San Bartolomé de Tirajana,** the administrative center of the south coast, is an attractive town planted with pink geraniums. Its Sunday-morning market in front of the church is popular with tourists, who come for the tropical produce and island crafts.

Detour east to visit the village of **Santa Lucía,** with its crafts shops and museum devoted to Guanche artifacts. Then rejoin GC520 and climb to the **Cruz Grande** summit. On the left you can see several of the island's reservoirs, known as the lakes of Gran Canaria. They are stocked with trout, and you can fish in them if you obtain a permit from the forest service (ICONA, tel. 928/24–87–35).

Continue in the direction of Tejeda, past mountain villages where farmers carry burlap sacks of freshly dug potatoes and just-picked watercress. On the right is the spike-shaped **Roque Nublo,** an eroded volcanic chimney worshiped by the Guanches. At the village of **Tejeda,** the road begins an 8-km (5-mi) ascent through a pine forest dotted with picnic spots to the parador.

Time Out Housed in a stone-and-stucco building, the **Parador Cruz de Tejeda** is dedicated to introducing Canarian cooking to tourists. There are great views from the terrace outside the dining room. Inside you can feast on watercress soup and swordfish, lamb, or pork served with mojo sauces. Canarian cheeses and homemade fig ice cream are on the dessert menu. A parking lot has been turned into a sidewalk café, with more familiar fare like hamburgers, chicken, and omelets at reasonable prices.

From the parador continue uphill about 21 km (13 mi) to the **Mirador Los Pechos,** the highest viewing point on the island, which offers more panoramic vistas.

Backtrack toward the parador and take the second road on the right winding tortuously down to **San Mateo,** which has the Casa Cho Zacarias museum of rural life and a winery (open Mon.–Sat. 9–1). Pass **Santa Brigida** and turn right toward the golf club on the rim of the Bandama crater. Continue to the village of **Atalaya,** where there are cave houses and pottery workshops.

Back on the main road leading into Las Palmas, you will pass through **Tafira Alta,** an exclusive enclave of the city's wealthy families. The **Jardín Canario Viero y Clavijo** (open daily 9–12 and 3–6) botanical gardens are here, with a respected collection of plants from all the Atlantic islands in their natural habitats.

Tour 3: North Coast

Leave Las Palmas by the northern road, passing the grim shanty-towns to the banana plantations of the coastal route. At Bañaderos ⑨ turn inland to **Arucas,** an agricultural center and the island's third-largest town. Its great gray stone Gothic church looks wildly out of place among the small white houses.

Continue uphill through the most verdant vegetation on Gran ⑩ Canaria to the village of **Teror,** an obligatory stop on all island tours. In the 18th-century church, **Nuestra Señora del Pino** (Our Lady of the Pine Tree), Gran Canaria's patron saint, the Virgen del Pino, is seated on a silver throne above the altar, flanked by heavy silver chandeliers. The statue, said to have been found in a pine tree in the 15th century, is now taken out for special fiestas. Wind your way west through the hillside villages of **Firgas** and **Moya** to take in the tropical foliage, then head back to the coast.

After the coastal highway crosses a deep ravine, turn left to visit the ⑪ **Cenobio de Valerón** (Monastery of Valerón), a group of caves cut out of the rockface of a cliff, and one of the islands' few accessible Guanche archaeological sites. Some believe that the caves were used for food storage; others, that the site was a type of convent for training the young daughters of noble families from nearby **Gáldar,** capital of the Guanche kingdom.

⑫ Continue through the banana plantations to **Agaete,** a town famous for the annual fiesta of the *rama* (branch). During the August 4 fiesta, pine branches from the island's upper slopes are carried by dancing throngs of people to the town. The ritual is a variation on a rain dance dating to pre-Christian days that was used by the Guanches in times of drought.

⑬ Just beyond Agaete is the port of **Puerto de las Nieves,** where painted boats bob in the tiny harbor and fresh fish is served in a few small restaurants. The short Avenida de las Poetas leads to an old windmill on the point, which is a good picnic spot. Look for the rocky point called the **Dedo de Dios** (Finger of God).

Time Out The **Cápita** restaurant (tel. 928/89–82–72) is a favorite with Canary residents, who often head to Puerto de las Nieves for Sunday lunch. The simple plant-filled dining room has wide windows on the harbor and classical music.

What to See and Do with Children

There are plenty of attractions to catch the eye of children along the south coast of Gran Canaria.

AquaSur water park has chutes and tubes for splashing the day away. *Carretera Palmitos Park, Km 3, tel. 928/76–99–18. Admission: 1,500 pesetas. Open daily 10–6.*

Holiday World amusement park has roller coasters and a Ferris wheel that children can see from miles away. *Carretera General, tel. 928/76–70–99. Admission free; unlimited rides, 1,500 pesetas. Open evenings 5 PM–1 AM.*

Palmitos Park is part botanical garden, displaying 51 types of palm trees, and part zoo, with tropical birds and an open-air butterfly house. Trained parrots also perform. *Carretera Palmitos, about 6 km (4 mi) inland from Maspalomas; tel. 928/76–04–58. Admission: 1,000 pesetas. Open daily 9:30–7.*

Off the Beaten Track

If you want to avoid the crowds of tourists stopping for lunch at the Parador Cruz de Tejeda on your mountain tour, follow the signs to the village of **Artenara,** about 13 km (8 mi) west of the road leading to the parador. It is an unspoiled hamlet with many cave houses built right into the side of the mountain. The restaurant **Mirador de la Silla** is in one of these cave entrances, but the cavern opens up to the other side of the mountain, where you can sit in the sun and enjoy a spectacular view. Canarian specialties are served at bargain prices.

Shopping

Gran Canaria has the best duty-free shops in the islands; it also boasts the only department stores, **El Corte Inglés** and **Galerías Preciados,** which face each other on Avenida Mesa y Lopez in central Las Palmas. For more unusual gift items, try **Antiguedades Linares** or **La Fataga** in the Pueblo Canario. The shops have a good selection of crafts from all over Spain, including knives with carved-bone handles made in Gran Canaria.

Parfumes Oceano, near the church parking lot in the village of Teror, offers perfumes made locally from tropical flowers.

Beaches

The beaches along Gran Canaria's eastern and southern coasts are the island's major tourist attraction. **Las Canteras** beach in Las Palmas is made safe for swimming by an artificial offshore reef. It can be extremely crowded in the summer, but the sand is swept clean every night by the city.

Playa de Tarajalillo, with alternating areas of black sand and gravel, is the first beach of the southern resort area, and a popular choice of local families. **Playa de San Agustín** is a half-mile strip of black sand fringed with a palm garden. It has rental areas for sailboards, pedal boats, and lounge chairs. **Playa de las Burras** is a gray-sand beach surrounding a crescent-shape harbor sometimes used by local fishermen.

Playa del Inglés is the most famous of Gran Canaria's beaches. Its white sands, which extend over 3 km (2 mi), swarm with beach-chair rentals, ice-cream vendors, and fast-food restaurants. West of here is an area of sand dunes and a sign-posted nude beach. **Maspalomas Beach** comes next. Its 1-km stretch of golden sand is bordered by endless dunes that provide a sense of isolation and refuge from the hustle of other Canarian resorts. Dozens of varieties of native birds and plants also find refuge in a lagoon alongside the dunes. The western edge of Maspalomas is marked by a lighthouse and fringed by a stately oasis of 1,000-year-old palm trees. **Playa de la Mujer** is a rocky beach around the point from Maspalomas and a good place to watch the sunset.

Sports

Diving **Snorkeling** and **diving** are often practiced near the Maspalomas lighthouse. A diving school is located at Patalavaca.

Golf The island has two golf courses. The **Las Palmas Golf Club** (tel. 928/ 35–01–04), on the rim of the Bandama crater about 15 minutes outside the capital, was founded in 1891 and is Spain's oldest course. The 18-hole **Maspalomas Golf Course** (tel. 928/ 76–25–81) is near the dunes.

Horseback Riding To rent horses, contact the Las Palmas Golf Club (*see* Golf, *above*) or Palmitos Park (*see* What to See and Do With Children, *above*).

Sailing The famous **Escuela de Vela de Puerto Rico** sailing school (tel. 928/ 56–07–72), where Spain's gold medalists in the 1984 Olympics trained and teach, is at Puerto Rico.

Windsurfing **Windsurfing** equipment can be rented from the Club Mistral at the Hotel Bahia Feliz (*see* Dining and Lodging, *below*).

Dining and Lodging

Las Palmas **Julio.** Owner Jose Medina has been welcoming diners to this out-
Dining standing seafood restaurant for 47 years. In a small dining room dec-
★ orated with ropes, portholes, and polished wood, you can tuck into 12 different types of shellfish or local fish, such as *cherne* and *vieja* served in a white-wine clam sauce. A typical Canarian soup or stew is prepared each day. *La Naval 132, tel. 928/46–01–39. Reservations advised. Dress: casual. AE, V. $$–$$$*
Hamburg Restaurant. Tops for atmosphere, the Hamburg specializes in filet mignon cooked a dozen different ways. The walls of the tiny restaurant are crammed with crockery, photos, and silver pitchers. Also try the smoked-salmon salad and, for dessert, the homemade German cakes. *Mary Sanchez 54, tel. 928/22–27–45. Reservations advised. Dress: casual. AE, V. Closed Sun. evening. $$*
Mesón de la Paella. Green latticework window trim and lace curtains give the white stucco mesón a homey feel. The kitchen serves up rice dishes from Spain's Mediterranean coast, such as *arroz negro* (black rice) and seafood paella. Look for the big paella-pan sign one block from the Plaza España. *Jose María Duran 47, tel. 928/27–16–40. AE, V. Closed Sat. evening and Sun. $$*

Lodging **Melia Las Palmas.** Aimed at businesspeople, the Melia has a superb location and offers large, comfortable rooms with orange striped carpet and orange vinyl headboards. The balconies have sweeping views of Las Canteras beach, and there is a pool on a terrace overlooking the sea. A breakfast buffet is included in the room rate. *Gomera 6, 35008, tel. 928/26–80–50, fax 928/26–84–11. 316 rooms with bath. Facilities: restaurant, coffee shop, outdoor pool, piano bar, discothèque, business center. AE, DC, MC, V. $$$*
Hotel Imperial Playa. Renovated in 1991 with business travelers in mind, the hotel sits right on Las Canteras beach and provides bright rooms with Scandinavian furniture and marble baths. The small terraces have good beach views. *Ferreras 1, 35008, tel. 928/26–48–54, fax 928/26–94–42. 142 rooms with bath. Facilities: restaurant, snack bar, gym, sauna. AE, MC, V. $$*
Apartments Brisamar Canteras. The best-maintained of all the beach apartments, the Brisamar's are a favorite with tourists from Finland. The rooms are only functional but freshly painted and

cheerful. *Paseo de las Canteras 49, 35010, tel. 928/26–94–00. 52 studio apartments. No credit cards. $*

**Maspalomas/
South Coast
Dining**

Cho Pedro. Located across the highway from the Playa del Inglés area, Cho Pedro is simply decorated with checked tablecloths, farm implements, and local handicrafts. Emphasis is on Canarian specialities such as soups, rabbit, or goat in spicy *salmorejo* sauce, and local fish. The *sama* cooked *a la sal* (in rock salt) is superb. *Marcial Franco 12, tel. 928/76–20–92. Reservations advised. Dress: casual. AE, V. $$*

Loopy's Tavern. An island tradition that few visitors to the south coast of Gran Canaria can resist, Loopy's is modeled after a U.S.-style western steakhouse. It features friendly waiters, imaginative cocktails, and great meat. Try the shishkebabs, which are served dangling from a metal contraption over your table. *Las Retamas, San Agustín, tel. 928/76–28–92. Reservations advised. Dress: casual. V. $$*

★ **Tenderete II.** Canarian cuisine is cherished at Tenderete, one of the few restaurants in the islands where you can order *gofio*, made here with roasted corn flour and fish broth. Typical soups and stews are served for the first course, and the main course is always fish, grilled or baked in rock salt. Pick it out from the display hooks in the front window. Wines from Lanzarote, El Hierro, and Tenerife are available. *Av. de Tirajan, Edificio Aloe, tel. 928/76–14–60. Reservations advised. Dress: casual. AE, DC, MC, V. $$*

Lodging

★ **Hotel Palm Beach.** The most sophisticated and luxurious hotel in the Canary Islands, the Palm Beach is located on the edge of Maspalomas beach in the middle of a 1,000-year-old palm oasis. The lobby is elegantly striped with black-and-white marble. Spacious rooms are decorated with dark bamboo furniture and are equipped with huge closets and large marble baths. The terraces overlook the sea or the palms. *Av. del Oasis s/n, 35106, tel. 928/14–08–06, fax 928/14–51–08. 358 rooms with bath. Facilities: restaurant, bar, outdoor pool, tennis, sauna, gym, thermal pool, Jacuzzi, shops, beauty parlor. AE, DC, V. $$$$*

Hotel Don Gregory. Located on the crescent-shape Las Burras beach is this modern eight-story brown brick hotel with a relaxed atmosphere. The palm trees in the gardens are decorated with tiny white lights. The carpeted rooms are big and square, with blond-wood furniture, marble baths, and large terraces; all overlook the beach. *Las Tabaibas 11, 35100, tel. 928/76–26–58, fax 928/76–99–96. 241 rooms with bath. Facilities: restaurant, bar, outdoor pool, tennis, shops, discothèque. AE, MC, V. $$$*

Hotel Bahia Feliz. A sports-oriented high-rise hotel, the Bahia Feliz is decorated in an eclectic style that mixes Moorish tiles with Polynesian batiks. The bar is a romantic spot out of the *Arabian Nights*, and the swimming pool is the largest on the island. The split-level rooms have a tiled sitting area three steps down from the platform bed. The hotel sits on its own tiny private beach about 8 km (5 mi) north of Playa del Inglés. *Playa del Tarajalillo, Carretera del Sur, Km 44, 35479, tel. 928/76–46–00, fax 928/76–29–35. 255 rooms with bath. Facilities: restaurant, bar, outdoor pool, windsurfing school, minigolf, tennis. AE, V. $$*

Duna Flor. This new complex of two-story blue-and-white apartment buildings is located near the Maspalomas golf course on a free bus line to the beach. The large pool area is landscaped with bright bougainvillea. The units have twin beds and a small balcony upstairs, with a sitting area and kitchen downstairs. *Av. de Neckerman s/n, 35100, tel. 928/76–57–04, fax 928/76–62–28. 282*

units. Facilities: restaurant, 2 bars, outdoor pool, playground. AE,
V. $

The Arts and Nightlife

The Arts   The **Las Palmas Philarmonic Orchestra** (Bravo Murillo 2123, tel.
928/32–05–13), one of Spain's oldest, offers an ample program of
concerts between October and May. Its classical music festival in
January brings in leading musicians from around the world. Information on tickets is available at the box office of the Teatro Pérez
Galdós (Plaza Mercado, tel. 928/36–15–09).

Nightlife   For quiet conversation, stop in at **La Posada** (La Naval 8, tel. 928/
Bar   26–41–32), a tropical bar at the end of Las Canteras beach specializing in Irish coffee and 17 other coffee drinks.

Casinos   Gamblers can choose between two casinos, the **Gran Casino de Las
Palmas** in the Santa Catalina Hotel (León y Castillo 227, Parque
Doramus, tel. 928/24–30–40) and the **Casino Gran Canaria** in the Hotel Tamarindos in St. Agustín (La Retama 3, Playa de San Agustín,
tel. 928/76–27–24).

Discos   Las Palmas has a lively nightlife, with dancing for the disco crowd at
Ecu and **Utopia,** both on Calle Tómas Miller, and a salsa beat emanating from **Yuca** (Calle Nicolás Estébanez). The discothèque on the
eighth floor of the **Hotel Reina Isabel** (Alfred L. Jones 40, tel. 928/
26–01–00) is tops with a middle-age international crowd and offers
great views of the city. "In" discos on the south coast currently include **Spider** (Av. Italia s/n, Playa del Inglés, tel. 928/26–41–32) and
the **St. Agustín Beach Club** (Playa Cocoteros s/n, tel. 928/76–03–70).

Lanzarote

The fourth largest of the Canary Islands, Lanzarote is mostly solidified lava. There are no springs or lakes, and it rarely rains, so all
fresh water comes from desalination plants. Despite its inhospitable
volcanic landscape, however, the island has turned itself into an inviting resort through good planning and conservation.

Lanzarote was named for the Italian explorer Lancelotto Malocello,
who arrived in the 14th century. But the founder of modern-day
Lanzarote was unquestionably artist César Manrique, whose aesthetic hand is evident in the design of most of the island's attractions.

César Manrique, a painter, sculptor, and architect who died in 1992,
was the unofficial artistic guru of the Canary Islands. In Lanzarote
he designed most of the island's tourist attractions and convinced
authorities to require all new buildings to be painted white with
green trim to suggest coolness and fertility. He also led the fight
against overdevelopment and lobbied against high-rise construction
in the Puerto del Carmen area.

Tour 1: Northern Lanzarote

The capital city of **Arrecife,** with its cinderblock houses, is the most
unattractive part of the island. A stop at the well-organized **tourism
office** in the municipal park along the sea is a good way to begin a
tour.

From here, walk to the **Castillo San Gabriel,** a double-walled fortress once used to keep pirates at bay. An archaeology museum is

housed within, and you can see copies of some of the Guanche cave drawings found on the island. *Admission: 210 pesetas. Open Mon.– Fri. 10–2. Closed Sat. and Sun.*

Continue north by car along the waterfront past the harbor to the next fortress, the **Castillo San José.** It has been turned into the stunning **Museo de Arte Contemporaneo** (Museum of Contemporary Art) by Manrique, one of whose paintings is on exhibit, along with other modern Spanish works. Go down the space-tunnel staircase for a look at the sophisticated, glass-walled restaurant that faces the harbor. *Av. de Naos s/n, tel. 928/81–23–21. Admission free. Museum open Mon.–Sat. 11–9.*

Head inland a few blocks, then follow the signs to **Costa Teguise,** a tasteful green-and-white development of apartments and a few large hotels. Notice how the chimneys on the bungalows all have different decorative shapes. King Juan Carlos owns a villa here near the Melia Salinas hotel (*see* Dining and Lodging, *below*). Costa Teguise has several small beaches; the best is **Las Cucharas.**

The **Jardín de Cactus** (Cactus Garden), just north of Costa Teguise between Guatiza and Mala, is the latest Manrique-designed addition to the island. The giant green metal cactus that marks the entrance comes perilously close to tacky, but the gardens artfully display nearly 10,000 cacti on a series of terraces. There is also a restored, functioning windmill that grinds and sells gofio. *Tel. 928/52–93–97. Admission: 400 pesetas. Open daily 10–6.*

Playa de la Garita, on the way north again, is a wide bay favored by surfers in winter, while snorkelers enjoy the crystal water and nearby rocky coves during the summer. The next stop, **Jameos del Agua** (water cavern), is a natural wonder created when molten lava streamed through an underground tunnel and hissed into the sea. Eerie music creates a mysterious atmosphere as you explore the cavern. Look for the tiny white crabs on the rocks in the underground lake. This species of blind, albino crab is found nowhere else in the world, and there is talk of closing the jameos to save the crabs from extinction. The cave entrance has been beautifully landscaped with tropical plants. *Rte. GC710, 22 km (13 mi) north of Arrecife, tel. 928/83–50–10. Admission: 750 pesetas days, 1,050 pesetas nights. Open daily 10–6; Tues., Fri., and Sat., also 7 PM–3 AM.*

The nearby **Cuevas Verdes** are for more adventurous cave explorers. A humorous, multilingual guide leads walks through a 2-km (1-mi) section of underground volcanic passageway. There is so little humidity in Lanzarote that no stalactites have formed, but the walk is one of the best tours on the island. *Rte. GC710, 22 km (13 mi) north of Arrecife, tel. 928/83–50–10. Admission: 650 pesetas. Open daily 10–6 (last tour at 5).*

Continue north as far as the little fishing village of **Orzola.** A small excursion boat leaves from here each morning for the neighboring islet of **La Graciosa,** where there are only 500 people and plenty of solitary beaches.

Time Out Stop at the sunny harborside restaurant **Perla del Atlantico** (Av. Marítima, tel. 928/83–51–46) for a drink or a lunch you'll remember long after your suntan has faded.

Make your way back to the center of the island through **Haria,** with its palm oasis, and the well-preserved colonial town of **Teguise,** once the island's capital. The windswept and empty **Famara Beach,** northwest of Teguise, is 3 km (2 mi) long with a half-sunken ship in the surf, evidence of the ocean's power on this part of the island.

South of Teguise in **Tahíche,** the unusual former home of artist Manrique has been opened to visitors as the **Fundación César Manrique.** On display are a collection of his paintings and sculptures, as well as works by other 20th-century artists. But the real attraction is the house itself, designed by Manrique to blend in with the volcanic landscape. The lower level is built in a series of caves. *Carretera Tahíche-San Bartolomé, 2 km west of Tahíche, tel. 928/ 81–01–38. Admission: 500 pesetas. Open weekdays 10–7, Sat. 10–2; closed Sun. and holidays.*

Tour 2: Timanfaya National Park and Southern Lanzarote

The **Parque National Timanfaya,** popularly known as the fire mountains, takes up much of the volcanic southern part of the island. To get there, drive inland from Arrecife on GC740 toward San Bartolomé. The strange metal sculpture at the top of the hill is the **Monument to the Campesino,** constructed out of old water tanks by Manrique to honor the island's farmers, who have struggled to scrape a living from the land despite scorching sun, no rain, and volcanic eruptions.

Lanzarote's agricultural belt can be seen as you head south from here. Notice the way grapes in **La Geria** are grown in cinder pits surrounded by a ring of volcanic rock. The rocks provide protection from the wind, and the cinders allow dew to drip through to the roots.

At **Yaiza** follow the signs to Timanfaya. The first thing you'll see is the staging area for the **camel rides.** Many of the Canary Islands offer camel rides, but these are the most famous and a big attraction for tourists. The brief rides are so bumpy you'll be glad they're not longer.

The volcanic landscape inside **Timanfaya** is a violent jumble of exploded craters, cinder cones, lava formations, and heat fissures. The park is strictly protected, and you can visit it only on a bus tour. Taped commentary in English points out the volcanoes and explains how the parish priest of Yaiza watched and took notes as the earth opened up in 1730 and spewed lava that buried two villages. *4 km (3 mi) north of Yaiza, tel. 928/84–00–57. Admission: 850 pesetas. Open daily 9–5.*

Time Out   Timanfaya is the site of one of the world's most unusual restaurants, **El Diablo,** where chicken, steaks, and spicy sausages are cooked over the crater of the volcano using the earth's natural heat. If you're not hungry, you can still watch the phenomenon, and there are additional heat vents below the restaurant if you want to have your own volcanic barbecue.

Continue south past the salt pans to **Playa Blanca,** Lanzarote's newest resort area. The ferry for Fuerteventura leaves from here, but there's not much more to the town. Tourists come for the exquisite white-sand beaches, reached down hard-packed dirt roads on **Punta de Papagayo.** The most popular beach is **Playa Papagayo.** Bring your own picnic; there's one bar and nothing else but sand and surf.

What to See and Do with Children

Children will be fascinated by the natural wonders of Lanzarote. Give them flashlights, and they can pretend to be Tom Sawyer or Huck Finn as the guide leads you through the **Cuevas Verdes** (*see* Tour 1, *above*). The volcanic heat vents and the camel rides at **Timanfaya National Park** (*see* Tour 2, *above*) are also intriguing for the little ones. **Guinate Tropical Park,** in the northern part of the island, is a 200-acre park with 1,300 species of exotic birds and animals. *Open daily 10–5.*

Shopping

For a good selection of island crafts, spend your Sunday morning between 10 and 2 at the open market in **Teguise.** Some vendors set up stalls in the plaza; others simply lay out a blanket in the street and sell embroidered tablecloths, leather goods, costume jewelry, African masks, and thousands of other items.

The **Montaña Tropical** is a complex of restaurants and shops built around a tropical-bird park and model-boat lake just outside Puerto de la Cruz. There is a crafts fair on Wednesday afternoon and demonstrations of flamenco dancing on Monday, Wednesday, and Friday.

Beaches

In addition to the beaches described above, Lanzarote has good sandy strands in the Puerto del Carmen area, and this is where most tourists head. **Playa Grande,** the main beach of Puerto del Carmen, is a long strip of yellow sand where you can rent sailboards, jet skis, skates, and lounge chairs. It is backed by a 3-km (2-mi) stretch of souvenir shops and restaurants of every national persuasion. **Playa de los Pocillos** is slightly north of Puerto del Carmen, and the site of most of the area's new development. Hotels and apartments are restricted, however, to the other side of the highway, leaving the 2-km-long beach of yellow sand surprisingly untamed. **Playa Matagorda,** the northern extension of Playa de los Pocillos, has alternating sections of gravel and gray sand. It is favored by surf fishermen.

Sports

Cycling   Mountain biking has become very popular here in the last few years. It's actually a very practical way to tour the island: Lanzarote is not particularly hilly, so you don't have to be a veteran of bike marathons to enjoy the ride. Rentals are available at **Fire Mountain Biking** (tel. 928/51–22–67) in Puerto del Carmen and at **Zafari Cycle** (tel. 928/51–76–91) in Playa Blanca.

Diving   The island's only official diving center is at Las Cucharas. The **N.A.U.I. España Diving Association** (tel. 928/59–04–07) is run by a German who speaks perfect English. He rents equipment, leads guided dives, and offers a certification course.

Golf   Lanzarote's 18-hole **Campo de Golf Costa Teguise** (tel. 928/59–05–12) is just outside the Costa Teguise development and features unusual sand traps filled with black-lava cinders.

Windsurfing   Water-sports fanatics can arrange windsurfing lessons and rent equipment from the **Lanzarote Surf Company** (tel. 928/59–19–74) at Las Cucharas beach.

Dining and Lodging

Arrecife
Dining

Castillo San Jose. Black and white furniture, glass walls, and modern art give the remodeled fortress an elegant feel. The restaurant features cuisine to match the sophisticated setting. Try the cold avocado soup with caviar, or salmon steak wrapped in cured ham. El Grifo is the most popular of the white Lanzarote wines. *Tel. 928/81-23-21. Reservations not required. Jacket and tie advised. AE, V. $$$*

Costa Teguise
Dining

La Jordana. This unpretentious restaurant with beamed ceiling and white walls is one of Lanzarote's most popular dining spots. The menu features international fare with French touches. Try the homemade pâté, veal with apples, or locally caught cherne in orange sauce. *Los Geranios 10–11, tel. 928/59–03–28. Reservations not accepted. Jacket and tie advised. AE, V. Closed Sun. and Sept. $$$*

Grill Casa Blanca. Inside a tiny octagonal house not far from the Teguise Playa hotel, this restaurant has the atmosphere of an English country cottage, with stained wood floors and wreaths of dried flowers. There is an open kitchen in the main dining room where you can watch the chef cook up Spanish and international specialties. Try the avocado and shrimp salad, steak with green peppercorns, or local fish dishes. *Las Olas 4, tel. 928/59–01–55. Reservations recommended for first seating. Dinner only. Dress: casual. AE, MC, V. $$*

*Dining and
Lodging*
★

Melia Salinas. A stunning hotel built around an interior tropical garden with hanging vines, palms, waterfalls, and songbirds, the Melia Salinas offers a chance to rub elbows with vacationing businesspeople and political leaders from Europe. The guest rooms have a tropical feel thanks to louvered closets and doors, and all have large flower-filled terraces that face the sea. The hotel's gourmet restaurant, **La Graciosa,** is Lanzarote's swankiest dining spot and enjoys a privileged location overlooking the garden. A German chef prepares international cuisine with fresh island ingredients such as giant prawns, duck breast in plum sauce, and halibut wrapped in chard. *Costa Teguise 35509, tel. 928/59–00–40, fax 928/59–03–90. 310 rooms with bath. Facilities: 2 restaurants, 2 bars, outdoor pool, semiprivate beach, tennis, squash, sauna, gym, shops, beauty parlor, 5-hole golf and putting green, basketball, football, archery, olympic shooting range. AE, DC, MC, V. $$$$*

Lodging

Teguise Playa. Don't be put off by the cold glass exterior of this hotel; the six-story lobby is filled with plants, and the staff is friendly. The rooms have white tile floors and bamboo furniture. Each has a geranium-filled terrace with a sea view over the hotel's private beach. *35509 Urbanización Costa Teguise, tel. 928/59–06–54, fax 928/59–09–79. 325 rooms with bath. Facilities: restaurant, bar, 2 outdoor pools, tennis, squash, sauna, gym, shops, beauty parlor. AE, MC, V. $$–$$$*

★

Apartamentos Las Cucharas. Housed in attractive three-story buildings with decorative chimneys, these new apartments sit right on Las Cucharas beach. They have knotty-pine furniture and terraces, with one or two bedrooms. The pool area is beautifully landscaped. *35509 Urbanización Costa Teguise, tel. 928/59–07–00. 66 units. Facilities: restaurant, bar, outdoor pool, children's pool. AE, V. $*

Playa Blanca
Lodging

Lanzarote Princess. Located near the virgin beaches of Lanzarote's south shore, the Lanzarote Princess is housed in a modern, white, three-story building with an airy plant-filled lobby. The rooms are a bit small and have linoleum floors; bright flowered bedspreads compensate a little for the somewhat sterile effect. The grounds, on the other hand, are vast and have good sports facilities and a huge pool with a bar on an island in the middle (in case you want to take a break from swimming laps). *Playa Blanca, Yaiza 35570, tel. 928/51–71–08, fax 928/51–70–11. 439 rooms with bath. Facilities: restaurant, bar, tennis, squash, minigolf, playground, hairdresser. AE, MC, V. $$*

Puerto del Carmen
Dining

Grill La Cascada. Named for the gushing waterfall in the middle of the spacious dining room, La Cascada is a favorite with local families as well as tourists, all attracted by the ambitious food at moderate prices. Start with stuffed avocados, then the brochette of fish and prawns. *Roque Nublo 5, tel. 928/51–17–31. Reservations advised. Dress: casual. AE, V. $$*

El Varadero. This converted fishermen's warehouse on the tiny harbor features a honky-tonk piano player and an informal, cheerful atmosphere. The food is typically Canarian with fresh fish and papas arrugadas, but steaks, chicken, and spaghetti are available as well. The tapas bar at the entrance is also popular. *Varadero 22, tel. 928/82–57–11. Reservations not necessary. Dress: casual. AE, V. $$*

Lodging

Los Farriones. The granddaddy of Lanzarote's resorts has retained an exclusive, elegant atmosphere as its tropical gardens designed by César Manrique have matured. The rooms are smallish with rattan furniture and linoleum flooring, but each has a terrace with views of the gardens and sea. *Roque del Oeste 1, 35510, tel. 928/51–01–75, fax 928/51–02–08. 237 rooms with bath. Facilities: restaurant, bar, outdoor pool, tennis, minigolf, gym, sauna. AE, V. $$*

La Geria. You enter on the third floor, where a marble staircase leads to lower floors. The rooms are carpeted and decorated with a sophisticated color scheme of slate blue and gray. Each has a little terrace with views of the beach across the street. *Playa de los Pocillos, Tias, 35510, tel. 928/51–04–41, fax 928/51–19–19. 244 rooms with bath. Facilities: restaurant, bar, outdoor pool, tennis, sauna, gym, playground, minigolf, shops, beauty parlor. AE, DC, MC, V. $$*

Yaiza
Dining

La Era. One of only three buildings that survived the eruption of the volcano that wiped out the town of Yaiza in 1730, this farmhouse restaurant offers simple dining rooms with blue-and-white checkered tablecloths on tables arranged around a center patio. This is a great place to try regional dishes such as goat stew, *cherne* in cilantro sauce, or Canarian cheeses. *Barranco 3, tel. 928/83–00–16. Reservations not necessary. Dress: casual. AE, DC, MC, V. $–$$*

Nightlife

Most nightlife in Lanzarote centers on the hotel bars, all of which feature live music. The island's most popular bar and meeting place is the **Hawaiian Pub** (Av. Marítima 74) in Puerto del Carmen. For dancing, try **Tiffany's** (Av. de Suiza 2, Playa de los Pocillos, tel. 928/51–13–44), an upscale disco for all ages; or **Jokers** (Av. de las Playas, tel. 928/51–02–42), a disco with a giant aquarium on the strip in Puerto del Carmen. The Costa Teguise has a new casino in the **Oasis Hotel** (tel. 928/59–25–25).

Fuerteventura

The dry island of Fuerteventura is a beachcomber's dream come true. It's the second largest of the Canary Islands, but the least inhabited, with only 20,000 people. Nearly all the visitors are Germans, brought in by large tour operators.

The two main resort areas are Corralejo, known for its acres of sand dunes, and the Jandia peninsula, with dozens of beaches, including one that's 26 km (16 mi) long. Tourism is relatively new to Fuerteventura, and both areas are in the midst of an uncontrolled building craze.

Touring the Island

Fuerteventura's capital, **Puerto del Rosario,** has long suffered from an image problem. It used to be called Puerto de Cabra (Goat Port), but the improved name has not changed the fact that it is a poor city with little of interest.

Take the coastal road north from Puerto del Rosario through red volcanic badlands to the dunes of **Corralejo,** a protected natural park. These hills of sand have blown across the sea from the Sahara Desert, just 96 km (60 mi) away, and it's not hard to imagine all of Fuerteventura as a piece of Africa that's broken away from the continent.

La Oliva, south on the inland road, boasts the island's principal historic building, the **Casa de los Coroneles.** Military governors built the immense house in the 1700s and ruled the island from it until the turn of the century. It is not open to the public.

Continue south and at the fork head south again toward **Antigua,** rather than east to Puerto Rosario. In Antigua you can visit a restored, white, Don Quixote–style windmill that was once used for grinding gofio. The modern, metal windmills you see throughout the island have been imported from the United States and are used for pumping water.

Betancuria, 8 km (5 mi) west of Antigua, was once the capital but now is almost a ghost town, with only 150 residents. Tourists come to visit the weather-worn colonial church of **Santa María de Betancuria,** built to large proportions because it was originally intended to be the cathedral of the Canary Islands. The **Museo de la Iglesia** (church museum; admission: 100 pesetas; open Mon.–Sat. 11–5) contains a replica of the banner carried by the Norman conqueror Juan de Bethancourt when he seized Fuerteventura in the 15th century. Be sure to see the small wooden statue of Santiago in the museum. Most of the artwork was salvaged from the convent now in ruins nearby. A **Museo Arqueológico** (Archaeology Museum) and a crafts workshop are on the other side of the ravine that cuts through the tiny hamlet.

The back way out of Betancuria toward Pájara is a lonely road that hugs the side of the mountain. At **Vega del Río de Palmas** you may see an old woman swathed in black driving a herd of goats through the palm oasis, but that's where civilization ends. Intense sun beats down, and it feels like the end of the earth. This desolate stretch of road is one of the best places to experience the essence of Fuerteventura.

Pájara is the administrative center of the booming Jandia peninsula and sports a two-block strip of boulevard, pretty wrought-iron street lamps, and a brand-new city hall.

Time Out Typical Fuerteventura lunches are served at **El Brasero,** an attractive patio-style grill along the highway in Tarajalejo. The island specialties are roast goat and goat cheese.

Fuerteventura was once divided into two kingdoms, and a wall was built across the Jandia peninsula to mark the border. Remnants of that wall are still visible today inland from **Matas Blancas,** 42 km (26 mi) south of Pájara on highway GC640.

As you continue south along the coast, the beaches become larger, the sand whiter, and the water bluer. The famous **Playas de Sotavento** (Sotavento Beaches) begin near the Costa Calma developments and extend gloriously for 26 km (16 mi). Around the bend is the old fishing port of **Morro Jable,** well on its way to becoming the next Tenerife. Many more miles of virgin coast exist beyond here— down a dirt road that eventually leads to the lighthouse—and beaches along the entire windward side of the peninsula remain untouched.

Beaches

There are more than 150 beaches on Fuerteventura and 65% of the coastline of the Jandia peninsula is rimmed in white sand. **Playa de Corralejo,** about a mile south of the town, is fringed by mountains of sand dunes and faces Los Lobos Island across the channel. Nude sunbathing is the norm on the more remote stretches of the beach. **Playa el Algibe de la Cueva,** on the northwest side of the island, has a castle once used to ward off pirates and is mainly frequented by locals. **Playa del Sotovento** is the popular 26-km- (16-mi-) long strand on the Jandia peninsula, where nude sunning is also favored except for directly in front of hotels. Beyond the town of Morro Jable, a dirt road leads to the isolated beaches of Juan Gomez and **Playa de las Pillas.** Following the dirt tracks across the narrow strip of land, you can visit the equally empty **Playa de Cofete** and **Playa de Barlovento de Jandia.**

Sports

Diving   For **scuba diving** and **snorkeling,** head for rocky outcroppings on the windward side of Jandia. The channel between Corralejo and the tiny Isla de Lobos is also rich in undersea life and favored by sport fishermen as well as divers.

Windsurfing   The island's other big tourist attraction is **windsurfing.** Boards are for rent at most hotels, and there are two main schools: **Ventura Surf** (tel. 928/86–60–40) in Corralejo and **Windsurf Urlaub** (tel. 928/87– 08–25) at the Sol Gorriones hotel on Sotavento Beach.

Dining and Lodging

Corralejo   **Tres Islas.** This luxury resort sits right on the empty white beach
Lodging   near the Corralejo dunes. The hotel is built around a central swimming pool complex decorated with yellow-and-white striped tents that add a festive feel. The bedrooms are more formal, with soft green carpeting, dark wood furniture, and floral prints. All have terraces. *Grandes Playas, 35660 Corralejo, tel. 928/86–60–00, fax 928/86–61–50. 365 rooms with bath. Facilities: restaurant, piano bar, 2 outdoor pools, children's pool, tennis, playground, gym, sauna, shops, beauty parlor. AE, V. $$$$*
Oliva Beach. The boxy, eight-story Oliva Beach is next door to Tres Islas and owned by the same company. The rooms are smallish with linoleum floors and orange drapes, but each has a furnished terrace with views of the undulating sand dunes or endless beach. There is an Olympic-size swimming pool, and the friendly staff runs a miniclub to keep youngsters busy all day. *Grandes Playas, 35660,*

tel. 928/86–61–00, fax 928/86–61–54. 410 rooms with bath. Facilities: restaurant, bar, outdoor pool, tennis, playground, shops, beauty parlor, discothèque. AE, V. $$

Costa Calma   **La Taberna Costa Calma.** Usually packed with locals and tourists, **Dining**   La Taberna serves Mexican specialties such as guacamole, as well as typical Canarian dishes, in several small dining rooms with stone archways and checked tablecloths. Try the *pescado a la sal* (fish baked to moist perfection in a crust of rock salt that is chipped away before eating). Garlic soup and goat cheese with mojo sauce are other specialties. *Carretera Jandía s/n. No phone. Dress: casual. No credit cards. $*

Lodging   **Fuerteventura Playa.** This sophisticated low-slung hotel, built around a large kidney-shape pool and thatch-roof bar, is located at the north end of the 26-km (16-mi) Sotovento beach. The rooms have slate-blue carpet and modern white furnishings with extra-large beds. Plant-filled terraces overlook the beach. *Urbanización Canal del Río Poligono C1, 35627, tel. 928/87–03–44 or 928/87–00–97. 300 rooms with bath. Facilities: restaurant, bar, outdoor pool, tennis, windsurfing, gym, sauna, beauty parlor, shops. AE, V. $$$*

Sol Gorriones. All by itself in the middle of the Sotavento coast, the Sol Gorriones, Jandía's first resort, is beginning to show its age. Most guests ignore the shag carpeting and '60s-style room decor, preferring to spend all their time outdoors. *Playa Barca, Gran Tarajal 35620, tel. 928/54–70–25, fax 928/54–70–00. 309 rooms with bath. Facilities: restaurant, bar, 3 outdoor pools, tennis, minigolf, playground, windsurfing, beauty parlor, shops, dancing. AE, MC, V. $$–$$$*

Barlovento Hotel. Opened in 1990, the Barlovento is a full-service all-suite hotel and an excellent value. The three-story building with blue metal railings looks a bit like a ship run aground on Sotovento beach. The suites include separate bedrooms, sitting areas, and kitchenettes. All have simple bleached-pine furniture, white tile floors, and terraces. *Costa Calma, 35627, tel. 928/87–07–38. 226 suites. Facilities: restaurant, piano-bar, outdoor pool, tennis, squash, gym, sauna, minigolf, video movies. AE, V. $$*

Morro Jable   **Casa Emilio.** The best of the new restaurants blossoming along **Dining**   Morro Jable's harbor, Casa Emilio has a wood-burning grill in the dining room where fresh fish is cooked as you watch. The kitchen also turns out delicious crab cocktail, pepper steak, and paella. *1 block uphill from harbor (sign is visible from harbor), tel. 928/54–00–54. Reservations not necessary. Dress: casual. No credit cards. $$*

La Palma

La Palma is a green and prosperous island that managed to exist quite successfully in the past without tourism. But now that it has been "discovered," La Palma is handling the new visitors with good taste by emphasizing the island's natural beauty, traditional crafts, and cuisine. The local residents, called Palmeros, are especially friendly; of all the Canary Islands, La Palma is likely to leave a visitor with the most positive impression.

Tour 1: The Capital

Santa Cruz de la Palma was an important port and bustling shipbuilding center in the 16th century. Then in 1533 a band of buccaneers led by French pirate François le Clerc raided the city and burned it to the ground. With money from the Spanish king, La Palma was rebuilt, which is why the city today has such a unified colonial appearance.

Start your tour by walking up the cobblestone main street, Calle O'Daly, which everyone calls Calle Real. Take a peek inside the patio of the **Palacio Salazar,** where the tourist office is located, to see an elegant example of Canarian architecture.

The triangular **Plaza de España** in front of the **Iglesia El Salvador** is the focus of city social life and fills with people in the early evening. The church is the only building that survived the pirate fire; it has a handsome Moorish carved ceiling. Bring a flashlight if you want to see the religious art on the walls.

Note the stone shields on the **city hall,** across the plaza. One is the coat of arms of Spain's Habsburg kings, and the other is the emblem of La Palma.

Walk uphill to the corner of Calle de la Puente, then look back at one of the most charming streets in the Canaries.

Time Out	The **Cafe La Placeta,** in the small plaza on Avenida Perez de Brito, is a good place for a break. You can sit under the striped umbrellas next to the splashing stone fountain.

Farther along you'll come to the **Museo Insular** (admission free; open weekdays 9–1 and 4–7) in the cloisters of the church of San Francisco. Exhibits are devoted to the navigational and trading history of La Palma, as well as to collections of Guanche pottery and tools. The **Museo Bellas Artes** (Fine Arts Museum) next door (admission free; same hours as Museo Insular) has a good collection of Flemish and Spanish paintings.

You can't miss the life-size cement replica of **Columbus's ship** *Santa María,* at the end of the Plaza Alameda. A tiny naval museum (admission free; open weekdays 9–1 and 3–6) is belowdecks. On the way back, stroll past the star-shape **Castillo Real,** a fortress that dates to the 16th century. Return to the center of town along **Avenida Marítima** and you'll pass a much-photographed row of Canarian houses with the typical green balconies. Stop in at **Tabacos Vargas** (Av. Marítima 55) to see the famous palmero cigars being rolled by hand. The cigar industry is a result of constant migration between the Canary Islands and Cuba. Those with a taste for fine cigars claim hand-rolled palmeros are better than the cigars now being manufactured in Cuba.

Tour 2: Around the Island

The village of **Las Nieves** has a beautifully preserved colonial plaza and the opulent church of **Nuestra Señora de las Nieves** (Our Lady of the Snows), which houses La Palma's patron saint, the Virgin of the Snows. The virgin, credited with saving many a ship from disaster, sits on a gold altar wearing vestments studded with pearls and emeralds.

Head south from here to the **Mirador de la Concepción** for a great view of the capital and its harbor. Continuing on through **Breña Alta,** you'll see tobacco growing alongside fruit trees on the terraced gardens. At **El Hoyo,** the vanes of an old windmill mark a ceramics workshop where reproductions of Guanche pots in the island museum are made.

The scenery becomes dry as you reach the volcanic southern tip of the island. Near Fuencaliente, visit the **San Antonio volcano** and the **Teneguía volcano,** the site of the most recent eruption in the Canary Islands. In 1971 Teneguía burst open, sending rivers of lava toward the sea and extending the length of the island by 3 km (2 mi). There are good beaches in the cinders below the volcano, reached over unpaved roads. At **Fuencaliente,** the heart of La Palma's wine region, the modern Teneguía cooperative winery can be visited. Also notice the solar-powered streetlights recently installed by the ecologically sensitive community.

Time Out | A restaurant in a cave awaits you 16 km (10 mi) north of Fuencaliente. Look for the door in the side of a mountain and a sign that says **Restaurant Tamanco.**

Next drive down through the banana plantations to **Tazacorte,** the old Guanche capital, or explore **Puerto Naos,** where a sunny, black-sand bay created by a volcanic eruption in 1947 has now been turned into a beach resort.

You can also head toward **El Paso** to return across the center of the island. Three km (2 mi) east of El Paso, a visitor center is being built for the **Parque Nacional de La Caldera de Taburiente.** The park is inside what looks like a huge crater in the middle of the island, but modern geologists do not think it was ever one giant volcano. They say the crater was formed by a series of small eruptions that pulled the center of the mountain apart; the gaping hole you see was caused by erosion.

A narrow paved road leads through pine forests to the **Mirador Cumbrecita** at 1,864 meters (6,014 ft) on the crater's rim. It's often raining or snowing up here, and bright rainbows span the canyon. The white dome and tower on the opposite side are the **Observatono Roque de los Muchachos,** home of Europe's largest telescope. Astronomers say the Canary Island peaks have some of the cleanest air and darkest skies in the world, just right for discovering the far reaches of the universe.

Canarian pine trees are especially adapted to fire and volcanic eruptions, taking only four years to regenerate themselves. There are lots of interesting hiking trails in the park, and camping is allowed on the valley floor with a permit obtainable at the visitor center.

Off the Beaten Track

A small group of **silk weavers** in the El Paso area are trying to keep the traditional island craft alive. They are happy to demonstrate the process. Head up the street that runs along the right side of El Paso's church. Keep going uphill, and at every fork in the road ask for directions to *seda* (silk) or Doña Bertila; they ask only that you phone first so that someone will be there to meet you. *Workshop of Doña Maruca, Barrial de Abajo 9, tel. 922/48–56–92 or 922/48–55–32.*

Shopping

The best crafts and food products La Palma has to offer can be found at **La Graja Centro de Artesania,** near the Mirador de la Concepción. Listen to the folk music on the stereo and sample the local wine. Embroidery, baskets, pottery, cookbooks, bottled mojo sauce, cigars, and other locally produced items are available.

Beaches

While La Palma is not known for its beaches, two black sand coves are popular with summertime swimmers. **Los Cancajos,** 5 km (2 mi) south of the capital, is a small crescent-shaped beach with crystaline water. **Puerto Naos** lies on the opposite side of the island (*see* Tour 2, *above*).

Sports

Hiking in the Parque Nacional de la Caldera de Taburiente is the principal sport on La Palma (*see* Tour 2, *above*).

Dining and Lodging

Playa de los Cancajos
Dining

Tres Chimineas. An outgoing Palmero married to an Englishwoman runs this attractive restaurant just outside Los Cancajos. Three decorative chimneys mark the building; inside you'll find fresh flowers and a sunny yellow decor. Local fish are the specialty—vieja is the best. *Carretera de Los Llanos de Aridane, Km 8, tel. 922/43-73-52. Reservations advised. Dress: casual. AE, V. $$*

Lodging
★

Hacienda San Jorge. Built to resemble a Canarian village, the San Jorge offers apartment units grouped in pastel-colored bungalows with turquoise balconies. The apartments have functional summer-house furniture, and all feature separate bedrooms, living area, kitchenette, bath, and terrace. The complex is built on several different levels surrounding a lake-size swimming pool just a few steps up from the black-sand beach. *38700, tel. 922/43-40-75, fax 922/43-45-28. 155 apartments. Facilities: restaurant, bar, outdoor pool, Jacuzzi, sauna, gym, playground. AE, V. $$*

Puerto Naos
Dining and Lodging

Sol La Palma. Perched at the end of La Palma's best beach, the Sol hotel, the island's first real resort, opened in November 1990. It has a flashy marble lobby with crystal chandeliers and fountains. The hotel rooms are huge, with understated beige furnishings, gray tile floors, sun terraces, and extra-large baths. A section of apartments is attached to the hotel. The restaurant buffet is bountiful with expensive treats (such as fresh shrimp and papaya) not normally found at moderately priced resorts. *38760, tel. 922/48-04-00, fax 922/48-09-04. 308 rooms with bath, 163 apartments. Facilities: restaurant, 3 bars, 2 outdoor pools, tennis, gym, disco. AE, V. $$*

San Andrés y Sauces
Dining

Mesón del Mar. Follow the road down to the tiny fishing harbor at Puerto Espindola and you'll end up on the doorstep of this popular seafood house. Fish couldn't be any fresher than it is here. A narrow wooden balcony holds tables overlooking the sea, and there are some respectable Canarian wines on the menu. *Puerto Espindola, tel. 922/45-03-05. No reservations. Dress: casual. No credit cards. $$*

Santa Cruz de la Palma
Dining
★

El Brasero. Located along the seafront, this is where native Palmeros head for a special meal of grilled steaks or fish served by especially friendly waiters. *Av. Marítima 54, tel. 922/41-20-33. Reservations not needed. Dress: casual. MC, V. $$*

Chipi Chipi. In the hills above Santa Cruz and 3 km (2 mi) beyond the church in Las Nieves is this restaurant, tucked away behind dense tropical gardens with chirping parrots. Each party of diners is seated in a private stone hut, decorated with turquoise furniture and more plants. The food is strictly local and portions are huge. You can start with salad or garbanzo-bean soup, followed by grilled meats washed down with local red wine. The *queso de almendras* (almond cheese) is a cookielike almond pastry. *Carretera de las*

Nieves, tel. 922/41–76–00. Reservations advised Sun. lunch. Dress: casual. MC, V. Closed Wed. $

Lodging **Castolete Aparthotel.** Right on the seafront but down the street from the heavy traffic, this new hotel is the best choice if you want to stay in the city. Most of the units are studios with divided sitting and sleeping areas and small kitchens. White wood and natural pine furniture give the rooms a clean, modern look. *Av. Marítima 75, 38700, tel. 922/42–08–40. 42 apartments. Facilities: restaurant, outdoor pool, Jacuzzi. AE, MC, V. $*

Tazacorte **Restaurant Playa Mont.** Looking like an upscale beach shack and
Dining open on one side to the ocean breezes, the Playa Mont serves some of
★ the best seafood in the islands. The secret is the sauces: traditional mojos and a delicious lemon butter. Fish is priced by weight, and the day's catch is listed on a chalkboard. *Puerto de Tazacorte, tel. 922/ 48–04–43. Reservations advised weekends. Dress: casual. AE, V. Closed Thurs. $$*

La Gomera

One of the least developed of the Canary Islands, tiny La Gomera attracts scores of denim-clad backpackers on shoestring budgets, as well as other travelers who care little for the disco beat of the more touristy islands. The mossy central peaks make up the Garajonay National Park and include a virgin forest of fragrant laurel trees, the likes of which have all but disappeared from less remote parts of the planet. The mountains fan out into six steep-sided valleys called *barrancos*. Villages in the barrancos are chiefly dedicated to small-scale banana growing, and you'll see three or four stalks of bananas outside each house in the morning awaiting pickup. The serpentine roads leading in and out of the valleys are so filled with switchbacks that traveling is slow and villages remain isolated.

Tour 1: San Sebastián

La Gomera's scraggly capital makes the most of its historical links with Christopher Columbus, who made his last stop on charted territory at **San Sebastián** before setting out for the edge of the Earth in 1492.

Begin with a visit to the **Torre del Conde** (Tower of the Count), built by the Spanish in 1450 for protection from the Guanche tribes. It came in handy in 1487 when the conde's wife, Beatriz de Bobadillo, took refuge in the tower after island chieftains killed her husband. But the beautiful, black-haired widow is better known for her love affair with Columbus, which began when both were back in Queen Isabella's court in Castile.

On his way to discover America, Columbus spent an idyllic 10 days with Beatriz while the rudder of the *Pinta* was being repaired in Gran Canaria. Then, after fetching the ship, he detoured his sailors back to La Gomera for one last fling.

The **Pozo de la Aduana** (Customs House Well; open Mon.–Fri. 8:30–2 and 4:30–6), at the head of Calle del Medio, is the well that Columbus used to resupply his ships with water, which was also used to baptize the New World. **Nuestra Señora de la Asunción** (Our Lady of the Assumption) church was just a tiny chapel when Columbus prayed there. Since then it has been enlarged in a variety of styles. Farther up the street you can visit the **Casa Colón** (admission free; open weekdays 9–1 and 4–7:30), the simple Canarian house where the explorer supposedly stayed during his time on the island with Beatriz. It is now devoted to exhibits by local artists.

Tour 2: Around the Island

Allow plenty of time for a drive around La Gomera, two days if possible. The distances are short, but travel takes a long time, and the island's roads are not for those who are afraid of heights.

The **Degollada de Peraza,** 14½ km (9 mi) south of San Sebastián, has a lookout with great views. Guanche chiefs pushed Beatriz's cruel husband, Fernan Peraza, to his death from this cliff after using a pretty princess to lure him to a nearby cave.

Playa de Santiago, with its fishing port and banana plantations, is down the steep canyon on the next road to the left. Until very recently the people who lived on the almost vertical slopes of the island's canyons used a mysterious whistling language called silbo to communicate across the canyons. Although the language is dying out, most of the older generation in the rural areas still understands silbo, and the gardeners at the parador in San Sebastián (*see* Dining and Lodging, *below*) sometimes give demonstrations. Boat excursions leave several times a week from Playa de Santiago to view **Los Organos,** a cliff made up of hundreds of tall basalt columns that resemble the pipes of an organ.

Make your way back to the central highway heading west through the fantastic geological formations. As you enter **Parque Nacional de Garajonay,** the road heads into the forest, and the air is filled with the spicy smell of laurel and pine trees. Much of the year this area is in the clouds, and the mossy trees drip with mist. The highest point on the island, Garajonay peak (1,498 meters [4,832 ft]), is to the right.

To learn more about Garajonay National Park, take the turnoff at Las Rosas for the **Juego de Bolas Visitor's Center** (tel. 922/80–09–93; admission free; open Tues.–Sat. 9:30–4:30). Exhibits explain the rare laurel forest, which UNESCO has designated part of the "patrimony of mankind." In crafts shops alongside the visitor's center, you can watch artisans at work (*see* Shopping, *below*).

Keep heading west to **Valle Gran Rey.** The terraced farms planted with bananas and palms look like something out of a Gauguin painting. The valley is home to a number of young German families who have followed the artist's example and fled to this earthly paradise.

As you head north around the island, you come to the town of **Alojera,** with a beautiful little black-sand beach. This area is known for its palm syrup. At night the syrup trees, which have a metal collar around them, produce up to 10 liters (3 gallons) of sap each, which is boiled down into syrup over wood fires the following day.

Off the Beaten Track

Take your taste buds on a trip off the beaten track with a stop at the **Casa Efigenia** in the hamlet of Las Hayas, about 30 minutes uphill from Valle Gran Rey. The plain, whitewashed walls of this restaurant are decorated with a few cobs of dried corn and a dusty case of citations that Doña Efigenia has received for her efforts at keeping traditional Gomeran cookery alive. It's simple food, prepared and served by Doña Efigenia herself, definitely not gourmet but certainly authentic. Gofio, here a paste of corn and barley flour with chunks of fresh corn and garbanzo beans, is served with mojo sauce and tangy goat cheese. The main course is a vegetable stew, and dessert is a heavy raisin-and-almond cake, to be smothered in palm tree syrup. The inexpensive restaurant is only open for lunch.

Shopping

There is a refreshing lack of shops in La Gomera. If you are looking for typical souvenirs, buy a bottle of palm syrup or a bag of macaroons from the little market on the Plaza de América in San Sebastián; paintings of Gomeran landscapes are for sale at **La Luna Art Gallery** (Calle del Medio 28). Typical ceramics, formed without the use of a potter's wheel, are still made and sold by village women in El Cercado. Other handicrafts, including rag rugs, baskets, and Gomeran drums, are available in the workshops at the **Juego de Bolas Visitor's Center** in Garajonay National Park.

Beaches

A strong current makes La Gomera's northern beaches dangerous for swimming. If you want sun, head for the volcanic sands of the island's southern shores. **San Sebastián**'s black-sand beach near the ferry dock is clean and popular with local families. **Playa de Santiago** is a rocky black beach that surrounds a small fishing bay. It has the sunniest weather on the island and is destined to become La Gomera's major resort area. In Valle Gran Rey, **Playa del Inglés** is a sandy black crescent of a beach favored by young people in search of an offbeat, inexpensive hideaway, while **Las Vueltas** beach, with its lagoon, is a favorite with local residents.

Sports

Hiking **Garajonay National Park** provides miles of interesting hikes. A trail map can be obtained at the visitor's center or the San Sebastián tourist office.

Water Sports Water-sports equipment is not available for rent in La Gomera yet; windsurfers and divers should bring their own gear.

Dining and Lodging

Playa de **Hotel Tecina.** La Gomera's only real resort hotel, the Tecina sprawls
Santiago luxuriously over a series of terraces high above the sea. There's an
Lodging elevator down to the beach. The rooms, grouped in hillside bungalows, all have summery green and pine furniture with big wooden terraces for sunbathing. Their baths are decorated with Spanish tile. Most guests arrive on package tours and eat all their meals in the hotel. *38800, tel. 922/89–50–50, fax 922/89–51–88. 326 rooms with bath. Facilities: restaurant, outdoor pool, swim-up bar, tennis, squash, gym, sauna, disco. AE, MC, V. $$$*
Apartamentos Tapahuga. This newest and most attractive building in Playa de Santiago sits right on the fishing harbor, and apartments have Canarian carved-pine balconies overlooking it. Kitchens and country-style Spanish furnishings give the apartments a homey feel, and there's a swimming pool on the roof. *Av. Marítima, 38800, tel. 922/89–51–59. 20 apartments. Facilities: outdoor pool. No credit cards. $*

San Sebastián **Marques de Oristano.** Step into the garden and climb to the second
Dining floor to enter the cheerful dining room of this restored Canarian house. Foreign residents on La Gomera come for the carpaccio, made with fish or beef. Other Italian-accented specialties include

mushroom salad, pastas, veal piccata, and hake in garlic sauce. *Calle del Medio 26, tel. 922/87–00–22. Reservations not necessary. Dress: casual. AE, V. Closed May and Nov. $$*

Dining and Lodging ★

Parador Conde de la Gomera. Built in 1970 in the style of an old island manor house, the parador has palm-filled courtyards and breeze-ways decorated with Spanish antiques. The large rooms combine bare wood floors with French provincial furniture and have big lou-vered shutters that open onto interior patios. The dining room has a barnlike Canarian ceiling but an elegant atmosphere thanks to the brass-and-frosted-glass chandeliers. The kitchen specializes in such local dishes as rabbit in salmorejo with papas arrugadas. *38800, tel. 922/87–11–00, fax 922/87–11–16. 42 rooms with bath. Facilities: restaurant, bar, garden, outdoor pool. AE, V. $$$*

Hostal El Pajar. This small hotel in the center of San Sebastián is aimed at local residents and offers basic rooms arranged around a typical Canarian patio. *Calle del Medio 23, 38800, tel. 922/87–02–07. Facilities: restaurant, bar. $*

Valle Gran Rey Dining

Charco del Conde. Sit on the sunny deck to enjoy the view of the *charco* (lagoon) and beach across the street. It's named for the Conde (Count) of La Gomera, because this is where the Guanche chiefs hatched the plot to toss him off the cliff. The restaurant serves good fish, steaks, and chicken with papas arrugadas and mojo sauces. *Carretera Puntilla Vueltas, tel. 922/80–54–03. Reserva-tions not necessary. Dress: casual. No credit cards. Closed Thurs. $*

Lodging

Apartamentos Charco del Conde. These low-rise flower-bedecked apartments across from Las Vueltas beach are a good place to go to escape from the world. Each apartment offers simple pine furnish-ings, a kitchen, and a private terrace. *Av. Marítima s/n, 38870, tel. 922/80–53–80, fax 922/80–55–02. 24 apartments. Facilities: out-door pool. No credit cards. $*

El Hierro

The smallest of the Canary Islands, El Hierro is strictly for those who enjoy nature and plenty of solitude. Most residents live in cool mountain villages that have little in common with the tropical beach towns of the other islands. The few visitors who do find their way to El Hierro usually come for the hiking, the diving, or the relaxation of being in a place where there is very little to do.

Touring the Island

The island's capital, **Valverde,** sits on a hillside at 620 meters (2,000 ft), about 10 km (6 mi) uphill from the airport on the coast. To pro-tect it from pirate raids, the town was located inland in the clouds, where its cobblestone streets always seem to be wet with mist. The church, with its balconied bell tower, was once a lookout for spotting pirates.

Head north around El Hierro toward Mocanal, passing terraced farms still plowed with mules. The **Mirador de la Peña,** at 682 meters (2,200 ft), offers a spectacular view of El Golfo on the back side of the island. El Golfo (the Bay) is formed by what looks like a huge, half-submerged volcanic crater. The part above water is a fertile, steep-sided valley where farmers grow pineapples, grapes, and many oth-er fruits.

Time Out The mirador's brand-new garden restaurant, **Mirador de la Peña,** designed by Cesar Manrique, is surely the island's most elegant eating spot. Glass walls allow a panoramic view of El Golfo below.

From here you can drive down to explore El Golfo. At the far end is a health spa with salty medicinal waters, called **Pozo de la Salud;** those who prefer tastier medicine can visit the island's **winery** in the big beige building near Frontera. The rocky coast along El Golfo is safe for swimming only during the summer.

A fragrant pine forest covers the middle of the island. Make a right turn into the forest on the paved road and you'll come to the **Hoya del Morcillo** picnic area, with barbecue pits, rest rooms, and a playground. Camping is permitted, and this is a good starting point for forest hikes.

At El Pinar the road starts to descend toward the sea, and about halfway down the terrain becomes volcanic. **La Restinga** is a small, rather ugly fishing port on the southern tip of the island. There's a gravel and black-sand beach crowded with painted fishing boats. The tourists who occasionally come here in the summer are generally scuba fanatics who say the diving is some of the best in the Canary Islands.

Dining and Lodging

Frontera **Club El Submarino.** Created by and for sports fans, this ultramod-
Lodging ern, isolated hotel offers diving, hiking, cave exploring, hang gliding, windsurfing, mountain biking, deep-sea fishing, and a few more mundane sports. *Frontera, 38915, tel. and fax 922/55–92–02. 10 rooms with bath. Facilities: outdoor pool, snack bar. AE, V. $$*

Las Playas **Parador Nacional El Hierro.** The road to the parador takes you
Dining and around a point jutting into the sea and deposits you at the bottom of
Lodging a 1,085-meter (3,500-ft) cliff of raw rock. Inside the parador you'll find a friendly staff and comfortable sitting rooms furnished with country antiques. The guest rooms are large, with Castilian furniture, hardwood floors, and heavy folk-art spreads. The parador is so isolated that meals must be eaten in its dining room. Delicious tidbits of island specialties are set out for appetizers, but the rest of the gourmet menu goes way beyond the chef's abilities, so it's best to stick to grilled fish and steak. *38915 Las Playas, tel. 922/55–80–36. 47 rooms with bath. Facilities: restaurant, bar, outdoor pool. AE, V. $$*

Punta Grande **Club Puntagrande.** Built on an old dock that extends out into the sea,
Dining and the four-room Puntagrande boasts a certificate on the wall from the
Lodging *Guinness Book of World Records* naming it the world's smallest hotel. The rooms have exposed rock walls and a nautical decor, with porthole windows turned into nightstands. An old diving suit and ship's lanterns hang in the dining room, which serves fresh fish and local wine. Don't worry about the tiny hotel being full; the owner also has apartments for rent up the road. *38911 Las Puntas, Frontera, tel. 922/55–90–81. 4 rooms with bath. Facilities: restaurant, bar, sun terrace. AE, V. $*

La Restinga **Casa Juan.** The two plain dining rooms have large tables to accom-
Dining modate families who come from all over the island for the delicious seafood soup. Their mojo sauces, served with papas arrugadas, are also outstanding. *Juan Gutierrez Monteverde 23, tel. 922/55–80–02. No credit cards. $*

Lodging **Apartamentos La Marina.** A brand-new three-story building on the harbor houses these tourist apartments. The furnishings are basic but clean, and all units have kitchens and balconies that offer unbeatable sunset viewing. *Av. Marítima 10, 38915, tel. 922/55–81–60. 12 apartments. No credit cards. $*

Valverde **Hotel Boomerang.** Owned by a local man who once worked in Aus-
Lodging tralia, the Boomerang is in the middle of town and offers clean and comfortable rooms with country pine furniture and tile baths. *Dr. Gost 1, 38900, tel. 922/55–02–00. 19 rooms with bath. Facilities: restaurant, bar. AE, DC, V. $*

Spanish Vocabulary

Words and Phrases

	English	Spanish	Pronunciation
Basics	Yes/no	Sí/no	see/no
	Please	Por favor	pohr fah-**vohr**
	May I?	¿Me permite?	meh pehr-**mee**-teh
	Thank you (very much)	(Muchas) gracias	(**moo**-chas) **grah**-see-as
	You're welcome	De nada	deh **nah**-dah
	Excuse me	Con permiso	con pehr-**mee**-so
	Pardon me/what did you say?	¿Perdón?/Mande?	pehr-**dohn/mahn**-deh
	Could you tell me?	¿Podría decirme?	po-**dree**-ah deh-**seer**-meh
	I'm sorry	Lo siento	lo see-**en**-to
	Good morning!	¡Buenos días!	**bway**-nohs **dee**-ahs
	Good afternoon!	¡Buenas tardes!	**bway**-nahs **tar**-dess
	Good evening!	¡Buenas noches!	**bway**-nahs **no**-chess
	Goodbye!	¡Adiós!/¡Hasta luego!	ah-dee-**ohss**/**ah**-stah-**lwe**-go
	Mr./Mrs.	Señor/Señora	sen-**yor**/sen-**yohr**-ah
	Miss	Señorita	sen-yo-**ree**-tah
	Pleased to meet you	Mucho gusto	**moo**-cho **goose**-to
	How are you?	¿Cómo está usted?	**ko**-mo es-**tah** oo-**sted**
	Very well, thank you.	Muy bien, gracias.	**moo**-ee bee-**en**, **grah**-see-as
	And you?	¿Y usted?	ee oos-**ted**
	Hello (on the telephone)	Diga	**dee**-gah
Numbers	1	un, uno	oon, **oo**-no
	2	dos	dohs
	3	tres	tress
	4	cuatro	**kwah**-tro
	5	cinco	**sink**-oh
	6	seis	saice
	7	siete	see-**et**-eh
	8	ocho	**o**-cho
	9	nueve	new-**eh**-veh
	10	diez	dee-**es**
	11	once	**ohn**-seh
	12	doce	**doh**-seh
	13	trece	**treh**-seh
	14	catorce	ka-**tohr**-seh
	15	quince	**keen**-seh
	16	dieciséis	dee-es-ee-**saice**
	17	diecisiete	dee-**es**-ee-see-**et**-eh
	18	dieciocho	dee-**es**-ee-**o**-cho
	19	diecinueve	dee-**es**-ee-new-**ev**-eh
	20	veinte	**vain**-teh

21	veinte y uno/veintiuno	**vain**-te-oo-noh
30	treinta	**train**-tah
32	treinta y dos	train-tay-**dohs**
40	cuarenta	kwah-**ren**-tah
43	cuarenta y tres	kwah-**ren**-tay-**tress**
50	cincuenta	seen-**kwen**-tah
54	cincuenta y cuatro	seen-**kwen**-tay kwah-tro
60	sesenta	sess-**en**-tah
65	sesenta y cinco	sess-**en**-tay **seen**-koh
70	setenta	set-**en**-tah
76	setenta y seis	set-**en**-tay **saice**
80	ochenta	oh-**chen**-tah
87	ochenta y siete	oh-**chen**-tay see-**yet**-eh
90	noventa	no-**ven**-tah
98	noventa y ocho	no-**ven**-tay-**o**-choh
100	cien	see-**en**
101	ciento uno	see-en-toh **oo**-noh
200	doscientos	doh-see-**en**-tohss
500	quinientos	keen-**yen**-tohss
700	setecientos	set-eh-see-**en**-tohss
900	novecientos	no-veh-see-**en**-tohss
1,000	mil	meel
2,000	dos mil	dohs meel
1,000,000	un millón	oon meel-**yohn**

Colors	black	negro	**neh**-groh
	blue	azul	ah-**sool**
	brown	café	kah-**feh**
	green	verde	**ver**-deh
	pink	rosa	**ro**-sah
	purple	morado	mo-**rah**-doh
	orange	naranja	na-**rahn**-hah
	red	rojo	**roh**-hoh
	white	blanco	**blahn**-koh
	yellow	amarillo	ah-mah-**ree**-yoh

Days of the Week	Sunday	domingo	doh-**meen**-goh
	Monday	lunes	**loo**-ness
	Tuesday	martes	**mahr**-tess
	Wednesday	miércoles	me-**air**-koh-less
	Thursday	jueves	hoo-**ev**-ess
	Friday	viernes	vee-**air**-ness
	Saturday	sábado	**sah**-bah-doh

Months	January	enero	eh-**neh**-roh
	February	febrero	feh-**breh**-roh
	March	marzo	**mahr**-soh
	April	abril	ah-**breel**
	May	mayo	**my**-oh
	June	junio	**hoo**-nee-oh
	July	julio	**hoo**-lee-yoh
	August	agosto	ah-**ghost**-toh
	September	septiembre	sep-tee-**em**-breh
	October	octubre	ok-**too**-breh
	November	noviembre	no-vee-**em**-breh
	December	diciembre	dee-see-**em**-breh

Useful Phrases	Do you speak English?	¿Habla usted inglés?	**ah**-blah oos-**ted** in-**glehs**
	I don't speak Spanish	No hablo español	no **ah**-bloh es-pahn-**yol**
	I don't understand (you)	No entiendo	no en-tee-**en**-doh
	I understand (you)	Entiendo	en-tee-**en**-doh
	I don't know	No sé	no seh
	I am American/ British	Soy americano/ (americana) inglés(a)	soy ah-meh-ree-**kah**-no (ah-meh-ree-**kah**-nah)/ in-**glehs**(ah)/
	What's your name?	¿Cómo se llama usted?	**koh**-mo seh **yah**-mah oos-**ted**?
	My name is . . .	Me llamo . . .	meh **yah**-moh
	What time is it?	¿Qué hora es?	keh **o**-rah es?
	It is one, two, three . . . o'clock.	Es la una. . . . Son las dos, tres	es la **oo**-nah/sohn lahs dohs, tress
	Yes, please/No, thank you	Sí, por favor/No, gracias	see pohr fah-**vor**/no **grah**-see-ahs
	How?	¿Cómo?	**koh**-mo?
	When?	¿Cuándo?	**kwahn**-doh?
	This/Next week	Esta semana/ la semana que entra	es-tah seh-**mah**-nah/lah seh-**mah**-nah keh en-trah
	This/Next month	Este mes/el próximo mes	es-teh mehs/el **prok**-see-moh mehs
	This/Next year	Este año/el año que viene	es-teh **ahn**-yo/el **ahn**-yo keh vee-**yen**-ay
	Yesterday/today/ tomorrow	Ayer/hoy/mañana	ah-**yehr**/oy/mahn-**yah**-nah
	This morning/ afternoon	Esta mañana/tarde	es-tah mahn-**yah**-nah/**tar**-deh
	Tonight	Esta noche	es-tah **no**-cheh
	What?	¿Qué?	keh?
	What is it?	¿Qué es esto?	keh es **es**-toh
	Why?	¿Por qué?	por keh
	Who?	¿Quién?	kee-**yen**
	Where is . . . ? the train station?	¿Dónde está . . . ? la estación del tren?	**dohn**-deh es-**tah** la es-tah-see-**on** del **train**
	the subway station?	la estación del Metro?	la es-ta-see-**on** del **meh**-tro
	the bus stop?	la parada del autobus?	la pah-**rah**-dah del oh-toh-**boos**

the post office?	la oficina de correos?	la oh-fee-**see**-nah deh-koh-**reh**-os
the bank?	el banco?	el **bahn**-koh
the . . . hotel?	el hotel . . . ?	el oh-**tel**
the store?	la tienda . . . ?	la tee-**en**-dah
the cashier?	la caja?	la **kah**-hah
the . . . museum?	el museo . . . ?	el moo-**seh**-oh
the hospital?	el hospital?	el ohss-pee-**tal**
the elevator?	el ascensor?	el ah-**sen**-sohr
the bathroom?	el baño?	el **bahn**-yoh
Here/there	Aquí/allá	ah-**key**/ah-**yah**
Open/closed	Abierto/cerrado	ah-bee-**er**-toh/ ser-**ah**-doh
Left/right	Izquierda/derecha	iss-key-**er**-dah/ dare-**eh**-chah
Straight ahead	Derecho	dare-**eh**-choh
Is it near/far?	¿Está cerca/lejos?	es-**tah** sehr-kah/ **leh**-hoss
I'd like . . .	Quisiera . . .	kee-see-**ehr**-ah
a room	un cuarto/una habitación	oon **kwahr**-toh/ **oo**-nah ah-bee-tah-see-**on**
the key	la llave	lah **yah**-veh
a newspaper	un periódico	oon pehr-ee-**oh**-dee-koh
a stamp	un timbre de correo	oon **teem**-breh deh koh-**reh**-oh
I'd like to buy . . .	Quisiera comprar . . .	kee-see-**ehr**-ah kohm-**prahr**
cigarette	cigarrillo	cee-ga-**ree**-yoh
matches	cerillos	ser-**ee**-ohs
a dictionary	un diccionario	oon deek-see-oh-**nah**-ree-oh
soap	jabón	hah-**bohn**
a map	un mapa	oon **mah**-pah
a magazine	una revista	**oon**-ah reh-**veess**-tah
paper	papel	pah-**pel**
envelopes	sobres	**so**-brehs
a postcard	una tarjeta postal	**oon**-ah tar-**het**-ah post-**ahl**
How much is it?	¿Cuánto cuesta?	**kwahn**-toh **kwes**-tah
It's expensive/ cheap	Está caro/barato	es-**tah kah**-roh/ bah-**rah**-toh
A little/a lot	Un poquito/ mucho . . .	oon poh-**kee**-toh/ **moo**-choh
More/less	Más/menos	mahss/**men**-ohss
Enough/too much/too little	Suficiente/ demasiado/ muy poco	soo-fee-see-**en**-teh/ deh-mah-see-**ah**-doh/ **moo**-ee poh-koh
Telephone	Teléfono	tel-**ef**-oh-no
Telegram	Telegrama	teh-leh-**grah**-mah

	I am ill	Estoy enfermo(a)	es-**toy** en-**fehr**-moh(mah)
	Please call a doctor	Por favor llame un medico	pohr fah-**vor** ya-meh oon **med**-ee-koh
	Help!	¡Auxilio! ¡Ayuda! ¡Socorro!	owk-**see**-lee-oh/ ah-**yoo**-dah/ soh-**kohr**-roh
	Fire!	¡Encendio!	en-**sen**-dee-oo
	Caution!/Look out!	¡Cuidado!	kwee-**dah**-doh
On the Road	Avenue	Avenida	ah-ven-**ee**-dah
	Broad, tree-lined boulevard	Paseo	pah-**seh**-oh
	Fertile plain	Vega	**veh**-gah
	Highway	Carretera	car-reh-**ter**-ah
	Mountain pass, port	Puerto	poo-**ehr**-toh
	Street	Calle	**cah**-yeh
	Waterfront promenade	Paseo marítimo	pah-**seh**-oh mahr-**ee**-tee-moh
	Wharf	Embarcadero	em-bar-cah-**deh**-ro
In Town	Arab souk or market	Zoco	**thoh**-koh
	Cathedral	Catedral	cah-teh-**dral**
	Church	Templo/Iglesia	**tem**-plo/ee-**glehs**-see-ah
	City hall	Ayuntamiento	ah-yoon-tah-me-**yen**-toh
	Door, gate	Puerta	poo-**ehr**-tah
	Float (in a procession)	Paso	**pah**-soh
	Inn, rustic bar, or restaurant	Mesón	meh-**sohn**
	Main square	Plaza mayor	plah-thah mah-**yohr**
	Market	Mercado	mer-**kah**-doh
	Neighborhood	Barrio	**bahr**-ree-o
	Traffic circle	Glorieta	glor-ee-**eh**-tah
	Wine cellar, wine bar, or wine shop	Bodega	boh-**deh**-gah
Dining Out	A bottle of . . .	Una bottella de . . .	**oo**-nah bo-**teh**-yah deh
	A cup of . . .	Una taza de . . .	**oo**-nah **tah**-thah deh
	A glass of . . .	Un vaso de . . .	oon **vah**-so deh
	Ashtray	Un cenicero	oon sen-ee-**seh**-roh
	Bill/check	La cuenta	lah **kwen**-tah
	Bread	El pan	el pahn
	Breakfast	El desayuno	el deh-sah-**yoon**-oh
	Butter	La mantequilla	lah man-teh-**key**-yah
	Cheers!	¡Salud!	sah-**lood**
	Cocktail	Un aperitivo	oon ah-pehr-ee-**tee**-voh
	Dinner	La cena	lah **seh**-nah
	Dish	Un plato	oon **plah**-toh

Menu of the day	Menú del día	meh-**noo** del **dee**-ah
Enjoy!	¡Buen provecho!	bwehn pro-**veh**-cho
Fixed-price menu	Menú fijo o turistico	meh-**noo fee**-hoh oh too-**ree**-stee-coh
Fork	El tenedor	ehl ten-eh-**dor**
Is the tip included?	¿Está incluida la propina?	es-**tah** in-cloo-**ee**-dah lah pro-**pee**-nah
Knife	El cuchillo	el koo-**chee**-yo
Large portion of savory snacks	Raciónes	rah-see-**oh**-nehs
Lunch	La comida	lah koh-**mee**-dah
Menu	La carta, el menú	lah **cart**-ah, el meh-**noo**
Napkin	La servilleta	lah sehr-vee-**yet**-ah
Pepper	La pimienta	lah pee-me-**en**-tah
Please give me	Por favor déme	pohr fah-**vor deh**-meh
Salt	La sal	lah sahl
Savory snacks	Tapas	**tah**-pahs
Spoon	Una cuchara	**oo**-nah koo-**chah**-rah
Sugar	El azúcar	el ah-**thu**-kar
Waiter!/Waitress!	¡Por favor Señor/Señorita!	pohr fah-**vor** sen-**yor**/sen-yor-**ee**-tah

Glossary

Alcazaba (Al-**ka**-tha-ba) Moorish fortress.

Alcázar (Al-**ka**-thar) Moorish fortified palace.

Aljibe (Al-**hee**-beh) Cistern, or water supply. Usually of Moorish, though sometimes Roman, origin.

Artesonado (Ar-teh-so-**nah**-doh) Intricate wooden inlaid ceiling of Moorish or Mudéjar inspiration.

Azulejo (Ah-thoo-**leh**-ho) Glazed ceramic tiles, often of Moorish inspiration and much used in ornamental decoration of patios, fountains, and benches.

Capilla mayor (Ka-**pee**-yah mah-**yor**) Chapel or chancel containing high altar in a cathedral.

Cartuja (Kar-**too**-ha) Carthusian monastery.

Churrigueresque (Choor-ree-gher-**esk**) Highly ornate Spanish Baroque of the late 17th and early 18th centuries as exemplified in Granada's Cartuja. The term derives from the Churriguera family of architects and sculptors. Its leading exponent was José Churriguera (1650–1725).

Ciudadela (See-oo-dah-**deh**-lah); in Catalan, **Ciutadella** (See-oo-tah-**deh**-yah) Citadel.

Coro (**Koh**-roh) Part of church built for the choir, usually walled-in in Spanish cathedrals.

Custodia (Koos-**toh**-dee-ah) Monstrance in which the Host is kept or carried in processions.

Esgrafiado (Ehs-grah-fee-**ah**-doh) Style of decorating a facade, by either etching patterns in stucco or implanting small pieces of coal, as in Segovia's Alcázar.

Isabelline (Ee-sah-beh-**leen**) Ornamental Gothic style developed during the reign of Isabel la Católica (1474–1504). An example is San Juan de los Reyes, Toledo.

Judería (Hoo-dehr-**ee**-ah) Jewish Quarter.

Lonja (**Lon**-hah); in Catalan, **Llotja** (**yoh**-hah) Merchants' or Stock Exchange.

Mezquita (Meth-**kee**-tah) Mosque.

Mihrab (**Meeh**-rab) Prayer niche in a mosque; faces Mecca.

Mocarabes (Moh-ka-rah-bess) Ornamental Moorish ceiling decoration, usually of painted stucco.

Mozarabe (Moh-**tha**-rah-beh) Christian living under Moorish rule, normally allowed freedom of worship. Also, term applied to the architecture of such Christians (Mozarabic).

Mudéjar (Moo-**deh**-har) Moor (Muslim) living under Christian rule, normally allowed freedom of worship. Also the term applied to the architecture of such Moors. The best example is Seville's Alcázar. The 1920s and 1930s saw a revival of Mudéjar art and architecture, especially in public buildings.

Plateresque (Plah-ter-**esk**) From *platero* (silversmith). Architectural term for Late-Gothic, Early Renaissance style and stonework carved so finely it resembles silverwork.

Reja (**Reh**-hah) Wrought-iron screen or grille, guarding either a chapel in a church or a house window, usually in Andalucía.

Retablo or **Reredos** (Reh-**tah**-bloh/Reh-**reh**-dos) Large altarpiece, sculptured, carved, or painted.

Sacristía or **Sagrario** (Sah-krees-**tee**-ah/Sah-**grah**-ree-oh) Sacristy or sanctuary of a church.

Sala capitular (**Sah**-lah kah-pee-too-**lahr**) Chapter house.

Silleria (See-yer-**ee**-ah) Choir stalls.

Index

Personal Itinerary

Departure *Date*

Time

Transportation

Arrival *Date*　　　*Time*

Departure *Date*　　　*Time*

Transportation

Accommodations

Arrival *Date*　　　*Time*

Departure *Date*　　　*Time*

Transportation

Accommodations

Arrival *Date*　　　*Time*

Departure *Date*　　　*Time*

Transportation

Accommodations

Personal Itinerary

Arrival *Date*   *Time*

Departure *Date*   *Time*

Transportation

Accommodations

Arrival *Date*   *Time*

Departure *Date*   *Time*

Transportation

Accommodations

Arrival *Date*   *Time*

Departure *Date*   *Time*

Transportation

Accommodations

Arrival *Date*   *Time*

Departure *Date*   *Time*

Transportation

Accommodations

Personal Itinerary

Arrival *Date*   *Time*

Departure *Date*   *Time*

Transportation

Accommodations

Arrival *Date*   *Time*

Departure *Date*   *Time*

Transportation

Accommodations

Arrival *Date*   *Time*

Departure *Date*   *Time*

Transportation

Accommodations

Arrival *Date*   *Time*

Departure *Date*   *Time*

Transportation

Accommodations

At last — a guide for Americans with disabilities that makes traveling a delight

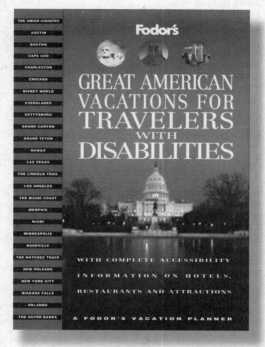

0-679-02591-X $18.00 ($24.00 Can)

This is the first and only complete guide to great American vacations for the 35 million North Americans with disabilities, as well as for those who care for them or for aging parents and relatives. Provides:

- Essential trip-planning information for travelers with mobility, vision, and hearing impairments
- Specific details on a huge array of facilities, along with solid descriptions of attractions, hotels, restaurants, and other destinations
- Up-to-date information on ISA-designated parking, level entranceways, and accessibility to pools, lounges, and bathrooms

At bookstores everywhere, or call **1-800-533-6478**

Fodor's Travel Guides

Available at bookstores everywhere, or call 1–800–533–6478, 24 hours a day.

U.S. Guides

Alaska

Arizona

Boston

California

Cape Cod, Martha's Vineyard, Nantucket

The Carolinas & the Georgia Coast

Chicago

Colorado

Florida

Hawaii

Las Vegas, Reno, Tahoe

Los Angeles

Maine, Vermont, New Hampshire

Maui

Miami & the Keys

New England

New Orleans

New York City

Pacific North Coast

Philadelphia & the Pennsylvania Dutch Country

The Rockies

San Diego

San Francisco

Santa Fe, Taos, Albuquerque

Seattle & Vancouver

The South

The U.S. & British Virgin Islands

USA

The Upper Great Lakes Region

Virginia & Maryland

Waikiki

Walt Disney World and the Orlando Area

Washington, D.C.

Foreign Guides

Acapulco, Ixtapa, Zihuatanejo

Australia & New Zealand

Austria

The Bahamas

Baja & Mexico's Pacific Coast Resorts

Barbados

Berlin

Bermuda

Brittany & Normandy

Budapest

Canada

Cancún, Cozumel, Yucatán Peninsula

Caribbean

China

Costa Rica, Belize, Guatemala

The Czech Republic & Slovakia

Eastern Europe

Egypt

Euro Disney

Europe

Florence, Tuscany & Umbria

France

Germany

Great Britain

Greece

Hong Kong

India

Ireland

Israel

Italy

Japan

Kenya & Tanzania

Korea

London

Madrid & Barcelona

Mexico

Montréal & Québec City

Morocco

Moscow & St. Petersburg

The Netherlands, Belgium & Luxembourg

New Zealand

Norway

Nova Scotia, Prince Edward Island & New Brunswick

Paris

Portugal

Provence & the Riviera

Rome

Russia & the Baltic Countries

Scandinavia

Scotland

Singapore

South America

Southeast Asia

Spain

Sweden

Switzerland

Thailand

Tokyo

Toronto

Turkey

Vienna & the Danube Valley

Special Series

Fodor's Affordables

Caribbean

Europe

Florida

France

Germany

Great Britain

Italy

London

Paris

Fodor's Bed & Breakfast and Country Inns Guides

America's Best B&Bs

California

Canada's Great Country Inns

Cottages, B&Bs and Country Inns of England and Wales

Mid-Atlantic Region

New England

The Pacific Northwest

The South

The Southwest

The Upper Great Lakes Region

The Berkeley Guides

California

Central America

Eastern Europe

Europe

France

Germany & Austria

Great Britain & Ireland

Italy

London

Mexico

Pacific Northwest & Alaska

Paris

San Francisco

Fodor's Exploring Guides

Australia

Boston & New England

Britain

California

The Caribbean

Florence & Tuscany

Florida

France

Germany

Ireland

Italy

London

Mexico

New York City

Paris

Prague

Rome

Scotland

Singapore & Malaysia

Spain

Thailand

Turkey

Fodor's Flashmaps

Boston

New York

Washington, D.C.

Fodor's Pocket Guides

Acapulco

Bahamas

Barbados

Jamaica

London

New York City

Paris

Puerto Rico

San Francisco

Washington, D.C.

Fodor's Sports

Cycling

Golf Digest's Best Places to Play

Hiking

The Insider's Guide to the Best Canadian Skiing

Running

Sailing

Skiing in the USA & Canada

USA Today's Complete Four Sports Stadium Guide

Fodor's Three-In-Ones (guidebook, language cassette, and phrase book)

France

Germany

Italy

Mexico

Spain

Fodor's Special-Interest Guides

Complete Guide to America's National Parks

Condé Nast Traveler Caribbean Resort and Cruise Ship Finder

Cruises and Ports of Call

Euro Disney

France by Train

Halliday's New England Food Explorer

Healthy Escapes

Italy by Train

London Companion

Shadow Traffic's New York Shortcuts and Traffic Tips

Sunday in New York

Sunday in San Francisco

Touring Europe

Touring USA: Eastern Edition

Walt Disney World and the Orlando Area

Walt Disney World for Adults

Fodor's Vacation Planners

Great American Learning Vacations

Great American Sports & Adventure Vacations

Great American Vacations

Great American Vacations for Travelers with Disabilities

National Parks and Seashores of the East

National Parks of the West

The Wall Street Journal Guides to Business Travel

The only guide to explore a *Disney World®* you've never seen before:
The one for grown-ups.

0-679-02490-5 $14.00 ($18.50 Can)

This is the only guide written specifically for the millions of adults who visit Walt Disney World® each year <u>without</u> kids. Upscale, sophisticated, packed full of facts and maps, *Walt Disney World® for Adults* provides up-to-date information on hotels, restaurants, sports facilities, and health clubs, as well as unique itineraries for adults. With *Walt Disney World® for Adults* in hand, you'll get the most out of one of the world's most fascinating, most complex playgrounds.

At bookstores everywhere, or call **1-800-533-6478.**

AT LAST

YOUR OWN PERSONALIZED LIST
OF WHAT'S GOING ON IN THE
CITIES YOU'RE VISITING.

KEYED TO THE DAYS WHEN
YOU'LL BE THERE, CUSTOMIZED
FOR YOUR INTERESTS,
AND SENT TO YOU BEFORE YOU
LEAVE HOME.

GET THE INSIDER'S
PERSPECTIVE. . .

UP-TO-THE-MINUTE
ACCURATE
EASY TO ORDER
DELIVERED WHEN YOU NEED IT

Now there is a revolutionary way to get customized, time-sensitive travel information just before your trip.

Now you can obtain detailed information about what's going on in each city you'll be visiting <u>before</u> you leave home—up-to-the-minute, objective information about the events and activities that interest you most.

Your Itinerary:
Customized reports available for 160 destinations

Travel Updates contain the kind of time-sensitive insider information you can get only from local contacts – or from city magazines and newspapers once you arrive. But now you can have the same information before you leave for your trip.

The choice is yours: current art exhibits, theater, music festivals and special concerts, sporting events, antiques and flower shows, shopping, fitness, and more.

The information comes from hundreds of correspondents and thousands of sources worldwide. Updated continuously, it's like having your own personal concierge or friend in the city.

You specify the cities and when you'll be there. We'll do the rest — personalizing the information for you the way no guidebook can.

It's the perfect extension to your Fodor's guide and the best way to make the most of your valuable travel time.

Use Order Form on back or call 1-800-799-9609

air
tour
9902
Regent's
The annu
in this an
domain of
tion as Joe Pa
worthwhile. It'
the performances
Tickets are usually
venue. Alternate
mances are cancelled
given. For more inform
Open-Air Theatre, Inner
NW1 4NP Open Air Thea
Tel: 935-5756. Ends: 9-11-93.
International Air Tattoo
Held biennially, the
military air displ
demost
tions

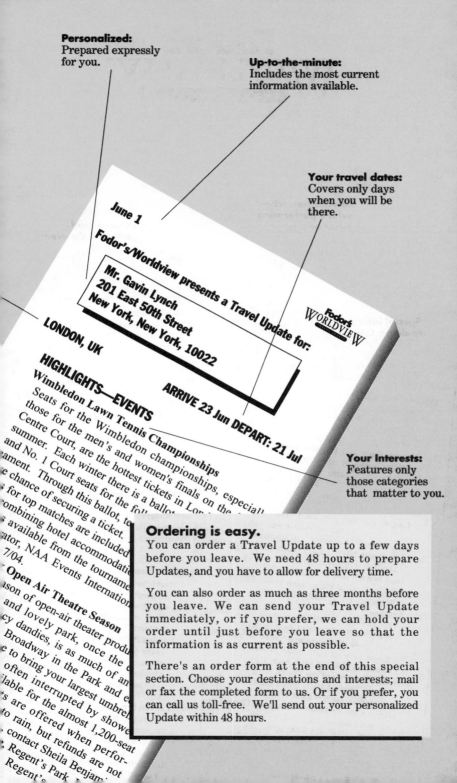

Personalized:
Prepared expressly for you.

Up-to-the-minute:
Includes the most current information available.

Your travel dates:
Covers only days when you will be there.

June 1

Fodor's/Worldview presents a Travel Update for:

Mr. Gavin Lynch
201 East 50th Street
New York, New York, 10022

Fodor's
WORLDVIEW

LONDON, UK

ARRIVE 23 Jun DEPART: 21 Jul

HIGHLIGHTS—EVENTS

Wimbledon Lawn Tennis Championships

Seats for the Wimbledon championships, especiall
those for the men's and women's finals on the
Centre Court, are the hottest tickets in Lon
summer. Each winter there is a ballo
and No. 1 Court seats for the foll
ament. Through this ballot, te
e chance of securing a ticket.
s for top matches are included
ombining hotel accommodati
s available from the tourname
ator, NAA Events Internation
7/04.

Open Air Theatre Season

ason of open-air theater produ
and lovely park, once the
cy dandies, is as much of an
Broadway in the Park and e
e to bring your largest umbrel
often interrupted by showe
lable for the almost 1,200-seat
s are offered when perfor-
o rain, but refunds are not
, contact Sheila Benjam
, Regent's Park
Regent's

Your Interests:
Features only those categories that matter to you.

Ordering is easy.

You can order a Travel Update up to a few days before you leave. We need 48 hours to prepare Updates, and you have to allow for delivery time.

You can also order as much as three months before you leave. We can send your Travel Update immediately, or if you prefer, we can hold your order until just before you leave so that the information is as current as possible.

There's an order form at the end of this special section. Choose your destinations and interests; mail or fax the completed form to us. Or if you prefer, you can call us toll-free. We'll send out your personalized Update within 48 hours.

**Special concerts—
who's performing
what and where**

**One-of-a-kind,
one-time-only events**

**Special interest,
in-depth listings**

Children — Events
Angel Canal Festival
The festivities include a children's funfair, entertainers, a boat rally and displays on the water. Regent's Canal. Islington. N1. Tube: Angel. Tel: 267 9100. 11:30am-5:30pm. 7/04.

Blackheath Summer Kite Festival
Stunt kite displays with parachuting teddy bears and trade stands. Free admission. SE3. BR: Blackheath. 10am. 6/27.

Megabugs
Children will delight in this infestation of giant robotic insects, including a praying mantis 60 times life size. Mon-Sat 10am-6pm; Sun 11am-6pm. Admission 4.50 pounds. Natural History Museum, Cromwell Road. SW7. Tube: South Kensington. Tel: 938 9123. Ends 10/01.

Childminders
This establishment employs only women, providing nurses and qualified nannies to

Music — Jazz & Blues
Tito Puente's Golden Men of Latin Jazz
The father of mambo and Cuban rumba king comes to town. Royal Festival Hall. South Bank. SE1. Tube: Waterloo. Tel: 928 8800. 8pm. 7/15.

Georgie Fame and The New York Band
Riding a popular tide with his latest album, the smoky-voiced Fame and his keyboard are on a tour yet again. The Grand. Clapham Junction. SW11. BR: Clapham Junction. Tel: 738 9000. 7:30pm. 7/07.

Jacques Loussier Play Bach Trio
The French jazz classicist and colleagues. Kenwood Lakeside. Hampstead Lane. Kenwood. NW3. Tube: Golders Green, then bus 210. Tel: 413 1443. 7pm. 7/10.

Tony Bennett and Ronnie Scott
Royal Festival Hall. South Bank. SE1. Tube: Waterloo. Tel: 928 8800. 8pm. 7/11.

Santana
Royal Festival Hall. South Bank. SE1. Tube: Waterloo. Tel: 928 8800. 8pm. 7/12.

Count Basie Orchestra and Nancy Wilson Trio
Royal Festival Hall. South Bank. SE1. Tube: Waterloo. Tel: 928 8800. 8pm. 7/14.

King Pleasure and the Biscuit Boys
Royal Festival Hall. South Bank. SE1. Tube: Waterloo. Tel: 928 8800. 6:30 and 9pm. 7/16.

Al Green and the London Community Gospel Choir
Royal Festival Hall. South Bank. SE1. Tube: Waterloo. Tel: 928 8800. 8pm. 7/13.

BB King and Linda Hopkins
Mother of the blues and successor to Bessie Smith, Hopkins meets up with "Blues Boy" King. Royal Festival Hall. South Bank. SE

Music — Classical
Marylebone Sinfonia
Kenneth Gowen conducts music by Puccini and Rossini. Queen Elizabeth Hall. South Bank. SE1. Tube: Waterloo. Tel: 928 8800. 7:45pm. 7/16.

London Philharmonic
Franz Welser-Moest and George Benjamin conduct selections by Alexander Goehr, Messiaen, and some of Benjamin's own compositions. Queen Elizabeth Hall. South Bank. SE1. Tube: Waterloo. Tel: 928 8800. 8pm.

London Pro Arte Orchestra and Forest Choir
Murray Stewart conducts selections by Rossini, Haydn and Jonathan Willcocks. Queen Elizabeth Hall. South Bank. SE1. Tube: Waterloo. Tel: 928 8800. 7:45pm.

Kensington Symphony Orchestra
Russell Keable conducts Dvorak's D

Here's what you get . . .

Detailed information about what's going on — precisely when you'll be there.

Reviews by local critics

Show openings during your visit

Handy pocket-size booklet

Exhibitions & Shows—Antique & Flower
Westminster Antiques Fair
Over 50 stands with pre-1830 furniture and other Victorian and earlier items. Thu-Fri 11am-8pm; Sat-Sun 11am-6pm. Admission 4 pounds, children free. Old Royal Horticultural Hall. Vincent Square. SW1. Tel: 0444/48 25 14. 6-24 thru 6/27.

Royal Horticultural Society Flower Show
The show includes displays of carnations, summer fruit and vegetables. Tue 11am-7pm; Wed 10am-5pm. Admission Tue 4 pounds, Wed 2 pounds. Royal Horticultural Halls. Greycoat Street and Vincent Square. SW1. Tube: Victoria. 7/20 thru 7/21.

Hampton Court Palace International Flower Show
Major international garden and flower show taking place in conjunction with

Theater — Musical
Sunset Boulevard
In June, the four Andrew Lloyd Webber musicals which dominated London's stages in the 1980s (Cats, Starlight Express, Phantom of the Opera and Aspects of Love) are joined by the composer's latest work, a show rumored to have his best music to date. The 1950 Billy Wilder film about a helpless young writer who is drawn into the world of a possessive, aging silent screen star offers rich opportunities for Webber's evolving style. Soaring, aching melodies, lush technical effects and psychological thrills are all expected. Patti Lupone stars. Mon-Sat at 8pm; matinee Thu-Sat at 3pm. In-person sales only at the box office; credit card bookings, Tel: 344 0055. Admission 15-32.50 pounds. Adelphi Theatre. The Strand. WC2. Tube: Charing Cross. Tel: 836 7611. Starts: 6/21.

Leonardo A Portrait of Love
A new musical about the great Renaissance artist and inventor comes in for a London pre-... tested by a brief run at Oxford's Old ... The work explores ...

Spectator Sports — Other Sports
Greyhound Racing: Wembley Stadium
This dog track offers good views of greyhound racing held on Mon, Wed and Fri. No credit cards. Stadium Way. Wembley. HA9. Tube: Wembley Park. Tel: 902 8833.

Benson & Hedges Cricket Cup Final
Lord's Cricket Ground. St. John's Wood Road. NW8. Tube: St. John's Wood. Tel: 289 1611. 11am. 7/10.

Business-Fax & Overnight Mail
Post Office, Trafalgar Square Branch
Offers a network of fax services, the Intelpost system, throughout the country and abroad. Mon-Sat 8am-8pm, Sun 9am-5pm. William IV Street. WC2. Tube: Charing Cross. Tel: 930 9580.

Fodor's
WORLDVIEW
TRAVEL UPDATE

London, England
Arriving: June 23
Departing: July 21

Interest Categories

For your personalized Travel Update, choose the categories you're most interested in from this list. Every Travel Update automatically provides you with *Event Highlights* - the best of what's happening during the dates of your trip.

1.	**Business Services**	Fax & Overnight Mail, Computer Rentals, Photocopying, Protocol, Secretarial, Messenger, Translation Services
	Dining	
2.	**All Day Dining**	Breakfast & Brunch, Cafes & Tea Rooms, Late-Night Dining
3.	**Local Cuisine**	In Every Price Range—from Budget Restaurants to the Special Splurge
4.	**European Cuisine**	Continental, French, Italian
5.	**Asian Cuisine**	Chinese, Far Eastern, Japanese, Other
6.	**Americas Cuisine**	American, Mexican & Latin
7.	**Nightlife**	Bars, Dance Clubs, Casinos, Comedy Clubs, Ethnic, Pubs & Beer Halls
8.	**Entertainment**	Theater—Comedy, Drama, English Language, Musicals, Dance, Ticket Agencies
9.	**Music**	Country/Western/Folk, Classical, Traditional & Ethnic, Opera, Jazz & Blues, Pop, Rock
10.	**Children's Activities**	Events, Attractions
11.	**Tours**	Local Tours, Day Trips, Overnight Excursions, Cruises
12.	**Exhibitions, Festivals & Shows**	Antiques & Flower, History & Cultural, Art Exhibitions, Fairs & Craft Shows, Music & Art Festivals
13.	**Shopping**	Districts & Malls, Markets, Regional Specialities
14.	**Fitness**	Bicycling, Health Clubs, Hiking, Jogging
15.	**Recreational Sports**	Boating/Sailing, Fishing, Golf, Ice Skating, Skiing, Snorkeling/Scuba, Swimming, Tennis & Racquet
16.	**Spectator Sports**	Auto Racing, Baseball, Basketball, Boating & Sailing, Football, Golf, Horse Racing, Ice Hockey, Rugby, Soccer, Tennis, Track & Field, Other Sports

Please note that interest category content will vary by season, destination, and length of stay.

Destinations

The Fodor's/Worldview Travel Update covers more than 160 destinations world-wide. Choose the destinations that match your itinerary from this list. (Choose bulleted destinations only.)

Europe
- Amsterdam
- Athens
- Barcelona
- Berlin
- Brussels
- Budapest
- Copenhagen
- Dublin
- Edinburgh
- Florence
- Frankfurt
- French Riviera
- Geneva
- Glasgow
- Istanbul
- Lausanne
- Lisbon
- London
- Madrid
- Milan
- Moscow
- Munich
- Oslo
- Paris
- Prague
- Provence
- Rome
- Salzburg
* Seville
- St. Petersburg
- Stockholm
- Venice
- Vienna
- Zurich

United States (Mainland)
- Albuquerque
- Atlanta
- Atlantic City
- Baltimore
- Boston
* Branson, MO
* Charleston, SC
- Chicago
- Cincinnati
- Cleveland
- Dallas/Ft. Worth
- Denver
- Detroit
- Houston
* Indianapolis
- Kansas City
- Las Vegas
- Los Angeles
- Memphis

- Miami
- Milwaukee
- Minneapolis/ St. Paul
* Nashville
- New Orleans
- New York City
- Orlando
- Palm Springs
- Philadelphia
- Phoenix
- Pittsburgh
- Portland
* Reno/ Lake Tahoe
- St. Louis
- Salt Lake City
- San Antonio
- San Diego
- San Francisco
* Santa Fe
- Seattle
- Tampa
- Washington, DC

Alaska
- Alaskan Destinations

Hawaii
- Honolulu
- Island of Hawaii
- Kauai
- Maui

Canada
- Quebec City
- Montreal
- Ottawa
- Toronto
- Vancouver

Bahamas
- Abaco
- Eleuthera/ Harbour Island
- Exuma
- Freeport
- Nassau & Paradise Island

Bermuda
- Bermuda Countryside
- Hamilton

British Leeward Islands
- Anguilla

- Antigua & Barbuda
- St. Kitts & Nevis

British Virgin Islands
- Tortola & Virgin Gorda

British Windward Islands
- Barbados
- Dominica
- Grenada
- St. Lucia
- St. Vincent
- Trinidad & Tobago

Cayman Islands
- The Caymans

Dominican Republic
- Santo Domingo

Dutch Leeward Islands
- Aruba
- Bonaire
- Curacao

Dutch Windward Island
- St. Maarten/ St. Martin

French West Indies
- Guadeloupe
- Martinique
- St. Barthelemy

Jamaica
- Kingston
- Montego Bay
- Negril
- Ocho Rios

Puerto Rico
- Ponce
- San Juan

Turks & Caicos
- Grand Turk/ Providenciales

U.S. Virgin Islands
- St. Croix
- St. John
- St. Thomas

Mexico
- Acapulco
- Cancun & Isla Mujeres
- Cozumel
- Guadalajara
- Ixtapa & Zihuatanejo
- Los Cabos
- Mazatlan
- Mexico City
- Monterrey
- Oaxaca
- Puerto Vallarta

South/Central America
* Buenos Aires
* Caracas
* Rio de Janeiro
* San Jose, Costa Rica
* Sao Paulo

Middle East
* Jerusalem

Australia & New Zealand
- Auckland
- Melbourne
* South Island
- Sydney

China
- Beijing
- Guangzhou
- Shanghai

Japan
- Kyoto
- Nagoya
- Osaka
- Tokyo
- Yokohama

Pacific Rim/Other
* Bali
- Bangkok
- Hong Kong & Macau
- Manila
- Seoul
- Singapore
- Taipei

* Destinations available by 1/1/95

Fodor's
WORLDVIEW TRAVEL UPDATE
Order Form

THIS TRAVEL UPDATE IS FOR (Please print):

Name _____

Address _____

City	State	Country	ZIP

Tel # ( ) - Fax # ( ) -

Title of this Fodor's guide: _____

Store and location where guide was purchased: _____

INDICATE YOUR DESTINATIONS/DATES: You can order up to three (3) destinations from the previous page. Fill in your arrival and departure dates for each destination. **Your Travel Update itinerary (all destinations selected) cannot exceed 30 days from beginning to end.**

		Month	Day		Month	Day
(Sample) LONDON	From:	6 /	21	To:	6 /	30
1	From:	/		To:	/	
2	From:	/		To:	/	
3	From:	/		To:	/	

CHOOSE YOUR INTERESTS: Select up to eight (8) categories from the list of interest categories shown on the previous page and circle the numbers below:

1 2 3 4 5 6 7 8 9 10 11 12 13 14 15 16

CHOOSE WHEN YOU WANT YOUR TRAVEL UPDATE DELIVERED (Check one):
❏ Please send my Travel Update immediately.
❏ Please hold my order until a few weeks before my trip to include the most up-to-date information.
Completed orders will be sent within 48 hours. Allow 7-10 days for U.S. mail delivery.

ADD UP YOUR ORDER HERE. *SPECIAL OFFER FOR FODOR'S PURCHASERS ONLY!*

	Suggested Retail Price	Your Price	This Order
First destination ordered	$ 9.95	$ 7.95	$ 7.95
Second destination (if applicable)	$ 6.95	$ 4.95	+
Third destination (if applicable)	$ 6.95	$ 4.95	+

DELIVERY CHARGE (Check one and enter amount below)

	Within U.S. & Canada	Outside U.S. & Canada
First Class Mail	❏ $2.50	❏ $5.00
FAX	❏ $5.00	❏ $10.00
Priority Delivery	❏ $15.00	❏ $27.00

ENTER DELIVERY CHARGE FROM ABOVE: + _____

TOTAL: $ _____

METHOD OF PAYMENT IN U.S. FUNDS ONLY (Check one):
❏ AmEx ❏ MC ❏ Visa ❏ Discover ❏ Personal Check (U. S. & Canada only)
❏ Money Order/ International Money Order
Make check or money order payable to: Fodor's Worldview Travel Update

Credit Card —/—/—/—/—/—/—/—/—/—/—/—/—/—/—/—/ Expiration Date:___/___

Authorized Signature _____

SEND THIS COMPLETED FORM WITH PAYMENT TO:
Fodor's Worldview Travel Update, 114 Sansome Street, Suite 700, San Francisco, CA 94104

OR CALL OR FAX US 24-HOURS A DAY
Telephone **1-800-799-9609** • Fax **1-800-799-9619** (From within the U.S. & Canada)
(Outside the U.S. & Canada: Telephone 415-616-9988 • Fax 415-616-9989)

(Please have this guide in front of you when you call so we can verify purchase.)
Code: FTG Offer valid until 12/31/95.